VOLUME 2: 1500 TO PRESENT

TRADITIONS THIRD EDITION
& ENCOUNTERS
A BRIEF GLOBAL HISTORY

Jerry H. Bentley
UNIVERSITY OF HAWAI'I

Herbert F. Ziegler
UNIVERSITY OF HAWAI'I

Heather E. Streets-Salter
NORTHEASTERN UNIVERSITY

McGraw Hill

Connect
Learn
Succeed™

Traditions and Encounters
Guarantees Better Course Performance

Better-prepared students

Imagine the dynamic class discussions you could have or lively lectures you could give if your students came to class prepared.

Enter **LearnSmart™,** the online adaptive learning system that guarantees that students come to class prepared. As part of McGraw-Hill's **Connect® History** program, LearnSmart assesses students' knowledge of the chapter content and identifies gaps in understanding. Students come to class with a better understanding of the course material.

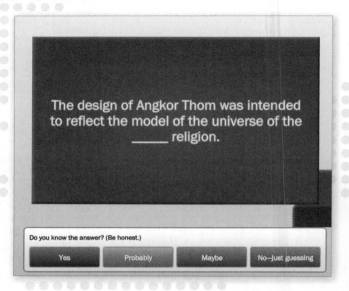

The design of Angkor Thom was intended to reflect the model of the universe of the _____ religion.

Do you know the answer? (Be honest.)

| Yes | Probably | Maybe | No—Just guessing |

Students tell us:

◆ I just wanted to let you know that **I love this Connect thing.** The LearnSmart modules are great and really help me to learn the material. I even downloaded their app for my phone." —Colorado State University

And the instructors say:

◆ "Five weeks into the semester, students in my three [course] sections have averages of 99.93, 99.97, and 100% respectively on the LearnSmart modules. **I would NEVER get that kind of learning and accuracy if I just assigned them to 'read the chapter and take notes'** or 'read the chapter and reflect' or some other reading-based assignment." —Florida State College at Jacksonville

◆ "LearnSmart has won my heart." —McLennan Community College

Better critical thinking skills

Traditions and Encounters moves students beyond memorization of names and dates and promotes critical thinking.

◆ **NEW Reverberations** help students draw connections between chapters. In showing how historical events like the Columbian exchange or industrialization affected different parts of the world, *Traditions and Encounters* helps students think about cause and effect.

Reverberations ● ● ● ● ● ● ● ● ●

The Diffusion of Technologies

Between about 1000 and 1500 c.e., the ever-increasing pace of human interaction in many parts of the world led to a spectacular diffusion of technologies. Technologies include both tools and techniques that humans use to adapt the natural environment to their needs, and thus can range from items like plows and horseshoes to irrigation systems or ideas about which crops to plant. Of course, both the existence of technologies and their diffusion were hardly unique to the period between 1000 and 1500 c.e.—indeed, we have already seen numerous examples of technological diffusion (such as the spread of horse-drawn chariots and iron smelting, among many others) in Parts I–III. But during the period between 1000 and 1500 c.e., increased inter-cultural interactions—especially across and between Eurasia and Africa—led not only to the more rapid diffusion of technologies, but also to the diffusion of particular technologies that would impact the world's history for centuries to come. One of the reasons for the increased pace of interactions across Eurasia and Africa was because of the spread of the *dar-al-Islam* after the eighth century, which we read about in Part III, and especially because of the Muslim merchants who established stable trade routes within and beyond its bounds. Another reason was the huge conquests made by nomadic Turks and Mongols from the eleventh to the thirteenth centuries. In the thirteenth century, Mongol conquests alone provided stable trade routes that connected Eurasia all the way from China to eastern Europe. Each of these developments provided the pathways not only for the introduction of new trade items and spiritual beliefs, but also for the diffusion of technologies from distant regions. Here, we discuss two types of technologies that were widely diffused in this period: technologies of warfare and technologies of transportation.

Technologies of Warfare

In this chapter, we have already seen that Mongols learned about gunpowder from the Chinese during the thirteenth century. Gunpowder, of course, was not new to the Chinese: as we saw in chapter 12, Chinese alchemists discovered the compound during the Han dynasty,

and by the eighth century Chinese strategists were using it for military purposes. But when Mongol invaders were introduced to gunpowder['s] destructive powers into the as 1214, for example, Ch an artillery unit. Faced w especially its usefulness i over Eurasia quickly sou Since the Mongols used g Persia and other parts thirteenth century, Musli incorporate the technolo selves. By the mid-thirte nology had also reached early fourteenth century cannons. Although early accurate, the diffusion o manently altered the nat eight centuries since Mo use of gunpowder techn of the globe in profound

Technologies of T

The period from around the widespread diffusion both animal and maritim that, in turn, allowed for tion across long distance growth. For example, Isl rica utilized camels to cro eighth century c.e. (chap els across the Sahara le changes in a variety of which included both the growing wealth resultin much larger Eurasian mar diffusion of the horse co tral Asia and north Africa helped to fuel European horses to pull much heavi ter 16). The result was for plowing and for trans

Siege of a North African Town, Fourteenth Century.

much slower oxen, which increased the amount of land that could be plowed as well as the rapidity with which goods could be brought to market. Maritime technologies also diffused widely in this period. For example, the magnetic compass was invented by the Chinese during the Tang or Song dynasties, but by the mid-eleventh century it was being used by mariners throughout the Indian Ocean basin. By the mid-twelfth century, Europeans were also using compasses in the Mediterranean and Atlantic—devices that helped Portuguese mariners find their way into the Indian Ocean in the fifteenth century (chapter 18). In subsequent centuries, European mari-

ners adopted many other maritime technologies from distant cultures—including the astrolabe—which were eventually used to cross the Atlantic to the Americas. Maritime technologies were not only important in Eurasia, however: during the twelfth and thirteenth centuries, voyages using sophisticated maritime techniques between the Hawaiian Islands and Tahiti allowed for the transfer of improved fishhook technologies to Hawaii (chapter 17).

When reading subsequent chapters, consider the effects that the diffusion of technologies have had on societies around the world over the very long term.

◆ **NEW Connecting the Sources** invites students to compare two primary sources—documents or images—and consider how information can be interpreted in different ways.

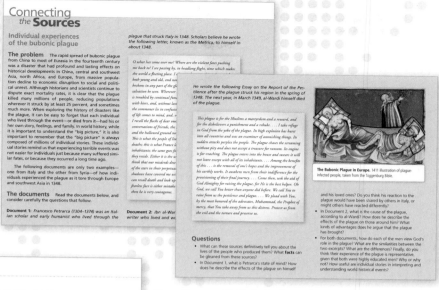

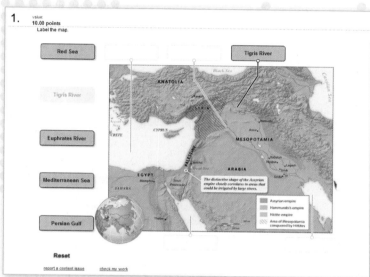

◆ **NEW CONNECT online activities** place students in a more active environment where they develop analytical skills.

◆ *Connect History* builds advanced thinking and writing skills through **"Critical Missions"** projects that place students in a pivotal moment in time and ask them to develop a historical argument.

◆ **Thinking about Traditions** and **Thinking about Encounters** ask thought-provoking questions that reinforce the narrative's central themes.

Better grades

Research shows that students' grades improve using Connect History and LearnSmart. Imagine being able to document this type of grade improvement through easily run reports.

Listen to instructors:

◆ "My class that is **using Connect scored higher than any other class in my 25 years of teaching."** — University of Colorado Denver

◆ "The students really love Connect. **They also got the best test scores on their first exam that I have ever seen in my teaching career."** — Georgia Southern University

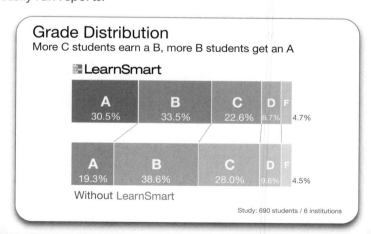

Grade Distribution
More C students earn a B, more B students get an A

LearnSmart

A	B	C	D	F
30.5%	33.5%	22.6%	8.7%	4.7%

A	B	C	D	F
19.3%	38.6%	28.0%	9.6%	4.5%

Without LearnSmart

Study: 690 students / 6 institutions

Traditions and Encounters: the digital and print program that Connects students to Success!

TRADITIONS AND ENCOUNTERS: A BRIEF GLOBAL HISTORY, VOLUME 2, THIRD EDITION
Published by McGraw-Hill, a business unit of The McGraw-Hill Companies, Inc., 1221 Avenue of the Americas, New York, NY 10020.

Some ancillaries, including electronic and print components, may not be available to customers outside the United States.

This book is printed on acid-free paper.

1 2 3 4 5 6 7 8 9 0 DOW/DOW 1 0 9 8 7 6 5 4 3

ISBN 978-0-07-741206-7
MHID 0-07-741206-0

Senior Vice President, Products & Markets: *Kurt L. Strand*
Vice President, General Manager, Products & Markets: *Michael Ryan*
Vice President, Content Production & Technology Services:
   Kimberly Meriwether David
Managing Director: *Gina Boedeker*
Director: *Matthew Busbridge*
Director of Development: *Rhona Robbin*
Managing Development Editor: *Nancy Crochiere*
Development Editor: *Nomi Sofer*
Editorial Coordinator: *Kaelyn Schulz*
Marketing Manager: *Stacy Ruel*
Digital Product Analyst: *John Brady*

Digital Development Editor: *Meghan Campbell*
Content Project Manager: *Jolynn Kilburg*
Senior Buyer: *Laura Fuller*
Senior Designer: *Laurie B. Janssen*
Cover/Interior Designer: *Elise Lansdon*
Cover Image: *Education Images/UIG Getty Images, Ian McKin/*
   Getty Images
Lead Content Licensing Specialist: *Carrie K. Burger*
Photo Research: *Danny Meldung/PhotoAffairs, Inc.*
Compositor: *Thompson Type*
Typeface: *10.5/12.5 Adobe Garamond Pro*
Printer: *R. R. Donnelley*

Page ii: © *SuperStock/Getty Images; p. iii:* © *bpk, Berlin/Kupferstichkabinett, Staatliche Museen/Joerg P. Anders/Art Resource, NY; p. vi:* © *Collection Rijksmuseum, Amsterdam; p. ix:* © *Bettmann/Corbis; p. x: Courtesy of the Australian War Memorial.*

The Library of Congress lists the Cataloging-in-Publication Data in the main title as follows:

Bentley, Jerry H., 1949–
   Traditions and encounters : a brief global history / Jerry H. Bentley, University of Hawaii–Manoa; Herbert F. Ziegler, University of Hawaii–Manoa; Heather Streets-Salter, Northeastern University. — Third Edition.
   pages cm
  Rev. ed. of: Traditions & encounters : a brief global history. Second edition. New York : McGraw-Hill, 2010.
  Includes index.
  ISBN 978–0–07–340697–8 — ISBN 0–07–340697–X (hard copy : alk. paper)   1. World history–Textbooks.
2. Intercultural communication–History–Textbooks.   I. Ziegler, Herbert F., 1949-, author. II. Streets-Salter, Heather, author.   III. Title.
  D20.B419 2014
  909–dc23   2012040755

BriefContents

Contents

PART 6

AN AGE OF REVOLUTION, INDUSTRY, AND EMPIRE, 1750–1914   464

PART **7**
CONTEMPORARY GLOBAL REALIGNMENTS   554

CHAPTER **29**
The Great War: The World in Upheaval   556

CHAPTER **30**
An Age of Anxiety   576

Preface

How do the themes of traditions and encounters help make sense of the entire human past?

World history is about both diversity and connections. We began this text with a simple goal: to help our students understand the unique histories of the world's rich variety of peoples, while at the same time allowing them to see the long histories of connections and interactions that have shaped all human communities for millennia. To do this, we have written a story around the dual themes of traditions and encounters, so that we can highlight the many different religions and customs embraced by the world's peoples while also exploring the encounters with other cultures that brought about inevitable change.

It is the interaction of these traditions and encounters that provides the key to making sense of our past. Human communities furthered themselves not by remaining isolated, but by interacting with others and exploring the benefits and risks of reaching out. The vitality of history—and its interpretation—lies in understanding the nature of individual traditions and the scope of encounters that punctuated every significant event in human history.

Traditions & Encounters: A Brief Global History provides a global vision of history that is increasingly meaningful in a shrinking world. The theme of **traditions** draws attention to the formation, maintenance, and sometimes collapse of individual societies. Because the world's peoples have also interacted regularly with one another since the earliest days of human history, the theme of **encounters** directs attention to communications, interactions, networks, and exchanges that have linked individual societies to their neighbors and others in the larger world.

The themes of traditions and encounters are at the heart of every chapter in the text. They provide a lens through which to interpret the affairs of humankind and the pressures that continue to shape history. All aspects of the text support these themes—from the organization of chapters, engaging stories of the world's peoples, to the robust map program and critical-thinking features.

Organization: Seven Eras of Global History

We discuss the world's development through time by organizing it into seven eras of global history. These eras, treated successively in the seven parts of this book, represent coherent epochs that form the larger architecture of world history as we see it. Every region of the world is discussed in each of the seven eras. The eras owe their coherence in large part to the networks of transportation, communication, and exchange that have linked peoples of different societies at different times in the past. This structure allows us to make cross-cultural comparisons that help frame world history for students to put events in a perspective that renders them more understandable.

Changes for the THIRD Edition

In preparing this third edition of *Traditions & Encounters: A Brief Global History,* we have revised, updated, and reorganized the text to stay current with recent world historical scholarship and to remain true to the goals of a brief textbook.

Significant modifications to the third edition include:

REVERBERATIONS This new feature appears once in every part and uses information from multiple chapters to discuss an overarching topic such as technological change, the Columbian exchange, or industrialization in order to help students think about cause and effect over the long term. The Reverberations feature appears in the first chapter of every part, and then reappears as a smaller boxed feature in the subsequent chapters, reminding students to consider how the "reverberations" relate to the specific material they are now reading.

CONNECTING THE SOURCES This new feature helps students recognize that historiography is based on scholars' interpretation of historical information. It focuses on two documents or images and asks students to think critically about the different ways the given information can be interpreted. This feature occurs once per part.

The Table of Contents has been reordered to place Chapter 29, "The Great War: The World in Upheaval" and Chapter 31, "Nationalism and Political Identities in Asia, Africa, and Latin America" together, and to place Chapter 30, "An Age of Anxiety" and Chapter 32, "New Conflagrations: World War II" together.

Chapter 24: The Islamic Empires has been thoroughly revised to take a more global view of Islam.

Chapter 25: Revolutions and National States in the Atlantic World has been revised to include coverage of the Enlightenment and a revised discussion of the French Revolution.

6 Ways to Improve
Your Course Outcomes

Connect

Connect® History is a highly interactive learning environment designed to help students connect to the resources they will need to achieve success. Map activities, primary source exercises, image analysis, key term quizzes, and review questions provide a wealth of assignments to ensure that students are comprehending the reading and will succeed in the course.

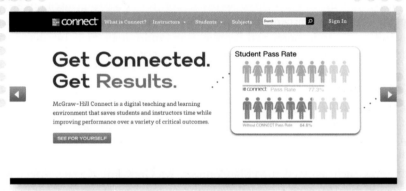

ConnectPlus® History offers all this with the addition of an integrated, interactive e-book. Optimized for the Web, the e-book immerses students in a flexible, interactive environment.

LearnSmart

LearnSmart, McGraw-Hill's adaptive learning system, helps assess student knowledge of course content and maps out a personalized study plan for success. Accessible within **Connect History, LearnSmart** uses a series of adaptive questions to pinpoint the concepts students understand—and those they don't. The result is an online tool that helps students learn faster and study more efficiently and enables instructors to customize classroom lectures and activities to meet their students' needs.

Create

Design your ideal course materials with McGraw-Hill's **Create**, **www.mcgrawhill-create.com!** Rearrange or omit chapters, combine material from other sources, and/or upload your syllabus or any other content you have written to make the perfect resources for your students. Search thousands of leading McGraw-Hill textbooks to find the best content for your students, then arrange it to fit your teaching style. You can even personalize your book's appearance by selecting the cover and adding your name, school, and course information. When you order a **Create** book, you receive a complimentary review copy. Get a printed copy in three to five business days or an electronic copy (eComp) via e-mail in about an hour. Register today at **www.mcgrawhillcreate.com** and craft your course resources to match the way you teach.

CourseSmart

CourseSmart offers thousands of the most commonly adopted textbooks across hundreds of courses from a wide variety of higher education publishers. It is the only place for faculty to review and compare the full text of a textbook online, providing immediate access without the environmental impact of requesting a printed exam copy. At **CourseSmart,** students can save up to 50 percent off the cost of a printed book, reduce their impact on the environment, and gain access to powerful Web tools for learning, including full text search, notes and highlighting, and e-mail tools for sharing notes among classmates. Learn more at **www.coursesmart.com.**

McGraw-Hill Campus

McGraw-Hill Campus is the first of its kind institutional service providing faculty with true single sign-on access to all of McGraw-Hill's course content, digital tools, and other high-quality learning resources from any learning management system (LMS). This innovative offering allows for secure and deep integration and seamless access to any of our course solutions such as McGraw-Hill Connect, McGraw-Hill Create, McGraw-Hill LearnSmart, or Tegrity. **McGraw-Hill Campus** includes access to our entire content library, including e-books, assessment tools, presentation slides, and multimedia content, among other resources, providing faculty open and unlimited access to prepare for class, create tests/quizzes, develop lecture material, integrate interactive content, and much more.

Online Learning Center for *Traditions & Encounters*

The **Online Learning Center (OLC)** at www.mhhe.com/bentleybrief3e contains a wealth of instructor resources, including an Instructor's Manual, Test Bank, and Power-Point presentations for each chapter. All maps and the vast majority of images from the print text are included.

- A **Computerized Test Bank,** McGraw-Hill's EZ Test, allows you to quickly create a customized test using the publisher's supplied test banks or your own questions. You decide the number, type, and order of test questions with a few simple clicks. EZ Test runs on your computer without a connection to the Internet.

Acknowledgments

Many individuals have contributed to this book, and the authors take pleasure in recording deep thanks for all the comments, criticism, advice, and suggestions that helped to improve the work. Special thanks to the editorial, marketing, and production teams at McGraw-Hill: Matthew Busbridge, Nancy Crochiere, Stacy Ruel, Nomi Sofer, and Jolynn Kilburg, who provided crucial support by helping the authors work through difficult issues and solving the innumerable problems of content, style, organization, and design that arise in any project to produce a history of the world.

Academic Reviewers

This edition continues to reflect many discerning suggestions made by instructors of the world history course. We would like to acknowledge the contributions of the following reviewers who suggested many of the changes implemented in this print and digital program:

Heather J. Abdelnur
Blackburn College

Wayne Ackerson
Salisbury University

Patrick Albano
Fairmont State University

William H. Alexander
Norfolk State University

Michael Balyo
Chemeketa Community College

Diane Barefoot
Caldwell Community College, Watauga Campus

Gene Barnett
Calhoun Community College

Christopher M. Bellitto
Kean University

John Boswell
San Antonio College

Beau Bowers
Central Piedmont Community College

Jeff Bowersox
University of Southern Mississippi

W. H. Bragg
Georgia College and State University

Kathryn Braund
Auburn University

David Brosius
U.S. Air Force Academy/ USAFA

Robert Brown
UNC Pembroke

Gayle Brunelle
California State University, Fullerton

Samuel Brunk
University of Texas, El Paso

Marybeth Carlson
University of Dayton

Kay J. Carr
Southern Illinois University

Robert Carriedo
U.S. Air Force Academy/ USAFA

Annette Chamberlin
Virginia Western Community College

Patricia Colman
Moorpark College

John Davidann
Hawaii Pacific University

Kevin Dougherty
University of Southern Mississippi

Tim Dowling
Virginia Military Institute

Christopher Drennan
Clinton Community College

Mitch Driebe
Andrew College

Shawn Dry
Oakland Community College

Shannon Duffy
Loyola University of New Orleans

Peter Dykema
Arkansas Technical University

Ken Faunce
Washington State University

Robert J. Flynn
Portland Community College

Deanna D. Forsman
North Hennepin Community College

Sarah Franklin
University of Southern Mississippi

Kristine Frederickson
Brigham Young University

James Fuller
University of Indianapolis

Jessie Ruth Gaston
California State University, Sacramento

George W. Gawrych
Baylor University

Deborah Gerish
Emporia State University

Gary G. Gibbs
Roanoke College

Philip Grace
Grand Valley State University

Candace Gregory
California State University, Sacramento

Ernie Grieshaber
Minnesota State University-Mankato

Casey Harison
University of Southern Indiana

Jillian Hartley
Arkansas Northeastern College

James M. Hastings
Wingate University

Gregory Havrilcsak
The University of Michigan, Flint

Timothy Hawkins
Indiana State University

John K. Hayden
Southwest Oklahoma State University

Susan M. Hellert
University of Wisconsin, Platteville

Mark C. Herman
Edison State College

Paul Isherwood
Ohio University

Theodore Kallman
San Joaquin Delta Community College

David Katz
Mohawk Valley Community College

Richard Kennedy
Mount Olive College

Janine Lanza
Wayne State University

Jodie N. Mader
Thomas More College

David Massey
Bunker Hill Community College

Eileen Moore
Miles College

Kelli Yoshie Nakamura
Kapiolani Community College

Anne Osborne
Rider University

Charles Parker
Saint Louis University

Brian Plummer
Asuza Pacific University

William Rodner
Tidewater Community College

Pamela Sayre
Henry Ford Community College

David Schmidt
Bethel College

Jerry Sheppard
Mount Olive College

Brett S. Shufelt
Copiah-Lincoln Community College

Kyle Smith
Grand Valley State University

Michael Snodgrass
Indiana University–Purdue University Indianapolis

Paul Steeves
Stetson University

Kurt Stiegler
Nicholls State University

Clif Stratton
Washington State University

Elisaveta Todorova
University of Cincinnati

Sarah Trembanis
Immaculata University

Judith Walden
College of the Ozarks

Ron Wallenfels
Kean University

Kathleen Warnes
Grand Valley State University

Kurt Werthmuller
Azusa Pacific University

Sherri West
Brookdale Community College

Kenneth Wilburn
East Carolina University

Jeffrey Wilson
University of New Orleans

Mary Clingerman Yaran
Grand Valley State University

William Zogby
Mohawk Valley Community College

In addition, we would like to thank the following individuals who participated in McGraw-Hill history symposia and focus groups and on the Connect Board of Advisors; these individuals helped shape our digital program:

Gisela Ables
Houston Community College

Sal Anselmo
Delgado Community College

Simon Baatz
John Jay College

Mario A. J. Bennekin
Georgia Perimeter College

Manu Bhagavan
Hunter College

C. J. Bibus
Wharton County Junior College

Olwyn M. Blouet
Virginia State University

Michael Botson
Houston Community College

Cathy Briggs
Northwest Vista College

Brad Cartwright
University of Texas at El Paso

Roger Chan
Washington State University

June Cheatham
Richland College

Karl Clark
Coastal Bend College

Bernard Comeau
Tacoma Community College

Kevin Davis
North Central Texas College

Michael Downs
Tarrant County College–Southeast

Laura Dunn
Brevard Community College

Arthur Durand
Metropolitan Community College

David Dzurec
University of Scranton

Amy Forss
Metropolitan Community College

Jim Good
Lone Star College–North Harris

R. David Goodman
Pratt Institute

Wendy Gunderson
Colin County Community College

Debbie Hargis
Odessa College

John Hosler
Morgan State University

James Jones
Prairie View A & M University

Mark Jones
Central Connecticut State University

Philip Kaplan
University of North Florida

Stephen Katz
Philadelphia University

Carol A. Keller
San Antonio College

Greg Kelm
Dallas Baptist University

Michael Kinney
Calhoun Community College

Jessica Kovler
John Jay College

David Lansing
Ocean County College

Benjamin Lapp
Montclair State University

Julian Madison
Southern Connecticut State University

David Marshall
Suffolk County Community College

Meredith R. Martin
Collin College

Linda McCabe
North Lake College

George Monahan
Suffolk County Community College

Tracy Musacchio
John Jay College

Mikal Nash
Essex County College

Sandy Norman
Florida Atlantic University

Michelle Novak
Houston Community College–Southeast

Veena Oldenburg
Baruch College

Jessica Patton
Tarrant County College–Northwest

Edward Paulino
John Jay College

Craig Pilant
County College of Morris

Robert Risko
Trinity Valley Community College

Esther Robinson
Lone Star College–Cyfair

Geri Ryder
Ocean County College

Linda Scherr
Mercer County Community College

Jessica Kovler
John Jay College

Susan Schmidt-Horning
St. John's University

Donna Scimeca
College of Staten Island

Jeffrey Smith
Lindenwood University

Rachel Standish
San Joaquin Delta College

Matthew Vaz
City College of New York

Roger Ward
Colin County Community College–Plano

Christian Warren
Brooklyn College

Don Whatley
Blinn College

Scott M. Williams
Weatherford College

Carlton Wilson
North Carolina Central University

Geoffrey Willbanks
Tyler Junior College

Chad Wooley
Tarrant County College

Connect Board of Advisors

Michael Downs
University of Texas–Arlington

Jim Halverson
Judson University

Reid Holland
Midlands Technical College

Stephen Katz
Rider University

David Komito
Eastern Oregon University

Wendy Sarti
Oakton Community College

Linda Scherr
Mercer County Community College

Eloy Zarate
Pasadena City College

Connect Survey Respondents

Allison Beth Barr
Baylor University

David Burden
Indiana Wesleyan University

Daniel Christensen
California State University, Fullerton

Julie deGraffenried
Baylor University

Jim Halverson
Judson University

Jeffrey S. Hamilton
Baylor University

Stephen Katz
Rider University

David Komito
Eastern Oregon University

Scott Lebowitz
Florida Atlantic University

Paul Lococo Jr.
Leeward Community College

Christine Lovasz-Kaiser
University of Southern Indiana

David Meskill
Dowling College

Eric Nelson
Missouri State University

Matthew Placido
Florida Atlantic University

Anne Quartararo
U.S. Naval Academy

Linda Scherr
Mercer County Community College

Martin Spence
Cornerstone University

Kate Transchel
California State University, Chico

Carey Watt
St. Thomas University

Leonard R. Winogora
Mercer County Community College

Eloy Zarate
Pasadena City College

About The Authors

Jerry H. Bentley was professor of history at the University of Hawai'i and editor of the *Journal of World History*. His research on the religious, moral, and political writings of Renaissance humanists led to the publication of *Humanists and Holy Writ: New Testament Scholarship in the Renaissance* (Princeton, 1983) and *Politics and Culture in Renaissance Naples* (Princeton, 1987). More recently, his research was concentrated on global history and particularly on processes of cross-cultural interaction. His book *Old World Encounters: Cross-Cultural Contacts and Exchanges in Pre-Modern Times* (New York, 1993) examines processes of cultural exchange and religious conversion before the modern era, and his pamphlet *Shapes of World History in Twentieth-Century Scholarship* (Washington, D.C., 1996) discusses the historiography of world history. His most recent publication is *The Oxford Handbook of World History* (Oxford, 2011), and he served as a member of the editorial team preparing the forthcoming *Cambridge History of the World*. Jerry Bentley passed away in July 2012.

Herbert F. Ziegler is an associate professor of history at the University of Hawai'i. He has taught world history since 1980 and currently serves as director of the world history program at the University of Hawai'i. He also serves as book review editor of the *Journal of World History*. His interest in twentieth-century European social and political history led to the publication of *Nazi Germany's New Aristocracy* (1990). He is at present working on a study that explores from a global point of view the demographic trends of the past ten thousand years, along with their concomitant technological, economic, and social developments. His other current research project focuses on the application of complexity theory to a comparative study of societies and their internal dynamics.

Heather E. Streets-Salter is an associate professor of history at Northeastern University, where she is the director of world history programs. She is the author of *Martial Races: The Military, Martial Races, and Masculinity in British Imperial Culture, 1857–1914* (2004), and *Modern Imperialism and Colonialism: A Global Perspective* (2010) with Trevor Getz. Her current research explores imperialism and colonialism as global phenomena through a focus on the administrative, political, and ideological networks that existed among French Indochina, the Dutch East Indies, and British Malaya between 1890 and 1940.

PART 5

THE ORIGINS OF GLOBAL INTERDEPENDENCE, 1500–1800

By 1500 C.E. peoples throughout the world had built well-organized societies with distinctive cultural traditions. Powerful agricultural societies dominated most of Asia, the Mediterranean basin, Europe, much of sub-Saharan Africa, Mexico, and the central Andean region. By 1500 peoples of the world had also established intricate transportation networks that supported travel, communication, and exchange. Although pioneered by merchants in the interests of trade, these routes also enabled the diffusion of religion, food crops, animal stocks, and disease pathogens.

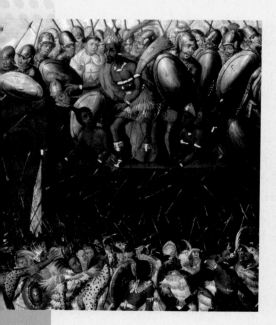

This late-sixteenth-century painting idealized the Spanish conquest of the Aztec empire. Shown on the wall is Motecuzoma, captured by the Spaniards attacking his palace, and he is pleading with the Aztecs to surrender.

Global Interactions

Yet the commercial, cultural, and biological exchanges of premodern times prefigured much more intense cross-cultural interactions after 1500. Beginning in the fifteenth century, European mariners established trade routes linking the lands of the Indian, Atlantic, and Pacific Ocean basins. These routes in turn fostered direct contact between the peoples of the eastern hemisphere, the western hemisphere, and Oceania.

The Early Modern Era

The establishment of links between all the world's regions and peoples gave rise to the early modern era of world history, approximately 1500 to 1800 C.E. The early modern era differed from the period from 1000 to 1500, when there were only sporadic contacts between peoples of the eastern hemisphere, the western hemisphere, and Oceania. It also differed from the modern era, from 1800 to the present, when national states, heavy industry, powerful weapons, and efficient technologies of transportation and communication enabled peoples of European ancestry to achieve political and economic dominance in the world.

New Exchanges

During the early modern era, several global processes touched peoples in all parts of the world and influenced the development of their societies. One involved biological exchange: plants, animals, diseases, and human communities crossed the world's oceans and established themselves in new lands, where they dramatically affected both the natural environment and established societies. Another involved commercial exchange: merchants took advantage of newly established sea-lanes to inaugurate a genuinely global economy. Yet another process involved the diffusion of

Mining operations at Potosí in South America gave rise to a large settlement that housed miners and others who supplied food, made charcoal, fashioned tools, and supported the enterprise. In this illustration from the mid-1580s, llamas laden with silver ore descend the mountain (background) while laborers work in the foreground to crush the ore and extract pure silver from it.

technologies and cultural traditions: printing and gunpowder spread throughout the world, and Christianity and Islam attracted increasing numbers of converts.

Consequences of Global Exchange

These global processes had different effects for different peoples. In the Americas and Oceania, diseases introduced from the eastern hemisphere ravaged indigenous populations and sometimes led to the collapse of whole societies. In contrast, Europeans claimed vast stretches of land in the Americas, where they founded colonies and cultivated crops for sale on the open market. In sub-Saharan Africa, millions of enslaved individuals underwent a forced migration to the western hemisphere, where they suffered both physical and psychological abuse. Meanwhile, east Asian and Islamic peoples prospered from increased trade but restricted the introduction of foreign ideas and technologies into their societies.

Although European peoples benefited from global processes of the period 1500 to 1800, by no means did they dominate world affairs in early modern times. Indeed, most of the western hemisphere and Africa lay beyond their control until the nineteenth century. Nevertheless, European peoples played a more prominent role in world affairs than any of their ancestors, and their efforts helped foster the development of an increasingly interdependent world.

In this anonymous painting produced about 1670, Dutch and English ships lie at anchor in the harbor of the busy port of Surat in northwestern India. Surat was the major port on the west coast of India, and it served as one of the chief commercial cities of the Mughal empire.

1. *What was it that distinguished this early modern period from the period 1000–1500, and from the modern period after 1800?*

2. *What were some of the global processes of the early modern era that affected peoples all over the world?*

Transoceanic Encounters and Global Connections

CHAPTER 19

This 16th century tapestry depicts the arrival of Portuguese mariner Vasco da Gama in the city of Calcutta, India, in May, 1498. © Banco Nacional Ultramarino, Portugal/Giraudon/ The Bridgeman Art Library

PART 5

EYEWITNESS:
Vasco da Gama's Spicy Voyage

On 8 July 1497 the Portuguese mariner Vasco da Gama led a small fleet of four armed merchant vessels with 170 crewmen out of the harbor at Lisbon. His destination was India, which he planned to reach by sailing around the continent of Africa and through the Indian Ocean. He carried letters of introduction from the king of Portugal as well as cargoes of gold, wool textiles, and other goods that he hoped to exchange for pepper and spices in India.

Before there would be an opportunity to trade, however, da Gama and his crew had a prolonged voyage through two oceans. They sailed south from Portugal to the Cape Verde Islands off the west coast of Africa, where they took on fresh provisions. On 3 August they headed southeast into the Atlantic Ocean to take advantage of the prevailing winds. For the next ninety-five days, the fleet saw no land. By October, da Gama had found westerly winds in the southern Atlantic, rounded the Cape of Good Hope, and entered the Indian Ocean. The fleet slowly worked its way up the east coast of Africa as far as Malindi, where da Gama secured the services of an Indian Muslim pilot to guide his ships across the Arabian Sea. On 20 May 1498—more than ten months after its departure from Lisbon—the fleet anchored at Calicut in southern India.

In India the Portuguese fleet found a wealthy, cosmopolitan society. The markets of Calicut offered not only pepper, ginger, cinnamon, and other spices but also rubies, emeralds, gold jewelry, and fine cotton textiles. Alas, apart from gold and some striped cloth, the goods that da Gama had brought attracted little interest among merchants at Calicut. Nevertheless, da Gama managed to exchange gold for a cargo of pepper and cinnamon that turned a handsome profit when the fleet returned to Portugal in August 1499. Da Gama's expedition also opened the door to direct maritime trade between European and Asian peoples and helped to establish permanent links between the world's various regions.

Cross-cultural interactions have been a persistent feature of historical development. Even in ancient times mass migration, campaigns of imperial expansion, and long-distance trade deeply influenced societies throughout the world. Yet after 1500 C.E. cross-cultural interactions took place on a much larger geographic scale than ever before, and encounters were often more disruptive than in earlier centuries. Equipped with advanced technologies and a powerful military arsenal, western European peoples began to cross the world's oceans in large numbers during the early modern era. At the same time, Russian adventurers built an enormous Eurasian empire and ventured tentatively into the Pacific Ocean.

Europeans were not the only peoples who actively explored the larger world during the early modern era. In the early fifteenth century, the Ming emperors of China sponsored a series of seven enormous maritime expeditions that visited all parts of the Indian Ocean basin. In the sixteenth century Ottoman mariners also ventured into the Indian Ocean. Following the Ottoman conquest of Egypt in 1517, both merchant and military

---

Vasco da Gama (VAS-koh duh GAM-uh)

1394–1460	Life of Prince Henry the Navigator of Portugal
1488	Bartolomeu Dias's voyage around the Cape of Good Hope into the Indian Ocean
1492	Christopher Columbus's first voyage to the western hemisphere
1497–1499	Vasco da Gama's first voyage to India
1519–1522	Ferdinand Magellan's circumnavigation of the world
1565–1575	Spanish conquest of the Philippines
1768–1780	Captain James Cook's voyages in the Pacific Ocean

vessels established an Ottoman presence throughout the Indian Ocean basin.

Although other peoples also made their way into the larger world, only Europeans linked the lands and peoples of the eastern hemisphere, the western hemisphere, and Oceania. Because of that, European peoples benefited from unparalleled opportunities to increase their power, wealth, and influence. As a result, after 1500, European peoples became much more prominent in the larger world than before.

The expansion of European influence resulted in the establishment of global networks of transportation, communication, and exchange. Indeed, a worldwide diffusion of plants, animals, diseases, and human communities followed European ventures across the oceans, and intricate trade networks eventually gave birth to a global economy. Although epidemic diseases killed millions of people, the spread of food crops and domesticated animals contributed to a dramatic surge in global population. The establishment of global trade networks ensured that interactions between the world's peoples would continue and intensify.

THE EUROPEAN RECONNAISSANCE OF THE WORLD'S OCEANS

Between 1400 and 1800, European mariners launched a remarkable series of exploratory voyages that took them to nearly all the earth's waters. Those voyages were very expensive affairs. Yet private investors and government authorities had strong motives to underwrite the expeditions and outfit them with the latest nautical technology. The voyages of exploration paid large dividends: they enabled European mariners to chart the world's ocean basins and develop an accurate understanding of world geography. On the basis of that knowledge, European merchants and mariners established global networks of communication, transportation, and exchange—and profited handsomely from their efforts.

Motives for Exploration

A complex combination of motives prompted Europeans to explore the world's oceans. Most important of those motives were the search for basic resources and lands suitable for the cultivation of cash crops, the desire to establish new trade routes to Asian markets, and the aspiration to expand the influence of Christianity.

Portuguese Exploration Mariners from the relatively poor kingdom of Portugal were most prominent in the search for fresh resources and lands. Beginning in the thirteenth century, Portuguese seamen ventured away from the coasts and into the open Atlantic Ocean to supplement their own meager resources. By the early fourteenth century, they had discovered the uninhabited Azores and Madeiras Islands and called frequently at the Canary Islands, inhabited by the indigenous Guanche people. These Atlantic islands proved ideal for the cultivation of sugar, a product that enjoyed a strong European demand. In the fifteenth century, Italian investors—who had organized sugar plantations in the Mediterranean since the twelfth century—helped Portuguese mariners establish plantations in the Atlantic islands. Continuing Portuguese voyages also led to the establishment of plantations on the Cape Verde Islands, São Tomé, Principe, and Fernando Po.

The Lure of Trade Even more alluring than the exploitation of fresh lands and resources was the goal of establishing maritime trade routes to the markets of Asia. During the era of the Mongol empires, European merchants often traveled over land as far as China to trade for Asian goods. When the Mongol empires collapsed and bubonic plague spread across Eurasia in the fourteenth century, however, travel on the silk roads became much more dangerous. As a result, Europeans relied on Muslim mariners to bring Asian goods through the Indian Ocean and the Red Sea to Cairo, where Italian merchants purchased them for distribution in western Europe. But prices at Cairo were high, and Europeans sought ever-larger quantities of Asian goods, particularly spices.

By the fourteenth century the wealthy classes of Europe regarded Indian pepper and Chinese ginger as expensive necessities, and they especially prized cloves and nutmeg from

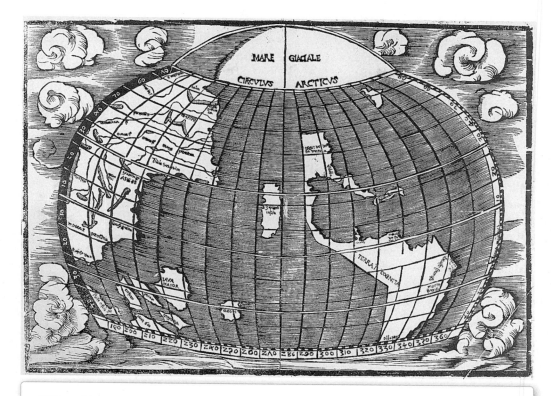

1512 world map.
This map, prepared about 1512 by the Polish cartographer Jan Stobnicza, shows eloquently that it took a long time for geographers to realize the extent of the Americas and the Pacific Ocean. Here "Cipangu" (Japan) lies just west of Mexico, with the Asian mainland nearby.

the spice islands of Maluku. Merchants and monarchs alike realized that by gaining direct access to Asian markets and eliminating Muslim intermediaries, they could increase the quantities of spices and other Asian goods available in Europe while making enormous profits.

African trade also beckoned to Europeans and called them to the sea. Since the twelfth century, Europeans had purchased west African gold, ivory, and slaves brought to north African ports by Muslim merchants. West African gold was especially important to Europeans because it was their principal form of payment for Asian luxury goods. As in the case of Asian trade, Europeans realized that they could profit from eliminating Muslim middlemen and establishing maritime routes that offered direct access to African markets.

Missionary Efforts Alongside material incentives, the goal of expanding the boundaries of Christianity drove Europeans into the larger world. Like Buddhism and Islam, Christianity is a missionary religion that directs believers to spread the faith. Sometimes such efforts were attempted through peaceful persuasion. At other times the expansion of Christianity could be quite violent. Beginning in the

eleventh century, for example, western Europeans launched a series of crusades against Muslims in Palestine, the Mediterranean islands, and Iberia. In Iberia, in fact, the Muslim kingdom of Granada fell to Spanish Christian forces just weeks before Christopher Columbus set sail on his famous first voyage to the western hemisphere in 1492. Whether through persuasion or violence, overseas voyages offered fresh opportunities for western Europeans to spread their faith.

In practice, the various motives for exploration combined and reinforced one another. When the Portuguese mariner Vasco da Gama reached the Indian port of Calicut in 1498, local authorities asked him what he wanted there. His reply: "Christians and spices." The goal of spreading Christianity thus became a powerful justification and reinforcement for the more material motives for the voyages of exploration.

The Technology of Exploration

Without advanced nautical technology and navigational skills, even the strongest motives would not have enabled European mariners to reconnoiter the world's oceans. They also needed sturdy ships, good navigational equipment, and knowledge of sailing techniques. These they devised by combining Chinese and Arabic technologies with their own inherited nautical technologies from the Mediterranean and northern Europe.

Ships and Sails

From their experiences in the rough coastal waters of the Atlantic, European sailors learned to construct ships strong enough to brave most adverse conditions. Beginning about the twelfth century, they increased the maneuverability of their craft by building a rudder onto the stern. (The sternpost rudder was a Chinese invention that had diffused across the Indian Ocean.) They outfitted their vessels with two types of sails: square sails (which enabled them to take full advantage of a wind blowing from behind) and triangular lateen sails (which could catch winds from the side as well as from behind). With a combination of square and lateen sails, European ships were able to use whatever winds arose. Their ability to tack—to advance against the wind by sailing across it—was crucial for the exploration of regions with uncooperative winds.

Navigational Instruments

The most important navigational equipment on board these vessels were magnetic compasses (which determined heading) and astrolabes (which determined latitude). The compass was a Chinese invention that had diffused throughout the Indian Ocean basin in the eleventh century and had reached European mariners by the mid–twelfth century. The astrolabe was a simplified version of an instrument used by Greek and Persian astronomers to measure the angle of the sun or the pole star above the horizon. In the late fifteenth century, however, Portuguese mariners encountered Arab sailors in the Indian Ocean using

---

astrolabe (AS-truh-leyb)

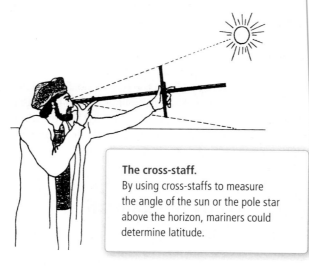

The cross-staff.
By using cross-staffs to measure the angle of the sun or the pole star above the horizon, mariners could determine latitude.

---

simpler and more serviceable instruments for determining latitude, which the Portuguese then used as models for the construction of cross-staffs and back-staffs.

Knowledge of Winds and Currents

European mariners' ability to determine direction and latitude enabled them to assemble a vast body of data about the earth's

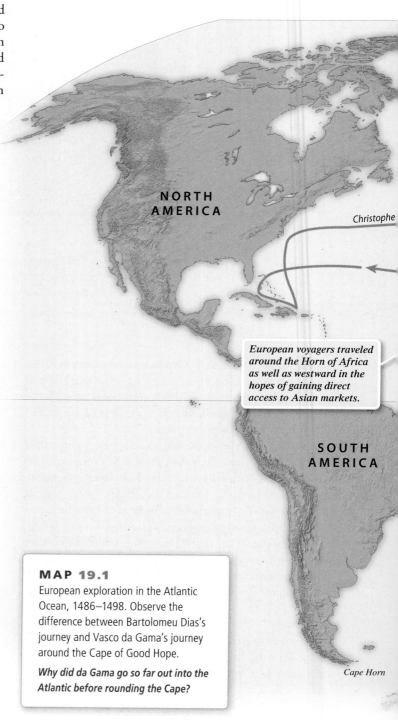

European voyagers traveled around the Horn of Africa as well as westward in the hopes of gaining direct access to Asian markets.

MAP 19.1
European exploration in the Atlantic Ocean, 1486–1498. Observe the difference between Bartolomeu Dias's journey and Vasco da Gama's journey around the Cape of Good Hope.

Why did da Gama go so far out into the Atlantic before rounding the Cape?

geography and to find their way around the world's oceans with tolerable accuracy and efficiency. Equipped with advanced technological hardware, European mariners ventured into the oceans and gradually compiled a body of practical knowledge about winds and currents. Critical to this body of knowledge was the strategy devised by Portuguese mariners called the *volta do mar* ("return through the sea"), which involved using prevailing winds and currents to reach destinations across the oceans. Although the *volta do mar* forced mariners to take indirect routes to their destinations—which at times required going hundreds of miles out of their way—experience soon taught that sailing around contrary winds was more reliable than butting up against them. When Vasco da Gama sailed for India

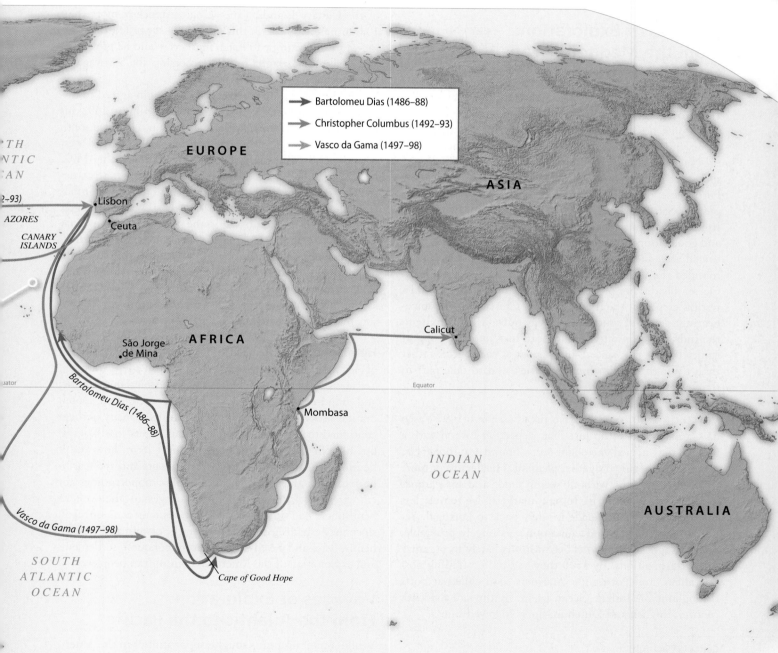

in 1497, for example, he sailed south to the Cape Verde Islands and then allowed the trade winds to carry him southwest into the Atlantic Ocean until he approached the coast of Brazil. Only then did da Gama catch the prevailing westerlies that allowed him to sail east around the Cape of Good Hope. As they became familiar with the wind systems of the world's oceans, European mariners developed variations on the *volta do mar* that enabled them to travel reliably to coastlines throughout the world.

Voyages of Exploration: From the Mediterranean to the Atlantic

Prince Henry of Portugal   Although European exploratory voyaging began as early as the thirteenth century, the pace quickened decisively after 1415. In that year, Prince Henry of Portugal (1394–1460), often called Prince Henry the Navigator, conquered the Moroccan port of Ceuta and sponsored a series of voyages down the west African coast. Portuguese merchants soon established fortified trading posts at São Jorge da Mina (in modern Ghana) and other strategic locations. There they exchanged European horses and goods for gold and slaves. Portuguese explorations continued after Henry's death, and in 1488 Bartolomeu Dias rounded the Cape of Good Hope and entered the Indian Ocean. He did not proceed farther because of storms and a restless crew, but the route to India, China, and the spice-bearing islands of southeast Asia lay open. The sea route to the Indian Ocean offered European merchants the opportunity to buy silk, spices, and pepper at the source, rather than through Muslim intermediaries, and to take part in the flourishing trade of Asia.

Vasco da Gama   As we have already seen, in 1497 Vasco da Gama sought to do just that, departing Lisbon with a fleet of four armed merchant ships bound for India. His experience was not altogether pleasant. His fleet went more than three months without seeing land, and his cargoes excited little interest in Indian markets. Moreover, less than half of his crew made it safely back to Portugal. Yet his cargo of pepper and cinnamon was hugely profitable, and Portuguese merchants began immediately to organize further expeditions. By 1500 they had built a trading post at Calicut, and Portuguese mariners soon called at ports throughout the Indian Ocean basin. By the late sixteenth century, English and Dutch mariners followed suit.

Ceuta (SYOO-tuh)
São Jorge de Mina (sou hor-hay day meena)
Bartolomeu Dias (bahr-tol-uh-MEY-oh dee-as)
Taino (tah-EE-no)
Guanahaní (Gwah-nah-nee)

Christopher Columbus   While Portuguese navigators plied the sea route to India, the Genoese mariner Cristoforo Colombo, known in English as Christopher Columbus (1451–1506), proposed sailing to the markets of Asia by a western route. On the basis of wide reading in the existing geographical literature, Columbus believed that the earth was a relatively small sphere with a circumference of about 17,000 nautical miles. (In fact, the earth's circumference is almost 25,000 nautical miles.) By Columbus's calculations, Japan should have been less than 2,500 nautical miles west of the Canary Islands. (The actual distance is more than 10,000 nautical miles.) This geography suggested that sailing west from Europe to Asian markets would be profitable, and Columbus sought royal sponsorship for a voyage to prove his ideas.

Eventually Fernando and Isabel of Spain agreed to underwrite Columbus's expedition, and in August 1492 his fleet of three ships departed southern Spain. He sailed south to the Canaries, picked up supplies, and then turned west with the trade winds. On the morning of 12 October 1492, he made landfall at an island in the Bahamas that the native Taino inhabitants called Guanahaní and that Columbus rechristened San Salvador (also known as Watling Island). Thinking that he had arrived in the spice islands known familiarly as the Indies, Columbus called the Tainos "Indians." He sailed around the Caribbean for almost three months in search of gold, and at the large island of Cuba he sent a delegation to seek the court of the emperor of China. When Columbus returned to Spain, he reported to his royal sponsors that he had reached islands just off the coast of Asia.

Hemispheric Links   Columbus never reached the riches of Asia, and he obtained very little gold in the Caribbean. Yet news of his voyage spread rapidly throughout Europe, and hundreds of Spanish, English, French, and Dutch mariners soon followed in his wake. Initially, many of them continued to seek the passage to Asian waters that Columbus himself had pursued. Over a longer term, however, it became clear that the American continents and the Caribbean islands themselves held abundant opportunities for entrepreneurs. Thus Columbus's voyages to the western hemisphere had unintended but momentous consequences, since they established links between the eastern and western hemispheres and paved the way for the conquest, settlement, and exploitation of the Americas by European peoples.

Voyages of Exploration: From the Atlantic to the Pacific

While some Europeans sought opportunities in the Americas, others continued to seek a western route to Asian markets. However, in the early sixteenth century no one suspected the vast size of the Pacific Ocean, which covers one-third of the earth's surface.

SourcesfromthePast

Christopher Columbus's First Impressions of American Peoples

Christopher Columbus kept journals of his experiences during his voyages to the western hemisphere. The journal of his first voyage survives mostly in summary, but it clearly communicates Columbus's first impressions of the peoples he met in the Caribbean islands. The following excerpts show that Columbus, like other European mariners, had both Christianity and commerce in mind when exploring distant lands.

Thursday, 11 October [1492]. . . .

I . . . in order that they would be friendly to us—because I recognized that they were people who would be better freed [from error] and converted to our Holy Faith by love than by force—to some of them I gave red caps, and glass beads which they put on their chests, and many other things of small value, in which they took so much pleasure and became so much our friends that it was a marvel. Later they came swimming to the ships' launches where we were and brought us parrots and cotton thread in balls and javelins and many other things, and they traded them to us for other things which we gave them, such as small glass beads and bells. In sum, they took everything and gave of what they had willingly.

But it seemed to me that they were a people very poor in everything. All of them go as naked as their mothers bore them; and the women also, although I did not see more than one quite young girl. And all those that I saw were young people, for none did I see of more than 30 years of age. They are very well formed, with handsome bodies and good faces. Their hair [is] coarse—almost like the tail of a horse—and short. They wear their hair down over their eyebrows except for a little in the back which they wear long and never cut. . . .

They do not carry arms nor are they acquainted with them, because I showed them swords and they took them by the edge and through ignorance cut themselves. They have no iron. Their javelins are shafts without iron and some of them have at the end a fish tooth and others of other things. All of them alike are of good-sized stature and carry themselves well. I saw some who had marks of wounds on their bodies and I made signs to them asking what they were; and they showed me how people from other islands nearby came there and tried to take them, and how they defended themselves and I believed and believe that they come here from *tierra firme* [the continent] to take them captive. They should be good and intelligent servants, for I see that they say very quickly everything that is said to them; and I believe that they would become Christians very easily, for it seemed to me that they had no religion. . . .

Monday, 12 November. . . .

They are very gentle and do not know what evil is; nor do they kill others, nor steal; and they are without weapons and so timid that a hundred of them flee from one of our men even if our men are teasing them. And they are credulous and aware that there is a God in heaven and convinced that we come from the heavens; and they say very quickly any prayer that we tell them to say, and they make the sign of the cross. So that Your Highnesses ought to resolve to make them Christians: for I believe that if you begin, in a short time you will end up having converted to our Holy Faith a multitude of peoples and acquiring large dominions and great riches and all of their peoples for Spain. Because without doubt there is in these lands a very great quantity of gold; for not without cause do these Indians that I bring with me say that there are in these islands places where they dig gold and wear it on their chests, on their ears, and on their arms, and on their legs; and they are very thick bracelets. And also there are stones, and there are precious pearls and infinite spicery. . . . And also here there is probably a great quantity of cotton; and I think that it would sell very well here without taking it to Spain but to the big cities belonging to the Grand [Mongol] Khan.

For Further Reflection

■ On the basis of Columbus's account, what inferences can you draw about his plans for American lands and peoples?

Source: Christopher Columbus. *The Diario of Christopher Columbus's First Voyage to America.* Trans. by Oliver Dunn and James E. Kelley Jr. Norman: University of Oklahoma Press, 1989, pp. 65–69, 143–45.

Ferdinand Magellan The reconnaissance of the Pacific Ocean basin began with the Portuguese navigator Fernão de Magalhães (1480–1521), better known as Ferdinand Magellan. While sailing in the service of Portugal, Magellan had visited ports throughout the Indian Ocean basin and had traveled east as far as the spice islands of Maluku.

He believed that the spice islands and Asian markets lay fairly close to the western coast of the Americas, and he decided to pursue Christopher Columbus's goal of establishing a western route to Asian waters. Because Portuguese

Ferdinand Magellan (FUR-dih-nand muh-JEHL-uhn)

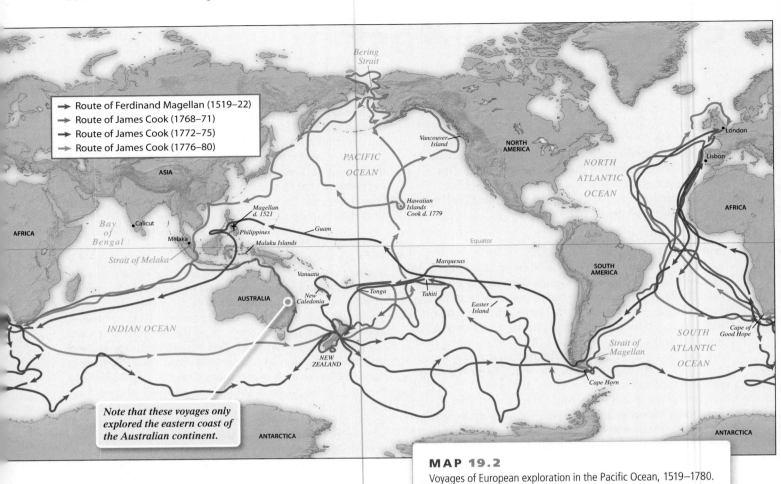

Route of Ferdinand Magellan (1519–22)
Route of James Cook (1768–71)
Route of James Cook (1772–75)
Route of James Cook (1776–80)

Note that these voyages only explored the eastern coast of the Australian continent.

MAP 19.2

Voyages of European exploration in the Pacific Ocean, 1519–1780.

What made exploration of the Pacific Ocean so daunting? What fate befell Magellan and Cook?

mariners had already reached Asian markets through the Indian Ocean, they had little interest in Magellan's proposed western route. Thus, on his Pacific expedition and circumnavigation of the world (1519–1522), Magellan sailed in the service of Spain.

The Circumnavigation Magellan's voyage was an exercise in endurance. He began by probing the eastern coast of South America in search of a strait leading to the Pacific. Eventually he found and sailed through the treacherous Strait of Magellan near the southern tip of South America. His fleet then sailed almost four months before taking on fresh provisions at Guam. During that period crewmen survived on worm-ridden biscuits, ship's rats, leather they had softened in the ocean, and water gone foul. Lacking fresh fruits and vegetables in their diet, many of the crew fell victim to the dreaded disease of scurvy, which caused painful rotting of the gums, loss of teeth, abscesses, hemorrhaging, and in most cases death. Scurvy killed 29 members of Magellan's crew during the Pacific crossing.

Conditions improved after the fleet called at Guam, but its ordeal had not come to an end. From Guam, Magellan proceeded to the Philippine Islands, where he and 40

of his crew were killed in a local political dispute. The survivors continued on to the spice islands of Maluku, where they took on a cargo of cloves. They then sailed home through the familiar waters of the Indian Ocean—and thus completed the first circumnavigation of the world—returning to Spain after a voyage of almost exactly three years. Of Magellan's five ships and 280 men, only one ship with 18 of the original crew returned. (An additional 17 crewmen returned later by other routes.)

Exploration of the Pacific The Pacific Ocean is so vast that it took European explorers almost three centuries to chart its features. Spanish merchants built on information gleaned from Magellan's expedition and established a trade route between the Philippines and Mexico, but they did not continue to explore the ocean basin itself. English navigators, however, ventured into the Pacific in search of a northwest passage from Europe to Asia. While searching for a passage, English mariners established many of the details of Pacific geography. In the sixteenth century, for example, Sir Francis Drake scouted the west coast of North America as far north as Vancouver Island.

Russian expansion was mostly a land-based affair in early modern times, but by the eighteenth century Russians also were exploring the Pacific Ocean. Russian officials commissioned the Danish navigator Vitus Bering to undertake two maritime expeditions (1725–1730 and 1733–1742) in search of a northeast passage to Asian ports. Bering sailed through the icy Arctic Ocean and the Bering Strait, which separates Siberia from Alaska.

Other Russian explorers made their way from Alaska down the western Canadian coast to northern California. By 1800 Russian mariners were scouting the Pacific Ocean as far south as the Hawaiian Islands. Indeed, they built a small fort on the island of Kaua'i and engaged in trade there for a few years in the early nineteenth century.

Captain James Cook Alongside Magellan, however, the most important of the Pacific explorers was Captain James Cook (1728–1779), who led three expeditions to the Pacific and died in a scuffle with the indigenous people of Hawai'i. Cook charted eastern Australia and New Zealand, and he added New Caledonia, Vanuatu, and Hawai'i to European maps of the Pacific. He probed the frigid waters of the Arctic Ocean and spent months at a time in the tropical islands of Tahiti, Tonga, and Hawai'i. By the time Cook's voyages had come to an end, European geographers had compiled a reasonably accurate understanding of the world's ocean basins, their lands, and their peoples.

Captain James Cook.
A portrait of Captain James Cook painted by William Hodges about 1775 depicts a serious and determined man.

What physical prop is included in the portrait, and why?

TRADE AND CONFLICT IN EARLY MODERN ASIA

The voyages of exploration taught European mariners how to sail to almost any coastline in the world and return safely. Once they arrived at their destinations, they sought commercial opportunities. In the eastern hemisphere they built a series of fortified trading posts that offered footholds in regions where established commercial networks had held sway for centuries. They even attempted to control the spice trade in the Indian Ocean, but with limited success. For the most part, they did not have the human numbers or the military power to impose their rule in the eastern hemisphere. In a parallel effort involving expansion across land rather than the sea, Russian explorers and adventurers established a presence in central Asia and Siberia, thus laying the foundations for a vast Eurasian empire. Commercial and political rivalries in both the eastern and the western hemispheres also led to conflict between European peoples, which resulted in numerous wars between competing powers for both territory and resources.

Trading-Post Empires

Portuguese Trading Posts Portuguese mariners built the earliest trading-post empire. Their goal was not to conquer territories but to control trade routes by forcing merchant vessels to call at fortified trading sites and pay duties there. Vasco da Gama obtained permission from local authorities to establish a trading post at Calicut when he arrived there in 1498. By the mid–sixteenth century, Portuguese merchants had built more than fifty trading posts between west Africa and east Asia.

Afonso d'Alboquerque Equipped with heavy artillery, Portuguese vessels were able to overpower most other craft they encountered, and they sometimes trained their cannon effectively onshore. The architect of their aggressive policy was Afonso d'Alboquerque, commander of Portuguese forces in the Indian Ocean during the early sixteenth century. Alboquerque's fleets seized Hormuz in 1508, Goa

Afonso d'Alboquerque (al-FAWN-soo d'AL-buh-kur-kee)

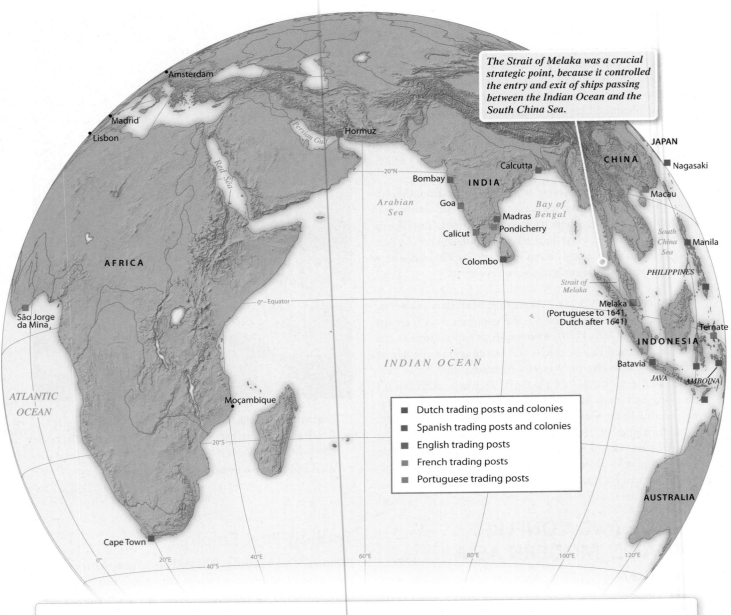

The Strait of Melaka was a crucial strategic point, because it controlled the entry and exit of ships passing between the Indian Ocean and the South China Sea.

■ Dutch trading posts and colonies
■ Spanish trading posts and colonies
■ English trading posts
■ French trading posts
■ Portuguese trading posts

MAP 19.3

European trading posts in Africa and Asia, ca. 1700. Note how many more trading posts there were in Asia than in Africa.

What accounts for the difference?

in 1510, and Melaka in 1511. From these strategic sites, Alboquerque sought to control Indian Ocean trade by forcing all merchant ships to purchase safe-conduct passes and present them at Portuguese trading posts. Ships without passes were subject to confiscation, along with their cargoes. Alboquerque's forces punished violators of his policy by executing them or cutting off their hands. Alboquerque was confident of Portuguese naval superiority and its ability to control trade in the Indian Ocean.

In reality, however, Portuguese forces did not have enough vessels to enforce their commander's orders. Arab, Indian, and Malay merchants continued to play prominent roles in Indian Ocean commerce, usually without taking the precaution of securing a safe-conduct pass. Indeed, Arab vessels continued to deliver shipments of pepper and spices through the Red Sea, which Portuguese forces never managed to control, to Cairo and Mediterranean trade routes.

Thinking about ENCOUNTERS

Trading Post Empires

Trading-post empires provided the most prominent spaces for cross-cultural interactions between Europeans, Africans, and Asians. Trading posts also limited European intrusion into Africa and Asia, especially in contrast to the settlement empires of the Americas. *What characterized the relations between, for example, the Portuguese and the inhabitants of the Indian Ocean basin? Why were Europeans confined to such posts?*

By the late sixteenth century, Portuguese hegemony in the Indian Ocean was growing weak. Portugal was a small country with a small population—about one million in 1500—and was unable to sustain its large seaborne trading empire. In addition, by the late sixteenth century, investors in other lands began to organize expeditions to Asian markets. Most prominent of those who followed the Portuguese into the Indian Ocean were English and Dutch mariners.

English and Dutch Trading Posts Like their predecessors, English and Dutch merchants built trading posts on Asian coasts and sought to channel trade through them, but they did not attempt to control shipping on the high seas. They also occasionally seized Portuguese sites, although Portuguese authorities held many of their trading posts into the twentieth century. Meanwhile, English and Dutch entrepreneurs established parallel networks. English merchants concentrated on India and built trading posts at Bombay, Madras, and Calcutta, while the Dutch operated more broadly from Cape Town, Colombo, and Batavia (modern Jakarta on the island of Java).

English and Dutch merchants enjoyed two main advantages over their Portuguese predecessors. They sailed faster, cheaper, and more powerful ships, which offered both an economic and a military edge over their competitors. Furthermore, they conducted trade through an exceptionally efficient form of commercial organization—the joint-stock company—which enabled investors to realize handsome profits while limiting the risk to their investments.

The Trading Companies English and Dutch merchants formed two especially powerful joint-stock companies: the English East India Company, founded in 1600, and its Dutch counterpart, the United East India Company, known from its initials as the VOC (Vereenigde Oost-Indische Compagnie), established in 1602. Private merchants advanced funds to launch these companies, outfit them with ships and crews, and provide them with commodities and money to trade. Although they enjoyed government support, the companies were privately owned enterprises. Unhampered by political oversight, company agents concentrated strictly on profitable trade. Their charters granted them the right to buy, sell, build trading posts, and even make war.

The English and Dutch companies experienced immediate financial success. In 1601, for example, five English ships set sail from London with cargoes mostly of gold and silver coins valued at thirty thousand pounds sterling. When they returned in 1603, the spices that they carried were worth more than one million pounds sterling. Because of their advanced nautical technology, powerful military arsenal, efficient organization, and relentless pursuit of profit, the English East India Company and the VOC contributed to the early formation of a global network of trade.

European Conquests in Southeast Asia

Following voyages of exploration to the western hemisphere, Europeans conquered indigenous peoples, built territorial empires, and established colonies settled by European migrants. In the eastern hemisphere, however, they were mostly unable to force their will on large Asian populations and powerful centralized states. With the decline of the Portuguese effort to control shipping in the Indian Ocean, Europeans mostly traded peacefully in Asian waters alongside Arab, Indian, Malay, and Chinese merchants.

Yet in two island regions of southeast Asia—the Philippines and Indonesia—Europeans conquered existing authorities and imposed their rule. Though densely populated, neither the Philippines nor Indonesia had a powerful state when Europeans arrived there in the sixteenth century. Nor did imperial authorities in China or India lay claim to the island regions. Heavily armed ships enabled Europeans to bring overwhelming force to bear and to establish imperial regimes that favored the interests of European merchants.

Conquest of the Philippines Spanish forces approached the Philippines in 1565 under the command of Miguel López de Legazpi, who named the islands after King Philip II of Spain. Because the Philippines had no central government, there was no organized resistance to the intrusion. By 1575 Spanish forces controlled the coastal regions of the central and northern islands, and during the

Miguel López de Legazpi (mee-GEHL LOH-pess de le-GAHS-pee)

The spice trade.
Harvesting mace on the island of Lontor in the Banda Islands.

seventeenth century they extended their authority to most parts of the archipelago except the southern island of Mindanao, where a large Muslim community stoutly resisted Spanish expansion.

Manila Spanish policy in the Philippines revolved around trade and Christianity. Manila soon emerged as a bustling, multicultural port city—an entrepôt for trade, particularly in silk—and it quickly became the hub of Spanish commercial activity in Asia. Chinese merchants were especially prominent in Manila. They occupied a specially designated commercial district of the city and supplied silk goods that Spanish traders shipped to Mexico in the Manila galleons. Their commercial success brought suspicion on the Chinese community, however, and resentful Spanish and Filipino residents massacred Chinese merchants in several eruptions of violence over the next few hundred years. Meanwhile, the Spanish also sought to Christianize the Philippines. Spanish rulers and missionaries pressured prominent Filipinos to convert to Christianity in hopes of persuading

others to follow their example. They opened schools to teach the fundamentals of Christian doctrine, along with basic literacy, in densely populated regions throughout the islands. Although Spanish missionaries initially faced resistance, over the long term Filipinos turned increasingly to Christianity, and by the nineteenth century the Philippines had become one of the most fervent Roman Catholic lands in the world.

Conquest of Java Dutch mariners who imposed their rule on the islands of Indonesia did not worry about seeking converts to Christianity but concentrated instead on the trade in spices, particularly cloves, nutmeg, and mace. The architect of Dutch policy was Jan Pieterszoon Coen, who in 1619 founded Batavia on the island of Java to serve as an entrepôt for the VOC. Coen's plan was to establish a VOC monopoly over spice production and trade, thus enabling Dutch merchants to reap enormous profits in European markets. Coen brought his naval power to bear on the small Indonesian islands and forced them to deliver spices only to VOC merchants. By the late seventeenth century, the VOC controlled all the ports of Java as well as most of the important spice-bearing islands throughout the Indonesian archipelago.

Dutch numbers were too few for them to rule directly over their whole southeast Asian empire. They made alliances with local authorities to maintain order in most regions, reserving only Batavia and the most important spice-bearing islands for direct Dutch rule. The Dutch did not embark on campaigns of conquest for purposes of adding to their holdings, but they uprooted spice-bearing plants on islands they did not control and mercilessly attacked peoples who sold their spices to merchants not associated with the VOC. Monopoly profits from the spice trade not only enriched the VOC but also made the Netherlands the most prosperous land in Europe throughout most of the seventeenth century.

Foundations of the Russian Empire in Asia

While western European peoples were building maritime empires, Russians were laying the foundations for a vast land empire that embraced most of northern Eurasia. This round of expansion began in the mid–sixteenth century, as Russian forces took over several Mongol khanates in central Asia. Those acquisitions resulted in Russian control over the Volga River and offered opportunities for trade with the Ottoman empire, Iran, and even India through the Caspian Sea. In the eighteenth century, Russian forces extended their presence in the Caspian Sea region by absorbing much of the Caucasus, a vibrant multiethnic region embracing the modern-day states of Georgia, Armenia, and Azerbaijan.

Mindanao (min-duh-NAH-oh)
Jan Pieterszoon Coen (yahn PEE-tuhr-sohn KOH-uhn)

Siberia Far more extensive were Russian acquisitions in northeastern Eurasia. The frozen tundras and dense forests of Siberia posed formidable challenges, but explorers and merchants made their way into the region in a quest for fur. In the late sixteenth century, Russian explorers pushed into the interior regions of Siberia by way of the region's great rivers. By 1639 they had made their way across the Eurasian landmass and reached the Pacific Ocean.

Native Peoples of Siberia Siberia was home to about twenty-six major ethnic groups that lived by hunting, trapping, fishing, or herding reindeer. These indigenous peoples varied widely in language and religion, and they responded in different ways to the arrival of Russian adventurers who sought to exact tribute from them by coercing them to supply animal pelts on a regular basis. Some groups readily accepted iron tools, woven cloth, flour, tea, and liquor for the skins of fur-bearing animals such as otter, lynx, and especially sable. Others resented the ever-increasing demands for tribute and resisted Russian encroachment on their lands. For example, the Yakut people of the Lena and Aldan river valleys in central Siberia mounted a revolt against Russian oppression in 1642. The Russian response was brutal: over a period of forty years, Russian forces drove many Yakut out of their settlements and reduced their population by an estimated 70 percent. Quite apart from military violence, the peoples of Siberia reeled from epidemic diseases that reduced many populations by more than half.

The Russian Occupation of Siberia Despite the region's harsh climate, Russian migrants—some of whom were social misfits or convicted criminals—gradually filtered into Siberia and thoroughly altered its demographic complexion. Small agricultural settlements grew up near many trading posts, particularly in the fertile Amur River valley. Over time, Siberian trading posts developed into Russian towns with Russian-speaking populations attending Russian Orthodox churches. By 1763 some 420,000 Russians lived in Siberia, nearly double the number of indigenous inhabitants. In the nineteenth century, large numbers of additional migrants moved east to mine Siberian gold, silver, copper, and iron, and the Russian state was well on the way toward consolidating its control over the region.

European Commercial Rivalries

Exploration and imperial expansion led to conflicts not only between Europeans and Asians but also among the Europeans. Mariners competed vigorously for trade in Asia and the Americas, and their efforts to establish markets—and sometimes monopolies—led frequently to clashes with their counterparts from different lands.

Competition and Conflict Indeed, throughout the seventeenth and early eighteenth centuries, commercial and political rivalries led to running wars between ships flying different flags. Dutch vessels were most numerous in the Indian Ocean, and they enabled the VOC to dominate the spice trade. Dutch forces expelled most Portuguese merchants from southeast Asia and prevented English mariners from establishing secure footholds there. By the early eighteenth century, trade in Indian cotton and tea from Ceylon had begun to overshadow the spice trade, and English and French merchants working from trading posts in India became the dominant carriers in the Indian Ocean. Fierce competition again generated violence: in 1746 French forces seized the English trading post at Madras, one of the three principal centers of British operations in India.

Commercial competition led to conflict also in the Caribbean and the Americas. English pirates and privateers preyed on Spanish shipping from Mexico, often seizing vessels carrying cargoes of silver. English and French forces constantly skirmished and fought over sugar islands in the Caribbean while also contesting territorial claims in North America. In addition, almost all conflicts between European states in the eighteenth century spilled over into the Caribbean and the Americas.

ECOLOGICAL EXCHANGES

European explorers and those who followed them established links between all lands and peoples of the world. Interaction between peoples in turn resulted in an unprecedented volume of exchange across the boundary lines of societies and cultural regions. Some of that exchange involved biological species: plants, food crops, animals, human populations, and disease pathogens all spread to regions they had not previously visited. These biological exchanges had differing and dramatic effects on human populations, destroying some of them through epidemic diseases while enlarging others through increased food supplies and richer diets. Commercial exchange also flourished in the wake of the voyages of exploration as European merchants traveled to ports throughout the world in search of trade. Indeed, by the mid–eighteenth century they had established globe-girdling networks of trade and communication.

The Columbian Exchange

Biological Exchanges Processes of biological exchange were prominent features of world history well before modern times. The early expansion of Islam, for example, had facilitated the diffusion of plants and food crops throughout much of the eastern hemisphere during the period from about 700 to 1100 C.E., some of which helped spark demographic and economic growth in the lands where they took

MAP 19.4
Russian expansion, 1462–1795. Observe how vast the empire became after it added the territory of Siberia.

How did Russians exert their control over such a huge and unforgiving territory?

The distance from Moscow to Yakutsk in Siberia is approximately 3,050 miles.

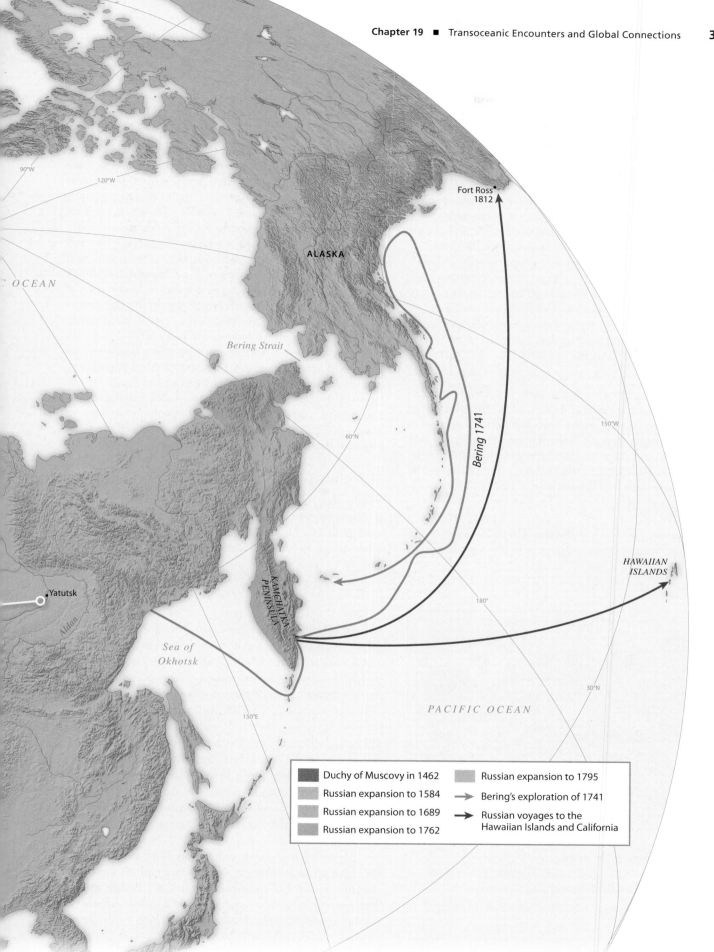

PART 5

Fort Ross•
1812

ALASKA

Bering Strait

Bering 1741

90°W

120°W

...C OCEAN

60°N

150°W

HAWAIIAN
ISLANDS

Yatutsk

KAMCHATKA
PENINSULA

Aldan

180°

30°N

Sea of
Okhotsk

150°E

PACIFIC OCEAN

	Duchy of Muscovy in 1462		Russian expansion to 1795
	Russian expansion to 1584	→	Bering's exploration of 1741
	Russian expansion to 1689	→	Russian voyages to the Hawaiian Islands and California
	Russian expansion to 1762		

Reverberations ●●●●●●●●

Short-Term and Long-Term Effects of the Columbian Exchange

Some events or processes in the global past are so momentous that they produce social, political, economic, or environmental changes for centuries— even in places thousands of miles from their points of origin. In other words, we can see the *reverberations* of these events or processes in multiple places and in multiple timelines after they occur. Understanding the spectrum of consequences spurred by such momentous events and processes can help us trace the historical connections between the world's people and places, even when such connections may not have been obvious to people living at the time.

Although the European mariners who first came into contact with the people, flora, and fauna of the Americas could not have understood it at the time, their encounters set in motion a process that permanently transformed not just the Americas but the entire world in ways that are still relevant today. Two facets of the exchange demonstrate how this was so: disease and the transfer of flora and fauna.

Disease

In this chapter we have already seen the devastating effect of disease on populations indigenous to the Americas, with scholars estimating between 50 and 90 percent mortality across the entire region. Such high mortality was a key factor in allowing European invaders to conquer, settle, and expand throughout the Americas—a process discussed in chapter 21. In other words, if disease had not ravaged indigenous populations, it seems likely that Europeans would not have been able to use American lands for their own purposes on such a large scale, and also that the population of the present-day Americas would be composed of many more peoples whose ancestors were native to the area. A longer-term consequence of disease during the Columbian exchange was that there were simply not enough laborers in large parts of the Americas to carry out the work required by large-scale agricultural enterprises developed by Europeans after conquest. As a result, first the Portuguese and then many other Europeans began to import African labor to the Americas, a process discussed in chapter 22. The Atlantic slave trade, in turn, had profound effects on enslaved individuals, the African states involved, and the eventual composition of populations in the Americas.

Flora and Fauna

In this chapter we have seen that the Columbian exchange involved extensive movement of plants and animals between Eurasia and the Americas. Over the long term, these exchanges transformed landscapes around

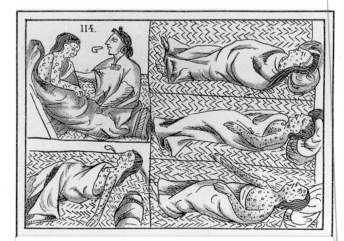

Epidemic disease in the Americas.
Smallpox victims in the Aztec empire. The disease killed most of those it infected and left disfiguring scars on survivors.

According to this depiction, what were the symptoms of smallpox?

root. Yet the *Columbian exchange*—the global diffusion of plants, food crops, animals, human populations, and disease pathogens that took place after voyages of exploration by Christopher Columbus and other European mariners— had consequences much more profound than earlier rounds of biological exchange. Unlike earlier processes, the Columbian exchange involved lands with radically different flora, fauna, and diseases. For thousands of years the various species of the eastern hemisphere, the western hemisphere, and Oceania had evolved along separate lines. By creating links between these biological zones, the European voyages of exploration set off a round of biological exchange that permanently altered the world's human geography and natural environment.

Beginning in the early sixteenth century, infectious and contagious diseases brought sharp demographic losses to indigenous peoples of the Americas and the Pacific islands. The worst scourge was smallpox, but measles, diphtheria, whooping cough, and influenza also took heavy tolls. Before

the world by introducing plant and animal species that became invasive in their new environments (such as dandelions in the Americas or pigs on the island of Barbados). Some introductions to the Americas, like the horse, brought about fundamental cultural changes. For example, Plains Indians adopted horses in order to hunt wild game more effectively, resulting in dramatic changes in gender ideologies and lifestyle (chapter 21). Products that originated in the Americas also had a profound impact on other parts of the world. For example, nutritional foods native to the Americas—including potatoes, corn, and sweet potatoes—helped spur population growth in places like China (chapter 23) that were not involved in the initial process of exchange at all. Nonfood crops were important to the Columbian exchange as well: tobacco, introduced from the Americas, was widely and quickly integrated into the cultures of both Europe (chapter 20) and the Islamic empires (chapter 24). In fact, in just a little more than one hundred years after being introduced to tobacco for the first time, Europeans had introduced tobacco to Europe, Asia, west Africa, and the Near East. In the present, approximately 1.1 billion of the world's people are smokers, and about 25 percent of smokers die from smoke-related causes.

These are only a small sampling of the historical reverberations of the Columbian exchange, both through time and across space. When reading subsequent chapters, try to identify additional developments that may have their origins in this truly momentous process.

Tabacum latifolium.

Tobacco. Tobacco was long used for religious and spiritual purposes in the Americas. After their arrival in the Americas, Europeans quickly popularized tobacco as a trade item and as a recreational drug to be smoked, snuffed, or chewed.

the voyages of exploration, none of the peoples of the western hemisphere or Oceania possessed inherited or acquired immunities to those pathogens. In the eastern hemisphere, these diseases were endemic: they claimed a certain number of victims from the ranks of infants and small children, but survivors gained immunity to the diseases through exposure at an early age. In some areas of Europe, for example, smallpox was responsible for 10 to 15 percent of deaths, but most victims were age ten or younger. Although its individual effects were tragic, smallpox did not pose a threat to European society as a whole because it did not carry away economically and socially productive adults.

Epidemic Diseases and Population Decline When infectious and contagious diseases traveled to previously unexposed populations, however, they touched off ferocious epidemics that sometimes destroyed entire societies. Beginning in 1519, epidemic smallpox ravaged the Aztec empire in combination with other diseases. Although scholars do not agree about the scale of mortality because preconquest population data are incomplete, many believe that within a century the indigenous population of Mexico had declined by as much as 90 percent, from about 17 million to 1.3 million. By that time Spanish conquerors had imposed their rule on Mexico, and the political, social, and cultural traditions of the indigenous peoples had either disappeared or fallen under Spanish domination.

Imported diseases took their worst tolls in densely populated areas such as the Aztec and Inca empires, but they did not spare other regions. Smallpox and other diseases were so easily transmissible that they raced to remote areas of North and South America and sparked epidemics well before the first European explorers arrived in those regions. By the 1530s smallpox may have spread as far from Mexico as the Great Lakes in the north and the pampas of Argentina in the south.

When introduced to the Pacific islands, infectious and contagious diseases struck vulnerable populations with the

Thinking about **TRADITIONS**

Local Foodways

For millennia, humans had generally relied on locally tended crops and foraged foods for their sustenance. *How did the Columbian exchange alter those traditional foodways? What new crops and animals traveled between the eastern and western hemispheres—and what were the consequences?*

same horrifying effects as in the Americas. All told, disease epidemics sparked by the Columbian exchange probably caused the worst demographic calamity in all of world history. Between 1500 and 1800, upward of 100 million people may have died of diseases imported into the Americas and Pacific islands.

Food Crops and Animals Over a longer term, however, the Columbian exchange increased rather than diminished human population because of the global spread of food crops and animals that it sponsored. In the long term, a better-nourished world was an important contributing factor in the growth of the world's population, which began in the eighteenth century and has continued to the present. Out of Eurasia to the western hemisphere traveled wheat, rice, sugar, bananas, apples, cherries, peaches, peas, and citrus fruits. Africa contributed yams, okra, collard greens, and coffee. Animals like horses, cattle, pigs, sheep, goats, and chickens also went from Europe to the Americas, where they sharply increased supplies of food and animal energy.

Food crops native to the Americas also played prominent roles in the Columbian exchange. American crops that took root in Africa, Asia, and Europe include maize, potatoes, beans, tomatoes, peppers, peanuts, manioc, papayas, guavas, avocados, tobacco, pineapples, and cacao, to name only a few. Residents of the eastern hemisphere only gradually developed a taste for American crops, but by the eighteenth century maize and potatoes had contributed to a sharply increased number of calories in Eurasian diets. In tropical regions, peanuts and manioc flourished in soils that otherwise would not produce large yields or support large populations.

Population Growth The Columbian exchange of plants and animals fueled a surge in world population. In 1500, as Eurasian peoples were recovering from epidemic bubonic plague, world population stood at about 425 million. By 1600 it had increased more than 25 percent, to 545 million. By 1750 human population stood at 720 million, and by

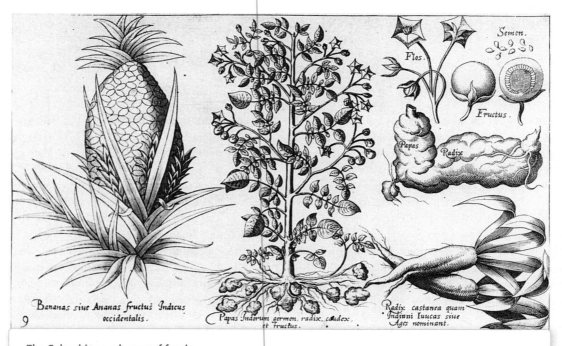

The Columbian exchange of foods.
Illustrations in an early-seventeenth-century book depict pineapple, potatoes, and cassava—all plants native to the Americas and unknown to Europeans before the sixteenth century.

1800 it had surged to 900 million, having grown by almost 50 percent during the previous century. Much of the rise was due to the increased nutritional value of diets enriched by the global exchange of food crops and animals.

Migration Alongside disease pathogens and plant and animal species, the Columbian exchange involved the spread of human populations through transoceanic migration, whether voluntary or forced. During the period from 1500 to 1800, the largest contingent of migrants consisted of enslaved Africans transported involuntarily to the Americas. A smaller migration involved Europeans who traveled to the Americas and settled in lands depopulated by infectious and contagious diseases. During the nineteenth century, European peoples traveled in huge numbers to the western hemisphere and also to south Africa, Australia, and Pacific islands, and Asian peoples migrated to tropical and subtropical destinations throughout much of the world. In combination, those migrations have profoundly influenced modern world history.

The Manila galleons
An artist's rendering of a Spanish galleon. Galleons were large, multidecked, highly stable and maneuverable sailing ships used by Europeans for war or commerce. The Spanish and the Portuguese built the largest types for their profitable overseas trade.

The Origins of Global Trade

The trading-post empires established by Portuguese, Dutch, and English merchants linked Asian markets with European consumers and offered opportunities for European mariners to participate in the carrying trade within Asia. Indeed, by the late sixteenth century, European merchants carrying carpets, spices, silks, and silver were as prominent as Arabs in the trading world of the Indian Ocean basin.

Transoceanic Trade Besides stimulating commerce in the eastern hemisphere, the voyages of European merchant mariners encouraged the emergence of a genuinely global trading system. As Europeans established colonies in the Caribbean and the Americas, for example, trade networks extended to all corners of the Atlantic Ocean basin. European manufactured goods traveled west across the Atlantic in exchange for silver from Mexican and Peruvian mines and agricultural products such as sugar and tobacco, both of which were in high demand among European consumers. Trade in human beings also figured in Atlantic commerce. European manufactured goods went south to west Africa, where merchants exchanged them for African slaves, who then went to the tropical and subtropical regions of the western hemisphere to work on plantations.

The Manila Galleons The experience of the Manila galleons illustrates the early workings of the global economy in the Pacific Ocean basin. For 250 years, from 1565 to 1815, Spanish galleons—sleek, fast, heavily armed ships capable of carrying large cargoes—regularly plied the waters of the Pacific Ocean between Manila in the Philippines

and Acapulco on the west coast of Mexico. From Manila they took Asian luxury goods to Mexico and exchanged them for silver. Most of the precious metal made its way to China, where a thriving domestic economy demanded increasing quantities of silver. Meanwhile, some of the Asian luxury goods from Manila remained in Mexico or went to Peru, where they contributed to a comfortable way of life for Spanish ruling elites. Most, however, went overland across Mexico and then traveled by ship across the Atlantic to Spain and European markets.

Environmental Effects of Global Trade As silver lubricated growing volumes of global trade, pressures increased on several animal species that had the misfortune to become commodities on the world market. Fur-bearing animals came under particularly intense pressure, as hunters sought their pelts for sale to consumers in China, Europe, and North America. During the seventeenth century, an estimated two hundred to three hundred thousand sable pelts flowed annually from Siberia to the global market, and during the eighteenth century, more than sixteen million North American beaver pelts fed consumers' demands for fur hats and cloaks. Wanton hunting of fur-bearing animals soon drove many species into extinction or near extinction, permanently altering the environments they had formerly inhabited. Early modern hunters also harvested enormous numbers of deer, codfish, whales, walruses, and seals as merchants sought to supply animal products for global consumers.

In the seventeenth and eighteenth centuries, the volume of global trade expanded rapidly. During the seventeenth century, for example, Dutch merchants imported, among other commodities, wheat from south Africa, cowry shells from India, and sugar from Brazil. The wheat fed domestic consumers, who increasingly worked as merchants, bankers, or manufacturers rather than as cultivators. English, Dutch, and other merchants eagerly purchased the cowry shells—which served as currency in much of sub-Saharan Africa—and exchanged them for slaves destined for plantations in the western hemisphere. The sugar went on the market at Amsterdam and found its way to consumers throughout Europe. And that was just the beginning. By 1750 all parts of the world except Australia participated in global networks of commercial relations in which European merchant mariners played prominent roles.

SUMMARY

Global commercial and biological exchanges arose from the efforts of European mariners to explore the world's waters and establish sea-lanes that would support long-distance trade. Their search for sea routes to Asia led them to the western hemisphere and the vast expanse of the Pacific Ocean. The geographic knowledge that they accumulated enabled them to link the world's regions into a finely articulated network of trade. But commercial exchange was not the only result of this global network. Food crops, animal stocks, disease pathogens, and human migrants also traveled the sea-lanes and dramatically influenced societies throughout the world. Transplanted crops and animal species led to improved nutrition and increasing populations throughout the eastern hemisphere. Epidemics sparked by unfamiliar disease pathogens ravaged indigenous populations in the Americas and the Pacific islands. Mass migrations of human communities transformed the social and cultural landscape of the Americas and encouraged increased mingling of the world's peoples. The European voyages of exploration, transoceanic trade networks, and the Columbian exchange pushed the world's regions toward interdependence and global integration.

STUDY TERMS

Afonso d'Alboquerque (357)
astrolabe (352)
Bartolomeu Dias (354)
Captain James Cook (357)
Ceuta (354)
Christopher Columbus (354–355)
Columbian exchange (361–364)
cross-staff (352)
East India Company (359)
epidemic disease (361, 365)
Ferdinand Magellan (355)
Guanahani (354)
Jan Pieterszoon Coen (360)

joint-stock company (359)
magnetic compass (352)
Manila galleons (367)
Miguel López de Legazpi (359)
Mindanao (360)
Prince Henry the Navigator (354)

São Jorge de Mina (354)
Taino (354)
Vasco da Gama (354)
Vitus Bering (357)
VOC (359–361)
Volta do mar (353–354)

FOR FURTHER READING

David R. Abernathy. *The Dynamics of Global Dominance: European Overseas Empires, 1415–1980*. New Haven, 2000. A survey of the rise and decline of European overseas empires during a period of more than five hundred years.

Rene J. Barendse. *The Arabian Seas*. Eastgate, N.Y., 2002. A path-breaking and complex work that emphasizes the long predominance of Asia in the world economy.

Francisco Bethencourt and Diogo Curto, eds. *Portuguese Overseas Expansion*. New York, 2007. A collection of essays provides an overview of Portuguese maritime expansion between 1400 and 1800.

K. N. Chaudhuri. *Trade and Civilisation in the Indian Ocean: An Economic History from the Rise of Islam to 1750*. Cambridge, 1985. A brilliant analysis that places the European presence in the Indian Ocean in its larger historical context.

Christopher Columbus. *The Diario of Christopher Columbus's First Voyage to America*. Trans. by Oliver Dunn and James E. Kelley Jr. Norman, Okla., 1989. A careful translation.

Alfred W. Crosby. *The Columbian Exchange: Biological and Cultural Consequences of 1492*. Westport, Conn., 1972. Focuses on early exchanges of plants, animals, and diseases between Europe and America.

Antonio Pigafetta. *Magellan's Voyage: A Narrative Account of the First Circumnavigation*. 2 vols. Trans. by R. A. Skelton. New Haven, 1969. Valuable account by a crewman on Magellan's circumnavigation of the world.

John F. Richards. *The Unending Frontier: An Environmental History of the Early Modern World*. Berkeley, 2003. Thoroughly explores the environmental effects of the global historical processes that shaped the early modern world.

Stuart B. Schwartz, ed. *Implicit Understandings: Observing, Reporting, and Reflecting on the Encounters between Europeans and Other Peoples in the Early Modern Era*. Cambridge, 1994. Fascinating collection of essays by specialists on cross-cultural perceptions in early modern times.

Yuri Slezkine. *Arctic Mirrors: Russia and the Small Peoples of the North*. Ithaca, N.Y., 1994. Thoughtful analysis of Russian relations with the hunting, fishing, and herding peoples of Siberia.

The Transformation of Europe

CHAPTER 20

This detail from a sixteenth-century painting by François Dubois depicts the brutal murder of French Protestants in Paris during the St. Bartholomew's Day Massacre on August 23, 1572.

EYEWITNESS:
Martin Luther Challenges the Church

In 1517 an obscure German monk posed a challenge to the Roman Catholic church. Martin Luther of Wittenberg denounced the church's sale of indulgences, a type of pardon that excused individuals from doing penance for their sins. Indulgences had been available since the eleventh century, but to raise funds for the reconstruction of St. Peter's basilica in Rome, church authorities began to market indulgences aggressively in the early sixteenth century. From their point of view, indulgences were splendid devices: they encouraged individuals to reflect piously on their behavior while also bringing large sums of money into the church's treasury.

To Martin Luther, however, indulgences were signs of greed, hypocrisy, and moral rot in the Roman Catholic church. Luther believed that no human being had the power to absolve individuals of their sins and grant them admission to heaven, so for him the sale of indulgences constituted a vast fraud. In October 1517, following academic custom, he offered to debate publicly with anyone who wished to dispute his views, and he denounced the sale of indulgences in a document called the *Ninety-five Theses*.

Luther did not nail his work to the church door in Wittenberg, although a popular legend credits him with that gesture, but news of the *Ninety-five Theses* spread instantly: within a few weeks, printed copies were available throughout Europe. Luther's challenge galvanized both strong support and severe criticism. Religious and political authorities seeking to maintain the established order were especially critical. Church officials judged Luther's views erroneous, and in 1520 Pope Leo X excommunicated him. In 1521 the Holy Roman emperor Charles V, a devout Roman Catholic, summoned Luther and demanded that he recant his views. Luther's response: "I cannot and will not recant anything, for it is neither safe nor right to act against one's conscience. Here I stand. I can do no other. God help me. Amen."

Martin Luther's challenge held enormous religious and political implications. Though expelled from the church, Luther still considered himself Christian, and he held religious services for a community of devoted followers. By the 1520s, religious dissent had spread through much of Germany and Switzerland. During the 1530s dissidents known as Protestants—because of their protest against the established order—organized movements also in France, England, the Low Countries, Italy, and Spain. By mid-century Luther's act of individual rebellion had mushroomed into the Protestant Reformation, which shattered the religious unity of western Christendom.

For all its unsettling effects, the Protestant Reformation was only one of several powerful movements that transformed European society during the early modern era. Another was the consolidation of strong centralized states, which took shape partly because of the Reformation. Between the sixteenth and eighteenth centuries, monarchs in western Europe took advantage of religious quarrels to tighten control over their societies. By the mid–eighteenth century, some rulers had concentrated so much power in their own hands that historians refer to them as absolute monarchs.

Alongside religious conflict and the building of powerful states, capitalism and early modern science profoundly influenced western European society in early modern times. Early capitalism encouraged European merchants

CHRONOLOGY

1473–1543	Life of Nicolaus Copernicus
1478	Foundation of the Spanish Inquisition
1483–1546	Life of Martin Luther
1517	Publication of the *Ninety-five Theses*
1540	Foundation of the Society of Jesus
1545–1563	Council of Trent
1564–1642	Life of Galileo Galilei
1571–1630	Life of Johannes Kepler
1618–1648	Thirty Years' War
1642–1727	Life of Isaac Newton
1643–1715	Reign of King Louis XIV
1648	Peace of Westphalia
1694–1778	Life of Voltaire
1723–1790	Life of Adam Smith

and manufacturers to reorganize their businesses in search of maximum efficiency. Early modern science challenged traditional ways of understanding the world and the universe and prompted European intellectuals to seek an entirely rational understanding of the natural world.

Thus between 1500 and 1800, western Europe underwent a thorough transformation. Although the changes were unsettling and often disruptive, they also strengthened European society. Indeed, by 1800 several European states had become especially powerful, wealthy, and dynamic. They stood poised to play major roles in world affairs during the nineteenth and twentieth centuries.

THE FRAGMENTATION OF WESTERN CHRISTENDOM

Although the peoples of western Europe spoke different languages and observed different customs, the church of Rome provided them with a common religious and cultural heritage. During the sixteenth and seventeenth centuries, however, revolts against the Roman Catholic church shattered the religious unity of western Europe. Followers of Martin Luther and other Protestant reformers established a series of churches independent of Rome, and Roman Catholic leaders strengthened their own church against the challengers. Throughout early modern times, religious controversies fueled social tensions.

The Protestant Reformation

Martin Luther Martin Luther (1483–1546) quickly attracted enthusiastic support from others who resented the policies of the Roman church. Luther was a talented writer, and he published scores of works condemning the Roman church. His cause benefited enormously from the printing press, which had first appeared in Europe in the mid–fifteenth century. A sizable literate public inhabited European cities and towns, and readers eagerly consumed printed works on religious as well as secular themes. Printed editions of Luther's writings appeared throughout Europe and sparked spirited debates on theological issues. His supporters

and his critics took their own works to the printers, and religious controversies kept the presses busy churning out pamphlets and treatises for a century and more. Luther attacked the Roman church for a wide range of abuses and called for thorough reform of Christendom. He advocated the closure of monasteries, translation of the Bible from Latin into vernacular languages, and an end to priestly authority, including the authority of the pope himself. Most important, Luther believed that salvation could never be earned through good works or through the prayers of others. Instead, he argued, humans could be saved only through faith in the promises of God as revealed in the Bible. This idea of "justification by faith alone" became the core of Protestant belief. When opponents pointed out that Luther's reform program ran counter to church policy, he rejected the authority of the church hierarchy and proclaimed that the Bible was the only source of Christian religious authority.

Reform outside Germany Luther's works drew an enthusiastic popular response, and in Germany they fueled a movement to reform the church along the lines of Luther's teachings. Lay Christians flocked to hear Luther preach in Wittenberg, and several princes of the Holy Roman Empire warmed to Luther's views—partly because of personal conviction but partly also because religious controversy offered opportunities for them to build their own power bases. Although German enthusiasm for Lutheranism was not monolithic, nevertheless many of the most important German cities—Strasbourg, Nuremberg, and Augsburg, among others—passed laws requiring all religious services

---

vernacular (ver-NA-kyoo-lar)

to follow Protestant doctrine and procedures during the 1520s and 1530s. By the mid–sixteenth century about half the German population had adopted Lutheran Christianity, and reformers had launched Protestant movements and established alternative churches in other lands as well. By the late 1520s the prosperous cities of Switzerland—Zurich, Basel, and Geneva—had fledgling Protestant churches. The heavily urbanized Low Countries also responded enthusiastically to Protestant appeals. Protestants appeared even in Italy and Spain, although authorities in those lands handily suppressed their challenge to the Roman church.

John Calvin Meanwhile, an even more influential reformation was taking shape in France and French-speaking Switzerland. The initiator was a French lawyer, John Calvin (1509–1564), who in the 1530s converted to Protestant Christianity. Because the French monarchy sought to suppress Protestants, Calvin moved to French-speaking Geneva in Switzerland, where he organized a tight-knit Protestant community. Calvin also composed an influential treatise, *Institutes of the Christian Religion* (first published in 1536), that presented Protestant teachings as a coherent and organized package. Although Calvin believed in the basic elements of Luther's Protestant teachings, his ideas differed from those of Luther in important ways. Most fundamentally, Calvin emphasized the awesome power of God more than Luther did. Indeed, he believed not only that humans could never earn salvation but also that God had in fact already determined which individuals would be saved from damnation before they were even born. These individuals, known as "the elect," were predestined to salvation regardless of their deeds on earth. This doctrine of "predestination," as it became known, grew increasingly important to the Calvinist church in the generations after Calvin's death.

Calvin's Geneva was based on a strict code of morality and discipline. Calvinists were supposed to dress simply, to study the Bible regularly, and to refrain from activities such as playing cards and dancing. It was, in effect, a model Protestant community. Geneva also became an important missionary center from which Calvinist doctrine spread to other parts of Europe. Calvinist missionaries were most active in France, where they attracted strong interest in the cities, but they ventured also to Germany, the Low Countries, England, Hungary, and—most successfully—the Netherlands and Scotland.

The English Reformation In England a reformation took place for political as well as religious reasons. Lutherans and other Protestants worked to build a following in England from the 1520s on, but they faced stout government resistance until King Henry VIII (reigned 1509–1547) came into conflict with the pope. Henry wanted to divorce his wife, who had not borne a male heir, but the pope refused to allow him to do so. Henry's response was to sever relations with the Roman church and make himself supreme head of the Anglican church—an English pope, as it were. While Henry reigned, the theology of the English church changed little, but his successors replaced Roman Catholic with Protestant doctrines and rituals. By 1560 England had permanently left the Roman Catholic community. Indeed, by the late sixteenth century, Lutherans, Calvinists, and Anglicans in Europe had built communities large enough that a return to religious unity in western Christendom was inconceivable.

The Catholic Reformation

In response to the Protestant Reformation, Roman Catholic authorities undertook a wide-ranging reform effort of their own. Their purpose was to clarify differences between Roman and Protestant churches, to correct abuses within the church (such as the ability of wealthy men to purchase clerical offices), to persuade Protestants to return to the Roman church, and to deepen the sense of spirituality and religious commitment in their own community. Taken together, their efforts constituted the Catholic Reformation.

The Council of Trent Two institutions were especially important for defining the Catholic Reformation and advancing its goals—the Council of Trent and the Society of Jesus. The Council of Trent was an assembly of high church officials who met intermittently between 1545 and 1563 to address matters of doctrine and reform. During the meetings, the council defined the elements of Roman Catholic theology in detail. The council also took steps to reform the church by demanding that church authorities observe strict standards of morality and requiring them to establish schools and seminaries to prepare priests properly for their roles.

St. Ignatius of Loyola While the Council of Trent dealt with doctrine and reform, the Society of Jesus sought to extend the boundaries of the reformed Roman church. The society's founder was St. Ignatius Loyola (1491–1556), a Basque nobleman and soldier who in 1521 suffered a leg wound that ended his military career. While recuperating he read spiritual works and popular accounts of saints' lives, and he resolved to put his energy into religious work. In 1540, together with a small band of disciples, he founded the Society of Jesus.

The Society of Jesus Ignatius required that members of the society, known as Jesuits, complete a rigorous and advanced education in theology, philosophy, languages, history, literature, and science. As a result of that preparation, the Jesuits made extraordinarily effective missionaries. They also acquired a reputation for discipline and determination, and often served as counselors to kings and other rulers.

Thinking about TRADITIONS

The Creation of New Traditions

Until the early sixteenth century, most of Europe was culturally united by the common practice of Roman Christianity. As a result of the Reformation, however, European peoples formed new identities and traditions based on their practice of either reformed Roman Catholicism or the various Protestant faiths. *What makes it possible for well-established traditions to change over time, and how are new traditions created?*

They also were the most prominent of the early Christian missionaries outside Europe: in the wake of the European reconnaissance of the world's oceans, Jesuits attracted converts in India, China, Japan, the Philippines, and the Americas, thus making Christianity a genuinely global religion.

Witch Hunts and Religious Wars

Europeans took religion seriously in the sixteenth century, and religious divisions helped to fuel social and political conflict. Apart from wars, the most destructive violence that afflicted early modern Europe was the hunt for witches, which was especially prominent in regions, such as the Rhineland, where tensions between Protestants and Roman Catholics ran high.

Like many other peoples, Europeans had long believed that certain individuals possessed unusual or supernatural powers. During the late fifteenth century, theologians developed a theory that some of these people were witches who derived their powers—such as the ability to fly through the night on brooms or pitchforks—from the devil. Theorists believed that witches regularly flew off to distant places to attend the witches' Sabbath, a gathering that featured devil worship and the concoction of secret potions and culminated in sexual relations with the devil himself. Indeed, witchcraft became a convenient explanation for any unpleasant turn of events—failure of a crop, an unexpected death, or inability to conceive a child.

Witch-Hunting In the sixteenth and seventeenth centuries, fears that individuals were making alliances with the devil sparked a widespread hunt for witches. About 110,000 individuals underwent trial as suspected witches, and about 60,000 of them died either by hanging or by burning at the stake. Most of the victims—perhaps 95 percent—were poor, old, single, or widowed women who lived on the margins of their societies and thus were easy targets for accusers. Although the fear of witches had largely diminished by 1700, the intermittent pursuit of witches for the better part of two centuries revealed clearly the stresses and strains—both secular and religious—that afflicted European society during early modern times.

Religious Wars Religious tensions also led to outright war between Protestant and Roman Catholic communities. Religious wars wracked France for thirty-six years (1562–1598), for example, and they also complicated relations between Protestant and Roman Catholic states. In 1588 King Philip II of Spain (reigned 1556–1598) attempted to force England to return to the Roman Catholic church by sending the Spanish Armada—a huge flotilla consisting of 130 ships and 30,000 men—to dethrone the Protestant Queen Elizabeth. The effort collapsed, however, when English forces disrupted the Spanish fleet by

Witches' sabbath.
In this etching from 1620 c.e., the artist portrays women cavorting with the devil and concocting potions in a nocturnal gathering of witches.

sending blazing, unmanned ships into its midst. Then a ferocious gale scattered Spanish vessels throughout the North Sea.

Religious convictions also aggravated relations between the Netherlands and Spain by fueling the revolt of the Dutch provinces from their overlord, the king of Spain. In 1567 resistance escalated into a full-scale rebellion. By 1610 the seven northern provinces (the modern Netherlands) had won their independence and formed a republic known as the United Provinces, leaving ten southern provinces (modern Belgium) under Spanish and later Austrian rule until the late eighteenth century.

The Thirty Years' War The religious wars culminated in a great continental conflict known as the Thirty Years' War (1618–1648). The war opened after the Holy Roman emperor attempted to force his Bohemian subjects to return to the Roman Catholic church, and the main battleground was the emperor's territory in Germany. By the time the war ended, however, Spanish, French, Dutch, German, Swedish, Danish, Polish, Bohemian, and Russian forces had taken part in the conflict. The war itself was the most destructive European conflict before the twentieth century. Quite apart from violence and brutalities committed by undisciplined soldiers, the war damaged economies and societies throughout Europe and led to the deaths of about one-third of the German population. And though religious differences were not the only issues of the war, they complicated other issues and made them more difficult to resolve.

THE CONSOLIDATION OF SOVEREIGN STATES

Although fundamentally a religious movement, the Reformation had strong political implications, and centralizing monarchs readily made use of religious issues in their efforts to strengthen their states and enhance their authority. Indeed, after the devastation of the Thirty Years' War, rulers of these states devised a diplomatic system that sought to maintain order among the many independent and competitive European states.

The Attempted Revival of Empire

After the dissolution of the Carolingian empire in the ninth century C.E., there was no effective imperial government in western Europe. The Holy Roman Empire emerged in the tenth century, but its authority extended only to Germany and northern Italy, and even there its power was contested. During the early sixteenth century, it seemed that Emperor Charles V (reigned 1519–1556) might establish the Holy Roman Empire as the preeminent political authority in Europe, but by midcentury it was clear that there would be no revival of empire. Thus, unlike China, India, and the Ottoman empire, early modern Europe developed as a region of independent states.

Charles V After 1438 the Habsburg family, with extensive dynastic holdings in Austria, dominated the Holy Roman Empire. Through marriage alliances, the Habsburgs accumulated rights and titles to lands throughout Europe and beyond. Indeed, when Charles V became emperor in 1519, his empire stretched from Vienna in Austria to Cuzco in Peru. In spite of his far-flung holdings, Charles did not extend his authority throughout Europe. Part of the reason was that throughout his reign Charles had to devote much of his attention and energy to the Lutheran movement and to putting down imperial princes who took advantage of religious controversy to assert their independence. Foreign difficulties also played a role, because Charles's neighbors to the west and east—in France and the Ottoman empire, respectively—actively opposed the creation of a powerful Holy Roman Empire.

To ensure that Charles's territories remained in disarray, for example, the Roman Catholic French kings aided German Lutherans in their rebellion against the Holy Roman Empire. The French kings even allied with the Muslim Ottoman Turks against the emperor, who did not want a powerful Christian empire to threaten their holdings in eastern Europe and the Mediterranean basin.

Thus domestic and foreign problems prevented Charles V from establishing his vast empire as the supreme political authority in Europe. In 1556, disappointed especially in his inability to suppress the Lutherans in his territories, the emperor abdicated his throne and retired to a monastery in Spain. His empire did not survive. Charles bestowed his holdings in Spain, Italy, the Low Countries, and the Americas on his son, King Philip II of Spain, and his brother Ferdinand inherited the Habsburg family lands in Austria and the imperial throne.

The New Monarchs

In the absence of effective imperial power, public affairs fell to the various regional states that had emerged during the middle ages. In this period, however, the most powerful European states were the kingdoms of England, France, and Spain. During the late fifteenth and sixteenth centuries, rulers of these lands, known as the "new monarchs," marshaled their resources, curbed the nobility, and built strong centralized regimes.

Carolingian (kar-uh-LIHN-jee-uhn)

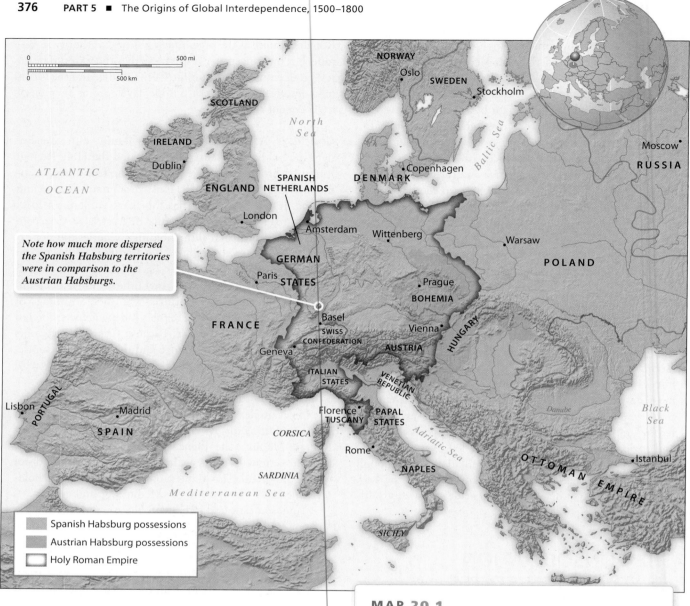

> Note how much more dispersed the Spanish Habsburg territories were in comparison to the Austrian Habsburgs.

Legend:
- Spanish Habsburg possessions
- Austrian Habsburg possessions
- Holy Roman Empire

MAP 20.1

Sixteenth-century Europe. Note the extent of Habsburg territories and the wide boundaries of the Holy Roman Empire.

With such powerful territories, what prevented the Habsburgs from imposing imperial rule on most of Europe?

Finance The new monarchs included Henry VIII of England, Louis XI and Francis I of France, and Fernando and Isabel of Spain. All the new monarchs sought to enhance their treasuries by developing new sources of finance. The French kings levied direct taxes on sales, households, and the salt trade. A new sales tax dramatically boosted Spanish royal income in the sixteenth century, and English kings increased revenues by raising fines and fees for royal services. Moreover, after Henry VIII severed ties between the English and Roman churches, he confiscated all church properties in England, which dramatically increased the size and wealth of the state.

State Power With their increased income the new monarchs enlarged their administrative staffs, which enabled them to collect taxes and implement royal policies more reliably than before. Increased wealth also allowed the new

monarchs to raise powerful armies when the need arose. That, in turn, resulted in increased control over the nobility, who could no longer compete with the power and wealth of the state.

The Spanish Inquisition The debates and disputes launched by the Protestant Reformation also helped monarchs increase their power. Whereas monarchs in Protestant lands—including England, much of Germany, Denmark, and Sweden—expropriated church wealth to expand their powers, others relied on religious justifications to advance

The Spanish Inquisition.

When the Spanish Inquisition detected traces of Protestant heresy, the punishment could be swift and brutal. In this engraving of about 1560, a large crowd observes the execution of heretics (top right) by burning at the stake.

Why were heretics burned rather than hung?

state ends. The Spanish Inquisition was the most distinctive institution of that kind. Fernando and Isabel founded the Spanish Inquisition in 1478, and they obtained papal license to operate the institution as a royal agency. Its original task was to ferret out those who secretly practiced Judaism or Islam, but Charles V charged it with responsibility also for detecting Protestant heresy in Spain.

Inquisitors had broad powers to investigate suspected cases of heresy. Popular legends have created an erroneous impression of the Spanish Inquisition as an institution running amok, framing innocent victims and routinely subjecting them to torture. In fact, inquisitors usually observed rules of evidence, and they released many suspects after investigation. Yet when they detected heresy, inquisitors could be ruthless. They sentenced hundreds of victims to hang from the gallows or burn at the stake and imprisoned many others for extended periods of time. Fear of the Inquisition deterred nobles from adopting Protestant views out of political ambition, and inquisitors also used their influence to silence those who threatened the Spanish monarchy. From 1559 to 1576, for example, inquisitors

imprisoned the archbishop of Toledo—the highest Roman Catholic church official in all of Spain—because of his political independence.

Constitutional States

During the seventeenth and eighteenth centuries, as they sought to restore order after the Thirty Years' War, European states developed along two lines. Rulers in England and the Netherlands shared authority with representative institutions and created constitutional states, whereas monarchs in France, Spain, Austria, Prussia, and Russia concentrated power in their own hands and created a form of state known as absolute monarchy.

Constitutional States During the seventeenth century the island kingdom of England and the maritime Dutch republic evolved governments that recognized rights pertaining to individuals and representative institutions. Their constitutional states took different forms: in England a constitutional monarchy emerged, whereas in the Netherlands a republic based on representative government emerged. In neither land did constitutional government come easily into being: in England it followed a civil war (1642–1649), and in the Netherlands it followed a long struggle for independence in the late sixteenth century. In both lands, however, constitutional government strengthened the state and provided a political framework that enabled merchants to flourish as never before in European experience.

The English Civil War Constitutional government came to England after political and religious disputes led to the English civil war. Politically, disputes arose between the king and the parliament over the king's ability to institute new taxes without parliamentary approval, while religious tensions between the Anglican king and a vocal group of zealous, reform-minded Calvinists in Parliament created a deep rift between the two branches of government. By 1641 King Charles I and Parliament were at loggerheads. Both sides raised armies. In the conflicts that followed, Parliamentary forces captured Charles and in 1649 executed him for tyranny. Yet English problems of government continued through a dictatorial Puritan regime as well as the restoration of the monarchy in 1660, until in 1688 Parliament deposed King James II and invited his daughter Mary and her Dutch husband, William of Orange, to assume the throne. The resulting arrangement provided that kings would rule in cooperation with Parliament, thus guaranteeing that nobles, merchants, and other constituencies would enjoy representation in government affairs. It also provided a momentous precedent in European affairs about the power of a people to replace its government if it is not perceived to be acting in the best interests of its people.

The Dutch Republic As in England, a combination of political and religious tensions led to conflict from which constitutional government emerged in the Netherlands. In the mid–sixteenth century, authority over the Low Countries, including modern-day Belgium as well as the Netherlands, rested with King Philip II of Spain. In 1566 Philip, a devout Roman Catholic, moved to suppress an increasingly popular Calvinist movement in the Netherlands—a measure that provoked large-scale rebellion against Spanish rule. In 1581 a group of Dutch provinces proclaimed themselves the independent United Provinces. Representative assemblies organized local affairs in each of the provinces,

The execution of King Charles I.
In this contemporary painting, the executioner holds up the just-severed head of King Charles I of England. The sight of a royal execution overcomes one woman, who faints (at bottom). © The Granger Collection, New York.

and on that foundation political leaders built a Dutch republic. Although Spain did not officially recognize the independence of the United Provinces until 1648, the Dutch republic was effectively organizing affairs in the northern Low Countries by the early seventeenth century.

In both England and the Dutch republic, merchants were especially prominent in political affairs, and state policy in both lands favored maritime trade and the building of commercial empires overseas. The constitutional states allowed entrepreneurs to pursue their economic interests with minimal interference from public authorities, and during the late seventeenth and eighteenth centuries both states experienced extraordinary prosperity as a result of those policies. Indeed, in many ways the English and Dutch states represented an alliance between merchants and rulers that worked to the benefit of both. Merchants supported the state with the wealth that they generated through trade—especially overseas trade—and rulers followed policies that looked after the interests of their merchants.

Absolute Monarchies

Whereas constitutional states devised ways to share power and authority, absolute monarchies stood on a theoretical foundation known as the divine right of kings. This theory held that kings derived their authority from God and served as "God's lieutenants upon earth." There was no role in divine-right theory for common subjects or even nobles in public affairs: the king made law and determined policy. In fact, absolute monarchs always relied on support from nobles and other social groups, but the claims of divine-right theory clearly reflected efforts at royal centralization.

The most conspicuous absolutist state was the French monarchy. The architect of French absolutism was a prominent church official, Cardinal Richelieu, who served as chief minister to King Louis XIII from 1624 to 1642. Richelieu worked systematically to undermine the power of the nobility and enhance the authority of the king. He destroyed nobles' castles and ruthlessly crushed aristocratic conspiracies. As a counterweight to the nobility, Richelieu built a large bureaucracy staffed by commoners loyal to the king. He also appointed officials to supervise the implementation of royal policy in the provinces.

The Sun King   The ruler who best epitomized royal absolutism was King Louis XIV (reigned 1643–1715). In fact, Louis XIV once reportedly declared that he was himself the state: "*l'état c'est moi.*" Known as *le roi soleil*—"the sun king"—Louis surrounded himself with splendor befitting one who ruled by divine right. During the 1670s he built a magnificent residence at Versailles, and in the 1680s he moved his court there. Louis's palace at Versailles was the largest building in Europe, with 230 acres of formal gardens and 1,400 fountains. All prominent nobles established residences at Versailles for their families and entourages. Louis strongly encouraged them to live at court, where he and his staff could keep an eye on them, and ambitious nobles gravitated there anyway in hopes of winning influence with the king. While nobles living at Versailles mastered the intricacies of court ritual and attended banquets, concerts, operas, balls, and theatrical performances, Louis and his ministers ran the state, maintained a huge army, waged war, and promoted economic development. In effect, Louis provided the nobility with luxurious accommodations and endless entertainment in exchange for absolute rule.

Richelieu (RISH-uh-loo)
Louis (LOO-ee)
Versailles (vehr-SEYE)

Versailles.
King Louis XIV and his entourage approach the main gate of Versailles (bottom right). Though only partially constructed at the time of this painting (1668), Versailles was already a spacious and luxurious retreat for Louis and his court.

Absolutism in Russia under Peter I Louis XIV was not the only absolute monarch of early modern Europe: Spanish, Austrian, and Prussian rulers embraced similar policies. Yet the potential of absolutism to increase state power was particularly conspicuous in the case of Russia, where tsars of the Romanov dynasty (1613–1917) tightly centralized government functions. Most important of the Romanov tsars was Peter I (reigned 1682–1725), widely known as Peter the Great, who inaugurated a thoroughgoing process of state transformation. Peter had a burning desire to transform Russia, a huge but underpopulated land, into a great military power like those that had recently emerged in western Europe. In 1697–1698 he led a large party of Russian observers on a tour of Germany, the Netherlands, and England to learn about western European administrative methods and military technology. His traveling companions often behaved crudely by western European standards: they consumed beer, wine, and brandy in quantities that astonished their hosts, and King William III sent Peter a bill for damages done by his entourage at the country house where they lodged in England.

On his return to Moscow, Peter set Russia spinning. He reformed the army by providing his forces with extensive training and equipping them with modern weapons. He ordered aristocrats to study mathematics and geometry so that they could calculate how to aim cannons accurately, and he began the construction of a navy. He also overhauled the government bureaucracy to facilitate tax collection and improve administrative efficiency. He even commanded his aristocratic subjects to wear western European fashions and ordered men to shave their traditional beards. These measures provoked spirited protest among those who resented the influence of western European ways. Yet Peter was so insistent on the observance of his policies that he reportedly went into the streets and personally hacked the beards off recalcitrants' faces. Perhaps the best symbol of his policies was St. Petersburg, a newly built seaport that Peter opened in 1703 to serve as a magnificent capital city and a haven for Russia's fledgling navy.

Catherine II and the Limits of Reform The most able of Peter's successors was Catherine II (reigned 1762–1796), also known as Catherine the Great. Like Peter, Catherine sought to make Russia a great power. She worked to improve governmental efficiency, and she promoted economic development in Russia's towns. For a while, she even worked to improve the conditions of Russia's oppressed peasantry by restricting the punishments—such as torture, beating, and mutilation—that noble landowners could inflict on the serfs who worked their lands.

Romanov (ruh-MAH-nuhf)
Yemelian Pugachev (yehm-eel-ian puh-gah-chehf)
Westphalia (west-FEY-lee-uh)

However, Catherine's interest in social reform cooled rapidly when it seemed to inspire challenges to her rule. She faced a particularly unsettling trial in 1773 and 1774, when a disgruntled former soldier named Yemelian Pugachev mounted a rebellion in the steppe lands north of the Caspian Sea. Pugachev raised a motley army of adventurers, exiles, peasants, and serfs who killed thousands of noble landowners and government officials before imperial forces crushed the uprising. Government authorities took the captured Pugachev to Moscow in chains, beheaded him, quartered his body, and displayed his parts throughout the city as a warning against rebellion. Thereafter, Catherine's first concern was the preservation of autocratic rule rather than the transformation of Russia according to western European models.

Thus, in Russia as in other European lands, absolutist policies resulted in tight centralization and considerable strengthening of the state. The enhanced power that flowed from absolutism became dramatically clear in the period 1772 to 1797, when Austria, Prussia, and Catherine II's Russia picked the weak kingdom of Poland apart. In a series of three "partitions," the predatory absolutist states seized Polish territory and absorbed it into their own realms, ultimately wiping Poland entirely off the map. The lesson of the partitions was clear: any European state that hoped to survive needed to construct an effective government that could respond promptly to challenges and opportunities.

The European States System

Whether they relied on absolutist or constitutional principles, European governments of early modern times built states much more powerful than those of their medieval predecessors. This round of state development led to difficulties within Europe, since conflicting interests fueled interstate competition and war. In the absence of an imperial authority capable of imposing and maintaining order in Europe, sovereign states had to find ways to resolve conflicts by themselves.

The Peace of Westphalia The Thirty Years' War demonstrated the chaos and devastation that conflict could bring. In an effort to avoid tearing their society apart, European states ended the Thirty Years' War with the Peace of Westphalia (1648), which laid the foundations for a system of independent, competing states. By the treaty's terms, the European states regarded one another as sovereign and equal. They also mutually recognized their rights to organize their own domestic and religious affairs and agreed that political and diplomatic affairs were to be conducted by states acting in their own interests. European religious unity had disappeared, and the era of the sovereign state had arrived.

The Peace of Westphalia did not bring an end to war. Indeed, war was almost constant in early modern Europe.

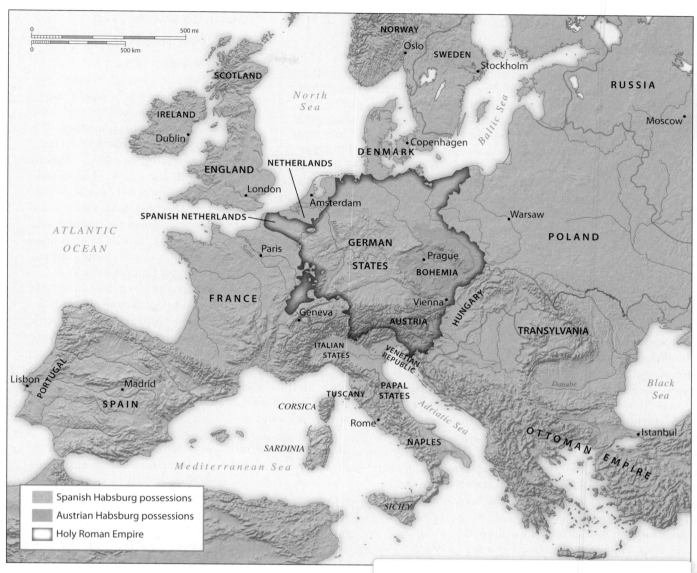

MAP 20.2

Europe after the Peace of Westphalia, 1648. Both England and the Netherlands became constitutional states with strong commercial interests. Compare this map with map 20.1.

How have the boundaries of the Holy Roman Empire changed, and why?

Most conflicts were minor affairs, but some grew to sizable proportions. Most notable among them were the wars of Louis XIV and the Seven Years' War. Between 1668 and 1713, the sun king sought to expand his borders east into Germany and to absorb Spain and the Spanish Netherlands into his kingdom. That prospect prompted England, the United Provinces, and Austria to mount a coalition against Louis. Later the Seven Years' War (1756–1763) pitted France, Austria, and Russia against Britain and Prussia, and it merged with conflicts between France and Britain in India and North America to become a global war for imperial supremacy.

The Balance of Power These shifting alliances illustrate the principal foundation of European diplomacy in early modern times—the balance of power. No ruler wanted to see another state dominate all the others. Thus, when any particular state began to wax strong, others formed coalitions against it. By playing balance-of-power politics, statesmen prevented the building of empires and ensured that Europe would be a land of independent, sovereign, competing states.

Military Development Frequent wars and balance-of-power diplomacy drained the resources of individual states but strengthened European society as a whole. European states competed vigorously and sought to develop the most

Reverberations of ● ● ● ● ● ● ● ●
The Columbian Exchange

In Europe, the Columbian exchange introduced new food crops that provided vital nutrition to ordinary people, which in turn helped fuel an impressive round of population growth across the region at precisely the same time indigenous American societies were devastated by European diseases. Yet European reliance on certain American food crops—especially the potato—would, over time, result in a dangerous dependency that led to famine when the crop failed, as it did in Ireland in 1845. Consider the ways that the exchange of items as seemingly mundane as new food crops can help shape historical developments over the long term, in both positive and negative ways.

expert military leadership and the most effective weapons for their arsenals. States organized military academies where officers received advanced education in strategy and tactics. Demand for powerful weapons stimulated the development of a sophisticated armaments industry. Gun foundries manufactured cannons of increasing size, range, power, and accuracy as well as small arms that allowed infantry to unleash withering volleys against their enemies.

In China, India, and Islamic lands, imperial states had little incentive to encourage similar technological innovation in the armaments industry. These states possessed the forces and weapons they needed to maintain order within their boundaries, and they rarely encountered foreign threats backed up with superior armaments. In Europe, however, failure to keep up with the latest improvements in arms technology could lead to defeat on the battlefield and decline in state power. Thus Europeans continuously sought to improve their military arsenals, and as a result, by the eighteenth century European armaments outperformed all others.

EARLY CAPITALIST SOCIETY

While the Protestant Reformation and the emergence of sovereign states brought religious and political change, a rapidly expanding population and economy encouraged the development of capitalism, which in turn led to a restructuring of European economy and society. Technologies of communication and transportation enabled businessmen to profit from distant markets, and merchants and manufacturers increasingly organized their affairs with the market rather than local communities in mind. Although capitalism generated considerable wealth, its effects were uneven and sometimes unsettling. Even in western Europe, where development and prosperity were most noticeable, early capitalism sometimes required painful adjustments to new conditions.

Population Growth and Urbanization

American Food Crops The foundation of European economic expansion in early modern times was a rapidly growing population, which reflected improved nutrition and decreasing mortality. The Columbian exchange enriched European diets by introducing new food crops to European fields and tables. Most notable of the introductions was the potato, which provided a welcome and inexpensive source of carbohydrates for peasants and laborers all over Europe. Other American crops, such as tomatoes and peppers, added vitamins and tangy flavor to European diets.

Since better-nourished populations are less susceptible to illness, new food crops also improved the overall resistance of Europeans to old diseases such as smallpox, dysentery, influenza, and typhus. Bubonic plague, a devastating epidemic killer during the fourteenth and fifteenth centuries, also receded from European society. Although plague made periodic appearances throughout the early modern era, epidemics were rare and isolated events after the mid–seventeenth century.

Population Growth and Urbanization Although European birthrates did not rise dramatically in early modern times, decreasing mortality resulted in rapid population growth. In 1500 the population of Europe, including Russia, was about 81 million. By 1700 the population had risen to 120 million, and in the next century it reached 180 million. Such rapid population growth drove a process of equally rapid urbanization. In the mid–sixteenth century, for example, the population of Paris was about 130,000, and that of London was about 60,000. A century later the populations of both cities had risen to 500,000. Other European cities also experienced rapid growth, including Madrid, Amsterdam, Berlin, Copenhagen, Dublin, Stockholm, and Vienna, to name only a few.

Early Capitalism and Protoindustrialization

The Nature of Capitalism Population growth and rapid urbanization helped spur a round of remarkable economic development. That economic growth coincided with the emergence of capitalism—an economic system in which private parties make their goods and services available on a free market and seek to take advantage of market conditions to profit from their activities. Private parties own the land, machinery, tools, equipment, buildings, workshops,

Thinking about ENCOUNTERS

Gaining Strength Through Competition

During the sixteenth and seventeenth centuries, the peoples of different European states frequently encountered one another through long and bloody wars. *Although such wars caused widespread destruction, in what ways did the constant competition between states also strengthen European society?*

and raw materials needed for production. Private parties also hire workers and decide for themselves what to produce: economic decisions are the prerogative of capitalist businessmen, not governments or social superiors. The center of a capitalist system is the market in which businessmen compete with one another, and the forces of supply and demand determine the prices received for goods and services. The goal is to realize handsome profits from these activities.

Supply and Demand The desire to accumulate wealth and realize profits was by no means new. Indeed, for several thousand years before the early modern era, merchants in China, southeast Asia, India, southwest Asia, the Mediterranean basin, and sub-Saharan Africa had pursued commercial ventures in hopes of realizing profits. During early modern times, however, European merchants and entrepreneurs transformed their society in a way that none of their predecessors had done. The capitalist economic order developed as businessmen learned to take advantage of market conditions in distant places via efficient networks of transportation and communication. For example, Dutch merchants might purchase cheap grain from Poland, store it in Amsterdam until they learned about a famine in the Mediterranean, and then transport it and sell it in southern France or Spain at an enormous profit.

Private parties organized an array of institutions and services to support early capitalism. Banks, for example, appeared in all the major commercial cities of Europe: they held funds on account for safekeeping and granted loans to merchants or entrepreneurs launching new business ventures. Insurance companies mitigated financial losses from risky undertakings such

as transoceanic voyages, and stock exchanges provided markets where investors could buy and sell shares in joint-stock companies and trade in other commodities as well.

Joint-Stock Companies Joint-stock companies were especially important institutions in early capitalist society. Large trading companies such as the English East India Company and its Dutch counterpart, the Vereenigde Oost-Indische Compagnie (VOC), spread the risks attached to expensive business enterprises and also took advantage of extensive communications and transportation networks. The trading companies organized commercial ventures on a larger scale than ever before in world history. They were the principal foundations of the global economy that emerged in early modern times, and they were the direct ancestors of contemporary multinational corporations.

Politics and Empire Capitalism did not develop in a political vacuum. On the contrary, it emerged with the active support of government authorities who saw a capitalist order as the one best suited to their individual and

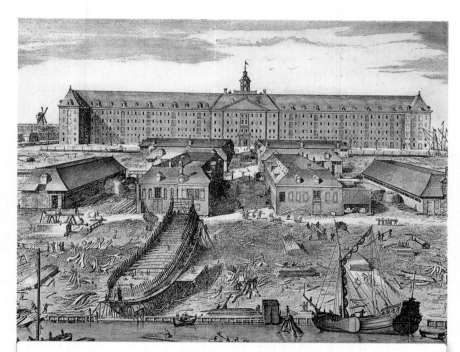

Dutch shipyard.
An anonymous engraving depicts workers building a massive, ocean-going sailing ship. In the seventeenth century, Dutch ships were inexpensive to operate, yet they accommodated abundant cargoes. © The Granger Collection, New York.

What kinds of cargoes were Dutch ships likely to carry in this period?

collective interests. Merchants were especially influential in the affairs of the English and Dutch states, so it is not surprising that these lands adopted policies that were most favorable to capitalist enterprises throughout the early modern era. The English and Dutch states recognized individuals' rights to possess private property and protected their financial interests. They also authorized joint-stock companies to explore and colonize distant lands in search of commercial opportunities. Indeed, imperial expansion and colonial rule were crucial for the development of capitalism, since they enabled European merchants to gain access to the natural resources and commodities that they distributed so effectively through their transportation networks.

The Putting-Out System Quite apart from its influence on trade and the distribution of goods, capitalism also encouraged European entrepreneurs to organize new ways to manufacture goods. For centuries, craft guilds had monopolized the production of goods such as textiles and metalwares in European towns and cities. Guilds fixed prices and wages, and sought not to realize profits so much as to protect markets and preserve their members' places in society. As a result, they actively discouraged competition. Because of this, capitalist entrepreneurs sidestepped the guilds and moved production into the countryside. There, they organized a "putting-out system" by which they delivered unfinished materials such as raw wool to rural households. Men and women in the countryside would spin and weave the wool into cloth and then cut and assemble the cloth into garments. The entrepreneur picked up the finished goods, paid the workers, and sold the items on the market for a handsome profit. The putting-out system represented an early effort to organize efficient industrial production, and some historians even refer to the seventeenth and eighteenth centuries as an age of "protoindustrialization."

Social Change in Early Modern Europe

Capitalist economic development brought unsettling change to European lands. In western Europe, the putting-out system introduced considerable sums of money into the countryside, which tended to undermine long-established patterns of rural life even as it brought material benefits such as improved food, clothing, and furnishings to rural households. Increased wealth meant that individuals suddenly acquired incomes that enabled them to become financially independent of their families and neighbors, and many feared that these individuals—especially young adults and women—might abandon their kin and way of life altogether as a result.

In eastern Europe, the putting-out system did not become a prominent feature of production, but early capitalism prompted deep social change there as well. Eastern Europe had very few cities in early modern times, so in agrarian states such as Poland, Bohemia, and Russia, most people had no alternative to working in the countryside. Landlords took advantage of this situation by forcing peasants to work under extremely harsh conditions.

Serfdom in Russia Russia in particular was a vast but sparsely populated empire with little trade or manufacturing. Out of a concern to retain the allegiance of the powerful nobles who owned most of Russia's land, the Romanov tsars restricted the freedoms of most Russian peasants and tied them to the land as serfs. The institution of serfdom had emerged in the early middle ages as a labor system that required peasants to provide labor services for landowners and prevented them from marrying or moving away without their landlords' permission. Although serfdom came to an end in western Europe after the fifteenth century, in eastern Europe landowners and rulers tightened restrictions on peasants during the sixteenth century. In Russia, for example, landlords commonly sold serfs to one another as if they were private property. In effect, the Romanovs won the support of the Russian nobles by ensuring them that laborers would be available to work their estates, which otherwise would have been worthless. Under these conditions, landlords operated estates with inexpensive labor and derived enormous incomes from the sale of agricultural products on the market.

These arrangements played crucial roles in the emergence of capitalism. In the larger economy of early modern Europe, eastern European lands produced agricultural products and raw materials based on semifree labor, which were then exported to western Europe to sustain its large and growing free wage labor force. Already by the early sixteenth century, consumers in the Netherlands depended for their survival on grains imported from Poland and Russia through the Baltic Sea. Thus it was possible for capitalism to flourish in western Europe only because the peasants and semifree serfs of eastern Europe provided inexpensive foods and raw materials that fueled economic development. From its earliest days, capitalist economic organization had implications for peoples and lands far removed from the centers of capitalism itself.

Profits and Ethics Capitalism also posed moral challenges. Medieval theologians had regarded profit making as morally dangerous, since profiteers looked to their own advantage rather than to the welfare of the larger community. But capitalism found advocates who sought to explain its principles and portray it as a socially beneficial form of economic organization. Most important of the early apostles of capitalism was the Scottish philosopher Adam Smith (1723–1790), who held that society would prosper when individuals pursued their own economic interests.

Nevertheless, prosperity was unattainable for all or even most early modern Europeans, which meant that the transition to capitalist economic practices was a long and painful process that generated deep social strains throughout Europe. Those strains often manifested themselves in violence: bandits plagued the countryside of early modern Europe, and muggers turned whole sections of large cities into danger zones. Some historians believe that witch-hunting activities reflected social tensions generated by early capitalism and that accusations of witchcraft represented hostility toward women who were becoming economically independent of their husbands and families.

The Nuclear Family In some ways capitalism favored the nuclear family as the principal unit of society. Although for centuries European couples had set up independent households, early capitalism offered further opportunities for independent families to increase their wealth by producing goods for sale on the market. As nuclear families became more important economically, they also became more socially and emotionally independent. Love between a man and a woman became a more important consideration in the making of marriages than the interests of the larger extended families, and affection between parents and their children became a more important ingredient of family life. Capitalism did not necessarily cause these changes in family life, but it may have encouraged developments that helped to define the nature and the role of the family in modern European society.

TRANSFORMATIONS IN SCIENTIFIC THINKING

While experiencing religious, political, economic, and social change, western Europe also underwent intellectual and cultural transformation. Astronomers and physicists rejected classical Greek and Roman authorities, whose theories had dominated scientific thought during the middle ages, and based their understanding of the natural world on direct observation and mathematical reasoning. During the seventeenth and eighteenth centuries, they elaborated a new vision of the earth and the larger universe in a process known as the scientific revolution. In the process, they weakened the influence of churches in western Europe and encouraged the development of secular values.

The Reconception of the Universe

The Ptolemaic Universe Until the seventeenth century, European astronomers based their understanding of the universe on the work of the Greek scholar Claudius Ptolemy of Alexandria. In the middle of the second century C.E., Ptolemy produced a work known as the *Almagest,* which envisioned a motionless earth surrounded by a series of nine hollow, concentric spheres that revolved around it.

Ptolemaic universe.
A woodcut illustration depicts the Ptolemaic universe with the earth at the center surrounded by spheres holding the planets and the stars.

Each of the first seven spheres had one of the observable heavenly bodies embedded in its shell. The eighth sphere held the stars, and an empty ninth sphere surrounded the whole cosmos and provided the spin that kept all the others moving. Beyond the spheres Christian astronomers located heaven, the realm of God.

Following Ptolemy, astronomers believed that the heavens consisted of a pure substance that did not experience change or corruption and was not subject to the physical laws that governed the world below the moon. They also held that heavenly bodies followed perfect circular paths in making their revolutions around the earth.

Planetary Movement This cosmology, however, did not mesh readily with the erratic movements of the planets, which sometimes slowed down, stopped, or even turned back on their courses. Astronomers went to great lengths to explain planetary behavior as the result of perfect circular movements. The result was an awkward series of adjustments

Ptolemaic (TAWL-oh-may-ihk)

Sources from the Past

Galileo Galilei, Letter to the Grand Duchess Christina

The Italian physicist and astronomer Galileo Galilei (1564–1642) was one of the most important European scientists in the early 1600s. His staunch defense of Nicolaus Copernicus' theory of a sun-centered universe threatened Catholic clergy, who were worried that such a theory threatened the authority of both the Bible and the Church. In 1615 Galileo, himself a devout Catholic, defended his scientific beliefs in a published letter to Christina, the grand duchess of Tuscany. Although the Church forced Galileo to publicly renounce his scientific beliefs in 1632, over the long term his writings contributed greatly to the reconception of the universe using the new scientific methodology.

Some years ago, as Your Serene Highness well knows, I discovered in the heavens many things that had not been seen before our own age. The novelty of these things, as well as some consequences which followed from them in contradiction to the physical notions commonly held among academic philosophers, stirred up against me no small number of professors—as if I had placed these things in the sky with my own hands in order to upset nature and overturn the sciences. They seemed to forget that the increase of known truths stimulates the investigation, establishment, and growth of the arts; not their diminution or destruction. . . .

Persisting in their original resolve to destroy me and everything mine by any means they can think of, these men are aware of my views in astronomy and philosophy. They know that as to the arrangement of the parts of the universe, I hold the sun to be situated motionless in the center of the revolution of the celestial orbs while the earth rotates on its axis and revolves around the sun. They know also that I support this position not only by refuting the arguments of Ptolemy and Aristotle, but by producing many counter-arguments; in particular, some which relate to physical effects whose causes can perhaps be assigned in no other way. In addition there are astronomical arguments derived from many things in my new celestial discoveries that confute the Ptolemaic system while admirably agreeing with and confirming the contrary hypothesis. Possibly because they are disturbed by the known truth of other propositions of mine which differ from those commonly held, and therefore mistrusting their defense so long as they confine themselves to the field of philosophy, these men have resolved to fabricate a shield for their fallacies out of the mantle of pretended religion and the authority of the Bible. These they apply, with little judgment, to the refutation of arguments that they do not understand and have not even listened to. . . .

. . . I think that in discussions of physical problems we ought to begin not from the authority of scriptural passages but from sense-experiences and necessary demonstrations; for the holy Bible and the phenomena of nature proceed alike from the divine Word, the former as the dictate of the Holy Ghost and the latter as the observant executrix of God's commands. It is necessary for the Bible, in order to be accommodated to the understanding of every man, to speak many things which appear to differ from the absolute truth so far as the bare meaning of the words is concerned. But Nature, on the other hand, is inexorable and immutable; she never transgresses the laws imposed upon her, or cares a whit whether her abstruse reasons and methods of operation are understandable to men. For that reason it appears that nothing physical which sense-experience sets before our eyes, or which necessary demonstrations prove to us, ought to be called in question (much less condemned) upon the testimony of biblical passages which may have some different meaning beneath their words. For the Bible is not chained in every expression to conditions as strict as those which govern all physical effects; nor is God any less excellently revealed in Nature's actions than in the sacred statements of the Bible.

For Further Reflection

■ Why did Galileo's critics, mentioned in the passage above, find fault with his scientific observations?

Source: Alfred J. Andrea and James H. Overfield. *The Human Record: Sources of Global History,* 3rd ed., vol. II: *Since 1500.* Boston and New York: Houghton Mifflin, 1998.

known as epicycles—small, circular revolutions that planets made around a point in their spheres, even while the spheres themselves revolved around the earth.

The Copernican Universe   In 1543, however, the Polish astronomer Nicolaus Copernicus published *On the Revolutions of the Heavenly Spheres,* which broke with Ptolemaic theory. Copernicus argued that the sun rather than the earth stood at the center of the universe and that the planets, including the earth, revolved around the sun. Although this new theory harmonized much better with observational data, it did not receive a warm welcome. Copernicus's ideas not only challenged prevailing scientific theories but also threatened cherished religious beliefs, which held that the earth and humanity were unique creations of God.

The Scientific Revolution

In time, though, Copernicus's theory inspired some astronomers to examine the heavens in fresh ways, using precise observational data and mathematical reasoning. Gradually, they abandoned the Ptolemaic in favor of the Copernican model of the universe. Some also began to apply their analytical methods to mechanics—the branch of science that deals with moving bodies—and by the mid–seventeenth century accurate observation and mathematical reasoning dominated both mechanics and astronomy. Indeed, reliance on observation and mathematics transformed the study of the natural world and brought about the scientific revolution.

Galileo Galilei The works of two mathematicians—Johannes Kepler of Germany and Galileo Galilei of Italy—rang the death knell for the Ptolemaic universe. Kepler (1571–1630) demonstrated that planetary orbits are elliptical, not circular as in Ptolemaic theory. Galileo (1564–1642) showed that the heavens were not the perfect, unblemished realm that Ptolemaic astronomers assumed. Using the recently invented telescope, Galileo was able to observe spots on the sun and mountains on the moon. He also caught sight of distant stars previously undetectable to the naked eye, which implied that the universe was much larger than anyone had previously suspected.

Isaac Newton The new approach to science culminated in the work of the English mathematician Isaac Newton (1642–1727), who depended on accurate observation and mathematical reasoning to construct a powerful synthesis of astronomy and mechanics. Newton outlined his views on the natural world in an epoch-making volume of 1687 titled *Mathematical Principles of Natural Philosophy.* Newton's work united the heavens and the earth in a vast, cosmic system. He argued that a law of universal gravitation regulates the motions of bodies throughout the universe, and he offered precise mathematical explanations of the laws that govern movements of bodies on the earth. His laws also allowed him to explain a vast range of seemingly unrelated phenomena, such as the ebb and flow of the tides and the eccentric orbits of planets and comets. Until the twentieth century, Newton's universe served as the unquestioned framework for the physical sciences.

Inspired by the dramatic discoveries of astronomers and physicists, other scientists began to construct fresh approaches to understanding the natural world. During the seventeenth and eighteenth centuries, anatomy, physiology, microbiology, chemistry, and botany underwent a thorough overhaul, as scientists tested their theories against direct observation of natural phenomena and explained them in rigorous mathematical terms.

Women and Science

In the sixteenth and seventeenth centuries, Europe's learned men challenged some of the most hallowed traditions concerning the nature of the physical universe and supplanted them with new scientific principles. Yet when male scientists studied female anatomy, female physiology, and women's reproductive organs, they were commonly guided not by scientific observation but by tradition, prejudice, and fanciful imagination. William Harvey (1578–1657), the English physician who discovered the principles of the circulation of human blood, also applied his considerable

Tycho Brahe's observatory.
In this specialized but eccentric observatory called Uraniborg, the scientist Tycho Brahe collected data related to astronomical phenomena. Although the castle was custom built for Brahe in 1584 on a Danish island, the withdrawal of support from the Danish king led Brahe to abandon it in 1597.

talents to the study of human reproduction. After careful dissection and observation of female deer, chickens, and roosters, he hypothesized that women, like hens, served as mere receptacles for the "vivifying" male fluid. According to him, it was the male semen—endowed with generative powers so potent that it did not even have to reach the uterus to work its magic—from which the unfertilized egg received life and form. Anatomy, physiology, and limited reproductive function seemed to confirm the innate inferiority of women, adding a "scientific" veneer to the traditionally limited images, roles, and functions of women. With the arrival of printing, men were able to disseminate more widely those negative conclusions about women.

Émilie du Châtelet Despite prevailing critical attitudes, some women found themselves drawn to the new intellectual currents of the time. One of the most notable female scientists of her age was Émilie du Châtelet (1706–1749), a French mathematician and physicist. Long famous for being the mistress of the celebrated French intellectual Voltaire (chapter 25), she was in fact a talented intellectual and scientist in her own right. A precocious child, du Châtelet was apparently fluent in six languages at the age of twelve, and she benefited from having an unusually enlightened father who provided his rebellious daughter with an education more typical for boys.

Du Châtelet's crowning achievement was her translation of Isaac Newton's monumental work *Principia Mathematica,* which has remained the standard French translation of the work. She did not simply render Newton's words into another language, however; rather, she explained his complex mathematics in graceful prose, transformed his geometry into calculus, and assessed the current state of Newtonian physics. She finished her work in the year of her death, at age forty-three, six days after giving birth to a child. Underscoring the difficulty of reconciling a woman's reproductive duties with her intellectual aspirations was her lover Voltaire's commentary. He declared in a letter to his friend Frederick II, king of Prussia (reigned 1740–1786), that du Châtelet was "a great man whose only fault was being a woman."

Science and Society

Newton's vision of the universe was so powerful and persuasive that its influence extended well beyond science. His work suggested that rational analysis of human behavior and institutions could lead to fresh insights about the human as well as the natural world. Thus from Scotland to Sicily and from Philadelphia to Moscow, European and Euro-American thinkers launched an ambitious project to use scientific principles and reason to transform the world. Like the early modern scientists, they abandoned Aristotelian philosophy, Christian theology, and other traditionally recognized authorities, and they sought to subject the human world to purely rational analysis. For example, the English philosopher John Locke (1632–1704) worked to discover natural laws of politics. He attacked divine-right theories that served as a foundation for absolute monarchy and advocated constitutional government on the grounds that sovereignty resides in the people rather than the state or its rulers. The Scottish philosopher Adam Smith (1723–1790) turned his attention to economic affairs and held that laws of supply and demand determine what happens in the marketplace. Using the techniques of scientific inquiry, thinkers like Locke and Smith helped constitute a movement called the Enlightenment (chapter 25), which itself provided the justification for momentous social and political change around the world.

SUMMARY

During the early modern era, European society experienced a series of profound and sometimes unsettling changes. The Protestant Reformation ended the religious unity of western Christendom and led to more than a century of religious conflict. Centralizing monarchs strengthened their realms and built a society of sovereign, autonomous, and intensely competitive states. Capitalist entrepreneurs reorganized the production and distribution of manufactured goods, and although their methods led to increased wealth, their quest for efficiency and profits clashed with traditional values. Modern science based on direct observation and mathematical explanations emerged as a powerful tool for the investigation of the natural world. Some people used scientific methods to investigate the human world and created a new moral thought based strictly on science and reason. At just the time that European merchants, colonists, and adventurers were seeking opportunities in the larger world, European society was becoming more powerful, more experimental, and more competitive than ever before.

STUDY TERMS

absolutism (379–380)
Anglicans (373)
Calvinists (373)
capitalism (382–385)
Carolingian (375)
Catherine the Great (380)
constitutional states (377–378)
Émilie du Châtelet (388)
Enlightenment (388)
Galileo Galilei (386–387)
Habsburgs (375–376)
Isaac Newton (387–388)
Johannes Kepler (387)
Louis XIV (379)
Martin Luther (371–372)
Nicolaus Copernicus (386)
Ninety-five Theses (371)
Peace of Westphalia (380)

Peter the Great (380)
Protestant Reformation (372)
protoindustrialization (382–384)
Ptolemaic system (385)
Richelieu (379)
Romanov (380)
scientific revolution (387)
Society of Jesus (373)
Spanish Inquisition (376–377)
Thirty Years' War (375)
vernacular (372)
Versailles (379)
Westphalia (380)
witch hunts (374)
Yemelian Pugachev (380)

FOR FURTHER READING

Paul Dukes. *The Making of Russian Absolutism, 1613–1801.* 2nd ed. London, 1990. A succinct study of two disparate centuries, the seventeenth and eighteenth, and two influential tsars, Peter and Catherine.

Robert S. Duplessis. *Transitions to Capitalism in Early Modern Europe.* Cambridge, 1997. A valuable synthesis of recent research on early capitalism and protoindustrialization.

Patricia Fara. *Pandora's Breeches: Women, Science, and Power in the Enlightenment.* London, 2004. An engaging account of the contributions women made to science in the seventeenth and eighteenth centuries.

Philip S. Gorski. *The Disciplinary Revolution: Calvinism and the Rise of the Early Modern State.* Chicago, 2003. Argues that the formation of strong European states was a result of religious and social control policies initiated by the Protestant Reformation.

Thomas S. Kuhn. *The Structure of Scientific Revolutions.* 3rd ed. Chicago, 1997. An influential theoretical work that views scientific thought in larger social and cultural context.

Jerry Z. Muller. *The Mind and the Market: Capitalism in Modern European Thought.* New York, 2002. Broad history of the development of capitalism through the eyes of major European thinkers, including Adam Smith, Joseph Schumpeter, and Karl Marx.

Andrew Pettegree. *Reformation and the Culture of Persuasion.* Cambridge, 2005. Investigates why people chose to support the Reformation in an era before mass literacy.

Eugene F. Rice Jr. and Anthony Grafton. *The Foundations of Early Modern Europe, 1460–1559.* 2nd ed. New York, 1994. Excellent introduction to political, social, economic, and cultural developments.

Paolo Rossi. *The Birth of Modern Science.* Malden, Mass., 2001. Explores specific seventeenth-century value systems and traditions that were central to the rise of modern science.

Simon Schama. *The Embarrassment of Riches: An Interpretation of Dutch Culture in the Seventeenth Century.* New York, 1987. A marvelous popular study of the wealthy Dutch republic at its height.

New Worlds: The Americas and Oceania

CHAPTER **21**

Doña Marina is depicted between a Tlaxcalan chief and Hernán Cortés.
© The Granger Collection, New York

EYEWITNESS:
The Mysterious Identity of Doña Marina

A remarkable young woman played a pivotal role in the Spanish conquest of Mexico. Originally called Malintzin, she is better known by her Spanish name, Doña Marina. Born about 1500 to a noble family in central Mexico, Doña Marina's mother tongue was Nahuatl, the principal language of the Aztec empire. When she was a girl, Doña Marina's family sent her to the Mexican coast as a slave. Her new family later passed her on to their neighbors on the Yucatan peninsula, where she also became fluent in the Maya language.

When Hernán Cortés arrived on the Mexican coast in 1519, only one of his soldiers could speak the Maya language spoken by coastal peoples. But he had no way to communicate with the Nahuatl-speaking peoples of central Mexico until a Maya chieftain presented him with twelve young women, including Doña Marina, as a token of alliance. Doña Marina's linguistic talents enabled Cortés to communicate through an improbable chain of languages—from Spanish to Maya to Nahuatl and then back again—while making his way to the Aztec capital of Tenochtitlan. (Doña Marina soon learned Spanish and thus eliminated the Maya link in the linguistic chain.)

Doña Marina provided Cortés with intelligence and diplomatic as well as linguistic services. On several occasions she learned of plans by native peoples to overwhelm and destroy the tiny Spanish army, and she alerted Cortés to the danger in time for him to forestall an attack. She also helped Cortés negotiate with emissaries from the major cities of central Mexico. Indeed, in the absence of Doña Marina's services, it is difficult to see how Cortés's small band could have survived to see the Aztec capital.

Apart from facilitating the Spanish conquest of the Aztec empire, Doña Marina also played a role in the formation of a new society in Mexico. In 1522 she gave birth to a son fathered by Cortés, and in 1526 she bore a daughter to a Spanish captain whom she had married. Her offspring thus symbolize the early emergence of a mestizo population in Mexico. Doña Marina died soon after the birth of her daughter, probably in 1527, but during her short life she contributed to the thorough transformation of Mexican society. Doña Marina's role in the Spanish conquest of Mexico underscored the existing divisions within sixteenth-century Mesoamerican society. Among some groups, she was remembered as the mother of the Mexican people, while recollection of her collaboration with Spaniards led other groups to call her La Malinche: the traitor.

Until 1492 the peoples of the eastern and western hemispheres had few dealings with one another. Sporadic encounters between Europeans and North Americans did occur, and it is likely that an occasional Asian or

Malintzin (mal-een-tzeen)
Nahuatl (na-watl)
Hernán Cortés (er-NAHN kawr-TEZ)
Tenochtitlan (teh-noch-tee-TLAHN)

CHRONOLOGY

1492	First voyage of Christopher Columbus to the western hemisphere
1494	Treaty of Tordesillas
1500	Brazil claimed for Portugal by Pedro Alvarez de Cabral
1518	Smallpox epidemic in the Caribbean
1519–1521	Spanish conquest of Mexico
1532–1540	Spanish conquest of Peru
1545	Spanish discovery of silver near Potosí
1604	Foundation of Port Royal (Nova Scotia)
1607	Foundation of Jamestown
1608	Foundation of Quebec
1623	Foundation of New Amsterdam
1630	Foundation of the Massachusetts Bay Colony
1688	Smallpox epidemic on Guam
1768–1779	Captain James Cook's exploration of the Pacific Ocean
1788	Establishment of the first European colony in Australia

Austronesian mariner reached the Pacific coast of the Americas before 1492. Yet travel between the eastern hemisphere, the western hemisphere, and Oceania was too irregular and infrequent to generate sustained interaction until the fifteenth century.

After 1492, however, the voyages of European mariners led to permanent and continuous contact between the peoples of all these areas. The resulting encounters brought profound and often violent change to both American and Pacific lands. European peoples possessed powerful weapons, horses, and ships that provided them with technological advantages over the peoples they encountered in the Americas and the Pacific islands. Moreover, most Europeans also enjoyed complete or partial immunity to diseases that caused devastating epidemics when introduced to the western hemisphere and Oceania. Because of their technological advantages and the depopulation that followed from epidemic diseases, European peoples were able to establish a presence throughout the Americas and much of the Pacific Ocean basin.

COLLIDING WORLDS

When European peoples first sought to establish their presence in the Americas, they brought technologies unavailable to the peoples they encountered in the western hemisphere. More important than technology, however, were the divisions between indigenous peoples that Europeans were able to exploit and the effects of epidemic diseases that devastated native societies. Soon after their arrival in the western hemisphere, Spanish conquerors toppled the Aztec and Inca empires and imposed their own rule in Mexico and Peru. In later decades Portuguese planters built sugar plantations on the Brazilian coastline. French, English, and Dutch migrants displaced indigenous peoples in North America and established settler colonies under the rule of European peoples.

The Spanish Caribbean

Tainos The first site of interaction between European and American peoples was the Caribbean. When Spanish mariners arrived there, the Tainos (also known as Arawaks) were the most prominent people in the region. The Tainos cultivated manioc and other crops, and they lived in small villages under the authority of chiefs who allocated land to families and supervised community affairs.

Spanish Arrival Christopher Columbus and his immediate followers made the island of Hispaniola (modern Haiti and the Dominican Republic) the base of Spanish operations in the Caribbean. Columbus's original plan was to build forts and trading posts where merchants could trade with local peoples for products desired by European consumers. However, it soon became clear that the Caribbean region offered no silks or spices for the European market. If Spanish settlers wanted to maintain their presence in the Caribbean, they would need to find some way to make a living.

The settlers first attempted to support their society by mining gold. Spanish settlers were few in number and were not inclined to perform heavy labor, so they recruited the labor they needed from the ranks of the Tainos. This was done through an institution known as the *encomienda,* which gave *encomenderos* (Spanish settlers) the right to compel Tainos to work in their mines or fields. In return for labor, *encomenderos* were supposed to look after their workers' welfare and encourage their conversion to Christianity.

Taino (tah-EE-noh)
encomienda (ehn-koh-MYEN-dah)

Die figur auzaigt vns das volck vnd insel die gefunden ist durch den christenlichen künig zů Portigal oder von seinen vnderthonen. Die leut sind also nacket hübsch, braun wolgestalt von leib. ir heübt halß.arm.scham.füß.frawen vnd mann ain wenig mit federn bedeckt. Auch haben die mann in iren angesichten vnd brust vil edel gestain. Es hat auch nyemann nichtz sunder sind alle ding gemai̇n Vnd die mann habende weyber welche in gefallen. es sey müter. schwester oder freündin. darjnn haben sy kain vnderschayd. Sy streyten auch mit einander. Sy essen auch ainander selbs die erschlagen werden. vnd henckeñ das selbig fleisch in den rauch. Sy werden alt hundert vnd fünnfzig iar. Vnd haben kain regiment.

Conscription of Taino labor was a brutal business. *Encomenderos* worked their charges hard and punished them severely. Tainos occasionally organized rebellions, but their bows, arrows, and slings had little effect against Spanish steel. By about 1515, social disruption and physical abuse caused Taino populations to decline on the large Caribbean islands—Hispaniola, Jamaica, Puerto Rico, and Cuba—favored by Spanish settlers.

Smallpox After 1518 serious demographic decline set in when smallpox reached the Caribbean and touched off devastating epidemics. To replace laborers lost to disease, *encomenderos* resorted to kidnapping and enslaving Tainos and other peoples. That tactic, however, only exposed additional victims to disease. As a result of epidemic disease, the native population of the Caribbean plummeted from about four million in 1492 to a few thousand in the 1540s. Entire native societies passed out of existence. By the middle of the sixteenth century, a few surviving words—*canoe, hammock, hurricane, barbecue, maize,* and *tobacco*—were all that was left of Taino society.

From Mining to Plantation Agriculture After the mid–sixteenth century, when it was clear that gold supplies in the region were thin, the Caribbean became a sleepy backwater of the Spanish empire. In the 1640s, French, English, and Dutch settlers began to take the place of the Spanish and flocked to the Caribbean with the intention of establishing plantations. Indeed, they found that the Caribbean offered ideal conditions for the cultivation of cash crops, particularly sugar and tobacco. Meanwhile, because indigenous populations were extinct, planters imported several million slaves to provide labor. By 1700 Caribbean society consisted of a small class of European administrators and large numbers of African slaves.

The Conquest of Mexico and Peru

Spanish interest shifted quickly from the Caribbean to the American mainland in the quest for resources. During the early sixteenth century, Spanish *conquistadores* ("conquerors") pressed west into Mexico and south into Panama and Peru. Between 1519 and 1521 Hernán Cortés and a small band of men brought down the Aztec empire in Mexico, and between 1532 and 1533 Francisco Pizarro and his followers toppled the Inca empire in Peru. Those conquests laid the foundations for colonial regimes that would transform the Americas.

In Mexico and Peru, Spanish explorers found societies quite different from those of the Caribbean islands. Both Mexico and Peru had been sites of agricultural societies, cities, and large states for more than a millennium. In the early fifteenth century, both lands fell under the sway of powerful imperial states: the Mexica people and their allies founded the Aztec empire, which expanded to embrace most of Mesoamerica, and the Incas imposed their rule on a vast realm extending from modern Ecuador in the north to modern Chile in the south. (See chapter 17.)

conquistadores (kon-kees-tah-DOH-rayz)

Reverberations of ● ● ● ● ● ● ● ● ●
The Columbian Exchange

Recall that the spread of epidemic diseases like smallpox and influenza from Eurasia to the Americas was one of the key features of the Columbian exchange—a process that began almost immediately after contact between Europeans and indigenous Americans in the late fifteenth century. Since indigenous Americans had no immunity to Eurasian diseases, they took a staggering toll: in some cases, as in colonial Mexico, the mortality rate may have been as high as 90 percent. If epidemic disease had not caused such high mortality among indigenous Americans, in what ways might the history of the Americas in the sixteenth and seventeenth centuries have been different?

Hernán Cortés The conquest of Mexico began in 1519 when Cortés led about 450 soldiers from Veracruz on the Gulf coast to the island city of Tenochtitlan, the stunningly beautiful Aztec capital situated in Lake Texcoco. They seized the emperor Motecuzoma II, who died in 1520 during a skirmish between Spanish forces and residents of Tenochtitlan. Aztec forces soon drove the conquistadores from the capital, but Cortés built a small fleet of ships, placed Tenochtitlan under siege, and in 1521 starved the city into surrender.

Spanish weapons and horses offered Cortés and his soldiers some advantage over the forces they met and help to account for the Spanish conquest of the Aztec empire. Yet weaponry alone clearly was not enough to overcome such a large, densely populated society. Indeed, Cortés's expedition also benefited from divisions among the indigenous peoples of Mexico and made important alliances with peoples who resented Aztec domination. Native allies reinforced the small Spanish army with thousands of veteran warriors and provided Spanish forces with logistical support and secure bases in friendly territory.

Epidemic Disease Epidemic disease also aided Spanish efforts. During the siege of Tenochtitlan, smallpox raged through the city, killing inhabitants by the tens of thousands. It then spread beyond the capital and raced through Mexico, carrying off so many people that Aztec society was unable to function. Only in the context of this enormous depopulation is it possible to understand the Spanish conquest of Mexico.

Francisco Pizarro Francisco Pizarro experienced similar results when he led a Spanish expedition from Central America to Peru. Pizarro set out in 1530 with 180 soldiers,

Motecuzoma (mo-tec-oo-ZO-ma)
Cuzco (KOOS-koh)
Atahualpa (ah-tah-WAHL-pah)

later joined by reinforcements to make a force of about 600. The conquistadores arrived in Peru just after a bitter dispute within the Inca ruling house, and it was easy for them to exploit differences between the factions. By 1533 they had taken the Inca capital at Cuzco. Under pretext of holding a conference, they called the Inca ruling elites together, seized them, and killed most of them. They spared the Inca ruler Atahualpa until he had delivered a large quantity of gold to Pizarro. Then they strangled him and decapitated his body. Pizarro and his conquistadores proceeded to loot gold and silver from Cuzco's temples and public buildings, and even to loot jewelry and ornaments from the embalmed bodies of deceased Inca rulers.

As Cortés's expedition had done to the Aztecs in Mexico, Pizarro's tiny force toppled the Inca empire by exploiting divisions among native peoples. Many Inca subjects despised their overlords and thus either allied with or did not resist Pizarro's forces. In addition, smallpox had spread

Hernán Cortés.
This portrait depicts Cortés, the Spanish conqueror of Mexico, in military armor.

SourcesfromthePast

First Impressions of Spanish Forces

The following document, based on indigenous accounts but filtered through imperial Spanish sensibilities, suggested that Motecuzoma reacted with fright when presented with reports that were less than reassuring since they focused on fearsome weapons and animals of the Spanish. Given the martial response of the Aztecs to the Spanish invasion, it seems highly unlikely that Motecuzoma or the Aztecs would have expressed terror in such a humiliating fashion.

And when [Motecuzoma] had heard what the messengers reported, he was terrified, he was astounded. . . .

Especially did it cause him to faint away when he heard how the gun, at [the Spaniards'] command, discharged [the shot]; how it resounded as if it thundered when it went off. It indeed bereft one of strength; it shut off one's ears. And when it discharged, something like a round pebble came forth from within. Fire went showering forth; sparks went blazing forth. And its smoke smelled very foul; it had a fetid odor which verily wounded the head. And when [the shot] struck a mountain, it was as if it were destroyed, dissolved. And a tree was pulverized; it was as if it vanished; it was as if someone blew it away.

All iron was their war array. In iron they clothed themselves. With iron they covered their heads. Iron were their swords. Iron were their crossbows. Iron were their shields. Iron were their lances.

And those which bore them upon their backs, their deer [that is, horses], were as tall as roof terraces.

And their bodies were everywhere covered; only their faces appeared. They were very white; they had chalky faces; they had yellow hair, though the hair of some was black. Long were their beards; they also were yellow. They were yellow-headed. [The black men's hair] was kinky, it was curly.

And their food was like fasting food—very large, white, not heavy like [tortillas]; like maize stalks, good-tasting as if of maize stalk flour; a little sweet, a little honeyed. It was honeyed to eat; it was sweet to eat.

And their dogs were very large. They had ears folded over; great dragging jowls. They had fiery eyes—blazing eyes; they had yellow eyes—fiery yellow eyes. They had thin flanks—flanks with ribs showing. They had gaunt stomachs. They were very tall. They were nervous; they went about panting, with tongues hanging out. They were spotted like ocelots; they were varicolored.

And when Motecuzoma heard all this, he was much terrified. It was as if he fainted away. His heart saddened; his heart failed him.

For Further Reflection

■ What did the Spanish and their indigenous allies hope to gain by presenting this image of Motecuzoma?

Source: Bernardino de Sahagún. *Florentine Codex: General History of the Things of New Spain,* 13 vols. Trans. by Arthur J. O. Anderson and Charles E. Dibble. Salt Lake City: University of Utah Press, 1950–1982, 13:19–20. (Translation slightly modified.)

to the Inca empire in the 1520s, long before Pizarro's arrival, and had already taken a heavy toll among Andean populations. As a result, by 1540 Spanish forces had established themselves securely as lords of the land.

Iberian Empires in the Americas

Spanish Colonial Administration The conquests of Mexico and Peru were the results not of Spanish royal policy but, rather, of individual efforts by freelance adventurers. Gradually, however, the Spanish monarchy extended its control over the growing American empire, and by about 1570 it had established formal rule under the Spanish crown. Spanish administrators established two main centers of authority in the Americas—Mexico (which they called New Spain) and Peru (known as New Castile)—each

governed by a viceroy who was responsible to the king of Spain. In Mexico they built a new capital, Mexico City, on top of Tenochtitlan. In Peru they moved the seat of government from the high-altitude Inca capital of Cuzco to the Peruvian coast and in 1535 founded the new capital of Lima.

The viceroys were the king's representatives in the Americas, and they wielded considerable power. The kings of Spain attempted to hold them in check by subjecting them to the review of courts known as *audiencias* staffed by university-educated lawyers. The *audiencias* heard appeals against the viceroys' decisions and policies and had the right to address their concerns directly to the Spanish king. Furthermore, the *audiencias* conducted reviews of viceroys'

audiencias (AW-dee-uhns-cee-ahs)

performance at the end of their terms, and negative reviews could lead to severe punishment.

In many ways, Spanish administration in the Americas was a ragged affair. Transportation and communication difficulties limited the ability of viceroys to supervise their own extensive territories. The jurisdiction of the viceroyalty of New Spain, for example, reached from Mexico City as far as St. Augustine in Florida (founded in 1565). Distance also prevented Spanish monarchs from exercising much influence on American affairs. It often took two years for the central government in Spain to respond to a query from Mexico or Peru, and when viceroys received clear orders that they did not like, it was easy to procrastinate.

Portuguese Brazil While the Spanish built a territorial empire in Mexico and Peru, Portuguese forces established an imperial presence in Brazil. The Portuguese presence came about by an odd twist of diplomatic convention. In 1494 Spain and Portugal signed the Treaty of Tordesillas, which divided the world along an imaginary north-south line 370 leagues west of the Azores and Cape Verde Islands. According to this agreement, Spain could claim any non-Christian lands west of that line, and Portugal gained the same rights for lands east of the line. Thus Portugal gained territory along the northeastern part of the South American continent, a region known as Brazil from the many brazilwood trees that grew along the coast, and the remainder of the western hemisphere fell under Spanish control. Brazil did not attract significant Portuguese interest, however, until entrepreneurs began establishing sugar plantations on the coast after the mid–sixteenth century. Once it was clear the plantations would be profitable, Portuguese interest—and settlement—surged.

Colonial American Society Both the Spanish and the Portuguese rapidly established cities throughout their territories. Like their compatriots in Europe, colonists preferred to live in cities even when they derived their income from the agricultural production of their landed estates, and they made every attempt to model their new cities along European lines. Away from urban areas, however, indigenous ways of life largely persisted. In places such as the Amazon basin and Paraguay, for example, where there were no mineral deposits to attract European migrants, European visitors learned to adapt to indigenous societies and customs: they ate bread made of manioc flour, made use of native hammocks and canoes, and communicated in the Guaraní and Tupí languages. Indeed, indigenous languages flourish even today throughout much of Latin America: among the

Quiché (keesh-AY)
Guaraní (gwahr-uh-NEE)
Quechua (keh-CHUA)

more prominent are Nahuatl in Mexico, Quiché in Mexico and Guatemala, Guaraní in Paraguay, and Quechua in the Andean highlands of Peru, Ecuador, and Bolivia.

Spanish and Portuguese peoples always saw the western hemisphere more as a land to exploit and administer than as a place to settle and colonize. Nevertheless, upward of five hundred thousand Spaniards and one hundred thousand Portuguese settled permanently in the Americas between 1500 and 1800. Their presence contributed to the making of a new world—a world characterized by intense interaction between the peoples of Europe, Africa, and the Americas—in the western hemisphere.

Settler Colonies in North America

Throughout the sixteenth century, Spanish explorers sought opportunities north of Mexico and the Caribbean. They established towns, forts, and missions from modern Florida as far north as Virginia, and they scouted shorelines off Maine and Newfoundland. On the west coast they established a fort on Vancouver Island in modern Canada. By midcentury, however, French, English, and Dutch mariners were dislodging Spanish colonists north of Florida. Originally, they came in a fruitless search for a northwest passage to Asia. Instead, they found immense quantities of codfish, which they exploited from the banks off Labrador, Newfoundland, Nova Scotia, and New England.

Foundation of Colonies More important, in the early seventeenth century they began to plant permanent colonies on the North American mainland. French settlers established colonies at Port Royal (Nova Scotia) in 1604 and Quebec in 1608, and English migrants founded Jamestown in 1607 and the Massachusetts Bay Colony in 1630. Dutch entrepreneurs built a settlement at New Amsterdam in 1623, but in 1664 an English fleet seized and rechristened it New York and absorbed it into English colonial holdings. During the seventeenth and eighteenth centuries, French migrants settled in eastern Canada, and French explorers and traders scouted the St. Lawrence, Ohio, and Mississippi rivers, building forts all the way to the Gulf of Mexico. Meanwhile, English settlers established colonies along the east coast of the present-day United States of America.

Life in those early settlements was extremely difficult. Most of the settlers hoped to sustain their communities not through farming but by producing valuable commodities such as fur, pitch, tar, or lumber, if not silver and gold. They relied heavily on provisions sent from Europe, and when supply ships did not arrive as expected, they sometimes avoided starvation only because indigenous peoples provided them with food. In Jamestown, food shortages and disease became so severe that only sixty of the colony's

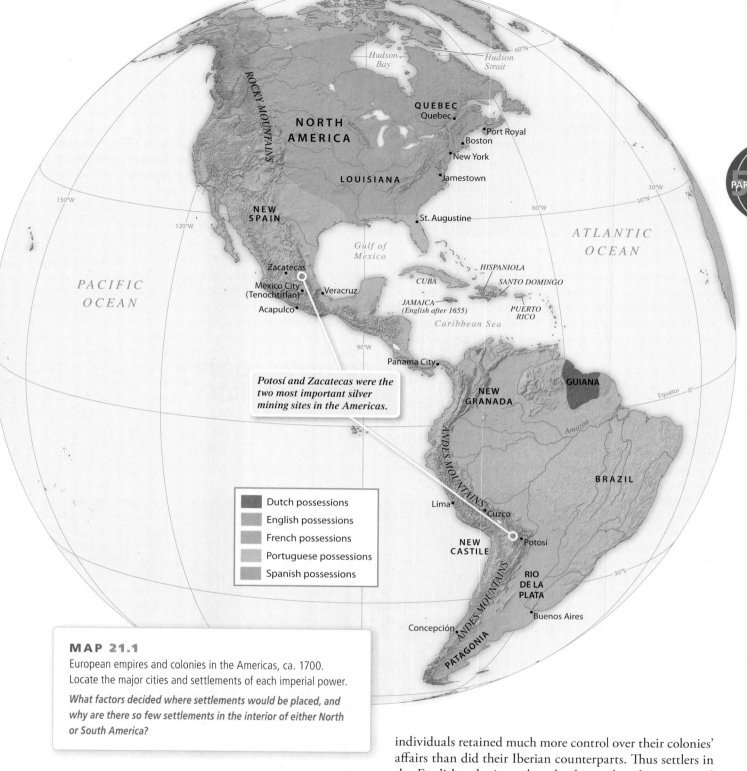

Potosí and Zacatecas were the two most important silver mining sites in the Americas.

Dutch possessions
English possessions
French possessions
Portuguese possessions
Spanish possessions

MAP 21.1

European empires and colonies in the Americas, ca. 1700. Locate the major cities and settlements of each imperial power.

What factors decided where settlements would be placed, and why are there so few settlements in the interior of either North or South America?

five hundred inhabitants survived the winter of 1609–1610. Some settlers went so far as to disinter corpses and consume the flesh of their departed neighbors.

Colonial Government The French and English colonies in North America differed in several ways from Iberian territories to the south. Whereas Iberian explorations had royal backing, private investors played larger roles in French and English colonial efforts. Because of that,

individuals retained much more control over their colonies' affairs than did their Iberian counterparts. Thus settlers in the English colonies—though ultimately subject to royal authority—maintained their own assemblies and influenced the choice of royal governors: there were no viceroys or *audiencias* in the North American colonies.

Relations with Indigenous Peoples French and English colonies differed from Iberian territories also in their relationships with indigenous peoples. French and English migrants did not find large, densely settled, centralized states like the Aztec and Inca empires. Although many of

Thinking about TRADITIONS

Preserving Traditions amid Turmoil

In spite of conquest and massive depopulation from epidemic disease, the peoples of the Americas managed to preserve aspects of their social, religious, and cultural identities. *In what specific ways did native American traditions persist, especially in terms of culture and religion?*

the native societies in eastern North America practiced agriculture, most also relied on hunting and consequently moved their villages frequently in pursuit of game. They did not claim ownership of precisely bounded territories, but they regularly migrated between well-defined regions.

When European settlers saw forested lands not bearing crops, they staked out farms for themselves. The availability of fertile farmland soon attracted large numbers of European migrants. Upward of 150,000 English migrants moved to North America during the seventeenth century alone, and sizable French, German, Dutch, and Irish contingents soon joined them.

European migrants took pains to justify their claims to American lands. Some, such as the English, sought to provide legal cover for their settlements by negotiating treaties with the peoples whose lands they colonized. Other migrants claimed that they were making productive use of lands that native peoples only used as hunting parks. Such justifications did not convince native peoples, who frequently clashed with colonists over the right to use their hunting grounds, whether treaties existed or not. In 1622, for example, native peoples angry over European intrusions massacred almost one-third of the English settlers in the Chesapeake region.

Such attacks did not stem the tide of European migrants, however. Between 1600 and 1800, about one million European migrants arrived in North America, many of whom actively sought to displace native peoples from their lands. Violent conflict, indeed, took a heavy toll on native populations. Yet as in the Iberian territories, epidemic disease also dramatically reduced the indigenous population of North America

in early modern times. In 1492 the native population of the territory now embraced by the United States was greater than five million, perhaps as high as ten million. By the mid–sixteenth century, however, smallpox and other diseases spread north from Mexico and ravaged native societies in the plains and eastern woodlands of North America. By 1800 only six hundred thousand indigenous peoples remained, as against almost five million settlers of European ancestry and about one million slaves of African ancestry. Although the settler colonies of North America differed markedly from the Iberian territorial empires, they too contributed greatly to the transformation of the western hemisphere.

COLONIAL SOCIETY IN THE AMERICAS

The European migrants who flooded into the western hemisphere interacted both with the native inhabitants and with African peoples whom they imported as enslaved laborers. Throughout the Americas, relations between individuals of

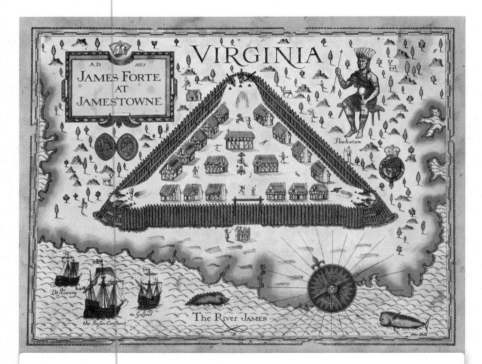

Jamestown.

A painting of the English settlement at Jamestown in the early seventeenth century illustrates the precarious relations between European settlers and indigenous peoples. Note the heavy palisades and numerous cannons deployed within the fort, as well as the imposing figure of the native chief Powhatan depicted outside the settlement's walls.

American, European, and African ancestry soon led to the emergence of mestizo populations. Yet European peoples and their Euro-American offspring increasingly dominated political and economic affairs in the Americas. They mined precious metals, cultivated cash crops such as sugar and tobacco, and trapped fur-bearing animals to supply capitalist markets that met the voracious demands of European and Asian consumers. Over time they also established their Christian religion as the dominant faith of the western hemisphere.

The Formation of Multicultural Societies

Many parts of the Americas remained outside European control until the nineteenth century. Only rarely did Europeans venture into the interior regions of the American continents in the sixteenth century, and those who did often found themselves at the mercy of the native inhabitants. But even though their influence reached the American interior only gradually, European migrants radically transformed the social order in the regions where they established colonies.

Mestizo Societies All European territories became multicultural societies where peoples of varied ancestry lived together under European or Euro-American dominance. Spanish and Portuguese territories soon became not only multicultural but ethnically mixed as well, largely because of migration patterns. Migrants to the Iberian colonies were overwhelmingly men: about 85 percent of the Spanish migrants were men, and the Portuguese migration was even more male-dominated than the Spanish. Because of the small numbers of European women, Spanish and Portuguese migrants entered into relationships with indigenous women, which soon gave rise to an increasingly *mestizo* ("mixed") society.

Most Spanish migrants went to Mexico, where there was soon a growing population of mestizos—those of Spanish and native parentage, like the children of Doña Marina. Women were more prominent among the migrants to Peru than to Mexico, and Spanish colonists there lived mostly in cities, where they maintained a more distinct community than did their counterparts in Mexico. In the colonial cities, Spanish migrants married among themselves and re-created a European-style society. In less settled regions, however, Spanish men associated with indigenous women and gave rise to mestizo society.

With few European women available in Brazil, Portuguese men readily entered into relations both with indigenous women and with African slave women. Brazil soon had large populations not only of mestizos but also of mulattoes born of Portuguese and African parents, *zambos* born of indigenous and African parents, and other combinations

Mestizo family.
Indigenous Zapotec painter Miguel Mateo Maldonado y Cabrera (1695–1768) created this domestic portrait of a multicultural family in the viceroyalty of New Spain, today's Mexico. A Spanish man gazes at his Mexican Indian wife and their mestizo daughter.

arising from these groups. Indeed, marriages between members of different racial and ethnic communities became common in colonial Brazil and generated a society even more thoroughly mixed than that of mestizo Mexico.

The Social Hierarchy In both the Spanish and the Portuguese colonies, migrants born in Europe known as *peninsulares* (people from the Iberian peninsula) stood at the top of the social hierarchy, followed by *criollos,* or creoles, individuals born in the Americas of Iberian parents. As the numbers of mestizos grew, they also became essential contributors to their societies, especially in Mexico and Brazil. Meanwhile, mulattoes, zambos, and other individuals of mixed parentage became prominent groups in Brazilian

mestizo (mehs-TEE-soh)
zambos (SAHM-bohs)
peninsulares (pehn-IHN-soo-LAH-rayz)
criollos (KRYO-yohs)

society, although they were usually subordinate to *peninsulares*, creoles, and even mestizos. In all the Iberian colonies, imported slaves and native peoples stood at the bottom of the social hierarchy.

Sexual Hierarchies   Race and ethnicity were crucial in shaping a person's position and role in colonial society. But the defining factor in both Spanish and Portuguese America was the existence of a clear sexual hierarchy that privileged men. Women lived in a patriarchal world, where men occupied positions of power and delineated the boundaries of acceptable female behavior. To the extent that women did exercise power, most of it was informal and limited to the confines of the home.

Gender alone, however, did not explain the diverse experiences of women in colonial society. Commonly, the ratio of men to women in a given community either enhanced or limited women's choices. Race and class also usually figured as powerful forces shaping women's lives. Women of European descent, though under strict patriarchal control and under pressure to conform to the stereotype of female dependence and passivity, sometimes used their elite position to their advantage. By necessity, women of color and low class became part of the colonial labor force, performing tasks such as food preparation, laundering, and weaving. Although poor, these women were freer to move about in public and to interact with others than were their elite counterparts. The most disadvantaged women were black, mulatta, and zamba slaves, who were required to perform hard physical tasks such as planting and cutting cane or working as laundresses.

North American Societies   The social structure of the French and English colonies in North America differed markedly from that of the Iberian colonies. Women were more numerous, especially among the English migrants, and settlers mostly married within their own groups. Although French fur traders often associated with native women and generated *métis* (the French equivalent of mestizos) in regions around trading posts, such arrangements were less common in French colonial cities such as Port Royal and Quebec.

Mingling between peoples of different ancestry was least common in the English colonies of North America. Colonists regarded the native peoples they encountered as lazy heathens who did not exert themselves to cultivate the land. Later they also scorned African slaves as inferior beings. Those attitudes fueled a virulent racism, and English settlers worked to maintain sharp boundaries between themselves and peoples of American and African ancestry.

métis (may-TEE)
Zacatecas (sah-kah-TEH-kahs)
Potosí (paw-taw-SEE)
quinto (KEEN-toh)

Yet English settlers readily borrowed useful cultural elements from other communities. From native communities, for example, they learned about American plants and animals, and they adapted moccasins and deerskin clothes. From their slaves they borrowed African food crops and techniques for the cultivation of rice. Yet, unlike their Iberian neighbors, English settlers strongly discouraged relationships between individuals of different ancestry and mostly refused to accept offspring of mixed parentage.

Mining and Agriculture in the Spanish Empire

From the Spanish perspective, the greatest attractions of the Americas were precious metals. Once the conquistadores had thoroughly looted the treasures of the Aztec and Inca empires, their followers opened mines to extract the mineral wealth of the Americas in a more systematic fashion.

Silver Mining   Silver was the most abundant American treasure, and much of Spain's American enterprise focused on its extraction. Silver production concentrated on two areas: the thinly populated Mexican north, particularly the region around Zacatecas, and the high central Andes, particularly the stunningly rich mines of Potosí. Both sites employed large numbers of indigenous laborers. Many laborers went to Zacatecas voluntarily to escape the pressures of conquest and disease. Over time they became professional miners, spoke Spanish, and lost touch with the communities of their birth.

Meanwhile, Spanish prospectors discovered a large vein of silver near Potosí in 1545 and began large-scale mining there in the 1580s. By 1600 Potosí had a booming population of 150,000. Such rapid growth created an explosive demand for labor. As in the Mexican mines, Spanish administrators relied mostly on voluntary labor, but they also adapted the Inca practice of requisitioning draft labor, known as the *mita* system, to recruit workers for particularly difficult and dangerous chores. Under the *mita* system, each native village was required to send one-seventh of its male population to work for four months in the mines at Potosí. Draft laborers received very little payment for their work, and conditions were extremely harsh. Death rates of draft laborers were high, and many native men sought to evade *mita* obligations by fleeing to cities or hiding in distant villages.

The Global Significance of Silver   The mining industries of Mexico and Peru powered the Spanish economy in the Americas and even stimulated the world economy of early modern times. Indeed, the Spanish government's share—one-fifth of all silver production, called the *quinto*—represented the principal revenue the crown derived from its American possessions. Most American silver made its way across the Atlantic to Spain, where it financed Spain's army and bureaucracy and lubricated markets throughout Europe. From Europe, merchants used it to trade for silk, spices, and porcelain in the markets of Asia. Silver also traveled from Acapulco on the west coast of Mexico across the Pacific in the Manila galleons, and from Manila it also made its way to Asian markets. No matter which direction it went, American silver powerfully stimulated global trade.

The Hacienda Apart from mining, the principal occupations in Spanish America were farming, stock raising, and craft production. By the seventeenth century the most prominent site of agricultural and craft production in Spanish America was the hacienda, or estate, which produced goods for sale to local markets in nearby mining districts, towns, and cities. Bordering the large estates were smaller properties owned by Spanish migrants or creoles as well as sizable tracts of land held by indigenous peoples who practiced subsistence agriculture.

Labor Systems The major source of labor for the haciendas was the indigenous population. As in the Caribbean, Spanish conquerors first organized native workforces under the *encomienda* system. Yet from the 1520s to the 1540s, this system led to rampant abuse, as Spanish landowners overworked their laborers and skimped on their maintenance. After midcentury, *encomenderos* in agriculturally productive regions increasingly required their subject populations to provide tribute but not labor. That didn't solve the problem of labor, however, so Spanish landowners resorted to a system of debt peonage to recruit workers for their haciendas. Under this system, landowners advanced loans to native peoples so that they could buy seeds, tools, and supplies for their farms. The debtors then repaid the loans with labor, but wages were so low that they were never able to pay off their debts. Thus, landowners helped create a cycle of debt that ensured them a dependent labor force to work their estates.

Resistance to Spanish Rule The Spanish regimes in the Americas met considerable resistance from indigenous peoples. Resistance took various forms: armed rebellion, halfhearted work, and retreat into the mountains and forests. On some occasions, indigenous peoples turned to Spanish law in search of aid against oppressive colonists. In 1615, for example, Felipe Guaman Poma de Ayala, a native of Peru, fired off a 1,200-page letter to King Philip III of Spain asking for protection for native peoples against rapacious colonists. He wrote passionately of men ruined by overtaxation and women driven to prostitution, of Spanish colonists who grabbed the lands of native peoples and Spanish priests who seduced the wives of native men. Guaman Poma warned the king that if Philip wanted anything to remain of his Andean empire, he should intervene and protect the indigenous peoples of the land. Unfortunately

for Guaman Poma, the king never saw the letter. Instead, it ended up in Denmark, where it remained unknown in a library until 1908.

Sugar and Slavery in Portuguese Brazil

Whereas the Spanish American empire concentrated on the extraction of silver, the Portuguese empire in Brazil depended on the production and export of sugar. The different economic and social foundations of the Spanish and Portuguese empires led to different patterns of labor recruitment. The Spanish forced native peoples to provide labor; the Portuguese relied instead on imported African slaves. Because of that, Africans and their descendants became the majority of the population in Brazil.

The Engenho Colonial Brazilian life revolved around the *engenho,* or sugar mill, which came to represent a complex of land, labor, buildings, animals, capital, and technical skills related to the production of sugar. Unlike other crops, sugarcane required extensive processing to yield molasses or refined sugar. Thus *engenhos* needed both heavy labor for the planting and harvesting of cane and specialized skills for the intricacies of processing.

The Search for Labor Like their Spanish counterparts, Portuguese colonists first tried to enlist local populations as laborers. Unlike the inhabitants of Mexico and Peru, however, the peoples of Brazil were not sedentary cultivators. They resisted efforts to commandeer their labor and evaded the Portuguese simply by retreating to interior lands. In addition, in Brazil as elsewhere in the Americas, epidemic diseases devastated indigenous populations. After smallpox and measles ravaged the Brazilian coast in the 1560s, Portuguese settlers had a hard time even finding potential laborers, let alone forcing them to work.

Slavery Faced with those difficulties, the colonists turned to another labor Source: African slaves. Portuguese plantation managers imported slaves as early as the 1530s, but they began to rely on African labor on a large scale only in the 1580s. The toll on slave communities was extremely heavy: arduous working conditions, mistreatment, poor nutrition, and inadequate housing combined to produce high rates of disease and mortality. Indeed, *engenhos* typically lost 5 to 10 percent of their slaves annually, so there was a constant demand for more slaves.

Owners had little economic incentive to improve conditions for slaves or to encourage them to reproduce naturally. If a slave lived five to six years, the investment of the average

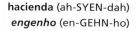

hacienda (ah-SYEN-dah)
engenho (en-GEHN-ho)

owner doubled and permitted him to purchase a new and healthy slave without taking a monetary loss. Children required financial outlays for at least twelve years, which from the perspective of the owner represented a financial loss. To them the balance sheet of sugar production was about profit, not about slaves' lives. All told, the business of producing Brazilian sugar was so brutal that every ton of the sweet substance cost one human life.

Fur Traders and Settlers in North America

The Fur Trade   European mariners first frequented North American shores in search of fish. Over time, though, trade in furs became far more lucrative. After explorers found a convenient entrance to rich fur-producing regions through the Hudson Strait and Hudson Bay, they began to connect large parts of the North American interior by a chain of forts and trading posts. Indigenous peoples trapped animals for Europeans and exchanged the pelts for manufactured goods. The hides went mostly to Europe, where there was strong demand for beaver skin hats and fur clothing.

Effects of the Fur Trade   The fur trade generated tremendous conflict between native groups. As overhunting caused American beaver populations to plummet, native trappers constantly had to push farther inland in search of hides. This frequently led native peoples to invade others' territories, which in turn often led to war. The fur trade also took place in the context of competition between European states. This competitive atmosphere contributed to further conflict, as indigenous peoples became embroiled in their patrons' rivalries.

Settler Society   European settler-cultivators posed an even more serious challenge to native ways of life than the fur traders, since they displaced indigenous peoples from the land and turned hunting grounds into plantations. And, as colonists' numbers increased, they sought to integrate their American holdings into the larger economy of the Atlantic Ocean basin by producing cash crops—such as tobacco, rice, and indigo—that they could market in Europe.

Tobacco   Tobacco farming quickly became critical to settler societies in eastern North America. Although originally hailed for its medicinal uses, this native American plant quickly became wildly popular with Europeans as a recreational drug. Indeed, just a few decades after English settlers cultivated the first commercial crop of tobacco in Virginia in 1612, Europeans were smoking tobacco socially in huge numbers. This widespread popularity was due to the addictive nature of nicotine, an oily, toxic substance

Tobacco use in Europe.
European moralists often denounced tobacco as a noxious weed, and they associated its use with vices such as drunkenness, gambling, and prostitution. Nevertheless, its popularity surged in Europe, and later in Africa and Asia as well, after its introduction from the Americas.

Does this engraving seem to promote or discourage the use of tobacco?

present in tobacco leaves. As a result, it was easy for tobacco users to become dependent on nicotine, which in turn kept demand for tobacco high. Moreover, merchants and mariners soon spread the use of tobacco throughout Europe and to all parts of the world that European ships visited—a process that helped, at least in the short term, to expand the markets for American tobacco.

Indentured Labor   Cash-crop plantations created high demand for cheap labor. Unlike their counterparts in the Spanish territories, indigenous peoples in North America could not be induced to labor in the colonists' fields. Instead, planters turned to indentured servants from Europe for their labor needs. Under this system, people who had little future in Europe—the chronically unemployed,

Plantation society.
The Goober-gatherers, 1890 (engraving), by Horace Bradley (fl. 1890).

orphans, criminals—received free passage across the Atlantic in exchange for providing four to seven years of labor. Although thousands of indentured servants came to the American colonies with high hopes for making a new start, the system was far from ideal—many died of disease or overwork before completing their terms of labor, and others found only marginal employment.

Slavery in North America English settlers in North America also found uses for African slaves. In 1619 a group of about twenty Africans reached Virginia, where they worked alongside European laborers as indentured servants. After about 1680, however, planters increasingly replaced indentured servants with African slaves. By 1750 some 120,000 black slaves tilled Chesapeake tobacco, and 180,000 others cultivated Carolina rice.

Slave labor was not prominent in the northern colonies, mostly because the land and the climate were not suitable for the cultivation of labor-intensive cash crops. Nevertheless, the economies of these colonies also profited handsomely from slavery. Many New England merchants traded in slaves destined for the West Indies: by the mid–eighteenth century, half the merchant fleet of Newport carried human cargo. The economies of New York and Philadelphia also benefited from the building and outfitting of slave vessels, and the seaports of New England

became profitable centers for the distillation of rum. The chief ingredient of that rum was slave-produced sugar from the West Indies, and merchants traded much of the distilled spirits for slaves on the African coast. Thus, although the southern plantation societies became most directly identified with slavery, all the North American colonies participated in and profited from the slave trade.

Christianity and Native Religions in the Americas

Like Buddhists and Muslims in earlier centuries, European explorers, conquerors, merchants, and settlers took their religious traditions with them when they traveled overseas. The desire to spread Christianity was a prominent motive behind European ventures overseas, and missionaries soon made their way to the Americas.

Spanish Missionaries From the beginning of Spanish colonization in Mexico and Peru, Franciscan, Dominican, and Jesuit missionaries campaigned to Christianize indigenous peoples. Over time, and despite considerable initial resistance, Christianity did win adherents in Spanish America. In the wake of conquest and epidemic disease, many native leaders in Mexico concluded that their gods had abandoned them and looked to the missionaries for spiritual guidance. When native peoples adopted Christianity, however, they blended their own interests and traditions with the faith taught by Spanish missionaries. When they learned about Roman Catholic saints, for example, they revered saints with qualities like those of their inherited gods or those whose feast days coincided with traditional celebrations.

The Virgin of Guadalupe

In Mexico, Christianity became especially popular after the mid–seventeenth century, as an increasingly mestizo society took the Virgin of Guadalupe almost as a national symbol. According to legends, the Virgin Mary appeared before a peasant near Mexico City in 1531. The site of the apparition soon became a popular local shrine visited mostly by Spanish settlers. By the 1640s the shrine attracted pilgrims from all parts of Mexico, and the Virgin of Guadalupe gained a reputation for working miracles on behalf of individuals who visited her shrine. The popularity of the Virgin of Guadalupe helped to ensure not only that Roman Catholic Christianity would dominate cultural and religious matters in Mexico but also that Mexican religious faith would retain strong indigenous influences.

French and English Missions

French and English missionaries did not attract nearly as many converts to Christianity in North America as their Spanish counterparts did in Mexico and Peru, partly because French and English colonists did not rule over sedentary cultivators: it was much more difficult to conduct missions among peoples who frequently moved about the countryside than among those who lived permanently in villages, towns, or cities. Even so, French missionaries did work actively among native communities in the St. Lawrence, Mississippi, and Ohio river valleys and experienced modest success for their efforts. English colonists, in contrast, displayed little interest in converting indigenous peoples to Christianity, nor did they welcome native converts into their agricultural and commercial society. Yet even without native conversion to Christianity, the growing settlements of French and especially English colonists guaranteed that European religious traditions would figure prominently in North American society.

The virgin of Guadalupe.
Famed Mexican painter Miguel Cabrera crafted this eighteenth-century depiction of the Virgin of Guadalupe. Recognized as the greatest painter in New Spain, he featured in this work one of Mexico's most powerful religious icons.

EUROPEANS IN THE PACIFIC

Though geographically distant from the Americas, Australia and the Pacific islands underwent experiences similar to those that transformed the western hemisphere in early modern times. Like their American counterparts, the peoples of Oceania had no inherited or acquired immunities to diseases that were common to peoples throughout the eastern hemisphere, and their numbers plunged when epidemic disease struck their populations. For the most part, however, Australia and the Pacific islands experienced epidemic disease and the arrival of European migrants later than did the Americas. European mariners thoroughly explored the Pacific basin between the sixteenth and eighteenth centuries, but only in Guam and the Mariana Islands did they establish permanent settlements before the late eighteenth century. Nevertheless, their scouting of the region laid a foundation for much more intense interactions between European, Euro-American, Asian, and Oceanic peoples during the nineteenth and twentieth centuries.

Australia and the Larger World

Dutch Exploration At least from the second century c.e., European geographers had speculated about *terra australis incognita*—"unknown southern land"—that they thought must exist in the world's southern hemisphere to balance the huge landmasses north of the equator. Although Portuguese mariners most likely charted much of the western and northern coasts of Australia as early as the 1520s, Dutch sailors based in the Indonesian islands made the first recorded European sighting of the southern continent in 1606. The Dutch VOC authorized exploratory voyages, but mariners found little to encourage further efforts. In 1623, after surveying the landscape of western Australia, the Dutch mariner Jan Carstenzs described the land as "the most arid and barren region that could be found anywhere on earth."

Virgin of Guadalupe (gwah-dah-LOO-pay)

Thinking about ENCOUNTERS

Disproportionate Disadvantages as a Result of Encounters

As in many other places and times, encounters between Europeans and the peoples of the Americas and Oceania spurred huge cultural, social, and economic changes for everyone involved. Yet the transformations that occurred among the peoples of the Americas and Oceania as a result of these encounters were disproportionately drastic and difficult. *Why did these encounters cause such hardship for both native Americans and Oceanians?*

Nevertheless, Dutch mariners continued to visit Australia. By the mid–seventeenth century they had scouted the continent's northern, western, and southern coasts and had fleeting encounters with indigenous populations. Yet because those peoples were nomadic foragers rather than sedentary cultivators, Europeans mostly considered them wretched savages. In the absence of tempting opportunities to trade, European mariners made no effort to establish permanent settlements in Australia.

British Colonists Only after James Cook charted the eastern coast in 1770 did European peoples become seriously interested in Australia. Cook dropped anchor for a week at Botany Bay (near modern Sydney) and reported that the region was suitable for settlement. In 1788 a British fleet arrived at Sydney carrying about one thousand passengers, eight hundred of them convicts, who established the first European settlement in Australia as a penal colony. For half a century Europeans in Australia numbered only a few thousand, most of them convicts. In fact, free settlers did not outnumber convicted criminal migrants until the 1830s. Thus, despite early fleeting encounters between European and aboriginal Australian peoples, it was only in the nineteenth and twentieth centuries that a continuing stream of European migrants and settlers linked Australia more directly to the larger world.

The Pacific Islands and the Larger World

The entry of European mariners into the Pacific Ocean basin did not bring immediate change to most of the Pacific islands. In these islands, as in Australia, European merchants and settlers did not arrive in large numbers until the late eighteenth century. However, in Guam and the Mariana Islands, dramatic change was already under way by the sixteenth century.

Spanish Voyages in the Pacific Ferdinand Magellan and his crew became the first Europeans to cross the Pacific Ocean, in 1521. Before reaching the Philippines, they encountered only one inhabited island group—the Marianas, dominated by Guam. In 1565 Spanish mariners inaugurated the Manila galleon trade between Manila and Acapulco. Because their primary goal was to link New Spain to Asian markets, they rarely went out of their way to explore the Pacific Ocean or to search for other islands. Although a few Spanish vessels visited some of the other Pacific islands in the sixteenth century, Spanish mariners found little to interest them and did not establish regular communications with island peoples.

Guam The only Pacific islands that attracted substantial Spanish interest in the sixteenth century were Guam and the Marianas. Manila galleons called regularly at Guam, which lay directly on the route from Acapulco to Manila. For more than a century, they took on fresh provisions and engaged in mostly peaceful trade with the indigenous Chamorro people. Then, in the 1670s and 1680s, Spanish authorities decided to bring the Mariana Islands under the control of the viceroy of New Spain in Mexico. They dispatched military forces to the islands to impose Spanish rule and subject the Chamorro to the spiritual authority of the Roman Catholic church. The Chamorro stoutly opposed those efforts, but a smallpox epidemic in 1688 severely reduced their numbers and crippled their resistance. By 1695 the Chamorro population had declined from about fifty thousand at midcentury to five thousand, mostly because of smallpox. By the end of the seventeenth century, Spanish forces had established garrisons throughout the Mariana Islands and relocated surviving Chamorro into communities supervised by Spanish authorities.

Visitors and Trade By the late eighteenth century, growing European and Euro-American interest in the Pacific Ocean basin led to sharply increased interactions between islanders and mariners. English and French mariners explored the Pacific basin in search of commercial opportunities and the elusive northwest passage from Europe to Asia. They frequently visited Tahiti after 1767, and they soon began to trade with the islanders: European mariners received provisions and engaged in sexual relations with Tahitian women in exchange for nails, knives, iron tools, and textiles.

Chamorro (chuh-MAWR-oh)

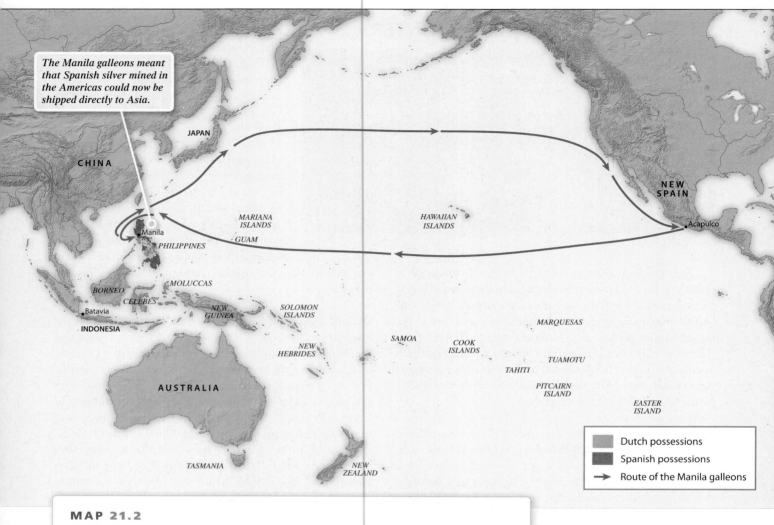

The Manila galleons meant that Spanish silver mined in the Americas could now be shipped directly to Asia.

Dutch possessions

Spanish possessions

→ Route of the Manila galleons

MAP 21.2

Manila galleon route and the lands of Oceania, 1500–1800. Note the route taken by the Manila galleons in relation to the majority of the Pacific islands.

Why weren't Spanish mariners more interested in exploring the rest of the Pacific as they made their way to the Philippines?

Captain Cook and Hawai'i After 1778 the published writings of Captain James Cook, who happened across the Hawaiian Islands in that year, galvanized even greater interest in the Pacific. European whalers, missionaries, and planters came in large numbers in search of opportunities. As a result, by the early nineteenth century, European and Euro-American peoples had become prominent figures in all the major Pacific island groups. In the next two centuries, interactions between islanders, visitors, and migrants brought rapid and often unsettling change to Pacific island societies.

SUMMARY

The Americas underwent thorough transformation in early modern times. Smallpox and other diseases sparked ferocious epidemics that devastated indigenous populations and undermined their societies. In the wake of severe depopulation, European peoples toppled imperial states, established mining and agricultural enterprises, imported enslaved African laborers, and founded colonies throughout much of the western hemisphere. Some indigenous peoples disappeared entirely as distinct groups. Others maintained their communities, identities, and cultural traditions but fell increasingly under the influence of European migrants and their Euro-American offspring. In Oceania only Guam and the Mariana Islands felt the full effects of epidemic disease and migration in the early modern era. By the late eighteenth century, however, European and Euro-American peoples with advanced technologies had thoroughly explored the Pacific Ocean basin, and epidemic diseases traveled with them to Australia and the Pacific islands. As a result, during the nineteenth and twentieth centuries, Oceania underwent a social transformation similar to the one experienced earlier by the Americas.

STUDY TERMS

Atahualpa (394)
audiencias (395)
Brazil (396, 399, 401–402)
Chamorro (405)
conquistadores (393)
criollos (399)
Cuzco (394)
Doña Marina (391)
encomienda (392)
engenho (401)
epidemic disease (394)
Francisco Pizarro (394)
fur trade (402)
Guaraní (396)
hacienda (401)
Hernán Cortés (391)
indentured labor (402)
James Cook (405–406)
Malintzin (391)
Manila galleons (405–406)

mestizo/métis (399/400)
mita system (400)
Motecuzoma II (394)
mulattoes (399)
Nahuatl (391)
New Spain (395–396)
peninsulares (399)
Peru (393–396)
Potosí (400)
Quechua (396)
Quiché (396)
quinto (400)
sugarcane (401)
Taino (392)
Tenochtitlan (391)
tobacco (393, 402)
viceroy (395–396)
Virgin of Guadalupe (404)
Zacatecas (400)
zambos (399)

FOR FURTHER READING

Rolena Adorno. *Guaman Poma: Writing and Resistance in Colonial Peru*. Austin, 2000. A native Andean, who came of age after the fall of the Inca empire, tells Philip III of Spain of the evils of colonialism and the need for reform.

Colin G. Callaway. *New Worlds for All: Indians, Europeans, and the Remaking of Early America*. Baltimore, 1997. Scholarly synthesis examining interactions and cultural exchanges between European and indigenous American peoples.

William Cronon. *Changes in the Land: Indians, Colonists, and the Ecology of New England*. New York, 1983. Brilliant study concentrating on the different ways English colonists and native peoples in colonial New England used the environment.

John H. Elliot. *Empires of the Atlantic World: Britain and Spain in America 1492–1830*. New Haven, 2006. Excellent comparative study of Spanish and English colonies in the Americas.

K. R. Howe. *Where the Waves Fall: A New South Sea Island History from First Settlement to Colonial Rule*. Honolulu, 1984. A thoughtful survey of Pacific island history emphasizing interactions between islanders and visitors.

John E. Kicza. *Resilient Cultures: America's Native Peoples Confront European Colonization, 1500–1800*. Upper Saddle River, N.J., 2002. A comprehensive comparative study assessing the impact of colonization on indigenous American peoples as well as native influences on American colonial history.

Karen Ordahl Kupperman. *Indians and English: Facing Off in Early America*. Ithaca, N.Y., 2000. Fascinating reconstruction of the early encounters between English and indigenous American peoples, drawing on sources from all parties to the encounters.

Kathleen Ann Meyers. *Neither Saints nor Sinners: Writing the Lives of Women in Spanish America*. New York, 2003. Examines female self-representation through the life writings of six seventeenth-century women in Latin America.

Matthew Restall, Lisa Sousa, and Kevin Terraciano, eds. *Mesoamerican Voices: Native Language Writings from Colonial Mexico, Yucatan, and Guatemala*. Cambridge, 2005. Composed between the sixteenth and eighteenth centuries, this collection of texts offers access to an important historical source.

David J. Weber. *Bárbaros: Spaniards and Their Savages in the Age of Enlightenment*. New Haven, 2005. Path-breaking and nuanced study of how Spanish administrators tried to forge a more enlightened policy toward native peoples.

Africa and the Atlantic World

CHAPTER 22

Armed escorts march a group of freshly captured Africans to the coast for sale in slave markets.
© North Wind Picture Archives

EYEWITNESS:
A Slave's Long, Strange Trip Back to Africa

Between 1760 and 1792, a west African man known as Thomas Peters crossed the Atlantic Ocean four times. In 1760 slave raiders captured Peters, whose original African name is unknown, marched him to the coast, and sold him to French slave merchants. He traveled in a slave ship to the French colony of Louisiana, where he probably worked on a sugar plantation. But Peters was not a docile servant. He attempted to escape at least three times, and his master punished him by beating him and branding him with a hot iron. During the 1760s his French master sold Peters to an English planter, and about 1770 a Scottish landowner in North Carolina bought him.

During the 1770s, as English colonists in North America prepared to rebel against the British government, slaves of African ancestry considered their own prospects and looked for ways to obtain personal freedom. Peters was among them. When war broke out, he made his way with his wife and daughter to British lines and joined the Black Pioneers, a company of escaped slaves who fought to maintain British rule in the colonies. When the colonists won the war, Peters escaped to Nova Scotia with his family and many other former slaves.

Blacks were legally free in Nova Scotia, but the white ruling elites forced them to till marginal lands and live in segregated villages. In hopes of improving their lot, some two hundred black families sent Peters to London in 1790, where he promoted the establishment of a colony for former slaves in Sierra Leone. His efforts succeeded, and the next year he returned to Nova Scotia to seek recruits for the colony. In 1792 he led 1,196 blacks aboard a convoy of fifteen ships and began his fourth crossing of the Atlantic Ocean. The colonists arrived safely at Freetown, and Peters served as a leader of the black community there. Although he lived less than four months after arriving in Sierra Leone, his life and experiences personified the links connecting the lands of the Atlantic Ocean basin.

For the most part, the peoples of sub-Saharan Africa continued to follow established patterns of life in early modern times. They built states and organized societies based on kinship groups, and in west Africa and coastal east Africa they continued to trade regularly with Muslim merchants from north Africa and southwest Asia.

Yet the establishment of global trade networks brought deep change to sub-Saharan Africa. Commercial opportunities drew Europeans to the coasts of west Africa, and maritime trade soon turned west African attention to the Atlantic. Maritime commerce also helped promote the emergence of prosperous port cities and the establishment of powerful coastal kingdoms that traded through the ocean rather than the desert. In central Africa and south Africa, European merchants brought the first substantial opportunities for long-distance trade, since Muslim merchants had not ventured to those regions in large numbers.

Trade through the Atlantic profoundly affected African society because it involved human beings. Slavery had been a part of African societies for centuries, and Africans had long supplied slaves to Muslim merchants involved in trans-Saharan trade networks. The Atlantic slave trade, however, was vastly larger than the African and Islamic

CHRONOLOGY

1441	Beginning of the Portuguese slave trade
1464–1493	Reign of Sunni Ali
1464–1591	Songhay empire
1506–1542	Reign of King Afonso I of Kongo
1623–1663	Reign of Queen Nzinga of Ndongo
1706	Execution of Doña Beatriz
1745–1797	Life of Olaudah Equiano
1793–1804	Haitian revolution
1807	End of the British slave trade
1865	Abolition of slavery in the United States

not only siphoned millions of people from their own societies but also provoked turmoil in much of sub-Saharan Africa.

The vast majority of Africans sold into the Atlantic slave trade went to the Caribbean or the Americas. Most worked on plantations cultivating cash crops for export, although some worked as domestic servants, miners, or laborers. Together they made up the largest migration in history before the nineteenth century and gave rise to an African diaspora in the western hemisphere. Under the restrictive conditions of slavery, they could not reconstitute African societies, but they preserved some African traditions and blended them with European and American traditions to create hybrid African-American societies.

slave trades, and it had more serious consequences for African society. Between the fifteenth and the nineteenth centuries, it

AFRICAN POLITICS AND SOCIETY IN EARLY MODERN TIMES

At the start of the early modern era, African peoples lived under a variety of political organizations, including clans governed by kinship groups, regional kingdoms, city-states, and large imperial states that drew their power from the trans-Saharan trade. Under the influence of maritime trade, however, African patterns of state development changed. In west Africa, regional kingdoms replaced imperial states as peoples organized their societies to take advantage of Atlantic as well as trans-Saharan commerce. In east Africa, Swahili city-states fell under the domination of Portuguese merchant-mariners seeking commercial opportunities in the Indian Ocean basin. The extension of trade networks also led to the formation of regional kingdoms in central Africa and south Africa. As the volume of long-distance trade grew, both Islam and Christianity became more prominent in sub-Saharan African societies.

The States of West Africa and East Africa

Between the eighth and the sixteenth centuries, powerful kingdoms and imperial states ruled the savannas of west Africa. The earliest was the kingdom of Ghana, which origi-

Ghana (GAH-nuh)
Songhay (song-AHY)
Sunni Ali (soon-ee ah-lee)
Timbuktu (tim-buhk-TOO)
Jenne (jehn-neh)

nated as early as the fourth or fifth century and established its dominance in the region in the eighth century. By controlling and taxing the trans-Saharan trade in gold, the kings of Ghana gained the resources they needed to field a large army and influence affairs in much of west Africa. In the thirteenth century the Mali empire replaced Ghana as the preeminent power in west Africa and continued the Ghana policy of controlling trans-Saharan trade.

The Songhay Empire In the fifteenth century the expansive state of Songhay emerged to take Mali's place as the dominant power of the western grasslands. Based in the trading city of Gao, Songhay rulers built a flourishing city-state as early as the eighth century. In the early fifteenth century, they rejected Mali authority, and in 1464 the Songhay ruler Sunni Ali (reigned 1464–1493) conquered his neighbors and consolidated the Songhay empire (1464–1591). He brought the important trading cities of Timbuktu and Jenne under his control and used their wealth to dominate the central Niger valley.

Songhay Administration Sunni Ali built an elaborate administrative and military apparatus to oversee affairs in his realm. He instituted a hierarchy of command that turned his army into an effective military force. He also created an imperial navy to patrol the Niger River, which was an extremely important commercial highway. Songhay military might enabled Sunni Ali's successors to extend their authority north into the Sahara, east toward Lake Chad, and west toward the upper reaches of the Niger River.

The Songhay emperors presided over a prosperous land. The capital city of Gao had about seventy-five thousand residents, many of whom participated in the lucrative trans-Saharan trade that brought salt, textiles, and metal goods south in exchange for gold and slaves. The emperors were all Muslims: they supported mosques, built schools to teach the Quran, and maintained an Islamic university at Timbuktu. Like the rulers of Ghana and Mali, the Songhay emperors valued Islam as a cultural foundation for cooperation with Muslim merchants and Islamic states in north Africa.

Fall of Songhay The Songhay empire dominated west Africa for most of the sixteenth century, but it was the last of the great imperial states of the grasslands. In 1591 a musket-bearing Moroccan army trekked across the Sahara and opened fire on the previously invincible Songhay military machine. Songhay forces withered under the attack, and subject peoples took the opportunity to revolt against Songhay domination.

As the Songhay empire crumbled, a series of small, regional kingdoms and city-states emerged in west Africa. On the coasts Diula, Mande, and other trading peoples established a series of states that entered into commercial relations with European merchant-mariners who called at west African ports after the fifteenth century. The increasing prominence of Atlantic trade in west African society worked against the interests of imperial states such as Mali and Songhay, which had relied on control of trans-Saharan trade to finance their empires.

Swahili Decline While regional states displaced the Songhay empire in west Africa, the Swahili city-states of east Africa fell on hard times. In 1505 a huge Portuguese naval expedition subdued all the Swahili cities from Sofala to Mombasa. Portuguese forces built administrative centers at Mozambique and Malindi and constructed forts throughout the region in hopes of controlling trade in east Africa. They did not succeed in that effort, but they disrupted trade patterns enough to send the Swahili cities into a decline from which they never fully recovered.

The Kingdoms of Central Africa and South Africa

The Kingdom of Kongo As trade networks multiplied and linked all regions of sub-Saharan Africa, an increasing volume of commerce encouraged state building in central and south Africa. In central Africa the principal states were the kingdoms of Kongo, Ndongo, Luba, and Lunda in the Congo River basin. Best known of them was the kingdom of Kongo, which emerged in the fourteenth century. Its rulers built a centralized state with officials overseeing

Timbuktu.
The city of Timbuktu, as sketched by a French traveler in 1828, was the commercial and cultural center of the Mali and Songhay empires. Though long in decline, the city's mosques, mud-brick dwellings, and crowds of people bespeak a prosperous community.

military, judicial, and financial affairs, and by the late fifteenth century Kongo embraced much of the modern-day Republic of the Congo and Angola.

In 1483 a small Portuguese fleet initiated commercial relations with the kingdom of Kongo. Within a few years, Portuguese merchants had established a close political and diplomatic relationship with the kings of Kongo. They supplied the kings with advisors, provided a military garrison to support the kings and protect Portuguese interests, and brought artisans and priests to Kongo.

The kings of Kongo converted to Christianity as a way to establish closer commercial and diplomatic relations with the Portuguese. The kings appreciated the fact that Christianity offered a strong endorsement of their monarchical rule and found similarities between Roman Catholic saints and the spirits recognized in Kongolese religion. King Nzinga Mbemba of Kongo, also known as King Afonso I (reigned 1506–1542), became a devout Roman Catholic and sought to convert all his subjects to Christianity. Portuguese priests in Kongo reported that he attended religious services daily and studied the Bible so zealously that he sometimes neglected to eat.

Diula (dih-uh-lah)
Mande (MAHN-dey)
Swahili (swah-HEE-lee)
Mozambique (moh-zam-BEEK)
Malindi (mah-LIN-dee)
Ndongo (n'DAWN-goh)
Nzinga Mbemba (IN-zinga MEHM-bah)

Slave Raiding in Kongo   Relations with Portugal brought wealth and foreign recognition to Kongo but also led eventually to the destruction of the kingdom. In exchange for their goods and services, Portuguese merchants sought high-value merchandise such as copper, ivory, and, most of all, slaves. They sometimes embarked on slaving expeditions themselves, but more often they made alliances with local authorities in interior regions and provided them with weapons in exchange for slaves. Such tactics undermined the authority of the kings, who appealed repeatedly for the Portuguese to cease or at least to limit their trade in slaves.

Over time, relations between Kongo and Portugal deteriorated, particularly after Portuguese agents began to pursue opportunities south of Kongo. In 1665 Portuguese colonists to the south even went to war with Kongo. Portuguese forces quickly defeated the Kongolese army and decapitated the king. Soon thereafter, Portuguese merchants began to withdraw from Kongo in search of more profitable business in the kingdom of Ndongo to the south. By the eighteenth century the kingdom of Kongo had largely disintegrated.

MAP 22.1

African states, 1500–1650. Locate the three largest states of Songhay, Kongo, and Kanem-Bornu.

What was it about their respective locations that favored the development of such large polities?

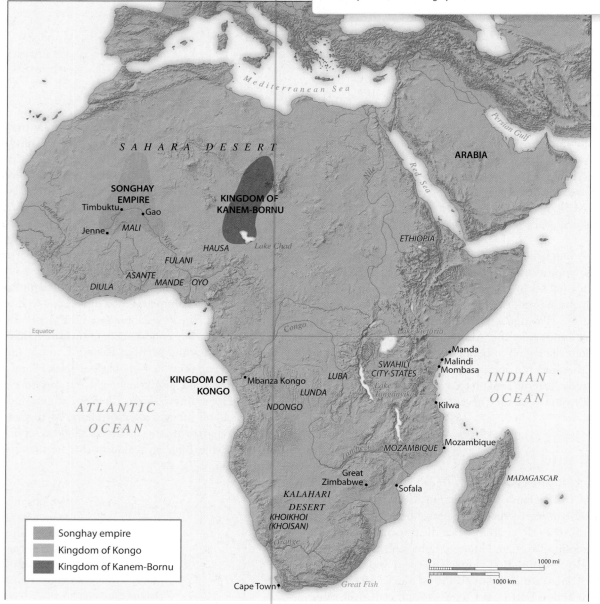

Thinking about TRADITIONS

Traditions in Africa and the Atlantic World
As a result of the Atlantic slave trade, millions of Africans from a wide variety of states and regions were forced to migrate to the Americas without the benefit of material possessions, family, or the freedom to live where and how they liked. In spite of these hardships, many African traditions survived in blended or creole forms of culture in the Americas. *What forms of culture best expressed this fusion? How did language and music in particular embody creole customs?*

The Kingdom of Ndongo Meanwhile, Portuguese explorers were developing a brisk slave trade to the south in the kingdom of Ndongo, which the Portuguese referred to as Angola from the title of the king, *ngola*. During the sixteenth century, Ndongo had grown from a small chiefdom subject to the kings of Kongo to a powerful regional kingdom, largely on the basis of the wealth it was able to attract by trading directly with Portuguese merchants rather than through Kongolese intermediaries. After 1611 the Portuguese steadily increased their influence inland by allying with neighboring peoples who delivered increasing numbers of war captives to feed the growing slave trade. Over the next several decades, Portuguese forces campaigned in Ndongo in an effort to establish a colony that would support large-scale trading in slaves.

Queen The conquest of Angola did not come easily. For forty years Queen Nzinga (reigned 1623–1663) led spirited resistance against Portuguese forces. Nzinga came from a long line of warrior-kings. She dressed as a male warrior when leading troops in battle and insisted that her subjects refer to her as king rather than queen. She mobilized central African peoples against her Portuguese adversaries, and she allied with Dutch mariners who also traded on the African coast. Her aim was to drive the Portuguese from her land, then expel the Dutch, and finally create a central African empire embracing the entire lower Congo basin.

The Portuguese Colony of Angola Although she was an effective military leader, Nzinga was unable to oust Portuguese forces from Ndongo.

When Nzinga died, Portuguese forces faced less capable resistance, and they both extended and tightened their control over Angola, the first European colony in sub-Saharan Africa.

Regional Kingdoms in South Africa

In south Africa, as in central Africa, regional kingdoms dominated political affairs. Kingdoms had begun to emerge as early as the eleventh century, largely under the influence of trade. Merchants from the Swahili city-states of coastal east Africa sought gold, ivory, and slaves from the interior regions of south Africa. By controlling local commerce, chieftains increased their wealth, enhanced their power, and extended their authority. By 1300 rulers of one such kingdom had built a massive, stone-fortified city known as Great Zimbabwe, near the city of Nyanda in modern Zimbabwe, and they dominated the gold-bearing plain between the Zambesi and Limpopo rivers until the late fifteenth century.

European Arrival in South Africa

After the fifteenth century a series of smaller kingdoms displaced the rulers of Great Zimbabwe, and Portuguese and Dutch mariners

---

Zimbabwe (zihm-BAHB-way)

Queen Nzinga of Ndongo.
In this engraving, the queen speaks with the Portuguese governor of Angola at his headquarters. The diplomat refused to provide Nzinga with a chair, so she seated herself on the back of a servant while her "concubines" looked on at the right.

began to play a role in south African affairs. They became especially active after Dutch mariners built a trading post at Cape Town in 1652. With the aid of firearms, they claimed lands for themselves and commandeered the labor of indigenous Khoikhoi peoples. By 1700 large numbers of Dutch colonists had begun to arrive in south Africa, and by midcentury they had established settlements in the region. Their conquests laid the foundation for a series of prosperous Dutch and British colonies in sub-Saharan Africa.

Islam and Christianity in Early Modern Africa

Indigenous religions remained influential throughout sub-Saharan Africa in early modern times. Although many African peoples recognized a supreme, remote creator god, they devoted most of their attention to powerful spirits who were thought to intervene directly in human affairs. Some of those spirits were associated with geographic features such as mountains, waters, or forests, and others were believed to be the spirits of ancestors who roamed the world.

Islam in Sub-Saharan Africa Although most Africans continued to observe their inherited religions, both Islam and Christianity attracted increasing interest in sub-Saharan Africa. Islam was most popular in the commercial centers of west Africa and the Swahili city-states of east Africa. In the sixteenth century the trading city of Timbuktu had a prominent Islamic university and 180 schools that taught the Quran. Students flocked to Timbuktu by the thousands from all parts of west Africa.

Most African Muslims blended Islam with indigenous beliefs and customs. The result was a syncretic brand of Islam that not only made a place for African beliefs but also permitted men and women to associate with one another on much more familiar terms than was common in north Africa and Arabia. This syncretic Islam frequently struck many devout Muslims as impure and offensive. Muslim merchants and travelers from north Africa and Arabia often commented on their shock at seeing women in tropical Africa who went out in public with bare breasts and socialized freely with men outside their own families.

The Fulani and Islam Some Muslims in sub-Saharan Africa also shared these concerns about the purity of Islam. Most important of them were the Fulani of the west African savannas, who observed a strict form of Islam like that practiced in north Africa and Arabia. Beginning about 1680 and continuing through the nineteenth century, the Fulani led a series of military campaigns to establish Islamic states and impose their own brand of Islam in west Africa. They

founded powerful states in what is now Guinea, Senegal, Mali, and northern Nigeria, and they promoted the spread of Islam beyond the cities to the countryside by establishing Islamic schools in remote towns and villages. Their campaigns did not stamp out African religions, but they strengthened Islam in sub-Saharan Africa and laid a foundation for new rounds of Islamic state-building and conversion efforts in the nineteenth and twentieth centuries.

Christianity in Sub-Saharan Africa Like Islam, Christianity blended with traditional beliefs and customs when it spread in sub-Saharan Africa and sometimes formed syncretic cults. A particularly influential syncretic cult was the Antonian movement in Kongo, which flourished in the early eighteenth century. The Antonian movement began in 1704 when an aristocratic woman named Doña Beatriz proclaimed that St. Anthony of Padua had possessed her and chosen her to communicate his messages. St. Anthony was a thirteenth-century Franciscan missionary and popular preacher, and he became the patron saint of Portugal. Doña Beatriz gained a reputation for working miracles and curing diseases, and she used her prominence to promote an African form of Christianity. She taught that Jesus Christ had been a black African man, that Kongo was the true holy land of Christianity, and that heaven was for Africans. She urged Kongolese to ignore European missionaries and heed her disciples instead, and she sought to harness the widespread popular interest in her teachings and use it to end the wars plaguing Kongo.

Doña Beatriz's movement was a serious challenge to Christian missionaries in Kongo. In 1706 they persuaded King Pedro IV of Kongo to arrest the charismatic prophetess on suspicion of heresy. After examining her, the missionaries determined that Doña Beatriz knowingly taught false doctrine. On their recommendation the royal government sentenced her to death and burned her at the stake. Yet the Antonian movement did not disappear: in 1708 an army of almost twenty thousand Antonians challenged King Pedro, whom they considered an unworthy ruler. Their efforts illustrate clearly the tendency of Kongolese Christians to fashion a faith that reflected their own needs and concerns as well as the interests of European missionaries.

Social Change in Early Modern Africa

Despite increased state-building activity and political turmoil, African society followed long-established patterns during the early modern era. Kinship groups, for example, continued to serve as the basis of social organization and sometimes political organization as well. Within agricultural villages throughout sub-Saharan Africa, clans under the leadership of prominent individuals organized the affairs of their kinship groups and disciplined those who

Khoikhoi (KOY-koy)
Fulani (foo-LAH-nee)

Sourcesfromthe Past

King Afonso I Protests Slave Trading in the Kingdom of Kongo

King Afonso I of Kongo wrote some twenty-four official letters to his fellow monarchs, the kings of Portugal. The letters touch on many themes—relations between Portugal and Kongo, Afonso's devotion to Christianity, and the slave trade. The following excerpts come from two letters of 1526, when Portuguese slave trading was causing serious disruption in Kongo, prompting Afonso to request help in controlling the activities of Portuguese merchants.

And we cannot reckon how great the damage [caused by Portuguese merchants] is, since the mentioned merchants are taking every day our natives, sons of the land and the sons of our noblemen and vassals and our relatives, because the thieves and men of bad conscience grab them wishing to have the things and wares of this Kingdom which they are ambitious of; they grab them and get them to be sold; and so great, Sir, is the corruption and licentiousness that our country is being completely depopulated, and Your Highness should not agree with this nor accept it as in your service. And to avoid it we need from [your] Kingdoms no more than some priests and a few people to teach in schools, and no other goods except wine and flour for the holy sacrament. That is why we beg of Your Highness to help and assist us in this matter, commanding your factors that they should not send here either merchants or wares, because it is *our will that in these Kingdoms there should not be any trade of slaves nor outlet for them.* Concerning what is referred [to] above, again we beg of Your Highness to agree with it, since otherwise we cannot remedy such an obvious damage. . . .

Moreover, Sir, in our Kingdoms there is another great inconvenience which is of little service to God, and this is that many of our people, keenly desirous as they are of the wares and things of your Kingdoms, which are brought here by your people, and in order to satisfy their voracious appetite, seize many of our people, freed and exempt men, and very often it happens that they kidnap even noblemen and the sons of noblemen, and our relatives, and take them to be sold to the white men who are in our Kingdoms. . . .

And as soon as they are taken by the white men they are immediately ironed and branded with fire, and when they are carried to be embarked, if they are caught by our guards' men the whites allege that they have bought them but they cannot say from whom, so that it is our duty to do justice and to restore to the freemen their freedom, but it cannot be done if your subjects feel offended, as they claim to be.

And to avoid such a great evil we passed a law so that any white man living in our Kingdoms and wanting to purchase goods [i.e., slaves] in any way should first inform three of our noblemen and officials of our court whom we rely upon in this matter, . . . who should investigate if the mentioned goods are captives or free men, and if cleared by them there will be no further doubt nor embargo for them to be taken and embarked. But if the white men do not comply with it they will lose the aforementioned goods. And if we do them this favor and concession it is for the part Your Highness has in it, since we know that it is in your service too that these goods are taken from our Kingdom, otherwise we should not consent to this.

For Further Reflection

■ On the basis of these letters, does it appear that King Afonso opposed all slave trading or only certain kinds of slave trading?

Source: Basil Davidson. *The African Past.* Boston: Little, Brown, 1964, pp. 191–93.

---

violated community standards. Even in lands ruled by formal states, clan leaders usually implemented state policy at the village level.

American Food Crops in Sub-Saharan Africa Yet interaction with European peoples brought change to African society in early modern times. Trade brought access to European textiles and metal goods, which became popular as complements to native African wares. Trade also brought new food crops to sub-Saharan Africa. In the mid–sixteenth century, American crops such as manioc, maize, and peanuts arrived in Africa aboard Portuguese ships. These crops supplemented bananas, yams, rice, and millet, the principal staple foods of sub-Saharan Africa. The most important American crop was manioc because of its high yield and because it thrived in tropical soils not well suited to cultivation of the other crops.

Population Growth By the eighteenth century, bread made from manioc flour had become a staple food in much of west Africa and central Africa, where it helped to underwrite steady population growth. In 1500 C.E. the population of sub-Saharan Africa was about thirty-four million. By 1600 it had increased to forty-four million, and it continued climbing to sixty million in 1800. This strong demographic expansion is all the more remarkable because it took place precisely when millions of Africans underwent an involuntary, forced migration to destinations in the Caribbean and the Americas.

THE ATLANTIC SLAVE TRADE

Of all the processes that linked Africa to the larger Atlantic world in early modern times, the most momentous was the Atlantic slave trade. From the fifteenth to the nineteenth century, European peoples looked to Africa as a source of labor for large plantations that they established in the western hemisphere. In exchange for slaves, African peoples received European manufactured products—most notably firearms. Only in the nineteenth century did the Atlantic slave trade and, in most places, slavery itself come to an end.

Foundations of the Slave Trade

Slavery in Africa Until the nineteenth century many settled peoples of the world utilized slave labor in some form. Slavery was common throughout Africa after the Bantu migrations spread agriculture to all parts of the continent. As in other societies, most slaves in Africa were war captives, although criminals and individuals expelled from their clans also fell into slavery. Once enslaved, an individual had no personal or civil rights. Owners could punish slaves at will and sell them as chattel. African slaves usually worked as cultivators in societies far from their homes, although some worked as administrators, soldiers, or even highly placed advisors. The Songhay emperors, for example, often employed slaves as administrators and soldiers, since the rulers distrusted free nobles, whom they considered excessively ambitious and undependable.

Law and society made African slavery different from bondage in Europe, Asia, and other lands. African law did not recognize private property but, rather, vested ownership of land in communities. Thus wealth and power in Africa came not from the possession of land but from control over the human labor that made land productive. Slaves were thus an important means of measuring wealth. Those who controlled large numbers of individuals were able to harvest more crops and accumulate more wealth than others. Africans routinely purchased slaves to enlarge their families, and they often assimilated slaves into their kinship groups so that within a generation a slave might obtain both freedom and an honorable position in a new family or clan.

Azores (uh-ZAWRZ)
Madeiras (muh-DEER-uhs)
São Tomé (SOU tuh-MEY)

The Islamic Slave Trade After the eighth century, Muslim merchants from north Africa, Arabia, and Persia sought African slaves for sale and distribution to destinations in the Mediterranean basin, southwest Asia, India, and even southeast Asia and China. When traditional sources proved insufficient to satisfy the demand for slaves, merchants created new supplies by raiding villages and capturing innocent individuals. Merchants then transported the freshly recruited slaves across the Sahara desert or boarded them on ships at the Swahili port cities of east Africa. Between the eighth and the twentieth centuries, as many as ten million Africans may have left their homeland to feed the Islamic slave trade.

By the time Europeans ventured to sub-Saharan Africa in the fifteenth and sixteenth centuries, traffic in slaves was a well-established feature of African society, and a system for capturing, selling, and distributing slaves had functioned effectively for more than five hundred years. After 1450 European peoples tapped existing networks and dramatically expanded commerce in African slaves even as they shifted its focus to the Atlantic Ocean basin. This Atlantic slave trade profoundly influenced the development of societies throughout the Atlantic Ocean basin.

Human Cargoes

The Atlantic slave trade began small, but it grew steadily and eventually reached enormous proportions. The earliest European slave traders were Portuguese explorers who, in 1441, seized twelve African men and took them to Portugal as slaves. Portuguese mariners encountered stiff resistance when they attempted to capture slaves, as African warriors fired thousands of poison-tipped arrows at gangs of would-be slave raiders. Soon, however, the mariners learned that they could purchase slaves rather than capture them. By 1460 they were delivering five hundred slaves per year to Portugal and Spain, where they usually worked as miners, porters, or domestic servants.

The Early Slave Trade Slave traders also delivered their human cargoes to Portuguese island colonies in the Atlantic. There was no supply of labor to work plantations in the Azores, the Madeiras, the Cape Verde Islands, and São Tomé, all of which were uninhabited when explorers discovered them in the fifteenth century. Sugar planters on the island of São Tomé in particular called for slaves in increasing quantities. By the 1520s some two thousand slaves per year went to São Tomé. By the 1530s Portuguese entrepreneurs had extended the use of slave labor to Brazil, which eventually became the wealthiest of the sugar-producing lands of the western hemisphere.

Spanish explorers and conquerors also sought laborers to work lands in the Caribbean and the Americas. As

Reverberations of ● ● ● ● ● ● ● ●
The Columbian Exchange

Think back to the effects of Eurasian diseases on the original inhabitants of the Americas after 1492. In what ways was the massive death toll among indigenous Americans related to the origins of the Atlantic slave trade?

imported diseases ravaged indigenous populations, the conquerors found themselves with few laborers to work the land. Gradually Spanish settlers began to rely on imported African slaves as laborers. In 1518 the first shipment of slaves went directly from west Africa to the Caribbean, where they worked on recently established sugar plantations. By the early seventeenth century, English colonists had introduced slaves also to the North American mainland.

Triangular Trade The demand for labor in the western hemisphere stimulated a profitable commerce known as the triangular trade, since European ships often undertook voyages of three legs. On the first leg they carried horses and European manufactured goods—especially firearms—which they exchanged in Africa for slaves. The second leg took Africans to Caribbean and American destinations.

On arrival merchants sold their human cargoes to plantation owners for two to three times what they had cost in Africa. In sugar-producing regions they often bartered slaves for sugar or molasses. Then they filled their vessels' hulls with American products before embarking on their voyage back to Europe.

At every stage of the process, the slave trade was a brutal and inhumane business. The original capture of slaves in Africa was almost always a violent affair. As European demand for slaves grew, some African chieftains organized raiding parties to seize individuals from neighboring societies. Others launched wars for the purpose of capturing victims for the slave trade. They often snatched individuals right out of their homes, fields, or villages: millions of lives changed instantly, as slave raiders grabbed their quarries and then immediately spirited them away in captivity. Bewilderment and anger was

the lot not only of the captives but also of their family members, who would never again see their kin.

The Middle Passage Following capture, enslaved individuals underwent a forced march to the coast, where they lived in holding pens until a ship arrived to transport them to the western hemisphere. Then they embarked on the dreadful middle passage, the trans-Atlantic journey aboard filthy and crowded slave ships. Enslaved passengers traveled belowdecks in hideously cramped quarters. Conditions were so bad that many slaves attempted to starve themselves to death or mounted revolts. Ship crews often treated the unwilling passengers with cruelty and contempt. Crew members used tools to pry open the mouths of those who refused to eat and pitched sick individuals into the ocean rather than have them waste limited supplies of food.

Middle passage.
Belowdecks on an illegal slave ship seized by a British antislavery patrol in 1846.

What kinds of conditions are depicted in this drawing?

Barring difficulties, the journey to Caribbean and American destinations took four to six weeks, during which heat, cold, and disease levied a heavy toll on the human cargo. During the early days of the slave trade, mortality could exceed 50 percent. As the volume of the trade grew, slavers provided better nourishment and facilities for their cargoes, and mortality eventually declined to about 5 percent per voyage. Over the course of the Atlantic slave trade, however, approximately 25 percent of individuals enslaved in Africa did not survive the middle passage.

The Impact of the Slave Trade in Africa

Volume of the Slave Trade Before 1600 the Atlantic slave trade operated on a modest scale: on average about two thousand slaves left Africa annually during the late fifteenth and sixteenth centuries. During the seventeenth century, slave exports rose dramatically to twenty thousand per year. The high point of the slave trade came in the eighteenth century, when the number of slaves exported to the Americas averaged fifty-five thousand per year. During the 1780s slave arrivals averaged eighty-eight thousand per year, and in some individual years they exceeded one hundred thousand. From beginning to end the Atlantic slave trade brought about twelve million Africans to the western hemisphere. An additional four million or more died before arriving.

The impact of the slave trade varied over time and from one African society to another. Some societies largely escaped the slave trade because their lands were distant from the major slave ports on the west African coast. Those societies that raided, took captives, and sold slaves to Europeans profited handsomely from the trade, as did the port cities and the states that coordinated trade with European merchants. Asante, Dahomey, and Oyo peoples, for example, took advantage of the slave trade to obtain firearms from European merchants and build powerful states in west Africa.

Social Effects of the Slave Trade On the whole, however, Africa suffered serious losses from the slave trade. The Atlantic slave trade alone deprived African societies of about sixteen million individuals, in addition to several million others consumed by the continuing Islamic slave trade during the early modern era. Although total African population rose during the early modern era, partly because American food crops enriched diets, several individual societies experienced severe losses because of the slave

Asante (uh-SAN-tee)
Dahomey (dah-HO-meh)
Oyo (OH-yoh)

> Over 80 percent of all slaves shipped across the Atlantic were sent to the Caribbean islands and Brazil.

trade. West African societies between Senegal and Angola were especially vulnerable to slave raiding because of their proximity to the most active slave ports.

While diverting labor from Africa to other lands, the slave trade also distorted African sex ratios, since approximately two-thirds of all exported slaves were males. Slavers preferred young men between ages fourteen and thirty-five, since they had the best potential to provide heavy labor over an extended period of time. This preference for male slaves had social implications for lands that provided slaves. By the late eighteenth century, for example, women made up more than two-thirds of the adult population of Angola. This sexual imbalance encouraged Angolans to practice polygamy and forced women to take on duties that in earlier times had been the responsibility of men.

Political Effects of the Slave Trade Apart from its demographic and social effects, the slave trade brought turmoil to African societies. Violence escalated especially after

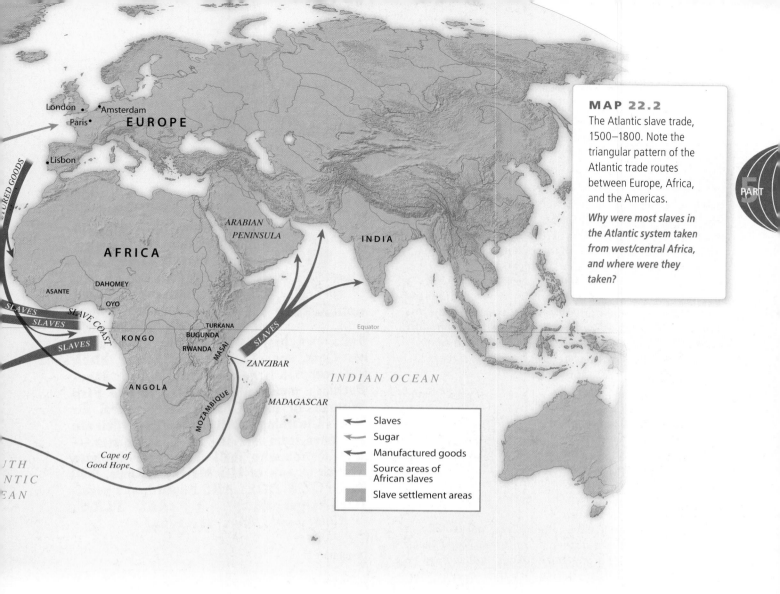

MAP 22.2
The Atlantic slave trade, 1500–1800. Note the triangular pattern of the Atlantic trade routes between Europe, Africa, and the Americas.

Why were most slaves in the Atlantic system taken from west/central Africa, and where were they taken?

- Slaves
- Sugar
- Manufactured goods
- Source areas of African slaves
- Slave settlement areas

Plantation life.
In an engraving of 1667, a European supervisor (lower right) directs slaves on a sugar plantation in Barbados as they haul cane, crush it to extract its juice, boil it to produce molasses, and distill the product into rum.

Connecting
the Sources

Using indirect sources to reconstruct the lives of slaves

In order to write about the past, historians must find and interpret **primary sources**. Primary sources can include material objects, archeological evidence, oral traditions, texts (including official documents, letters, accounts, newspapers), or images. They provide the evidence on which historical narratives rest. This exercise highlights some of the challenges of interpreting original primary sources by asking you to consider the kinds of contextual information you might need in order to interpret such documents accurately, and by asking you to consider what individual documents can and cannot tell you.

The problem

Sometimes historians want to find out about the experiences of groups that may not have had much power in the past, such as women, peasants, or slaves. This can be difficult, however, because such groups frequently did not leave many textual records behind. In the case of slaves who became part of the Atlantic slave trade, it is difficult to find primary sources created by individual slaves themselves, particularly in the seventeenth and eighteenth centuries. Many slaves were not literate in European languages, and even when slaves were literate the documents they created may not have been saved for later inclusion in historical archives. Some slave voices—like Olaudah Equiano's—have survived from that period, as we see in this chapter. But to understand the varieties of experiences slaves might have had, historians must use many primary sources written by others, including those written by slave traders, slave owners, courts, and governments. Let us consider two such sources as a way of thinking about what indirect sources can and cannot tell us about the experience of slavery in the eighteenth century.

The documents

Read the documents below, and consider carefully the questions that follow.

Document 1: *This advertisement comes from the* New London Summary *(Connecticut) on March 30, 1764.*

Document 1

The text reads:

Ran away from me the subscriber, the 14th instant, a Molatto named Bilhah, a tall, thick-built well-proportioned Wench; had on a brown short stuff Gown, batt'd with Yellow, a blue camblet Quilt, and check'd linnen Apron, black silk Bonnet, a large pair flower'd silver Shoe-Buckles; may possibly pretend to be a Free Woman, or may Change her Apparel for Men's Cloathing. All Masters of Vessels are cautioned from carrying off said Molatto— Any Person who shall secure said Molatto Wench in any of His Majesty's Goals, shall have FOUR DOLLARS Reward, and necessary Charges paid by Jared Eliot. Killingworth, Mar. 21, 1764.

Document 2: *This broadside advertisement was posted in Charlestown, South Carolina, in 1769.*

Document 2

ARRIVED in the Ship
Countess of Sussex, Thomas Davies,
Master, directly from Gambia, by
JOHN CHAPMAN, & Co.

THIS is the Vessel that had the Small-Pox on Board at the Time of her Arrival the 31st of March last: Every necessary Precaution hath since been taken to cleanse both Ship and Cargo thoroughly, so that those who may be inclined to purchase need not be under the least Apprehension of Danger from Infliction.

The NEGROES are allowed to be the likeliest Parcel that have been imported this Season.

Questions

- What can these advertisements definitively tell you about their respective situations? What **facts** can be gleaned from these brief sources?
- In Document 1, what might this advertisement imply about the experience of slavery from Bilhah's point of view? For example, does it imply that Bilhah was unhappy with her status as a slave, or is it simply impossible to know?
- Also in Document 1, what might this advertisement imply about Bilhah's treatment prior to her departure? Are there any clues that indicate how she lived under Jared Eliot's care?
- In Document 2, what kinds of information can you glean about the possible experience of the captive slaves held aboard the *Countess of Sussex*? For example, what might it have been like to cross the Atlantic with smallpox aboard?
- Taking both documents together, what kinds of contextual information would you need in order to understand these advertisements more fully? For example, would your conclusions about the meaning of Document 1 change if you knew that hundreds of slaves ran away every year or, alternatively, if Bilhah was a rare exception? Would your conclusions regarding Document 2 be different if you knew that the *Countess of Sussex* was one of many slave ships to arrive in port at Charlestown in 1769, or if you knew such a landing was a rare occurrence? What further information would you need in order to use these documents to interpret the experience of North American slaves in the eighteenth century?
- Sources such as these make up the building blocks on which historians base their interpretations of the past. In most cases, however, historians discover that they must use a variety of primary and secondary sources in order to make accurate interpretations.

The text reads:

CHARLESTOWN, April 27, 1769

TO BE SOLD,
On Wednesday the Tenth Day of
May next,

A CHOICE CARGO OF
Two Hundred & Fifty
NEGROES:

Source Website: **Document 1:** http://www.yale.edu/glc/citizens/stories/module1/documents/runaway_slave.html **Document 2:** http://www.pbs.org/wgbh/aia/part1/1h304.html

the late seventeenth century, when African peoples increasingly exchanged slaves for European firearms. When the kingdom of Dahomey obtained effective firearms, for example, its armies were able to capture slaves from unarmed neighboring societies and exchange them for more weapons. During the eighteenth century, Dahomey expanded rapidly and absorbed neighboring societies by increasing its arsenal of firearms and maintaining a constant flow of slaves to the coast. By no means did all African states take such advantage of the slave trade, but Dahomey's experience illustrates the potential of the slave trade to alter the patterns of African politics and society.

THE AFRICAN DIASPORA

Some slaves worked as urban laborers or domestic servants, and in Mexico and Peru many worked also as miners. The vast majority, however, provided agricultural labor on plantations in the Caribbean or the Americas. There they cultivated cash crops that made their way into commercial arteries linking lands throughout the Atlantic Ocean basin. Although deprived of their freedom, slaves often resisted their bondage, and they built hybrid cultural traditions compounded of African, European, and American elements. Most European and American states ended the slave trade and abolished slavery during the nineteenth century. By that time the African diaspora—the dispersal of African peoples and their descendants—had left a permanent mark throughout the western hemisphere.

Plantation Societies

Most African slaves went to plantations in the tropical and subtropical regions of the western hemisphere. Spanish colonists established the first of these plantations in 1516 on the island of Hispaniola (modern Haiti and the Dominican Republic) and soon extended them to Mexico as well. Beginning in the 1530s Portuguese entrepreneurs organized plantations in Brazil, and by the early seventeenth century English, Dutch, and French plantations had also appeared in the Caribbean and the Americas.

Cash Crops Many of these plantations produced sugar, which was one of the most lucrative cash crops of early modern times. But plantations produced other crops as well, including tobacco, rice, and indigo. By the eighteenth century many plantations concentrated on the cultivation of cotton, and coffee had begun to emerge as a plantation specialty.

diaspora (dahy-AS-per-uh)
Suriname (SOOR-uh-nahm)
Saramaka (sar-ah-MAH-kah)

Regardless of the crops they produced, Caribbean and American plantations had certain elements in common. All of them specialized in the production and export of commercial crops. They all also relied almost exclusively on slave labor. Plantations also featured a sharp, racial division of labor: small numbers of European or Euro-American supervisors governed plantation affairs, and large numbers of African or African-American slaves performed most of the community's physical labor.

Regional Differences In spite of their structural similarities, plantation societies differed considerably from one region to another. In the Caribbean and South America, slave populations usually were unable to sustain their numbers by natural means. This was due partly to the impact of tropical diseases such as malaria and yellow fever and partly to the brutal working conditions the slaves faced on the plantations. Moreover, since most slaves were male, slave communities did not reproduce quickly.

Thus, in the Caribbean and South America, plantation owners demanded a continuous supply of slaves to maintain their workforces. Of all the slaves delivered from Africa to the western hemisphere, about half went to Caribbean destinations, and a third more went to Brazil.

Only about 5 percent of enslaved Africans went to North American destinations. Diseases there were less threatening than in the Caribbean and Brazil. Moreover, North American planters imported larger numbers of female slaves and encouraged their slaves to form families and bear children. Their support for slave families was especially strong in the eighteenth century, when the prices of slaves direct from Africa rose dramatically.

Resistance to Slavery No matter where they lived, slaves did not meekly accept their status but, like Thomas Peters, resisted it in numerous ways. Some forms of resistance were mild but costly to slave owners: slaves often worked slowly for their masters but diligently in their own gardens, for example. Sometimes they sabotaged plantation equipment or work routines. More seriously, slaves resisted by running away. Runaways known as maroons gathered in remote regions and built their own self-governing communities. Many maroons had gained military experience in Africa, and they organized escaped slaves into effective military forces. Maroon communities flourished throughout slaveholding regions of the western hemisphere, and some of them survived for centuries. In present-day Suriname, for example, the Saramaka people maintain an elaborate oral tradition that traces their descent from eighteenth-century maroons.

Slave Revolts The most dramatic form of resistance to slavery was the slave revolt. Slaves far outnumbered others in most plantation societies, and thus slave revolts brought

self-governing republic (1804). The Haitian revolution terrified slave owners and inspired slaves throughout the western hemisphere, but no other slave rebellion matched its accomplishments.

Slavery and Economic Development

The physical labor of African and African-American slaves made crucial contributions to the building of new societies in the Americas and also to the making of the early modern world as a whole. Slave labor cultivated many of the crops and extracted many of the minerals that made their way around the world in the global trade networks of the early modern era. Although slaves themselves did not enjoy the fruits of their labors, without them it would have been impossible for prosperous new societies to emerge in the Americas during the early modern era.

Thinking about ENCOUNTERS

Encounters in Africa and the Atlantic World

Although many of the peoples of sub-Saharan Africa continued to follow established patterns of life in the early modern period, the opening of the Atlantic slave trade ushered in a new era of intense and destructive encounters between Africans and Europeans. *In what ways did these encounters shape African societies in Africa itself, and in what ways did they shape the emerging societies of the Americas?*

stark fear to plantation owners and supervisors. Yet slave revolts almost never brought slavery itself to an end, because the European and Euro-American ruling elites had access to military forces that extinguished most rebellions. Only in the French sugar colony of Saint-Domingue did a slave revolt abolish slavery as an institution (1793). Indeed, the slaves of Saint-Domingue declared independence from France, renamed the land Haiti, and established a

Saint-Domingue (san doe-MANG)

Treatment of slaves.
Slaves were vulnerable to cruel treatment that often provoked them to run away from their plantations or even mount revolts. A French visitor to Brazil in the early nineteenth century depicted a Portuguese overseer administering a brutal whipping to a bound slave on a plantation near Rio de Janeiro.

What function might the branch behind this slave's knees have had?

The Making of African-American Cultural Traditions

Enslaved Africans did not enjoy the luxury of maintaining their inherited cultural traditions in the western hemisphere. When packed in slave ships for the middle passage, they found themselves in the company of Africans from societies other than their own. When sold to masters in the Caribbean and the Americas, they joined societies shaped by European and American traditions. In those new circumstances, then, slaves constructed distinctive African-American cultural traditions.

African and Creole Languages European languages were the dominant tongues in the slave societies of the western hemisphere, but slave communities frequently spoke a creole tongue that drew on several African and European languages. In the low country of South Carolina and Georgia, for example, slaves made up about three-quarters of the population in the eighteenth century and regularly communicated in the creole languages Gullah and Geechee, respectively.

African-American Religions Like their languages, slaves' religions combined elements from different societies. Some slaves from Africa were Christians, and many others converted to Christianity after their arrival in the western hemisphere. Most Africans and African-Americans, however, practiced a syncretic faith that made considerable room for African interests and traditions. Because they developed mostly in plantation societies under conditions of slavery, these syncretic religions usually did not create an institutional structure or establish a hierarchy of priests and officials. Yet in several cases—most notably Voudou in Haiti, Santeria in Cuba, and Candomblé in Brazil—they became exceedingly popular.

All the syncretic African-American religions drew inspiration from Christianity: they met in parish churches, sought personal salvation, and made use of Christian paraphernalia such as holy water, candles, and statues. Yet they also preserved African traditions. They associated African deities with Christian saints and relied heavily on African

Gullah (GUHL-uh)
Geechee (GEE-chee)
Voudou (voo-doo)
Santeria (sahn-tuh-REE-uh)
Candomblé (kan-duhm-BLEH)
Olaudah Equiano (oh-LAU-duh ay-kwee-AHN-oh)

rituals such as drumming, dancing, and sacrificing animals. They also preserved beliefs in spirits and supernatural powers: magic, sorcery, witchcraft, and spirit possession all played prominent roles in African-American religions.

African-American Music As in their languages and religions, slaves relied on their African traditions in creating musical forms attuned to the plantation landscape. African slaves in the Americas adapted African musical traditions, including both their rhythmic and oratorical elements, to their new environments as a means of buffering the shock of transition, as a way to survive and to resist the horrid conditions of their new lives. In the process, they managed to create musical forms that made their influence felt not just in the slave quarters but also in the multicultural societies of the Caribbean and the Americas.

Slaves fashioned a new sense of identity and strength by adapting west African instruments and musical traditions to suit European languages, Christian religion, and the work routines of American plantations. Slave musicians played drums and stringed instruments like banjos that closely resembled traditional African instruments. They also adapted west African call-and-response patterns of singing to the rhythms of field work on plantations. Indeed, from work songs and spirituals to the blues, jazz, and soul, African-American music evolved to mirror the difficult and often chaotic circumstances of black life in the Americas.

African-American Cultural Traditions African traditions also made their effects felt throughout much of the western hemisphere. Slaves introduced African foods to Caribbean and American societies and helped give rise to distinctive hybrid cuisines. They combined African okra, for example, with European-style sautéed vegetables and American shellfish to produce magnificent gumbos, which found their way to Euro-American as well as African-American tables. Slaves introduced rice cultivation to tropical and subtropical regions. They also built houses, fashioned clay pots, and wove grass baskets in west African styles. In many ways the African diaspora influenced the ways all peoples lived in plantation societies.

The End of the Slave Trade and the Abolition of Slavery

Olaudah Equiano Almost as old as the Atlantic slave trade itself were voices calling for its abolition. The American and French revolutions, with their calls for liberty and universal human rights, stimulated the abolitionist cause.

Africans also took up the struggle to abolish commerce in human beings. Frequent slave revolts in the eighteenth and nineteenth centuries made the institution of slavery an expensive and dangerous business. Some freed slaves contributed to the abolitionist cause by writing books that exposed the brutality of institutional slavery. Most notable of them was the west African Olaudah Equiano (1745–1797), who in 1789 published an autobiography detailing his experiences as a slave and a free man. Captured at age ten in his native Benin (in modern Nigeria), Equiano worked as a slave in the West Indies, Virginia, and Pennsylvania. He accompanied one of his masters on several campaigns of the Seven Years' War before purchasing his freedom in 1766. The book became a best seller, and Equiano traveled throughout the British Isles giving speeches and denouncing slavery as an evil institution. He lobbied government officials and members of Parliament, and his efforts strengthened the antislavery movement in England, which after 1789 was spearheaded by the social reformer and Parliamentarian William Wilberforce.

Olaudah Equiano.
The abolitionist former slave as depicted in the first edition of his autobiography (1789).

The Economic Costs of Slavery Quite apart from moral and political arguments, economic forces contributed to the end of slavery and the slave trade. Indeed, it gradually became clear that slave labor did not come cheap. The possibility of rebellion forced slave societies to maintain expensive military forces. Even in peaceful times slaves were often unwilling and unproductive workers. Furthermore, in the late eighteenth century a rapid expansion of Caribbean sugar production led to declining prices. About the same time, African slave traders and European merchants sharply increased the prices they charged for fresh slaves.

As the profitability of slavery declined, Europeans began to shift their investments from sugarcane and slaves to newly emerging manufacturing industries. Investors soon found that wage labor in factories was cheaper than slave labor on plantations. As an additional benefit, free workers spent much of their income on manufactured goods. Meanwhile, European investors realized that leaving Africans in Africa, where they could secure raw materials and buy manufactured goods in exchange, was good business.

End of the Slave Trade Denmark abolished trade in slaves in 1803, and other lands followed suit: Great Britain in 1807, the United States in 1808, France in 1814, the Netherlands in 1817, and Spain in 1845. The end of the slave trade did not abolish the institution of slavery itself, however, and as long as plantation slavery continued, a clandestine trade shipped slaves across the Atlantic. British naval squadrons sought to prevent this trade by conducting search-and-seizure operations, and gradually the illegal slave trade ground to a halt. The last documented ship that carried slaves across the Atlantic arrived in Cuba in 1867.

The abolition of the institution of slavery itself was a long-drawn-out process: emancipation of all slaves came in 1833 in British colonies, 1848 in French colonies, 1865 in the United States, 1886 in Cuba, and 1888 in Brazil. Saudi Arabia and Angola abolished slavery in the 1960s. Officially, slavery no longer exists, but millions of people live in various forms of involuntary servitude even today. According to the Anti-slavery Society for the Protection of Human Rights, debt bondage, contract labor, sham adoptions, servile marriages, and other forms of servitude still oppress more than two hundred million people, mostly in Africa, south Asia, and Latin America. Meanwhile, the legacy of the Atlantic slave trade remains visible throughout much of the western hemisphere, where the African diaspora has given rise to distinctive African-American communities.

SUMMARY

During the early modern era, the peoples of sub-Saharan Africa built states and traded with Islamic societies as they had since the eighth century C.E. Yet African peoples also experienced dramatic changes as they participated in the formation of an integrated Atlantic Ocean basin. The principal agents of change were European merchant-mariners who sought commercial opportunities in sub-Saharan Africa. They brought European manufactured goods and introduced American food crops that fueled population growth throughout Africa. But they also encouraged vast expansion of existing slave-trading networks as they sought laborers for plantations in the western hemisphere. The Atlantic slave trade violently removed at least sixteen million individuals from their home societies and caused political turmoil and social disruption throughout much of sub-Saharan Africa. Enslaved Africans and their descendants were mostly unable to build states or organize societies in the western hemisphere. But they formed an African diaspora that maintained some African traditions and profoundly influenced the development of societies in all slave-holding regions of the Caribbean and the Americas. They also collaborated with others to bring about an end to the slave trade and the abolition of slavery itself.

STUDY TERMS

African diaspora (422–425)
Angola (413)
Antonian movement (414)
Asante (418)
Atlantic slave trade (416–422)
Azores (416)
Candomblé (424)
Cape Town (414)
creole language (424)
Dahomey (418)
Diaspora (422)
Diula (411)
Doña Beatriz (414)
Fulani (414)
Geechee (424)
Ghana (410)
Great Zimbabwe (413)
Gullah (424)
Haiti (422–423)
Islamic slave trade (416)
Jenne (410)
Khoikhoi (414)

King Afonso I (415)
kingdom of Kongo (411–412)
Madeiras (416)
Mali empire (410)
Malindi (411)
Mande (411)
manioc (415)
middle passage (417–418)
Mozambique (411)
Ndongo (411)
Nzinga Mbemba (411)
Olaudah Equiano (424)
Oyo (418)
plantation (422–423)
Queen Nzinga (413)
Saint-Domingue (423)
Santeria (424)
São Tomé (416)
Saramaka (422)
Songhay empire (410)
Sunni Ali (410)
Suriname (422)

Swahili (411)   Voudou (424)
Timbuktu (410)   Zimbabwe (413)
triangular trade (417)

FOR FURTHER READING

Michael L. Conniff and Thomas J. Davis. *Africans in the Americas: A History of the Black Diaspora.* New York, 1994. A comprehensive survey of African-European relations, the slave trade, and the African diaspora.

Philip D. Curtin. *The Rise and Fall of the Plantation Complex: Essays in Atlantic History.* 2nd ed. Cambridge, 1998. Examines plantation societies and slavery as institutions linking lands throughout the Atlantic Ocean basin.

Christopher Ehret. *The Civilizations of Africa: A History to 1800.* Charlottesville, Va., 2002. An important contribution that views Africa in the context of world history.

Olaudah Equiano. *Equiano's Travels.* Ed. by Paul Edwards. Oxford, 1967. An abridged and conveniently available edition of Equiano's autobiography.

Philip Gould. *Barbaric Traffic: Commerce and Antislavery in the Eighteenth-Century Atlantic World.* Cambridge, 2003. Compelling study of Anglo-American antislavery literature that suggests the discourse was less a debate over the morality of slavery than a concern with the commercial aspects of the slave trade.

Patrick Manning. *Slavery and African Life: Occidental, Oriental, and African Slave Trades.* Cambridge, 1990. Concentrates on the impact of the slave trade on Africa.

James H. Sweet. *Recreating Africa: Culture, Kinship, and Religion in the African-Portuguese World, 1441–1770.* Chapel Hill, 2006. Engaging study of African slave culture in Portuguese Brazil and the process of creolization.

John Thornton. *Africa and Africans in the Making of the Atlantic World, 1400–1800.* 2nd ed. New York, 1997. A rich analysis of African peoples and their roles in the Atlantic Ocean basin.

Dale W. Tomich. *Through the Prism of Slavery: Labor, Capital, and World Economy.* Lanham, Md., 2004. Brief overview of slavery's role in the development of global capitalism.

Jan Vansina. *Paths in the Rainforest: Toward a History of Political Tradition in Equatorial Africa.* Madison, 1990. A thoughtful analysis that considers both native traditions and external influences on African history.

Tradition and Change in East Asia

CHAPTER 23

Although the Great Wall of China had precedents as early as the fourth century B.C.E., this 2,500-kilometer (1,550-mile) stone and brick wall was built by the Ming emperors in the fifteenth and sixteenth centuries to protect China from invaders.

EYEWITNESS:
Matteo Ricci and Chiming Clocks in China

In January 1601 a mechanical clock chimed the hours for the first time in the city of Beijing. In the early 1580s, devices that Chinese called "self-ringing bells" had arrived at the port of Macau with Portuguese merchants. Reports of them soon spread to the emperor in Beijing. The Roman Catholic missionary Matteo Ricci conceived the idea of awing the emperor with mechanical clocks and then persuading him and his subjects to convert to Christianity. From his post at Macau, Ricci let imperial authorities know that he could supply the emperor with a chiming clock. When the emperor Wanli granted him permission to travel to Beijing and establish a mission, Ricci took with him a large mechanical clock intended for public display and a smaller clock for the emperor's personal use.

Chiming mechanical clocks enchanted Wanli and his court and soon became the rage in elite society throughout China. Wealthy Chinese merchants paid handsome sums for them, and Europeans often found that business went better if they presented clocks to the government officials they dealt with. By the eighteenth century the imperial court maintained a workshop to manufacture and repair mechanical clocks and watches. Although most Chinese could not afford to purchase mechanical clocks, commoners could admire the large, chiming clock Matteo Ricci installed outside his residence in Beijing.

Chiming clocks did not have the effect that Ricci desired. The emperor showed no interest in Christianity, and the missionaries attracted only small numbers of Chinese converts. Yet, by opening the doors of the imperial court to the missionaries, the self-ringing bells symbolized the increasing engagement between Asian and European peoples.

By linking all the world's regions and peoples, the European voyages of exploration inaugurated a new era in world history. Yet transoceanic connections influenced different societies in very different ways. In contrast to sub-Saharan Africa, where the Atlantic slave trade provoked turmoil, east Asian lands benefited greatly from long-distance trade, since it brought silver, which stimulated their economies. East Asian societies benefited also from American plant crops that made their way across the seas as part of the Columbian exchange.

Unlike societies in the Americas, where Europeans profoundly influenced historical development from the time of their arrival, east Asian societies largely controlled their own affairs until the nineteenth century. Because of its political and cultural preeminence, China remained the dominant power in east Asia. China was also a remarkably prosperous land. Indeed, with its huge population, enormous productive capacity, and strong demand for silver, China was a leading economic powerhouse driving world trade in early modern times. By the late eighteenth century, however, China was experiencing social and economic change that eventually caused instability.

Matteo Ricci (maht-TAY-oh REET-chee)
Wanli (wahn-LEE)

CHRONOLOGY

1368–1644	**Ming dynasty (China)**
1368–1398	**Reign of Hongwu**
1403–1424	**Reign of Yongle**
1552–1610	**Life of Matteo Ricci**
1572–1620	**Reign of Emperor Wanli**
1600–1867	**Tokugawa shogunate (Japan)**
1616–1626	**Reign of Nurhaci**
1642–1693	**Life of Ihara Saikaku**
1644–1911	**Qing dynasty (China)**
1661–1722	**Reign of Kangxi**
1736–1795	**Reign of Qianlong**
1793	**British trade mission to China**

During the seventeenth and eighteenth centuries, Japan also underwent major transformations. The Tokugawa shoguns unified the Japanese islands for the first time and laid a foundation for long-term economic growth. While tightly restricting contacts and relations with the larger world, Tokugawa Japan generated a distinctive set of social and cultural traditions. Those developments helped fashion a Japan that would play a decisive role in global affairs by the twentieth century.

THE QUEST FOR POLITICAL STABILITY

During the thirteenth and fourteenth centuries, China was ruled by the Yuan dynasty (1279–1368) of nomadic Mongol warriors. Mongol overlords ignored Chinese political and cultural traditions, and they displaced Chinese bureaucrats in favor of foreign administrators. When the Yuan dynasty came to an end, the Ming emperors who succeeded it sought to erase all signs of Mongol influence and restore traditional ways to China. Looking to the Tang and Song dynasties for inspiration, they built a powerful imperial state, revived the civil service staffed by Confucian scholars, and promoted Confucian thought. Rulers of the succeeding Qing dynasty were themselves Manchus of nomadic origin, but they too worked zealously to promote Chinese ways. Ming and Qing emperors alike were deeply conservative: their principal concern was to maintain stability in a large agrarian society, so they adopted policies that favored Chinese political and cultural traditions. The state they fashioned governed China for more than half a millennium.

The Ming Dynasty

Ming Government When the Yuan dynasty collapsed, the Ming dynasty (1368–1644) restored native rule to China.

Tokugawa (TOH-koo-GAH-wah)
shogun (SHOH-gun)
Qing (chihng)
Hongwu (hawng-woo)
eunuch (YOO-nuhk)
Yongle (yong-lay)

Hongwu (reigned 1368–1398), founder of the Ming ("brilliant") dynasty, built a tightly centralized state. As emperor, Hongwu made extensive use of mandarins, imperial officials who oversaw implementation of government policies throughout China. He also placed great trust in eunuchs on the assumption that they could not generate families who might one day challenge imperial authority. The emperor Yongle (reigned 1403–1424) launched a series of naval expeditions that went as far as Malindi in east Africa. Yongle's successors discontinued the expeditions but maintained the centralized state that Hongwu had established.

The Great Wall The Ming emperors were determined to prevent new invasions. In 1421 Yongle moved the capital from Nanjing in the south to Beijing to keep closer watch on the Mongols and other nomadic peoples in the north. The later Ming emperors sought to protect their realm by building new fortifications, including the Great Wall of China, along the northern border. The Great Wall had precedents dating back to the fourth century B.C.E., but its construction was a Ming-dynasty project. Workers by the hundreds of thousands labored throughout the late fifteenth and sixteenth centuries to build a stone and brick barrier that ran some 2,500 kilometers (1,550 miles). The Great Wall was 10 to 15 meters (33 to 49 feet) high, and it featured watch towers, signal towers, and accommodations for troops deployed on the border.

The Ming emperors also set out to eradicate Mongol and other foreign influences and to create a stable society in the image of the Chinese past. Respect for Chinese traditions facilitated the restoration of institutions that the Mongols had ignored or suppressed. The government sponsored study of Chinese cultural traditions, especially Confucianism and

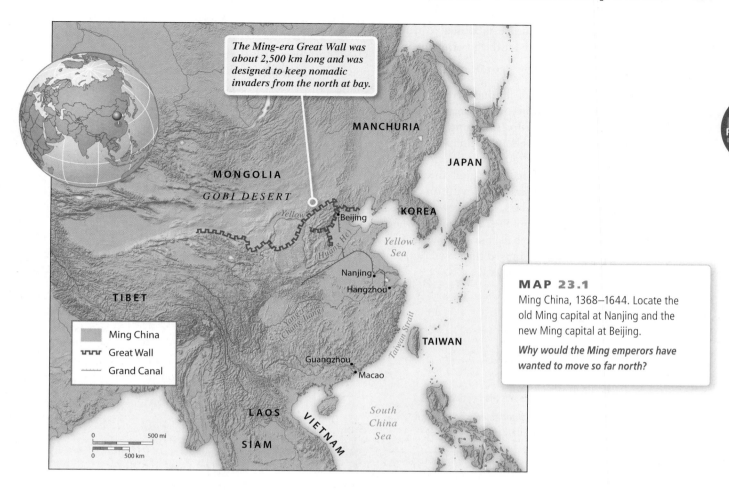

The Ming-era Great Wall was about 2,500 km long and was designed to keep nomadic invaders from the north at bay.

MAP 23.1

Ming China, 1368–1644. Locate the old Ming capital at Nanjing and the new Ming capital at Beijing.

Why would the Ming emperors have wanted to move so far north?

the reestablishment of imperial academies and regional colleges. Most important, the Ming state restored the system of civil service examinations that Mongol rulers had neglected.

Ming Decline The vigor of early Ming rule did not survive beyond the mid–sixteenth century, when a series of problems weakened the dynasty. From the 1520s to the 1560s, pirates and smugglers operated almost at will along the east coast of China. Suppression of pirates took more than forty years, partly because of an increasingly inept imperial government. The later Ming emperors lived extravagantly in the Forbidden City, a vast imperial enclave in Beijing, and received news about the outside world only from eunuch servants and administrators. The emperors sometimes ignored government affairs for decades on end, while powerful eunuchs won favor by providing for their

The Forbidden City.

The emperor Yongle designed the Forbidden City as a vast, walled imperial retreat in central Beijing. Here a sculptured lion guards the Forbidden City's Gate of Supreme Harmony.

amusement. As the eunuchs' influence increased, corruption and inefficiency spread throughout the government and weakened the Ming state.

Ming Collapse When a series of famines struck China during the early seventeenth century, the government was unable to organize effective relief efforts. During the 1630s peasants organized revolts throughout China. To complicate matters further, Manchu forces invaded from the north. In 1644 Chinese rebel forces captured the Ming capital at Beijing. Manchu invaders allied with an army loyal to the Ming, crushed the rebels, and recovered Beijing. The Manchus portrayed themselves as avengers who saved the capital from dangerous rebels, but they neglected to restore Ming rule. Instead, they moved their own capital to Beijing and displaced the Ming dynasty.

Nurhaci (NOOR-hacheh)

The Qing Dynasty

The Manchus When the Ming dynasty fell, Manchus poured south into China from their homeland of Manchuria. The victors proclaimed a new dynasty, the Qing ("pure"), which ruled China until the early twentieth century (1644–1911). The Manchus mostly were pastoral nomads whose remote ancestors had traded with China since the Qin dynasty. During the late sixteenth and early seventeenth centuries, an ambitious chieftain named Nurhaci (reigned 1616–1626) unified Manchu tribes into a centralized state and organized a powerful military force. During the 1620s and 1630s, the Manchu army captured Korea and Mongolia and launched small-scale invasions into China. After their seizure of Beijing in 1644, the Manchus moved to extend their authority throughout China. By the early 1680s they had consolidated the Qing dynasty's hold throughout the land.

The establishment of the Qing dynasty was due partly to Manchu military prowess and partly to Chinese support for the Manchus. During the 1630s and 1640s, many Chinese generals and Confucian scholar-bureaucrats deserted the Ming dynasty because of its corruption and inefficiency. The

MAP 23.2

The Qing empire, 1644–1911. Compare this map with Map 23.1.

Why would the Qing emperors have wanted to incorporate such extensive territories in Mongolia and Tibet into their empire?

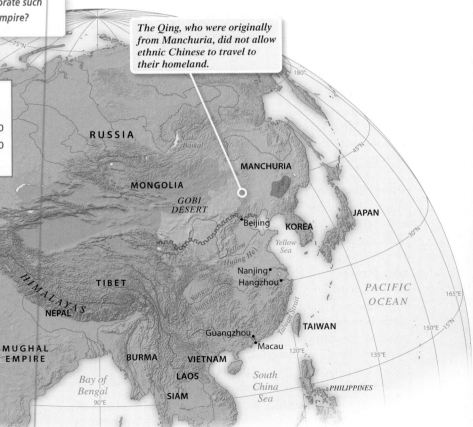

The Qing, who were originally from Manchuria, did not allow ethnic Chinese to travel to their homeland.

- Qing homeland
- Qing expansion to 1644
- Qing expansion, 1644–1690
- Qing expansion, 1690–1750
- Great Wall

Manchu ruling elites were schooled in Chinese language and Confucian thought, and they often enjoyed more respect from the scholar-bureaucrats than the high administrators of the Ming dynasty itself.

The Manchus were careful to preserve their own ethnic and cultural identity. They outlawed intermarriage between Manchus and Chinese and forbade Chinese to travel to Manchuria or to learn the Manchurian language. Qing authorities also forced Chinese men to shave the front of their heads and grow a Manchu-style queue as a sign of submission to the dynasty.

Kangxi and His Reign The long reigns of two particularly effective emperors, Kangxi (1661–1722) and Qianlong (1736–1795), helped mute the tensions between Manchus and Chinese and allowed the Manchus to consolidate their hold on China. Kangxi was a Confucian scholar as well as an enlightened ruler. He studied the Confucian classics and sought to apply their teachings through his policies. Thus, for example, he organized flood-control and irrigation projects on the Confucian precept that rulers should look after the welfare of their subjects and promote agriculture. He also generously patronized Confucian schools and academies.

Kangxi was also a conqueror, and he oversaw the construction of a vast Qing empire. He conquered the island of Taiwan, where Ming loyalists had retreated after their expulsion from southern China, and absorbed it into his empire. Like his predecessors of the Han and Tang dynasties, Kangxi sought to forestall problems with nomadic peoples by projecting Chinese influence into central Asia. His conquests in Mongolia and central Asia extended almost to the Caspian Sea, and he imposed a Chinese protectorate over Tibet. Kangxi's grandson Qianlong continued this expansion of Chinese influence by consolidating Kangxi's conquests in central Asia and by making Vietnam, Burma, and Nepal vassal states of the Qing dynasty.

Qianlong and His Reign Qianlong's reign marked the height of the Qing dynasty. Like Kangxi, Qianlong was a sophisticated and learned man. During his long, stable, and prosperous reign, the imperial treasury bulged so much

Kangxi.
Though painted in the nineteenth century, this portrait depicts Kangxi in his imperial regalia as he looked at about age fifty.

that on four occasions Qianlong canceled tax collections. Toward the end of his reign, however, Qianlong delegated many responsibilities to his favorite eunuchs. His successors continued that practice, and by the nineteenth century the Qing dynasty faced serious difficulties. Throughout the reign of Qianlong, however, China remained a wealthy and well-organized land.

The Son of Heaven and the Scholar-Bureaucrats

Although Qing rulers usually appointed Manchus to the highest political posts, they relied on the same governmental apparatus that the Ming emperors had established. Indeed, for more than five hundred years, the autocratic state created by the Ming emperor Hongwu governed China's fortunes.

The Son of Heaven If the emperor of China during the Ming and Qing dynasties was not quite a god, he certainly was more than a mere mortal. Chinese tradition held that he was the "Son of Heaven," the human being designated by heavenly powers to maintain order on the earth. He led a privileged life within the walls of the Forbidden City. Hundreds of concubines resided in his harem, and thousands of eunuchs looked after his desires. Everything about his person and the institution he represented conveyed a sense of awesome authority. The imperial wardrobe and personal effects bore designs forbidden to all others, for instance, and the written characters of the emperor's name were taboo throughout the realm. Individuals who had the rare privilege of a personal audience with the emperor had to perform the kowtow—three kneelings and nine head knockings. Those who gave even minor offense faced having their bare buttocks flogged with bamboo canes.

The Scholar-Bureaucrats Day-to-day governance of the empire fell to scholar-bureaucrats appointed by the emperor. With few exceptions these officials came from the class of well-educated and highly literate men known as the scholar-gentry. These men had earned academic degrees by

Kangxi (kahng-shee)
Qianlong (chyahn-lawng)
kowtow (kou-tou)

Thinking about TRADITIONS

The Importance of Tradition to Ming and Qing Dynasties

Between 1500 and 1800, the Ming and Qing dynasties in China sought to promote stability within their realms by encouraging Chinese people to restore and then maintain the cultural traditions of past eras. *What traditions were both dynasties particularly keen to encourage, and how did they promote their restoration?*

passing rigorous civil service examinations, and they dominated China's political and social life.

Preparations for the examinations began at an early age, either in local schools or with private tutors. By the time students were eleven or twelve years old, they had memorized several thousand characters that were necessary to deal with the Confucian curriculum, including the *Analects* of Confucius and other standard works. They followed those studies with instruction in calligraphy, poetry, and essay composition.

Civil Service Examinations The examinations consisted of a battery of tests administered at the district, provincial, and metropolitan levels. Stiff official quotas restricted the number of successful candidates in each examination—only three hundred students could pass metropolitan examinations—and students frequently took the examinations several times before earning a degree.

The Examination System and Chinese Society The possibility of bureaucratic service—with prospects for rich social and financial rewards—ensured that competition for degrees was ferocious at all levels. Yet a degree did not ensure government service. During the Qing dynasty the empire's one million degree holders competed for twenty thousand official civil service positions, and only those who passed the metropolitan examinations could look forward to powerful positions in the imperial bureaucracy.

Yet the examination system was a pivotal institution. By opening the door to honor, power, and rewards, the examinations encouraged serious pursuit of a formal education. Furthermore, since the system did not erect social barriers before its recruits, it provided an avenue for upward social mobility. Finally, in addition to selecting officials for government service, the education and examination system molded the personal values of those who managed day-to-day affairs in imperial China. By concentrating on Confucian classics and neo-Confucian commentaries, the examinations guaranteed that Confucianism would be at the heart of Chinese education and that Confucians would govern the state.

ECONOMIC AND SOCIAL CHANGES

By modeling their governmental structure on the centralized imperial states of earlier Chinese dynasties, the Ming and Qing emperors succeeded in their goal of restoring and maintaining traditional ways in China. They also sought to preserve the traditional hierarchical and patriarchal social order. Yet, while the emperors promoted conservative political and social policies, China experienced economic and social changes, partly as a result of influences from abroad. Agricultural production increased dramatically and fueled rapid population growth, and global trade brought China enormous wealth. These developments deeply influenced Chinese society and partly undermined the stability that the Ming and Qing emperors sought to preserve.

The Patriarchal Family

Filial Piety Moralists portrayed the Chinese people as one large family, and they extended family values to the larger society. Filial piety, for example, implied not only duties of children toward their fathers but also loyalty of subjects toward the emperor. Like the imperial government, the Chinese family was hierarchical, patriarchal, and authoritarian. The father was head of the household, and he passed leadership of the family to his eldest son. The veneration of ancestors, which the state promoted as a matter of Confucian propriety, strengthened the authority of the patriarchs by honoring the male line of descent. Filial piety was the cornerstone of family values. Children had the duty to look after their parents' happiness and well-being, especially in their old age. Young children heard stories of sons who went so far as to cut off parts of their bodies to ensure that their parents had enough to eat.

The social assumptions of the Chinese family extended into patrilineal descent groups such as the clan. Clans—whose members sometimes numbered in the thousands—assumed responsibilities such as the maintenance of local order, organization of local economies, and provision for welfare. Clan-supported education gave poor but promising relatives the opportunity to succeed in the civil service examinations. Finally, clans served as a means for the transmission of Confucian values from the gentry leaders to all social classes within the clan.

Gender Relations Within the family, Confucian principles subjected women to the authority of men. The subordination of females began at an early age. Chinese parents preferred boys over girls. Whereas a boy might have the opportunity to take the official examinations and become a

Reverberations of ● ● ● ● ● ● ● ●

The Columbian Exchange

Prior to the sixteenth century, crops such as corn, sweet potatoes, and peanuts had only been known in the Americas. As a result of the Columbian exchange, however, food crops native to the Americas were brought not only to Europe but also to Asia and Africa. The introduction of such crops to China during the sixteenth century not only changed Chinese cuisine, but also allowed more land to be cultivated. The result was dramatic population growth, which had both positive and negative effects for Chinese people over the long term. In this case, consider the ways that events and processes that occurred in the Americas played an important, but unforeseen, role in shaping historical developments in east Asia.

Population Growth and Economic Development

China was a predominantly agricultural society, a fact that meshed agreeably with the Confucian view that land was the source of everything praiseworthy. Yet only a small fraction of China's land is suitable for planting: even today only about 11 percent is in cultivation. To feed the country's large population, China's farmers relied on intensive, garden-style agriculture that was highly productive. On its strong agrarian foundation, China supported a large population and built the most highly commercialized economy of the preindustrial world.

government official, parents regarded a girl as a social and financial liability. Under those circumstances it was not surprising that girls were the primary victims of infanticide.

During the Ming and Qing dynasties, patriarchal authority over females probably became tighter than ever before in China. Since ancient times, relatives had discouraged widows from remarriage, but social pressures increased during the Ming dynasty. Friends and relatives not only encouraged widows to honor the memory of their departed husbands but also heaped posthumous honors on those who committed suicide and followed their spouses to the grave.

Foot Binding Moreover, foot binding, a custom that probably originated in the Song dynasty, became exceptionally popular during the late Ming and Qing dynasties. Tightly constrained and deformed by strips of linen, bound feet could not grow naturally and so would not support the weight of an adult woman. Bound feet were small and dainty, and they sometimes inspired erotic arousal among men. The practice of foot binding became most widespread among the wealthy classes, since it demonstrated an ability to support women who could not perform physical labor, but commoners sometimes bound the feet of especially pretty girls in hopes of arranging favorable marriages.

Marriage itself was a contractual affair whose principal purpose was to continue the male line of descent. A bride became a member of the husband's family, and her position there was one of unambiguous subservience. Women could not divorce their husbands, but men could put aside their wives in cases where there were no offspring or where the wife was guilty of adultery, theft, or disobedience.

Thus custom and law combined to strengthen patriarchal authority in Chinese families during the Ming and Qing dynasties. Yet, while family life continued to develop along traditional lines, the larger Chinese society underwent considerable change between the sixteenth and the eighteenth centuries.

American Food Crops By intensively cultivating every available parcel of land, Chinese peasants increased their yields of traditional food crops—especially rice, wheat, and millet—until the seventeenth century. As peasants approached the upper limits of agricultural productivity, Spanish merchants coming by way of the Philippines introduced American food crops to China. American maize, sweet potatoes, and peanuts permitted Chinese farmers to take advantage of soils that previously had gone uncultivated. The introduction of new crops increased the food supply and supported further population growth.

Population Growth In spite of recurring epidemic diseases such as plague, China's population rose rapidly from 100 million in 1500 to 160 million in 1600. By 1750 it had surged to 225 million. However, this rapid demographic growth set the stage for future economic and social problems, since agricultural production could not keep pace with population over a long term.

Although an increasing population placed pressure on Chinese resources, it offered opportunities for entrepreneurs. Indeed, entrepreneurs had access to a large labor force, which meant they were able to recruit workers readily at low cost. After the mid–sixteenth century the Chinese economy benefited also from the influx of Japanese and American silver, which stimulated trade and financed further commercial expansion.

Foreign Trade Global trade brought tremendous prosperity to China, especially during the early Qing dynasty. Chinese workers produced vast quantities of silk, porcelain, lacquerware, and tea for consumers in the Indian Ocean basin, central Asia, and Europe. Chinese imports were relatively few, and thus the most important form of compensation for exports was silver bullion, which supported the silver-based Chinese economy and fueled manufacturing.

Economic growth and commercial expansion took place mostly in an atmosphere of tight government regulation. Although the Ming emperor Yongle had sponsored a series of maritime expeditions (1405–1433) in the Indian Ocean basin, his successors withdrew their support for such activities and even tried to prevent Chinese subjects from dealing with foreign peoples. In its effort to pacify southern China during the later seventeenth century, the Qing government tried to end maritime activity altogether. An imperial edict of 1656 forbade "even a plank from drifting to the sea," and in 1661 the emperor Kangxi ordered evacuation of the southern coastal regions. Those policies had only a limited effect, and when Qing forces pacified southern China in the 1680s, government authorities rescinded the strictest measures. Thereafter, however, Qing authorities closely supervised the activities of foreign merchants in China. Portuguese merchants were allowed to operate only at the port of Macau, and British agents had to deal exclusively with the official merchant guild in Guangzhou.

Government policies also discouraged the organization of large-scale commercial ventures by Chinese merchants. As a result, it was impossible to maintain shipyards that could construct large sailing ships capable of traveling long distances. Similarly, it was impossible to organize large trading firms like the English East India Company or the Dutch VOC.

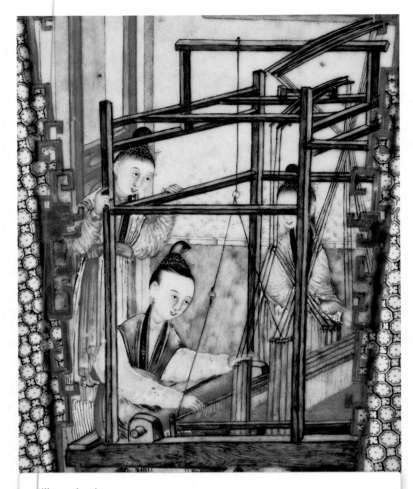

Silk production.
A Ming-era vase painting depicts a woman weaving silk as an attendant pours tea.

Trade and Migration to Southeast Asia

Nevertheless, thousands of Chinese merchants worked either individually or in partnerships, plying the waters of the China seas to link China with global trade networks. Chinese merchants were especially prominent in Manila, where they exchanged silk and porcelain for American silver that came across the Pacific Ocean from Mexico. They were also frequent visitors at the Dutch colonial capital of Batavia, where they supplied the VOC with silk and porcelain in exchange for silver and Indonesian spices. Entrepreneurial Chinese merchants ventured also to lands throughout southeast Asia in search of exotic tropical products for Chinese consumers. Indeed, the early modern era was an age when merchants established a prominent Chinese presence throughout southeast Asia.

Government and Technology

China's economic expansion took place largely in the absence of technological innovation. During the Tang and Song dynasties, Chinese engineers had produced a veritable flood of inventions, and China was the world's leader in technology. Yet by early Ming times, technological innovation had slowed. Part of the explanation for the slowdown has to do with the role of the government. During the Tang and Song dynasties, the imperial government had encouraged technological innovation as a foundation of military and economic strength. In contrast, the Ming and Qing regimes favored political and social stability over technological innovation.

Alongside government policy, the abundance of skilled workers discouraged technological innovation. When employers wanted to increase production, they found that hiring additional workers was less costly than making investments in new technologies. In the short run this tactic kept most of China's population gainfully employed. Over the longer term, however, it meant that China lost technological ground to European peoples, who embarked on a round of stunning technological innovation beginning about the mid–eighteenth century.

SourcesfromthePast

Qianlong on Chinese Trade with England

Qing administrators tightly restricted foreign trade. Foreign merchants had to deal with government-approved agents outside the city walls of Guangzhou and had to depart as soon as they had completed their business. In 1793 a British diplomat representing King George III of England bestowed gifts on the emperor Qianlong and petitioned for the right to trade at ports other than Guangzhou. In a letter to King George, Qianlong outlined his views on Chinese trade with England. His letter also bespeaks clearly the importance of government policy for commerce and economic affairs in China.

You, O king, from afar have yearned after the blessings of our civilization, and in your eagerness to come into touch with our influence have sent an embassy across the sea bearing a memorandum. I have already taken note of your respectful spirit of submission, have treated your mission with extreme favor and loaded it with gifts, besides issuing a mandate to you, O king, and honoring you with the bestowal of valuable presents. . . .

Yesterday your ambassador petitioned my ministers to memorialize me regarding your trade with China, but his proposal is not consistent with our dynastic usage and cannot be entertained. Hitherto, all European nations, including your own country's barbarian merchants, have carried on their trade with our Celestial Empire at Guangzhou. Such has been the procedure for many years, although our Celestial Empire possesses all things in prolific abundance and lacks no product within its own borders. There was therefore no need to import the manufactures of outside barbarians in exchange for our own produce. But as the tea, silk, and porcelain which the Celestial Empire produces are absolute necessities to European nations and to yourselves, we have permitted, as a signal mark of favor, that trading agents should be established at Guangzhou, so that your wants might be supplied and your country thus participate in our benefi-

cence. But your ambassador has now put forward new requests which completely fail to recognize our throne's principle to "treat strangers from afar with indulgence," and to exercise a pacifying control over barbarian tribes the world over. . . . Your England is not the only nation trading at Guangzhou. If other nations, following your bad example, wrongfully importune my ear with further impossible requests, how will it be possible for me to treat them with easy indulgence? Nevertheless, I do not forget the lonely remoteness of your island, cut off from the world by intervening wastes of sea, nor do I overlook your excusable ignorance of the usages of our Celestial Empire. I have consequently commanded my ministers to enlighten your ambassador on the subject, and have ordered the departure of the mission. . . .

If, after the receipt of this explicit decree, you lightly give ear to the representations of your subordinates and allow your barbarian merchants to proceed to Zhejiang and Tianjin, with the object of landing and trading there, the ordinances of my Celestial Empire are strict in the extreme, and the local officials, both civil and military, are bound reverently to obey the law of the land. Should your vessels touch the shore, your merchants will assuredly never be permitted to land or to reside there, but will be subject to instant expulsion. In that event your barbarian merchants will have had a long journey for nothing. Do not say that you were not warned in due time! Tremblingly obey and show no negligence! A special mandate!

For Further Reflection

■ What considerations might have prompted the Chinese government to take such a restrictive approach to foreign trade?

Source: J. O. P. Bland. *Annals and Memoirs of the Court of Peking.* Boston: Houghton Mifflin, 1914, pp. 325–31. (Translation slightly modified.)

Gentry, Commoners, Soldiers, and Mean People

Privileged Classes Besides the emperor and his family, scholar-bureaucrats and gentry occupied the most exalted positions in Chinese society. Scholar-bureaucrats had much in common with the gentry: they came largely from gentry ranks, and after leaving government service they usually rejoined gentry society. The scholar-bureaucrats and the

gentry functioned as intermediaries between the imperial government and local society. By organizing water-control projects and public security measures, they played a crucial role in the management of local society.

Scholar-bureaucrats and gentry were easy to identify. They wore distinctive clothing—black gowns with blue borders adorned with various rank insignia—and commoners addressed them with honorific terms. They also received favorable legal treatment and enjoyed immunity from corporal punishment as well as exemption from labor service and taxes.

Most of the gentry owned land, which was their major source of income. Some were also silent business partners of merchants and entrepreneurs. Their principal source of income, however, was the government service to which their academic degrees gave them access. In contrast to landed elites elsewhere, who often lived on rural estates, China's gentry resided largely in cities and towns, where they tended to political, social, and financial affairs.

Working Classes Confucian tradition ranked three broad classes of commoners below the gentry: peasants, artisans or workers, and merchants. By far the biggest class consisted of peasants: a designation that covered everyone from day laborers to petty landlords. Confucian principles regarded peasants as the most honorable of the three classes, since they performed honest labor and supplied the entire population with food.

The category of artisans and workers encompassed a wide spectrum of occupations. Despite their lower status, crafts workers, tailors, barbers, and physicians generally enjoyed higher income than peasants did. Artisans and workers were usually employees of the state or of gentry and merchant families, but they also pursued their occupations as self-employed persons.

Merchants Merchants, from street peddlers to individuals of enormous wealth and influence, ranked at the bottom of the Confucian social hierarchy. Because moralists looked on them as unscrupulous social parasites, merchants enjoyed little legal protection. Yet Chinese merchants often garnered official support for their enterprises through bribery of government bureaucrats or through profit-sharing arrangements with gentry families. Indeed, the participation of gentry families in commercial ventures such as warehousing, money-lending, and pawnbroking blurred the distinction between gentry and merchants. In addition, merchants blurred the distinction further by preparing their sons for government examinations, which could result in appointment to civil service positions and promotion to gentry status.

Although China was still a basically agricultural land under the Ming and the Qing, the increasing prominence of artisans and merchants demonstrated that manufacturing and commerce had become much more economically important than in ancient times. As a result, those who could exploit opportunities had the potential to lead comfortable lives and even to climb into the ranks of the privileged gentry class. Yet Chinese merchants and artisans did not forge cooperative relationships with government authorities as their counterparts in England and the Netherlands did.

The principal concern of late Ming and Qing authorities was to preserve the stability of a large agrarian society,

Chinese peasants.
This engraving depicts a peasant couple in harness pulling a plow. Note that the man wears the braided queue that Manchus required their male Chinese subjects to wear.

Why would the peasants have been pulling the plow themselves?

not to promote rapid economic development through trade. Thus Chinese authorities did not adopt policies designed to strengthen both merchants and the state by authorizing merchants to pursue their efforts aggressively in the larger world.

Lower Classes Beyond the Confucian social hierarchy were members of the military forces and the so-called mean people, such as slaves, indentured servants, entertainers, and prostitutes. Confucian moralists regarded armed forces as a wretched but necessary evil and attempted to avoid military dominance of society by placing civilian bureaucrats in the highest command positions, even at the expense of military effectiveness.

THE CONFUCIAN TRADITION AND NEW CULTURAL INFLUENCES

The Ming and Qing emperors looked to Chinese traditions for guidance in framing their cultural as well as their political and social policies. They provided generous support for Confucianism, and they ensured that formal education in China revolved around Confucian thought and values. Yet demographic and urban growth also encouraged the emergence of a vibrant popular culture in Chinese cities, and European missionaries acquainted the Chinese with Roman Catholic Christianity and European science and technology as well.

Neo-Confucianism and Pulp Fiction

Imperial sponsorship of Chinese cultural traditions meant primarily support for the Confucian tradition, especially as systematized by the Song dynasty scholar Zhu Xi, the most prominent architect of neo-Confucianism. Zhu Xi combined the moral, ethical, and political values of Confucius with the logical rigor and speculative power of Buddhist philosophy. He emphasized the values of self-discipline, filial piety, and obedience to established rulers, all of which appealed to Ming and Qing emperors seeking to maintain stability in their vast realm. To promote Confucian values, the Ming and Qing emperors supported educational programs at many levels throughout the land.

Popular Culture While the imperial courts promoted Confucianism, a lively popular culture took shape in the cities of China. Most urban residents did not have an advanced education and knew little about Confucius. Many were literate, however, and they found that popular novels met their needs for entertainment and diversion. Although Confucian scholars thought popular novels were crude, printing made it possible to produce them cheaply and in large numbers, and urban residents eagerly consumed them. Many of the novels had little literary merit, but their tales of conflict, horror, wonder, excitement, and sometimes unconcealed pornography appealed to readers.

Popular Novels Some popular novels, however, did offer thoughtful reflections on the world and human affairs. The historical novel *The Romance of the Three Kingdoms,* for example, explored the political intrigue that followed the collapse of the Han dynasty. *The Dream of the Red Chamber* told the story of cousins deeply in love who could not marry because of their families' wishes. Through the prism of a sentimental love story, the novel shed fascinating light on the dynamics of wealthy scholar-gentry families.

The Return of Christianity to China

Nestorian Christians had established churches and monasteries in China as early as the seventh century C.E., and Roman Catholic communities were prominent in Chinese commercial centers during the Yuan dynasty. After the outbreak of epidemic plague and the collapse of the Yuan dynasty in the fourteenth century, however, Christianity disappeared from China. When Roman Catholic missionaries returned in the sixteenth century, they had to start from scratch in their efforts to win converts.

Matteo Ricci Founder of the mission to China was the Italian Jesuit Matteo Ricci (1552–1610), who had the ambitious goal of converting China to Christianity, beginning with the Ming emperor Wanli. Ricci was a brilliant and learned man as well as a polished diplomat, and he became a popular figure at the Ming court. On arrival at Macau in 1582, Ricci immersed himself in the study of the Chinese language and the Confucian classics. By the time he first traveled to Beijing and visited the imperial court in 1601, Ricci was able to write learned Chinese and converse fluently with Confucian scholars.

Ricci's mastery of Chinese language and literature opened doors for the Jesuits, who then dazzled their hosts with European science, technology, and mechanical gadgetry such as glass prisms, harpsichords, and especially "self-ringing bells"—spring-driven mechanical clocks that chimed the hours.

Confucianism and Christianity The Jesuits sought to capture Chinese interest with European science and technology, but their ultimate goal was to win converts. Ricci, for example, tried to make Christianity seem familiar by arguing that the doctrines of Confucius and Jesus were very similar, if not identical. The Jesuits also held religious services in the Chinese language and allowed converts to continue the time-honored practice of venerating their ancestors.

In spite of their tolerance, flexibility, and genuine respect for their hosts, the Jesuits attracted few converts in China. By the mid–eighteenth century, Chinese Christians numbered about 200,000—a tiny proportion of the Chinese population of 225 million. Many Chinese hesitated to adopt Christianity partly because of its exclusivity: like Islam, Christianity claimed to be the only true religion, so conversion implied that the time-honored traditions of Confucianism, Daoism, and Buddhism were fallacious creeds—a proposition most Chinese were unwilling to accept.

End of the Jesuit Mission Ultimately, the Roman Catholic mission in China came to an end because of squabbles between the Jesuits and members of the Franciscan and Dominican orders, who also sought converts in China. Jealous of the Jesuits' presence at the imperial court, they complained to the pope about their rivals' tolerance of Chinese traditions. The pope sided with the critics and in the early eighteenth century issued several proclamations ordering missionaries in China to conduct services according to European standards. In response, the emperor Kangxi ordered an end to the preaching of Christianity in China. By the mid–eighteenth century, the mission had weakened so much that it had effectively come to an end.

The Roman Catholic mission to China did not attract large numbers of converts, but it nonetheless had important cultural effects. In letters, reports, and other writings

---

Zhu Xi (ZHOO SHEE)
neo-Confucianism (NEE-oh kuhn-FYEW-shuhn-iz'm)
Buddhism (BOO-diz'm)

distributed widely throughout Europe, the Jesuits described China as an orderly and rational society. The rational morality of Confucianism appealed to the Enlightenment intellectuals, who sought alternatives to Christianity as the foundation for ethics and morality. Thus for the first time since Marco Polo, strong European interest in east Asian societies was stimulated.

THE UNIFICATION OF JAPAN

During the late sixteenth and early seventeenth centuries, the political unification of Japan ended an extended period of civil disorder. Like the Ming and Qing emperors in China, the Tokugawa shoguns sought to lay a foundation for long-term political and social stability by promoting conservative values and tightly restricting foreign influence in Japan. As in China, however, demographic expansion and economic growth fostered social and cultural change in Japan, and merchants introduced Chinese and European influences into Japan.

The Tokugawa Shogunate

From the twelfth through the sixteenth century, a *shogun* ("military governor") ruled Japan through retainers who received political rights and large estates in exchange for military services. Theoretically, the shogun ruled as a temporary stand-in for the Japanese emperor. In fact, however, the emperor was nothing more than a figurehead. After the fourteenth century the conflicting ambitions of shoguns and retainers led to constant turmoil, and by the sixteenth century Japan was in a state of civil war. Japanese historians often refer to the sixteenth century as the era of *sengoku*—"the country at war."

Tokugawa Ieyasu Toward the end of the sixteenth century, a series of military leaders brought about the unification of the land. In 1600 the last of those leaders, Tokugawa Ieyasu (reigned 1600–1616), established a military government known as the Tokugawa *bakufu* ("tent government," since it theoretically was only a temporary replacement for the emperor's rule). Ieyasu and his descendants ruled the bakufu as shoguns from 1600 until the end of the Tokugawa dynasty in 1867.

The principal aim of the Tokugawa shoguns was to prevent the return of civil war. Consequently, the shoguns needed to control the *daimyo* ("great names"), powerful territorial lords who ruled most of Japan from their vast, hereditary landholdings. Each maintained a government,

Tokugawa (TAW-koo-GAH-wah)
Sengoku (sehn-goh-koo)
bakufu (bah-kuh-fuh)
daimyo (DEYEM-yoh)

an independent judiciary, and schools, and each circulated paper money. Moreover, after the mid–sixteenth century, many daimyo established relationships with European mariners, from whom they learned how to manufacture and use gunpowder weapons, which they turned against one another.

Control of the Daimyo From the castle town of Edo (modern Tokyo), the shogun sought to extend his control over the daimyo through the policy of "alternate attendance," which required daimyo to maintain their families at Edo and spend every other year at the Tokugawa court. This policy enabled the shoguns to keep an eye on the daimyo, and it encouraged daimyo to spend their money on comfortable lives in Edo rather than on military forces that could challenge the bakufu. The shoguns also discouraged the daimyo from visiting one another and even required daimyo to obtain permission to meet with the emperor.

Control of Foreign Relations In an effort to prevent European influences from destabilizing the land, the Tokugawa shoguns closely controlled relations between Japan and the outside world. A primary concern was that Europeans might threaten the bakufu by making alliances with daimyo and supplying them with weapons. Thus during the 1630s the shoguns issued a series of edicts sharply restricting Japanese relations with other lands.

The policy forbade Japanese to go abroad on pain of death and prohibited the construction of large ships. It expelled Europeans from Japan and prohibited foreign merchants from trading in Japanese ports. The policy did, however, allow carefully controlled trade with Asian lands, and it also permitted small numbers of Chinese and Dutch merchants to trade under tight restrictions at the southern port city of Nagasaki. As a result, Japan was never completely isolated from the outside world.

Economic and Social Change

By ending civil conflict and maintaining political stability, the Tokugawa shoguns set the stage for economic growth in Japan. Ironically, peace and a booming economy encouraged social change that undermined the order that the bakufu sought to preserve. Economic growth had its roots in increased agricultural production, especially of rice, cotton, silk, and indigo. In many parts of Japan, villages moved away from subsistence farming in favor of production for the market.

Population Growth Increased agricultural production brought about rapid demographic growth: during the seventeenth century the Japanese population rose by almost one-third, from twenty-two million to twenty-nine million. Thereafter, however, many families practiced population

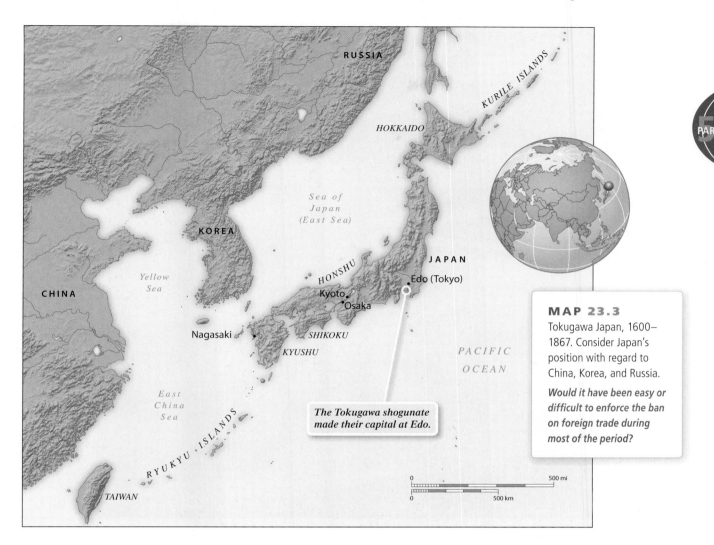

MAP 23.3
Tokugawa Japan, 1600–1867. Consider Japan's position with regard to China, Korea, and Russia.

Would it have been easy or difficult to enforce the ban on foreign trade during most of the period?

The Tokugawa shogunate made their capital at Edo.

control to maintain or raise their standard of living. Between 1700 and 1850 the Japanese population grew only moderately, from twenty-nine million to thirty-two million. Contraception, late marriage, and abortion all played roles in limiting population growth, but the principal method of control was infanticide, euphemistically referred to as "thinning out the rice shoots." Japanese families resorted to these measures primarily because Japan was land poor, which made it easy for populations to strain available resources.

Social Change The Tokugawa era was an age of social as well as demographic change in Japan. Because of Chinese cultural influence, the Japanese social hierarchy followed Confucian precepts in ranking the ruling elites—including the daimyo and samurai warriors—as the most privileged class of society, followed by peasants and artisans. As in China, merchants ranked at the bottom. Yet the extended period of peace ushered in by Tokugawa rule undermined the social position of the ruling elites, who found their traditional role as local administrators redundant.

Many of the ruling elite also fell into financial difficulty in this period because of rising prices and lavish lifestyles. As a result, many became indebted to rice brokers and gradually declined into genteel poverty.

Meanwhile, as in China, merchants in Japan became increasingly wealthy and prominent. Japanese cities flourished throughout the Tokugawa era—the population of Edo approached one million by 1700—and merchants prospered in the vibrant urban environment. Rice dealers, pawnbrokers, and sake merchants soon controlled more wealth than the ruling elites.

Neo-Confucianism and Floating Worlds

Neo-Confucianism in Japan Japan had gone to school in China, and the influence of China continued throughout the Tokugawa era. Formal education began with the study of Chinese language and literature. As late as the nineteenth century, many Japanese scholars wrote their

Nagasaki Harbor.
Dutch sailing ships and smaller Japanese vessels mingle in Nagasaki harbor. Dutch merchants conducted their business on the artificial island of Deshima, at left. © Carousel/Laurie Platt Winfrey, Inc.

Why was the island so densely populated?

philosophical, legal, and religious works in Chinese. The common people embraced Buddhism, which had come to Japan from China, and Confucianism was the most influential philosophical system. Indeed, by the early eighteenth century, neo-Confucianism had become the official ideology of the Tokugawa bakufu.

Native Learning Yet even with Tokugawa sponsorship, neo-Confucianism did not dominate intellectual life in Japan. Some scholars sought to establish a sense of Japanese identity that did not depend on cultural kinship with China. Particularly during the eighteenth century, scholars

of "native learning" scorned neo-Confucianism and even Buddhism as alien cultural imports and emphasized instead the importance of folk traditions and the indigenous Shinto religion for Japanese identity. Many scholars of native learning viewed Japanese people as superior to all others and glorified the supposed purity of Japanese society before its adulteration by Chinese and other foreign influences.

Meanwhile, the emergence of a prosperous merchant class encouraged the development of a vibrant popular culture. During the seventeenth and eighteenth centuries, an exuberant middle-class culture flourished in cities such as Kyoto, Edo, and Osaka. In those and other cities, Japan's finest creative talents catered to middle-class appetites.

Shintoism (SHIHN-toh-iz'm)

Thinking about ENCOUNTERS

Foreign Influences on China and japan

Although both the Chinese and Japanese states sought to minimize cultural contacts with outsiders from overseas, encounters with the wider world nevertheless affected each state in important ways. *Describe the ways encounters with foreign traders and missionaries shaped the internal development of China and Japan in economic, social, and cultural terms.*

Floating Worlds The centers of Tokugawa urban culture were the *ukiyo* ("floating worlds"), entertainment and pleasure quarters where teahouses, theaters, brothels, and public baths offered escape from the rigid rules of conduct that governed public behavior in Tokugawa society. In contrast to the solemn, serious proceedings of the imperial court and the bakufu, the popular culture of urban residents was secular, satirical, and even scatological. The main expressions of this lively culture were prose fiction and new forms of theater.

Ihara Saikaku (1642–1693), one of Japan's most prolific poets, helped create a new genre of prose literature, the "books of the floating world." Much of his fiction revolved around the theme of love. In *The Life of a Man Who Lived for Love*, for example, Ihara chronicled the experiences of a townsman who devoted his life to a quest for sexual pleasure. Ihara's treatment of love stressed the erotic rather than the aesthetic, and the brief, episodic stories that made up his work appealed to literate urban residents who were not inclined to pore over dense neo-Confucian treatises.

Beginning in the early seventeenth century, two new forms of drama became popular in Japanese cities. One was *kabuki* theater, which usually featured several acts consisting of lively and sometimes bawdy skits where stylized acting combined with lyric singing, dancing, and spectacular staging. The other new dramatic form was *bunraku,* the puppet theater. In bunraku, chanters accompanied by music told a story acted out by puppets. Manipulated by a team of three, each puppet could execute the subtlest and most intricate movements, such as brushing a tear

from the eye with the sleeve of a kimono. Both kabuki and bunraku attracted enthusiastic audiences in search of entertainment and diversion.

Christianity and Dutch Learning

Christian Missions Christian missionaries and European merchants also contributed their own distinctive threads to the cultural fabric of Tokugawa Japan. The Jesuit Francis Xavier opened the first Roman Catholic mission in 1549 and for a few decades experienced remarkable success. Several powerful daimyo adopted Christianity and ordered their subjects to do likewise. Many Japanese converts became enthusiastic Christians and worked to convert their compatriots to the new faith. By the 1580s about 150,000 Japanese had converted to Christianity, and by 1615 Japanese Christians numbered about 300,000.

Although Christians were only a tiny minority of the Japanese population, the popularity of Christianity generated a backlash among those seeking to preserve Japanese

kabuki (kah-BOO-kee)
bunraku (boon-RAH-koo)
Francis Xavier (fran-sis ZEY-vee-er)

Kabuki Theater.
A colored woodcut by Okumura Masanobu depicts the audience at a seventeenth-century kabuki theater. Enthusiastic actors often ran down wooden ramps and played their roles among the audience.

religious and cultural traditions. The Tokugawa shoguns restricted European access to Japan largely because of concerns that Christianity might serve as a cultural bridge for alliances between daimyo and European adventurers, which in turn could threaten the bakufu. Meanwhile, Buddhist and Confucian scholars resented the Christian conviction that their faith was the only true doctrine.

Anti-Christian Campaign   Between 1587 and 1639, shoguns promulgated several decrees ordering a halt to Christian missions and commanding Japanese Christians to renounce their faith. In 1612 the shoguns began rigorous enforcement of these decrees. They tortured and executed European missionaries who refused to leave the islands as well as Japanese Christians who refused to abandon their faith. The campaign was so effective that even some European missionaries abandoned Christianity. Most notable was the Portuguese Jesuit Christovão Ferreira, head of the Jesuit mission in Japan, who gave up Christianity under torture, adopted Buddhism, and interrogated many

---

Christovão Ferreira (chris-STOH-voh feh-RAY-rah)

Europeans who fell into Japanese hands in the mid–seventeenth century. By the late seventeenth century, the anti-Christian campaign had claimed tens of thousands of lives, and Christianity survived only as a secret, underground religion.

Dutch Learning   Tokugawa policies ensured that Christianity would not soon reappear in Japan, but they did not entirely prevent contacts between Europeans and Japanese. After 1639 Dutch merchants trading at Nagasaki became Japan's principal source of information about the world beyond east Asia. A small number of Japanese scholars learned Dutch to communicate with the foreigners. Their studies, which they called "Dutch learning," brought considerable knowledge of the outside world to Japan. After 1720 Tokugawa authorities lifted the ban on foreign books, and Dutch learning—especially European art and science—began to play a significant role in Japanese intellectual life. Indeed, by the mid–eighteenth century the Tokugawa shoguns themselves had become enthusiastic proponents of Dutch learning, and schools of European medicine and Dutch studies flourished in several Japanese cities.

SUMMARY

Both China and Japan controlled their own affairs throughout the early modern era and avoided the turmoil that afflicted societies in the Americas and much of sub-Saharan Africa. Rulers of the Ming dynasty built a powerful centralized state in China. They worked diligently to restore traditional ways by reviving Chinese political institutions and providing state sponsorship for neo-Confucianism. In the interest of stability, authorities also restricted foreign merchants' access to China and limited the activities of Christian missionaries. The succeeding Qing dynasty pursued similar policies. The Ming and Qing dynasties both brought political stability, but China experienced considerable social and economic change in early modern times. American food crops helped increase agricultural production, which fueled rapid population growth, and global trade stimulated the Chinese economy, which improved the position of merchants and artisans in society. The experience of the Tokugawa era in Japan was much like that of the Ming and Qing eras in China. The Tokugawa bakufu brought political order to the Japanese islands and closely controlled foreign relations, but a vibrant economy promoted social change that enhanced the status of merchants and artisans.

STUDY TERMS

bakufu (440)
Buddhism (439)
bunraku (443)
Christovão Ferreira (444)
civil service examinations (434)
daimyo (440)
Dutch learning (444)
eunuch (430)
filial piety (434)
floating worlds (443)
Forbidden City (431)
Francis Xavier (443)
Great Wall (430–431)
Hongwu (430)

Jesuits (439)
kabuki (443)
Kangxi (433)
kowtow (433)
Manchu (432–433)
Matteo Ricci (429)
Ming dynasty (430)
neo-Confucianism (439)
Nurhaci (432)
Qianlong (433)
Qing dynasty (430)
Sengoku (440)
Shinto (442)
Shintoism (442)
shogun (430)

Son of Heaven (433)
Tokugawa Ieyasu (430)
Tokugawa shogunate (440)

Wanli (429)
Yongle (430)
Zhu Xi (439)

FOR FURTHER READING

Timothy Brook. *The Chinese State in Ming Society.* London and New York, 2004. An important collection of essays on commercialism and social networks, and the role they played in the development of a stable society.

———. *The Confusions of Pleasure: Commerce and Culture in Ming China.* Berkeley, 1998. Fascinating social and cultural analysis of Ming China focusing on the role of commerce as an agent of social change.

Mark C. Elliott. *The Manchu Way: The Eight Banners and Ethnic Identity in Late Imperial China.* Stanford, 2001. Important scholarly study focusing on relations between Manchus and Chinese during the Qing dynasty.

Benjamin A. Elman. *A Cultural History of Civil Examinations in Late Imperial China.* Berkeley, 2000. A meticulous study of one of the most important institutions in Chinese history.

Ray Huang. *1587: A Year of No Significance.* New Haven, 1981. A very good history of the late Ming, with insights into daily life.

Susan Mann and Yu-Ying Cheng, eds. *Under Confucian Eyes: Writings on Gender in Chinese History.* Berkeley, 2001. A rich anthology of primary texts documenting the lives of women in imperial China.

Susan Naquin and Evelyn S. Rawski. *Chinese Society in the Eighteenth Century.* New Haven, 1987. A lucid and well-organized discussion of Chinese social history.

Kenneth Pomeranz. *The Great Divergence: China, Europe, and the Making of the Modern World Economy.* Princeton, 2000. Path-breaking scholarly study that illuminates the economic history of the early modern world through comparison of economic development in Asian and European lands.

Conrad Totman. *Early Modern Japan.* Berkeley, 1993. An outstanding survey of Tokugawa ecological, political, social, economic, and cultural history.

H. Paul Varley. *Japanese Culture.* 4th ed. Honolulu, 2000. Places the cultural history of the Tokugawa era in its larger historical context.

The Islamic Empires

CHAPTER 24

The Taj Mahal, a sumptuous mosque and tomb built between 1632 and 1649 by Shah Jahan in memory of his wife, Mumtaz Mahal.

EYEWITNESS:
Shah Jahan's Monument to Love and Allah

In 1635 Shah Jahan, the emperor of Mughal India, took his seat on the Peacock Throne. Seven years in the making, the Peacock Throne is probably the most spectacular seat on which any mortal human being has rested. Shah Jahan ordered the throne encrusted with ten million rupees' worth of diamonds, rubies, emeralds, and pearls. Atop the throne itself stood a magnificent, golden-bodied peacock with a huge ruby and a fifty-carat, pear-shaped pearl on its breast and a brilliant tail fashioned of sapphires and gems.

Yet, for all its splendor, the Peacock Throne ranks a distant second among Shah Jahan's artistic projects: pride of place goes to the incomparable Taj Mahal. Built over a period of eighteen years as a tomb for Shah Jahan's beloved wife, Mumtaz Mahal, who died during childbirth in 1631, the Taj Mahal is a graceful and elegant monument both to the departed empress and to Shah Jahan's Islamic faith.

The emperor and his architects conceived the Taj Mahal as a vast allegory in stone symbolizing the day when Allah would cause the dead to rise and undergo judgment. Its gardens represented the gardens of paradise, and the four water channels running through them symbolized the four rivers of the heavenly kingdom. The domed marble tomb of Mumtaz Mahal represented the throne of Allah. The main gateway to the structure features the entire text of the chapter promising that on the day of judgment, Allah will punish the wicked and gather the faithful into his celestial paradise.

The Peacock Throne and the Taj Mahal testify to the wealth of the Mughal empire, and the tomb of Mumtaz Mahal bespeaks also the fundamentally Islamic character of the ruling dynasty. But the Mughal realm was not the only well-organized Islamic empire of early modern times. The Ottoman dynasty ruled a powerful empire that expanded from its base in Anatolia to embrace much of eastern Europe, Egypt, and north Africa. The Safavid dynasty challenged the Ottomans for dominance in southwest Asia and prospered from its role in trade networks linking China, India, Russia, southwest Asia, and the Mediterranean basin. Between them, the Mughal, Ottoman, and Safavid empires ruled over most of the vast Islamic world in the early modern period, with the exception of Southeast Asia and parts of sub-Saharan Africa. Indeed, while Islam itself had continued to spread in many parts of the world since the fall of the Abbasid dynasty in 1258, the resurgence of Islamic empires beginning in the fifteenth century represented the most significant organization of Islamic peoples since the Mongol conquests of the thirteenth century.

All three Islamic empires of early modern times had dynasties that originated with nomadic, Turkish-speaking peoples from the steppes of central Asia—most of which had converted to Islam during the Abbasid period (750–1258). All three dynasties retained political and cultural traditions that their ancestors had adopted on the steppes, but they also adapted readily to the city-based agricultural societies that they conquered. The Ottoman dynasty

Shah Jahan (shah jah-han)
Mumtaz Mahal (moom-tahz muh-HAHL)

1289–1923	Ottoman dynasty
1451–1481	Reign of Mehmed the Conqueror
1453	Ottoman conquest of Constantinople
1501–1524	Reign of Shah Ismail
1501–1722	Safavid dynasty
1514	Battle of Chaldiran
1520–1566	Reign of Süleyman the Magnificent
1526–1858	Mughal dynasty
1556–1605	Reign of Akbar
1588–1629	Reign of Shah Abbas the Great
1659–1707	Reign of Aurangzeb

made especially effective use of gunpowder weapons, and the Safavids and the Mughals also incorporated gunpowder weapons into their arsenals. All three dynasties officially embraced Islam and drew cultural guidance from long-held Islamic values.

During the sixteenth and early seventeenth centuries, the three Islamic empires presided over expansive and prosperous societies. Each controlled important trade routes that linked peoples across thousands of miles, and each produced sought-after commodities that were traded in distant markets. About the mid–seventeenth century, however, they all began to weaken. Each empire waged long, costly wars that drained resources without bringing compensating benefits. The empires also faced domestic difficulties. Each of them was an ethnically and religiously diverse realm, and each experienced tensions when conservative Muslim leaders lobbied for strict observance of Islam while members of other communities sought greater freedom for themselves. Furthermore, the Islamic empires made little investment in economic and technological development. By the mid–eighteenth century the Safavid empire had collapsed, and the Ottoman and Mughal realms were rapidly falling under European influence. Yet even though the early modern Islamic empires declined in power, the cultural legacy of Islam has lived on in all of the areas that were once under their control.

FORMATION OF THE ISLAMIC EMPIRES

When the Mongols invaded the Islamic heartland in the thirteenth century and ultimately toppled the Abbasid dynasty in Baghdad in 1258, they wreaked enormous destruction on Muslim culture by burning libraries and destroying mosques. Yet within forty years, the Mongols who had destroyed the Abbasids had themselves converted to Islam. Mongols also established a tradition of employing large numbers of Turkic peoples from the steppes of central Asia in their militaries and administrations, and brought gunpowder technologies to Islamic areas from China—both of which were critical to the development of the early modern Islamic empires. Indeed, each of the early modern Islamic empires developed from small, Turkic warrior principalities in frontier areas of central Asia. As they grew, they devised elaborate administrative and military institutions and effectively employed gunpowder technologies they had learned from the Mongols. Under the guidance of talented and energetic rulers, each empire organized an effective governmental apparatus and presided over a diverse and prosperous society that maintained connections with distant lands ranging from east and southeast Asia to western Europe.

The Ottoman Empire

Osman The Ottoman empire was an unusually successful frontier state. The term *Ottoman* derived from Osman Bey, founder of the dynasty that continued in unbroken succession from 1289 until the dissolution of the empire in 1923. Osman was *bey* (chief) of a band of seminomadic Turks who migrated to northwestern Anatolia in the thirteenth century. Osman and his followers sought above all to become *ghazi*, Muslim religious warriors who fought on behalf of the faith.

Ottoman Expansion The Ottomans' location on the borders of the Byzantine empire afforded them ample opportunity to wage holy war. Their first great success came in 1326 with the capture of the Anatolian city of Bursa, which became the capital of the Ottoman principality. About 1352 they established a foothold in Europe when they seized the fortress of Gallipoli. The city of Edirne (Adrianople) became a second Ottoman capital and served as a base for further expansion into the Balkans. As warriors settled in frontier districts and pushed their boundaries forward, they

Osman Bey (oz-MAHN beh)
ghazi (GAH-zee)
Byzantine (BIHZ-uhn-teen)

took spoils and gathered revenues that enriched both the *ghazi* and the central government.

Driving Ottoman expansion was a formidable military machine, which included light cavalry, volunteer infantry, and—as the state grew larger—heavy cavalry. After expanding into the Balkans, the Ottomans created an important force composed of slave troops. Through an institution known as the *devshirme,* the Ottomans required the Christian population of the Balkans to contribute young boys to become slaves of the sultan. The boys received special training, learned Turkish, and converted to Islam. According to individual ability, they entered either the Ottoman civilian administration or the military. Those who became soldiers were known as Janissaries, from the Turkish *yeni cheri* ("new troops"). The Janissaries quickly gained a reputation for esprit de corps, loyalty to the sultan, and readiness to employ new military technology. The Ottomans also outfitted their forces with gunpowder weapons and used them effectively in battles and sieges.

Mehmed the Conqueror

The capture of Constantinople in 1453 by Mehmed II (reigned 1451–1481)—known as Mehmed the Conqueror—opened a new chapter in Otto-man expansion. With its superb location and illustrious heritage, Constantinople became the new Ottoman capital, subsequently known as Istanbul. With the capture of the great city behind him, Mehmed presented himself not just as a warrior-sultan but as a true emperor. He laid the foundations for a tightly centralized, absolute monarchy, and his army faced no serious rival. He completed the conquest of Serbia, moved into southern Greece and Albania, eliminated the last Byzantine outpost at Trebizond, captured Genoese ports in the Crimea, initiated a naval war with Venice in the Mediterranean, and reportedly hoped to march on Rome and capture the pope. Toward the end of his life, he launched an invasion of Italy and briefly occupied Otranto, but his successors abandoned plans for expansion in western Europe.

Süleyman the Magnificent

The Ottomans continued their expansion in the early sixteenth century by occupying Syria and Egypt. The occupation of both areas represented a shift in Ottoman expansionist goals from a focus on non-Muslim areas to areas that were governed by other Muslims. In Syria and Egypt, for example, Ottomans waged war against the Muslim Mamluks who had ruled the area

Istanbul (iss-TAHN-bull)
Süleyman (SOO-lehy-mahn)

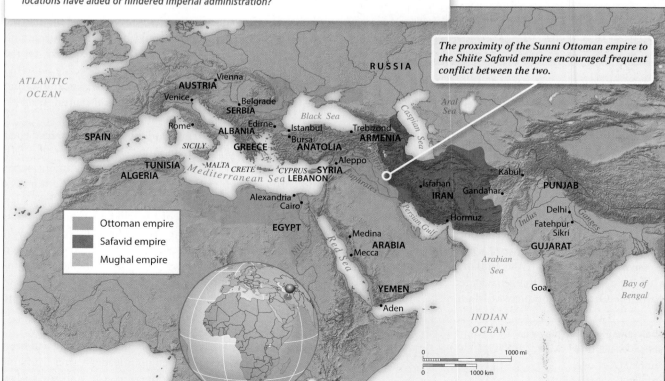

MAP 24.1

The Islamic empires, 1500–1800. Locate the Ottoman capital of Istanbul, the Safavid capital of Isfahan, and the Mughal capital of Delhi.

What strategic or commercial purposes did each of these capitals fulfill, and how would their locations have aided or hindered imperial administration?

The proximity of the Sunni Ottoman empire to the Shiite Safavid empire encouraged frequent conflict between the two.

Süleyman the Magnificent.
Sultan Süleyman (center, on horse) leads Ottoman forces as they march on Europe.

that it not only controlled Islam's holiest sites, but that it also controlled some of the wealthiest trade routes in Eurasia, particularly those that went through Cairo (in modern Egypt) and Damascus (in modern Syria).

Ottoman imperialism climaxed in the reign of Süleyman the Magnificent (reigned 1520–1566). In 1534 Süleyman conquered Baghdad and added the Tigris and Euphrates valleys to the Ottoman domain. In Europe he kept the rival Habsburg empire on the defensive throughout his reign. He captured Belgrade in 1521, defeated and killed the king of Hungary at the battle of Mohács in 1526, and in 1529 subjected the Habsburgs' prized city of Vienna to a brief but nonetheless terrifying siege.

Under Süleyman the Ottomans also became a major naval power. In addition to their own Aegean and Black Sea fleets, the Ottomans inherited the navy of the Mamluk rulers of Egypt. A Turkish corsair, Khayr al-Din Barbarossa Pasha, placed his pirate fleet under the Ottoman flag and became Süleyman's leading admiral. With such resources and leadership, Süleyman was able to challenge Christian vessels throughout the Mediterranean as well as Portuguese fleets in the Red Sea and the Indian Ocean, which had only recently become a threat to Islamic lands in those regions.

The Safavid Empire

In 1499 a twelve-year-old boy named Ismail left the swamps of Gilan near the Caspian Sea, where he had hidden from the enemies of his family for five years, to seek his revenge. Two years later he entered Tabriz at the head of an army and laid claim to the ancient Persian imperial title of shah. The young Shah Ismail (reigned 1501–1524) also proclaimed that the official religion of his realm would be Twelver Shiism, and he proceeded to impose it, by force when necessary, on the formerly Sunni population. Over the next decade he seized control of the Iranian plateau and launched expeditions into the Caucasus, Anatolia, Mesopotamia, and central Asia.

The Safavids   Shah Ismail and his successors traced their ancestry back to Safi al-Din (1252–1334), leader of a Sufi religious order in northwestern Persia. The famous tomb and shrine of Safi al-Din at Ardabil became the home of Shah Ismail's family (named "Safavids" after the holy man himself), the headquarters of his religious movement, and the center of a determined, deliberate conspiracy to win political power for his descendants. The Safavids changed their religious preferences several times in the hope of gaining popular support before settling on a form of Shiism that appealed to the nomadic Turkish tribes who were moving into the area.

Twelver Shiism   Twelver Shiism held that there had been twelve infallible imams (or religious leaders) after Muhammad, beginning with the prophet's cousin and son-in-law

for over two centuries. The reason the Ottomans gave for this campaign was that the Mamluks were no longer able to protect Muslim holy sites, particularly Mecca and Medina, from foreigners. Of special concern to the Ottomans were the Christian Portuguese, who had begun their aggressive style of trade in the Indian Ocean and Red Sea after Vasco da Gama circumnavigated Africa in 1498. By 1516, the Ottoman conquest of Mamluk territories meant

Shah Ismail (shah IZ-may-el)
Shiism (SHEE-izm)
Sunni (SOON-nee)
Safavid (SAH-fah-vihd)

SourcesfromthePast

Sultan Selim I, Letter to Shah Ismail of Persia

In 1514, the Ottoman Sultan Selim I (reigned 1512–1520) wrote the following letter to the founder of the Safavid Empire, Ismail I (reigned 1501–1524). Ismail had recently invaded Ottoman territory in eastern Anatolia, and war seemed certain. In addition, Ismail was the leader of the emerging Shi'ite interpretation of Islam, while Selim was a Sunni Muslim. This letter reveals the deep bitterness that developed between Shi'ites and Muslims in the early modern period. Although Selim's forces did in fact defeat Ismail's army at the battle of Chaldiran, Ismail retained control of Persia and thus helped to ensure the survival of Shi'ism.

The Supreme Being who is at once the sovereign arbiter of the destinies of men and the source of all light and knowledge, declares in the holy book [the Qur'an] that the true faith is that of the Muslims, and that whoever professes another religion, far from being hearkened to and saved, will on the contrary be cast out among the rejected on the great day of the Last Judgment. . . . Place yourself, O Prince, among the true believers, those who walk in the path of salvation, and who turn aside with care from vice and infidelity. . . .

I, sovereign chief of the Ottomans, master of the heroes of the age . . . address myself graciously to you, Amir Isma'il, chief of troops of Persia. . . . [M]an is the only being who can comprehend the attributes of the divinity and adore its sublime beauties; but he possesses this rare intelligence, he attains this divine knowledge only in our religion and by observing the precepts of the prince of prophets, the Caliph of Caliphs, the right arm of the God of Mercy; it is then only by practicing the true religion that man will prosper in this world and merit eternal life in the other. As to you, Amir Isma'il, such a recompense will not be your lot; because you have denied the sanctity of the divine laws; because you have deserted the path of salvation and the sacred commandments; because you have impaired the purity of the dogmas of Islam; because you have dishonoured, soiled and destroyed the altars of the Lord, usurped the sceptre of the

East by unlawful and tyrannical means, because coming forth from the dust, you have raised yourself by odious devices to a place shining with splendor and magnificence. . . . Now as the first duty of a Muslim and above all of a pious prince is to obey the commandment, "O, you faithful who believe, be the executors of the decrees of God!" the *ulama* and our doctors have pronounced sentence of death against you, perjurer and blasphemer, and have imposed on every Muslim the sacred obligation to arm in defense of religion and destroy heresy and impiety in your person and that of all your partisans.

. . . However, anxious to conform to the spirit of the law of the Prophet, we come, before commencing war, to set out before you the words of the Qur'an, in place of the sword, and to exhort you to embrace the true faith; this is why we address this letter to you. . . . We urge you to look into yourself, to renounce your errors, and to march towards the good with a firm and courageous step; we ask further that you give up possession of the territory violently seized from our state and to which you have only illegitimate pretensions. . . .

But if, to your misfortune, you persist in your past conduct . . . you will see in a few days your plains covered with our tents and inundated with our battalions. Then prodigies of valor will be done, and we shall see the decrees of the Almighty, Who is the God of Armies, and sovereign judge of the actions of men, accomplished. For the rest, victory to him who follows the path of salvation!

For Further Reflection

■ According to Selim I, why did Ismail's Shi'ite faith constitute a blasphemy against Islam? Why might Selim have viewed Shi'ism as such a threat?

Source: Reprinted with the permission of Simon & Schuster, Inc., from THE MUSLIM WORLD ON THE EVE OF EUROPE'S EXPANSION, translated and edited by John J. Saunders. Copyright © 1966 by Prentice Hall. All rights reserved.

Ali. The twelfth, or "hidden," imam had gone into hiding about 874 to escape persecution, but the Twelver Shiites believed he was still alive and would one day return to take power and spread the true religion. Ismail's father had instructed his Turkish followers to wear a distinctive red hat with twelve pleats in memory of the twelve Shiite imams, and they subsequently became known as the *qizilbash* ("red heads"). Safavid propaganda also suggested that Ismail was himself the hidden imam, or even an incarnation of

Allah. Although most Muslims would have regarded those pretensions as utterly blasphemous, the *qizilbash* enthusiastically accepted them, since they resembled traditional Turkish conceptions of leadership that associated military leaders with divinity. The *qizilbash* believed that Ismail would make them invincible in battle, and they became fanatically loyal to the Safavid cause.

---

qizilbash (gihZIHL-bahsh)

Shah Ismail's curious blend of Shiism and Turkish militancy created some powerful enemies. Foremost among them were the staunchly Sunni Ottomans, who detested the Shiite Safavids and feared the spread of Safavid propaganda among the nomadic Turks in their own territory. As a result, Ottomans launched a full-scale invasion of Safavid territory in the early sixteenth century.

Battle of Chaldiran At a battle on the plain of Chaldiran (1514), the Ottomans deployed heavy artillery and thousands of Janissaries equipped with firearms behind a barrier of carts. Although the Safavids knew about gunpowder technology, they declined to use devices that they saw as unreliable and unmanly. Trusting in the protective charisma of Shah Ismail, the *qizilbash* cavalry fearlessly attacked the Ottoman line and suffered devastating casualties. Ismail had to slip away, and the Ottomans temporarily occupied his capital at Tabriz. The Ottomans badly damaged the Safavid state but lacked the resources to destroy it, and the two empires remained locked in intermittent conflict for the next two centuries.

Shah Abbas the Great Later Safavid rulers prudently abandoned the extreme Safavid ideology that associated the emperor with Allah in favor of more conventional Twelver Shiism, from which they still derived legitimacy as descendants and representatives of the imams. In the late sixteenth century, Shah Abbas the Great (reigned 1588–1629) fully revitalized the Safavid empire. He moved the capital to the more central location of Isfahan, encouraged trade with other lands, and reformed the administrative and military institutions of the empire. With newly strengthened military forces, Shah Abbas led the Safavids to numerous victories. He attacked and defeated the nomadic Uzbeks in central Asia, expelled the Portuguese from Hormuz, and harassed the Ottomans mercilessly in a series of wars from 1603 to the end of his reign. His campaigns brought most of northwestern Iran, the Caucasus, and Mesopotamia under Safavid rule.

The Mughal Empire

Babur In 1523 Zahir al-Din Muhammad, known as Babur ("the Tiger"), a Chagatai Turk who claimed descent from both Chinggis Khan and Tamerlane, appeared in northern India. Unlike the Ottomans or Safavids, who fought on behalf of Islam, Babur made little pretense to be anything

Chaldiran (chahld-ih-rahn)
Mughal (MOO-guhl)
Babur (BAH-ber)
Zahir al-Din Muhammad (zah-here ahl-dihn muh-HAHM-mud)
Chagatai (chah-guh-TAHY)

Shah Ismail and the *qizilbash.*
This miniature painting from a Safavid manuscript depicts the shah and his *qizilbash* warriors wearing the distinctive red pleated cap that was their emblem of identity.

more than a soldier of fortune in the manner of his illustrious ancestors. His father had been the prince of Farghana, and Babur's great ambition was to transform his inheritance into a glorious central Asian empire. Yet envious relatives and Uzbek enemies frustrated his ambitions.

Unable to accomplish his goals in central Asia, Babur turned his attention to India. With the aid of gunpowder weapons, including artillery and firearms, Babur took Delhi in 1526. Ironically, Babur cared little for the land he had conquered. Many in his entourage wanted to take their spoils of war and leave the hot and humid Indian climate, which ruined their finely crafted compound bows, but Babur elected to stay. By the time of his death in 1530, Babur had built a loosely knit empire that stretched from

Kabul through the Punjab to the borders of Bengal. He founded a dynasty called the *Mughal* (a Persian term for "Mongol"), which expanded to embrace almost all the Indian subcontinent.

Akbar The real architect of the Mughal empire was Babur's grandson Akbar (reigned 1556–1605), a brilliant and charismatic ruler. During his reign, Akbar created a centralized administrative structure with ministries regulating the various provinces of the empire. His military campaigns consolidated Mughal power in Gujarat and Bengal. He destroyed the Hindu kingdom of Vijayanagar, thus lay-

ing the foundation for later Mughal expansion in southern India.

In addition to being an able ruler, Akbar was a thoughtful, reflective man deeply interested in religion and philosophy. He pursued a policy of religious toleration that he hoped would reduce tensions between Hindu and Muslim communities in India. Although illiterate (probably due to dyslexia), he was extremely intelligent and had books read to him daily. Instead of imposing Islam on his subjects, he encouraged the elaboration of a syncretic religion called the "divine faith" that focused attention on the emperor as a ruler common to all the religious, ethnic, and social groups of India.

Aurangzeb The Mughal empire reached its greatest extent under Aurangzeb (reigned 1659–1707). During his long reign, Aurangzeb waged a relentless campaign of expansion. By the early eighteenth century, Mughals ruled the entire subcontinent except for a small region at the southern tip. Although he greatly expanded Mughal boundaries, Aurangzeb presided over a troubled empire. Aurangzeb was a devout Muslim, and he broke with Akbar's policy of religious toleration. He demolished several famous Hindu temples and replaced them with mosques. He also imposed a tax on Hindus in an effort to encourage conversion to Islam. His promotion of Islam appealed strongly to Indian Muslims, but it provoked deep hostility among Hindus and enabled local leaders to organize movements to resist or even rebel against Mughal authority.

IMPERIAL ISLAMIC SOCIETY

Despite many differences, there were striking similarities in the development of Ottoman, Safavid, and Mughal societies. All relied on bureaucracies that drew inspiration from the steppe traditions of Turkish and Mongol peoples as well as from the heritage of Islam. They adopted similar economic policies and sought ways to maintain harmony in societies that embraced many different religious and ethnic groups. Rulers of all the empires also sought to enhance the legitimacy of their regimes by providing for public welfare and associating themselves with literary and artistic talent. Finally, all of the empires became centers of long-distance trade, and thus were areas of cross-cultural interaction.

The Dynastic State

The Ottoman, Safavid, and Mughal empires were all military creations, regarded by their rulers as personal possessions by right of conquest. The rulers exercised personal command of the armies, appointed and dismissed officials at will, and adopted whatever policies they wished. In theory, the emperors owned all land and granted use of it in

Akbar.

This manuscript illustration from about 1590 depicts Akbar (at top, shaded by attendants) inspecting construction of a new imperial capital at Fatehpur Sikri.

What kinds of projects are laborers working on?

Thinking about TRADITIONS

Religious Diversity

An overarching feature of all three Islamic empires was the ethnic and religious diversity of the subject populations. *What measures did the rulers of the Ottoman, Safavid, and Mughal states take to maintain harmony among the different ethnic and religious communities?*

return for the payment of fixed taxes. The emperors and their families derived revenues from crown lands, and revenues from other lands supported military and administrative officials.

The Emperors and Islam In the Ottoman, Safavid, and Mughal empires, the prestige and authority of the dynasty derived from the personal piety and the military prowess of the ruler and his ancestors. Devotion to Islam encouraged rulers to extend their faith to new lands. Moreover, the *ghazi* ideal of spreading Islam by fighting infidels or heretics resonated with the traditions of Turkish and Mongolian peoples, who were accustomed both to warfare and to leadership by warriors.

Steppe Traditions The autocratic authority wielded by the rulers of the Islamic empires also reflected steppe traditions. The early emperors largely did as they pleased, irrespective of religious and social norms. The Ottoman sultans, for example, unilaterally issued numerous legal edicts, and Safavid and Mughal rulers unabashedly asserted their spiritual authority over their subjects. Yet steppe practices also brought problems to the Islamic empires, especially regarding succession issues. In the steppe empires the ruler's relatives often managed components of the states, and succession to the throne became a hot contest between competing members of the family. This was reflected in the Mughal empire, where conflicts among princes and rebellions of sons against fathers were recurrent features throughout its history. The Safavids also engaged in murderous struggles for the throne. Shah Abbas himself lived in fear that another member of the family would challenge him. He kept his sons confined to the palace and killed or blinded relatives he suspected, almost wiping out his family in the process.

Succession issues also became a problem for the Ottomans. After the fifteenth century, the sultans increasingly moved to protect their position by eliminating family rivals. Mehmed the Conqueror decreed that a ruler could legally kill off his brothers after taking the throne. His successors observed that tradition in Turko-Mongol style—by strangling victims with a silk bow string so as not to shed royal blood—until 1595, when the new sultan executed

nineteen brothers, many of them infants, as well as fifteen expectant mothers. After that episode, sultans confined their sons in special quarters of the imperial harem and forbade them to go outside except to take the throne.

Women and Politics Even though Muslim theorists universally agreed that women should have no role in public affairs, women played important roles in managing the Islamic empires. Many Ottoman, Safavid, and Mughal emperors followed the example of Chinggis Khan, who revered his mother and his first wife. In the Islamic empires the ruler's mother and his chief wife or favorite concubine enjoyed special privileges and authority. Ottoman courtiers often complained loudly about the "rule of women," thus offering eloquent testimony to the power that women could wield. Süleyman the Magnificent, for example, became infatuated with Hürrem Sultana (also known as Roxelana), a concubine of Ukrainian origin. Süleyman elevated her to the status of a legal wife, consulted her on state policies, and deferred to her judgment even to the point of executing his eldest son when Hürrem wanted to secure the succession of her child.

Women also played prominent political roles in the Safavid and Mughal empires. In Safavid Persia, Mahd-e Olya, the wife of one shah, was the de facto ruler. Her efforts to limit the power of the *qizilbash* so enraged them that they murdered her. The aunt of another shah scolded the ruler for neglecting his duties and used her own money to raise an army to put down a revolt. The Mughal emperor Jahangir was content to let his wife Nur Jahan run the government, and even the conscientious Muslim Aurangzeb listened to his daughter's political advice.

Agriculture and Trade

Food Crops Productive agricultural economies were the foundations of all the Islamic empires. Each empire extracted surplus agricultural production and used it to finance armies and bureaucracies. Mostly the Islamic empires relied on crops of wheat and rice that had flourished for centuries in the lands they ruled. The Columbian exchange brought American crops to all the Islamic empires but without the same dramatic effects as in Europe, east Asia, and Africa. European merchants did introduce maize, potatoes, tomatoes, and other crops to the Islamic empires, however, and although the new arrivals did not become staples, they enlivened regional cuisines with new tastes and textures.

Two products of the Columbian exchange that caught on extremely well in both the Ottoman and the Safavid empires were coffee and tobacco. Although native to Ethiopia and cultivated in southern Arabia, coffee did not become

Reverberations of ● ● ● ● ● ● ● ●
The Columbian Exchange

Tobacco, a plant native to the Americas, had been used by indigenous groups for millennia as a sacred drug and for community rituals. Within a century after indigenous groups introduced Europeans to the plant, tobacco use had spread throughout Europe and reached most parts of Asia as well as the Islamic empires. Tobacco use became wildly popular in the Islamic empires, in part because Islamic restrictions against the use of alcohol made the stimulant effects of tobacco that much more attractive. Consider the long-term effects of tobacco use in the Islamic empires both in terms of the social and recreational functions that tobacco filled in the context of coffeehouses, and also in terms of the health effects for millions of smokers who suffered from respiratory and other tobacco-related diseases in the centuries after its introduction.

popular in Islamic lands until the sixteenth century. Like sugar, coffee had traveled to Europe and from there to the Americas, where plantations specialized in the production of both tropical crops for the world market. By the eighteenth century, American producers and European merchants supplied Muslim markets with coffee as well as sugar.

Tobacco According to the Ottoman historian Ibrahim Pechevi, English merchants introduced tobacco about 1600, claiming it was useful for medicinal purposes. Within a few decades it had spread throughout the Ottoman empire. The increasing popularity of coffee drinking and pipe smoking encouraged entrepreneurs to establish coffeehouses where customers could indulge their appetites for caffeine and nicotine at the same time. The popularity of coffeehouses provoked protest from moralists who worried that these popular attractions were dens of iniquity. Pechevi himself complained about the hideous odor of tobacco and the messy ashes, and religious leaders claimed that it was worse to frequent a coffeehouse than a tavern. Sultan Murad IV went so far as to outlaw coffee and tobacco and to execute those who continued to partake. That effort, however, was a losing battle. Both pastimes eventually won widespread acceptance, and the coffeehouse became a prominent social institution in the Islamic empires.

Population Growth American food crops had less demographic effect in the Islamic empires than in other parts of the

world. The population of India surged during early modern times, growing from 105 million in 1500 to 190 million in 1800. But population growth in India resulted more from intensive agriculture along traditional lines than from the influence of new crops. The Safavid population grew less rapidly, from 5 million in 1500 to 8 million in 1800. Ottoman numbers grew from 9 million in 1500 to about 24 million about 1800, but those numbers reflect territorial additions more than fertility increases. Even in the Ottoman heartland of Anatolia, population did not expand nearly as dramatically as it did in other lands in early modern times. From 6 million in 1500, the population of Anatolia rose to just 9 million in 1800.

Trade The Islamic empires ruled lands that had figured prominently in long-distance trade for centuries and participated actively in global trade networks in early modern times. In the Ottoman empire, for example, the early capital at Bursa was also the terminus of a caravan route that brought raw silk from Persia to supply the Italian market. The Ottomans also granted special trading concessions to merchants from England and France to cement alliances against common enemies in Spain and central Europe, and the city of Aleppo became an emporium for foreign merchants engaged primarily in the spice trade.

Ottoman coffeehouse.
This nineteenth-century depiction of a coffeehouse in Istanbul demonstrates the centrality of tobacco smoking to the experience. In the Ottoman empire, men socialized in coffeehouses while smoking from elaborate water pipes called hookahs.

In this picture, what seems most central—coffee or tobacco?

Shah Abbas promoted Isfahan as a commercial center and extended trading privileges to foreign merchants to help create a favorable environment for trade. European merchants sought Safavid raw silk, carpets, and ceramics. The English East India Company, the French East India Company, and the Dutch VOC all traded actively with the Safavids. To curry favor, the English company even sent military advisors to help introduce gunpowder weapons to Safavid armed forces and provided a navy to help them retake Hormuz in the Persian Gulf from the Portuguese.

The Mughals did not pay as much attention to foreign trade as the Ottomans and the Safavids, partly because of the enormous size and productivity of the domestic Indian economy and partly because the Mughal rulers had little interest in maritime affairs. Nevertheless, the Mughal treasury derived significant income from foreign trade. The Mughals allowed the creation of trading stations and merchant colonies by Portuguese, English, French, and Dutch merchants. Meanwhile, Indian merchants formed trading companies of their own, venturing both overland as far as Russia and by sea to ports all over the Indian Ocean. In fact, Indian merchants from Gujarat had been among the first to bring Islam to the island of Sumatra, in southeast Asia, in the late thirteenth century. By the middle of the fifteenth century, Indian merchants and southeast Asian Muslim converts had already spread the faith to Malacca and other surrounding areas even before the creation of the Mughal empire in the sixteenth century.

Religious Affairs in the Islamic Empires

Religious Diversity All the Islamic empires had populations that were religiously and ethnically diverse, and imperial rulers had the daunting challenge of maintaining harmony among different religious communities. The Ottoman empire included large numbers of Christians and Jews in the Balkans, Armenia, Lebanon, and Egypt. The Safavid empire embraced sizable Zoroastrian and Jewish communities as well as many Christian subjects in the Caucasus. The Mughal empire was especially diverse. Most Mughal subjects were Hindus, but large numbers of Muslims lived alongside smaller communities of Jains, Zoroastrians, Christians, and devotees of syncretic faiths such as Sikhism.

Akbar's Divine Faith In India, Akbar was especially tolerant of diverse religions and worked to find a religious synthesis that would serve as a cultural foundation for unity in his diverse empire. As part of that effort, he supported

Sikhs (SIHKS)
dhimmi (DIHM-mee)
jizya (JIHZ-yuh)

the early Sikhs, who combined elements of Hinduism and Islam in a new syncretic faith. He also attempted to elaborate his own "divine faith," which emphasized loyalty to the emperor while borrowing eclectically from different religious traditions. Akbar never explained his ideas systematically, but it is clear that they drew most heavily on Islam. The divine faith was strictly monotheistic, and it reflected the influence of Shiite and Sufi teachings. But it also glorified the emperor: Akbar even referred to himself as the "lord of wisdom," who would guide his subjects to an understanding of god. The divine faith was tolerant of Hinduism, and it even drew inspiration from Zoroastrianism in its effort to bridge the gaps between Mughal India's many cultural and religious communities.

Status of Religious Minorities The Islamic empires relied on a long-established model to deal with subjects who were not Muslims. They did not require conquered peoples to convert to Islam but extended to them the status of *dhimmi* (a protected people). In return for their loyalty and payment of a special tax known as *jizya,* dhimmi communities retained their personal freedom, kept their property, practiced their religion, and handled their own legal affairs. In the Ottoman empire, for example, autonomous religious communities known as *millet* retained their own civil laws, traditions, and languages. *Millet* communities usually also assumed social and administrative functions in matters concerning birth, marriage, death, health, and education.

The situation in the Mughal empire was different, since its large number of religious communities made a *millet* system impractical. Mughal rulers reserved the most powerful military and administrative positions for Muslims, but in the day-to-day management of affairs, Muslims and Hindus cooperated closely. Some Mughal emperors, such as Akbar, worked particularly hard to forge links between religious communities and to integrate Muslim and Hindu elites. Indeed, in an effort to build bridges between the different religious communities of his realm, he abolished the *jizya* and sponsored discussions and debates between Muslims, Hindus, Jains, Zoroastrians, and Christians.

Promotion of Islam Policies of religious tolerance were not popular with many Muslims, who worried that toleration might lead to their absorption into Hindu society. They therefore insisted that Mughal rulers create and maintain an Islamic state based on Islamic law. When Aurangzeb reached the Mughal throne in 1659, that policy gained strength. Aurangzeb reinstated the *jizya* and promoted Islam as the official faith of Mughal India. His policy satisfied zealous Muslims but at the cost of deep bitterness among his Hindu subjects. Tension between Hindu and Muslim communities in India persisted throughout the Mughal dynasty and beyond.

Cultural Patronage of the Islamic Emperors

As the empires matured, the Islamic rulers sought to enhance their prestige through public works projects and patronage of scholars. They competed to attract outstanding religious scholars, artists, and architects to their courts and lavished resources on public buildings.

Istanbul Capital cities and royal palaces were the most visible expressions of imperial majesty. The Ottomans took particular pride in Istanbul, which quickly revived after conquest and became a bustling, prosperous city of more than a million people. At its heart was the great Topkapi palace, which housed government offices and meeting places for imperial councils. At its core was the sultan's residence with its harem, gardens, pleasure pavilions, and a repository for the most sacred possessions of the empire, including the mantle of the prophet Muhammad. Sultan Süleyman the Magnificent was fortunate to be able to draw on the talents of the architectural genius Sinan Pasha (1489–1588) to create the vast religious complex called the Süleymaniye, which blended Islamic and Byzantine architectural elements. It combined tall, slender minarets with large domed buildings supported by half domes in the style of the Byzantine church Hagia Sofia (which the Ottomans converted into the mosque of Aya Sofya).

Isfahan Shah Abbas made his capital, Isfahan, into one of the most precious jewels of urban architectural development anywhere in the world. Abbas concentrated markets, the palace, and the royal mosque around a vast polo field and public square. Broad, shaded avenues and magnificent bridges linked the central city to its suburbs. Safavid architects made use of monumental entryways, vast arcades, spacious courtyards, and intricate, colorful decoration. Unlike the sprawling Ottoman and Mughal palaces, the Safavid palaces in Isfahan were relatively small and emphasized natural settings with gardens, pools, and large, open verandas. The point was not only to enable the shah to observe outside activities but also to emphasize his visibility and accessibility, qualities long esteemed in the Persian tradition of kingship.

In India, Mughal architects skillfully blended central Asian traditions with elements of Hindu architecture, and they built on a scale that left no doubt about their wealth and resources. They constructed scores of mosques, fortresses, and palaces and sometimes created entire cities.

Topkapi (TOHP-kah-pih)
Sinan Pasha (sih-NAHN pah-cha)

Isfahan Royal Mosque.
The Royal Mosque of Isfahan, centerpiece of the city as rebuilt by Shah Abbas at the end of the sixteenth century. With its combination of an open space flanked by markets, the palace, and religious structures, Isfahan stands as a unique example of urban planning in Islamic lands.

The Süleymaniye Mosque.
This massive mosque was built for Sultan Süleyman the Magnificent by the Ottoman architect Sinan Pasha in 1556.

Thinking about ENCOUNTERS

Islamic Mapmaking

Muslims evinced a generalized wariness about knowledge deriving from European contacts. One notable exception to this was Piri Reis, an Ottoman cartographer. *Why did he draw on European sources for his maps? Why were maps seen as so strategically useful in an age of cross-cultural contacts?*

Fatehpur Sikri The best example was Fatehpur Sikri, a city planned and constructed by Akbar that served as his capital from 1569 to 1585. With its mint, records office, treasury, and audience hall, the new city demonstrated Akbar's strength and imperial ambitions. Fatehpur Sikri was also a private residence and retreat for the ruler, reproducing in stone a royal encampment with exquisite pleasure palaces where Akbar indulged his passions for music and conversation with scholars and poets. At yet another level, it was a dramatic display of Mughal piety and devotion, centered on the cathedral mosque and the mausoleum of Akbar's Sufi spiritual teacher, Shaykh Salim Chishthi. Despite their intensely Islamic character, many of the buildings consciously incorporated Indian elements, such as verandas supported by columns and decorations of stone elephants. Unfortunately, Akbar had selected a poor site for the city and soon abandoned it because of its bad water supply.

Fatehpur Sikri (fah-teh-poor SIH-kree)
Shaykh Salim Chishthi
(sheyk sah-LEEM CHEESH-tee)

Fatehpur Sikri.
This city was built by Akbar in the 1570s to commemorate the emperor's military conquests and house the tomb of his religious guide. It included a palace, an audience hall where Akbar attended religious and philosophical debates, and a great mosque.

The Taj Mahal The most famous of the Mughal monuments—and one of the most prominent of all Islamic edifices—was the Taj Mahal. Shah Jahan had twenty thousand workers toil for eighteen years to erect the exquisite white marble mosque and tomb. He originally planned to build a similar mausoleum out of black marble for himself, but his son Aurangzeb deposed him before he could carry out the project. Shah Jahan spent his last years confined to a small cell with a tiny window, and only with the aid of a mirror was he able to catch the sight of his beloved wife's final resting place.

THE EMPIRES IN TRANSITION

The Islamic empires underwent dramatic change between the sixteenth and the eighteenth centuries. The Safavid empire disappeared entirely. In 1722 a band of Afghan tribesmen marched all the way to Isfahan, blockaded the city until its starving inhabitants resorted to cannibalism, forced the shah to abdicate, and executed thousands of Safavid officials as well as many members of the royal family. After the death of Aurangzeb in 1707, Mughal India experienced provincial rebellions and foreign invasions. By midcentury the subcontinent was falling under British imperial rule. By 1700 the Ottomans, too, were on the defensive: the sultans lost control over provinces such as Lebanon and Egypt, and throughout the eighteenth and nineteenth centuries European and Russian states placed political, military, and economic pressure on the shrinking Ottoman realm.

The Deterioration of Imperial Leadership

Strong and effective central authority was essential to the Islamic empires, and Muslim political theorists never tired of emphasizing the importance of rulers who were diligent, virtuous, and just. Weak, negligent, and corrupt rulers would allow the social order to break down. The Ottomans were fortunate in having a series of talented sultans for three centuries, and the Safavids and the Mughals produced their share of effective rulers as well.

Dynastic Decline Eventually, however, all three dynasties had rulers who were incompetent or irresponsible about tending to affairs of state. Moreover, all three dynasties faced difficulties because of suspicion and fighting among competing members of their ruling houses. In the Ottoman empire alone, notorious examples of problem rulers included Süleyman's successor, Selim the Sot (reigned 1566–1574) and Ibrahim the Crazy (reigned 1640–1648), who taxed and spent to such excess that government officials deposed and murdered him. Indeed, after the late seventeenth century, weak rule increasingly provoked mutinies in the army, provincial revolts, political corruption, and insecurity throughout the Ottoman realm.

Religious Tensions Political troubles often arose from religious tensions. Conservative Muslim clerics had considerable influence in the Islamic empires because of their monopoly on education and their deep involvement in the everyday lives and legal affairs of ordinary subjects. The clerics mistrusted the emperors' interests in unconventional forms of Islam such as Sufism, complained bitterly when women or subjects who were not Muslims played influential political roles, and protested any exercise of royal authority that contradicted Islamic law.

In the Ottoman empire, disaffected religious students often joined the Janissaries in revolt. A particularly serious threat came from the Wahhabi movement in Arabia, which denounced the Ottomans as dangerous religious innovators who were unfit to rule. Conservative Muslims fiercely protested the construction of an astronomical observatory in Istanbul and forced the sultan to demolish it in 1580. In 1742 they also forced the closure of the Ottoman printing press, which they regarded as an impious technology.

In the Safavid empire, rulers fell under the domination of conservative Shiite clerics. Shiite leaders pressured the shahs to persecute Sunnis, non-Muslims, and even the Sufis who had helped establish the dynasty. Religious tensions also afflicted Mughal India. In the mid–eighteenth century, as Aurangzeb struggled to claim the Mughal throne, he drew on conservative Islamic ideas when he required non-Muslims to pay the poll tax and ordered the destruction of Hindu temples. Those measures inflamed tensions between the various Sunni, Shiite, and Sufi branches of Islam and also fueled animosity among Hindus and other Mughal subjects who were not Muslims.

Economic and Military Decline

In the sixteenth century, all the Islamic empires had strong domestic economies and played prominent roles in global trade networks. By the eighteenth century, however, domestic economies were under great stress, and foreign trade had declined dramatically or had fallen under the control of European powers. The Islamic empires were well on their way to becoming marginal lands that depended on goods produced elsewhere.

Economic Difficulties The high cost of maintaining an expensive military and administrative apparatus helped to bring about economic decline in the Islamic empires. As

long as the empires were expanding, they were able to finance their armies and bureaucracies with fresh resources extracted from newly conquered lands. When expansion slowed, ceased, or reversed, however, they faced the problem of supporting their institutions with limited resources. The long, costly, and unproductive wars fought by the Ottomans with the Habsburgs in central Europe, by the Safavids and Ottomans in Mesopotamia, and by Aurangzeb in southern India exhausted the treasuries of the Islamic empires without making fresh resources available to them.

As expansion slowed and the empires lost control over remote provinces, officials reacted to the loss of revenue by raising taxes, selling public offices, accepting bribes, or resorting to simple extortion. All those measures did long-term economic damage. To make matters worse, the governments viewed foreign trade as just another opportunity to bring in revenue. The Ottomans expanded the privileges enjoyed by foreign merchants, and the Mughals encouraged the establishment of Dutch and English trading outposts and welcomed the expansion of their business in India. In other words, imperial authorities were content to have foreign traders come to them. None made serious efforts to establish commercial stations abroad, although Indian merchants organized their own private trading companies.

Military Decline As they lost initiative to western European peoples in economic and commercial affairs, the Islamic empires also did not seek actively to improve their military technologies. During the sixteenth and early seventeenth centuries, the Islamic empires were able to purchase European weapons in large numbers and attract European expertise that kept their armies supplied with powerful gunpowder weapons. By about the mid–seventeenth century, however, European military technology was advancing so rapidly that the Islamic empires could not keep pace. None of the empires had a large armaments industry, so they had to rely on foreign suppliers. They still were able to purchase European weapons and expertise, but their arsenals became increasingly dated, since they depended on technologies that European peoples had already replaced. By the late eighteenth century, even the once-influential Ottoman navy was closing its shipbuilding operations and ordering new military vessels from foreign shipyards.

Cultural Conservatism

While experiencing economic and military decline, the Islamic empires also neglected cultural developments in the larger world. Europeans who visited the Islamic empires attempted to learn as much as possible about the language, religion, social customs, and history of the host countries.

Wahhabi (wuh-HAH-bee)
Sufis (SOO-fees)

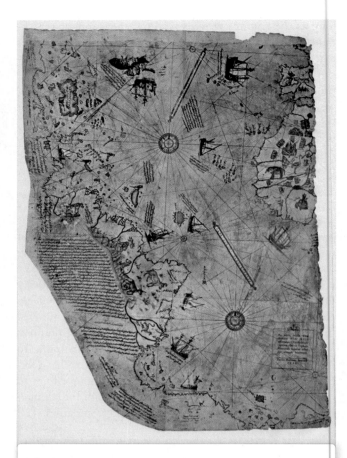

Ottoman map.
Ottoman cartographer Piri Reis drew on European charts when preparing this map of the Atlantic Ocean basin in 1513. Caribbean and South American coastlines are visible at left, and Iberian and west African coastlines appear in the upper right corner.

What function might the illustrations of ships and other figures have served on a map such as this?

They published accounts of their travels that became extremely popular in their homelands, and they advocated serious study of Islamic lands.

Piri Reis Meanwhile, the Islamic empires expressed only limited interest in world affairs. In the sixteenth century, just as European mariners were scouting Atlantic waters, Ottoman mariners did reconnoiter the Indian Ocean basin from east Africa to Indonesia. Ottoman geographers also manifested great interest in European knowledge of geography, some of which had considerable military value. The Ottoman admiral and cartographer Piri Reis produced several large-scale maps and a major navigational text, the *Book of Seafaring*, which drew on reports and maps from

Piri Reis (pir-ree reys)

European mariners and explorers. Some of Piri Reis's maps included the Atlantic coast of North America and the lands visited by Columbus, which the cartographer probably learned about from Spanish sailors captured in naval conflicts with Ottoman forces.

Cultural Conservatism On the whole, however, few Muslims traveled willingly to the infidel lands of "the Franks." Muslim rulers and their Muslim subjects were confident that they had nothing to learn from Europeans. As a result, most Muslims remained largely oblivious to European cultural and technological developments. Not until 1703 was there an attempt to introduce European scientific instruments such as the telescope into astronomical observatories. Then conservative Muslim clerics soon forced the removal of the foreign implements, which they considered impious and unnecessary.

The Printing Press The early experience of the printing press in the Islamic empires illustrates especially well the resistance of conservative religious leaders to cultural imports from western Europe. Jewish refugees from Spain introduced the first printing presses to Anatolia in the late fifteenth century. Ottoman authorities allowed them to operate presses in Istanbul and other major cities as long as they did not print books in the Turkish or Arabic language. Not until 1729 did government authorities lift the ban on the printing of such books. During the next thirteen years, a Turkish press published seventeen books dealing mostly with history, geography, and language before conservative Muslims forced its closure in 1742. Only in 1784 did a new Turkish press open.

Printing also caught on slowly in Mughal India. Jesuit missionaries in Goa published books, including translations of the Bible into Indian and Arabic languages, as early as the 1550s. Yet Mughal rulers displayed little interest in the press, and printing did not become prominent in Indian society until the establishment of British colonial rule in Bengal in the eighteenth century.

To some extent, aesthetic considerations stood in the way of the printing press: particularly in the Ottoman and Safavid empires, scholars and general readers alike preferred elegant handwritten books to cheaply produced printed works. Yet resistance to printing also reflected the concerns of conservative religious leaders that readily available printed books would introduce all manner of new and dangerous ideas to the public.

Thus, like imperial China and Tokugawa Japan, the Islamic empires resisted the introduction of cultural influences from western European societies. Rulers of the Islamic empires readily accepted gunpowder weapons as enhancements to their military and political power, but they and their subjects drew little inspiration from European religion, science, or ideas. Moreover, under the influence of conservative religious leaders, Islamic authorities actively discouraged the circulation of ideas that might pose unsettling challenges to the social and cultural order. Like the Ming, Qing, and Tokugawa rulers, the Ottoman, Safavid, and Mughal emperors preferred political and social stability to the risks that foreign cultural innovations might bring.

SUMMARY

Like China and Japan, the Islamic empires largely retained control of their own affairs throughout the early modern era. Ruling elites of the Ottoman, Safavid, and Mughal empires came from nomadic Turkish stock, and they all drew on steppe traditions in organizing their governments. But the rulers also devised institutions that maintained order over a long term. During the sixteenth and seventeenth centuries, all the Islamic empires enjoyed productive economies that enabled merchants to participate actively in the global trade networks of early modern times. By the early eighteenth century, however, these same empires were experiencing economic difficulties that led to political and military decline. Like the Ming, Qing, and Tokugawa rulers in east Asia, the Islamic emperors mostly sought to limit foreign and especially European influences in their realms. The Islamic emperors ruled lands that were religiously and ethnically diverse, and most of them worried that such influences would threaten political and social stability. They allowed their subjects to practice faiths other than Islam, and a few emperors actively worked to defuse religious tensions in their realms. For the most part, however, rulers of the Islamic empires followed the advice of conservative Muslim clerics, who promoted Islamic values and fought the introduction of foreign cultural imports that might undermine their authority. By the late eighteenth century, the Safavid empire had collapsed, and economic difficulties and cultural insularity had severely weakened the Ottoman and Mughal empires. Yet the cultural legacies of the Islamic empires continue to influence the regions where they once ruled even in the present day.

STUDY TERMS

Akbar (453, 456, 458)
Aurangzeb (453)
Babur (452)
Byzantine (448)
Chagatai (452)
Chaldiran (452)
devshirme (449)
dhimmi (456)
Fatehpur Sikri (458)
ghazi (448)
Hürrem Sultana (454)
Istanbul (449)
Jahangir (454)
Janissaries (449)
jizya (456)
Mehmed the Conqueror (449)
Mughals (452)
Mumtaz Mahal (447)
Osman Bey (448)
Ottomans (448–450)
Piri Reis (460)
qizilbash (451)
Safavids (450)
Shah Abbas the Great (452)
Shah Ismail (450)
Shah Jahan (447)
Shaykh Salim Chishthi (458)
Shiism (450)
Sikhs (456)
Sinan Pasha (457)
Sufis (459)
Süleyman the Magnificent (449)
Süleymaniye mosque (457)
Sunni (450)
Topkapi Palace (457)
Twelver Shiism (450)
Wahhabi (459)
Zahir al-Din Muhammad (452)

FOR FURTHER READING

Jonathan P. Berkey. *The Formation of Islam: Religion and Society in the Near East, 600–1800.* New York, 2002. Broad survey of the history of Islam and Islamic civilization.

Stephen Frederic Dale. *Indian Merchants and Eurasian Trade, 1600–1750.* Cambridge, 1994. Examines the workings of an Indian trading community that conducted business in Persia, central Asia, and Russia.

Carter Vaughn Findley. *The Turks in World History.* New York, 2005. A highly readable account that connects the two-thousand-year history of the Turkic peoples with larger global processes.

Halil Inalçik. *The Ottoman Empire: The Classical Age, 1300–1600.* New York, 1973. A reliable survey by the foremost historian of the early Ottoman empire.

Kemal H. Karpat. *The Politicization of Islam: Reconstructing Identity, State, Faith, and Community in the Late Ottoman State.* New York, 2001. Scholarly study of the Ottoman state's role in constructing Muslim identity.

Bernard Lewis. *The Muslim Discovery of Europe.* New York, 1982. An important study that charts Muslim interest in European affairs.

Leslie Pierce. *The Imperial Harem: Women and Sovereignty in the Ottoman Empire.* Oxford, 1993. Challenges many stereotypes about the role of women in the imperial Ottoman elite.

John F. Richards. *The Mughal Empire.* Cambridge, 1993. A concise and reliable overview of Mughal history, concentrating on political affairs.

Roger Savory. *Iran under the Safavids.* Cambridge, 1980. A rich and authoritative survey of Safavid history, especially interesting for its views on Safavid origins, culture, and commercial relations.

PART 5 THE ORIGINS OF GLOBAL INTERDEPENDENCE, 1500–1800

When European mariners made contact with the peoples of the Americas in the late fifteenth century, they initiated a process of interaction and exchange that had profound consequences for the whole world. Indeed, by 1800 few of the world's peoples remained untouched by the transformations wrought by early modern global exchanges in material items such as trade goods, plants, animals, people, and technologies as well as intangible items such as ideas and microbes.

Yet the impact of these exchanges was not uniform around the world. For the Europeans who established trade routes across the earth's oceans, who settled the Americas, and who founded trading posts in both Africa and Asia, the early modern era was one of unprecedented territorial expansion, population increase, and growing political and economic influence in the wider world.

For the peoples of the Americas, however, the establishment of global networks of exchange was nothing short of catastrophic. European diseases such as smallpox and influenza decimated indigenous communities, killing as much as 90 percent of the population. European conquerors then took advantage of weakened populations to claim, conquer, and settle huge tracts of valuable land for their own uses, relegating indigenous peoples to marginal lands or to providing labor for the conquerors. These same global networks of exchange also wreaked havoc on west African communities. Indeed, the labor shortages caused by population loss in the Americas led Europeans to force millions of Africans into crossing the Atlantic to serve as slaves on European plantations.

The new global exchanges of the early modern period also affected east, south, and southwest Asia in important but less dramatic ways. In China, American silver fueled the economy, while American food crops contributed to population growth. In the Islamic empires, European traders gained significant footholds in port cities, while American crops including tobacco became firmly enmeshed in Islamic culture. Yet—unlike the Americas, which had been overwhelmed by Europeans as a result of disease—the states of east, south, and southwest Asia remained strong and powerful in the early modern period.

Nevertheless, by 1800 the world was a different place than it had been in 1500. Contact and conquest in the Americas had created fundamentally new, hybrid societies that blended indigenous, European, and African populations. Moreover, while states in east, south, and southwest Asia remained powerful in this period, Europeans—via their role in connecting the world through trade—had become more prominent in world affairs than ever before.

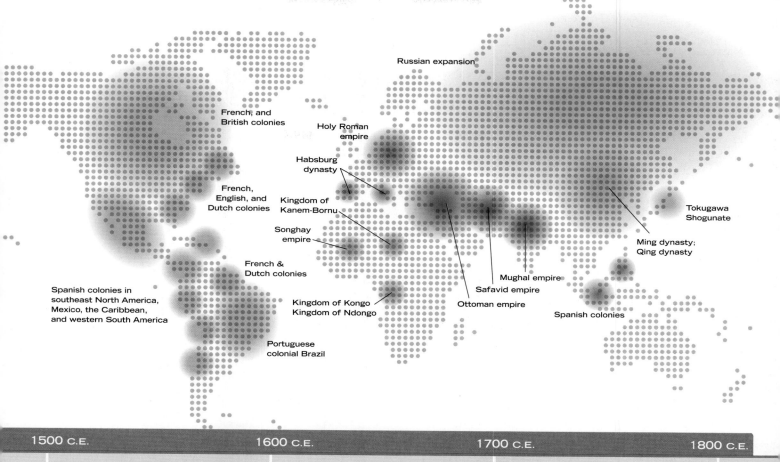

French, and British colonies

Holy Roman empire

Habsburg dynasty

Kingdom of Kanem-Bornu

French, English, and Dutch colonies

Songhay empire

French & Dutch colonies

Russian expansion

Tokugawa Shogunate

Ming dynasty; Qing dynasty

Spanish colonies in southeast North America, Mexico, the Caribbean, and western South America

Kingdom of Kongo Kingdom of Ndongo

Mughal empire

Safavid empire

Ottoman empire

Spanish colonies

Portuguese colonial Brazil

1500 C.E.	1600 C.E.	1700 C.E.	1800 C.E.	
China: Ming dynasty, 1368–1644 C.E. Russian expansion, 1462–1795 C.E.	Japan: Tokugawa Shogunate, 1600–1867 C.E. China: Qing dynasty, 1644–1911 C.E.			CENTRAL & EAST ASIA
Holy Roman Empire & Habsburg dynasty (including Spanish and Austrian territories), ca. 1519–1648 C.E.				EUROPE
Ottoman empire, 1289–1923 C.E. Safavid empire, 1501–1722 C.E. Mughal empire, 1526–1858 C.E.				SOUTH & SOUTHWEST ASIA
Songhay empire, 1464–1591 C.E. Decline of Swahili city-states after Portuguese raids, 1497–1505 C.E.	Kingdom of Ndongo, early 16th century to 1671 C.E.			AFRICA
Kingdom of Kongo, 1396–1910 C.E.				
Spanish colonies in Mexico, the Caribbean, southeast North America, and western South America, 1492–18th century Portuguese colonial Brazil, 1500–1822 C.E. French, English, and Dutch colonies in North America, ca. 1600–late 18th century				THE AMERICAS
Spanish colonies in the Pacific, 1500–1800 C.E.				OCEANIA

PART 6

AN AGE OF REVOLUTION, INDUSTRY, AND EMPIRE, 1750–1914

During the period from about 1750 to 1914, European peoples parlayed the profits they had gained from early modern trade, as well as their recent and advantageous domination of the Americas, into global hegemony. In stark contrast to the period from 1500 to 1800, by the late nineteenth century European powers controlled affairs in most of Asia and almost all of Africa, and their Euro-American cousins continued to dominate the Americas. Three historical developments—revolution,

industrialization, and imperialism—help to explain how European and Euro-American peoples came to dominate so much of the world.

Atlantic Revolutions

Revolution transformed societies in North America, France, Haiti, and South America during the late eighteenth and early nineteenth centuries. Although the results of each revolution were different, Enlightenment values of freedom, equality, and popular sovereignty played a large role in each. Revolutions also had a profound effect on the organization of societies in the Atlantic Ocean basin. First in Europe and later

Parisian women were the leaders of the crowd that marched to Versailles, protested high food prices, and forced the king and queen to return to Paris in October 1789.

in the Americas as well, revolutions and the conflicts that followed from them encouraged the formation of national identities.

Industrialization

The idea of organizing states around national communities eventually influenced political development throughout the world. While organizing themselves into national states, western European and North American peoples also embarked on processes of industrialization. Although industrialization initially caused a great deal of discomfort and dislocation for workers, over time industrial societies became economically much stronger than agricultural societies, and industrial production brought about general

Young woman at work in a mechanized mill in the 1830s.

improvement in material standards of living. After originating in Britain in the late eighteenth century, industrialization spread rapidly to western Europe and North America, and by the late nineteenth century to Russia and Japan as well.

Imperialism and Colonialism

Alongside increased material standards of living, industrialization brought political, military, and economic strength. In western Europe, the United States, and Japan, industrialization helped underwrite processes of imperialism and colonialism. Railroads, steamships, telegraphs, and lethal weapons enabled industrial powers to impose their rule in most of Asia and Africa in the nineteenth century, just as Euro-American settlers relied on industrial technologies to drive the indigenous peoples of North America and South America onto marginal lands.

Domination and Resistance

Revolution, industrialization, and imperialism had effects that were felt around the world. Western European and North American peoples vastly strengthened their position in the world by exercising political or economic influence over other societies. They also inspired sustained resistance among colonized peoples, which eventually led to the organization of anticolonial movements. Indeed, revolution, industry, and empire fueled conflict throughout the world in the nineteenth century, and in combination they forced the world's peoples to deal with one another more systematically than ever before in history.

1. *What factors allowed Europeans to assume global dominance between the late eighteenth and twentieth centuries?*

2. *What were some of the consequences of the revolutions, industrialization, and imperialism for non-Europeans?*

The battle of Omdurman on the Nile River, 2 September 1898.

465

Revolutions and National States in the Atlantic World

CHAPTER **25**

Liberty, personified as a woman, leads the French people in a famous painting by Eugène Delacroix.

EYEWITNESS:
Olympe de Gouges Declares the Rights of Women

Marie Gouze was a French butcher's daughter who educated herself by reading books, moved to Paris, and married a junior army officer. Under the name Olympe de Gouges she won some fame as a journalist, actress, and playwright. Gouges was as flamboyant as she was talented, and her well-publicized love affairs scandalized Parisian society.

Gouges was also a revolutionary and a strong advocate of women's rights. She responded enthusiastically when the French revolution broke out in July 1789, and she applauded in August when revolutionary leaders proclaimed freedom and equality for all citizens in the *Declaration of the Rights of Man and the Citizen*. It soon became clear, however, that freedom and equality pertained only to male citizens. Revolutionary leaders welcomed women's contributions to the revolution but refused to grant them political and social rights.

Gouges demanded that women share equal rights in family property and campaigned for equal education. She even appealed to Queen Marie Antoinette to use her influence to advance women's rights. In 1791 Gouges published a *Declaration of the Rights of Woman and the Female Citizen,* which claimed the same rights for women that revolutionary leaders had granted to men in August 1789. She insisted on the rights of women to vote, speak their minds freely, participate in the making of law, and hold public office.

Gouges's declaration attracted a great deal of attention but little support. Revolutionary leaders dismissed her appeal, and in 1793 they executed her because of her affection for Marie Antoinette and her persistent crusade for women's rights. Yet Gouges's campaign illustrated the power of the ideals of the eighteenth-century Enlightenment movement, which emphasized freedom and equality. Revolutionary leaders—themselves deeply influenced by Enlightenment ideals—stilled her voice, but once they had proclaimed freedom and equality as universal human rights, they were unable to suppress demands to extend them to new constituencies.

A series of violent revolutions based on Enlightenment principles brought dramatic political and social change to lands throughout much of the Atlantic Ocean basin in the late eighteenth and early nineteenth centuries. Revolution broke out first in the British colonies of North America, where colonists founded a new republic. A few years later, revolutionaries abolished the French monarchy and thoroughly reorganized French society. Revolutionary ideas soon spread, prompting Latin American peoples to seek independence from Spanish and Portuguese colonial rule. In Saint-Domingue, revolution led to the abolition of slavery as well as independence from French rule. By the 1830s, peoples had reorganized political and social structures throughout western Europe and the Americas.

The revolutions of the late eighteenth and early nineteenth centuries had two results of deep global significance. First, they helped to spread a cluster of Enlightenment ideas concerning freedom, equality, and popular sovereignty. Revolutionary leaders argued that political authority arose from the people rather than the

Olympe de Gouges (oh-LIM-peh de gouj)

CHRONOLOGY

1632–1704	Life of John Locke
1694–1778	Life of Voltaire
1712–1778	Life of Jean-Jacques Rousseau
1744–1803	Life of Toussaint Louverture
1748–1793	Life of Olympe de Gouges
1753–1811	Life of Miguel de Hidalgo
1769–1821	Life of Napoleon Bonaparte
1774–1793	Reign of King Louis XVI
1775–1781	American Revolution
1783–1830	Life of Simón Bolívar
1789–1799	French revolution
1791–1803	Haitian revolution
1799–1814	Reign of Napoleon
1810–1825	Wars of independence in Latin America
1814–1815	Congress of Vienna

justified their actions in general terms that prompted disenfranchised groups to seek freedom, equality, and a political voice as well. Indeed, such ideas spread globally in the nineteenth and twentieth centuries as social reformers and revolutionaries struggled to make freedom and equality a reality for oppressed groups throughout the world.

Second, while promoting Enlightenment values, revolutions encouraged the consolidation of national states as the principal form of political organization. As peoples defended their states from enemies and sometimes mounted attacks on foreign lands, they developed a powerful sense of identity with their compatriots. During the nineteenth century, strong national identities led to movements to build national states, which in turn profoundly influenced the political experiences of European states. During the late nineteenth and twentieth centuries, efforts to harness nationalist sentiments and form states based on national identity became one of the most powerful and dynamic movements in world history.

rulers and often sought to establish republican forms of government in which the people selected delegates to represent their interests. In fact, early revolutionaries extended political rights only to a privileged group of white men, but they

POPULAR SOVEREIGNTY AND POLITICAL UPHEAVAL

Drawing on Enlightenment ideals, revolutionaries of the eighteenth and nineteenth centuries sought to fashion equitable societies by instituting governments that were responsive to the peoples they governed. In justifying their policies, revolutionaries argued for popular sovereignty—the notion that legitimate political authority resides not in kings but, rather, in the people who make up a society. In North America, colonists declared independence from British rule and instituted a new government founded on the principle of popular sovereignty. Soon thereafter, French revolutionaries abolished the monarchy and revamped the social order. Yet revolutionaries in France were unable to devise a stable alternative to the monarchy. In the early nineteenth century, Napoleon Bonaparte imposed military rule on France and helped spread revolutionary ideas to much of western Europe.

philosophes (fil-uh-sofs)

The Enlightenment and Revolutionary Ideas

Isaac Newton's conception of the universe during the scientific revolution (discussed in chapter 20) had been so powerful and persuasive that its influence extended well beyond science and into the realm of politics and human relationships. Newton's work on the rationality of the laws of physics suggested that human behavior and institutions might also be guided by rational laws. Inspired by this idea, during the seventeenth and eighteenth centuries European and Euro-American thinkers launched an ambitious project to discover the laws that governed humanity. Some, such as John Locke (1632–1704), sought the natural laws of politics. Others, such as Adam Smith (1723–1790), sought to comprehend the laws of economics. Like the early modern scientists, however, they all abandoned Aristotelian philosophy and Christian religion as sources of authority in their quest to subject the human world to purely rational analysis. The result of their work was a movement known as the Enlightenment.

The center of Enlightenment thought was France, where prominent intellectuals known collectively as *philosophes* ("philosophers") advanced the cause of reason. The philosophes addressed their works more to the educated public than to scholars: instead of formal philosophical treatises, they mostly composed histories, novels, dramas, satires, and pamphlets on religious, moral, and political issues.

Voltaire   More than any other philosophe, François-Marie Arouet (1694–1778) epitomized the spirit of the Enlightenment. Writing under the pen name Voltaire, he championed individual freedom and attacked any institution sponsoring intolerant or oppressive policies. Targets of his often caustic wit included the French monarchy and the Roman Catholic church. When the king of France sought to save money by reducing the number of horses kept in royal stables, for example, Voltaire suggested that it would be more effective to get rid of the asses who rode the horses. Voltaire also waged a long literary campaign against the Roman Catholic church, which he held responsible for fanaticism, intolerance, and incalculable human suffering.

The Theory of Progress   Most philosophes were optimistic about the future of the world and humanity. In fact, they believed that rational understanding of human and natural affairs would bring about a new era of progress and individual freedom and would lead to the construction of a prosperous, just, and equitable society. Although those fond wishes did not come to pass, the Enlightenment did indeed help to bring about a thorough cultural transformation of European society. For one thing, it weakened the influence of organized religion by encouraging the replacement of Christian values with a new set of secular values based on reason. Furthermore, the Enlightenment encouraged political and cultural leaders to subject society to rational analysis and intervene actively in its affairs in the interests of promoting progress and prosperity. Perhaps most importantly, the Enlightenment encouraged thinkers and activists to question the social, political, and economic order around them, and offered concrete ideas about how societies could be reordered more effectively.

Popular Sovereignty   One of the notions that Enlightenment thinkers questioned most consistently was the long-held idea that European monarchs possessed a divine right to rule. Instead, philosophes and other advocates of Enlightenment ideas argued that kings should be responsible to the people they governed. The English philosopher John Locke, for example, regarded government as a contract between rulers and ruled. In his *Second Treatise of Civil Government,* published in 1690, Locke held that individuals granted political rights to their rulers but retained personal rights to life, liberty, and property. Furthermore, according to Locke, rulers derived their authority from the consent of those they governed. If rulers broke the contract,

the people had the right to replace their rulers. In effect, Locke's political thought relocated sovereignty, removing it from rulers as divine agents and vesting it in the people of a society.

Individual Freedom   Enlightenment thinkers addressed issues of freedom and equality as well as sovereignty. Philosophes resented the persecution of religious minorities as well as royal censorship. Philosophes called for religious toleration and freedom to express their views openly. Thus, when censors prohibited the publication of their writings in France, they often published their books in Switzerland or the Netherlands and smuggled them across the border into France.

Political and Legal Equality   Many Enlightenment thinkers also called for equality. They argued that privileged aristocrats made no more contribution to the larger society than peasants, artisans, or workers and recommended the creation of a society in which all individuals would be equal before the law. The most prominent advocate of political equality was the French-Swiss thinker Jean-Jacques Rousseau (1712–1778). In his influential book *The Social Contract* (1762), Rousseau argued that members of a society were collectively the sovereign. In an ideal society all individuals would participate directly in the formulation of policy and the creation of laws.

Global Influence of Enlightenment Values   Most Enlightenment thinkers were of common birth but comfortable means. Though seeking to limit the prerogatives of ruling and aristocratic classes, they did not envision a society in which they would share political rights with women, children, peasants, laborers, or slaves. Nevertheless, Enlightenment thought constituted a serious challenge to long-established notions of political and social order. Although arguments for freedom, equality, and popular sovereignty originally served the interests of relatively privileged European and Euro-American men, many other groups made effective use of them in seeking the extension of political rights. Indeed, Enlightenment ideas became the foundation and the justification for a series of revolutions that rocked the Atlantic world in the late eighteenth and early nineteenth centuries.

The American Revolution

In the mid–eighteenth century there was no sign that North America would become a center of revolution. Residents of the thirteen British colonies there regarded themselves as British subjects: they recognized British law, read

Voltaire (vohl-TAIR)

English-language books, and benefited handsomely from British rule. Trade brought prosperity to the colonies, and British military forces protected colonists' interests. From 1754 to 1763, for example, British forces waged an expensive conflict in North America known as the French and Indian War. That conflict merged with a larger contest for imperial supremacy, the Seven Years' War (1756–1763), in which British and French forces battled each other in Europe and India as well as North America. Victory in the Seven Years' War ensured that Britain would dominate global trade and that British North America would prosper.

Tightened British Control of the Colonies After the mid-1760s, however, North American colonists became increasingly disenchanted with British imperial rule.

Faced with staggering financial difficulties arising from the Seven Years' War, the British parliament expected that the North American colonies would bear a fair share of the cost through new taxes. But new taxes proved extremely unpopular in North America. Colonists especially resented the imposition of taxes on molasses by the Sugar Act (1764), on publications and legal documents by the Stamp Act (1765), on a variety of imported items by the Townshend Act (1767), and on tea by the Tea Act (1773). Colonists also took offense at the Quartering Act (1765), which required them to provide housing and accommodations for British troops.

Colonists argued that they should pay such taxes only if the North American colonies were represented in the British parliament, arguing that there should be "no taxation without representation." They boycotted British

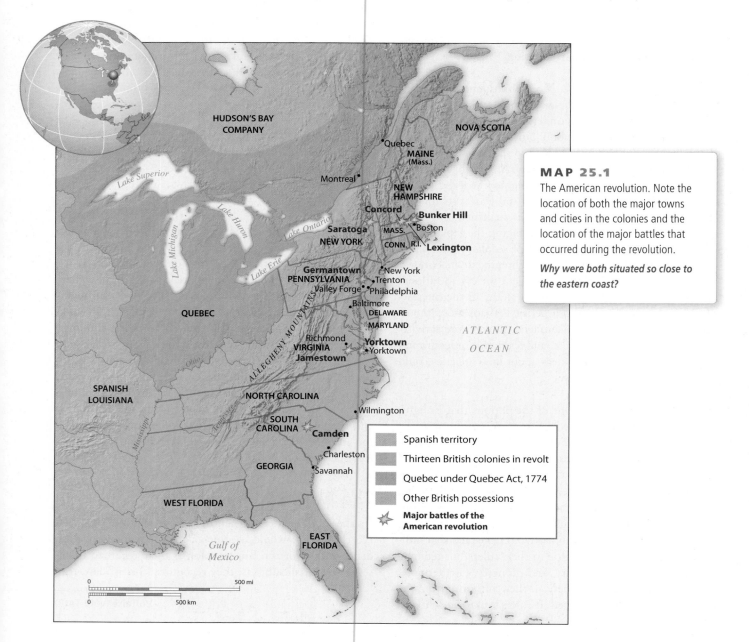

MAP 25.1

The American revolution. Note the location of both the major towns and cities in the colonies and the location of the major battles that occurred during the revolution.

Why were both situated so close to the eastern coast?

products, physically attacked British officials, and mounted protests. They also organized the Continental Congress (1774), which coordinated the colonies' resistance to British policies. By 1775 tensions were so high that British troops and a colonial militia skirmished at the village of Lexington, near Boston. The war of American independence had begun.

The Declaration of Independence On 4 July 1776 the Continental Congress adopted a document titled "The unanimous Declaration of the thirteen united States of America." This Declaration of Independence drew deep inspiration from Enlightenment political thought in its insistence "that all men are created equal, that they are endowed by their Creator with certain unalienable Rights, that among these are Life, Liberty, and the pursuit of Happiness." It echoed John Locke's contractual theory of government in arguing that governments derive their power and authority from "the consent of the governed." When any government infringes on individuals' rights, the document continued, "it is the Right of the People to alter or abolish it, and to institute new Government." The Declaration of Independence presented a long list of specific abuses charged to the British crown and concluded by proclaiming the colonies "Free and Independent States."

It was one thing to declare independence, but a different matter to make independence a reality. Britain enjoyed many advantages over the rebels: a strong government, the most powerful navy in the world, a competent army, and a sizable population of loyalists in the colonies. But the colonies were far away, and British opponents were many. In addition, many European states were eager to see Britain lose its colonies: France, Spain, the Netherlands, and several German principalities all contributed militarily and economically to the American quest for independence. Moreover, George Washington (1732–1799) provided strong and imaginative military leadership for the colonial army while local militias employed guerrilla tactics effectively against British forces.

By 1780 all combatants were weary of the conflict. In October 1781 British forces surrendered to American and French forces commanded by George Washington at Yorktown, Virginia. In September 1783 diplomats concluded the Peace of Paris, by which the British government formally recognized American independence.

Building an Independent State The leaders of the fledgling republic organized a state that reflected Enlightenment principles. In 1787 a constitutional convention drafted the Constitution of the United States, which emphasized the rights of individuals. American leaders based the federal government on popular sovereignty, and they agreed to guarantee individual liberties such as freedom of speech, of the press, and of religion. Full political and social rights, however, were accorded only to men of property: landless men, women, slaves, and indigenous peoples were not included. Over the long term, however, disenfranchised groups claimed and struggled for political and legal rights and helped broaden the implications of the Enlightenment values of freedom and equality as well as popular sovereignty.

The French Revolution

French revolutionaries also drew inspiration from Enlightenment political thought, but the French revolution was a more radical affair than its American counterpart. American revolutionary leaders sought independence from British imperial rule, but they were content to retain British law and much of their British social and cultural heritage. In contrast, French revolutionary leaders repudiated existing society, often referred to as the *ancien régime* ("the old order"), and sought to replace it with new political, social, and cultural structures. But, unlike their American counterparts, French revolutionaries lacked experience with self-government.

The Continental Congress.
In this painting by American artist John Trumbull, authors of the Declaration of Independence, including John Adams, Thomas Jefferson, and Benjamin Franklin, stand before a desk at the Continental Congress in Philadelphia.

The Estates General Serious financial, political, and social problems put France on the road to revolution. In the 1780s approximately half of the French royal government's revenue went to pay off war debts—some of them arising from French support for colonists in the war of American independence—and an additional quarter went to French armed forces. King Louis XVI (reigned 1774–1793) was unable to raise more revenue from the overburdened peasantry, so he sought to increase taxes on the French nobility, which had long been exempt from many levies. Aristocrats protested that effort and forced Louis to summon the Estates General, an assembly that represented the entire French population through groups known as estates. In the ancien régime there were three estates, or political classes. The first estate consisted of about one hundred thousand Roman Catholic clergy, and the second included some four hundred thousand nobles. The third estate embraced the rest of the population—about twenty-four million serfs, free peasants, and urban residents ranging from laborers, artisans, and shopkeepers to physicians, bankers, and attorneys. Though founded in 1303, the Estates General had not met since 1614. The third estate had as many delegates as the other two estates combined, but that numerical superiority offered no advantage when the assembly voted on issues, because voting took place by estate—one vote for each—not by individuals.

In May 1789 King Louis called the Estates General into session at the royal palace of Versailles in hopes that it would authorize new taxes. Louis never controlled the assembly. Representatives of the third estate arrived at Versailles demanding political and social reform. Although some members of the lower clergy and a few prominent nobles supported reform, the first and second estates stymied efforts to push measures through the Estates General.

The National Assembly On 17 June 1789, after several weeks of fruitless debate, representatives of the third estate took the dramatic step of seceding from the Estates General and proclaiming themselves to be the National Assembly. Three days later, meeting in an indoor tennis court, members of the new Assembly swore not to disband until they had provided France with a new constitution. On 14 July 1789 a Parisian crowd, fearing that the king sought to undo events of the previous weeks, stormed the Bastille, a royal jail and arsenal, in search of weapons. The military garrison protecting the Bastille surrendered to the crowd but only after killing many of the attackers. To vent their rage, members of the crowd hacked the defenders to death. One assailant used his pocketknife to sever the garrison commander's head, which the victorious crowd mounted

ancien régime (ahn-syan rey-ZHEEM)
Louis (LOO-ee)

on a pike and paraded around the streets of Paris. News of the event soon spread, sparking insurrections in cities throughout France.

Emboldened by popular support, the National Assembly undertook a broad program of political and social reform. The *Declaration of the Rights of Man and the Citizen,* which the National Assembly promulgated in August 1789, articulated the guiding principles of the program. Reflecting the influence of American revolutionary ideas, the *Declaration of the Rights of Man and the Citizen* proclaimed the equality of all men, declared that sovereignty resided in the people, and asserted individual rights to liberty, property, and security.

Liberty, Equality, and Fraternity Between 1789 and 1791 the National Assembly reconfigured French society. Taking the Enlightenment ideals of "liberty, equality, and fraternity" as its goals, the Assembly abolished the old social order. It seized church lands, abolished the first estate, defined clergy as civilians, and required clergy to take an oath of loyalty to the state. It also produced a constitution that left the king in place but deprived him of legislative authority. France became a constitutional monarchy in which men of property—about half the adult male population—had the right to vote in elections to choose legislators. Thus far, the French revolution represented an effort to put Enlightenment political thought into practice.

The Convention The revolution soon took a radical turn. Efforts by the French nobility to mobilize foreign powers in support of the king and the restoration of the ancien régime gave the Assembly the pretext to declare war against Austria and Prussia in April 1792. Adding to the military burden of France, revolutionary leaders declared war on Spain, Britain, and the Netherlands. Fearing military defeat and counterrevolution, revolutionary leaders created the Convention, a new legislative body elected by universal manhood suffrage, which abolished the monarchy and proclaimed France a republic. The Convention rallied the French population by instituting the *levée en masse,* a "mass levy" that drafted people and resources for use in the war against invading forces. The Convention also rooted out enemies at home by making frequent use of the guillotine. In 1793 King Louis XVI and his wife, Queen Marie Antoinette, themselves went to the guillotine when the Convention found them guilty of treason.

Revolutionary chaos reached its peak in 1793 and 1794 when Maximilien Robespierre (1758–1794) and the radical Jacobin party dominated the Convention. A lawyer by training, Robespierre had emerged during the revolution as a ruthless but popular radical known as "the Incorruptible," and he dominated the Committee of Public Safety, the executive authority of the Republic. The Jacobins believed

SourcesfromthePast

Declaration of the Rights of Man and the Citizen

While developing their program of reform, members of the National Assembly consulted closely with Thomas Jefferson, the principal author of the American Declaration of Independence, who was the U.S. ambassador to France in 1789. Thus it is not surprising that the Declaration of the Rights of Man and the Citizen reflects the influence of American revolutionary ideas.

First Article. Men are born and remain free and equal in rights. Social distinctions may be based only on common utility.

Article 2. The goal of every political association is the preservation of the natural and inalienable rights of man. These rights are liberty, property, security, and resistance to oppression.

Article 3. The principle of all sovereignty resides essentially in the nation. No body and no individual can exercise authority that does not flow directly from the nation.

Article 4. Liberty consists in the freedom to do anything that does not harm another. The exercise of natural rights of each man thus has no limits except those that assure other members of society their enjoyment of the same rights. These limits may be determined only by law.

Article 6. Law is the expression of the general will. All citizens have the right to participate either personally or through their representatives in the making of law. The law must be the same for all, whether it protects or punishes. Being equal in the eyes of the law, all citizens are equally eligible for all public honors, offices, and occupations, according to their abilities, without any distinction other than that of their virtues and talents.

Article 7. No person shall be accused, arrested, or imprisoned except in the cases and according to the forms prescribed by law. Any one soliciting, transmitting, executing, or causing to be executed, any arbitrary order, shall be punished. But any citizen summoned or arrested in virtue of the law shall submit without delay, as resistance constitutes an offense.

Article 9. As all persons are held innocent until they shall have been declared guilty, if arrest shall be deemed indispensable, all harshness not essential to the securing of the prisoner's person shall be severely repressed by law.

Article 11. The free communication of thoughts and opinions is one of the most precious rights of man: every citizen may thus speak, write, and publish freely, but will be responsible for abuse of this freedom in cases decided by the law.

Article 13. For the maintenance of public military force and for the expenses of administration, common taxation is necessary: it must be equally divided among all citizens according to their means.

Article 15. Society has the right to require from every public official an accounting of his administration.

Article 16. Any society in which guarantees of rights are not assured and separation of powers is not defined has no constitution at all.

Article 17. Property is an inviolable and sacred right. No one may be deprived of property except when public necessity, legally determined, clearly requires it, and on condition of just and prearranged compensation.

For Further Reflection

■ In what ways do the principles established in the Declaration reflect the political transformations taking place throughout the age of Atlantic revolutions?

Source: Déclaration des droits de l'homme et du citoyen. Translated by Jerry H. Bentley.

---

passionately that France needed complete restructuring, and they unleashed a campaign of terror to promote their revolutionary agenda. They sought to eliminate the influence of Christianity in French society by closing churches, forcing priests to take wives, and promoting a new, secular "cult of reason." They reorganized the calendar, replacing seven-day weeks with ten-day units that recognized no day of religious observance. The Jacobins also encouraged citizens to display their revolutionary zeal by wearing working-class clothes and granted increased rights to women by permitting them to inherit property and divorce their husbands. The Jacobins made especially frequent use of the guillotine: in a yearlong "reign of terror" between the summer of 1793 and the summer of 1794, they executed about forty thousand people and imprisoned three hundred thousand others as suspected enemies of the revolution.

The Directory Eventually, such political purges undermined confidence in the regime itself. In July 1794 the Convention arrested Robespierre and his allies, convicted them of tyranny, and sent them to the guillotine. A group of conservative men of property then seized power and ruled France under a new institution known as the Directory (1795–1799). However, the Directory was unable to resolve the economic and military problems that plagued revolutionary France. In seeking a middle way between the

The execution of King Louis XVI.
The guillotine was an efficient killing machine. In this contemporary print the executioner displays the just-severed head of King Louis XVI to the crowd assembled to witness his execution.

ancien régime and radical revolution, they lurched from one policy to another, and the Directory faced constant challenges to its authority. It came to an end in November 1799 when a young general named Napoleon Bonaparte staged a coup d'état and seized power.

The Reign of Napoleon

Born to a minor noble family on the Mediterranean island of Corsica, Napoleon Bonaparte (1769–1821) studied at French military schools and became an officer in the army of King Louis XVI. A brilliant military leader, he became a general at age twenty-four. He was a fervent supporter of the revolution and defended the Directory against a popular uprising in 1795. In a campaign of 1796–1797, he drove the Austrian

Napoleon Bonaparte (nuh-POH-lee-uhn BOH-nuh-pahrt)

army from northern Italy and established French rule there. In 1798 he mounted an invasion of Egypt, but the campaign ended in a French defeat. Politically ambitious, Napoleon returned to France in 1799 and joined the Directory. When Austria, Russia, and Britain formed a coalition to attack France and end the revolution, he overthrew the Directory, imposed a new constitution, and named himself first consul. In 1802 he became consul for life, and two years later he crowned himself emperor.

Napoleonic France Napoleon brought political stability to a land torn by revolution and war. He made peace with the Roman Catholic church and reversed the most radical religious policies of the Convention. In 1804 Napoleon promulgated the Civil Code, a revised body of civil law, which also helped stabilize French society. The Civil Code affirmed the political and legal equality of all adult men and established a merit-based society in which individuals advanced in education and employment because of talent rather than birth or social standing. The Civil Code confirmed many of the moderate revolutionary policies of the National Assembly but retracted measures passed by the more radical Convention. The code restored patriarchal authority in the family, for example, by making women and children subservient to male heads of households.

Although he approved of the Enlightenment ideal of equality, Napoleon was no champion of intellectual freedom or representative government. He limited free speech and routinely censored newspapers and other publications. He established a secret police force that relied heavily on spies and detained suspected political opponents by the thousands. He made systematic use of propaganda to manipulate public opinion. He ignored elective bodies and founded a dynasty that set his family above the people in whose name they ruled.

Napoleon's Empire While working to stabilize France, Napoleon also sought to extend his authority throughout Europe. Napoleon's armies conquered the Iberian and Italian peninsulas, occupied the Netherlands, and inflicted humiliating defeats on Austrian and Prussian forces. Napoleon sent his brothers and other relatives to rule the conquered and occupied lands, and he forced Austria, Prussia, and Russia to ally with him and respect French hegemony in Europe.

Napoleon's empire began to unravel in 1812, when he decided to invade Russia. Convinced that the tsar was conspiring with his British enemies, Napoleon led an army of six hundred thousand soldiers to Moscow. He captured the city, but the tsar withdrew and set Moscow ablaze, leaving Napoleon's vast army without adequate shelter or supplies. Napoleon ordered a retreat, but the bitter Russian winter destroyed his army, and only a battered remnant of thirty thousand soldiers managed to limp back to France.

The Fall of Napoleon Napoleon's disastrous Russian campaign emboldened his enemies. A coalition of British, Austrian, Prussian, and Russian armies converged on France

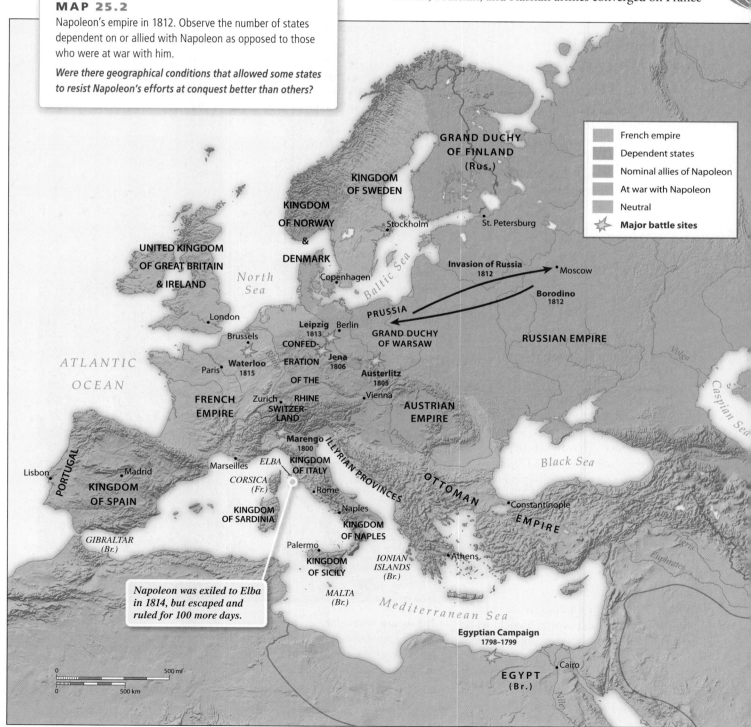

MAP 25.2

Napoleon's empire in 1812. Observe the number of states dependent on or allied with Napoleon as opposed to those who were at war with him.

Were there geographical conditions that allowed some states to resist Napoleon's efforts at conquest better than others?

French empire

Dependent states

Nominal allies of Napoleon

At war with Napoleon

Neutral

⭐ **Major battle sites**

GRAND DUCHY OF FINLAND (Rus.)

KINGDOM OF SWEDEN

KINGDOM OF NORWAY & DENMARK

Stockholm

St. Petersburg

UNITED KINGDOM OF GREAT BRITAIN & IRELAND

North Sea

Copenhagen

Baltic Sea

Invasion of Russia 1812

Moscow

Borodino 1812

PRUSSIA

GRAND DUCHY OF WARSAW

RUSSIAN EMPIRE

London

Brussels

Leipzig 1813

Berlin

ATLANTIC OCEAN

Waterloo 1815

Paris

CONFED-ERATION OF THE RHINE

Jena 1806

Austerlitz 1805

Vienna

Volga

Caspian Sea

FRENCH EMPIRE

Zurich

SWITZER-LAND

AUSTRIAN EMPIRE

Marengo 1800

ILLYRIAN PROVINCES

Danube

Black Sea

Lisbon

Madrid

Marseilles

ELBA

CORSICA (Fr.)

KINGDOM OF ITALY

Rome

OTTOMAN EMPIRE

Constantinople

PORTUGAL

KINGDOM OF SPAIN

KINGDOM OF SARDINIA

Naples

KINGDOM OF NAPLES

Athens

Tigris

Euphrates

GIBRALTAR (Br.)

Palermo

IONIAN ISLANDS (Br.)

KINGDOM OF SICILY

MALTA (Br.)

Mediterranean Sea

Napoleon was exiled to Elba in 1814, but escaped and ruled for 100 more days.

Egyptian Campaign 1798–1799

EGYPT (Br.)

Cairo

Nile

0   500 mi

0   500 km

and forced Napoleon to abdicate his throne in April 1814. The victors restored the French monarchy and exiled Napoleon to the tiny Mediterranean island of Elba. But in March 1815 Napoleon escaped from Elba, returned to France, and ruled France for a hundred days before a British army defeated him at Waterloo in Belgium. This time, European powers banished Napoleon to the remote and isolated island of St. Helena in the South Atlantic Ocean, where he died of natural causes in 1821.

THE INFLUENCE OF REVOLUTION

The Enlightenment ideals promoted by the American and French revolutions appealed to peoples throughout Europe and the Americas. In the Caribbean and Latin America, they inspired revolutionary movements: slaves in the French colony of Saint-Domingue rose against their overlords and established the independent republic of Haiti, and Euro-American leaders mounted independence movements in Mexico, Central America, and South America. The ideals of the American and French revolutions also encouraged social reformers to organize broader programs of liberation for women and slaves of African ancestry.

The Haitian Revolution

The only successful slave revolt in history took place on the Caribbean island of Hispaniola. The Spanish colony of Santo Domingo occupied the eastern part of the island (modern Dominican Republic), and the French colony of Saint-Domingue occupied the western part (modern Haiti). Saint-Domingue was one of the richest of all European colonies in the Caribbean: sugar, coffee, and cotton produced there accounted for almost one-third of France's foreign trade.

Saint-Domingue Society In 1790 the population of Saint-Domingue included about forty thousand white French settlers, thirty thousand *gens de couleur* (free people of color), and some five hundred thousand black slaves, most of whom were born in Africa. Led by wealthy planters, white residents stood at the top of society.

Gens de couleur farmed small plots of land, sometimes with the aid of a few slaves, or worked as artisans in the island's towns. Most of the colony's slaves toiled in the fields under brutal conditions. Many slaves ran away into the mountains to escape such treatment. By the late eighteenth century, Saint-Domingue had many large communities of maroons (escaped slaves).

The American and French revolutions prepared the way for a violent political and social revolution in Saint-Domingue. Because French policy supported North American colonists against British rule, colonial governors in Saint-Domingue sent about five hundred *gens de couleur* to fight in the American war of independence. They returned to Saint-Domingue with the intention of reforming society. When the French revolution broke out in 1789, white settlers in Saint-Domingue sought the right to govern themselves,

The Haitian Revolution.
The slave rebellion in Saint-Domingue struck fear in the hearts of European and Euro-American peoples. This French print depicts outnumbered white settlers under attack on a plantation. © The Granger Collection, New York

Does the artist of this sketch seem to favor the rebels or the Europeans?

Thinking about TRADITIONS

Nationalism and the Cultivation of Traditions
During the nineteenth century, nationalists sought to create distinctive identities for members of their political communities. *In what ways did nationalists utilize ideas about common cultural and historical traditions to bolster support for their causes?*

but they opposed proposals to grant political and legal equality to the *gens de couleur.* By May 1791 civil war had broken out between white settlers and *gens de couleur.*

Slave Revolt The conflict expanded dramatically when a charismatic Voudou priest named Boukman organized a slave revolt. In August 1791 some twelve thousand slaves began killing white settlers, burning their homes, and destroying their plantations. Within a few weeks the numbers of slaves in revolt grew to almost one hundred thousand. Saint-Domingue quickly descended into chaos as white, *gens de couleur,* and slave factions battled one another. Foreign armies soon complicated the situation: French troops arrived in 1792 to restore order, and British and Spanish forces intervened in 1793 in hopes of benefiting from France's difficulties.

Toussaint L'Ouverture Eventually, slave forces overcame white settlers, *gens de couleur,* and foreign armies. Their successes were due largely to the leadership of François-Dominique Toussaint (1744–1803), who after 1791 called himself Louverture—from the French *l'ouverture,* meaning "the opening." The son of slaves, he himself had been a free man since 1776. Toussaint was a skilled organizer, and by 1793 he had built a strong, disciplined army. He shrewdly played French, British, and Spanish forces against one another while also jockeying for power with other black and mulatto generals. By 1797 he led an army of twenty thousand that controlled most of Saint-Domingue. In 1801 he issued a constitution that granted equality and citizenship to all residents of Saint-Domingue. He stopped short of declaring independence from France, however, because he did not want to provoke Napoleon into attacking the island.

The Republic of Haiti Nevertheless, in 1802 Napoleon dispatched forty thousand troops to restore French authority in Saint-Domingue. Toussaint attempted to negotiate a peaceful settlement, but the French commander arrested him and sent him to France, where he died in jail of maltreatment in 1803. By the time he died, however, the black generals who succeeded Toussaint had defeated the remaining French troops and driven them out of the colony.

Late in 1803 they declared independence, and on 1 January 1804 they proclaimed the establishment of Haiti, meaning "land of mountains," which became the second independent republic in the western hemisphere.

Wars of Independence in Latin America

Latin American Society Revolutionary ideals traveled beyond Saint-Domingue to the Spanish and Portuguese colonies in the Americas. Though governed by *peninsulares* (colonial officials from Spain or Portugal), the Iberian colonies all had a large, wealthy, and powerful class of Euro-American *criollos,* or creoles, individuals born in the Americas of Spanish or Portuguese ancestry. In 1800 the *peninsulares* numbered about 30,000, and the creole population was 3.5 million. The Iberian colonies also had a large population—about 10 million in all—of less privileged classes such as black slaves, indigenous peoples, mestizos, and mulattoes.

Creoles prospered during the eighteenth century as they established plantations in the colonies and participated in trade with Spain and Portugal. Yet the creoles also had grievances. Like British colonists in North America, the creoles resented administrative control and economic regulations imposed by the Iberian powers. Although they drew inspiration from Enlightenment political thought, the creoles desired neither radical social reform nor the establishment of an egalitarian society. Instead, they sought to displace the *peninsulares* but retain their privileged position in society. Between 1810 and 1825, creoles led movements that brought independence to all Spanish colonies in the Americas—except Cuba and Puerto Rico—and established creole-dominated republics.

Mexican Independence The struggle for independence began in the wake of Napoleon's invasion of Spain and Portugal (1807), which weakened royal authority in the Iberian colonies. By 1810 revolts against Spanish rule had broken out in Argentina, Venezuela, and Mexico. The most serious was a peasant rebellion in Mexico led by a parish priest, Miguel de Hidalgo (1753–1811), who rallied indigenous peoples and mestizos against colonial rule. Conservative creoles who feared revolution by the masses soon captured Hidalgo and executed him, but his rebellion continued to flare for three years after his death. Hidalgo became the symbol of Mexican independence, and the day

---

peninsulares (peh-neen-soo-LAH-rehs)
criollos (kree-OH-lohs)
Miguel de Hidalgo (mee-GEL de hee-DHAHL-goh)

Miguel de Hidalgo.
Hidalgo was a priest and a leader of the Mexican War of Independence in 1810. This painting shows him celebrating after a victory at the Battle of Monte de las Cruces in 1810. Although he was executed by royalist forces in 1811, in Mexico he is seen as the father of the nation.

a fervent republican steeped in Enlightenment ideas about popular sovereignty. Inspired by the example of George Washington, he took up arms against Spanish rule in 1811. In 1819, after many reversals, he assembled an army that surprised and crushed the Spanish army in Colombia. Later he campaigned in Venezuela, Ecuador, and Peru, coordinating his efforts with other creole leaders such as José de San Martín (1778–1850) in Argentina and Bernardo O'Higgins (1778–1842) in Chile. By 1825 creole forces had overcome Spanish armies and deposed Spanish rulers throughout South America.

Bolívar's goal was to weld the former Spanish colonies of South America into a confederation like the United States. During the 1820s independent Venezuela, Colombia, and Ecuador formed a republic called Gran Colombia, and Bolívar attempted to bring Peru and Bolivia into the confederation. By 1830, however, strong political and regional differences led to the breakup of Gran Colombia. As the confederation disintegrated, a bitterly disappointed Bolívar—who died shortly afterward—pronounced South America "ungovernable."

Brazilian Independence Independence came to Portuguese Brazil at the same time as to Spanish colonies, but by a different process. When Napoleon invaded Portugal in 1807, the royal court fled Lisbon and established a government-in-exile in Rio de Janeiro. In 1821 the king returned to Portugal, leaving his son Pedro in Brazil as regent. The next year Brazilian creoles called for independence from Portugal, and Pedro agreed to their demands. In 1822 Pedro declared Brazil's independence and accepted appointment as Emperor Pedro I (reigned 1822–1834).

Creole Dominance In Brazil as in the former Spanish colonies, creole elites dominated both politics and society. Indeed, independence brought little social change in Latin America: although the *peninsulares* returned to Europe, Latin American society remained stratified and unequal. The newly independent states granted military authority to local strongmen, known as caudillos, allied with creole elites. The new states also allowed the continuation of slavery, confirmed the wealth and authority of the Roman Catholic church, and repressed the lower orders. The principal beneficiaries of independence in Latin America were the creole elites.

The Emergence of Ideologies: Conservatism and Liberalism

While inspiring revolutions and independence movements in other lands, the American and French revolutions also prompted political and social theorists to crystallize the modern ideologies of conservatism and liberalism. An *ideology* is a coherent vision of human nature, human society,

on which he proclaimed his revolt—16 September 1810—is Mexico's principal national holiday.

Colonial rule came to an end in 1821, when the creole general Augustín de Iturbide (1783–1824) declared independence from Spain. In the following year, he declared himself emperor of Mexico. Iturbide was an incompetent administrator, however, and in 1823 creole elites deposed him and established a republic. Two years later the southern regions of the Mexican empire declared their own independence. They formed a Central American Federation until 1838, then split into the independent states of Guatemala, El Salvador, Honduras, Nicaragua, and Costa Rica.

Simón Bolívar In South America, creole elites such as Simón Bolívar (1783–1830) led the movement for independence. Born in Caracas (in modern Venezuela), Bolívar was

caudillos (KAHW-dee-yohs)

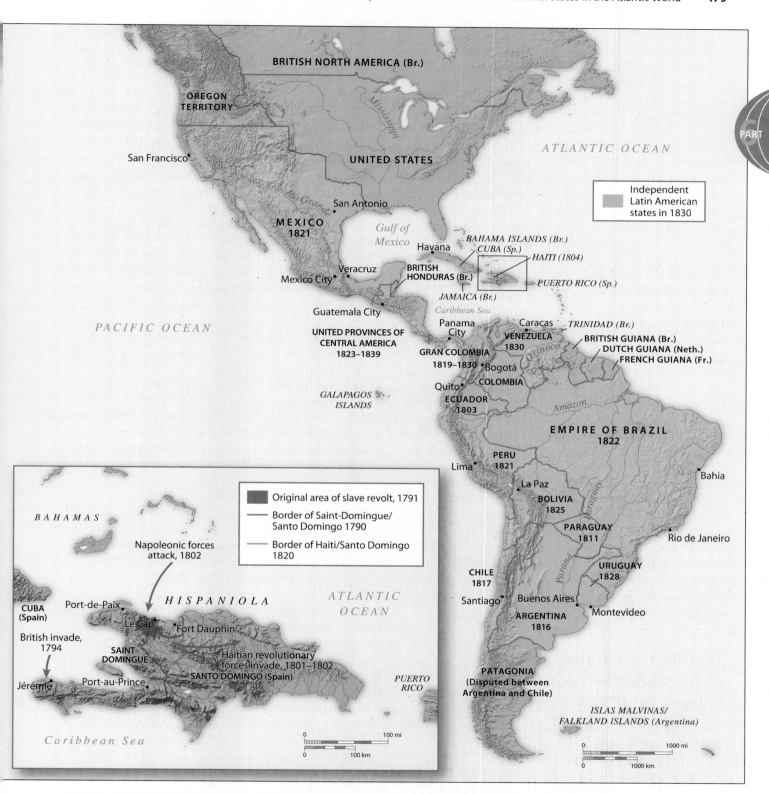

MAP 25.3

Latin America in 1830. Note the dates each state won its independence.

Since most states became independent in very close succession, what conditions prevented Latin American states from joining together in a federation like that in the United States?

and the larger world that proposes some particular form of political and social organization as ideal. People who promote a given ideology seek to design a political and social order for their communities.

Conservatism   The modern ideology of conservatism arose as political and social theorists responded to the challenges of the American and especially the French revolutions. Conservatives believed that social change, if necessary at all, must be undertaken gradually and with respect for tradition. The English political philosopher Edmund Burke (1729–1797), for example, condemned radical or revolutionary change, which in his view could only lead to anarchy. Thus Burke approved of the American revolution, which he viewed as a natural and logical change, but he denounced the French revolution as a chaotic and irresponsible assault on society.

Liberalism   In contrast to conservatives, liberals viewed change as the agent of progress. Conservatism, they argued, was just a means to justify the status quo and maintain the privileges enjoyed by favored classes. For liberals the trick was not to stifle change but, rather, to manage it in the best interests of society. Liberals such as the English political philosopher John Stuart Mill (1806–1873) championed the Enlightenment values of freedom and equality, which they believed would lead to higher standards of morality and increased prosperity for the whole society. They usually favored republican forms of government in which citizens elected representatives to legislative bodies, and they called for written constitutions that guaranteed freedom and equality for all citizens. Although some liberals, such as Mill, advocated universal suffrage (and in Mill's case even women's suffrage), many liberals during the nineteenth century did not go so far: for most, universal suffrage still seemed dangerous because it allowed the uneducated masses to participate in politics.

Testing the Limits of Revolutionary Ideals: Slavery and Women's Rights

The Enlightenment ideals of freedom and equality were watchwords of revolution in the Atlantic Ocean basin. Yet different revolutionaries understood the implications of freedom and equality in very different ways, and the Atlantic revolutions had produced widely varying results. Nevertheless, in the wake of the revolutions, social activists in Europe and the Americas considered the possibility that the ideals of freedom and equality would have further implications as yet unexplored. They turned their attention especially to the issues of slavery and women's rights.

Movements to End the Slave Trade   The campaign to end the slave trade and abolish slavery began in the eighteenth century. Only after the American, French, and Haitian revolutions, however, did the antislavery movement gain momentum. The leading spokesman of the movement was William Wilberforce (1759–1833), a prominent English philanthropist elected in 1780 to a seat in Parliament. There he tirelessly attacked slavery on moral and religious grounds. After the Haitian revolution he attracted supporters who feared that continued reliance on slave labor would result in more and larger slave revolts, and in 1807 Parliament passed Wilberforce's bill to end the slave trade. Under British pressure, other states also banned international commerce in slaves: the United States in 1808, France in 1814, the Netherlands in 1817, and Spain in 1845. The slave trade died slowly, but the British navy, which dominated the North Atlantic Ocean, patrolled the west coast of Africa to ensure compliance with the law.

Movements to Abolish Slavery   The abolition of slavery itself was a much bigger challenge than ending the slave trade because owners had property rights in their slaves and strongly resisted efforts to alter the system. In some places, revolution hastened slavery's end: Haiti abolished the institution in 1801 and Mexico in 1829, and in South America Simón Bolívar freed slaves who joined his forces and provided constitutional guarantees of free status for all residents of Gran Colombia. In other areas slavery was abolished as a result of extensive campaigns by antislavery activists such as Wilberforce. In 1833, one month after Wilberforce's death, Parliament provided twenty million pounds sterling as compensation to slave owners and abolished slavery throughout the British empire. Other states followed the British example: France abolished slavery in 1848, the United States in 1865, Cuba in 1886, and Brazil in 1888.

Freedom without Equality   Abolition brought legal freedom for African and African-American slaves, but it did not bring political equality. In most places, African-American peoples were prevented from voting through property requirements, literacy tests, and campaigns of intimidation. Nor did emancipation bring social and economic improvements for former slaves and their descendants. White creole elites owned most of the property in the Americas, and they kept blacks in subordination by forcing them to accept low-paying work.

Enlightenment Ideals and Women   Meanwhile, women who participated alongside men in the movement to abolish slavery came to believe that women suffered many of the same legal disabilities as slaves: they had little access to education, they could not enter professional occupations that required advanced education, and they were legally deprived of the right to vote. In making the case for their own rights, women drew on Enlightenment ideas about liberty and equality. For example, the English writer Mary Astell (1666–1731) used the political thought of John Locke to suggest that absolute sovereignty was no more appropriate in a family than in a state. Astell also reflected Enlightenment influence in asking why, if all men were born free, all women were born slaves? Mary Wollstonecraft (1759–1797), another British writer, similarly drew on Locke's ideas, especially in her 1792 essay titled *A Vindication of the Rights of Woman*. Like Astell, Wollstonecraft argued that women possessed all the rights that Locke had granted to men. She especially insisted on the right of women to education: it would make them better mothers and wives, she said, and would enable them to contribute to society by preparing them for professional occupations and participation in political life.

Women and Revolution Women played crucial roles in the revolutions of the late eighteenth and early nineteenth centuries, from making bandages to managing farms to actively taking up arms. Yet even so, they did not win political or social rights. In France, where women did gain rights to property, education, and divorce in the early years of the revolution, they were consistently denied the right to vote or to hold public office. In the later years of the revolution, under the Directory and Napoleon's rule, women lost even the limited rights they had won earlier. In other lands, women never gained as much as they did in revolutionary France. In the United States and the independent states of Latin America, revolution brought legal equality and political rights only for adult white men, who retained patriarchal authority over their wives and families.

Women's Rights Movements Nevertheless, throughout the nineteenth century social reformers pressed for women's rights as well as the abolition of slavery. The American feminist Elizabeth Cady Stanton (1815–1902) was an especially prominent figure in this movement. In 1840 Stanton went to London to attend an antislavery conference but found that the organizers barred women from participation. Infuriated, Stanton returned to the United States and organized a conference of feminists who met at Seneca Falls, New York, in 1848. The conference passed twelve resolutions demanding that lawmakers grant women the right to vote, to attend public schools, to enter professional occupations, and to participate in public affairs. The women's rights movement experienced only limited success in the nineteenth century: some women gained access to education, but nowhere did they win the right to vote. Yet, by seeking to extend the promises of Enlightenment political thought to blacks and women as well as white men,

social reformers of the nineteenth century laid a foundation that would lead to large-scale social change in the twentieth century.

THE CONSOLIDATION OF NATIONAL STATES IN EUROPE

The Enlightenment ideals of freedom, equality, and popular sovereignty inspired political revolutions in much of the Atlantic Ocean basin, and the revolutions in turn helped spread Enlightenment values. The wars of the French revolution and the Napoleonic era also inspired the development of a particular type of community identity that had little to do with Enlightenment values—nationalism. Revolutionary wars involved millions of French citizens in the defense of their country against foreign armies and the extension of French influence to neighboring states. Wartime experiences encouraged peoples throughout Europe to think of themselves as members of distinctive national communities. Throughout the nineteenth century, European nationalist leaders worked to fashion states based on national identities and mobilized citizens to work in the interests of their own national communities, sometimes by fostering jealousy and suspicion of other national groups. By the late nineteenth century, national identities were so strong that peoples throughout Europe responded enthusiastically to ideologies of nationalism, which promised glory and prosperity to those who worked in the interests of their national communities.

Nations and Nationalism

One of the most influential concepts of modern political thought is the idea of the nation. At various times and places in history, individuals have associated themselves primarily with families, clans, cities, regions, and religious faiths. Yet, during the nineteenth century, European peoples came to identify strongly with communities they called nations. Members of a nation considered themselves a distinctive people that spoke a common language, observed common customs, inherited common cultural traditions, held common values, and shared common historical experiences.

Intense feelings of national identity fueled ideologies of nationalism. Advocates of nationalism insisted that the nation must be the focus of political loyalty. Zealous nationalist leaders maintained that members of their national communities had a common destiny that they could best advance by organizing independent national states. Ideally, in their view, the boundaries of the national state embraced the territory occupied by the national community, and its government promoted the interests of the national group, sometimes through conflict with other peoples.

Cultural Nationalism Early nationalist thought often sought to deepen appreciation for the historical experiences of the national community and foster pride in its cultural accomplishments. During the late eighteenth century, for example, Johann Gottfried von Herder (1744–1803) sang the praises of the German *Volk* ("people") and their powerful and expressive language. In reaction to Enlightenment thinkers and their quest for a scientific, universally valid understanding of the world, early cultural nationalists such as Herder emphasized the uniqueness of their societies through the study of history, literature, and song.

Political Nationalism During the nineteenth century, nationalist thought became much more strident. In lands where they were minorities or where they lived under foreign rule, nationalists demanded loyalty and solidarity from the national group and sought to establish independent states. In Italy, for example, the nationalist activist Giuseppe Mazzini (1805–1872) formed a group called Young Italy that promoted independence from Austrian and Spanish rule and the establishment of an Italian national state. Austrian and Spanish authorities forced Mazzini to lead much of his life in exile, but he used the opportunity to encourage the organization of nationalist movements in new lands. By the mid–nineteenth century, Young Italy had inspired the development of nationalist movements in Ireland, Switzerland, and Hungary.

Nationalism and Anti-Semitism While it encouraged political leaders to work toward the establishment of national states for their communities, nationalism also had strong potential to stir up conflict between different groups of people. The more nationalists identified with their own national communities, the more they distinguished themselves both from peoples in other lands and from minority groups within their own societies. This divisive potential of nationalism helps to explain the emergence of Zionism, a political movement that holds that the Jewish people constitute a nation and have the right to their own national homeland. Unlike Mazzini's Italian compatriots, Jews did not inhabit a well-defined territory but, rather, lived in states throughout Europe. As national communities tightened their bonds, nationalist leaders often became distrustful of minority populations. Suspicion of Jews fueled

violent anti-Semitism in many parts of Europe. In Russia and in the Russian-controlled areas of Poland, the persecution of Jews climaxed in a series of anti-Jewish riots called pogroms, which claimed the lives and property of thousands of Jews.

During the late nineteenth and twentieth centuries, millions of Jews migrated to other European lands or to North America to escape persecution and violence. Anti-Semitism was not as severe in France as in central and eastern Europe, but it reached a fever pitch there after a military court convicted Alfred Dreyfus, a Jewish army officer, of spying for Germany in 1894. Although he was innocent of the charges and eventually had the verdict reversed on appeal, Dreyfus was the focus of bitter debates about the trustworthiness of Jews in French society. The trial also became a key event in the evolution of Zionism.

Zionism Among the reporters at the Dreyfus trial was a Jewish journalist from Vienna, Theodor Herzl (1860–1904). As Herzl witnessed mobs shouting "Death to the Jews" in the land of enlightenment and liberty, he concluded that

Theodor Herzl.
A determined Theodor Herzl founded the Zionist movement, which sought to confront anti-Semitism in Europe by establishing a home for the Jews in Palestine.

Johann Gottfried von Herder (YOH-hahn GAWT-freet fuhn HER-duhr)

Giuseppe Mazzini (joo-ZEP-pe maht-TSEE-nee)

Theodor Herzl (TEY-aw-dohr HER-tsuhll)

Thinking about ENCOUNTERS

Nationalism on the March

The Napoleonic wars that followed the French revolution brought both French troops and revolutionary ideals to the regions of Europe involved in those wars. *What ideals were exported from France? How did clashes between the French and other peoples of Europe, such as the Italians and the Germans, reshape the nationalist sentiments of those peoples?*

anti-Semitism was a persistent feature of human society that assimilation could not solve. In 1896 Herzl published the pamphlet *Judenstaat,* which argued that the only defense against anti-Semitism lay in the mass migration of Jews from all over the world to a land that they could call their own. In the following year, Herzl organized the first Zionist Congress in Basel, Switzerland, which founded the World Zionist Organization. The delegates at Basel formulated the basic platform of the Zionist movement, declaring that "Zionism seeks to establish a home for the Jewish people in Palestine," the location of the ancient kingdom of Israel. During the next half century, Jewish migrants trickled into Palestine, and in 1948 they won recognition for the Jewish state of Israel. Although it arose in response to exclusive nationalism in Europe, Zionism in turn provoked a resentful nationalism among Palestinians displaced by Jewish settlers. Conflicts between Jews and Palestinians continue to the present day.

The Emergence of National Communities

The French revolution and the wars that followed it heightened feelings of national identity throughout Europe. In France the establishment of a republic based on liberty, equality, and fraternity inspired patriotism and encouraged citizens to rally to its defense when foreign armies threatened it. Revolutionary leaders took the tricolored flag as a symbol of the French nation, and they adopted a rousing marching tune, the "Marseillaise," as an anthem that inspired pride and identity with the national community. In Spain, the Netherlands, Austria, Prussia, and Russia, national consciousness surged in reaction to the arrival of revolutionary and Napoleonic armies. Opposition to Napoleon and his imperial designs also inspired national feeling in Britain.

The Congress of Vienna After the fall of Napoleon, conservative political leaders feared that heightened national consciousness and ideas of popular sovereignty would undermine European stability. Meeting as the Congress of Vienna (1814–1815), representatives of Britain, Austria, Prussia, and Russia attempted to restore the prerevolutionary order. Under the guidance of the influential foreign minister of Austria, Prince Klemens von Metternich (1773–1859), the Congress dismantled Napoleon's empire, returned sovereignty to Europe's royal families, restored them to the thrones they had lost during the Napoleonic era, and created a diplomatic order based on a balance of power that prevented any one state from dominating the others. A central goal of Metternich himself was to suppress national consciousness, which he viewed as a serious threat to the multicultural Austrian empire. Yet the efforts of the Congress of Vienna to restore the ancien régime had limited success. Although the European balance of power established at Vienna survived for almost a century, it had become impossible to suppress national consciousness and ideas of popular sovereignty.

Nationalist Rebellions From the 1820s through the 1840s, a wave of rebellions inspired by nationalist sentiments swept through Europe. The first uprising occurred in 1821 in the Balkan Peninsula, where the Greek people sought independence from the Ottoman Turks. With the aid of Britain, France, and Russia, the rebels won formal recognition of Greek independence in 1830. In the same year, liberal revolutionaries in France, Spain, Portugal, and some of the German principalities called for constitutional government based on popular sovereignty. In Belgium, Italy, and Poland, they demanded independence and the formation of national states as well as popular sovereignty. Revolution in Paris drove Charles X from the throne, and uprisings in Belgium resulted in independence from the Netherlands. In 1848 a new round of rebellions shook European states, where they brought down the French monarchy and seriously threatened the Austrian empire. Uprisings also rocked cities in Italy, Prussia, and German states in the Rhineland.

By the summer of 1849, the veteran armies of conservative rulers had put down the last of the rebellions. However, advocates of national independence and popular sovereignty remained active, and the potential of their ideals to mobilize popular support were crucial in the unification of two new European states: Italy by 1870 and Germany by 1871.

Judenstaat (juh-dehn-STAHT)
Klemens von Metternich (kleh-men fuhn MET-er-nik)

Reverberations ● ● ● ● ● ● ● ● ●

The Birth of Nationalism

The consequences of the birth of nationalism for world history have been enormous, beginning in the period 1750–1914 and continuing right down to the present. From its beginnings, nationalism was intimately linked with powerful emotive phenomena such as folk traditions, songs, and literature that symbolized common heritage and common values. As a result, nationalism had the power to awaken deep feelings of love and unity, and also of hatred and ferocity, among its adherents. Such feelings often spurred individuals to work on behalf of the nation even at the expense of their own interests. They also encouraged individuals to exclude—sometimes brutally—those they defined as "outside the nation," and to see the interests of their own nation in competition with the interests of others. As a result, people around the world have done extraordinary things—both altruistic and cruel—in the name of nationalism.

In this chapter, we have already seen some of the first instances (in Italy and Germany) of individuals using the power of nationalism to create unified state governments where there were none before—a process that has been attempted multiple times (e.g., Greater Serbia, Palestine) since then. We have also seen that nationalism was used from its beginnings as a tool to exclude unwelcome groups, in this case European Jews. In fact, nationalism has often served as the double-edged sword of unity. On the one side, its symbols and myths have been used by diverse populations as the glue uniting them into one people, as in many of the newly formed North, South, and Central American nations during the nineteenth century (chapter 27). On the other side, by emphasizing particular languages and heritages, nationalism often inspires some groups to seek the exclusion of others, as people of European ancestry tried to do to Native Americans throughout the Americas (chapter 27). Nationalism has also spurred deep feelings of animosity or competition between people of different nations, which has increased the incidence of serious conflict between states (chapters 28 and 29).

One of the hallmarks of nationalism is that its emotive power has often been exploited by state governments for self-interested purposes. In late-nineteenth-century

The Unifications of Italy and Germany

The most striking demonstration of the power that national sentiments could unleash involved the unifications of Italy and Germany. Since the fall of the Roman empire, Italy and Germany had been disunited lands. A variety of regional kingdoms, city-states, and ecclesiastical states ruled the Italian peninsula for more than a thousand years, and princes divided Germany into more than three hundred semi-autonomous jurisdictions.

Cavour and Garibaldi The unification of Italy came about when practical political leaders such as Count Camillo di Cavour (1810–1861), prime minister to King Vittore Emmanuele II of Piedmont and Sardinia, combined forces with nationalist advocates of independence. Cavour was a cunning diplomat, and the kingdom of Piedmont and Sardinia was the most powerful of the Italian states. In alliance with France, Cavour expelled Austrian authorities—who

had gained control of the region through the Congress of Vienna—from most of northern Italy in 1859. Then he turned his attention to southern Italy, where Giuseppe Garibaldi (1807–1882), a dashing soldier of fortune and a passionate nationalist, led the unification movement. With an army of about one thousand men outfitted in distinctive red shirts, Garibaldi swept through Sicily and southern Italy, outmaneuvering government forces and attracting enthusiastic recruits. In 1860 Garibaldi met King Vittore Emmanuele near Naples. Not ambitious to rule, Garibaldi delivered southern Italy into Vittore Emmanuele's hands, and the kingdom of Piedmont and Sardinia became the kingdom of Italy. During the next decade the new monarchy absorbed several additional territories, including Venice, Rome, and their surrounding regions.

Otto von Bismarck In Germany as in Italy, unification came about when political leaders harnessed nationalist aspirations. The Congress of Vienna created a German Confederation composed of thirty-nine states dominated by Austria. In 1862 King Wilhelm I of Prussia—one of the thirty-nine states—appointed a wealthy landowner, Otto von Bismarck (1815–1898), as his prime minister. Bismarck was a master of realpolitik ("the politics of reality") who

---

Vittore Emmanuele (vih-tor-reh i-MAHN-yoo-uhl)
Giuseppe Garibaldi (juh-SEP-eh gar-uh-BAWL-dee)
Otto von Bismarck (oht-toh fuhn BIZ-mahrk)

Japan, for example, reformers tried to inculcate a strong sense of national pride in Japanese citizens in order to garner support for a rapid program of industrialization that would allow Japan to be competitive on the world stage (chapter 26). While the process did foster national identification among ordinary Japanese people as well as rapid industrialization, the result was a far stronger state buttressed by a handful of extremely powerful corporations. In Europe, meanwhile, states played upon nationalist sentiments among their citizens—especially the specter of being bested by other nations—to garner support for imperial expansion in Asia and Africa (chapter 28). Indeed, by framing expansionist programs in terms of national aggrandizement, states were able to

The Sans-Culottes. A French Sans-Culottes holding the French tricolor flag. Behind him is the countryside of France, and his clothes indicate his common status. Images like these were used to evoke emotions in viewers about their national identity.

win the support for imperial conquests. Somewhat ironically, European imperial expansion ensured that people all over the world would be introduced to the concept of nationalism during the nineteenth and twentieth centuries—with consequences that would ultimately bring all of the European empires down (chapter 31).

The birth of nationalism profoundly shaped identities, loyalties, and both individual and state actions around the world from the late eighteenth century onward, with effects that continue to reverberate in the present. In subsequent chapters, think about the many and varied ways that the force of nationalism—born in the context of the Atlantic revolutions—has shaped the world we live in today.

The Coronation of Wilhelm I. Wearing a white jacket, Otto von Bismarck (center) witnesses the crowning of King Wilhelm I of Prussia as German emperor. The coronation followed the victory of Prussia over France in 1871, and it took place in the royal palace at Versailles.

Why would it have been symbolically significant to stage the coronation at Versailles?

argued that "the great questions of the day will not be settled by speeches or majority votes . . . but by blood and iron." It was indeed blood and iron that brought about the unification of Germany. As prime minister, Bismarck reformed and expanded the Prussian army. Between 1864 and 1870 he intentionally provoked three wars—with Denmark, Austria, and France—and whipped up German sentiment against the enemies. In all three conflicts Prussian forces quickly shattered their opponents, swelling German pride. In 1871 the Prussian king proclaimed himself emperor of the Second Reich—meaning the second German empire, following the Holy Roman Empire—which embraced almost all German-speaking peoples outside Austria and Switzerland in a powerful and dynamic national state.

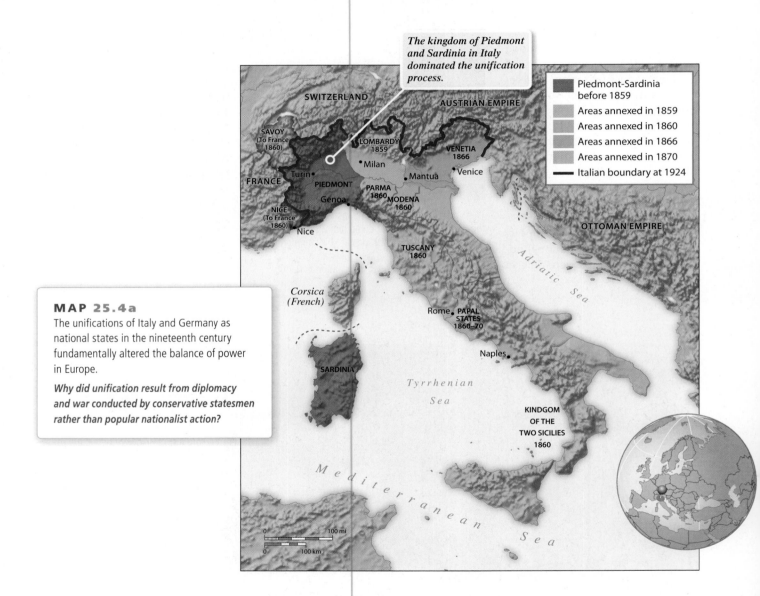

The kingdom of Piedmont and Sardinia in Italy dominated the unification process.

Piedmont-Sardinia before 1859
Areas annexed in 1859
Areas annexed in 1860
Areas annexed in 1866
Areas annexed in 1870
Italian boundary at 1924

MAP 25.4a
The unifications of Italy and Germany as national states in the nineteenth century fundamentally altered the balance of power in Europe.

Why did unification result from diplomacy and war conducted by conservative statesmen rather than popular nationalist action?

The unifications of Italy and Germany made it clear that when coupled with strong political, diplomatic, and military leadership, nationalism had enormous potential to mobilize people who felt a sense of national kinship. Italy, Germany, and other national states went to great lengths to foster a sense of national community. They adopted national flags to serve as symbols of unity, national anthems to inspire patriotism, and national holidays to focus public attention on individuals and events of special importance for the national community. They established bureaucracies that took censuses of national populations and tracked vital national statistics involving birth, marriage, and death. They built schools that instilled patriotic values in students, and they recruited young men into armies that defended national interests and sometimes went on the offensive to enhance national prestige. By the end of the nineteenth century, the national state had proven to be a powerful model of political organization in Europe.

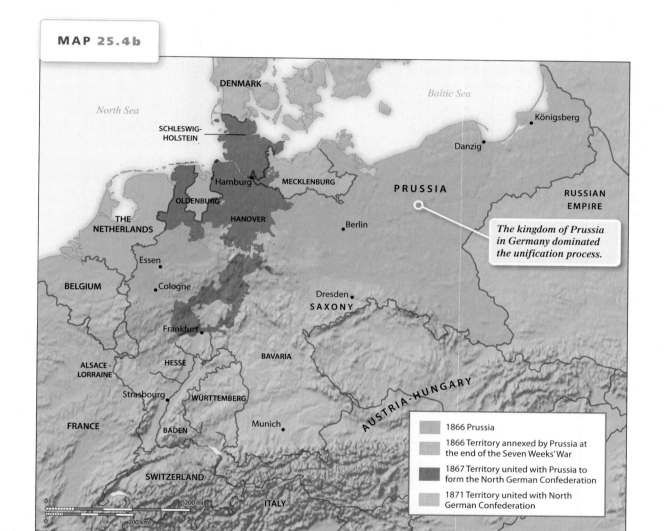

MAP 25.4b

The kingdom of Prussia in Germany dominated the unification process.

- 1866 Prussia
- 1866 Territory annexed by Prussia at the end of the Seven Weeks' War
- 1867 Territory united with Prussia to form the North German Confederation
- 1871 Territory united with North German Confederation

SUMMARY

The Enlightenment ideals of freedom, equality, and popular sovereignty inspired revolutionary movements throughout much of the Atlantic Ocean basin in the late eighteenth and early nineteenth centuries. In North America colonists threw off British rule and founded an independent federal republic. In France revolutionaries abolished the monarchy, established a republic, and refashioned the social order. In Saint-Domingue rebellious slaves threw off French rule, established an independent Haitian republic, and granted freedom and equality to all citizens. In Latin America creole elites led movements to expel Spanish and Portuguese colonial authorities and found independent republics. During the nineteenth century, adult white men were the main beneficiaries of movements based on Enlightenment ideals, but social reformers launched campaigns to extend freedom and equality to African-Americans and women.

Meanwhile, as they fought one another in wars sparked by the French revolution, European peoples developed strong feelings of national identity and worked to establish states that advanced the interests of national communities. Nationalist thought was often divisive: it pitted national groups against one another and fueled tensions, especially in large multicultural states. But nationalism also contributed to state-building movements that had the potential to unite. During the nineteenth and twentieth centuries, peoples throughout the world drew inspiration from Enlightenment ideals and national identities when seeking to build or restructure their societies.

STUDY TERMS

American revolution (469–471)
ancien regime (472)
anti-Semitism (482–483)
caudillos (478)
Civil Code (474)
conservatism (480)
Continental Congress (471)
criollos (477)
Elizabeth Cady Stanton (481)
Estates General (472)
French revolution (471–472)
gens de couleur (476–477)
George Washington (471)
German unification (484–486)
Gran Colombia (478)
Guiseppe Gariboladi (484)
Guiseppe Mazzini (482)
Haitian revolution (476)
Italian unification (484–486)
Jean-Jacques Rousseau (469)
Johann Gottfried von Herder (482)
John Locke (469)

Judenstaat (483)
Klemens von Metternich (483)
liberalism (480)
Louis XVI (472)
Mary Wollstonecraft (481)
Maximilien Robespierre (472–473)
Miguel de Hidalgo (477)
Napoleon Bonaparte (474)
National Assembly (472–474)
nationalism (481–484)
Olympe de Gouges (467)
Otto von Bismarck (484)
peninsulares (477)
philosophes (468)
reign of terror (473)
Seven Years' War (470)
Simón Bolívar (478)
Theodor Herzl (482)
Toussaint Louverture (477)
Vittore Emmanuele (484)
Voltaire (469)
Waterloo (476)
William Wilberforce (480)
Young Italy (482)
Zionism (482–483)

FOR FURTHER READING

Benedict Anderson. *Imagined Communities: Reflections on the Origin and Spread of Nationalism.* Rev. ed. London, 1991. A pioneering work that analyzes the means and the processes by which peoples came to view themselves as members of national communities.

Bernard Bailyn. *The Ideological Origins of the American Revolution.* 2nd ed. Cambridge, Mass., 1992. A fundamental study of pamphlets and other publications that criticized British colonial policy in North America.

David A. Bell. *The Cult of the Nation in France: Inventing Nationalism, 1680–1800.* Cambridge, Mass., 2001. Looks at how patriotism and national sentiment were grafted onto religious forms of community in the context of the eighteenth century and the French revolution.

Aviva Chomsky and Aldo Lauria-Santiago, eds. *Identity and Struggle at the Margins of the Nation-State: The Laboring Peoples of Central America and the Hispanic Caribbean.* Durham, 1998. Discusses the impact that peasant action had on political and cultural development in different societies.

Linda Colley. *Britons: Forging the Nation, 1707–1837.* New Haven, 1992. A detailed analysis of the emergence of British national identity.

Laureant Dubois. *Avengers of the New World: The Story of the Haitian Revolution.* Cambridge, Mass., 2005. Comprehensive study of how the French slave colony of Saint-Domingue became a unique example of a successful black revolution that challenged the boundaries of freedom, citizenship, and empire.

Susan Dunn. *Sister Revolutions: French Lightning, American Light.* New York, 1999. An accessible and stimulating work that traces the different legacies of the American and French revolutions of the eighteenth century.

François Furet. *Revolutionary France, 1770–1880.* Trans. by A. Nevill. Oxford, 1992. An influential interpretation emphasizing the ideological dimension of the French revolution.

Lester D. Langley. *The Americas in the Age of Revolution, 1750–1850.* New Haven, 1997. A comparative study of revolutions and wars of independence in the western hemisphere.

Eric Van Young. *The Other Rebellion: Popular Violence, Ideology, and the Mexican Struggle for Independence, 1810–1821.* Stanford, 2001. An exhaustive account of Mexico's movement toward independence from Spain that stresses the importance of domestic struggles that pitted classes and ethnic groups against one another.

The Making of Industrial Society

CHAPTER 26

This 19th-century photograph of Manchester, England depicts densely packed urban buildings alongside smokestacks, both of which were characteristic of cities during the industrial revolution.

EYEWITNESS:
Betty Harris: A Woman Chained in the Coal Pits

In 1827, shortly after marrying at age twenty-three, Betty Harris took a job as a drawer in a coal pit near Manchester, England. A drawer's job involved crawling down narrow mine shafts and hauling loads of coal from the bottom of the pit to the surface. Drawers performed unskilled labor for low wages, but their work was essential for obtaining the coal that fueled the factories and mills of early industrial society.

While working, Harris wore a heavy belt around her waist. Hitched to the belt was a chain that passed between her legs and attached to the coal cart that she pulled through the steep and slippery mine shafts, often on hands and knees. Every workday, even when she was pregnant, Harris strapped on her belt and chain at 6:00 A.M., removing her bindings only at the end of the shift twelve hours later.

Harris reported that drawing coal was "very hard work for a woman," and she did not exaggerate. The belts and chains worn by drawers often chafed their skin raw, and miners contributed to their physical discomfort by beating them for slow or clumsy work. The miners, many of whom worked naked in the hot, oppressive coal pits, also took sexual liberties with the women and girl drawers: Harris personally knew several illegitimate children conceived during forced sexual encounters in the mines.

Betty Harris faced her own sexual problems once she arrived home. Exhausted from twelve hours of work, with only a one-hour break for a lunch consisting of bread and butter, she often tried to discourage her husband's advances. Her husband had little patience, however, and Harris remarked that "my feller has beaten me many a time for not being ready." Harris's work schedule made comfortable family life impossible. A cousin had to care for her two children during the day, and Harris tended to them and her husband at night. At age thirty-seven, after fourteen years in the mines, Harris admitted that "I am not so strong as I was."

Not all industrial workers worked in such difficult conditions, but Betty Harris's experience nonetheless illustrates some of the deep changes that industrialization wrought in patterns of work and family life. First in Britain, then in western Europe, North America, Russia, and Japan, machines and factories transformed agricultural societies into industrial societies. At the heart of this transformation were technological changes that led to the extensive use of machinery in manufacturing. Industrial machinery transformed economic production by turning out high-quality products quickly, cheaply, and efficiently. The process of industrialization encouraged rapid technological innovation and over the long term raised material standards of living in much of the world.

But the impact of industrialization went beyond economics, generating widespread and often unsettling social change as well. Early industrialists created a new work environment, the factory, which concentrated large numbers of workers under one roof to operate complicated machinery. By moving work outside the home, however, factories drew fathers, mothers, and children in different directions, altered traditional patterns of domestic life, and strained family relations in the industrial era.

CHRONOLOGY

1733	John Kay develops the flying shuttle
1765	James Watt patents an improved steam engine
1779	Samuel Crompton develops the spinning mule
1785	Edmund Cartwright develops the power loom
1797	Eli Whitney introduces interchangeable parts to the manufacturing process
1829	George Stephenson's locomotive, the Rocket, attains a speed of 45 kilometers (28 miles) per hour
1848	Karl Marx and Friedrich Engels publish *Manifesto of the Communist Party*
1849–1915	Life of Sergei Witte
1851	Crystal Palace exhibition in London
1853	Arrival of Commodore Perry in Japan
1853–1856	Crimean War
1855–1881	Reign of Tsar Alexander II
1856	Bessemer converter developed
1861	Emancipation of the Russian serfs
1868	Meiji restoration
1913	Henry Ford introduces the assembly line to the manufacture of automobiles

Industrialization encouraged rapid urbanization and migration. New cities mushroomed to house workers who left the countryside for jobs in factories. Millions of migrants even crossed the seas in search of opportunities in new lands. Often, however, early industrial workers found themselves living in squalor and laboring under dangerous conditions.

Social critics and reformers worked to alleviate the problems of early industrial society. Despite their appeals, however, capitalism and industrialization flourished and spread rapidly from Britain to continental Europe, North America, and Asia. In some areas, notably western Europe and North America, industrialization was encouraged so that states could gain the economic advantages of industrialization. In other places, including Russia and Japan, industrialization was undertaken as part of a larger program of social, political, and economic reform to avoid domination by western European and American powers. Elsewhere, industrialization created a new international division of labor that made most of Africa, Asia, and Latin America economically dependent on the export of raw materials that supplied the factories and cities of the industrialized world. Thus, although industrialization and its effects spread unevenly and for different reasons, they profoundly influenced social and economic conditions all over the globe.

PATTERNS OF INDUSTRIALIZATION

Industrialization refers to a process that transformed agrarian and handicraft-centered economies into economies distinguished by industry and machine manufacture. The principal features of that process were technological and organizational changes that transformed manufacturing and led to increased productivity. Critical to industrialization were technological developments that made it possible to produce goods by machines rather than by hand and that harnessed inanimate sources of energy such as coal and petroleum. Also critical was the development of factory production, wherein workers assembled under one roof to produce goods in mass quantities. The need to invest in expensive factory equipment in turn encouraged the formation of large businesses: by the mid–nineteenth century many giant corporations had joined together to control trade through trusts and cartels.

Foundations of Industrialization

By the mid–eighteenth century, several areas of the world—Great Britain in western Europe, the Yangzi Delta in China, Japan—exhibited dynamic economies that shared many common features. High agricultural productivity resulted in significant population growth, and high population densities encouraged occupational specialization outside of agriculture. Navigable rivers and networks of canals facilitated trade and transport, and cities and towns supported sophisticated banking and financial institutions. At the same time, these sophisticated economies ran up against difficult ecological obstacles—especially soil depletion and deforestation—that threatened continued population growth and consumption levels. Despite their common features, Great Britain was the first to transcend these ecological constraints by exploiting coal deposits fortuitously found at home and natural resources found abroad.

Coal and Colonies Until the eighteenth century, wood had served as Great Britain's primary source of fuel for iron production, home heating, and cooking. Such extensive use of wood had resulted in serious wood shortages. However, geographic luck had placed some of western Europe's largest coal deposits in Great Britain, within easy reach of water transport, centers of commerce, and pools of skilled labor. That fortunate conjunction encouraged the substitution of coal for wood, thus creating a promising framework for industrialization. Indeed, without easily accessible coal deposits, it was unlikely that the economy could have supported expanding iron production and the application of steam engines to mining and industry—both crucial to the industrial process in Great Britain. In that respect Britain's experience differed from that of China, because the main coal-producing regions of northwest China were quite distant from the Yangzi Delta, China's most economically promising region for the development of industrialization. Thus, geography conspired against an important early shift from wood to coal in China.

The unique economic relationship between Europe and the Americas gave Great Britain additional ecological relief. The colonized lands of the Americas lifted European land constraints by supplying European societies with a growing volume of primary products. During the eighteenth century slave-based plantations supplied Europe with huge amounts of sugar and cotton; the former increased available food calories, and the latter kept emerging textile industries going. Neither of those products could have been grown in Europe. The significance of valuable American resources grew after 1830, when large amounts of grain, timber, and beef grown on colonial acreage traveled across the Atlantic to European destinations. In addition, American lands served as outlets for European manufactured goods as well as Europe's surplus population. Access to such overseas resources, in addition to coal deposits at home, provided a context—one not available to societies such as China—that increased the odds for an industrial breakthrough.

Industrial expansion in Britain began in the mid–eighteenth century with the textile industry, when consumer demand spurred a transformation of the British cotton industry. During the seventeenth century, English consumers had become fond of calicoes—inexpensive, brightly printed cotton textiles from India. Cotton cloth came into demand because it was lighter and easier to wash than wool, which was the principal fabric of European clothes before the nineteenth century. Although British wool producers tried to protect their industry through a series of laws designed to prohibit imports of cotton cloth in 1720 and 1721, they could not stifle public demand.

Mechanization of the Cotton Industry In fact, demand for cotton was so strong that producers had to speed up spinning and weaving to supply growing markets. To increase production they turned to inventions that rapidly mechanized the cotton textile industry. The first important technological breakthrough came in 1733 when Manchester mechanic John Kay invented the flying shuttle, which sped up the weaving process. Within a few years, inventors created several mechanical spinning devices, the most important of which was Samuel Crompton's spinning "mule," built in 1779. In 1790 the mule was adapted for steam power, and it became the device of choice for spinning cotton. A worker using a steam-driven mule could produce a hundred times more thread than a worker using a manual spinning wheel.

The new spinning machines necessitated new weaving machines so that weavers could keep up with the production of thread. In 1785 Edmund Cartwright, a clergyman without experience in either mechanics or textiles, patented a water-driven power loom. Within two decades steam moved the power loom, and by the 1820s hand weavers were nearly obsolete. A young boy working on two power looms could produce fifteen times more cloth than the fastest hand weaver. Collectively, these technological developments permitted the mass production of inexpensive textile goods. By 1830 half a million people worked in the cotton business, Britain's leading industry, which accounted for 40 percent of exports.

Steam Power The most crucial technological breakthrough of the early industrial era was the development of a general-purpose steam engine in 1765 by James Watt, an instrument maker at the University of Glasgow in Scotland. Even before Watt's time, primitive steam engines had powered pumps that drew water out of coal mines, but those devices consumed too much fuel to be useful for other purposes. Watt's version relied on steam to force a piston to turn a wheel, whose rotary motion converted a simple pump into an engine. By 1800 more than a thousand of Watt's steam engines were in use in the British Isles. They were especially prominent in the textile industry, where they allowed greater productivity for manufacturers and cheaper prices for consumers.

Iron and Steel The iron and steel industries also benefited from technological refinement, and the availability of inexpensive, high-quality iron and steel reinforced the move toward mechanization. After 1709 British smelters began to use coke (a purified form of coal) rather than more expensive charcoal as a fuel to produce iron. As a result, British iron production skyrocketed during the eighteenth century, and prices to consumers fell. Inexpensive iron fittings and parts made industrial machinery stronger, and iron soon became common in bridges, buildings, and ships.

Steel is much harder, stronger, and more resilient than iron, but until the nineteenth century it was very expensive to produce. In 1856, however, Henry Bessemer built a

The steam locomotive.
George Stephenson's North Star engine of 1837.

refined blast furnace known as the Bessemer converter that made it possible to produce large quantities of steel cheaply. Steel production rose sharply, and steel quickly began to replace iron in tools, machines, and structures that required high strength.

Transportation Steam engineering and metallurgical innovations both contributed to improvements in transportation technology. In 1815 George Stephenson, a self-educated Englishman, built the first steam-powered locomotive. In 1829 his Rocket won a contest by reaching a speed of 45 kilometers (28 miles) per hour. By the mid–nineteenth century, refined steam engines of high efficiency also began to drive steamships.

Because they had the capacity to carry huge cargoes, railroads and steamships dramatically lowered transportation costs. They also contributed to the creation of transportation networks that linked remote interior regions and distant shores more closely than ever before in history. Between 1830 and 1870, British entrepreneurs laid about 20,000 kilometers (13,000 miles) of railroads, which carried some 322 million passengers as well as cargoes of raw materials and manufactured goods. Meanwhile, steamships proved their versatility by advancing up rivers to points that sailboats could not reach because of inconvenient twists or turns.

The Factory System

The Factory The factory system became the characteristic method of production in industrial economies. It emerged in the late eighteenth century, when technological advances transformed the British textile industry, and by the mid–nineteenth century most cotton production took place in factories. Many of the newly developed machines were too large and expensive for home use, so it became necessary to move work to centralized locations. That centralization of production brought together more workers doing specialized tasks than ever before.

Working Conditions The factory system with its new machines demanded a rational organization of job functions. Thus, the factory became associated with a new division of labor that called for a production process in which each worker performed a single task, rather than one in which a single worker completed the entire job, as was typical of handicraft traditions. This new division of labor allowed managers to improve worker productivity and realize spectacular increases in the output of manufactured goods. But the new environment also had unsettling effects on the nature of work. For instance, the factory system led to the emergence of an owner class whose capital financed equipment and machinery that were too expensive for workers to acquire. As a result, industrial workers became mere wage earners who depended on their employers for their livelihood. The repetitive and boring nature of many industrial jobs, moreover, left many workers alienated from their work and the products of their labor. In addition, any broad-range skills that workers might have previously acquired as artisans often became obsolete in the factory work environment. Between 1811 and 1816, that situation prompted organized bands of English handicraft workers known as Luddites to destroy textile machines that they blamed for their low wages and unemployment. Nevertheless, by hanging fourteen Luddites in 1813, the government served notice that it was unwilling to tolerate violence even against machines, and the movement gradually died out.

Equally disturbing was the new work discipline and the pace of work. Those accustomed to rural labor found that the seasons and fluctuations in the weather no longer dictated work routines. Instead, clocks, machines, and shop rules established new rhythms of work. Industrial workers commonly labored six days a week, twelve to fourteen hours a day. The factory whistle sounded the beginning and the end of each working day, and throughout the day workers had to keep pace with the movements of machines. At the same time, they faced strict and immediate supervision. Floor managers pressured men, women, and children to speed up production and punished them when they did not meet expectations. In addition, dangerous work conditions often meant that early industrial workers faced the possibility of maiming or fatal accidents.

The Early Spread of Industrialization

For fifty years industrialization occurred only in Britain. Aware of their head start, British entrepreneurs and government officials forbade the export of machinery,

Working conditions.
Workers tend to a massive steam hammer under dangerous conditions.

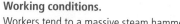

manufacturing techniques, and skilled workers to other lands. Yet Britain's monopoly on industrialization did not last, because enterprising entrepreneurs ignored government regulations and sold machinery and technical know-how abroad. Moreover, European and North American businesspeople did not hesitate to bribe or even kidnap British engineers to learn the secrets of industrialization, and they also smuggled advanced machinery out of the British Isles.

Industrialization in Western Europe As a result, by the mid–nineteenth century industrialization had spread to France, Germany, Belgium, and the United States. The earliest Continental center of industrial production was Belgium, where coal, iron, textile, glass, and armaments production flourished in the early nineteenth century. About the same time, France also moved toward industrialization. By the mid–nineteenth century, French engineers and inventors were devising refinements and innovations that led to greater efficiencies, especially in metallurgical industries. Although German industrialization started off more slowly than in France or Belgium, German coal and iron production soared after the 1840s, and by the 1850s an extensive railroad network was under

construction. After unification in 1871, Bismarck's government sponsored rapid industrialization in Germany, especially of heavy industry.

Industrialization in North America Industrialization transformed North America as well as western Europe in the nineteenth century. American industrialization began in the 1820s when entrepreneurs lured British crafts workers to New England and built a cotton textile industry. By midcentury well over a thousand mills were producing fabrics from raw cotton grown in the southern states, and New England had emerged as a site for the industrial production also of shoes, tools, and handguns. In the 1870s heavy iron and steel industries emerged in areas such as western Pennsylvania and central Alabama where there were abundant supplies of iron ore and coal. By 1900 the United States had become an economic powerhouse, and industrialization had begun to spill over into southern Canada.

Industrial Capitalism

Mass Production Cotton textiles were the major factory-made products during the early phase of industrialization, but the factory system soon spread to other industries. An

MAP 26.1

Industrial Europe ca. 1850. Locate the places marked as emerging industrial areas.

Are there any features those areas have in common? If so, what are they?

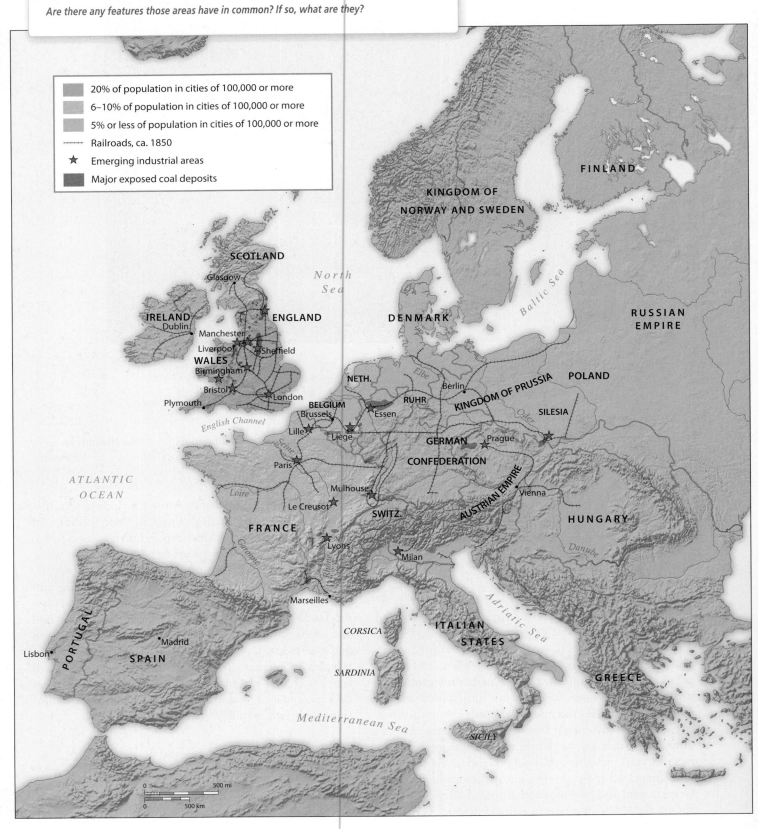

important contribution to the evolving factory system came from the American inventor Eli Whitney (1765–1825). Though best remembered as the inventor of the cotton gin (1793), Whitney also developed the technique of using machine tools to produce interchangeable parts in the making of firearms. This method meant that unskilled workers made only a particular part that fit every musket of the same model. Before long, entrepreneurs applied Whitney's method to the manufacture of everything from clocks and sewing machines to uniforms and shoes. By the middle of the nineteenth century, mass production of standardized articles was becoming the hallmark of industrial societies.

In 1913 Henry Ford improved manufacturing techniques further when he introduced the assembly line to automobile production. Instead of organizing production around a series of stations where workers assembled whole cars using standardized parts, Ford designed a conveyor system that allowed each worker to perform a specialized task at a fixed point on the assembly line. With the assembly line, workers churned out a complete chassis every 93 minutes instead of every 728 minutes under the old system. Such huge gains in productivity meant that car prices plummeted, allowing millions of ordinary people to purchase automobiles. The age of the motor car had arrived.

The Corporation As the factory evolved, so too did the organization of business. Industrial machinery and factories were expensive investments, and they encouraged businesses to organize on a large scale. During the 1850s and 1860s, government authorities in Britain and France laid the legal foundations for the modern corporation, which quickly became the most common form of business organization in industrial societies. A corporation was a private business owned by many investors who financed the business through the purchase of stocks representing shares in the company. When a corporation flourished, investors received dividends in proportion to their stake in the company. But if a corporation went bankrupt, laws protected shareholders from liability or financial loss beyond the extent of their investments—which made them extremely attractive to investors. By the late nineteenth century, corporations controlled most businesses requiring large investments in land, labor, or machinery.

Monopolies, Trusts, and Cartels To protect their investments, some big businesses of the late nineteenth century sought not only to outperform their competitors in the capitalist marketplace but also to eliminate competition.

The Crystal Palace exhibition.
Exhibitors from around the world displayed fine handicrafts and manufactured goods at the Crystal Palace exhibition of 1851 in London. Industrial products from Britain and the United States particularly attracted the attention of visitors to the enchanting and futuristic exhibition hall.

Business firms formed associations to restrict markets or establish monopolies in their industries. Large-scale business organizations formed trusts and cartels, both of which aimed to control the supply of a product and hence its price in the marketplace. Trusts commonly sought control of industries through vertical organization, by which they would dominate all facets of a single industry. John D. Rockefeller's Standard Oil Company and Trust, for example, controlled almost all oil drilling, processing, refining, marketing, and distribution in the United States.

Cartels, in contrast, tried to eliminate competition by means of horizontal organization, which involved the consolidation or cooperation of independent companies in the same business. Thus cartels sought to ensure the prosperity of their members by absorbing competitors, fixing prices, regulating production, or dividing up markets. By the end of the nineteenth century, some governments outlawed trusts and cartels. However, monopolistic practices continued well into the twentieth century.

INDUSTRIAL SOCIETY

Industrialization brought material benefits in its train: inexpensive manufactured products, rising standards of living, and population growth. Yet industrialization also unleashed dramatic social change. Immense internal and external migrations took place as people moved from the countryside to work in new industrial cities, and as Europeans crossed the Atlantic to seek opportunities in the western hemisphere.

Industrialization also encouraged the emergence of new social classes and forced men, women, and children to adjust to distinctly new patterns of family and work life. Reformers sought to alleviate the social and economic problems that accompanied industrialization and worked toward the building of a more equitable and just society.

The Fruits of Industry

Industrialization brought efficiencies in production that flooded markets with affordable manufactured goods. Indeed, industrialization raised material standards of living in many ways. Industrial production led to dramatic reductions in the cost of clothing, for example, so by the early nineteenth century all but the desperately poor could afford several changes of clothes. Industrial factories turned out tools that facilitated agricultural work, and steam-powered locomotives delivered produce quickly and cheaply to distant markets. Consumers in early industrial Europe also filled their homes with more furniture, porcelain, and decorative objects than any but the most wealthy of their ancestors.

Population Growth   The populations of European and Euro-American peoples rose sharply during the eighteenth and nineteenth centuries, reflecting the rising prosperity and standards of living that came with industrialization. Between 1700 and 1900 the population of Europe increased from 105 to 390 million. Demographic growth in the western hemisphere—fueled by migration from Europe—was even more remarkable. Between 1700 and 1900 the population of North America and South America rose from 13 million to 145 million.

The rapid population growth in Europe and the Americas reflected changing patterns of fertility and mortality. In most preindustrial societies fertility was high, but so was child mortality, which held population growth in check. High birthrates were common also in early industrializing societies, but death rates fell markedly because better diets and improved disease control reduced child mortality. By the late nineteenth century, better diets and improved sanitation led to declining levels of adult as well as child mortality. In combination, these two factors allowed populations to expand rapidly.

The Demographic Transition   Beginning in the nineteenth century, however, industrializing lands experienced a social change known as the *demographic transition*. As industrialization transformed societies, fertility began a marked decline. In the short run, mortality fell even faster than fertility, so the populations of industrial societies continued to increase. Over time, however, declining birthrates led to lower population growth and relative demographic

stability. The principal reason for declining fertility in industrial lands was voluntary birth control through contraception, perhaps because raising children cost more in industrial societies or because more children were likely to survive to adulthood than in the past.

Urbanization and Migration

Industrialization and population growth strongly encouraged migration and urbanization. Within industrial societies, migrants flocked from the countryside to urban centers in search of work. For example, in 1800 about one-fifth of the British population lived in towns and cities of 10,000 or more inhabitants. By 1900 three-fourths of the population worked and lived in cities. That pattern repeated itself elsewhere: by 1900 at least half of the population in industrialized lands lived in towns with populations of 2,000 or more. The increasing size of cities reflected this internal migration. In 1800 there were barely twenty cities in Europe with populations as high as 100,000, and there were none in the western hemisphere. By 1900 there were more than 150 large cities in Europe and North America combined.

The Urban Environment   With urbanization came intensified environmental pollution. Although cities have always been unsanitary places, the rapid increase in urban populations during the industrial age dramatically increased the magnitude and severity of water and air pollution. The widespread burning of fossil fuels fouled the air with vast quantities of chemicals and particulate matter. This pollution led to occupational diseases in some trades. Chimney sweeps, for instance, contracted cancer of the scrotum from hydrocarbon deposits found in soot. Effluents from factories and mills as well as untreated sewage dirtied virtually every major river. No part of a city was immune to the constant stench coming from air and water pollution. Worse, tainted water supplies and unsanitary living conditions led to periodic epidemics of cholera and typhus. Until the latter part of the nineteenth century, urban environments remained dangerous places in which death rates commonly exceeded birthrates, and only the constant stream of new arrivals from the country kept cities growing.

Income determined the degree of comfort and security offered by city life. The wealthy typically tried to insulate themselves from urban discomforts by retreating to their elegant homes in newly growing suburbs. The working poor, in contrast, occupied overcrowded tenements lacking in comfort and amenities. The cramped spaces in apartments obliged many to share the same bed, increasing the ease of disease transmission. The few open spaces outside the buildings were usually home to herds of pigs living in their own dung or were depositories for pools of stagnant water and human waste.

SourcesfromthePast

Testimony for the Factory Act of 1833: Working Conditions in England

During the 1830s and 1840s, deplorable conditions in England's factories and mines led the British Parliament to conduct a series of investigations on the subject. Investigators asked doctors, workers, and factory owners many questions about working conditions and their effects on laborers. The results of these investigations led to parliamentary legislation designed to protect workers from the worst effects of industrialization, such as the Factory Act of 1833. The following section relates to child labor as presented by John Wright, who was a steward in a silk factory.

Testimony of John Wright.

How long have you been employed in a silk-mill?—More than thirty years.

Did you enter it as a child?—Yes betwixt five and six.

How many hours a day did you work then?—The same thirty years ago as now.

What are those hours?—Eleven hours per day and two over-hours: over-hours are working after six in the evening until eight. The regular hours are from six in the morning to six in the evening, and two others are two over-hours. . . .

Why, then, are those employed in them said to be in such a wretched condition?—In the first place, the great number of hands congregated together, in some rooms forty, in some fifty, in some sixty, and I have known some as many as 100, which must be injurious to both health and growing. In the second place, the privy is in the factory, which frequently emits an unwholesome smell; and it would be worth while to notice in the future erection of mills, that there be betwixt the privy door and the factory wall a kind of a lobby of cage-work. 3dly, The tediousness and the everlasting sameness in the first process preys much on the spirits, and makes the hands spiritless. 4thly, the extravagant number of hours a child is compelled to labour and confinement, which for one week is seventy-six hours. . . . 5thly, About six months in the year

we are obliged to use either gas, candles, or lamps, for the longest portion of that time, nearly six hours a day, being obliged to work amid the smoke and soot of the same; and also a large portion of oil and grease is used in the mills.

What are the effects of the present system of labor?—From my earliest recollections, I have found the effects to be awfully detrimental to the well-being of the operative; I have observed frequently children carried to factories, unable to walk, and that entirely owing to excessive labour and confinement. The degradation of the workpeople baffles all description: frequently have two of my sisters been obliged to be assisted to the factory and home again, until by-and-by they could go no longer, being totally crippled in their legs. And in the next place, I remember some ten or twelve years ago working in one of the largest firms in Macclesfield, . . . with about twenty-two men, where they were scarce one half fit for His Majesty's service. Those that are straight in their limbs are stunted in their growth; much inferior to their fathers in point of strength. 3dly, Through excessive labour and confinement there is often a total loss of appetite; a kind of langour steals over the whole frame—enters to the very core—saps the foundation of the best constitution—and lays our strength prostrate in the dust. In the 4th place, by protracted labour there is an alarming increase of cripples in various parts of this town, which has come under my own observation and knowledge.

Are all these cripples made in the silk factories?—Yes, they are, I believe. . . .

For Further Reflection

■ In Wright's opinion, what aspect of labor in the silk factories is the most damaging for children?

Source: Dennis Sherman et al. *World Civilizations: Sources, Images, and Interpretations,* 3rd ed., Vol. II. Boston: McGraw-Hill, 2002, pp. 119–120.

By the later nineteenth century, though, government authorities were tending to the problems of the early industrial cities. They improved municipal water supplies, expanded sewage systems, and introduced building codes that outlawed the construction of rickety tenements to accommodate poorly paid workers. Those measures made city life safer and brought improved sanitation. City authorities also built parks and recreational facilities to make cities more livable.

Transcontinental Migration Rapid population growth in Europe also encouraged massive migration to the Americas, especially to the United States. During the nineteenth and early twentieth centuries, about fifty million Europeans migrated to the western hemisphere, which accounts for much of the stunning demographic growth of the Americas. Many of the migrants intended to stay for only a few years and fully expected to return to their homelands with a modest fortune made in the Americas. The vast

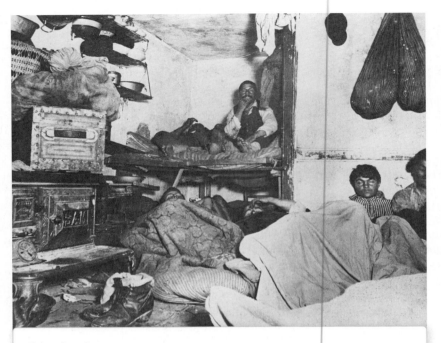

Urban housing.
Squalid living conditions, ca. 1885. A group of people live in crowded conditions in one room in New York.

majority, however, remained in the western hemisphere. They and their descendants transformed the Americas into Euro-American lands.

Industry and Society

New Social Classes Industrialization radically altered traditional social structures and helped bring new social classes into being. Enterprising businesspeople became fabulously wealthy and powerful enough to overshadow the traditionally privileged classes. Less powerful than this new elite was the middle class, consisting of small business owners, factory managers, engineers, and professionals such as teachers, physicians, and attorneys. A large portion of industrial wealth flowed to the middle class, which benefited greatly from industrialization. Meanwhile, laborers who toiled in factories and mines constituted a new working class. Less skilled than the artisans and crafts workers of earlier times, the new workers tended to machines or provided heavy labor for low wages.

Industrial Families The most basic unit of social organization—the family—also underwent fundamental change during the industrial age. In preindustrial societies the family was the basic productive unit. Whether engaged in agriculture, domestic manufacturing, or commerce, family members worked together and contributed to the welfare of the larger group. Industrialization challenged the family

economy and reshaped family life by moving economic production outside the home and introducing a sharp distinction between work and family life. Workers left their homes each day to labor an average of fourteen hours in factories, and family members led increasingly separate lives.

Men and the Industrial Revolution
Men gained increased stature and responsibility in the industrial age as work dominated public life. Upper-class and middle-class men enjoyed especially increased prestige at home, since they usually were the sole providers who made their families' comfortable existence possible. Working-class men also enjoyed increased prestige because they tended to make wages far in excess of those of working-class women. As a result, their earnings usually constituted the bulk of their families' income.

Women and the Industrial Revolution Industrialization dramatically changed the terms of work for women. When industry moved production from the home to the factory, married women were unable to work unless they left their homes and children in someone else's care. Millions of working-class women had no choice but to work under such terms, but by the late nineteenth century middle-class society promoted the idea that respectable women should devote themselves to raising children, managing the home, and preserving family values rather than to paid labor.

For middle-class women, then, industrialization brought stringent confinement to the domestic sphere and pressure to conform to new models of behavior revolving around their roles as mothers and wives. Popular books such as *Woman in Her Social and Domestic Character* (1833) insisted that the ideal woman "knows that she is the weaker vessel" and takes pride in her ability to make the home a happy place. Meanwhile, in addition to working in factories, millions of working-class women worked as domestic servants for the growing middle class. In fact, one of every three European women became a domestic servant at some point in her life.

Child Labor Industrialization profoundly influenced the childhood experience. Children in preindustrial societies had always worked in and around the family home. However, industrial work, which took children away from home and parents for long hours with few breaks, made child labor seem especially pitiable and exploitative. Early reports from British textile mills described sensational abuses by

Thinking about **TRADITIONS**

Family and Factory

Most families had for long centuries lived according to the rhythms of nature and agrarianism. The age of industrialization introduced a machine-driven world and radically altered family life. *What transformations occurred once factories organized life and work? Did changes equally affect men, women, and children?*

overseers who forced children to work from dawn until dark and beat them to keep them awake. In the 1840s the British parliament began to pass laws regulating child labor and ultimately restricted or removed children from the industrial workforce. In the long term, urban industrial societies redefined the role of children. Motivated in part by the recognition that modern society demanded a skilled and educated labor force, governments established the legal requirement that education, and not work for monetary gain, was the principal task of childhood. In England, for instance, education for children ages five to ten became mandatory by 1881.

The Socialist Challenge

Among the most vocal and influential critics of early industrial society were the socialists, who worked to alleviate the social and economic problems generated by capitalism and industrialization. Socialists deplored economic inequalities, as represented by the vast difference in wealth between a captain of industry and a factory laborer, and they condemned the system that permitted the exploitation of laborers, especially women and children. Early socialists sought to expand the Enlightenment understanding of equality: they understood equality to have an economic as well as a political, legal, and social dimension, and they looked to the future establishment of a just and equitable society. Although most

Women at work.
This 1909 photograph shows a young girl being instructed by a male supervisor on how to use a spinning machine. Women, not men, made up the bulk of the early labor force in the textile industry, principally because women were presumed easier to discipline than men and because women's smaller hands allegedly made them better suited for working with machines.

socialists shared this general vision, they held very different views on the best way to establish and maintain an ideal socialist society.

Utopian Socialists The term *socialism* first appeared around 1830, when it referred to the thought of social critics such as Robert Owen (1771–1858). Often called utopian socialists, these reformers and their followers worked to establish ideal communities that would point the way to an equitable society. Owen, for example, was a successful businessman who transformed a squalid Scottish cotton mill town called New Lanark into a model industrial community. At New Lanark, Owen raised wages, reduced the workday from seventeen to ten hours, built spacious housing, and opened a store that sold goods at fair prices. Despite the costs of those reforms, the mills of New Lanark generated profits. Owen also kept young children out of the factories and sent them to a school that he opened in 1816. Owen's indictment of competitive capitalism, his stress on cooperative control of industry, and his advocacy of improved educational standards for children left a lasting imprint on the socialist tradition.

The ideas of the utopian socialists resonated widely in the nineteenth century, and their disciples established experimental communities from the United States to Romania. Despite the enthusiasm of the founders, most of the communities soon encountered economic difficulties and political problems that forced them to fold. By the mid-nineteenth century, most socialists looked not to utopian communities but to large-scale organization of working people as the best means to bring about a just and equitable society.

Marx and Engels Most prominent of the nineteenth-century socialists were the German theorists Karl Marx (1818–1883) and Friedrich Engels (1820–1895). Marx and Engels believed that social problems of the nineteenth century were inevitable results of a capitalist economy. They held that capitalism divided people into two main classes, each with its own economic interests and social status: the capitalists, who owned industrial machinery and factories (which Marx and Engels called the means of production), and the proletariat, consisting of wageworkers who had only their labor to sell. Intense competition between capitalists trying to realize a profit resulted in ruthless exploitation of the working class. Moreover, according to Marx and Engels, the state and its coercive institutions, such as police forces and courts of law, functioned to enable capitalists to continue their exploitation of the proletariat. Even music, art, literature, and religion served the purposes of capitalists, according to Marx and Engels, since they amused the working classes and diverted attention from their misery.

The Communist Manifesto Marx developed those views fully in a long, theoretical work called *Capital.* Together with Engels, Marx also wrote a short, spirited tract titled *Manifesto of the Communist Party* (1848). In the *Manifesto* Marx and Engels aligned themselves with the communists, who worked toward the abolition of private property and the institution of a radically egalitarian society. The *Manifesto* asserted that all human history had been the history of struggle between social classes. It also argued that the future lay with the working class. Crises of overproduction, underconsumption, and diminishing profits would shake the foundations of the capitalist order. Meanwhile, members of the proletariat would come to view the forcible overthrow of the existing system as the only alternative available to them. Marx and Engels believed that a socialist revolution would result in a "dictatorship of the proletariat," which would abolish private property and destroy the capitalist order. After the revolution was secure, the state would wither away. Coercive institutions would also disappear, since there would no longer be an exploiting class. Thus socialism would lead to a fair, just, and egalitarian society infinitely more humane than the capitalist order.

The doctrines of Marx and Engels came to dominate European and international socialism, and socialist parties grew rapidly throughout the nineteenth century. Political parties, trade unions, newspapers, and educational associations all worked to advance the socialist cause. Yet socialists disagreed strongly on the best means to reform society. Revolutionary socialists such as Marx and Engels urged workers to forcibly seize control of the state. In contrast, evolutionary socialists placed their hopes in representative governments and called for the election of legislators who supported socialist reforms.

Social Reform Although socialists did not win control of any government until the Russian revolution of 1917, their critiques helped persuade government authorities to attack the abuses of early industrialization and provide more security for the working classes. In Britain, for example, Parliament prohibited underground employment for women and stipulated that children under age nine not work more than nine hours a day. Beginning in 1832, a series of parliamentary acts also expanded the franchise for men by reducing property qualifications, preparing the way for universal male suffrage. In Germany in the 1880s, Otto von Bismarck introduced medical insurance, unemployment compensation, and retirement pensions to provide social security for working people in industrial society. Yet Bismarck's reforms were hardly universal: they did not apply to women or agricultural workers, and they were paid for by expensive contributions from employers as well as from workers' salaries.

Trade Unions Trade unions also sought to advance the quest for a just and equitable society. As governments regulated businesses and enhanced social security, trade unions struggled to improve workers' lives by seeking higher wages and better working conditions for their members. Through

Industrial conflict.
Robert Koehler's painting *The Strike* depicts a situation verging on violence as workers mill about in a confrontation with factory owners and one angry laborer crouches to pick up a stone.

most of the nineteenth century, both employers and governments considered trade unions illegal associations whose purpose was to restrain trade. Yet trade unions persisted, and over the long run they improved the lives of working people and reduced the likelihood that a disgruntled proletariat would mount a revolution to overthrow industrial capitalist society.

GLOBAL EFFECTS OF INDUSTRIALIZATION

Although early industrialization was a British, western European, and North American affair, it had deep global implications. In part this was because industrial powers used their tools, technologies, business organization, financial influence, and transportation networks to obtain raw materials from preindustrial societies around the world. Many lands that possessed natural resources were unable to maintain control over them because representatives of industrial countries dominated the commercial and financial

institutions associated with their trade. Other societies, in particular Russia and Japan, saw the writing on the wall and embarked on huge industrialization programs of their own to stave off Euro-American domination.

The International Division of Labor

Industrialization influenced the economic and social development of many societies because it promoted a new international division of labor. Industrial societies needed minerals, agricultural products, and other raw materials to supply their factories, and they frequently obtained them from distant regions of the world.

Although large-scale global trade in agricultural products such as sugar, tea, and cotton was nothing new, industrial society fueled the demand for additional products as industrialists sought the natural resources and agricultural products of Africa, the Americas, Asia, Australia, and eastern Europe. The mechanization of the textile industry, for example, produced a demand for large quantities of raw cotton, which came mostly from India, Egypt, and the southern rim of the United States. Similarly, new industrial technologies increased demand for products such as rubber, the principal ingredient of the belts and tires that were essential to industrial machinery, which came from Brazil, Malaya, and the Congo River basin.

Economic Development In some lands specialization in the production and export of primary goods paved the way for economic development and eventual industrialization. That pattern was especially noticeable in lands settled by European colonists, including Canada, Argentina, Uruguay, South Africa, Australia, and New Zealand, each of which experienced economic growth through the export of primary products and the infusion of foreign capital and labor. The same societies had an additional advantage in that they were high-wage economies. High incomes fostered economic development in two ways: they created flourishing markets, and they encouraged entrepreneurs to counteract high wages and labor security by inventing new labor-saving technologies.

Economic Dependence In most of Latin America, sub-Saharan Africa, south Asia, and southeast Asia, however, dependence on exporting primary products such as sugar, cotton, and rubber resulted in little or no industrialization. Foreign investors owned and controlled the plantations that produced those crops, and most of the profits generated went abroad, depriving domestic economies of funds that might have contributed to the building of markets and industries. The low wages of plantation workers made the situation worse by dampening demand for manufactured goods. The result was the concentration of wealth in the hands of a small group of people, whether local or foreign, who contributed little to the creation of a domestic market. To compound the problem, both native and foreign financial interests adopted a free-trade policy that permitted unrestricted entry of foreign manufactures, further limiting opportunities for indigenous industrialization. Thus, although industrialization linked all the world's peoples in increasingly complex ways, its benefits and rewards went primarily to those who controlled the tools, capital, and trade rather than to those who provided the raw materials that made production possible.

The Continuing Spread of Industrialization: Russia and Japan

Industrialization brought great economic and military strength to societies that reconfigured themselves and relied on mechanized production. Their power encouraged

Romanov (ROH-muh-nawf)
tsar (zahr)

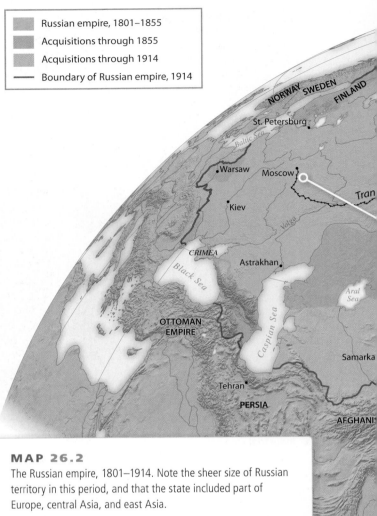

MAP 26.2

The Russian empire, 1801–1914. Note the sheer size of Russian territory in this period, and that the state included part of Europe, central Asia, and east Asia.

How would straddling so much space and so many cultures have affected the process of industrialization and nationalism in Russia?

Legend:
- Russian empire, 1801–1855
- Acquisitions through 1855
- Acquisitions through 1914
- Boundary of Russian empire, 1914

other societies to seek their own paths to industrialization. Indeed, by the late nineteenth century it had become clear to leaders in many preindustrial lands that unless they undertook programs of social, political, and economic reform, they would grow progressively weaker in relation to industrial powers. Faced with such a reality, after 1870 both Russia and Japan embarked on campaigns of rapid industrialization to strengthen their societies and enable them to resist military and economic pressures from western Europe and the United States.

Russia in 1870 was a multiethnic, multilingual, multicultural empire that stretched from Poland to the Pacific Ocean. The Romanov tsars ruled their diverse and sprawling realm through an autocratic regime in which all initiative came from the central administration. The tsars enjoyed the support of a powerful class of nobles who owned most of the land and were exempt from taxes and military duty.

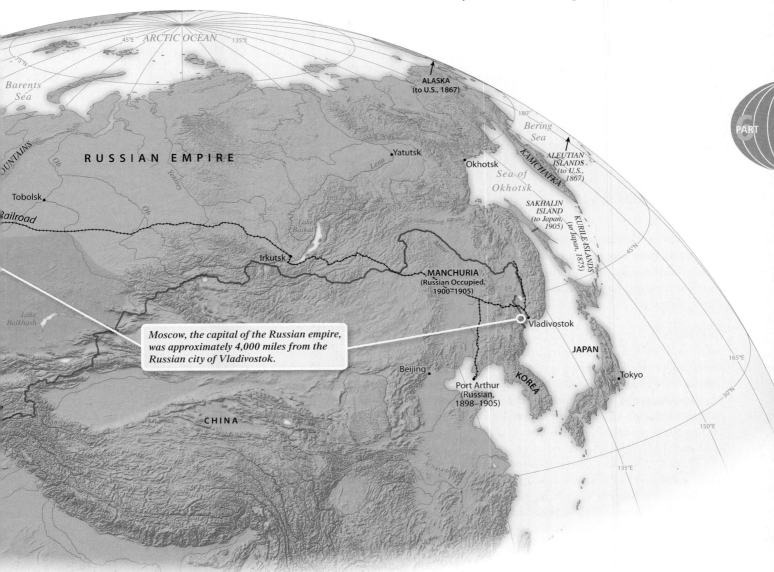

Moscow, the capital of the Russian empire, was approximately 4,000 miles from the Russian city of Vladivostok.

Peasants made up the vast majority of the population, and most of them were serfs bound to the lands that they cultivated.

Although the Russian army in the nineteenth century was huge, conflict with France and Britain in the Crimean War (1853–1856) clearly revealed the inability of Russian forces—based as they were on an agrarian economy—to compete with the industrial powers of western Europe. Military defeat compelled the tsarist autocracy to reevaluate the Russian social order and undertake an extensive program of reform along western European lines.

Tsar Alexander II of Russia.
After signing the Treaty of Paris in 1856, ending the Crimean War, Alexander abolished serfdom in the Russian empire.

Emancipation of the Serfs The key to social reform in Russia was emancipation of the serfs (1861), an institution many believed had become an obstacle to economic development. Indeed, Tsar Alexander II (reigned 1855–1881) emancipated the serfs partly with the intention of creating a mobile labor force for emerging industries, and the tsarist government encouraged industrialization as a way of strengthening the Russian empire. Thus, although Russian industrialization took place within a framework of capitalism, it differed from western European industrialization in that the

Thinking about ENCOUNTERS

Who Reaped the Benefits of Industrialization?

Over the course of the nineteenth century, industrialization increasingly linked the world's societies through the dual processes of technology transfer and the exploitation of natural resources. Yet the benefits of industrialization were not uniform throughout the world. *Why is it that some societies were able to industrialize on the British model while others were not?*

motivation for development was political and military and the driving force was government policy rather than entrepreneurial initiative. Industrialization proceeded slowly at first, but it surged during the last two decades of the nineteenth century.

Railroads In Russia the tsarist government promoted industrialization by encouraging the construction of railroads to link the distant regions of the far-flung empire. In 1860 Russia had fewer than 1,100 kilometers (700 miles) of railroads, but by 1900 there were more than 58,000 kilometers (36,000 miles). Most impressive of the Russian railroads was the trans-Siberian line, constructed between 1891 and 1904, which stretched more than 9,000 kilometers (5,600 miles) and linked Moscow with the port of Vladivostok on the Pacific Ocean. Apart from drawing the regions of the Russian empire together, railroads stimulated the development of coal, iron, and steel industries and enabled Russia to serve as a commercial link between western Europe and east Asia.

The Witte System Russian industry experienced explosive growth when Count Sergei Witte served as finance minister (1892–1903). Witte oversaw construction of the trans-Siberian railroad, and he worked to push Russian industrialization by reforming commercial law, protecting infant industries, supporting steamship companies, and promoting nautical and engineering schools. He invited foreign investors to bring their capital and expertise to Russia, and he encouraged the establishment of savings banks to raise additional investment funds at home. By 1900 Russia produced half the world's oil, and Russian steel production ranked fourth in the world, behind that of the United States, Germany, and Britain. As a result of Witte's efforts,

Russia also had enormous coal and iron industries, and government demand for weapons also supported a huge armaments industry.

Industrial Discontent Although Russia successfully began a program of industrialization, such efforts came at a high cost. As in other lands, industrial growth generated an urban working class, which endured miserable working and living conditions. Employers kept wages of overworked and poorly housed workers at the barest minimum. Moreover, economic exploitation and the lack of political freedom made workers increasingly receptive to socialist and revolutionary propaganda, which—when combined with further military defeat and political oppression—eventually undermined the Russian state itself in the early twentieth century.

Foreign Pressure In Japan, too, imperial authorities pushed industrialization, although under very different circumstances from those in Russia. Until 1853 Japan had largely closed itself off from interaction with European and American traders. The situation changed abruptly in that year, however, with the arrival of a U.S. naval squadron in Tokyo Bay. The American commander, Commodore Matthew C. Perry, trained his guns on the bakufu capital of Edo (modern Tokyo) and demanded that the shogun open Japan to diplomatic and commercial relations and sign a treaty of friendship. The shogun had no good alternative and so acquiesced to Perry's demands. Representatives of Britain, the Netherlands, and Russia soon won similar rights, all of which opened Japanese ports to foreign commerce, deprived the government of control over tariffs, and granted foreigners extraterritorial rights.

The sudden intrusion of foreign powers precipitated a domestic crisis in Japan that eventually resulted in the collapse of the Tokugawa bakufu and the restoration of imperial rule. After years of conflict and a brief civil war, the boy emperor Mutsuhito—known by his regnal name, Meiji ("Enlightened Rule")—took the reins of power on 3 January 1868.

The Meiji Restoration The Meiji restoration returned authority to the Japanese emperor and marked the birth of a new Japan. Determined to gain parity with foreign powers, a conservative coalition of daimyo, imperial princes, court nobles, and samurai formed a new government dedicated to the twin goals of prosperity and strength: "rich country, strong army." The Meiji government looked to the industrial lands of Europe and the United States to obtain the knowledge and expertise to strengthen Japan. The Meiji

---

Sergei Witte (SAYR-gay VIHT-tee)

Tokugawa (TOH-koo-GAH-wah)

Mutsuhito (MOO-tsoo-HE-taw)

Meiji (MAY-jee)

daimyo (DEYEM-yoh)

Reverberations of ● ● ● ● ● ● ● ● ● ●
The Birth of Nationalism

Nationalism came to Japan as a result of contact with the aggressive trade policies of the United States and other European nations. An elite group of reformers believed that in order to avoid domination by western powers, they had to modernize and industrialize on the western model—which included embracing the idea of a Japanese nation whose citizens would work together to promote the interests of the new state. In this case, then, the idea of creating a strong nation was initiated from the top down rather than from a groundswell of popular sentiment. Part of the way this was accomplished was through mandatory, state-funded education programs to teach both literacy as well as an appreciation of state-sanctioned national values. Consider the role mandatory public education has played in building nationalist feelings among populations around the world. Do such programs always serve the interests of states?

government sent many students and officials abroad to study everything from technology to constitutions, and it also hired foreign experts to facilitate economic development and the creation of indigenous expertise.

Economic Development Economic initiatives were critical to the process of Meiji reconstruction. Convinced that a powerful economy was the foundation of national strength, the Meiji government created a modern transportation, communications, and educational infrastructure. The establishment of telegraph, railroad, and steamship lines tied local and regional markets into a national economic network. Aiming to improve literacy rates, the government introduced a system of universal primary and secondary education.

Japanese industrialization.
The Tomioka silk factory, established in the 1870s, was one of the earliest mechanized textile factories in Japan. In this factory, as in many textile mills in Europe and North America, male managers oversaw female factory workers. © The Granger Collection, New York

What are most of the women in this drawing doing?

Universities provided advanced instruction for the best students, especially in scientific and technical fields. This infrastructure supported rapid industrialization and economic growth. Although most economic enterprises were privately owned, the government controlled military industries and established pilot programs to stimulate industrial development. During the 1880s the government sold most of its enterprises to private investors who had close ties to government officials. The result was a concentration of enormous economic power in the hands of a small group of people, collectively known as *zaibatsu*, or financial cliques. By the early twentieth century, Japan had joined the ranks of the major industrial powers.

Costs of Economic Development As in Russia, economic development came at a price, as the Japanese people

bore the social and political costs of rapid industrialization. During this period, hundreds of thousands of rural families lived in destitution, haunted by malnutrition, starvation, and infanticide. In addition, those who took up work in the burgeoning industries learned that working conditions were difficult and that the state did not tolerate labor organizations that promoted the welfare of workers.

Nevertheless, the desire to achieve political and economic equality with Euro-American industrial powers—and to avoid the domination and dependence experienced by preindustrial societies elsewhere—transformed Japan into a powerful industrial society in a single generation. Serving as symbols of Japan's remarkable development were the conclusion of an alliance with Britain as an equal power in 1902 and convincing displays of military prowess in victories over the Chinese empire (1894–1895) and the Russian empire (1904–1905).

---

zaibatsu (zeye-BAHT-soo)

SUMMARY

The process of industrialization involved the harnessing of inanimate sources of energy, the replacement of handicraft production with machine-based manufacturing, and the generation of new forms of business and labor organization. Along with industrialization came demographic growth, large-scale migration, and rapid urbanization, which increased the demand for manufactured goods by the masses of working people. Societies that underwent industrialization enjoyed sharp increases in economic productivity: they produced large quantities of high-quality goods at low prices, and their increased productivity translated into higher material standards of living. Yet industrialization brought costs as well as benefits. Family life changed dramatically in the industrial age as men, women, and children increasingly left their homes to work in factories and mines, often under appalling conditions. Socialist critics sought to bring about a more just and equitable society, and government authorities curtailed the worst abuses of the early industrial era. Meanwhile, industrialization increasingly touched the lives of peoples around the world. To avoid being dominated, Russia and Japan followed the lead of Britain, western Europe, and North America into industrialization, whereas many African, Asian, and Latin American lands became dependent on the export of raw materials to industrial societies.

STUDY TERMS

Bessemer converter (494)
cartels (497)
child labor (500)
Commodore Matthew C. Perry (506)
Communist Manifesto (502)
corporations (492)
daimyo (506)
demographic transition (498)
Eli Whitney (497)
factory system (494)
flying shuttle (493)
Friedrich Engels (502)
George Stephenson (494)
Henry Ford (497)
James Watt (493)

Karl Marx (502)
Luddites (494)
Meiji (506)
middle class (500)
Mutsuhito (506)
power loom (493)
Robert Owen (502)
Romanov (504)
Sergei Witte (506)
socialism (502)
spinning mule (493)
Tokugawa (506)
trade unions (502)
trusts (497)
Tsar Alexander II (505)
working class (500)
zaibatsu (508)

FOR FURTHER READING

Daniel R. Headrick. *The Tentacles of Progress: Technology Transfer in the Age of Imperialism, 1850–1940.* New York, 1988. Concentrates on the political and cultural obstacles that hindered transfer of European technologies to colonial lands.

Marius B. Jansen and Gilbert Rozman, eds. *Japan in Transition: From Tokugawa to Meiji.* Princeton, 1986. Important collection of essays exploring economic and social change during the era of the Meiji restoration.

Penelope Lane, Neil Raven, and K. D. M. Snell, eds. *Women, Work and Wages in England, 1600–1850.* Rochester, N.Y., 2004. Study of women's contributions to British industrialization and how it was rewarded.

Karl Marx and Friedrich Engels. *The Communist Manifesto.* Trans. by Samuel Moore. Harmondsworth, 1967. English translation of the most important tract of nineteenth-century socialism, with an excellent introduction by historian A. J. P. Taylor.

David R. Meyer. *The Roots of American Industrialization.* Baltimore, 2003. Interdisciplinary study that ties America's industrialization to increasing agricultural productivity of the antebellum period.

Kenneth Pomeranz. *The Great Divergence: China, Europe, and the Making of the Modern World Economy.* Princeton, 2000. Argues that the fortuitous location of coal deposits and access to the resources of the Americas created a uniquely advantageous framework for English industrialization.

Hans Rogger. *Russia in the Age of Modernisation and Revolution, 1881–1917.* New York, 1983. An important study of Russian social and economic development.

Peter N. Stearns. *The Industrial Revolution in World History.* Boulder, 1993. An excellent overview of industrialization, its European origins, its spread, and its effects in the larger world.

E. P. Thompson. *The Making of the English Working Class.* New York, 1966. A classic work that analyzes the formation of working-class consciousness in England from the 1790s to the 1830s.

Louise A. Tilly. *Industrialization and Gender Inequality.* Washington, D.C., 1993. A brief historiographical survey of debates on gender and industrialization in England, France, Germany, the United States, Japan, and China.

The Americas in the Age of Independence

CHAPTER **27**

Chinese immigrants employed to build the California railroads in the 1890s.

EYEWITNESS:
Fatt Hing Chin Searches for Gold from China to California

A village fish peddler, Fatt Hing Chin often roamed the coast of southern China in search of fish to sell at market. One day at the wharves, he heard a tale of mysterious but enticing mountains of gold beckoning young Chinese to cross the ocean. At age nineteen, Chin longed for the glittering mountains. He learned that he could purchase passage on a foreign ship, and in 1849 he boarded a Spanish ship to sail to California and join the gold rush.

Once at sea, Chin was surprised at the large number of young Chinese men crammed in with him in the ship's vomit-laden hold. Ninety-five difficult days and nights passed before the hills of San Francisco came into view. On arrival the travelers met Chinese veterans of life in the United States who explained the need to stick together if they were to survive and prosper.

Chin hired out as a gold miner, and after two years he accumulated his own little pile of gold. He wrote to his brothers and cousins, urging them to join him, and thus helped fuel the large-scale overseas migration of workers. Having made his fortune, though, Chin decided to return to China. Indeed, California gold provided him with the means to take a wife, build a house, and buy some land in his home country.

Although settled and prosperous, Chin longed for the excitement of California. Leaving his pregnant wife, he sailed for California again after only a year in China. He returned to mining with his brother, but the gold was more difficult to find. Inspired by the luck of another migrant, Tong Ling, who managed to get one dollar for each meal he sold, Chin's cousins in San Francisco decided to open a restaurant. Chin found the city much more comfortable than the mountains. "Let the others go after the gold in the hills," he said. "I'll wait for the gold to come to the city."

Fatt Hing Chin was one of the earliest Chinese migrants to settle in the Americas. His career path—from a miner in search of quick riches to an urban resident committed to a new homeland—was quite typical of Chinese migrants to the United States. Along with millions of others from Europe and Asia, Chinese migrants increased the ethnic diversity of American populations and stimulated political, social, and economic development in the western hemisphere.

During the late eighteenth and early nineteenth centuries, almost all the lands of the western hemisphere won their independence from European colonial powers. American peoples then struggled throughout the nineteenth century to build their own states and societies. The United States built the most powerful state in the western hemisphere and embarked on a westward push that brought most of the temperate regions of North America under U.S. control. Canada built a federal state under British Canadian leadership. The varied lands of Latin America built smaller states that often fell under the sway of local military leaders. One issue that most American peoples wrestled with, regardless of their region, was the legacy of the Enlightenment. The effort to build societies based on freedom, equality, and constitutional government was a monumental challenge that remained only partially

CHRONOLOGY

1803	Louisiana Purchase
1804–1806	Lewis and Clark expedition
1812–1814	War of 1812
1838–1839	Trail of Tears
1845–1848	Mexican-American War
1848	Seneca Falls Convention
1849	California gold rush
1850s	*La Reforma* in Mexico
1861–1865	U.S. Civil War
1867	Establishment of the Dominion of Canada
1867	French troops withdraw from Mexico
1867–1877	Reconstruction in the United States
1869	Completion of the transcontinental railroad line in the United States
1876	Battle of Little Big Horn
1876–1911	Rule of Porfirio Díaz in Mexico
1885	Completion of the Canadian Pacific Railroad
1885	Northwest Rebellion
1890	Massacre at Wounded Knee
1911–1920	Mexican revolution

realized. Indeed, Asian and European migrants joined freed slaves and native-born workers in labor systems—from plantations and factories to debt peonage—that often betrayed American promises of welcome and freedom.

The age of independence for the United States, Canada, and Latin America was a contentious era characterized by continuous mass migration and explosive economic growth, occasionally followed by deep economic stagnation, and punctuated with civil war, ethnic violence, class conflict, and battles for racial and sexual equality. Goals to build effective states, enjoy economic prosperity, and attain cultural cohesion were elusive throughout the nineteenth century and in many ways remain so even in the present day. Nevertheless, the histories of these first lands to win independence from colonial powers inspired other peoples who later sought freedom from imperial rule.

THE BUILDING OF AMERICAN STATES

After winning independence from Britain, the United States fashioned a government and began to expand rapidly to the west. Yet the United States was an unstable society composed of varied regions with diverse economic and social structures. Differences over slavery and the rights of individual states as opposed to the federal government sparked a bloody civil war in the 1860s. That conflict resulted in the abolition of slavery and the strengthening of the federal state. The experience of Canada was very different from that of the United States. Canada gained independence from Britain without fighting a war, and even though Canada also was a land of great diversity, it avoided falling into a civil war. Canada established a relatively weak federal government, which presided over provinces that had considerable power over local affairs. Latin American lands were even more diverse than their counterparts to the north, and there was never any real possibility that they could join together in a confederation. Throughout the nineteenth century Latin America was a politically fragmented region, and many individual states faced serious problems and divisions within their own societies.

The United States: Westward Expansion and Civil War

After gaining independence the United States faced the need to construct a government. During the 1780s leaders from the rebellious colonies drafted a constitution that entrusted responsibility for general issues to a federal government, reserved authority for local issues for individual states, and provided for the admission of new states and territories to the confederation. Originally, most states limited the vote to men of property, but the Enlightenment ideal of equality encouraged political leaders to extend the franchise: by the mid–nineteenth century almost all adult white men were eligible to vote.

Westward Expansion and Manifest Destiny While working to settle constitutional issues, Americans also began to expand to the west. After the American Revolution, Britain ceded to the new republic all lands between the Appalachian Mountains and the Mississippi River, and the United States doubled in size. In 1803 Napoleon Bonaparte allowed the United States to purchase France's Louisiana Territory, which extended from the Mississippi River to the

Thinking About TRADITIONS

Vanishing Ways of Life

For millennia indigenous peoples throughout the Americas had established their own cultural and economic patterns of life. *What happened to those traditions once the consolidating nation-states in North America and Latin America committed to an expansion of their territories? How did indigenous peoples resist such conquest?*

Rocky Mountains. Overnight the United States doubled in size again. Between 1804 and 1806 a geographic expedition led by Meriwether Lewis and William Clark mapped the territory and surveyed its resources. Settlers soon began to flock west in search of cheap land to cultivate. By the 1840s many Americans spoke of a "manifest destiny" to occupy all of North America from the Atlantic to the Pacific Ocean.

Conflict with Indigenous Peoples Westward expansion brought settlers and government forces into conflict with the indigenous peoples of North America, who resisted efforts to push them from their ancestral lands

and hunting grounds. However, U.S. officials and military forces supported Euro-American settlers and gradually forced the continent open to white expansion. With the Indian Removal Act of 1830, the United States government determined to move all Native Americans west of the Mississippi River into "Indian Territory" (Oklahoma). Among the tribes affected by this forced removal from the east were the Cherokees, who suffered a harrowing 800-mile migration from the eastern woodlands to Oklahoma on the Trail of Tears (1838–1839), so known because thousands died from disease, starvation, and the difficulties of relocation.

After 1840 the site of conflict between Euro-American and indigenous peoples shifted to the plains region west of

MAP 27.1

Westward expansion of the United States during the nineteenth century. Note the large land claims ceded by Britain, France, and Mexico.

Why were there no portions of North America purchased from or ceded by native Americans?

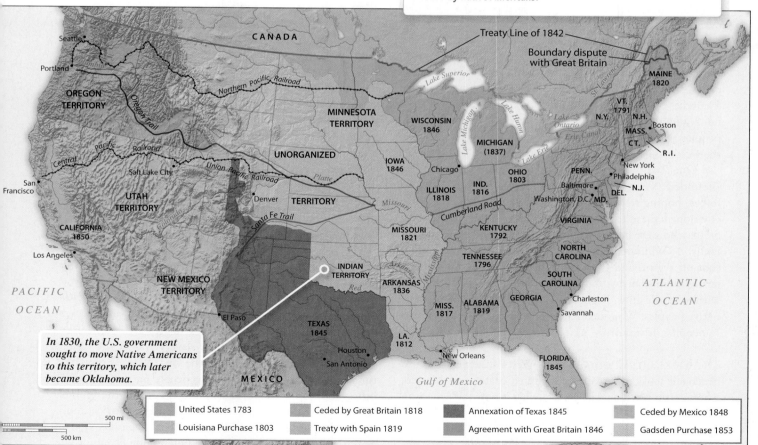

In 1830, the U.S. government sought to move Native Americans to this territory, which later became Oklahoma.

| United States 1783 | Ceded by Great Britain 1818 | Annexation of Texas 1845 | Ceded by Mexico 1848 |
| Louisiana Purchase 1803 | Treaty with Spain 1819 | Agreement with Great Britain 1846 | Gadsden Purchase 1853 |

Plains indian camp.
This photograph from the 1890s in South Dakota offers an idealized, pastoral, and peaceful image of the disappearing indigenous societies in the United States.

the Mississippi River. Settlers and ranchers in the trans-Mississippi west encountered peoples such as the Sioux, the Comanche, the Pawnee, and the Apache, who possessed firearms and outstanding equestrian skills. The native peoples of the plains offered effective resistance to encroachment by white settlers and at times won powerful victories over U.S. forces. In 1876, for example, thousands of Lakota Sioux and their allies annihilated an army under the command of Colonel George Armstrong Custer in the battle of Little Big Horn (in southern Montana). Ultimately, however, Native Americans on the plains lost the war against the forces of U.S. expansionism. U.S. forces employed cannons and deadly, rapid-fire Gatling guns against native peoples, which helped break native resistance and opened the western plains to U.S. conquest.

One last symbolic conflict took place in 1890 at Wounded Knee Creek in South Dakota. U.S. cavalry forces, hoping to suppress Sioux religious ceremonies that envisioned the disappearance of white people, chased the Sioux who were fleeing to safety in the South Dakota Badlands. At Wounded Knee Creek, a Sioux man accidentally shot off a gun, and the cavalry overreacted badly, slaughtering more than two hundred men, women, and children with machine guns. Emblematic of harsh U.S. treatment of native peoples, Wounded Knee represented the place where "a people's dream died," as a later native leader put it.

The Mexican-American War Westward expansion also generated tension between the United States and Mexico, whose territories included most of what is now the American

southwest. Texas declared independence from Mexico in 1836, largely because the many American migrants who had settled there wanted to run their own affairs. In 1845 the United States accepted Texas as a new state—against vigorous Mexican protest—and moved to consolidate its hold on the territory. Those moves led to conflicts that rapidly escalated into the Mexican-American War (1845–1848). U.S. forces instigated the war and then inflicted a punishing defeat on the Mexican army. By the Treaty of Guadalupe Hidalgo (1848), the United States took possession of approximately one-half of Mexico's territory, paying a mere fifteen million dollars in exchange for Texas north of the Rio Grande, California, and New Mexico. Thousands of U.S. and Mexican soldiers died in this conflict, and thousands of Mexican families found themselves stranded in territories annexed by the United States. Some returned to Mexico, while most stayed put and attained U.S. citizenship. This conflict nonetheless fueled Mexican nationalism, as well as Mexican disdain for the United States.

Westward expansion also created problems within the republic by aggravating tensions between regions. The most divisive issue had to do with slavery, which had vexed American politics since independence. The Enlightenment ideal of equality clearly suggested that the appropriate policy was to abolish slavery, but the framers of the Constitution recognized the sanctity of private property, including slaves. American independence initially promoted a surge of antislavery sentiment, and states from Delaware north abolished slavery within their jurisdictions. That move hardened divisions between slave and free states. Westward expansion aggravated tensions further by raising the question of whether settlers could extend slavery to newly acquired territories.

Sectional Conflict The election of Abraham Lincoln to the presidency in 1860 was the spark that ignited war between the states (1861–1865). Lincoln was an explicitly sectional candidate who was convinced that slavery was immoral and who was committed to free soil—territories without slavery. Fundamentally, slavery was at the center of the conflict that erupted into the Civil War. At the same time, the issue of slavery was also deeply intertwined with other important issues such as the nature of the Union, states' rights as opposed to the federal government's authority, and the needs of a budding industrial-capitalist system against those of an export-oriented plantation economy.

Sioux (soo)
Guadalupe Hidalgo (gwahd-l-OOP hee-DAHL-goh)

The U.S. Civil War Eleven southern states withdrew from the Union in 1860 and 1861, affirming their right to dissolve the Union and their support for states' rights. Northerners saw the situation differently. They viewed secession as illegal insurrection and an act of betrayal. They fought not only against slavery but also against the concept of a state subject to blackmail by its constituent parts. They also fought for a way of life—their emerging industrial society—and an expansive western agricultural system based on free labor.

The U.S. Civil War.
The grotesquely twisted bodies of dead Confederate soldiers lay near a fence outside Antietam, Maryland, in 1862. The Civil War was the most costly in U.S. history in number of lives lost.

Ultimately, the northern states prevailed. They brought considerable resources to the war effort—some 90 percent of the country's industrial capacity and approximately two-thirds of its railroad lines—but still they fought four bitter years against a formidable enemy. The consequences of that victory were enormous, for it ended slavery in the United States. Indeed, once Abraham Lincoln signed the Emancipation Proclamation on 1 January 1863, which made the abolition of slavery an explicit goal of the war, it was clear that a northern victory would entail radical changes in southern life. Moreover, the victory of the northern states ensured that the United States would remain politically united, and it enhanced the authority of the federal government in the American republic. Thus, as European lands were building powerful states on the foundations of revolutionary ideals, liberalism, and nationalism, the United States also forged a strong central government to supervise westward expansion and deal with the political and social issues that divided the American republic.

The Canadian Dominion: Independence without War

Autonomy and Division Canada did not fight a war for independence, and in spite of deep regional divisions, it did not experience bloody internal conflict. Instead, Canadian independence came gradually as Canadians and the British government agreed on general principles of autonomy. The distinctiveness of the two dominant ethnic groups, the British Canadians and the French Canadians, ensured that the process of building an independent society would not be smooth, but intermittent fears about the possibility of a U.S. invasion from the south helped submerge ethnic differences. By the late nineteenth century, Canada was a land in control of its own destiny.

Originally colonized by trappers and settlers from both Britain and France, the colony of New France passed into the British empire after the British victory in the Seven Years' War (1756–1763). Until the late eighteenth century, however, French Canadians outnumbered British Canadians, so imperial officials made large concessions to their subjects of French descent to forestall unnecessary strife. After 1781, however, large numbers of British loyalists fled the newly formed United States and sought refuge in Canada, thus greatly enlarging the size of the English-speaking community there.

The War of 1812 Ethnic divisions and political differences could easily have splintered Canada, but the War of 1812 stimulated a sense of unity against an external threat. The United States declared war on Britain in retaliation for encroachments on U.S. rights during the Napoleonic wars, and the British colony of Canada formed one of the front lines of the conflict. U.S. military leaders assumed that they could easily invade and conquer Canada to pressure Britain. Despite the greater resources of the United States, however, Canadian forces repelled U.S. incursions. Their victories promoted a sense of Canadian pride, and anti-U.S. sentiments became a means for covering over differences among French and British Canadians.

After the War of 1812, Canada experienced an era of rapid growth. Expanded business opportunities drew English-speaking migrants, who swelled the population. This influx threatened the identity of Quebec, and discontent in Canada reached a critical point in the 1830s. The British imperial governors of Canada did not want a repeat of the American Revolution, so between 1840 and 1867 they defused tensions by expanding home rule in Canada and permitting the provinces to govern their internal affairs.

Dominion Fear of U.S. expansion helped stifle internal conflicts among Canadians and prompted Britain to grant independence to Canada. The British North America Act of 1867 joined Quebec, Ontario, Nova Scotia, and New Brunswick and recognized them as the Dominion of Canada. Other provinces joined the Dominion later. Each province had its own seat of government, provincial legislature, and lieutenant governor representing the British crown. The act created a federal government headed by a governor-general, who acted as the British representative. An elected House of Commons and an appointed Senate rounded out the framework of governance. Without waging war, the Dominion of Canada had won control over all Canadian internal affairs, and Britain retained jurisdiction over foreign affairs until 1931.

John A. Macdonald (1815–1891) became the first prime minister of Canada, and he moved to incorporate all of British North America into the Dominion. He negotiated the purchase of the huge Northwest Territories from the Hudson Bay Company in 1869, and he persuaded Manitoba, British Columbia, and Prince Edward Island to join the Dominion. Then, to strengthen the union, he oversaw construction of a transcontinental railroad, completed in 1885. The railroad facilitated transportation and communications

MAP 27.2

The Dominion of Canada in the nineteenth century. Note the provinces that make up the modern state of Canada and the dates in which they were incorporated into the Dominion.

At what date were eastern and western Canada geographically united?

The Canadian Pacific Railroad was crucial for connecting eastern and western Canada.

throughout Canada and eventually helped bring new provinces into the Dominion: Alberta and Saskatchewan in 1905 and Newfoundland in 1949. Although maintaining ties to Britain and struggling to forge an identity distinct from its powerful neighbor to the south, Canada developed as a culturally diverse yet politically unified society.

Latin America: Fragmentation and Political Experimentation

Political unity was short-lived in Latin America. Simón Bolívar (1783–1830), hailed as the region's liberator, worked for the establishment of a large confederation that would provide Latin America with the political, military, and economic strength to resist encroachment by foreign powers. The wars of independence that he led encouraged a sense of solidarity in Latin America. But Bolívar once admitted, "I fear peace more than war," and after the defeat of the common colonial enemy, most of Latin America fragmented into numerous independent states. An important exception was the state of Brazil which, under the leadership of Dom Pedro I (1798–1834) and his son, Dom Pedro II (1825–1891), managed to maintain stability and economic prosperity through most of the nineteenth century.

Creole Elites and Political Instability Following the example of the United States, creole elites usually established republics with written constitutions for the newly independent states of Latin America. Yet Latin American leaders had less experience with self-government because Spanish and Portuguese colonial regimes were far more autocratic than was the British imperial government in North America. As a result, several Latin American lands lurched from one constitution to another as leaders struggled to create a machinery of government that would lead to political and social stability.

Creole elites also dominated the newly independent states and effectively prevented mass participation in public affairs. Less than 5 percent of the male population was active in Latin American politics in the nineteenth century, and millions of indigenous peoples lived entirely outside the political system. Those disillusioned with the system, then, had little choice beyond rebellion. To make matters worse, elites were divided by vocation—urban merchants versus rural landowners—as well as by ideology, whether liberalism, conservatism, secularism, or Roman Catholicism.

Conflicts with Indigenous Peoples One thing elites agreed on was the policy of claiming land for agriculture and ranching by pushing aside indigenous peoples. Conflict was most intense on the plains of Argentina and Chile. During the mid–nineteenth century, as the United States was crushing native resistance to western expansion in North America, Argentine and Chilean forces brought modern weapons to bear in their campaign to conquer the indigenous peoples of the South American plains. By the 1870s colonists had pacified the most productive lands and forced indigenous peoples either to assimilate to Euro-American society or to retreat to marginal lands that were unattractive to cultivators and ranchers.

Caudillos Although creole elites agreed on the policy of conquering native peoples, division in the newly independent states helped *caudillos,* or regional military leaders, come to power in much of Latin America. The wars of independence had lasted well over a decade, and they provided Latin America with military rather than civilian heroes. After independence, military leaders took to the political stage by exploiting the discontent of the masses. One of the most notable caudillos was Juan Manuel de Rosas, who from 1835 to 1852 ruled an Argentina badly divided between the cattle-herding society of the pampas (the interior grasslands) and the urban elite of Buenos Aires. Rosas called for regional autonomy in an attempt to reconcile competing interests, but he worked to centralize the government he usurped. He quelled rebellions, but he did so in bloody fashion: one writer counted 22,404 victims murdered under Rosas's rule.

Rosas did what caudillos did best: he restored order. In doing so, however, he made terror a tool of the government, and he ruled as a despot through his own personal army. Yet although caudillo rule limited freedom and undermined republican ideals, it also sometimes gave rise to liberal opposition movements in favor of democratic forms of government.

Mexico: War and Reform Independent Mexico was a case in point. The Mexican-American War caused political turmoil in Mexico and helped the caudillo General Antonio López Santa Anna (1797–1876) come to power. After the defeat and disillusion of the war, however, a liberal reform movement attempted to reshape Mexican society. Led by President Benito Juárez (1806–1872), a Mexican of indigenous ancestry, *La Reforma* of the 1850s aimed to limit the power of the military and the Roman Catholic church in Mexican society. The Constitution of 1857 set forth the ideals of *La Reforma*. It curtailed the prerogatives of priests and military elites, and it guaranteed universal male suffrage and other civil liberties, such as freedom of speech.

Mexico: Revolution *La Reforma* challenged the conservatism of Mexican elites, who led spirited opposition against it. In fact, divisions were so deep that conservatives forced

---

caudillos (KAHW-dee-yohs)
Juan Manuel de Rosas (HWAHN mahn-WEL de roh-sahs)
Buenos Aires (BWE-naws AHY-res)
Benito Juárez (beh-nee-toh WAHR-ez)

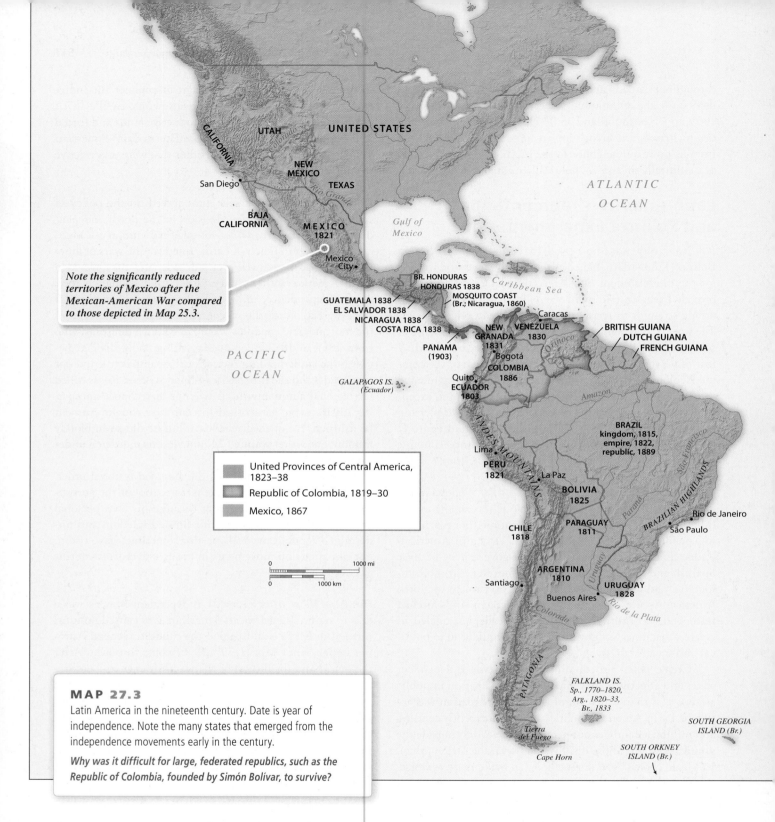

Note the significantly reduced territories of Mexico after the Mexican-American War compared to those depicted in Map 25.3.

United Provinces of Central America, 1823–38

Republic of Colombia, 1819–30

Mexico, 1867

MAP 27.3

Latin America in the nineteenth century. Date is year of independence. Note the many states that emerged from the independence movements early in the century.

Why was it difficult for large, federated republics, such as the Republic of Colombia, founded by Simón Bolívar, to survive?

the Juárez government out of Mexico City until 1861. During those difficult times, Juárez chose to suspend loan payments to foreign powers to lessen Mexico's financial woes, and that led to French, British, and Spanish intervention as Europeans sought to protect their investments in Mexico. France's Napoleon III even sent tens of thousands of troops to Mexico and proclaimed a Mexican empire. However, he was forced to withdraw French forces in 1867, and in the

same year a Mexican firing squad killed the man he had appointed emperor, the Austrian archduke Maximilian (1832–1867). Juárez managed to restore a semblance of liberal government, but Mexico remained beset by political divisions.

By the early twentieth century, Mexico was a divided land moving toward civil war. The Mexican revolution (1911–1920), a bitter and bloody conflict, broke out when

Emiliano Zapata.
Zapata, hailing from the southern state of Morelos, was the very picture of a revolutionary leader, heavily armed and sporting his dashing, trademark moustache.

In what ways did Zapata's clothing reflect his Mexican identity?

hacienda lands and began distributing the lands to the peasants, while Villa attacked and killed U.S. citizens in retaliation for U.S. support of Mexican government officials.

Despite the power and popularity enjoyed by Zapata and Villa, they did not command the resources and wealth of the government. The Mexican revolution came to an end soon after government forces ambushed and killed Zapata in 1919. Villa likewise was assassinated, on his ranch in 1923. Government forces regained control over a battered and devastated Mexico: as many as two million Mexicans may have died in the revolution. Although radicals such as Zapata and Villa were ultimately defeated, the Mexican Constitution of 1917 had already addressed some of the concerns of the revolutionaries by providing for land redistribution, universal suffrage, state-supported education, minimum wages and maximum hours for workers, and restrictions on foreign ownership of Mexican land and resources.

In the form of division, rebellion, caudillo rule, and civil war, instability and conflict plagued Latin America throughout the nineteenth century. Many Latin American peoples lacked education, profitable employment, and political representation. Simón Bolívar himself once said that "independence is the only blessing we have gained at the expense of all the rest."

AMERICAN ECONOMIC DEVELOPMENT

During the nineteenth and early twentieth centuries, two principal influences—mass migration and British investment—shaped economic development throughout the Americas. But American states reacted in different ways to migration and foreign investment. The United States and Canada absorbed waves of migrants, exploited British capital, built industrial societies, and established economic independence. The fragmented states of Latin America were unable to follow suit, as they struggled with the legacies of colonialism, slavery, and economic dependence on single export crops. Throughout the Americas, however, life and labor for freed slaves, migrants, or industrial workers often proved arduous and at times heartbreaking, even as these American workers contributed to the economic development of the region.

Migration to the Americas

Underpinning the economic development of the Americas was the mass migration of European and Asian peoples to the United States, Canada, and Latin America. Gold

middle-class Mexicans joined with peasants and workers to overthrow the powerful dictator Porfirio Díaz (1830–1915). The revolt, which attempted to topple the grossly unequal system of landed estates—whereby fully 95 percent of all peasants remained landless—turned increasingly radical as rebels engaged in guerrilla warfare against government forces. The lower classes took up weapons and followed the revolutionary leaders Emiliano Zapata (1879–1919) and Francisco (Pancho) Villa (1878–1923), charismatic agrarian rebels who organized huge armies fighting for *tierra y libertad* (land and liberty). Zapata, the son of a mestizo peasant, and Villa, the son of a field worker, embodied the ideals and aspirations of the indigenous Mexican masses and enjoyed tremendous popular support. They discredited timid governmental efforts at reform and challenged governmental political control; Zapata himself confiscated

Porfirio Díaz (pawr-FEER-eeo DEE-ahs)
Emiliano Zapata (eh-mee-LYAH-no zuh-PAH-tuh)
Francisco Villa (frahn-SEES-kow VEE-uh)

Thinking about ENCOUNTERS

Mass Migration

The nineteenth century witnessed a mass migration of Asians and Europeans to the Americas. *How did those migrants contribute to a redefinition of work and culture in the Americas? How in turn did their experience in the Americas—North, Central, and South—change migrants and their cultural practices?*

discoveries in California and Canada drew prospectors hoping to make a quick fortune, but outnumbering gold prospectors were millions of European and Asian migrants who made their way to the factories, railroad construction sites, and plantations of the Americas. Following them were others who offered the support services that made life for migrant workers more comfortable and at the same time transformed the ethnic and cultural landscape of the Americas.

Industrial Migrants After the mid–nineteenth century, European migrants flocked to North America, where they filled the factories of the growing industrial economy of the United States. Their lack of skills made them attractive to industrialists seeking workers to operate machinery or perform heavy labor at low wages. By keeping labor costs down, migrants helped increase the profitability and fuel the expansion of U.S. industry. In the 1850s alone European migrants to the United States numbered 2.3 million—almost as many as had crossed the Atlantic during the half century from 1800 to 1850—and the volume of migration surged until the early twentieth century. In the first half of the century, migrants came mostly from Ireland, Scotland, Germany, and Scandinavia to escape high rents and indebtedness. By the late nineteenth century, most European migrants came from southern and eastern Europe and included Poles, Russian Jews, Slavs, Italians, Greeks, and Portuguese. Without their labor, the remarkable industrial expansion that the United States experienced in the late nineteenth century would have been inconceivable.

Chinese migration grew rapidly after the 1840s, when British gunboats opened China to foreign influences. Between 1852 and 1875 some two hundred thousand Chinese migrated to California. Some, like Fatt Hing Chin, negotiated their own passage, but most traveled on indentured labor contracts that required them to cultivate crops or work on the Central Pacific Railroad. An additional five thousand Chinese entered Canada to search for gold in British Columbia or work on the Canadian Pacific Railroad.

Plantation Migrants Whereas migrants to the United States contributed to the development of an industrial society, those who went to Latin American lands mostly worked on agricultural plantations. Some Europeans figured among these migrants. About four million Italians sought

Immigrants to the United States.
These immigrants catch their first glimpse of the Statue of Liberty as they approach New York Harbor.

What might these immigrants have been thinking as they completed their long journeys?

opportunities in Argentina in the 1880s and 1890s, for example, and the Brazilian government paid Italian migrants to cross the Atlantic and work for coffee growers after the abolition of slavery there (1888).

Other migrants who worked on plantations in the western hemisphere came from Asia. More than fifteen thousand indentured laborers from China worked in the sugarcane fields of Cuba during the nineteenth century, and Indian migrants traveled to Jamaica, Trinidad, Tobago, and Guyana. Laborers from both China and Japan migrated to Peru, where they worked on cotton plantations, mined guano deposits, and helped build railroad lines. After the middle of the nineteenth century, expanding U.S. influence in the Pacific islands also led to Chinese, Japanese, Filipino, and Korean migrations to Hawai'i, where planters sought indentured laborers to tend sugarcane. About twenty-five thousand Chinese went to Hawai'i during the 1850s and 1860s, and later 180,000 Japanese also made their way to island plantations.

Economic Expansion in the United States

British Capital British investment capital in the United States proved crucial to the early stages of industrial development by helping businesspeople establish a textile industry. In the late nineteenth century, it also helped spur a vast expansion of U.S. industry by funding entrepreneurs who opened coal and iron ore mines, built iron and steel factories, and constructed railroad lines. The flow of investment monies was a consequence of Britain's own industrialization, which generated enormous wealth and created a need for investors to find profitable outlets for their funds.

Railroads Perhaps the most important economic development of the later nineteenth century was the construction of railroad lines that linked all U.S. regions and helped create an integrated national economy. Because of its enormous size and environmental diversity, the United States offered an abundance of natural resources for industrial exploitation. But vast distances made it difficult to maintain close economic ties between regions until a boom in railroad construction created a dense transportation, communication, and distribution network. Before the Civil War the United States had about 50,000 kilometers (31,000 miles) of railroad lines, most of them short routes east of the Mississippi River. By 1900 there were more than 320,000 kilometers (200,000 miles) of track, and the American rail network stretched from coast to coast.

Railroads decisively influenced American economic development. They provided cheap transportation for agricultural commodities, manufactured goods, and individual travelers. Railroads hauled grain, beef, and hogs from the plains states, cotton and tobacco from the south, lumber from the northwest, iron and steel from Pittsburgh, and finished products from the eastern industrial cities. Quite apart from the transportation services they provided, railroads spurred the development of other industries: they required huge amounts of coal, wood, glass, and rubber, and by the 1880s some 75 percent of U.S. steel went to the railroad industry. Railroads also required the development of new managerial skills to operate large, complicated businesses with multiple employees.

Space and Time Railroads led to drastic changes in the landscape. Indeed, the westward expansion driven by the railroad led to large-scale land clearing and the extension of farming and mining lands and brought about both human suffering for indigenous peoples and environmental damage through soil erosion and pollution. Railroads even shaped the American sense of time. Until rapid and regular rail transportation became available, communities set their clocks by the sun. As a result, New York time was eleven minutes and forty-five seconds behind Boston time. Those differences in local sun times created scheduling nightmares as well as the potential for train

The railroad.

In this lithograph of Frances F. Palmer's well-known painting *American Express Train* (ca. 1864), the railroad demonstrates its domination of the natural landscape and its role as the harbinger of change and industry.

accidents. To simplify matters, in 1883 railroad companies divided the North American continent into four zones in which all railroad clocks read precisely the same time. The general public quickly adopted "railroad time," and in 1918 the U.S. government legally established the four time zones as the national standard.

Economic Growth Led by railroads, the U.S. economy expanded at a blistering pace between 1870 and 1900. Inventors designed new products and brought them to market: electric lights, telephones, typewriters, phonographs, film photography, motion picture cameras, and electric motors all made their appearance during this era. Indeed, by the early twentieth century the United States had emerged as one of the world's major industrial powers.

Canadian Prosperity

British investment deeply influenced the development of the Canadian as well as the U.S. economy in the nineteenth and early twentieth centuries. Canadian leaders, like U.S. leaders, took advantage of British capital to industrialize without allowing their economy to fall under British control.

The National Policy After the establishment of the Dominion, politicians started a program of economic development known as the National Policy. The idea was to attract migrants, protect nascent industries through tariffs, and build national transportation systems. The centerpiece of the transportation network was the transcontinental Canadian Pacific Railroad, built largely with British investment capital and completed in 1885. The Canadian Pacific Railroad opened the western prairie lands to commerce, stimulated the development of other industries, and promoted the emergence of a Canadian national economy. The National Policy created some violent altercations with indigenous peoples who resisted encroachment on their lands and with trappers who resented disruption of their way of life, but it also promoted economic growth and independence.

As a result of the National Policy, Canada experienced booming agricultural, mineral, and industrial production in the late nineteenth and early twentieth centuries. Canadian population surged as a result of both migration and natural increase. Migrants flocked to Canada's shores from Asia and especially from Europe: between 1903 and 1914 some 2.7 million eastern European migrants settled in Canada. Fueled in part by this population growth, Canadian economic expansion took place on the foundation of rapidly increasing wheat production and the extraction of rich mineral resources, including gold, silver, copper, nickel, and asbestos. Industrialists also tapped Canadian rivers to produce the hydroelectric power necessary for manufacturing.

U.S. Investment Canada remained wary of its powerful neighbor to the south but did not keep U.S. economic influence entirely at bay. By 1918, Americans owned 30 percent of all Canadian industry, and thereafter the U.S. and Canadian economies became increasingly interdependent. Canada began to undergo rapid industrialization after the early twentieth century, as the province of Ontario benefited from the spillover of U.S. industry in the northeast.

Latin American Dependence

Latin American states did not undergo industrialization or enjoy economic development as did the United States and Canada. Colonial legacies are part of the explanation. Even when Spain and Portugal controlled the trade and investment policies of their American colonies, their home economies were unable to supply sufficient quantities of the manufactured goods that colonial markets demanded. As a result, they opened the colonies to British, French, and German trade, which in turn snuffed out local industries that could not compete with British, French, and German producers of inexpensive manufactured goods. Moreover, both in colonial times and after independence, Latin American elites retained control over local economies. Elites profited handsomely from European trade and investment and thus had little incentive to work toward economic diversification.

British Investment Foreign influence in Latin America generally took the form of investment, which brought handsome profits and considerable control over Latin American economic affairs. In Argentina, for example, British investors encouraged the development of cattle and sheep ranching. After the 1860s and the invention of refrigerated cargo ships, meat became Argentina's largest export. British investors controlled the industry and reaped the profits, however, as Argentina became Britain's principal supplier of meat.

Attempted Industrialization In a few lands, ruling elites made attempts to encourage industrialization, but with only limited success. The most notable of those efforts came when the dictatorial general Porfirio Díaz ruled Mexico (1876–1911). Díaz represented the interests of large landowners, wealthy merchants, and foreign investors. Under his rule, railroad tracks and telegraph lines connected all parts of Mexico and the production of mineral resources surged. A small steel industry produced railroad track and construction materials, and entrepreneurs also established glass, chemical, and textile industries. The capital, Mexico City, underwent a transformation during the Díaz years: it acquired paved streets, streetcar lines, and electric streetlights. But the profits from Mexican enterprises did not support continuing industrial development. Instead, they went into the pockets of the Mexican oligarchy and foreign investors who supported Díaz while a growing and discontented urban working class seethed with resentment at low wages, long hours, and foreign managers. Even as agriculture, railroad construction, and mining were booming, the standard of living for average Mexicans was declining in the late nineteenth century. Frustration with that state of affairs helps explain the sudden outbreak of violent revolution in 1911.

Despite a large proportion of foreign and especially British control, Latin American economies expanded rapidly in the late nineteenth century. Exports drove this growth: copper and silver from Mexico, bananas from Central America, rubber and coffee from Brazil, beef and wheat from Argentina, copper from Chile, and tobacco and sugar from Cuba. Other areas in the world also developed many of these same products for export, however, and competition for markets tended to drive prices down. As in the United States and Canada, foreign investment in Latin America provided capital for development, but unlike the situation in the northern lands, control over industries and exports remained in foreign hands. Latin American economies were thus subject to decisions made in the interests of foreign investors, and unstable governments could do little in the face of strong foreign intervention. Controlled by the very elites who profited from foreign intervention at the expense of their citizens, Latin American governments helped promote the region's economic dependence, despite growth in industrial and export economies.

AMERICAN CULTURAL AND SOCIAL DIVERSITY

Much of the allure of the Americas derived from their vast spaces and diverse populations. While diversity distinguished the Americas, it also provided abundant fuel for conflicts between ethnic groups, social classes, and those segregated by race or gender. The social and cultural diversity of American societies challenged their ability to achieve cultural cohesion as well as democratically inclusive states. The lingering legacies of European conquest, slavery, migration, and patriarchy highlighted contradictions between the Enlightenment ideals of freedom and equality and the realities of life for native and African-American peoples as well as recent migrants and women. In efforts to maintain their own position and preserve social stability, the dominant political forces in the Americas often repressed demands for recognition by dispossessed groups.

Multicultural Society in the United States

By the late nineteenth century, the United States had become a boisterous multicultural society whose population included indigenous peoples, Euro-American settlers, African-American laborers, and growing numbers of migrants from Europe and Asia. The poet Walt Whitman described the United States as "not merely a nation but a teeming nation of nations." Yet political and economic power rested almost exclusively with white male elites of European ancestry. The United States experienced tension and occasional conflict as members of various constituencies worked for dignity, prosperity, and a voice in society.

Native Peoples   As they expanded to the west, Euro-American settlers and ranchers pushed indigenous peoples onto reservations. Begrudging Native Americans even those meager lands, the United States embarked in the latter half of the nineteenth century on a policy designed to reduce native autonomy even further through laws and reforms aimed at assimilating tribes to the white way of life. The U.S. government and private citizens acted to undermine or destroy outright the bases of native cultural traditions. For example, government officials removed native children from their families and tribes and enrolled them in white-controlled boarding schools. These schools, such as the Carlisle Indian School and the Toledo Indian School, illustrated the extent

Assimilation programs for Native Americans.
The Apache youths at the Carlisle Indian School offer stark faces to the camera, suggesting their discontent with reform efforts directed at assimilation through education.

Reverberations of ● ● ● ● ● ● ● ● ●

The Birth of Nationalism

The most powerful group of people in the United States during the nineteenth century—white males of European ancestry—defined the nation in terms of the legacies of the American Revolution and a common western European heritage. This group often resisted incorporating other peoples from different traditions into the nation, including former slaves, immigrants from Asia and southern Europe, and Native Americans. Think about the methods that people of western European ancestry used to exclude people from other traditions from full participation in national life, and about the consequences of such exclusionary practices on the development of the United States from the nineteenth century all the way to the present. Why do ideas about who belongs in the nation have the potential to generate so much conflict?

to which white society sought to eliminate tribal influences and inculcate Christian, U.S. values. Tribal languages as well as native dress and hair fashions were banned, further distancing the children from their cultures. Native Americans, however, resisted those forms of assimilation, and over the following decades tribes rebuilt and reaffirmed native identities.

Freed Slaves The Civil War ended slavery, but it did not bring about equality for freed slaves and their African-American descendants. In an effort to establish a place for freed slaves in American society, northern forces sent armies of occupation to the southern states and forced them to undergo a program of social and political reconstruction (1867–1877). They extended civil rights to freed slaves and provided black men with voting rights. People in southern states elected biracial governments for the first time in U.S. history, and freed slaves participated actively in the political affairs of the republic.

After Reconstruction, however, the armies of occupation went home, and a violent backlash soon dismantled the reforms of Reconstruction. By the turn of the century, U.S. blacks faced violence and intimidation when they tried to vote. Southern states fashioned a rigidly segregated society that deprived the African-American population of educational, economic, and political opportunities. Although freedom was better than slavery, it was far different from the hopeful visions of the slaves who had won their emancipation.

Women Even before the Civil War, a small but growing women's movement had emerged in the United States. At the Seneca Falls Convention in 1848, feminists issued a declaration arguing "that all men and women are created equal" and demanding equal political and economic rights.

Women fought for equal rights throughout the nineteenth century, and new opportunities for education and employment offered alternatives to marriage and domesticity. Women's colleges, reform activism, and professional industrial jobs allowed some women to pursue careers over marriage. Yet meaningful economic and political opportunities for women awaited the twentieth century.

Migrants Between 1840 and 1914 some twenty-five million European migrants landed on American shores, and in the late nineteenth century most of them hailed from southern and eastern European countries. Migrants introduced new foods, music, dances, holidays, sports, and languages to U.S. society and contributed to the cultural diversity of the western hemisphere. Yet white, native-born citizens of the United States began to feel swamped by the arrival of so many migrants. Indeed, concerns about growing numbers of migrants with different cultural and social traditions eventually led to the

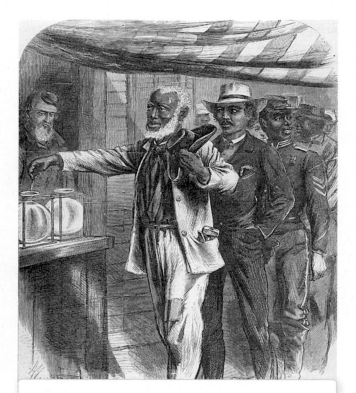

Voting rights for free blacks.
A lithograph from *Harper's Weekly* after the Civil War. An artisan, a middle-class African-American, and a black Union soldier are in the process of voting, perhaps for the first time in their lives.

What message might this image have been trying to convey?

exclusion of new arrivals from Asian lands: the U.S. government ordered a complete halt to migration from China in 1882 and Japan in 1908.

Canadian Cultural Contrasts

Ethnic Diversity British and French settlers each viewed themselves as Canada's founding people. That cleavage, which profoundly influenced Canadian political development, masked much greater cultural and ethnic diversity in Canada. French and British settlers displaced the indigenous peoples, who remain a significant minority of Canada's population today. Slavery likewise left a mark on Canada. Slavery was legal in the British empire until 1833, and many early settlers brought their slaves with them to Canada. After emancipation, blacks in Canada were free but not equal, segregated and isolated from the political and cultural mainstream. Chinese migrants also came to Canada: lured by gold rushes such as the Fraser River rush of 1858 and by opportunities to work on the Canadian Pacific Railway in the 1880s, Chinese migrants lived mostly in segregated Chinatowns in the cities of British Columbia, and like blacks they had little voice in public affairs. Between 1896 and 1914 three million migrants from Britain, the United States, and eastern Europe arrived in Canada, bringing even greater ethnic diversity with them.

Despite the heterogeneity of Canada's population, communities descended from British and French settlers dominated Canadian society, and conflict between the two communities was the most prominent source of ethnic tension throughout the nineteenth and twentieth centuries. After 1867, as British Canadians led the effort to settle the Northwest Territories and incorporate them into the Dominion, frictions between the two groups intensified. Westward expansion brought British Canadian settlers and cultivators into conflict with French Canadian fur traders, lumberjacks, and métis of mixed French and Indian ancestry.

The Métis and Louis Riel Indeed, a major outbreak of civil strife took place in the 1870s and 1880s. Native peoples and métis had moved west throughout the nineteenth century to preserve their land and trading rights, but the drive of British Canadians to the west threatened them. Louis Riel (1844–1885), who was himself a métis, emerged as the leader of the métis and indigenous peoples of western Canada. Of particular importance was his leadership in the resistance to the Canadian Pacific Railroad—and the white settlement it promised to bring—during the 1880s. In 1885 he organized a military force of métis and native peoples in the Saskatchewan river country and led an insurrection known as the Northwest Rebellion. Canadian forces quickly subdued the makeshift army, and government authorities executed Riel for treason. Although the Northwest Rebellion never had a chance of success, the execution of Riel nonetheless threatened to undermine the beginnings of Canadian national unity and foreshadowed a long term of cultural conflict between Canadians of British, French, and indigenous ancestry.

Ethnicity, Identity, and Gender in Latin America

The heritage of Spanish and Portuguese colonialism and the legacy of slavery inclined Latin American societies toward the establishment of hierarchical distinctions based on ethnicity and color. At the top of society stood the creoles, individuals of European ancestry born in the Americas; indigenous peoples, freed slaves, and their black descendants occupied the lowest rungs of the social ladder. In between were various groups of mixed ancestry. Although most Latin American states ended the legal recognition of these groups, the distinctions themselves persisted and limited their opportunities.

Migration and Cultural Diversity Large-scale migration brought cultural diversity to Latin America in the nineteenth century. Indentured laborers who went from Asian lands to Peru, Brazil, Cuba, and other Caribbean destinations carried with them many of their native cultural practices. When their numbers were relatively large, as in the case of Indian migrants to Trinidad and Tobago, they formed distinctive communities in which they observed their inherited cultural and social traditions. Migration of European workers to Argentina brought a lively diversity to the capital of Buenos Aires, which was perhaps the most cosmopolitan city of nineteenth-century Latin America. With its broad avenues, smart boutiques, and handsome buildings graced with wrought iron, Buenos Aires enjoyed a reputation as "the Paris of the Americas."

Gauchos One prominent symbol of Latin American identity was Argentina's gauchos (cowboys). Most gauchos were of mixed-race ancestry, but there were also white and black gauchos. In fact, anyone who adopted gaucho ways became a gaucho, and gaucho society acquired an ethnic egalitarianism rarely found elsewhere in Latin America. Gauchos were most prominent in the Argentine pampas, but their cultural practices linked them to the cowboys, or vaqueros, found throughout the Americas. As pastoralists herding cattle and horses on the pampas, gauchos stood apart from both the indigenous peoples and the growing urban and agricultural elites who gradually displaced them with large landholdings and cattle ranches that spread to the pampas.

gauchos (GAHW-chohs)
vaqueros (bah-KEH-rohs)

Sources from the Past

The Meaning of Freedom for an Ex-Slave

Even before the conclusion of the Civil War brought slavery to an end in the United States, Jourdan Anderson had taken the opportunity to run away and claim his freedom. After the war his former master, Colonel P. H. Anderson, wrote a letter asking him to return to work on his Tennessee plantation. In responding from his new home in Dayton, Ohio, Anderson respectfully referred to the colonel as "my old master" and addressed him as "sir." Yet Anderson's letter makes it clear that his family's freedom and welfare were his principal concerns.

I want to know particularly what the good chance is you propose to give me. I am doing tolerably well here; I get $25 a month, with victuals and clothing; have a comfortable home for Mandy (the folks here call her Mrs. Anderson), and the children, Milly, Jane and Grundy, go to school and are learning well; the teacher says Grundy has a head for a preacher. They go to Sunday-School, and Mandy and me attend church regularly. We are kindly treated; sometimes we overhear others saying, "Them colored people were slaves" down in Tennessee. The children feel hurt when they hear such remarks, but I tell them it was no disgrace in Tennessee to belong to Col. Anderson. Many darkies would have been proud, as I used to was, to call you master. Now, if you will write and say what wages you will give me, I will be better able to decide whether it would be to my advantage to move back again.

As to my freedom, which you say I can have, there is nothing to be gained on that score, as I got my freepapers in 1864 from the Provost-Marshal-General of the Department at Nashville. Mandy says she would be afraid to go back without some proof that you are sincerely disposed to treat us justly and kindly—and we have concluded to test your sincerity by asking you to send us our wages for the time we served you. This will make us forget and forgive old scores, and rely on your justice and friendship in the future. I served you faithfully for thirty-two years and Mandy twenty years. At $25 a month for me, and $2 a week for Mandy, our earnings would amount to $11,680. Add to this the interest for the time our wages has been kept back and deduct what you paid for our clothing and three doctor's visits to me, and pulling a tooth for Mandy, and the balance will show what we are in justice entitled to. Please send the money by Adams Express, in care of V. Winters, esq, Dayton, Ohio. If you fail to pay us for faithful labors in the past we can have little faith in your promises in the future. We trust the good Maker has opened your eyes to the wrongs which you and your fathers have done to me and my fathers, in making us toil for you for generations without recompense. Here I draw my wages every Saturday night, but in Tennessee there was never any pay day for the negroes any more than for the horses and cows. Surely there will be a day of reckoning for those who defraud the laborer of his hire.

In answering this letter please state if there would be any safety for my Milly and Jane, who are now grown up and both good-looking girls. You know how it was with poor Matilda and Catherine. I would rather stay here and starve and die if it comes to that than have my girls brought to shame by the violence and wickedness of their young masters. You will also please state if there has been any schools opened for the colored children in your neighborhood, the great desire of my life now is to give my children an education, and have them form virtuous habits.

For Further Reflection

■ In what clever ways does Jourdan Anderson test the seriousness of his former owner's offer of employment, and what does his approach say about the meaning of black freedom?

Source: Leon F. Litwack. *Been in the Storm So Long: The Aftermath of Slavery.* New York: Knopf, 1979, pp. 334–35.

Male Domination Even more than in the United States and Canada, male domination was a central characteristic of Latin American society in the nineteenth century. Women could not vote or hold office, nor could they work or manage estates without permission from their male guardians. In rural areas, women were liable to rough treatment and assault by gauchos and other men steeped in the values of *machismo*—a social ethic that honored male strength, courage, aggressiveness, assertiveness, and cunning. Women did carve spaces for themselves outside or alongside the male world of machismo, and this was especially true in the home and in the marketplace, where Latin American women exerted great influence and control. In addition, although Latin American lands did not generate a strong women's movement, they did begin to expand educational opportunities for girls and young women after the mid–nineteenth century. In large cities most girls received some formal schooling, and women usually filled teaching positions in the public schools that proliferated throughout Latin America in the late nineteenth century.

SUMMARY

After gaining independence from European colonial powers, the states of the western hemisphere worked to build stable and prosperous societies. The independent American states faced difficult challenges as they sought to construct viable societies on the Enlightenment principles of freedom, equality, and constitutional government. The United States and Canada built large federal societies in North America, whereas a series of smaller states governed affairs in Latin America. Throughout the hemisphere descendants of European settlers subdued indigenous American peoples and built societies dominated by Euro-American peoples. They established agricultural economies, exploited natural resources, and in some lands launched processes of industrialization. They accepted streams of European and Asian migrants, who contributed to American cultural diversity. All American lands experienced tensions arising from social, economic, cultural, and ethnic differences, which led occasionally to violent civil conflict and often to smoldering resentments and grievances. The making of independent American societies was not a smooth process, but it reflected the increasing interdependence of all the world's peoples.

STUDY TERMS

Abraham Lincoln (514)
Antonio Lopez Santa Anna (517)
Battle of Little Big Horn (514)
Benito Juárez (517)
British North America Act (516)
Buenos Aires (517)
Canadian Pacific railroad (522)
caudillos (517)
Emancipation Proclamation (515)
Emiliano Zapata (519)
Francisco (Pancho) Villa (519)
gauchos (525)
Guadalupe Hidalgo (514)
Indian Removal Act of 1830 (513)
John A. Macdonald (516)

Juan Manuel de Rosas (517)
La Reforma (517)
manifest destiny (512)
massacre at Wounded Knee (514)
Mexican-American War (514)
National Policy (522)
Northwest Rebellion (525)
Porfirio Díaz (519)
railroad time (522)
Reconstruction (524)
Seneca Falls Convention (524)
Sioux (514)
Trail of Tears (513)
United States Civil War (515)
vaqueros (525)
War of 1812 (515)

FOR FURTHER READING

Victor Bulmer-Thomas, John H. Coatsworth, and Robert Cortés Conde, eds. *The Cambridge Economic History of Latin America. Vol. I: The Colonial Era and the Short Nineteenth Century.* Cambridge, 2006. Scholarly collection of essays that outlines the region's main economic trends and developments.

Ellen C. DuBois. *Feminism and Suffrage: The Emergence of an Independent Women's Movement in America, 1848–1869.* Ithaca, 1984. Traces the rise and character of the U.S. women's movement in the nineteenth century.

Eric Foner. *Reconstruction: America's Unfinished Revolution.* New York, 2002. Chronicles how black and white Americans responded to the changes brought about by the end of slavery in the aftermath of the Civil War.

David Barry Gaspar and Darlene Clark Hine, eds. *Beyond Bondage: Free Women of Color in the Americas.* Chicago, 2004. Collection of essays on free black women and their unique abilities to negotiate social and legal institutions in the era of slavery.

Tom Holm. *The Great Confusion in Indian Affairs: Native Americans and Whites in the Progressive Era.* Austin, 2005. Study of Native American resistance to the American government's attempts at subjugation.

Patricia Nelson Limerick. *The Legacy of Conquest: The Unbroken Past of the American West.* New York, 1987. A provocative work exploring the influences of race, class, and gender in the conquest of the American west.

J. R. Miller. *Skyscrapers Hide the Heavens: A History of Indian-White Relations in Canada.* Toronto, 1989. An important study of Canadian policies toward indigenous peoples.

Walter Nugent. *Crossings: The Great Transatlantic Migrations, 1870–1914.* Bloomington, 1992. Provides an overview and analysis of the mass migrations to North America in the nineteenth and twentieth centuries.

Robert L. Scheina. *Latin American Wars.* Vol. 1: *The Age of the Caudillos, 1791–1899.* Washington, D.C., 2003. By examining the wars of independence, this work uncovers the reasons behind the failures of Latin American state building.

Ronald Takaki. *A Different Mirror: A History of Multicultural America.* Boston, 1993. A spirited account of the contributions made by peoples of European, African, Asian, and Native American ancestry to the modern American society.

The Building of Global Empires
CHAPTER 28

A British husband and wife sit at the breakfast table attended by Indian servants.

EYEWITNESS:
Cecil John Rhodes Discovers Imperial Diamonds Are Forever

Few Europeans had traveled to south Africa by the mid–nineteenth century, but the discovery of diamonds and rich gold deposits brought European settlers to the region in large numbers. Among the arrivals was Cecil John Rhodes, an eighteen-year-old student at Oxford University, who in 1871 went to south Africa in search of a climate that would relieve his tuberculosis. While there, Rhodes bought claims in the diamond fields, and he bought the rights to others' claims when they looked promising. By 1889, at age thirty-five, he had almost monopolized diamond mining in south Africa, and he controlled 90 percent of the world's diamond production. With ample financial backing, Rhodes also built up a healthy stake in the gold-mining business and entered politics, serving as prime minister (1890–1896) of the British Cape Colony.

Yet Rhodes's ambitions went far beyond business and local politics. In his vision the Cape Colony would serve as a base of operations for the extension of British control to all of Africa. Under Rhodes's guidance, Cape Colony annexed Bechuanaland (modern Botswana) in 1885, and in 1895 it added Rhodesia (modern Zambia and Zimbabwe) to its holdings. But Rhodes's plan did not stop with Africa: he urged the expansion of the British empire until it embraced all the world, including the United States of America. Rhodes considered British imperial expansion as a duty to humankind: "We are the finest race in the world," he said in 1877, "and the more of the world we inhabit, the better it is for the human race." In his sense of superiority to other peoples, his compulsion to expand, and his craving to extract wealth from distant parts of the world, Rhodes represented well the views of European imperialists who carved the world into colonies during the nineteenth century.

From the days of ancient Mesopotamia and Egypt to the present, strong societies have often sought to dominate their weaker neighbors by subjecting them to imperial rule. Yet during the second half of the nineteenth century, a handful of western European states wrote a new chapter in the history of imperialism. Strong nationalist sentiments enabled them to mobilize their populations for purposes of overseas expansion. Industrialization equipped them with the most effective tools and the most lethal weapons available anywhere in the world. Three centuries of experience with maritime trade in Asia, Africa, the Americas, and Oceania provided them with unparalleled knowledge of the world and its peoples. With those advantages, western European peoples conquered foreign armies, dominated foreign economies, and imposed their hegemony throughout the world. Toward the end of the century, the United States and Japan joined European states as imperial powers.

The establishment of global empires had far-reaching effects. In many ways, imperialism tightened links between the world's societies. Imperial powers encouraged trade between dominant states and their overseas colonies, for example, and they organized mass migrations of laborers to work in agricultural and industrial ventures. Yet imperialism also fostered divisions between the world's peoples. Powerful tools, deadly weapons, and global

Cecil Rhodes (see-sihl rhohdz)
Bechuanaland (bech-oo-AH-nuh-land)

529

CHRONOLOGY

1805–1848	**Reign of Muhammad Ali in Egypt**
1808–1839	**Reign of Sultan Mahmud II**
1809–1882	**Life of Charles Darwin**
1816–1882	**Life of Count Joseph Arthur de Gobineau**
1824	**Founding of Singapore by Thomas Stamford Raffles**
1839–1842	**Opium War**
1839–1876	**Tanzimat era**
1850–1864	**Taiping rebellion**
1853–1902	**Life of Cecil Rhodes**
1857	**Sepoy Rebellion**
1859–1869	**Construction of the Suez Canal**
1860–1864	**Land wars in New Zealand**
1860–1895	**Self-Strengthening Movement**
1884–1885	**Berlin West Africa Conference**
1894–1895	**Sino-Japanese War**
1897–1901	**Term of office of U.S. president William McKinley**
1898–1899	**Spanish-Cuban-American War**
1899–1902	**South African War (Boer War)**
1901–1909	**Term of office of U.S. president Theodore Roosevelt**
1904–1905	**Russo-Japanese War**
1904–1914	**Construction of the Panama Canal**
1905–1906	**Maji-Maji rebellion**
1908–1918	**Young Turk era**

hegemony tempted European peoples to consider themselves superior to their subjects throughout the world: modern racism is one of the legacies of imperialism. Another effect of imperialism was the development of both resistance and nationalism in subject lands. Thus, although formal empires almost entirely dissolved in the twentieth century, the influence of global imperialism continues to shape the contemporary world.

FOUNDATIONS OF EMPIRE

In nineteenth-century Europe, proponents of empire advanced a variety of political, economic, and cultural arguments to justify the conquest or economic control of foreign lands. The imperialist ventures that they promoted enjoyed dramatic success partly because of the increasingly sophisticated technologies developed by European industry.

Motives of Imperialism

Modern Imperialism The building of empires is an old story in world history. By the nineteenth century, however, European observers recognized that empires of their day were different from those of earlier times. Accordingly, about midcentury they began to speak of *imperialism,* and by the 1880s the recently coined term had made its way into popular speech and writing throughout western Europe. In contemporary usage, imperialism refers to the domination over subject lands in the larger world. Sometimes that domination came through formal imperialism, which involved military conquest and the establishment of political control. Frequently, however, it arose through what is known as informal imperialism: that is, the domination of trade, investment, and business activities that enabled imperial powers to profit from subject societies and influence their affairs without going to the trouble of exercising direct political control.

Modern Colonialism Like the building of empires, the establishment of colonies in foreign lands is a practice dating from ancient times. In modern times, however, colonialism refers not just to the settlement of colonists in new lands but also to the political, social, economic, and cultural structures that enabled imperial powers to dominate subject lands. In some places, such as North America, Chile,

Reverberations of ● ● ● ● ● ● ● ● ● ●

The Birth of Nationalism

State governments sometimes used popular nationalist sentiment for their own purposes when it came to imperial expansion. One characteristic feature of nationalism is that nationalists often define their common bonds in opposition to other peoples and traditions: thus, national unity tends to be most strongly expressed when members feel threatened by outside forces. During the nineteenth century, some governments sought to capitalize on this characteristic of nationalism to gain popular support for imperial expansion, and also to manipulate political opinion at home. The Abyssinian campaign of 1862 is but one example of this phenomenon: during an election year, the British Conservative party used an incident in which several British citizens had been taken hostage by the Ethiopian king as a way to whip up nationalist outrage against both the Ethiopians and the ruling British Liberal party. In part because of this nationalist fervor, the Liberals were defeated and the Conservatives were voted into power. What might be the short- and long-term consequences of manipulating nationalist feeling for political purposes?

Argentina, Australia, New Zealand, and South Africa, European powers established settler colonies populated largely by migrants from the home societies. Yet contemporary scholars also speak of European colonies in India, southeast Asia, and sub-Saharan Africa, even though European migrants did not settle there in large numbers. In such places, European agents and officials established political control and controlled domestic and foreign policy, integrated local economies into the network of global capitalism, and promoted European educational and cultural preferences. Contemporary scholars also speak of areas, particularly in the Ottoman Empire and China, where Europeans did not establish formal colonies but nevertheless dominated finances, economy, and foreign policies to such a degree that they represented a form of imperial domination known as informal imperialism.

Economic Motives of Imperialism During the second half of the nineteenth century, many Europeans came to believe that imperial expansion and colonial domination were crucial for the survival of their societies. A wide range of motives encouraged European peoples to launch campaigns of domination, conquest, and control. Some advocates argued that imperialism was in the economic interests of European societies as well as individuals. They pointed out that overseas colonies could serve as reliable sources of raw materials: rubber, tin, and copper were vital industrial products, for example, and by the late nineteenth century petroleum had also become a crucial industrial resource.

Political Motives of Imperialism Geopolitical arguments were also important for justifying imperialism. Even if colonies were not economically beneficial, imperialists held that it was crucial for political and military reasons to maintain them. Some overseas colonies occupied strategic sites on the world's sea-lanes, and others offered harbors or supply stations for commercial and naval ships. Advocates of imperialism sought to gain those advantages for their own states and to deny them to rivals.

Imperialism had its uses also for domestic politics. In an age when socialists and communists directly confronted industrialists, European politicians and national leaders sought to defuse social tension and inspire patriotism by focusing public attention on foreign imperialist ventures. Even spiritual motives fostered imperialism. Like the Jesuits in the early modern era, missionaries flocked to African and Asian lands in search of converts to Christianity, and their spiritual campaigns provided a powerful religious justification for imperialism. Furthermore, missionaries often facilitated communications between imperialists and subject peoples, and they sometimes provided European officials with information they needed to maintain control of overseas colonies.

Cecil Rhodes.
Here, Rhodes rests in the goldfields of South Africa, about 1897.

Thinking about TRADITIONS

New Imperialism?

The building of empires stretched back historically as far as the beginning of written history. *How did the so-called new imperialism of the nineteenth and twentieth centuries differ from earlier imperial traditions?*

Cultural Motives of Imperialism While missionaries sought to introduce Christianity to subject peoples, their goals were compatible with those of other Europeans who sought to bring them "civilization" in the form of political order and social and cultural enlightenment. French imperialists routinely invoked the *mission civilisatrice* ("civilizing mission") as justification for their expansion into Africa and Asia, and other European powers routinely justified foreign intervention as their duty to civilize "backward" peoples.

Tools of Empire

Even the strongest motives would not have enabled imperialists to impose their rule throughout the world without the powerful technological advantages of industrialization. During the nineteenth century, industrialists devised effective technologies of transportation, communication, and war that enabled European imperialists to have their way in the larger world.

Transportation Technologies The most important innovations in transportation involved steamships and railroads. During the 1830s British naval engineers adapted steam power to military uses and built large, ironclad ships equipped with powerful guns. These steamships traveled much faster than any sailing vessel, and as an additional advantage they could ignore the winds and travel in any direction. Because of that, they could travel much farther upriver than sailboats, which enabled imperialists to project power deep into the interior regions of foreign lands.

The construction of new canals enhanced the effectiveness of steamships. Both the Suez Canal (constructed 1859–1869) and the Panama Canal (constructed 1904–1914) facilitated the building and maintenance of empires by enabling naval vessels to travel rapidly between the world's seas and oceans. They also lowered the costs of trade between imperial powers and subject lands.

mission civilisatrice (mee-see-on sih-vihl-ihs-a-trihs)
Omdurman (om-door-MAHN)
Khartoum (khar-TOOM)

Once imperialists had gained control of overseas lands, railroads helped them to maintain their hegemony and organize local economies to their own advantage. Rail transportation enabled colonial officials and armies to travel quickly through the colonies. It also facilitated trade in raw materials and the distribution of European manufactured goods in the colonies.

Military Technologies European industrialists also churned out enormous quantities of increasingly powerful weapons. By the middle of the nineteenth century, European armies were using breech-loading firearms with rifled bores that were far more accurate and reliable than any other firearm. By the 1870s Europeans were experimenting with rifled machine guns, and in the 1880s they adopted the Maxim gun, a light and powerful weapon that fired eleven bullets per second.

These firearms provided European armies with an arsenal vastly stronger than any other in the world. Accurate rifles and machine guns devastated opposing overseas forces, enabling European armies to impose colonial rule against far more numerous opponents. In 1898, for example, a British army with twenty machine guns and six gunboats encountered a Sudanese force at Omdurman, near Khartoum on the Nile River. During five hours of fighting, the British force lost 368 men, whereas machine guns and explosive charges fired from gunboats killed some 11,000 Sudanese. The battle of Omdurman opened the door for British colonial rule in Sudan.

Communications Technologies Communications also benefited from industrialization. In the 1830s it took as long as two years for a British correspondent to receive a reply to a letter sent to India by sailing ship. By the 1850s, after the introduction of steamships, correspondence could make the round-trip between London and Bombay in four months. With the opening of the Suez Canal in 1869, steamships traveled from Britain to India in less than two weeks.

The invention of the telegraph made it possible to exchange messages even faster. By 1870 submarine cables carried messages between Britain and India in about five hours. By 1902 cables linked all parts of the British empire throughout the world, and other European states maintained cables to support communications with their own colonies. Their monopoly on telegraphic communications allowed imperial officials to rapidly mobilize forces to deal with troubles, and the telegraph allowed merchants to respond quickly to developments of economic and commercial significance. Rapid communication was an integral structural element of empire.

EUROPEAN IMPERIALISM

Aided by powerful technologies, European states launched an unprecedented round of empire building in the second half of the nineteenth century. Imperial expansion began with the British conquest of India. Competition between imperial powers led to European intrusion into central Asia, the establishment of colonies in southeast Asia, and interference in the Ottoman and Qing empires in southwest and east Asia. Fearful that rivals might gain control over remaining regions, European states embarked on a campaign of frenzied expansion in the 1880s that brought almost all of Africa and Pacific Ocean territories into their empires. Throughout this period, Europeans were engaged simultaneously in projects of settler colonialism, formal imperialism without large numbers of settlers, and informal imperialism in which sovereignty was compromised by widespread economic interference.

Sepoy Rebellion of 1857.
Troops loyal to the British hang two participants of the Sepoy Rebellion on a makeshift gallows. During the Rebellion, British forces frequently resorted to summary execution without trial for those they suspected of involvement.

What kind of message was the placement of such gallows intended to convey?

Whether European powers engaged in one kind or another of imperial project depended largely on rivalries with other European powers, the strategic or economic importance of a given area, and the level and type of resistance offered by indigenous peoples.

The British Empire in India

The British empire in south Asia and southeast Asia grew out of the mercantile activities of the English East India Company, which enjoyed a monopoly on English trade with India. The East India Company obtained permission from the Mughal emperors of India to build fortified posts on the coastlines. In the seventeenth century, company merchants traded mostly for Indian pepper and cotton, Chinese silk and porcelain, and spices from southeast Asia. During the eighteenth century, tea and coffee became the most prominent trade items, and European consumers acquired a permanent taste for both beverages.

Company Rule After the death of the emperor Aurangzeb in 1707, the Mughal state entered a period of decline. The East India Company took advantage of Mughal weakness to strengthen and expand its trading posts. In the 1750s company merchants began campaigns of outright conquest in India, largely to protect their commercial interests. From

their forts at Calcutta, Madras, and Bombay, the merchants extended their authority inland and won official rights to rule from the Mughal emperors and local authorities. They enforced their rule with armies composed mostly of Indian troops known as sepoys.

In 1857, following widespread campaigns of conquest that left most of the subcontinent under British control, the Indian sepoys of the Bengal army revolted. The Sepoy Rebellion, as it became known, was quickly augmented by civilian peasants and disgruntled elites in north-central India who were deeply dissatisfied with recent British policies regarding taxation and law. To regain control, the British waged a bloody campaign of retribution in which many thousands of Indians—including civilians not directly involved in the rebellion—lost their lives through summary hangings and the destruction of villages. Once order was restored in 1858, the British government abolished the East India Company and assumed direct rule over the subcontinent.

British Imperial Rule Under the new administration, Queen Victoria (reigned 1837–1901) assigned responsibility for Indian policy to the newly established office of secretary of state for India. A viceroy represented British royal

Mughal (MOO-guhl)
Qing (ching)

authority and administered the colony through an elite Indian civil service staffed almost exclusively by the English. Indians served in low-level bureaucratic positions, but British officials formulated all domestic and foreign policy in India.

Under both company rule and direct colonial administration, British rule transformed India. To profit from India's enormous size and wealth, British officials cleared forests and encouraged the cultivation of crops, such as tea, coffee, and opium, that were especially valuable trade items. They restructured landholdings and ensured that land taxes financed the costs of British rule. They built extensive railroad and telegraph networks that tightened links between India and the larger global economy. They also constructed new canals, harbors, and irrigation systems to support commerce and agriculture.

Especially after 1857, British colonial authorities made little effort to promote Christianity. They did, however, establish English-style schools for the children of Indian

sati (suh-TEE)

elites, and they suppressed Indian customs that conflicted with European law or values. Most prominent of those customs were sati (the practice of widows burning themselves on their husbands' funeral pyres), infanticide, and slavery.

Imperialism in Southeast Asia

The Dutch East Indies As the East India Company and British colonial agents tightened their grip on India, competition among European states kindled further empire-building efforts. In southeast Asia, Dutch officials tightened their control and extended their authority throughout the Dutch East Indies, the archipelago that makes up the modern state of Indonesia. Along with cash crops of sugar, tea, coffee, and tobacco, exports of rubber and tin made the Dutch East Indies a valuable and productive colony.

British Colonies in Southeast Asia In the interests of increasing trade between India, southeast Asia, and China, British imperialists moved in the nineteenth century to

MAP 28.1

Imperialism in Asia, ca. 1914. Date is year of conquest. Note the claims made by various industrial powers.

Which territories remained unclaimed, and why? Which power claimed the most imperial territory in Asia?

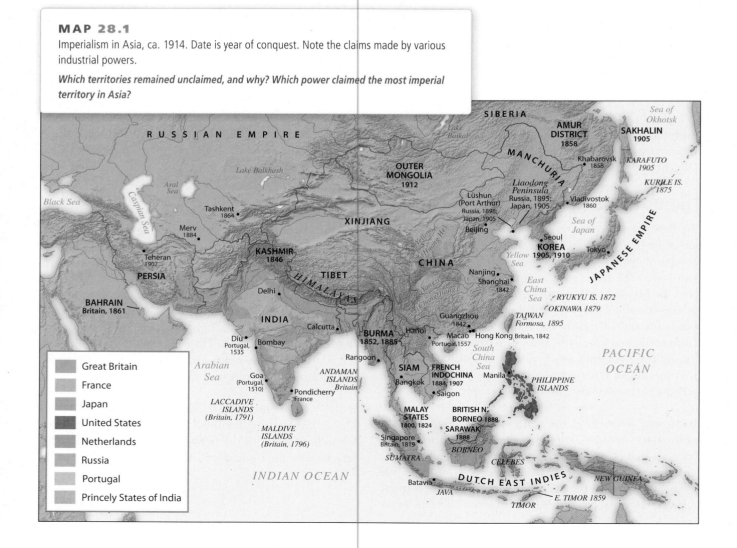

establish a presence in southeast Asia. By the 1880s they had established colonial authority in Burma, which became a source of teak, ivory, rubies, and jade. In 1824 Thomas Stamford Raffles founded the port of Singapore, which soon became the busiest center of trade in the Strait of Melaka. Administered by the colonial regime in India, Singapore served as the base for the British conquest of Malaya (modern Malaysia) in the 1870s and 1880s. Besides offering ports that enabled the British navy to control sea-lanes linking the Indian Ocean with the South China Sea, Malaya provided abundant supplies of tin and rubber.

French Indochina   French imperialists built the large southeast Asian colony of French Indochina, consisting of the modern states of Vietnam, Cambodia, and Laos, between 1859 and 1893. Like their British counterparts in India, French colonial officials introduced European-style schools and sought to establish close connections with native elites. Unlike their rivals, French officials also encouraged conversion to Christianity, and as a result the Roman Catholic church became prominent throughout French Indochina, especially Vietnam. By century's end, all of southeast Asia had come under European imperial rule except for the kingdom of Siam (modern Thailand), which preserved its independence largely because colonial officials regarded it as a convenient buffer state between British-dominated Burma and French Indochina.

Informal Imperialism in the Ottoman and Qing Empires

As in India, the Indonesian islands, and Vietnam, European powers in the nineteenth century frequently seized territories outright and ruled them as colonies. More frequently, however, European (and later U.S.) forces used their economic and military power to force concessions out of militarily weak societies. They won rights for businesses to seek opportunities on favorable terms, gained influence in political affairs, and enabled industrial capitalists to realize huge profits without going to the trouble and expense of establishing formal colonies. In the last half of the nineteenth century, two formerly powerful societies—the Ottoman and the Qing empires—increasingly came under such informal imperialism as each struggled with military weakness and internal problems in contrast to the industrialized and competitive nation-states of Europe. Although reform movements emerged in both lands, the results were inadequate, and by the early twentieth century both empires were still firmly in the grip of foreign domination.

Military Decline   By the late seventeenth century, it was already clear that Ottoman forces lagged behind European armies in strategy, tactics, weaponry, and training. Loss of military power translated into declining effectiveness of the central government, which was losing power in the provinces to its own officials. In addition, although the Ottoman government managed to maintain its authority in Anatolia as well as in Iraq, it suffered serious territorial losses in the Caucasus, central Asia, and the Balkan provinces of Greece (independent 1830) and Serbia (independent 1867).

Most significant, however, was the loss of Egypt. In 1798 the ambitious French general Napoleon invaded Egypt in hopes of using it as a springboard for an attack on the British empire in India. His campaign was a miserable failure, but the invasion sparked turmoil in Egypt, as local elites battled to seize power after Napoleon's departure. The ultimate victor was the energetic general Muhammad Ali, who built a powerful army modeled on European forces and ruled Egypt from 1805 to 1848. He also launched a program of industrialization, concentrating on cotton textiles and armaments. Although he remained nominally subordinate to the Ottoman sultan, by 1820 he had established himself as the effective ruler of Egypt, which was the most powerful land in the Muslim world. He even invaded Syria and Anatolia, threatening to capture Istanbul and topple the Ottoman state. Indeed, the Ottoman dynasty survived only because British forces intervened out of fear that Ottoman collapse would result in a sudden and dangerous expansion of Russian influence.

Economic Difficulties   Meanwhile, European textiles and manufactured goods began to flow into the Ottoman empire in the eighteenth and nineteenth centuries. Because these items were inexpensive and high-quality products, they placed considerable pressure on Ottoman artisans and crafts workers. Gradually, the Ottoman empire moved toward financial dependency on Europe. After the middle of the nineteenth century, economic development in the Ottoman empire depended heavily on foreign loans, as European capital financed the construction of railroads, utilities, and mining enterprises. Interest payments grew to the point that they consumed more than half of the empire's revenues. In 1882 the Ottoman state was unable to pay interest on its loans and had no choice but to accept European administration of its debts.

The Capitulations   Nothing symbolized foreign influence more than the capitulations, agreements that exempted European visitors from Ottoman law and provided European powers with extraterritoriality—the right to exercise jurisdiction over their own citizens according to their own laws. Capitulations also served as instruments of economic penetration by European businesspeople who established tax-exempt banks and commercial enterprises in the Ottoman empire, and they permitted foreign governments to levy duties on goods sold in Ottoman ports.

Caucasus (KAW-kuh-suhs)

The Reforms of Mahmud II In response to recurring and deepening crises, Ottoman leaders launched a series of reforms designed to strengthen and preserve the state. In the early nineteenth century, a significant period of reform occurred under the leadership of Sultan Mahmud II (reigned 1808–1839). Mahmud's program remodeled Ottoman institutions along western European lines, especially in the creation of a more effective army. Before long, Ottoman recruits wore European-style uniforms and studied at military and engineering schools that taught European curricula. Equally important, Mahmud's government created a system of secondary education for boys to facilitate the transition from mosque schools, which provided primary education, to newly established scientific, technical, and military academies. To make his authority more effective, the sultan established European-style ministries, constructed new roads, built telegraph lines, and inaugurated a postal service. By the time of Mahmud's death in 1839, the Ottoman empire had shrunk in size, but it was also more manageable and powerful than it had been since the early seventeenth century.

The Tanzimat Era Continuing defeats on the battlefield and the rise of separatist movements among subject peoples, however, prompted the ruling classes to undertake even more radical reforms during the Tanzimat ("reorganization") era (1839–1876). In designing their program, Tanzimat reformers drew considerable inspiration from Enlightenment thought and the constitutional foundations of western European states. One of their primary aims was to make Ottoman law more acceptable to Europeans so

Mahmud II (mah-MOOD)
Tanzimat (TAHNZ-ee-MAT)

MAP 28.2

Territorial losses of the Ottoman empire, 1800–1923. Compare the borders of the Ottoman empire in 1800 with what was left of the empire in 1914.

What might have been the strategic value of the remaining Ottoman territories?

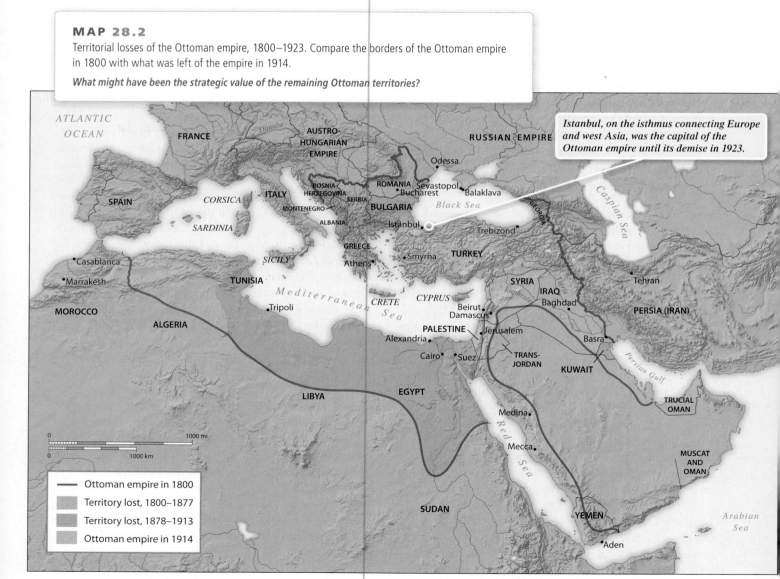

Istanbul, on the isthmus connecting Europe and west Asia, was the capital of the Ottoman empire until its demise in 1923.

Legend:
- Ottoman empire in 1800
- Territory lost, 1800–1877
- Territory lost, 1878–1913
- Ottoman empire in 1914

they could have the capitulations lifted and recover Ottoman sovereignty. Among the most important Tanzimat reforms were those that guaranteed public trials, rights of privacy, and equality before the law for all Ottoman subjects, whether Muslim or not. By 1869 educational reforms also provided free and compulsory primary education for all children. Yet even though reform and reorganization strengthened Ottoman society, the Tanzimat also provoked spirited opposition. Harsh criticism came from religious conservatives, who argued that reformers posed a threat to the empire's Islamic foundation. Perhaps most dangerously, the Ottoman bureaucracy itself criticized Tanzimat reforms because they believed that too much power was concentrated in the hands of the sultan.

The Young Turks

The despotic reign of Abdül Hamid II (reigned 1876–1909) only seemed to confirm such criticisms, and a variety of liberal groups grew up to oppose his rule. Among the most articulate were those whose members were familiar with European society, and who believed above all else that Ottoman society was in dire need of a written constitution that defined and limited the sultan's power. The most active dissident organization was the Ottoman Society for Union and Progress, better known as the Young Turk Party. Founded in 1889 by exiled Ottoman subjects living in Paris, the Young Turk Party vigorously called for universal suffrage, equality before the law, freedom of religion, free public education, secularization of the state, and the emancipation of women. In 1908 the Young Turks inspired an army coup that forced Abdül Hamid to reinstate a constitution he had abandoned at the start of his reign. In 1909 they dethroned him and established Mehmed V. Rashid (reigned 1909–1918) as a puppet sultan. Throughout the Young Turk era (1908–1918), Ottoman sultans reigned but no longer ruled.

Yet in spite of their efforts to shore up the ailing empire, reformers could not turn the tide of decline: Ottoman armies continued to lose wars, and subject peoples continued to seek autonomy or independence. By the early twentieth century, the Ottoman empire survived principally because European diplomats could not agree on how to dispose of the empire without upsetting the European balance of power.

The Opium Trade

The Chinese empire experienced even more difficulties than the Ottoman empire in the nineteenth century. Qing problems became serious in the early nineteenth century

when officials of the British East India Company began to trade in opium—rather than silver—in exchange for the Chinese silks, porcelains, and teas so coveted by Europeans. Trade in opium was illegal in China, but it expanded rapidly for decades because Chinese authorities made little effort to enforce the law. By the late 1830s, however, government officials had become aware that China had a trade problem and a drug problem as well. In 1839 the government took active steps to halt the trade, which included the destruction of some twenty thousand chests of opium.

The Opium War

Outraged, British commercial agents pressed their government into a military retaliation designed to reopen the opium trade. The ensuing conflict, known as the Opium War (1839–1842), made plain the military power differential between Europe and China. The Chinese navy and infantry were no match for their British counterparts, who relied on steam power and modern firearms, and in 1842 the Chinese government sued for peace. China experienced similar military setbacks throughout the second half of the nineteenth century in conflicts with Britain and France (1856–1858), France (1884–1885), and Japan (1894–1895).

Unequal Treaties

In the wake of those confrontations came a series of pacts collectively known in China as unequal treaties, which curtailed China's sovereignty. The Treaty of Nanjing (1842), which ended the British war against the Chinese, ceded Hong Kong Island in perpetuity to Britain, opened five Chinese ports to commerce and residence,

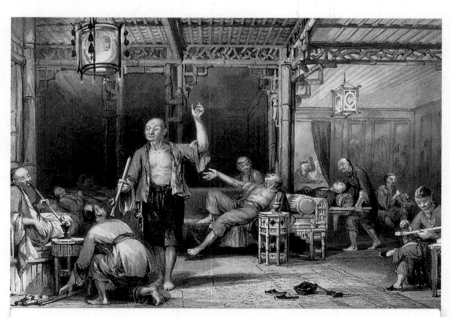

Chinese opium smokers.
Chinese efforts to stop opium imports led to a humiliating defeat in the Opium War.

What do the physical effects of opium seem to have been?

compelled the Qing government to extend most-favored-nation status to Britain, and granted extraterritoriality to British subjects. In later years France, Germany, Denmark, the Netherlands, Spain, Belgium, Austria-Hungary, the

United States, and Japan concluded similar unequal treaties with China. By 1900 ninety Chinese ports were under the effective control of foreign powers, foreign merchants controlled much of the Chinese economy, Christian missionaries sought converts throughout China, and foreign gunboats patrolled Chinese waters.

To make matters more difficult, China was convulsed by several large-scale rebellions in the nineteenth century, all of which reflected the increasing poverty and discontent of the Chinese peasantry. After 1850, rebellions erupted throughout China: the Nian rebellion (1851–1868) in the northeast, the Muslim rebellion (1855–1873) in the southwest, and the Tungan rebellion (1862–1878) in the

Nian (neen)

Tungan (tuhn-gahn)

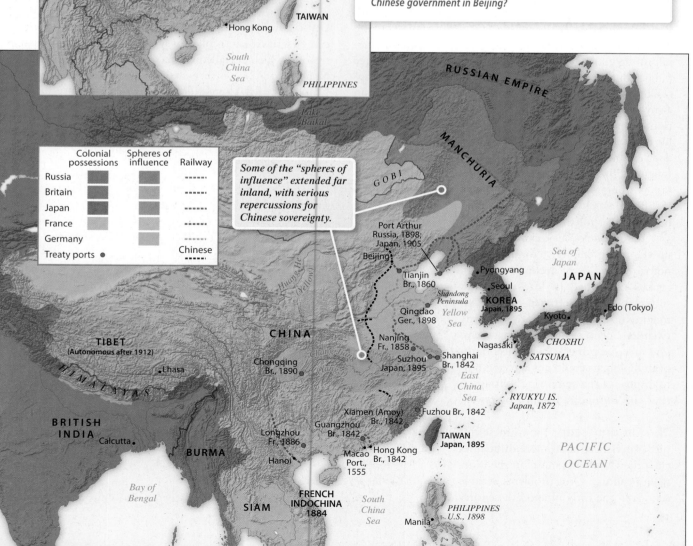

MAP 28.3

East Asia in the nineteenth century. Notice the division of China, which technically remained a sovereign nation, into spheres of influence by various European nations and Japan.

What impact would such spheres of influence have had on the Chinese government in Beijing?

northwest. Most dangerous of all was the Taiping rebellion (1850–1864), which raged throughout most of China and brought the Qing dynasty to the brink of collapse.

The Taiping Rebellion The village schoolteacher Hong Xiuquan provided both inspiration and leadership for the Taiping rebellion. He called for the destruction of the Qing dynasty and for the radical transformation of Chinese society, including the abolition of private property, the creation of communal wealth to be shared according to needs, the prohibition of foot binding and concubinage, free public education, simplification of the written language, literacy for the masses, and equality of the sexes. After sweeping through southeastern China, Hong and his followers in the Society of God Worshipers took Nanjing in 1853 and made it the capital of their Taiping ("Great Peace") kingdom. In 1855 a million Taipings were poised to attack Beijing, and in 1860 they threatened Shanghai. Although the rebellion was eventually crushed in 1864 with the aid of European advisors and weapons, in all it claimed between twenty and thirty million lives and devastated part of the Chinese countryside.

The Self-Strengthening Movement The Taiping rebellion altered the course of Chinese history. Contending with aggressive foreign powers and lands ravaged by domestic rebellion, Qing rulers recognized that reforms were necessary for the empire to survive. Most imaginative of these programs was the Self-Strengthening Movement (1860–1895). While holding to Confucian values and seeking to reestablish a stable agrarian society, movement leaders built modern shipyards, constructed railroads, established weapons industries, opened steel foundries with blast furnaces, and founded academies to develop scientific expertise.

Yet the Self-Strengthening Movement did not introduce enough industry to bring real military and economic strength to China. It also did not prevent continuing foreign intrusion into Chinese affairs. During the latter part of the nineteenth century, foreign powers began to dismantle the Chinese system of tributary states. In 1885 France incorporated Vietnam into its colonial empire, and in 1886 Great Britain detached Burma from Chinese control. In 1895 Japan forced China to recognize the independence of Korea and cede the island of Taiwan and the Liaodong peninsula in southern Manchuria. By 1898 foreign powers had carved China itself into spheres of economic influence, and only distrust among them prevented the total dismemberment of the Middle Kingdom.

The Hundred Days Reforms These setbacks sparked the ambitious but abortive Hundred Days reforms of 1898, whose purpose was to turn China into a powerful modern industrial society. Impressed by the ideas of reform-minded scholars, the young and open-minded Emperor Guangxu

launched a sweeping program to transform China into a constitutional monarchy, guarantee civil liberties, root out corruption, remodel the educational system, modernize military forces, and stimulate economic development. Yet these reform efforts produced a violent reaction from members of the imperial household, from their allies in the gentry, and especially from the young emperor's aunt, the ruthless and powerful empress dowager Cixi. After a period of 103 days, Cixi nullified the reform decrees, imprisoned the emperor in the Forbidden City, and executed six leading reformers.

The Boxer Rebellion Cixi then threw her support behind an antiforeign uprising known as the Boxer rebellion, a violent movement spearheaded by militia units calling themselves the Society of Righteous and Harmonious Fists. The foreign press referred to the rebels as Boxers. In 1899 the Boxers organized to rid China of "foreign devils" and their influences. With the empress dowager's encouragement, the Boxers went on a rampage in northern China, killing foreigners and Chinese who had ties to foreigners. Confident that foreign weapons could not harm them, some 140,000 Boxers besieged foreign embassies in Beijing in the summer of 1900. They were crushed, however, by a heavily armed force of British, French, Russian, U.S., German, and Japanese troops. After the rebellion, the Chinese government was forced to allow foreign powers to station troops at their embassies in Beijing and along the route to the sea. When Cixi died in 1908, anti-Qing revolutionary movements that sought alternative methods to deal with foreign and domestic crises were rife throughout China. Indeed, revolution broke out in the autumn of 1911, and by early 1912 the child Puyi—the last emperor of the Qing dynasty—had abdicated his throne.

The Scramble for Africa

Even as European powers sponsored informal imperialism in the Ottoman and Qing empires in the last half of the nineteenth century, they also embarked on a striking outburst of formal imperialism in Africa. This was all the more remarkable, since as late as 1875 European peoples maintained a limited presence in Africa: their only sizable possessions were the Portuguese colonies of Angola and Mozambique, the French settler colony in northern Algeria, and a cluster of settler colonies populated by British and Dutch migrants in south Africa.

Between 1875 and 1900, however, the relationship between Africa and Europe dramatically changed. Within a quarter century European imperial powers partitioned

Taiping (TEYE-pihng)
Hong Xiuquan (hoong shee-OH-chew-an)
Liaodong (lyou-dawng)
Guangxu (wang-soo)

and colonized almost the entire African continent. Prospects of exploiting African resources and nationalist rivalries between European powers help to explain this frenzied quest for empire, often referred to as the "scramble for Africa."

The Belgian Congo In the 1870s King Leopold II of Belgium (reigned 1865–1909) employed the American journalist Henry Morton Stanley to help develop commercial ventures and establish a colony called the Congo Free State (modern-day Democratic Republic of the Congo) in the basin of the Congo River. To forestall competition from Belgium's much larger and more powerful European neighbors, Leopold announced that the Congo region would be a free-trade zone accessible to merchants and businesspeople from all European lands. In fact, however, he carved out a personal colony with the sole purpose of extracting lucrative rubber using forced labor. Working conditions in the Congo Free State were so brutal, taxes so high, and abuses so many that four to eight million Africans died under Leopold's personal rule. Once those abuses became public, humanitarian pressure induced the Belgian

Physical mutilation in the Belgian Congo.
This 1912 photograph shows a stark portrait of the Belgian king's inhumane treatment of Africans in the Congo. When Africans in the Congo did not collect their allotted quotas of rubber for the state, they or their relatives were liable to have their hands or feet amputated as punishment.

government to take control away from Leopold in 1908 and administer the colony directly.

As Leopold colonized central Africa, Britain established an imperial presence in Egypt. In an effort to build up their army, strengthen the economy, and distance themselves from Ottoman authority, Egypt's leaders had borrowed heavily from European lenders in the mid–nineteenth century. By the 1870s crushing debt forced Egyptian officials to impose high taxes, which provoked popular unrest and a military rebellion. Concerned over the status of their financial interests and the security of the Suez Canal, British forces occupied Egypt in 1882.

The Berlin Conference The British occupation of Egypt intensified tensions between those European powers who were seeking African colonies. To avoid war, delegates from fourteen European states and the United States—not a single African was present—met at the Berlin West Africa Conference (1884–1885) to devise ground rules for the colonization of Africa. According to those rules, any European state could establish African colonies after notifying the others of its intentions and occupying previously unclaimed territory.

During the 1890s European imperialists sent armies to impose colonial rule on the African territories they claimed. Although resistance to colonial rule was often fierce, European cannons and machine guns rarely failed to defeat African forces. By the turn of the century, European colonies embraced all of Africa except for Ethiopia, where native forces fought off Italian efforts at colonization in 1896, and Liberia, a small republic in west Africa that was effectively a dependency of the United States.

Direct and Indirect Rule In the wake of rapid conquest, Europeans struggled to identify the most cost-effective and efficient system of rule in Africa. By the early twentieth century, after some experimentation, most European governments sought to establish their own rule, which took the form of either direct rule, typical of French colonies, or indirect rule, characteristic of British colonies. Under direct rule, colonies were headed by European personnel who assumed responsibility for tax collection, labor and military recruitment, and the maintenance of law and order. Administrative boundaries intentionally cut across existing African political and ethnic boundaries to divide and weaken potentially powerful indigenous groups. In contrast, indirect rule sought to exercise control over subject populations through indigenous institutions such as "tribal" authorities and "customary laws." Both methods of government were flawed: under direct rule, imperial powers struggled with a constant shortage of European personnel, which undermined the effectiveness of rule, and indirect rule imposed erroneous and rigid European ideas about what constituted tribal categories and boundaries onto African societies.

Sourcesfromthe**Past**

The Royal Niger Company Mass-Produces Imperial Control in Africa

The 1880s proved a crucial time for sub-Saharan African societies and European imperial adventurers. European nations at the Berlin Conference set forth the rules by which they would partition and rule African states, and then those nations—such as Great Britain—commissioned companies like the Royal Niger Company to assert imperial prerogatives. To fend off French competitors in the Niger River delta, the British-controlled Royal Niger Company had local rulers sign its "standard treaty," a mass-produced, fill-in-the-blank document that essentially ceded trade and political control to the company, and thus to Britain, in what became the British colony of Nigeria.

We, the undersigned Chiefs of _____, with the view to the bettering of the condition of our country and our people, do this day cede to the Royal Niger Company, forever, the whole of our territory from _____.

We also give to the said Royal Niger Company full power to settle all native disputes arising from any cause whatever, and we pledge ourselves not to enter into any war with other tribes without the sanction of the said Royal Niger Company.

We understand that the said Royal Niger Company have full power to mine, farm, and build in any portion of our country.

We bind ourselves not to have any intercourse with any strangers or foreigners except through the said Royal Niger Company.

In consideration of the foregoing, the said Royal Niger Company (Chartered and Limited) bind themselves not to interfere with any of the native laws or customs of the country, consistently with the maintenance of order and good government.

The said Royal Niger Company agree to pay native owners of land a reasonable amount for any portion they may require.

The said Royal Niger Company bind themselves to protect the said Chiefs from the attacks of any neighboring aggressive tribes.

The said Royal Niger Company also agree to pay the said Chiefs _____ measures native value.

We, the undersigned witnesses, do hereby solemnly declare that the _____ Chiefs whose names are placed opposite their respective crosses have in our presence affixed their crosses of their own free will and consent, and that the said _____ has in our presence affixed his signature.

Done in triplicate at _____, this _____ day of _____, 188__.

Declaration by interpreter I, _____, of _____, do hereby solemnly declare that I am well acquainted with the language of the country, and that on the _____ day of _____, 188__, I truly and faithfully explained the above Agreement to all the Chiefs present, and that they understood its meaning.

For Further Reflection

■ What did this "standard treaty" promise to Nigerian leaders, and what was expected in return? Given language barriers and imperial greed, do you believe Nigerians received true and faithful explanations of the treaty's meaning?

Source: Alfred J. Andrea and James H. Overfield, eds. The Human Record: Sources of Global History, 3rd ed., vol. 2. Boston: Wadsworth, 1998, pp. 299–300.

South Africa Although already inhabited by Europeans long before the scramble for Africa, still the southern tip of the African continent did not escape conflict at the close of the nineteenth century. In this case, however, the main antagonists were both of European descent: one side was composed of the descendants of Dutch settlers who had founded Cape Town in 1652 (called "Boers" or "Afrikaners"), and the other of British settlers who had taken control of the Cape in 1815. Relations between the two groups had never been good. When the British established themselves at the Cape, they subjected Afrikaners to British language

and law—including the abolition of slavery when it became law in 1833. The abolition of slavery was particularly contentious, as Afrikaners believed that God had given them the right to exploit both the people and the resources of the Cape—the results of which left the indigenous Khoikhoi and Xhosa peoples decimated and virtually landless. Chafing under British rule, Afrikaners left their farms in Cape Colony and gradually migrated east in what they called the

Khoikhoi (KOI-koi)
Xhosa (KOH-suh)

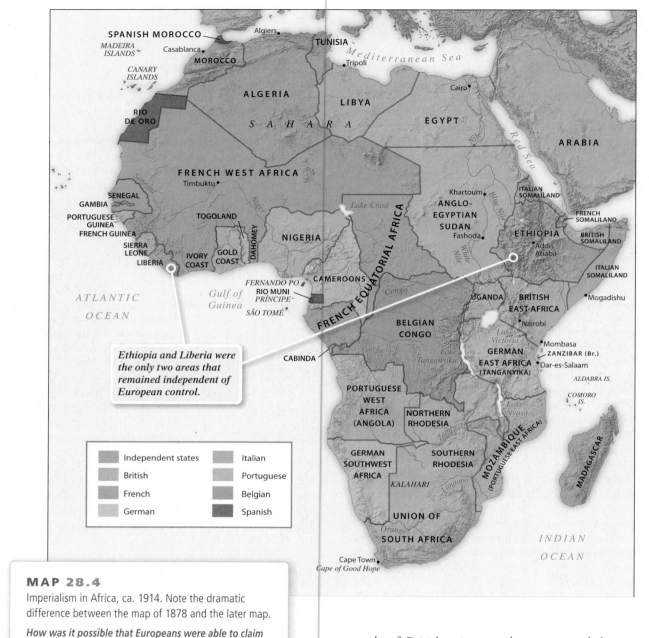

MAP 28.4

Imperialism in Africa, ca. 1914. Note the dramatic difference between the map of 1878 and the later map.

How was it possible that Europeans were able to claim so much territory in such a short span of time?

Great Trek. By the mid–nineteenth century, after fierce conflict with the Ndebele and Zulu peoples indigenous to the interior of the region, the Afrikaners created several independent republics: the Republic of Natal, annexed by the British in 1843; the Orange Free State in 1854; and in 1860 the South African Republic (Transvaal territories).

Britain's lenient attitude toward Afrikaner statehood took a drastic turn with the discovery of diamonds (1867) and gold (1886) in Afrikaner territories. The influx of thou-

sands of British miners and prospectors led to tensions between British authorities and Afrikaners, culminating in the South African War (1899–1902; sometimes called the Boer War). Although the brutal conflict pitted whites against whites, it also took a large toll on black Africans, who served both sides as soldiers and laborers. The internment of 100,000 black Africans in British concentration camps, for example, left more than 10,000 dead. The Afrikaners conceded defeat in 1902, and by 1910, the British government had reconstituted the four former colonies as provinces in the Union of South Africa, a largely autonomous British dominion. British attempts at improving relations between English speakers and Afrikaners centered on shoring up the privileges of white colonial society and the domination of black Africans.

Ndebele (uhn-duh-BEE-lee)

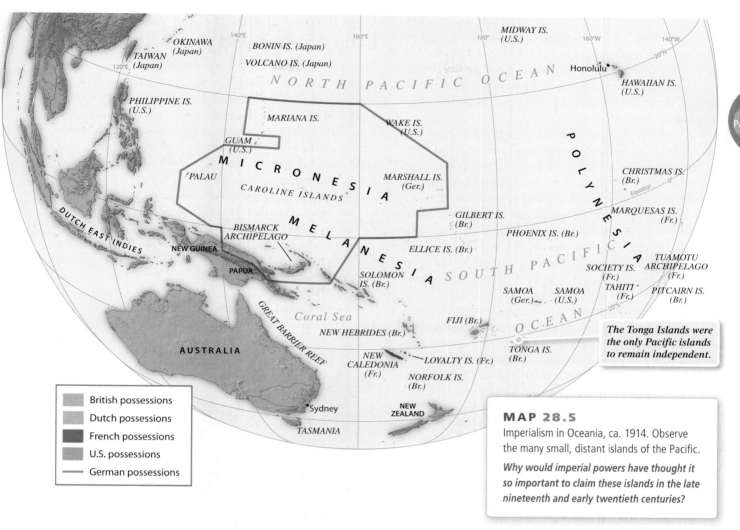

MAP 28.5

Imperialism in Oceania, ca. 1914. Observe the many small, distant islands of the Pacific.

Why would imperial powers have thought it so important to claim these islands in the late nineteenth and early twentieth centuries?

The Tonga Islands were the only Pacific islands to remain independent.

Legend:
- British possessions
- Dutch possessions
- French possessions
- U.S. possessions
- German possessions

European Imperialism in the Pacific

While scrambling for Africa, European imperial powers did not overlook opportunities to establish their presence in the Pacific Ocean basin. Imperialism in the Pacific took two main forms. In Australia and New Zealand, European powers established settler colonies and dominant political institutions. In most of the Pacific islands, however, they sought commercial opportunities and reliable bases for their operations but did not wish to go to the trouble or expense of outright colonization. Only in the late nineteenth century did they begin to impose direct colonial rule on the islands.

Settler Colonies in the Pacific Settlers began to arrive in Australia in 1788, nearly two decades after Captain James Cook reported that the region would be suitable for settlement. In that year, a British fleet with about one thousand settlers, most of them convicted criminals, arrived at Sydney harbor and established the colony of New South Wales. By the 1830s voluntary migrants outnumbered convicts, and the discovery of gold in 1851 brought a surge in migration to Australia. European settlers established communities also in New Zealand, where the islands' fertile soils and abundant stands of timber drew large numbers of migrants.

European migration rocked the societies of Australia and New Zealand. Diseases such as smallpox and measles devastated indigenous peoples at the same time that European migrants flooded into their lands. The aboriginal population of Australia fell from about 650,000 in 1800 to 90,000 in 1900, whereas the European population rose from a few thousand to 3.75 million during the same period. Similarly, the population of indigenous Maori in New Zealand fell from about 200,000 in 1800 to 45,000 a century later, while European numbers climbed to 750,000.

Increasing migration also fueled conflict between European settlers and native populations. Large settler societies pushed indigenous peoples from their lands, often following violent confrontations. Because the nomadic foraging

Maori (MAY-oh-ree)

peoples of Australia did not occupy lands permanently, British settlers considered the continent *terra nullius*—"land belonging to no one"—that they could seize and put to their own uses. Despite native resistance, by 1900 the British had succeeded in brutally displacing most indigenous Australians from their traditional lands and dispersing them throughout the continent.

A similarly disruptive process transpired in New Zealand, where Maori leaders organized effective and long-lasting opposition to British attempts to usurp their land and sovereignty. Conflicts over land confiscations and disputed land sales, for example, helped to spark the New Zealand Wars, a series of confrontations between the Maori and the British that flared from the mid- to late nineteenth century. Despite that resistance, by the end of the century the British had managed to force many Maori into poor rural communities separated from European settlements.

Imperialists in Paradise   On the smaller Pacific islands, the picture was quite different. Although indigenous peoples were ravaged by European diseases, the imperial powers had little interest in establishing direct colonial rule over the islands. Rather, they were content to use the islands as naval ports, as coaling stations, and sometimes as producers of primary products. The situation changed, however, in the late nineteenth century, as European nationalist rivalries encouraged the imperial powers to stake their claims in the Pacific as they had done in Africa. Thus, although France had established a protectorate in Tahiti, the Society Islands, and the Marquesas as early as 1841, it only imposed direct colonial rule in 1880. Britain made Fiji a crown colony in 1874, and Germany annexed several of the Marshall Islands in 1876 and 1878. At the Berlin Conference, European diplomats agreed on a partition of Oceania as well as Africa, and Britain, France, Germany, and the United States proceeded to claim almost all the Pacific islands. By 1900 only the kingdom of Tonga remained independent, and even Tonga accepted British protection against the possibility of encroachments by other imperial powers.

THE EMERGENCE OF NEW IMPERIAL POWERS

Nineteenth-century imperialism was mostly a European affair until the end of the century. At that point, two new imperial powers appeared on the world stage: the United States and Japan. Both lands experienced rapid industrialization in the late nineteenth century, and both built powerful armed forces. As European imperial powers planted their flags throughout the world, leaders of the United States and Japan decided that they too needed to establish a global imperial presence.

Lili'uokalani (lee-lee-oo-oh-kah-lah-nee)

U.S. Imperialism in Latin America and the Pacific

The very existence of the United States was due to European imperialism. After the new republic had won its independence, U.S. leaders brought almost all the temperate regions of North America under their authority. In the process, they pushed indigenous peoples onto marginal lands and reservations. This domination of the North American continent was part of the larger story of European and Euro-American imperialism.

The fledgling United States also tried to wield power outside North America. In 1823 President James Monroe (in office 1817–1825) issued a proclamation that warned European states against imperialist designs in the western hemisphere. The Monroe Doctrine, as it came to be known, later served as a justification for U.S. intervention in hemispheric affairs.

As the United States consolidated its continental holdings, U.S. leaders became interested in acquiring territories

Queen Lili'uokalani, last monarch of Hawai'i.
In this picture, taken before her deposition in 1893, the queen wears a European dress and sits on a throne covered with a traditional royal cape made of bird feathers.

Thinking about ENCOUNTERS

Imperial Connections

During the nineteenth and twentieth centuries, European, American, and Japanese imperialism helped connect the world's peoples ever more tightly through resource exploitation, trade relationships, and migration patterns. *What technologies, ideologies, and institutions made it possible for imperial powers to maintain these connections, even in the face of resistance?*

beyond the temperate regions of North America. The United States purchased Alaska from Russia in 1867 and in 1875 claimed a protectorate over the islands of Hawai'i, where U.S. entrepreneurs had established highly productive sugarcane plantations. The Hawaiian kingdom survived until 1893, when a group of planters and businesspeople overthrew the last monarch, Queen Lili'uokalani (reigned 1891–1893), and invited the United States to annex the islands. In 1898 the pro-expansion president William McKinley (in office 1897–1901) agreed to acquire the islands.

The Spanish-Cuban-American War

The United States emerged as a major imperial and colonial power after the brief Spanish-Cuban-American War (1898–1899). War broke out as anticolonial tensions mounted in Cuba and Puerto Rico—the last remnants of Spain's American empire—where U.S. business interests had made large investments. In 1898 the U.S. battleship *Maine* exploded and sank in Havana harbor. U.S. leaders claimed sabotage and declared war on Spain. The United States easily defeated Spain and took control and possession of Cuba and Puerto Rico. After the U.S. navy destroyed the Spanish fleet at Manila in a single day, the United States also took possession of Guam and the Philippines to prevent them from falling under German or Japanese control.

The consolidation of U.S. authority in the Philippines was an especially difficult affair. The Spanish-Cuban-American War coincided with a Filipino revolt against Spanish rule, and U.S. forces promised to support independence of the Philippines in exchange for an alliance against Spain. After the victory over Spain, however, President McKinley decided to bring the Philippines under American control instead. In response, Filipino rebels—led by Emilio Aguinaldo—turned their arms against the new intruders. The result was a bitter insurrection that raged until 1902 and claimed the lives of 4,200 American soldiers, 15,000 rebel troops, and some 200,000 Filipino civilians.

Instability and disorder also prompted the United States to intervene in the affairs of Caribbean and Central American lands, even those that were not U.S. possessions, to prevent rebellion and protect American business interests. In

the early twentieth century, U.S. military forces occupied Cuba, the Dominican Republic, Nicaragua, Honduras, and Haiti.

The Panama Canal To facilitate communication and transportation between the Atlantic and the Pacific oceans, the United States sought to build a canal across the Isthmus of Panama in northern Colombia. However, Colombia was unwilling to cede land for the project. Under President Theodore Roosevelt (in office 1901–1909), an enthusiastic champion of imperial expansion, the United States supported a rebellion against Colombia in 1903 and helped rebels establish the breakaway state of Panama. In exchange for that support, the United States won the right to build a canal across Panama and to control the adjacent territory, known as the Panama Canal Zone. Roosevelt then added a corollary to the Monroe Doctrine in 1904, which stated that the United States has the right to intervene in the domestic affairs of nations within the hemisphere if they demonstrate an inability to maintain the security deemed necessary to protect U.S. investments. The Roosevelt Corollary, along with the Panama Canal when it opened in 1914, strengthened U.S. military and economic claims.

Imperial Japan

Strengthened by the rapid industrialization during the Meiji era, Japan joined the ranks of imperial powers in the late nineteenth century. Indeed, while founding representative political institutions to demonstrate their trustworthiness to American and European diplomats, Japanese leaders also made a bid to stand alongside the world's great powers by launching a campaign of imperial expansion.

Early Japanese Expansion The Japanese drive to empire began in the east Asian islands. During the 1870s Japanese leaders consolidated their hold on Hokkaido and the Kurile Islands to the north, and they encouraged Japanese migrants to populate the islands to forestall Russian expansion there. By 1879 they had also established their hegemony over Okinawa and the Ryukyu Islands to the south.

The Sino-Japanese War In 1876 Japan purchased modern warships from Britain, and the newly strengthened Japanese navy immediately began to flex its muscles in Korea. In 1894 conflict erupted between Japan and China over the status of Korea. When an antiforeign rebellion broke out in Korea in 1893, Qing rulers sent an army to restore order and reassert Chinese authority in Korea. However, Japanese

Emilio Aguinaldo (ee-MEE-lyaw AH-gee-NAHL-daw)

businesses had built substantial interests in Korea, and Meiji leaders were unwilling to recognize Chinese control over such an economically important land. Thus in August 1894 they declared war on China. The Japanese navy quickly gained control of the Yellow Sea and demolished the Chinese fleet in a battle lasting a mere five hours. Within a few months the conflict was over. When the combatants made peace in April 1895, Qing authorities recognized the independence of Korea, thus making it essentially a dependency of Japan. They also ceded Taiwan, the Pescadores Islands, and the Liaodong peninsula, which strengthened Japanese control over east Asian waters. Alongside territorial acquisitions, Japan gained unequal treaty rights in China like those enjoyed by European and American powers.

The Russo-Japanese War The unexpected Japanese victory startled European imperial powers, especially Russia. Tensions between Japan and Russia soon mounted, because both imperial powers had territorial ambitions in the Liaodong peninsula, Korea, and Manchuria. War broke out in 1904, and Japanese forces overran Russian installations before reinforcements could arrive from Europe. The Japanese navy destroyed the Russian Baltic fleet, which had

The Russo-Japanese War.
In this painting, Japanese infantry charge into battle. Note the distinctly western uniforms worn by the soldiers.

sailed halfway around the world to support the war effort. By 1905 the war was over, and Japan won international recognition of its colonial authority over Korea and the Liaodong peninsula. Furthermore, Russia ceded the southern half of Sakhalin island to Japan, along with a railroad and economic interests in southern Manchuria. Victory in the Russo-Japanese War transformed Japan into a major imperial power.

LEGACIES OF IMPERIALISM

Imperialism and colonialism profoundly influenced the development of world history. In some ways they tightened links between the world's peoples: trade and migration increased dramatically as imperial powers exploited the resources of subject lands and recruited labor forces to work in colonies throughout the world. Yet imperialism and colonialism also brought peoples into conflict and heightened senses of difference between peoples. European, Euro-American, and Japanese imperialists all came to think of themselves as superior to the peoples they overcame. Meanwhile, foreign intrusion stimulated the development of resistance in colonized lands, which over time served as a foundation for anticolonial independence movements.

Empire and Economy

One of the principal motives of imperialism was the desire to gain access to natural resources and agricultural products. As imperial powers consolidated their hold on foreign lands, colonial administrators reorganized subject societies so they would become efficient suppliers of timber, rubber, petroleum, gold, silver, diamonds, cotton, tea, coffee, cacao, and other products. As a result, global trade in those commodities surged during the nineteenth and early twentieth centuries. The advantages of this trade went mostly to the colonial powers, whose policies encouraged subject lands to provide raw materials for processing in the industrialized societies of Europe, North America, and Japan.

Introduction of New Crops In some cases, colonial rule led to the introduction of new crops that transformed both the landscape and the social order of subject lands. In the early nineteenth century, for example, British colonial officials introduced tea bushes from China to Ceylon and India. The effect on Ceylon was profound. British planters felled trees on much of the island, converted rain forests into tea plantations, and recruited Ceylonese women by the thousands to carry out the labor-intensive work of harvesting mature tea leaves.

Consumption of tea in India and Ceylon was almost negligible, but increased supplies met the growing demand for tea in Europe, where the beverage became accessible to individuals of all social classes. The value of south Asian tea exports rose from about 309,000 pounds sterling in 1866 to 6.1 million pounds sterling in 1900. Malaya and Sumatra underwent a similar social transformation after British colonial agents planted rubber trees there in the 1870s and established plantations to meet the growing global demand for rubber products.

Labor Migrations

Efforts to exploit the natural resources and agricultural products of subject lands led imperial and colonial powers to encourage mass migrations of workers during the nineteenth and early twentieth centuries. Two patterns of labor migration were especially prominent during the imperial and colonial era. European migrants went mostly to temperate lands, where they worked as free cultivators or industrial laborers. In contrast, migrants from Asia, Africa, and the Pacific islands moved largely to tropical and subtropical lands, where they worked as indentured laborers on plantations or manual laborers for mining enterprises or large-scale construction projects.

European Migration Between 1800 and 1914 some fifty million European migrants left their homes and sought opportunities overseas. Most of those migrants left the relatively poor agricultural societies of southern and eastern Europe, especially Italy, Russia, and Poland, although sizable numbers came also from Britain, Ireland, Germany, and Scandinavia. A majority of the migrants—about thirty-two million—went to the United States. Settler colonies in Canada, Argentina, Australia, New Zealand, and south Africa also drew large numbers of European migrants.

Indentured Labor Migration In contrast to their free European counterparts, migrants from Asia, Africa, and the Pacific islands generally traveled as indentured laborers. As the institution of slavery went into decline, planters sought laborers from poor and densely populated lands who could replace slaves. Between 1820 and 1914 about 2.5 million indentured laborers left their homes to work in distant parts of the world. Labor recruiters generally offered workers free passage to their destinations and provided them with food, shelter, clothing, and modest compensation for their services in exchange for a commitment to work for five to seven years.

The majority of the indentured laborers came from India, but sizable numbers also came from China, Japan, Java, Africa, and the Pacific islands. Indentured laborers went mostly to tropical and subtropical lands in the Americas, the Caribbean, Africa, and Oceania. Large numbers of Indian laborers went to work on rubber plantations in Malaya and sugar plantations in south Africa, the Pacific

island of Fiji, the Guianas, and the Caribbean islands of Trinidad, Tobago, and Jamaica. After the Opium War, large numbers of Chinese laborers went to sugar plantations in Cuba and Hawai'i, guano mines in Peru, tin mines in Malaya, gold mines in south Africa and Australia, and railroad construction sites in the United States, Canada, and Peru. After the Meiji restoration in Japan, a large contingent of Japanese laborers migrated to Hawai'i to work on sugar plantations, and a smaller group went to work in guano mines in Peru. Indentured laborers from Africa went mostly to sugar plantations in Réunion, the Guianas, and Caribbean islands. Those from Pacific islands went mostly to plantations on other Pacific islands and in Australia.

Empire and Migration All the large-scale migrations of the nineteenth century reflected the global influence of imperial powers. European migrations were possible only because European and Euro-American peoples had established settler societies in temperate regions around the world. Movements of indentured laborers were possible because colonial officials were able to recruit workers and dispatch them to distant lands where their compatriots had already established plantations or opened mines. In combination the nineteenth-century migrations profoundly influenced societies around the world by depositing large communities of people with distinctive ethnic identities in lands far from their original homes.

Empire and Society

Colonial Conflict The policies adopted by imperial powers and colonial officials forced peoples of different societies to deal with one another on a regular and systematic basis. Their interactions often led to violent conflicts between colonizers and subject peoples. Indeed, the Sepoy Rebellion was only one among many insurrections organized by discontented Indian subjects between the mid–nineteenth and the mid–twentieth centuries. Colonized lands in southeast Asia and Africa also became hotbeds of resistance, as subject peoples revolted against foreign rule, the tyrannical behavior of colonial officials, the introduction of European schools and curricula, high taxation, and requirements that subject peoples provide compulsory labor for colonists' enterprises.

Many rebellions drew strength from traditional religious beliefs, and priests or prophets often led resistance to colonial rule. In Tanganyika, for example, a local prophet organized the huge Maji-Maji rebellion (1905–1906) to expel German colonial authorities from east Africa. Rebels sprinkled themselves with *maji-maji* ("magic water"), which they believed would protect them from German weapons. Although the rebellion failed and resulted in the deaths of as many as seventy-five thousand insurgents, it testified to

Connecting
the Sources

Thinking about colonized peoples' responses to colonization

The problem   For many years, the history of imperialism and colonialism was written from the point of view of the various colonizing powers. Colonial officials produced copious amounts of official and unofficial documents about colonial policies, their own experiences, and their opinions of colonized people. Not surprisingly, the histories written about colonialism using such sources tended to be biased in favor of the colonizers, and frequently marginalized the experiences of colonized peoples themselves. In the last four decades, however, a plethora of histories have appeared that explore the colonial past from the point of view of colonized peoples, relying on previously underutilized sources such as court records, letters, memoirs, oral interviews, and fiction. Such sources have altered the way historians understand the massive imperial expansion that occurred in Asia and Africa in the nineteenth and first half of the twentieth centuries, as they have allowed historians to understand not only the actions of colonizers but the responses of colonized people to colonialism and conquest.

Let us consider two sources generated by people responding to British policies—one from China, the other from southern Africa—in order to think about what sources generated by the people who experienced colonialism can and cannot tell us.

Opium War. The British Ironclad steamship HMS *Nemesis* destroying Chinese ships during the Opium War in 1841.

The documents   Read the documents below, and consider carefully the questions that follow.

Document 1: *The following resolution was produced in 1842—just after the defeat of the Chinese empire by the British in the Opium War—by Chinese citizens at a large public meeting in the city of Canton (Guangzhou).*

Behold that vile English nation! Its ruler is at one time a woman, then a man, and then perhaps a woman again; its people are at one time like vultures, and then they are like wild beasts, with dispositions more fierce and furious than the tiger or wolf, and natures more greedy than anacondas or swine. These people having long steadily devoured all the western barbarians, and like demons of the night, they now suddenly exalt themselves here.

During the reigns of the emperors Kien-lung [Qianlong] and Kia-king [Jiaqing] these English barbarians humbly besought an entrance and permission to deliver tribute and presents; they afterwards presumptuously asked to have Chu-san [the city of Zhoushan]; but our sovereigns, clearly perceiving their traitorous designs, gave them a determined refusal. From that time, linking themselves with traitorous Chinese traders, they have carried on a large trade and poisoned our brave people with opium.

Verily, the English barbarians murder all of us that they can. They are dogs, whose desires can never be satisfied. Therefore we need not inquire whether the peace they have now made be real or pretended. Let us all rise, arm, unite, and go against them.

We do here bind ourselves to vengeance, and express these our sincere intentions in order to exhibit our high principles and patriotism. The gods from on high now look down upon us; let us not lose our just and firm resolution.

Document 2: *The following letter was written in 1858 by Moshweshewe I, founder of Basutoland and chief of the Basuto people in South Africa. It was directed to Sir George Grey, then governor of the Cape Colony and high commissioner of South Africa, regarding Moshweshewe's treatment at the hands of white South African Boers.*

. . . About twenty-five years ago my knowledge of the White men and their laws was very limited. I knew merely that mighty

Moshweshewe I, 1786–1870.

nations existed, and among them was the English. These, the blacks who were acquainted with them, praised for their justice. Unfortunately it was not with the English Government that my first intercourse with the whites commenced. People who had come from the Colony first presented themselves to us, they called themselves Boers. I thought all white men were honest. Some of these Boers asked permission to live upon our borders. I was led to believe they would live with me as my own people lived, that is, looking to me as to a father and a friend.

About sixteen years since, one of the [British] Governors of the [Cape] Colony, Sir George Napier, marked down my limits on a treaty he made with me. I was to be ruler within those limits. A short time after, another Governor came, it was Sir P. Maitland. The Boers then began to talk of their right to places I had then lent to them. Sir P. Maitland told me those people were subjects of the Queen, and should be kept under proper control; he did not tell me that he recognized any right they had to land within my country, but as it was difficult to take them away, it was proposed that all desiring to be under the British rule should live in that part near the meeting of the Orange and Caledon rivers.

Then came Sir Harry Smith, and he told me not to deprive any chief of their lands or their rights, he would see justice done to all, but in order to do so, he would make the Queen's Laws extend over every white man. He said the Whites and Blacks were to live together in peace. I could not understand what he would do. I thought it would be something very just, and that he was to keep the Boers in my land under proper control, and that I should hear no more of their claiming the places they lived on as their exclusive property. But instead of this, I now heard that the Boers consider all those farms as their own, and were buying and selling them one to the other, and driving out by one means or another my own people.

In vain I remonstrated. Sir Harry Smith had sent Warden to govern in the Sovereignty. He listened to the Boers, and he proposed that all the land in which those Boers' farms were should be taken from me. . . . One day he sent me a map and said, sign that, and I will tell those people . . . to leave off fighting: if you do not sign the map, I cannot help you in any way. I thought the Major was doing very improperly and unjustly. I was told to appeal to the Queen to put an end to this injustice. I did not wish to grieve Her Majesty by causing a war with her people. I was told if I did not sign the map, it would be the beginning of a great war. I signed, but soon after I sent my cry to the Queen. I begged Her to investigate my case and remove "the line," as it was called, by which my land was ruined. I thought justice would soon be done, and Warden put to rights. [Hostilities then broke out between the Boers and Moshweshewe's people, and Moshweshewe was thus requesting arbitration by Grey, the high commissioner]

Questions

- What can these documents definitively tell you about their respective writers' situations? What **facts** can be gleaned from these brief sources?

- In Document 1, how do the Chinese who produced the resolution feel about the recent British victory? What have the British done to deserve such condemnation, in the group's view? How does the group propose to remedy the problem of the British in China?

- In Document 2, why does Moshweshewe carefully recount his interactions with the various British officials who oversee the area in which Basutoland is situated? What kind of tone does Moshweshewe take in this letter, and why? Do you think Moshweshewe believes he has been treated fairly by the Boers and the British? What do you think happened when he signed the map?

- What can these two documents tell us about the experience of colonialism in general? Do you imagine that the responses to domination suggested by these documents were common reactions to colonial expansion, or do you think responses would differ depending on the interests of the colonized group?

- Sources such as these make up the building blocks on which historians base their interpretations of the past. In most cases, however, historians discover that they must use a variety of primary and secondary sources in order to make accurate interpretations.

Source Website: **Document 1:** http://www.fordham.edu/halsall/mod/1842canton.asp **Document 2:** http://www.fordham.edu/Halsall/mod/1858basuto.asp

the fact that rebellion was a constant threat to colonial rule. Even when subject peoples dared not revolt, they resisted colonial rule by boycotting European goods, organizing political parties and pressure groups, and pursuing anticolonial policies through churches and religious groups.

Scientific Racism Social and cultural differences were the foundation of an academic pursuit known as scientific racism, which became prominent especially after the 1840s. Theorists such as the French nobleman Count Joseph Arthur de Gobineau (1816–1882) took race as the most important index of human potential. In fact, there is no such thing as a biologically pure race, but nineteenth-century theorists assumed that the human species consisted of several distinct racial groups. In his dense, four-volume *Essay on the Inequality of the Human Races* (1853–1855), Gobineau divided humanity into four main racial groups. Gobineau characterized Africans as unintelligent and lazy; Asians as smart but docile; the native peoples of the Americas as dull and arrogant; and Europeans as intelligent, noble, and morally superior to others. Throughout the later nineteenth and early twentieth centuries, racist thinkers sought to identify racial groups on the basis of skin color, bone structure, nose shape, cranial capacity, and other physical characteristics.

After the 1860s scientific racists drew heavily from the writings of Charles Darwin (1809–1882), an English biologist whose book *On the Origin of Species* (1859) argued that all living species had evolved over thousands of years in a ferocious contest for survival. Species that adapted well to their environment survived, reproduced, and flourished, according to Darwin, whereas others declined and went into extinction. The slogan "survival of the fittest" soon became a byword for Darwin's theory of evolution. Theorists known as social Darwinists seized on those ideas, which Darwin had applied exclusively to biological matters, and adapted them to explain the development of human societies. The English philosopher Herbert Spencer (1820–1903) relied on theories of evolution to explain differences between the strong and the weak: successful individuals and races had competed better in the natural world and consequently evolved to higher states than did other, less fit, peoples. On the basis of that reasoning, Spencer and others justified the domination of European imperialists over subject peoples as the inevitable result of natural scientific principles.

Racist views were by no means a monopoly of European imperialists: U.S. and Japanese empire builders also developed a sense of superiority over the peoples they conquered and ruled. U.S. forces in the Philippines disparaged the rebels they fought there as "gooks," and they did not hesitate to torture enemies in a conflict that was supposed to "civilize and Christianize" the Filipinos. In the 1890s

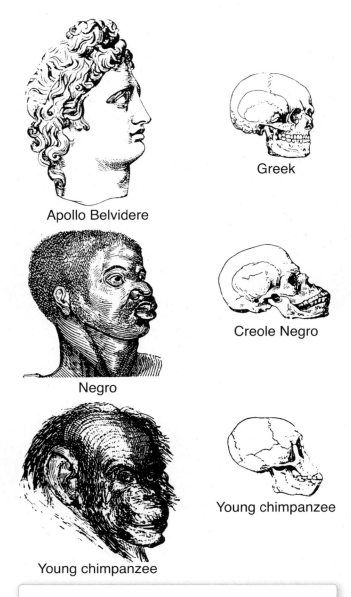

Apollo Belvidere

Greek

Negro

Creole Negro

Young chimpanzee

Young chimpanzee

Scientific racism.
Scientific racists often argued that Europeans had reached a higher stage of evolution than other peoples. An illustration from a popular book by Josiah Clark Nott and G. R. Glidden, *Indigenous Races of the Earth*, deliberately distorted facial and skull features to suggest a close relationship between African peoples and chimpanzees.

Japanese newspapers portrayed Chinese and Korean peoples as dirty, backward, stupid, and cowardly. After their victory in the Russo-Japanese War, political and military leaders came to believe that Japan had an obligation to oversee the affairs of their backward neighbors and help civilize their little Asian brothers.

SUMMARY

The construction of global empires in the nineteenth century noticeably increased the tempo of world integration. Armed with powerful transportation, communication, and military technologies, European peoples imposed their rule on much of Asia and almost all of Africa. They wielded enormous influence throughout the world, even where they did not establish imperial control, because of their wealth and economic power. Toward the end of the nineteenth century, the United States and Japan joined European states as global imperialists. All the imperial powers profoundly influenced the development of the societies they ruled. They shaped the economies and societies of their colonies by pushing them to supply natural resources and agricultural commodities in exchange for manufactured products. They created multicultural societies around the world by facilitating the movement of workers to lands where there was high demand for labor on plantations or in mines. They also provoked subject peoples to resist colonial expansion, which over time led them to develop a sense of national identity. From the early twentieth century forward, much of global history has revolved around issues stemming from the world order of imperialism and colonialism.

STUDY TERMS

Bechuanaland (529)
Boxer rebellion (539)
capitulations (535)
Caucasus (535)
Cecil Rhodes (529)
direct rule (540)
East India Company (533)
Emilio Aguinaldo (545)
formal imperialism (530)
Guangxu (539)
Hong Xiuquan (539)
Hundred Days reforms (539)
indentured labor (537)
indirect rule (540)
informal imperialism (531, 533, 535)
Khartoum (532)
Khoikhoi (541)
King Leopold II (540)
Liaodong (539)

Lili'uokalani (544)
Mahmud II (536)
Maji-Maji rebellion (547)
Maori (543)
mission civilisatrice (532)
Monroe Doctrine (544)
Mughal (533)
Ndebele (542)
New Zealand Wars (544)
Nian (538)
Omdurman (532)
Opium War (537)
Panama Canal (545)
Qing (533)
Roosevelt Corollary (545)
Russo-Japanese War (546)
sati (534)
scientific racism (550)
Self-Strengthening Movement (539)
Sepoy Rebellion (533)

South African War (542)
Spanish-Cuban-American War (545)
Suez Canal (532)
Taiping rebellion (539)
Tanzimat (536)
Tungan (538)
unequal treaties (537)
Xhosa (541)
Young Turk Party (537)

FOR FURTHER READING

W. G. Beasley. *Japanese Imperialism, 1894–1945*. Oxford, 1987. The best study of the topic, emphasizing the relationship between Japanese industrialization and imperialism.

Sugata Bose. *A Hundred Horizons: The Indian Ocean in the Age of Global Empires*. Cambridge, Mass., 2006. A bold interregional history that argues that the peoples of the Indian Ocean littoral shared a common historical destiny.

Jane Burbank and Frederick Cooper. *Empires in World History: Power and the Politics of Difference*. Princeton, 2010. A major study that considers modern empires in historical context.

Ken S. Coates. *A Global History of Indigenous Peoples: Struggle and Survival*. Houndmills, 2004. Stressing the active role of indigenous peoples, this work examines the dynamics of colonial encounters.

Philip D. Curtin. *The World and the West: The European Challenge and the Overseas Response in the Age of Empire*. Cambridge and New York, 2000. A work that focuses on cultural change as it examines how various peoples have responded to the establishment of European empires.

Trevor Getz and Heather Streets-Salter. *Modern Imperialism and Colonialism: A Global Perspective*. New York, 2010. Explores the structures and ideologies of imperialism and colonialism since 1400 from a global perspective.

Adam Hochschild. *King Leopold's Ghost: A Story of Greed, Terror, and Heroism in Colonial Africa*. Boston, 1998. A ghastly story of nearly forgotten greed and crime.

Zine Magubane. *Bringing the Empire Home: Race, Class, and Gender in Britain and Colonial South Africa*. Chicago, 2004. Study of the ways that colonial England used racial stereotypes to justify its own social hierarchies as well as the colonial project.

Thomas Pakenham. *The Scramble for Africa, 1876–1912*. New York, 1991. Detailed popular history of empire building in sub-Saharan Africa.

H. L. Wesseling. *The European Colonial Empires: 1815–1919*. New York, 2004. Puts the process of colonization into a comparative and long-term perspective.

PART 6 AN AGE OF REVOLUTION, INDUSTRY, AND EMPIRE, 1750–1914

Since the end of the fifteenth century, the world's peoples grew increasingly interconnected as a result of transoceanic networks of trade and migration. Indeed, the forces unleashed by multiple revolutions, rapid industrialization, and widespread imperialism in this period radically intensified earlier patterns of intercultural exchange.

The Atlantic revolutions clearly demonstrate the multiple threads that connected people and places across the oceans even at the beginning of this period. The first revolution to occur, in the thirteen North American English colonies, was fed by Enlightenment ideals of liberty and equality that traveled from Europe to the Americas along with trade items and migrants. From there, the success of the American Revolution inspired French thinkers. Both American and French success then inspired Haitian and Latin American revolutionaries to sever their colonial ties. Meanwhile, revolutionaries began to form identities on the basis of nation-states—an idea that, once formed, reverberated around the Atlantic basin and, later, the world.

By the nineteenth century, new technologies produced by industrialization—including the railroad, the steamship, and the telegraph—allowed ideas, trade goods, and people to travel far faster and over far greater distances than in the past. As a result, huge geographical expanses across oceans as well as continents were knitted together into new relationships.

Moreover, the global impact of industrialization increased as new states in western Europe, North America, Russia, and Japan undertook their own programs of industrialization. These powers then spread industrial technologies to every continent in the world.

Although the impact of industrial technologies was global by 1914, the world's peoples did not realize the benefits of industrialization equally. Instead, industrial powers—especially Europeans and their North American descendants—used their technological advantages to conquer and dominate vast territories in Asia, Africa, and Oceania. As a result, by the start of the twentieth century the leading industrial powers had carved the world into vast empires—each connected by networks of trade, resource exploitation, and migration.

The global webs of connection forged via industry and empire did not breed harmony. Rather, the growth of nationalism around the world encouraged intense competition for natural resources, strategic ports, and international prestige. In addition, industrial and imperial powers increasingly justified their domination of the world in terms of racial superiority, which bred discontent among the conquered and dominated peoples of the world. Such discontent, when combined with disputes between the great powers, led to explosive conflicts that would make the twentieth century the most violent in the history of humankind.

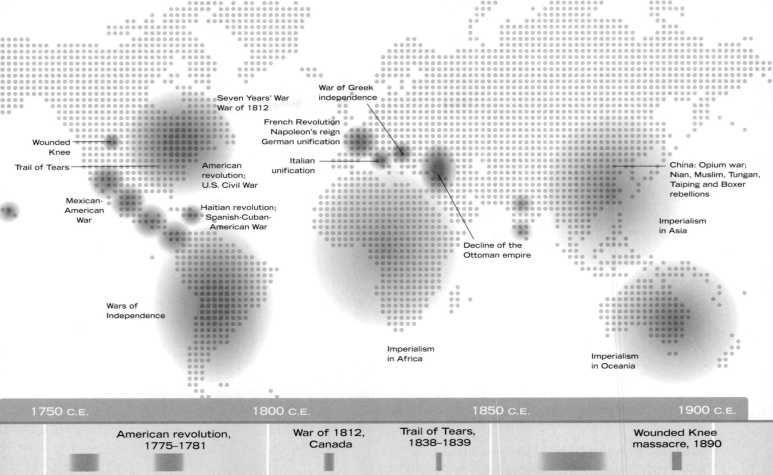

1750 C.E.	1800 C.E.	1850 C.E.	1900 C.E.

American revolution, 1775–1781

War of 1812, Canada

Trail of Tears, 1838–1839

Wounded Knee massacre, 1890

Seven Years' War, 1756–1763

U.S. Civil War & Reconstruction, 1861–1865; 1867–1877

Haitian revolution, 1791–1803

THE AMERICAS

Wars of independence in Latin America, 1810–1825

Mexican-American War, 1846–1848

Spanish-Cuban-American War, 1898–1899

EUROPE

French revolution, 1789–1799
Napoleon's reign, 1799–1814

Italian unification, 1859–1870
German unification, 1864–1871

War of Greek independence, 1821–1827

SOUTHWEST ASIA

Decline of Ottoman empire, 1800–1923 (southwest Asia & northern Africa)

China: Opium War, 1839–1842; Nian, Muslim, Tungan and Taiping rebellions, 1851–1878; Boxer rebellion, 1898–1901;

EAST ASIA

Meiji Japan, 1868–1912; Imperialism in Asia, ca. 1914. Territories claimed by Britain, France, the U.S., Japan, Russia, and Portugal.

AFRICA

Imperialism in Africa, ca. 1914. Territories claimed by Belgium, Britain, France, Germany, Italy, Portugal, and Spain.

OCEANIA

Imperialism in Oceania, ca. 1914. Territories claimed by Britain, France, Germany and the U.S.

PART 7
CONTEMPORARY GLOBAL REALIGNMENTS

At the time the Great War erupted in 1914, Europeans and their descendants in North America dominated global affairs to an unprecedented extent, exercising political and economic control over peoples and their lands in most of Asia, nearly all of Africa, the Americas, and the Pacific islands. This global dominance was the outcome of three interconnected historical developments that took place between 1750 and 1914: the formation of national states, industrialization, and imperial expansion.

The Road to World War

Those same historical developments, which encouraged national rivalries, colonial disputes, and nationalist aspirations, plunged Europe—and then much of the world—into war in 1914. By the time the war ended in 1918, all the major European powers had ex-

Australian recruiting poster. The British were keen to augment their forces by recruiting Australians and others to help defeat the Ottoman empire, which had allied itself with the Central Powers.

hausted much of their economic wealth and global political primacy.

Global Instability in the Interwar Years

Global interdependence ensured that economic instability after the Great War affected much of the world.

This was especially true in the Great Depression, when political turmoil and social misery paved the way to fascist dictatorships in Italy and Germany and to nationalist movements in Asia. Meanwhile, the Soviet Union embarked on a state-sponsored program of rapid industrialization that transformed it into a major international power.

World War II

Sparked as a result of the Great War and the Great Depression, World War II began in China in 1931 when Japanese forces established a colonial empire in Manchuria. The conflict spread to Europe in the late 1930s when the Nazi regime embarked on a policy of territorial expansion. By 1941 all the world's major powers had been sucked into a maelstrom of violence and suffering that engulfed most European societies, almost all of Asia and the Pacific, and parts of Africa.

The Cold War

World War II completed the economic and political weakening of European societies and led to the immediate outbreak of the cold war and the dismantling of colonial empires, both of which realigned the world of the late twentieth and twenty-first centuries. The cold war conflict between the forces of capitalism and communism produced a new set of global

Smokestacks in Siberia releasing carbon dioxide emissions into the atmosphere. Most scientists argue that emissions such as these, along with other hydrocarbon emissions and methane, contribute to global warming, the increases of world temperatures that are having a negative impact on the world's economy and natural environment.

relationships, shaping the foreign policies, economic systems, and political institutions of nations throughout the world until its abrupt end in the late 1980s.

Decolonization

In the three decades after World War II, an irresistible wave of independence movements swept away colonies and empires and led to the establishment of new nations in Africa and Asia. However, the initial euphoria that accompanied freedom from imperial control was tempered by neocolonial and postcolonial problems such as interference by the superpowers, lack of economic development, and regional and ethnic conflicts.

Global Contemporary Issues

Other forces that reshaped the twentieth- and twenty-first-century world include globalization, a process that widened the extent and the forms of cross-cultural interaction among the world's peoples. Technological advances dissolved old political, social, and economic barriers. The resulting global integration encouraged similar economic and political preferences and fostered common cultural values, but forces promoting distinct cultural traditions and political identities also arose to challenge the universalizing effects of globalization.

1. *What historical developments caused the eruption of the intense violence of the two world wars in the twentieth century?*

2. *Is the globalization of the contemporary period a radical break with the past, or an acceleration of existing patterns?*

EAST-AFRICAN TRANSPORT–NEW STYLE

This poster, produced by the Empire Marketing Board, presented an idealized image of the dominant European role in forwarding African economic progress.

The Great War:
The World in Upheaval

CHAPTER 29

This painting by C. R. W. Nevinson, called *Harvest of Battle*, testifies to the appalling scale of death and destruction during the battles of WWI.

EYEWITNESS:
A Bloodied Archduke and a Bloody War

Archduke Francis Ferdinand (1863–1914) was aware that his first official visit to Sarajevo in 1914 was fraught with danger. That ancient city was the capital of Bosnia-Herzegovina, twin provinces that had been under Ottoman rule since the fifteenth century, then occupied in 1878, and finally annexed by Austria-Hungary in 1908. These provinces became the hotbed of pan-Serbian nationalism. Most Serbian nationalists hated the Austro-Hungarian dynasty and the empire represented by Ferdinand, the heir to the throne.

It was a warm and radiant Sunday morning when Ferdinand's motorcade made its way through the narrow streets of Sarajevo. Waiting for him along the designated route were seven assassins armed with bombs and revolvers, one of whom threw a bomb into the open car. Glancing off Ferdinand's arm, the bomb exploded near another vehicle and injured dozens of spectators.

Undeterred, Ferdinand went on to a reception at city hall; after the reception he instructed his driver to take him to the hospital where those wounded in the earlier attack were being treated. While Ferdinand was on his way to the hospital, a young Bosnian Serb named Gavrilo Princip (1894–1918) lunged at the archduke's car and fired a revolver. The first bullet blew a gaping hole in the side of Ferdinand's neck. A second bullet intended for the governor of Bosnia went wild and entered the stomach of the expectant Duchess Sophie, the wife of the archduke. Turning to his wife, the archduke pleaded: "Sophie, dear! Don't die! Stay alive for our children!" By the time medical aid arrived, however, the archduke and the duchess were dead.

The assassination of the archduke and his wife brought to a head the tensions between the Austro-Hungarian empire and the neighboring kingdom of Serbia. As other European powers took sides, the stakes far outgrew Austro-Serbian conflicts. Nationalist aspirations, international rivalries, and an inflexible alliance system transformed that conflict into a general European war and ultimately into a global struggle involving thirty-two nations. Twenty-eight of those nations, collectively known as the Allies and the Associated Powers, fought the coalition known as the Central Powers, which consisted of Germany, Austria-Hungary, the Ottoman empire, and Bulgaria. The shell-shocked generation that survived the carnage called this clash of arms the Great War. A subsequent generation of survivors renamed the conflict World War I, because it was, sadly, only the first of two wars that engulfed the world in the first half of the twentieth century.

Although the Great War only lasted four years, from August 1914 to November 1918, it deserves special attention because the processes of nationalism, industrialization, and imperialism all coalesced in one massive explosion of global violence, ushering in history's most violent century. In geographic extent the conflict surpassed all previous wars, compelling men, women, and children on five continents to participate directly or indirectly in a struggle that many did not understand. The Great War also had the distinction of being the first total war in human history, as governments mobilized every available human and material resource for the conduct of war. Moreover, the industrial nature of the conflict meant that it was the bloodiest in the annals of organized violence.

CHRONOLOGY

1914	Assassination of Archduke Francis Ferdinand
1915	Japan makes twenty-one demands on China
1915	Gallipoli campaign
1916	Battles at Verdun and the Somme
1917	German resumption of unrestricted submarine warfare
1917	United States declaration of war on Germany
1917	Bolshevik Revolution
1918	Treaty of Brest-Litovsk
1918	Armistice suspends hostilities
1919	Paris Peace Conference
1920	First meeting of the League of Nations

The military casualties passed a threshold beyond previous experience: approximately fifteen million soldiers died, and an additional twenty million combatants suffered injuries.

The war of 1914–1918 did more than destroy individual lives. It seriously damaged national economies, it led to the redrawing of European boundaries, and it caused the demise of four dynasties and their empires—the Ottoman empire, the Russian empire, the Austro-Hungarian empire, and the German empire. The war also helped unleash the Bolshevik Revolution of 1917, which set the stage for an ideological conflict between capitalism and communism that endured to the end of the twentieth century. Finally, the Great War was responsible for an international realignment of power. It undermined the preeminence and prestige of European society, signaling an end to Europe's global primacy.

THE DRIFT TOWARD WAR

Although the catalyst for war was the assassination of Archduke Francis Ferdinand, the assassin's bullets would have had limited effect if there had not been deeper reasons for war. Indeed, the underlying causes for the war of 1914–1918 were many, including intense nationalism, abrasive colonial rivalries, and a general struggle over the balance of power in Europe and in the world at large. Between 1871 and 1914, European governments adopted foreign policies that increased steadily the danger of war. So as to not find themselves alone in a hostile world, national leaders sought alignments with other powers. The establishment and maintenance in Europe of two hostile alliances—the Allies and the Central Powers—helped spread the war from the Balkans.

Nationalist Aspirations

The nationalist fervor that spread throughout most of Europe in the nineteenth century had led many Europeans to rally behind the idea of *self-determination,* or the idea that peoples with the same ethnic origins, language, and political ideals had the right to form sovereign states. In fact, that idea helped inspire the nationalist movements that led to the creation of the new nations of Belgium (1830), Italy (1861), and Germany (1871). Yet at the end of the nineteenth century, the issue of nationalism remained unresolved in other areas of Europe, most notably in eastern Europe and the Balkans. There the nationalist aspirations of subject minorities threatened to tear apart the multinational empires of the Ottoman and Habsburg dynasties and with them the regional balance of power.

The Ottoman empire had controlled the Balkan peninsula since the fifteenth century, but after 1829 the Turkish empire shriveled, largely because of nationalist revolts. Greece was the first to gain independence (in 1830), but within a few decades Serbia, Romania, and Bulgaria followed suit. Austria-Hungary also confronted nationalism within its realms, especially the aspirations of Slavic peoples—Poles, Czechs, Slovaks, Serbs, Croats, and Slovenes. Most menacing and militant were the Serbs, who pressed for unification with the independent kingdom of Serbia. Russia and Germany added fuel to this volatile situation by supporting opposing sides. Russia supported Serbia and the notion of Slavic cultural unity, while Germany backed Austria-Hungary. Thus the stage was set for international conflict.

National Rivalries

Aggressive nationalism was also manifest in economic competition and colonial conflicts, fueling dangerous rivalries among the major European powers. All the industrialized nations of Europe competed for foreign markets and engaged in tariff wars, but the most unsettling economic rivalry involved Great Britain and Germany. By the twentieth century, Germany's rapid industrialization threatened Britain's long-standing economic predominance. Indeed, by 1914 Britain's share of global industrial output had declined to a level roughly equal to Germany's 13 percent. British reluctance to accept the relative decline of British industry vis-à-vis German industry strained relations between the two economic powers.

Thinking about TRADITIONS

Nationalism and Self-Determination

At the beginning of the twentieth century, the force of nationalism had led many European groups who were part of larger state or imperial structures to insist on their right to national self-determination. *In what ways did the idea of tradition inform and justify their various calls for separate nationhood?*

The Naval Race An expensive naval race further exacerbated tensions between the two nations. When Germany's political and military leaders announced their program to build a fleet with many large battleships, they seemed to undermine Britain's longtime mastery of the seas. The British government moved to meet the German threat through the construction of super battleships known as *dreadnoughts*. Rather than discouraging the Germans, the British determination to retain naval superiority stimulated the Germans to build their own flotilla of dreadnoughts. As the two nations raced to outdo each other, international hostilities boiled under the surface.

Colonial Disputes National rivalries also fomented colonial competition. During the late nineteenth and early twentieth centuries, European nations searched aggressively for new colonies or dependencies to bolster economic performance. In their haste to conquer and colonize, the imperial powers stumbled over one another, repeatedly clashing in one or another corner of the globe: Britain and Russia faced off in Persia (modern-day Iran) and Afghanistan; Britain and France in Siam (modern-day Thailand) and the Nile valley; Britain and Germany in east and southwest Africa; Germany and France in Morocco and west Africa.

Between 1905 and 1914, a series of international crises and two local wars raised tensions and almost precipitated a general European war. The first crisis resulted from a French-German confrontation over Morocco in 1905. When the German government announced its support of

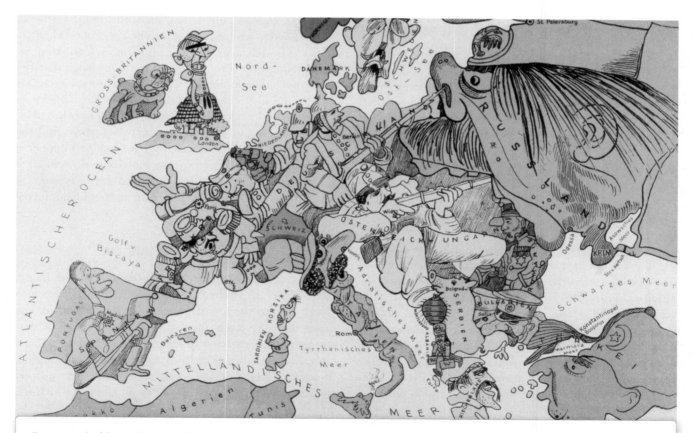

European rivalries at the start of WWI.
This satirical map was created by dissident cartoonist Walter Trier.

What message was Trier trying to convey with this map?

Moroccan independence, which French encroachment endangered, the French responded by threatening war. An international conference in the following year prevented a clash of arms, but similar crises threatened the peace in subsequent years. Contributing to the growing tensions in European affairs were the Balkan wars. Between 1912 and 1913, the states of the Balkan peninsula—including Bulgaria, Greece, Montenegro, Serbia, and Romania—fought two wars for possession of European territories held by the Ottoman empire. The Balkan wars strained European diplomatic relations and helped shape the tense circumstances that led to the outbreak of the Great War.

Public Opinion   Public pressure also contributed to national rivalries. New means of communication—especially cheap, mass-produced newspapers—nourished the public's desire to see their country "come in first," whether in the competition for colonies or in the race to the South Pole. However, public pressure calling for national greatness placed policymakers and diplomats in an awkward situation. Compelled to achieve headline-grabbing foreign policy successes, these leaders ran the risk of paying for short-lived triumphs with long-lasting hostility from other countries.

Understandings and Alliances

In addition to a basic desire for security, escalating national rivalries and nationalist aspirations of subject minorities spawned a system of entangling alliances. The complexity of those obligations could not hide the common characteristic underlying all the alliances: they outlined the circumstances under which countries would go to war to support one another. Intended to preserve the peace, rival alliance systems created a framework whereby even a small international crisis could set off a chain reaction leading to global war. By 1914 Europe's major powers had transformed themselves into two hostile camps—the Triple Alliance and the Triple Entente.

The Central Powers   The Triple Alliance, also known as the Central Powers, grew out of the close relationship that developed between the leaders of Germany and Austria-Hungary during the last three decades of the nineteenth century. In 1879 the governments of the two empires formed the Dual Alliance, a defensive pact that ensured reciprocal protection from a Russian attack and neutrality in case of an attack from any other power. Fear of a hostile France motivated Germans to enter into this pact, whereas Austrians viewed it as giving them a free hand in pursuing their Balkan politics without fear of Russian intervention. Italy, fearful of France, joined the Dual Alliance in 1882, thereby transforming it into the Triple Alliance.

Triple Entente (ahn-TAHNT)
Schlieffen (SHLEE-fn)

The Allies   Meanwhile, the leaders of other nations viewed this new constellation of power with suspicion. This response was especially true of French leaders, who still remembered France's humiliating defeat during the Franco-Prussian War of 1870–1871. The tsarist regime of Russia was equally disturbed by the new alignment of powers, especially by Germany's support of Austria, and British leaders were traditionally suspicious of any arrangement that seemed to threaten the balance of power on the Continent. The result was that, in a series of agreements between 1904 and 1914, the most unlikely bedfellows formed the Triple Entente, a combination of nations commonly referred to as the Allies. The construction of such alliances made it difficult for diplomats to contain what otherwise might have been relatively small international crises.

War Plans   The preservation of peace was also difficult because the military staffs of each nation had devised inflexible military plans and timetables to be carried out in the event of war. German war plans in particular played a crucial role in the events leading to the Great War. Germany's fear of encirclement by France and Russia encouraged its military planners to devise a strategy that would avoid a war on two fronts. It was based on a strategy developed in 1905 by General Count Alfred von Schlieffen (1833–1913). The Schlieffen plan called for a swift knockout of France, followed by defensive action against Russia. German planners predicated their strategy on the knowledge that the Russians could not mobilize their soldiers and military supplies as quickly as the French, thus giving German forces a few precious weeks during which they could concentrate their full power on France. However, Germany's military strategy was a serious obstacle to those seeking to preserve the peace. In the event of Russian mobilization, Germany's leaders would feel compelled to stick to their war plans by attacking France first, thereby setting in motion a military conflict of major proportions.

GLOBAL WAR

In the capitals of Europe, people danced in the streets when their governments announced formal declarations of war. When the first contingents of soldiers left for the front, jubilant crowds threw flowers at the feet of departing men, who expected to return victorious after a short time. However, reality crushed any expectations of a short and triumphant war. On most fronts the conflict quickly bogged down and became a war of attrition in which the firepower of modern weapons slaughtered soldiers by the millions. For the first time in history, belligerent nations engaged in total war. Even in democratic societies, governments assumed dictatorial control to marshal the human and material resources required for continuous war. One result was increased participation of women in the labor force. Total war had repercussions that went beyond the borders of Europe.

Imperial ties drew millions of Asians, Africans, and residents of the British dominions into the war to serve as soldiers and laborers. Struggles over far-flung colonies further underlined the global dimension of this war. Last, the war gained a global flavor through the entry of Japan, the United States, and the Ottoman empire, nations whose leaders professed little direct interest in European affairs.

The Guns of August

Declarations of War   The shots fired from Gavrilo Princip's revolver on that fateful day of 28 June 1914 set in motion a flurry of diplomatic activity that quickly escalated into war. Austrian leaders in Vienna were determined to teach the unruly Serbs a lesson, and on 23 July the Austrians issued an ultimatum to the government of Serbia. When the Serbian government rejected one of its terms, Austria-Hungary declared war on Serbia. The war had begun. The subsequent sequence of events was largely determined by two factors: complex mobilization plans and the grinding logic of the alliance system. Military planners were convinced that the timing of mobilization orders and adherence to precise timetables were crucial to the successful conduct of war.

On 29 July the Russian government mobilized its troops to defend its Serbian ally and itself from Austria. The tsar of Russia then ordered mobilization against Germany. Nicholas II (1868–1918) took that decisive step reluctantly and only after his military experts had convinced him that a partial mobilization might invite defeat should the Germans enter the war on the side of Austria. His action precipitated a German ultimatum to Russia on 31 July, demanding that the Russian army cease its mobilization immediately. Another ultimatum addressed to France demanded to know what France's intentions were in case Germany and Russia went to war. The Russians replied with a blunt "impossible," and the French never answered. Thus on 1 August the German government declared war on Russia, and France started to mobilize.

On 3 August the Germans declared war on France. On the same day, German troops invaded Belgium in accordance with the Schlieffen plan. Key to this plan was an attack on the weak left flank of the French army by an imposing German force through neutral Belgium. On 4 August the British government sent an ultimatum to Germany demanding that Belgian neutrality be respected.

When Germany's wartime leaders refused, the British immediately declared war. A local conflict had become a general European war.

Mutual Butchery

Everyone expected the war to be brief. In the first weeks of August 1914, twenty million young men donned uniforms, took up rifles, and left for the front. Many of them looked forward to heroic charges, rapid promotions, and a quick homecoming. Some dreamed of glory and honor, and they believed that God was on their side. Similar attitudes prevailed among the political and military leaders of the belligerent nations, who were preoccupied by visions of sweeping assaults, envelopments, and, above all, swift triumphs. Their visions could hardly have been more wrong.

The Western Front   The initial German thrust toward Paris in August 1914 came to a grinding halt along the river Marne, after which each side tried to outflank the other in a race to the Atlantic coast. For the next three years, the battle lines remained virtually stationary, as both sides dug in and slugged it out in a war of attrition that lasted until the late autumn of 1918. Each belligerent tried to wear down the enemy by inflicting continuous damage and casualties, only to have its own forces suffer heavy losses in return. Trenches on the western front ran from the English Channel to Switzerland. Farther south, Italy left the Triple Alliance to enter the war on the side of the Allies in 1915. Allied hopes that the Italians would pierce Austrian defenses quickly faded. After a disastrous defeat at Caporetto in 1917, Italian forces maintained a defensive line only with the help of the French and the British.

Stalemate and New Weapons   The stalemate on the western and southern fronts reflected technological developments that favored defensive tactics. Barbed wire proved highly effective in frustrating the advance of soldiers across "no-man's-land," the deadly territory between opposing trenches. In addition, the rapid and continuous fire of machine guns turned infantry charges across no-man's-land into suicide missions. Both sides developed weapons to break the deadly stalemate and reintroduce movement into the war. Gas often proved lethal, and it caused its victims excruciating pain. Mustard gas, for example, rotted the body from both within and without.

Poison gas.
Air raid warden in helmet and gas mask, holding a wooden gas attack rattle in his gloved hand.

Caporetto (kap-uh-RET-oh)

Reverberations ● ● ● ● ● ● ● ●

The Destructive Potential of Industrial Technologies

By the last half of the nineteenth century, a variety of European and American intellectuals believed that industrialization—which resulted in mass-produced goods, new and more rapid forms of communication, and all manner of mechanized devices—had led to a marked improvement in the human condition. Moreover, these same intellectuals were optimistic that industrialization would continue to contribute to the overall progress of humanity into the distant future. In many ways their expectations were realized: during the twentieth century industrial machinery made it possible to feed billions of people, build vast networks of roads, and create hundreds of millions of cars and airplanes. Mass-produced medicines made it possible to virtually eliminate smallpox, the plague, and a variety of other health scourges from much of the world, while mass-produced consumer goods allowed people to purchase, at relatively low cost, a bewildering variety of items designed to make them more comfortable. At an aggregate level, humans in the twentieth century lived longer, were less poor, were more connected to one another, and had access to more everyday comforts than their predecessors in previous centuries.

The Machinery of War

Yet the twentieth century also revealed the enormous costs of industrialization—costs that reverberate right up to the present. Indeed, although industrialization allowed the manufacture of goods and materials that brought people together or made life more convenient, it also allowed for the manufacture of items designed for destruction on a hitherto unimaginable scale. In this chapter we have already seen how the belligerent European nations involved in World War I marshaled their industrial power to manufacture deadly weapons, ammunition, chemical gases, tanks, and submarines. Few humans alive even in 1900 could have imagined the devastation—in both life and property—made possible when industrial powers put their energies toward destruction. In fact, disillusion with the destructive capacities of industrial technologies played an important role in the widespread atmosphere of anxiety that permeated intellectual and popular circles after the war—a process discussed in chapter 30. Such anxieties did not prevent industrialized nations from continuing to develop more and better ways to destroy their enemies, however. During World War II, opposing sides used industrial technology to kill ever more efficiently and quickly. In the case of Germany, Adolf Hitler took industrialized killing to a chilling new level when he authorized the use of advanced industrial techniques to kill millions of Jews, Gypsies, Slavs, dissidents, and homosexuals (chapter 32). After the war, the creation of the atom bomb used with such devastating effect in Hiroshima and Nagasaki made it clear that scientists had designed industrial weaponry capable of destroying entire populations in one blow. From that point until the dissolution of the

After blistering the skin and damaging the eyes, the gas attacked the bronchial tubes, stripping off the mucous membrane. Death could occur in four to five weeks. Yet although both sides suffered heavy casualties, totaling about 800,000 soldiers, gas attacks failed to deliver the promised strategic breakthroughs. Other novel weapons developed during the war included tanks and airplanes. Other weapons systems, such as the submarine, had made earlier appearances in warfare but were most effectively used by the German navy against Allied commercial shipping in the Great War.

War casualties on the Western front.
This photograph depicts a mutilated body among barbed wire in no-man's-land.

No-Man's-Land The most courageous infantry charges, even when preceded by pulverizing artillery barrages and clouds of poisonous gas, were no match for determined defenders. Shielded by the dirt of their trenches and by barbed wire and gas masks, they unleashed a torrent of lethal metal with their machine guns and repeating rifles. In every sector of the front, those who fought rarely found the glory they sought. Instead, they encountered death. No-man's-land was strewn with shell craters, cadavers, and body parts. The grim realities of trench warfare—the wet, cold, waist-deep mud, gluttonous lice,

Soviet Union in 1991, people all over the world were subjected to the threat of nuclear annihilation if the "cold" war between the U.S. and the U.S.S.R. ever erupted into a "hot" war (chapter 33). During the twentieth century, indeed, the threat of mass destruction via industrial technologies was a reality that significant segments of the world's population learned to live with.

Environmental Impact

Industrial technologies also proved to be destructive during the twentieth century in terms of their environmental impact. Since the nineteenth century, industrial economies relied on fossil fuels to function. In addition, industrial manufacturing required the widespread exploitation of raw materials such as cotton and timber. During the nineteenth and much of the twentieth centuries, industrializing states operated as though fossil fuels and raw materials would be endlessly available. Over time, however, it became clear that large-scale industrialization resulted in air and water pollution as well

Munitions. Women at work in an English munitions factory. The Great War drew huge numbers of men out of the workforce at a time of great industrial need. Women replaced them, for the first time assuming traditionally "male" jobs.

as in deforestation, erosion, and the loss of biodiversity. During the post–World War II period, these problems intensified as a variety of new states sought to establish industrialized economies of their own—a process discussed in chapter 33. By the end of the twentieth century, moreover, the majority of the world's scientists concluded that the pollution generated by more than a century of industrialization had caused changes in climate on a planetary scale (chapter 34). The ultimate impact of these changes remain unclear, although some scientists fear that it may be too late to undo the damage that has been set in motion from industrialization.

These are only a small sampling of the historical reverberations of the destructive potential of industrial technologies, both through time and across space. When reading subsequent chapters, try to identify additional developments whose origins can be traced to the consequences of industrialization, whether of a positive or destructive nature.

and corpse-fed rats—contrasted sharply with the ringing phrases of politicians and generals justifying the unrelenting slaughter.

Bloodletting   Many battles took place, but some were so horrific, so devastating, and so futile that their names are synonymous with human slaughter. The casualty figures attested to this bloodletting. In 1916 the Germans tried to break the deadlock with a huge assault on the fortress of Verdun. The French rallying cry was "They shall not pass," and they did not—but at a tremendous cost: while the victorious French counted 315,000 dead, the defeated Germans suffered a loss of 280,000. To relieve the pressure on Verdun, British forces counterattacked at the Somme, and by November they had gained a few thousand yards at the cost of 420,000 casualties. The Germans suffered similar losses, although in the end neither side gained any strategic advantage.

The Eastern Front   In eastern Europe and the Balkans, the battle lines were more fluid. After a staunch defense, a combination of Austrian and German forces overran Serbia, Albania, and Romania. Farther north, Russia took the offensive early by invading Prussia in 1914. The Central Powers recovered quickly, however, and in the summer of 1915, combined German-Austrian forces drove the Russian armies out of East Prussia and then out of Poland and established a defensive line extending from the Baltic to the Ukraine. Russian counterattacks in 1916 and 1917 collapsed in a sea of casualties. Those Russian defeats undermined the popularity of the tsar and his government and played a significant role in fostering revolutionary ferment within Russian society.

New Rules of Engagement   Dying and suffering were not limited solely to combatants: the Great War established rules of engagement that made civilians targets of warfare, both from air attacks and from naval blockades. Indeed, military leaders on both sides used blockades to deny food to whole populations, hoping that starving masses would force their governments to capitulate. The British blockade of Germany during the war contributed to the deaths of an estimated half million Germans.

Total War: The Home Front

As the Great War ground on, it became a conflict of attrition in which the organization of material and human resources was of paramount importance. War became total, fought between entire societies, and total victory was the only

acceptable outcome that might justify the terrible sacrifices made by all sides. The nature of total war created a military front and a home front. The term *home front* expressed the important reality that the outcome of the war hinged on how effectively each nation mobilized its economy and activated its noncombatant citizens to support the war effort.

MAP 29.1

The Great War in Europe and southwest Asia, 1914–1918. Note the locations of both the eastern and the western fronts in Europe during the war.

Why didn't the same kind of trench warfare immobilize opposing armies on the eastern front the way it did on the western front?

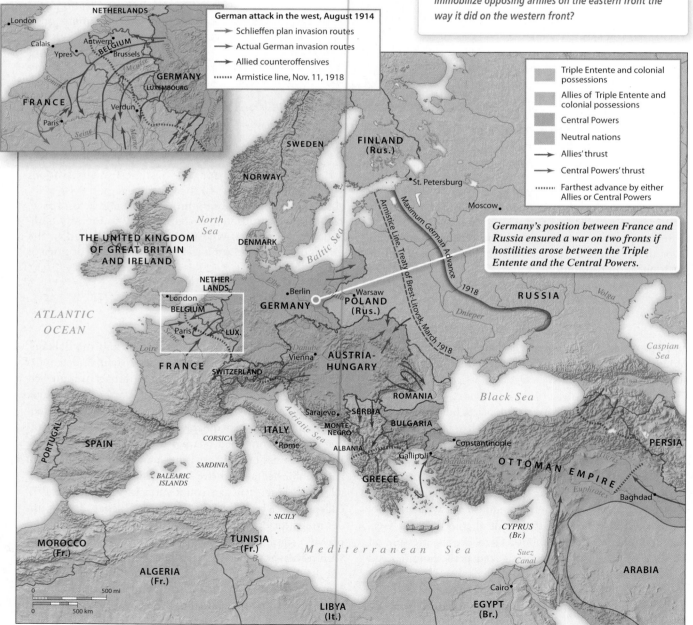

Triple Entente and colonial possessions

Allies of Triple Entente and colonial possessions

Central Powers

Neutral nations

Allies' thrust

Central Powers' thrust

Farthest advance by either Allies or Central Powers

Germany's position between France and Russia ensured a war on two fronts if hostilities arose between the Triple Entente and the Central Powers.

German attack in the west, August 1914

→ Schlieffen plan invasion routes

→ Actual German invasion routes

→ Allied counteroffensives

······ Armistice line, Nov. 11, 1918

The Home Front As the war continued beyond Christmas 1914 and as war weariness and a decline in economic capability set in, the response of all belligerents was to limit individual freedoms and give control of society increasingly to military leaders. Initially, ministers and generals shrank from compulsive measures, even conscription of recruits, but they quickly changed their minds. Each belligerent government eventually militarized civilian war production by subordinating private enterprises to governmental control and imposing severe discipline on the labor process.

Economic measures were foremost in the minds of government leaders because the war created unprecedented demands for raw materials and manufactured goods. Planning boards reorganized entire industries, set production quotas and priorities, and determined what would be produced and consumed. Government authorities also established wage and price controls, extended work hours, and in some instances restricted the movement of workers. Because bloody battlefields caused an insatiable appetite for soldiers, nations responded by extending military service. In Germany, for example, men between the ages of sixteen and sixty were eligible to serve at the front. By constantly tapping into the available male population, the war created an increasing demand for workers at home. Unemployment—a persistent feature of all prewar economies—vanished virtually overnight.

Women at War As men marched off to war, women marched off to work. Conscription took men out of the labor force, and wartime leaders exhorted women to fill the gaps in the workforce. A combination of patriotism and high wages drew women into many formerly "male" jobs in a wide variety of industries and public sectors. Perhaps the most crucial work performed by women during the war was the making of shells. Several million women, and sometimes children, put in long, hard hours in munitions factories. That work exposed them to severe dangers, not to mention death, from explosions and poisoning from long-term exposure to TNT.

Although some middle- and upper-class women reported that the war was a liberating experience in regard to personal and economic freedom, most working-class women found little that was liberating in war work. Most of the belligerent governments promised equal pay for equal work, but in most instances that promise remained unfulfilled. Moreover, substantial female employment was a transitory phenomenon. Once the war was over, many women workers—especially those in traditionally male occupations—found themselves forced to concede their jobs to men. Nevertheless, the extension of voting rights to women shortly after the war—in Britain (1918, for women thirty years and older), Germany (1919), and Austria (1919)—was in part due to the role women assumed during the Great War.

Propaganda To maintain the spirit of the home front and to counter threats to national unity, governments resorted to the restriction of civil liberties, censorship of bad news, and vilification of the enemy through propaganda campaigns. While some government officials busily censored war news, people who had the temerity to criticize their nation's war effort were prosecuted as traitors. Meanwhile, the propaganda offices of the belligerent nations tried to convince the public that military defeat would mean the destruction of everything worth living for, and to that end they did their utmost to discredit and dehumanize the enemy.

German propaganda depicted Russians as semi-Asiatic barbarians, and French authorities chronicled the atrocities committed by the German "Hun" in Belgium. In 1917 the *Times* of London published a story claiming that Germans converted human corpses into fertilizer and food. In Germany, one widely distributed poster invoked images of bestial black Allied soldiers raping German women to suggest the horrors that would follow if the nation's war effort failed. Most atrocity stories were patently false, and they eventually engendered public skepticism and cynicism.

War propaganda.
"The Heroes of Belgium, 1914." French propaganda poster expresses outrage at the German invasion of Belgium.

What are these "German" soldiers trampling underfoot?

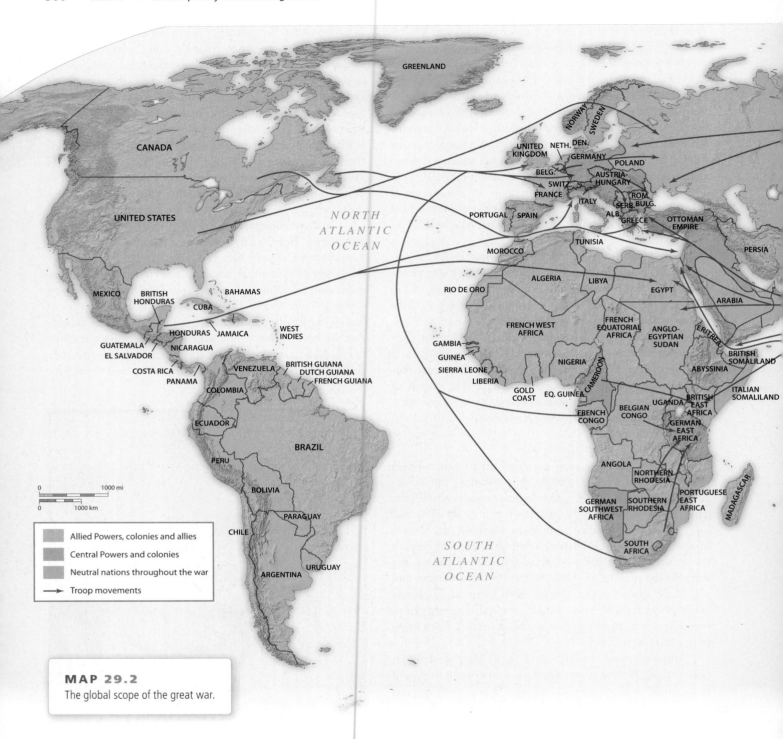

MAP 29.2
The global scope of the great war.

Map legend:
- Allied Powers, colonies and allies
- Central Powers and colonies
- Neutral nations throughout the war
- → Troop movements

Ironically, public disbelief of wartime propaganda led to an inability to believe in the abominations perpetrated in later wars.

Conflict in East Asia and the Pacific

The Great War quickly turned from a European war into a global conflict. There were three reasons for the war's expansion. First, European governments carried their animosities into their colonies, embroiling them—especially African societies—in their war. Second, because Europe's human reserves were not enough to satisfy the appetite of war, the British and the French augmented their ranks by recruiting men from their colonies. Millions of Africans and Asians were drawn into the war. Behind their trenches the French employed laborers from Algeria, China, and French Indochina, and the British did not hesitate to draft Indian and African troops for combat. The British in particular

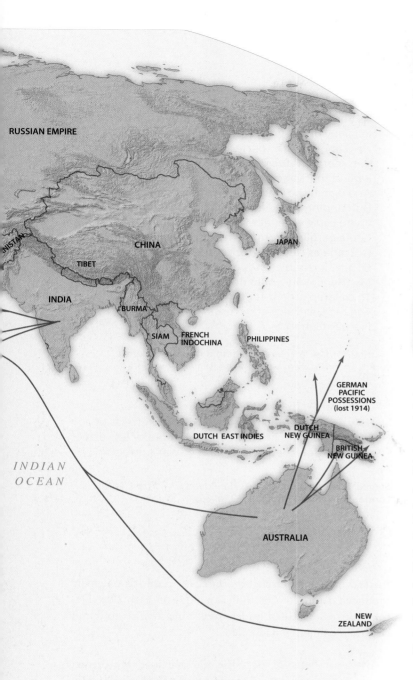

Colonial participation in WWI.
An Indian gun crew in the Somme area, 1916.

note also demanded that the German navy unconditionally withdraw its warships from Japanese and Chinese waters. When the Germans refused to comply, the Japanese entered the war on the side of the Allies on 23 August 1914. Japanese forces then proceeded to seize German territories in China and—aided by forces from New Zealand and Australia—in the Pacific. Next, Japan shrewdly exploited Allied support and European preoccupation to advance its own imperial interests in China. On 18 January 1915 the Japanese presented the Chinese government with twenty-one secret demands. The terms of that ultimatum, if accepted, would have reduced China to a protectorate of Japan. Chinese diplomats leaked the note to the British authorities, who spoke up for China, thus preventing total capitulation. The Twenty-one Demands reflected Japan's determination to dominate east Asia and served as the basis for future Japanese pressure on China.

Battles in Africa and Southwest Asia

The geographic extent of the conflict also broadened beyond Europe when the Allies targeted German colonies in Africa. When the war of 1914–1918 erupted in Europe, all of sub-Saharan Africa (except Ethiopia and Liberia) consisted of European colonies, with the Germans controlling four: Togoland, the Cameroons, German Southwest Africa, and German East Africa. Unlike the capture of German colonies in the Pacific, which Allied forces accomplished during the first three months of the war with relative ease, the conquest of German colonies in Africa was difficult.

relied on troops furnished by the dominion lands, including Australia, New Zealand, Canada, Newfoundland, and South Africa. Third, the Great War assumed global significance because of the entrance into the war of Japan, the United States, and the Ottoman empire.

On 15 August 1914 the Japanese government sent an ultimatum to Germany demanding the handover of the German-leased territory of Jiaozhou (northeastern China) to Japanese authorities without compensation. The same

Jiaozhou (jyou-joh)

SourcesfromthePast

Dulce et Decorum Est

The Great War produced a wealth of poetry. The poetic response to war covered a range of moods from early romanticism and patriotism to cynicism, resignation, and the angry depiction of horror. Perhaps the greatest of all war poets was Wilfred Owen (1893–1918), whose poems are among the most poignant of the war. Owen, who enlisted for service on the western front in 1915, was injured in March 1917 and sent home. Declared fit for duty in August 1918, he returned to the front. German machine-gun fire killed him on 7 November, four days before the armistice, when he tried to cross the Sambre Canal.

Bent double, like old beggars under sacks,
Knock-kneed, coughing like hags, we cursed
  through sludge,
Till on the haunting flares we turned our backs
And towards our distant rest began to trudge.
Men marched asleep. Many had lost their boots
But limped on, blood-shod. All went lame; all blind;
Drunk with fatigue; deaf even to the hoots
Of gas-shells dropping softly behind.
Gas! GAS! Quick, boys!—An ecstasy of fumbling,
Fitting the clumsy helmets just in time;
But someone still was yelling out and stumbling
And floundering like a man in fire or lime.—
Dim, through the misty panes and thick green light

As under a green sea, I saw him drowning.
In all my dreams, before my helpless sight,
He plunges at me, guttering, choking, drowning.
If in some smothering dreams you too could pace
Behind the wagon that we flung him in,
And watch the white eyes writhing in his face,
His hanging face, like a devil's sick of sin;
If you could hear, at every jolt, the blood
Come gargling from the froth-corrupted lungs,
Obscene as cancer, bitter as the cud
Of vile, incurable sores on innocent tongues,—
My friend, you would not tell with such high zest
To children ardent for some desperate glory,
The old Lie: Dulce et decorum est
Pro patria mori.*

*Author's note: "Sweet and fitting is it to die for one's country" comes from a line by the Roman poet Horace (65–8 B.C.E.)

For Further Reflection

■ How does Owen poetically describe the effects of a gas attack? Is his literary depiction more or less effective than detached descriptions of war's effects?

Source: Edmund Blunden, ed. *The Poems of Wilfred Owen.* London: Chatto & Windus, 1933, p. 66.

Fighting took place on land and sea; on lakes and rivers; in deserts, jungles, and swamps; and in the air. Indeed, the German flag did not disappear from Africa until after the armistice took effect on 11 November 1918.

The most extensive military operations outside Europe took place in the southwest Asian territories of the Ottoman empire, which was aligned with the Central Powers at the end of 1914. Seeking a way to break the stalemate on the western front, Winston Churchill (1874–1965), first lord of the Admiralty (British navy), suggested that an Allied strike against the Ottomans—a weak ally of the Central Powers—would hurt the Germans. Early in 1915 the British navy conducted an expedition to seize the approach to the Dardanelles Strait in an attempt to open a warm-water supply line to Russia through the Ottoman-controlled strait. The campaign was a disaster. Turkish defenders, ensconced in the cliffs above, quickly pinned down the Allied troops on the beaches. Trapped between the sea and the hills, Allied soldiers dug in and engaged in

their own version of trench warfare. The resulting stalemate produced a total of 250,000 casualties on each side. Despite the losses, Allied leaders took nine months to admit that their campaign had failed.

Armenian Massacres   The war provided the pretext for a campaign of extermination against the Ottoman empire's two million Armenians. Friction between Christian Armenians and Muslim Ottoman authorities went back to the nineteenth century, when distinct nationalist feelings stirred many of the peoples who lived under Ottoman rule.

After 1913, the Ottoman state adopted a new policy of Turkish nationalism intended to shore up the crumbling imperial edifice. The new nationalism stressed Turkish culture and traditions and regarded Christian minorities as obstacles to Turkism. During the Great War, the Ottoman government branded Armenians as traitorous internal enemies. The government then unleashed a murderous campaign against the Armenians, which included mass evacuations that were accompanied by starvation, dehydration, and exposure. Equally deadly were government-organized massacres that claimed victims through mass drowning, incineration, or assaults with blunt instruments.

Best estimates suggest that close to a million Armenians perished between 1915 and 1917 in what has become known as the Armenian genocide. Although it is generally agreed that the Armenian genocide did occur, the Turkish government denies the label of state-sponsored genocide, arguing instead that the deaths occurred as a result of communal warfare, disease, and famine.

THE END OF THE WAR

The war produced strains within all the belligerent nations, but most of them managed, often ruthlessly, to cope with food riots, strikes, and mutinies. In the Russian empire, the war amplified existing stresses to such an extent that the Romanov dynasty was forced to abdicate in favor of a provisional government in the spring of 1917. Eight months later, the provisional government yielded power to Bolshevik revolutionaries, who took Russia out of the war early in 1918. This blow to the Allies was more than offset by the entry of the United States into the conflict in 1917, which turned the tide of war in 1918. The resources of the United States finally compelled the exhausted Central Powers to sue for peace in November 1918.

In 1919 the victorious Allies gathered in Paris to hammer out a peace settlement that turned out to be a compromise that pleased few of the parties involved. The most significant consequence of the war was Europe's diminished role in the world. The war of 1914–1918 undermined Europe's power and simultaneously promoted nationalist aspirations among colonized peoples, who clamored for self-determination and national independence. For the time being, however, the major imperialist powers kept their grip on their overseas holdings.

Revolution in Russia

The Great War had undermined the Russian state. In the spring of 1917, disintegrating armies, mutinies, and food shortages provoked a series of street demonstrations and strikes in Petrograd (St. Petersburg). The inability of police forces to suppress the uprisings, and the subsequent mutiny of troops garrisoned in the capital, persuaded Tsar Nicholas II (reigned 1894–1917) to abdicate the throne.

The Struggle for Power After its success in Petrograd, this "February Revolution" spread throughout the country, and political power in Russia shifted to two new agencies: the provisional government and the Petrograd soviet of Workers' and Soldiers' Deputies. Soviets, which were

Vladimir Lenin.
In this photograph, Lenin makes a speech in Red Square on the first anniversary (1918) of the Bolshevik revolution.

revolutionary councils organized by socialists, surfaced all over Russia in 1917, wielding considerable power through their control of factories and segments of the military. The period between February and October witnessed a political struggle between the provisional government and the powerful Petrograd soviet. At first the new government enjoyed considerable public support as it eliminated the repressive institutions of the tsarist state, but it failed to satisfy popular demands for an end to war and for land reform. It claimed that, being provisional, it could not make fundamental changes such as confiscating land and distributing it among peasants. The government also promised to continue the war and to bring it to a victorious conclusion. The Petrograd soviet, in contrast, called for an immediate peace.

Lenin Into this tense political situation stepped Vladimir Ilyich Lenin (1870–1924), a revolutionary Marxist and the leader of the small but radical Bolshevik socialist party. Although Lenin had been living in enforced exile in Switzerland, early in 1917 the German High Command helped him return to Russia in the hope that he would foment revolution and bring about Russia's withdrawal from the war. He did. Already in April 1917 Lenin began calling for the transfer of legal authority to the soviets and advocated uncompromising opposition to the war.

Under Lenin's leadership, the Bolsheviks eventually gained control of the Petrograd soviet. Crucial to this development was the provisional government's insistence on

Romanov (ROH-mah-nahv)
Bolshevik (BOHL-shih-vehk)
Vladimir Ilyich Lenin (VLAD-uh-meer IL-yich LEHN-in)

continuing the war, its inability to feed the population, and its refusal to undertake land reform. Workers and peasants became increasingly convinced that their problems could be solved only by the soviets. In September, Lenin persuaded the Central Committee of the Bolshevik party to organize an armed insurrection and seize power in the name of the All-Russian National Congress of Soviets, which was then convening in Petrograd. During the night of 24 October and the following day, armed workers, soldiers, and sailors stormed the Winter Palace, the home of the provisional government. By the afternoon of 25 October, the virtually bloodless insurrection had run its course, and power passed from the provisional government into the hands of Lenin and the Bolshevik party.

Treaty of Brest-Litovsk   The Bolshevik rulers then ended Russia's involvement in the Great War by signing the Treaty of Brest-Litovsk with Germany on 3 March 1918. The treaty gave the Germans possession or control of one-third of Russia's territory (the Baltic States, the Caucasus, Finland, Poland, and the Ukraine) and one-quarter of its population. Although the terms of the treaty were harsh and humiliating, taking Russia out of the war gave the new government an opportunity to deal with internal problems. Russia's departure from the war also meant that Germany could concentrate all its resources on the western front.

U.S. Intervention and Collapse of the Central Powers

The year 1917 was crucial for another reason: it marked the entry of the United States into the war on the side of the Allies. In 1914 the American public firmly opposed intervention in a European war. That sentiment soon changed. After the outbreak of the war, the United States pursued a neutrality that favored the Allies, and as the war progressed, the United States became increasingly committed economically to an Allied victory.

America Declares War   The official factor in the United States' decision to enter the war, however, was Germany's resumption of unrestricted submarine warfare in February 1917—a practice that had aroused American outrage in the early years of the war. Germany's leaders took this decisive step because they were desperate to break the British blockade that threatened to starve the Central Powers and hoped to use their submarines to do so. German military experts calculated that submarine attacks against the ships of Great Britain and all the ships headed to Great Britain would bring about the defeat of Great Britain in six months. By that time, however, both the American public and its leadership were invested in an Allied victory, and thus Germany's decision brought the United States into the war in April 1917.

Collapsing Fronts   The corrosive effects of years of bloodletting showed. For the first two years of the conflict, most people supported their governments' war efforts, but the continuing ravages of war took their toll everywhere. The Central Powers suffered from food shortages as a result of the British blockade, and increasing numbers of people took to the streets to demonstrate against declining food rations. Food riots were complemented by strikes as prewar social conflicts reemerged. Governments reacted harshly to these challenges, pouncing on strikers, suppressing demonstrators, and jailing dissidents. Equally dangerous was the breakdown of military discipline on both sides. In France, for example, a mutiny in the spring of 1917 involved 50,000 soldiers, resulting in 23,385 courts-martial and 432 death sentences.

Against that grim background, Germany took the risk of throwing its remaining might at the western front in the spring of 1918. The gamble failed, and as the offensive petered out, the Allies—strengthened by fresh U.S. troops—broke through the front and started pushing the Germans back. By that time Germany had effectively exhausted its human and material means to wage war. Meanwhile, Bulgaria capitulated to the invading Allies on 30 September, the Ottomans concluded an armistice on 30 October, and

Prisoners of war.
German prisoners taken in France in the fall of 1918.

Austria-Hungary surrendered on 4 November. Finally, the Germans accepted an armistice, which took effect on 11 November 1918. At last the guns went silent.

After the War

The immediate effects of the Great War were all too obvious. Aside from the physical destruction, which was most visible in northern France and Belgium, the war had killed, disabled, orphaned, or rendered homeless millions of people. Conservative estimates suggest that the war killed fifteen million people and wounded twenty million others. Many of the combatant survivors were unable to adjust back into civilian life after the horrors of what they had seen in battle. Survivors frequently displayed symptoms that contemporaries labeled "shell shock" (know today as post-traumatic stress disorder), which ranged from horrific nightmares, to uncontrollable shaking, to an inability to interact with others. Moreover, in the immediate postwar years, millions of people—noncombatants as well as combatants—succumbed to the effects of starvation, malnutrition, and epidemic diseases.

The Influenza Pandemic of 1918 The end of the Great War coincided with the arrival of one of the worst pandemics ever recorded in human history. No one knows its origins or why it vanished in mid-1919, but by the time this virulent influenza disappeared, it had left more than 20 million dead. This exceptionally lethal virus hit young adults—a group usually not severely affected by influenza—with particular ferocity.

The Great War did not cause the flu pandemic of 1918–1919, but wartime traffic on land and sea probably contributed to the spread of the infection. From the remotest villages in Arctic climates and crowded cities in India and the United States to the battlefields of Europe, men and women were struck down by high fever. Within a few days they were dead. In Calcutta, India, the postal service and the legal system ground to a halt. The Pacific Islands suffered worst of all as the flu wiped out up to 25 percent of the entire population. Indeed, the influenza plague did not discriminate between the rich and poor, men and women, or the sick and healthy. Moreover, the presence of doctors and nurses made no difference. There was no cure for the flu of 1918.

Before the costs of the war were assessed fully, world attention shifted to Paris. There, in 1919, the victorious powers convened to arrange a postwar settlement and set terms for the defeated nations. At the outset, people on both sides of the war had high hopes for the settlement, but in the end it left a bitter legacy. Ultimately, Georges Clemenceau (1841–1929), David Lloyd George (1863–1945), and Woodrow Wilson—the representative leaders of France, Great Britain, and the United States—dominated the deliberations. The Allies did not permit representatives of the Central Powers to participate, and the Soviet Union was not invited to the conference. Throughout this time the British blockade of Germany remained in effect, adding a sense of urgency to the proceedings.

Wilson's Fourteen Points One year before the opening of the Paris Peace Conference, in January 1918, U.S. president Woodrow Wilson had forwarded a proposal for a just and enduring postwar peace settlement. Wilson's postwar vision subsequently prompted the defeated Central Powers to announce their acceptance of his so-called Fourteen Points as the basis for the armistice. They also expected the Allies to use them as the foundation for later peace treaties. Key among Wilson's Fourteen Points were the following recommendations: open covenants (agreements) of peace, openly arrived at; absolute freedom of navigation upon the seas in peace and war; the removal of all economic barriers and the establishment of an equality of trade conditions among all nations; adequate guarantees for a reduction in national armaments; adjustments of colonial disputes to give equal weight to the interests of the controlling government and the colonial population; and a call for "a general association of nations."

The idealism expressed in the Fourteen Points gave Wilson a position of moral leadership among the Allies. Those same allies also opposed various points of Wilson's peace formula, because those points compromised the secret wartime agreements by which they had agreed to distribute among themselves territories and possessions of the defeated nations. The defeated powers, in turn, later felt betrayed when they faced the harsh peace treaties that so clearly violated the spirit of the Fourteen Points.

The Peace Treaties The final form of the treaties represented a series of compromises among the victors. The hardest terms originated with the French, who desired the destruction or the permanent weakening of German power. Thus, in addition to requiring Germany to accept sole responsibility and guilt for causing the war, the victors demanded a reduction in the military potential of the former Central Powers. In addition, the Allies prohibited Germany and Austria from entering into any sort of political union. The French and the British agreed that the defeated Central Powers must pay for the cost of the war and required the payment of reparations either in money or in kind.

The Paris Peace Conference resulted in additional treaties with Bulgaria, Austria, Hungary, and the Ottoman empire. Whereas Bulgaria lost only small portions of territory as a result, the Austro-Hungarian empire was destroyed: in separate treaties both Austria and Hungary suffered severe territorial losses. Arrangements between the defeated Ottoman empire and the Allies proved to be a more complicated

Georges Clemenceau (jawrj klem-uhn-SOH)

Thinking about ENCOUNTERS

From Civil War to Total War

Many observers considered the Great War a civil war among Europeans. *How did the war draw in peoples outside Europe, and what form did contacts between Europeans, Asians, and Africans take?*

and protracted affair that involved two treaties. In 1920 the Treaty of Sèvres effectively dissolved the empire, calling for the surrender of Ottoman Balkan and Arab provinces and the occupation of eastern and southern Anatolia by foreign powers. However, Turkish nationalists—led by the war hero Mustafa Kemal—set out to defy those terms. Kemal organized a national army that drove out Allied occupation forces, abolished the sultanate, and replaced it with the Republic of Turkey, with Ankara as its capital. In a great diplomatic victory for Turkish nationalists, the Allied powers officially recognized the Republic of Turkey in a final peace agreement, the Treaty of Lausanne (1923).

The League of Nations Although the war was over, the peace settlement that resulted from it was weak. To be sure, some efforts to avoid future conflicts were made. At the urging of U.S. president Woodrow Wilson, the Covenant of the League of Nations was made an integral part of the peace treaties, and every signatory to a peace treaty had to accept this new world organization. However, the league suffered from fundamental weaknesses that made it unable to enforce its decisions. Over the next two decades, it became clear that the league could not stop the aggression that would lead to World War II, and the institution closed its doors in 1940. Nevertheless, the league did establish the pattern for a permanent international organization and served as a model for its successor, the United Nations.

Self-Determination Another weakness of the peace was the uneven way in which key ideas of the peacemaking process—especially the idea of national self-determination—were put into practice around the world. In Europe, the peacemakers in Paris did in fact try to apply the principle of self-determination and nationality to a variety of peoples, such as Slavs, Czechs, and Slovaks, although the results were far from perfect. Yet in other instances peacemakers pushed the principle aside for strategic and security reasons, such as in Austria and Germany, whose peoples were denied the right to form one nation.

Treaty of Sèvres (SEV-ruh)
Mustafa Kemal (MOOS-tah-fah kuh-MAHL)

The Mandate System However imperfect the results, the peacemakers at Paris tried to apply the principle of self-determination and nationality throughout Europe. Elsewhere, however, they did not do so. The unwillingness to apply the principle of self-determination became most obvious when the victors confronted the issue of what to do with Germany's former colonies and the Arab territories of the Ottoman empire. Because the United States rejected the establishment of old-fashioned colonies, the European powers came up with the enterprising idea of trusteeship. Article 22 of the Covenant of the League of Nations referred to the colonies and territories of the former Central Powers as areas "inhabited by peoples not yet able to stand by themselves under the strenuous conditions of the modern world." As a result, "The tutelage of such peoples should be entrusted to the advanced nations who . . . can best undertake this responsibility." The administration of the mandates fell to the victorious powers of the Great War.

The Germans interpreted the mandate system as a division of colonial booty by the victors, who had conveniently forgotten to apply the tutelage provision to their own colonies. German cynicism was more than matched by Arab outrage. The establishment of mandates in the former territories of the Ottoman empire violated promises (made to Arabs) by French and British leaders during the war. They had promised Arab nationalists independence from the Ottoman empire and had promised Jewish nationalists in Europe a homeland in Palestine. Where the Arabs hoped to form independent states, the French (in Lebanon and Syria) and the British (in Iraq and Palestine) established mandates. The Allies viewed the mandate system as a reasonable compromise between the reality of imperialism and the ideal of self-determination. To the peoples who were directly affected, the mandate system smacked of continued imperial rule draped in a cloak of respectability.

Challenges to European Preeminence

When the war ended, it seemed to most Europeans that their global hegemony was more secure than ever. But the Great War did irreparable damage to European power and prestige and set the stage for a process of decolonization that gathered momentum during and after the Second World War. The decline in European power was closely related to diminished economic stature, a result of the commitment to total war. Nothing was more indicative of Europe's reduced economic might than the reversal of the economic relationship between Europe and the United States. Whereas the United States was a debtor nation before 1914, owing

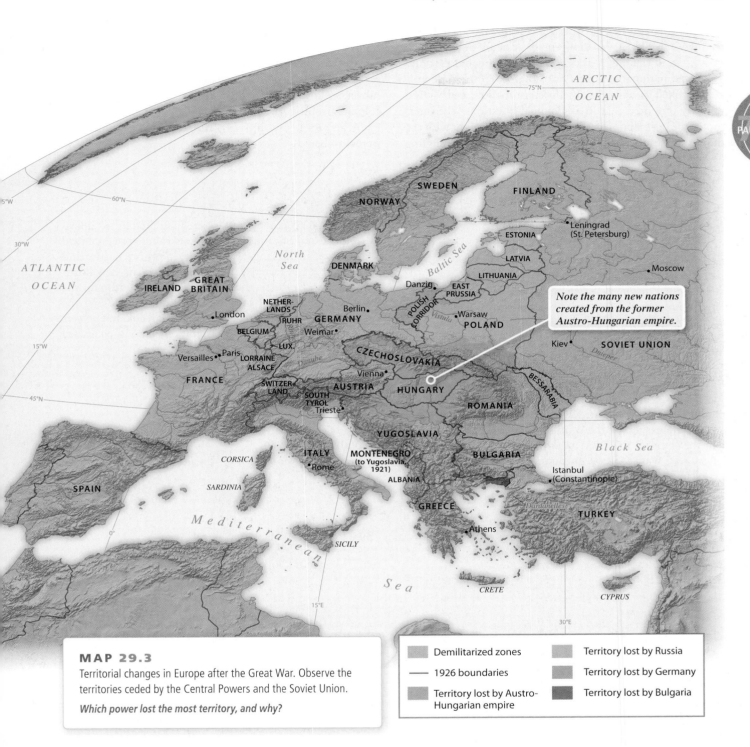

MAP 29.3

Territorial changes in Europe after the Great War. Observe the territories ceded by the Central Powers and the Soviet Union.

Which power lost the most territory, and why?

Demilitarized zones

—— 1926 boundaries

Territory lost by Austro-Hungarian empire

Territory lost by Russia

Territory lost by Germany

Territory lost by Bulgaria

billions of dollars to European investors, by 1919 it was a major creditor.

The war also weakened the European hold over colonial territories. Colonial subjects in Africa, Asia, and the Pacific tended to view the Great War as a civil war among the European nations, a bloody spectacle in which the haughty bearers of an alleged superior society vilified and

slaughtered one another. Because Europe seemed weak, divided, and vulnerable, the white overlords no longer appeared destined to rule over colonized subjects. The colonials who returned home from the war in Europe and southwest Asia reinforced those general impressions with their own firsthand observations. In particular, they were less inclined to be obedient imperial subjects.

The war also helped spread revolutionary ideas to the colonies. The U.S. war aims spelled out in the Fourteen Points raised the hopes of peoples under imperial rule and promoted nationalist aspirations. The peacemakers repeatedly invoked the concept of self-determination, and Wilson publicly proposed that in all colonial questions "the interests of the native populations be given equal weight with the desires of European governments." Nationalists struggling to organize anti-imperialist resistance also sought inspiration from the Soviet Union, whose leaders denounced all forms of imperialism and pledged their support to independence movements. Taken together, those messages were subversive to imperial control and had a great appeal for colonial peoples. Although nationalist movements endured many setbacks, the days of European global dominance were numbered.

SUMMARY

The assassination of the Austrian archduke Francis Ferdinand had a galvanizing effect on a Europe torn by national rivalries, colonial disputes, and demands for self-determination. In the summer of 1914, inflexible war plans and a tangled alliance system transformed a local war between Austria-Hungary and Serbia into a European-wide clash of arms. With the entry of the Ottoman empire, Japan, and the United States, the war of 1914–1918 became a global conflict. Although many belligerents organized their societies for total war and drew on the resources of their overseas empires, the war remained at a bloody stalemate until the United States entered the conflict in 1917. The tide turned, and the combatants signed an armistice in November 1918. The Great War, a brutal encounter between societies and peoples, inflicted ghastly human casualties, severely damaged national economies, and discredited established political and cultural traditions. The war also altered the political landscape of many lands as it destroyed four dynasties and their empires and fostered the creation of several new European nations. In Russia the war served as a backdrop for the world's first successful socialist revolution. In the end the Great War sapped the strength of European colonial powers while it promoted nationalist aspirations among colonized peoples.

STUDY TERMS

Allies (Triple Entente) (560)
Bolshevik revolution (569)
Caporetto (561)
Central Powers (Triple Alliance) (560)
dreadnoughts (559)
February Revolution (569)

Fourteen Points (571)
Francis Ferdinand (558)
Georges Clemenceau (571)
home front (565)
Jiaozhou (567)
League of Nations (572)
mandate system (572)
Mustafa Kemal (572)
no-man's-land (562)
Paris Peace Conference (571)
poison gas (561)
Romanov (569)
Schlieffen plan (560)
self-determination (558, 572)

soviets (569)
total war (564)
Treaty of Brest-Litovsk (570)
Treaty of Lausanne (572)
Treaty of Sèvres (572)
Twenty-one Demands (567)
unrestricted submarine warfare (570)
Vladimir Ilyich Lenin (569)
western front (561)
Winston Churchill (568)

FOR FURTHER READING

Joanna Bourke. *Dismembering the Male: Men's Bodies, Britain, and the Great War.* Chicago, 1996. A study that examines the most intimate site of the war—the bodies of the men who fought it.

Belinda Davis. *Home Fires Burning: Food, Politics, and Everyday Life in World War I Berlin.* Chapel Hill, 2000. Effectively covers daily life in wartime and also offers insights into how government policies during the war affected the reconstruction of society following it.

Niall Ferguson. *The Pity of War: Explaining World War I.* New York, 2000. A stimulating example of revisionist history that shifts the blame for the war away from Germany and onto England.

Paul Fussell. *The Great War and Modern Memory.* Oxford, 1975. An original and deeply moving piece of cultural history.

Peter Gatrell. *Russia's First World War: A Social and Economic History.* London, 2005. Traces the impact of World War I on Russian society before the revolution.

John Maynard Keynes. *The Economic Consequences of the Peace.* New York, 1920. A classic and devastating critique of the Versailles treaty.

John H. Morrow. *The Great War: An Imperial History.* New York, 2003. A global history of the Great War that places the conflict squarely in the context of imperialism.

Michael S. Neiberg. *Fighting the Great War.* Cambridge, Mass., 2005. A good blend of narrative and analysis, this work highlights the global reach of the conflict.

Erich Remarque. *All Quiet on the Western Front.* New York, 1958. A fictional account of trench warfare.

Hew Strachan. *The First World War.* Vol. 1: *To Arms.* New York, 2001. The first of three anticipated volumes, this is a masterly work that treats the war in global rather than European terms.

An Age of Anxiety

CHAPTER **30**

Edvard Munch, *Anxiety,* 1896.

EYEWITNESS:
The Early Life of a Dictator

Born on a lovely spring day in 1889, in a quaint Austrian village, he was the apple of his mother's eye. He basked in Klara's warmth and indulgence as a youth, enjoying the fine life of a middle-class child. As he grew older, however, he sensed a tension between the competing expectations of his parents. Contented with the dreamy indolence allowed by Klara, he bristled at the demands of his father, Alois, who expected him to study hard and enter the Austrian civil service. He had no desire to become a bureaucrat. In fact, he envisioned a completely different life for himself. He wanted to be an artist.

Alois's unexpected death in 1903 freed him from a future as a bureaucrat. He left school in 1905, not at all dissatisfied with having achieved only a ninth-grade education, because now he could pursue an education as an artist. He followed his ambitions to Vienna, only to find bitter disappointment when the Vienna Academy of Fine Arts rejected him as an art student in 1907. His beloved Klara died the following year, and he meandered the city streets of Vienna, admiring the architecture of the city and attending the opera when his funds permitted.

Eventually, he hit bottom and began staying at a homeless shelter. It was interesting, though, to hear the different political points of view spouted by the shelter's other inhabitants. They discussed compelling issues of the day, and he listened intently to those who hailed the supremacy of the Aryan race and the inferiority of the Jews. He came to hate Jews and Marxists, who he thought had formed an evil union with the goal of destroying the world. He also despised liberalism and democracy.

In 1913 he left his Austrian homeland and found refuge in Munich, Germany. In Germany he volunteered for service in the army, which had just embarked on the greatest war ever fought. He discovered in himself a real talent for military service, and he remained in the army for the duration of the war, 1914–1918. Twice wounded and decorated for bravery, he nonetheless found himself in despair at war's end. An impotent rage coursed through him when he learned of Germany's defeat. He knew with all his being that the Jews were responsible for this humiliation, and he also knew that he had to enter the political arena in his chosen fatherland and save the nation. Adolf Hitler had finally found his mission in life.

Hitler (1889–1945) stood as just one personification of Europe's age of anxiety in the early decades of the twentieth century. Embittered by a sense of dislocation and fear stemming from the enormous changes engulfing the society around him, Hitler dedicated himself to discovering a way out of the anxiety for Germany. Ultimately, his solutions brought about more rather than less anxiety, but the novelty and cruelty of his political and military agendas reflected brilliantly the traumatic consequences of the Great War and the Great Depression.

Just as Adolf Hitler changed as a result of his life experiences in the early twentieth century, so too did European society as a whole. Badly shaken by the effects of war, Europeans experienced a shock to their system of values, beliefs, and traditions. Profound scientific and cultural transformations in the postwar decades also contributed to a sense of loss and anxiety. Then, as peoples in Europe and around the world struggled to

CHRONOLOGY

1905	Einstein publishes special theory of relativity
1907	Picasso paints *Les demoiselles d'Avignon*
1918–1920	Civil war in Russia
1919	Mussolini launches fascist movement in Italy
1921–1928	Lenin's New Economic Policy
1927	Heisenberg establishes "uncertainty principle"
1928–1932	First Soviet Five-Year Plan
1929	U.S. stock market crash
1929	Beginning of Great Depression
1929	Hemingway and Remarque publish antiwar novels
1933–1945	Hitler is ruler in Germany
1935–1938	Stalin's "Great Purge" in the Soviet Union

come to terms with the aftermath of war, an unprecedented economic contraction gripped the international community.

Against the background of the Great Depression, dictators in Russia, Italy, and Germany tried to translate blueprints for utopias into reality. Those political innovations unsettled many Europeans and much of the world, contributing significantly to the anxiety of the age. Moreover, such innovations matched in their radicalness, however strangely, the vast alterations taking place in the intellectual and cultural realms of European society after the Great War.

PROBING CULTURAL FRONTIERS

The Great War discredited established social and political institutions and long-held beliefs about the superiority of European society. While some European intellectuals and leaders had been anxious about the future of their society since the end of the nineteenth century, in the aftermath of the Great War the tendency for writers, poets, theologians, and other intellectuals to lament the decline and imminent death of their society increased markedly. Yet not everyone was so pessimistic: indeed, while some wrote obituaries, others embarked on bold new cultural paths that established the main tendencies of contemporary thought and taste. Both trends, however, turned many established beliefs, traditions, and certainties on their heads in the years after the Great War.

The discoveries of physicists undermined the Newtonian universe, in which a set of inexorable natural laws governed events, with a new and disturbing cosmos. Equally discomfiting were the insights of psychoanalysis, which suggested that human behavior was fundamentally irrational. Disquieting trends in the arts paralleled developments in science and psychology. Especially in painting, an aversion to realism and a pronounced preference for abstraction heralded the arrival of new aesthetic standards.

Postwar Pessimism

"You are all a lost generation," noted Gertrude Stein (1874–1946) to her fellow American writer Ernest Hemingway (1899–1961). Stein had given a label to the group of American intellectuals and literati who congregated in Paris in the postwar years. This "lost generation" expressed in poetry and fiction the malaise and disillusion that characterized U.S. and European thought after the Great War. The brutal realities of industrialized warfare left no room for heroes or glory, and during the 1920s artists and intellectuals spat out their revulsion in a host of war novels, such as Hemingway's *A Farewell to Arms* (1929) and Erich Maria Remarque's *All Quiet on the Western Front* (1929)—works overflowing with images of meaningless death and suffering. Postwar writers lamented the decline of Western society. A retired German schoolteacher named Oswald Spengler (1880–1936) made headlines when he published *The Decline of the West* (1918–1922). In this work, which might have been seen as an obituary of civilization, Spengler proposed that all societies pass through a life cycle of growth and decay comparable to the biological cycle of living organisms. His analysis of the history of western Europe led him to conclude that European society had entered the final stage of its existence. All that remained was irreversible decline, marked by imperialism and warfare.

Theologians joined the chorus of despair. In 1919 Karl Barth (1886–1968), a notable Christian theologian, published a religious bombshell titled *Epistle to the Romans*. In his work Barth sharply attacked the liberal Christian theology that embraced the idea of progress, that is, the tendency of European thinkers to believe in limitless improvement as the realization of God's purpose. The Augustinian, Lutheran, and Calvinist message of original sin—the depravity of human nature—fell on receptive ears as many Christians refused to accept the idea that contemporary human society was in any way a realization of God's

Reverberations of ● ● ● ● ● ● ● ●

The Destructive Potential of Industrial Technologies

World War I is an instructive example of the long-term consequences of historical events on both intellectual and popular culture. Prior to the war, many Europeans believed that the technologies associated with industrialization—while not without their problems—would ultimately lead to greater human comfort, prosperity, and happiness. Yet the role of mass-produced war materiel in the huge scale of slaughter during the war caused Europeans to wonder with horror if, with industrial technologies, humans had created a monster that would ultimately bring about more death and destruction than happiness. In effect, the realities of the war made it impossible for Europeans to return to the optimism of the nineteenth century with regard to the benefits of modern technologies. Consider how this ambivalence, in turn, became an important feature of intellectual and popular culture not only in interwar Europe, but in many parts of the world right up to the present.

Adolf Hitler.
This is one of the few known photographic images of a young Hitler, taken in 1923.

purpose. The Russian orthodox thinker Nikolai Berdiaev (1874–1948) summed up those sentiments: "Man's historical experience has been one of steady failure, and there are no grounds for supposing it will be ever anything else."

The Great War destroyed long-cherished beliefs, such as belief in the universality of human progress. Many idols of nineteenth-century progress came under attack, especially science and technology. The scientists' dream of leading humanity to a beneficial conquest of nature seemed to have gone awry, because scientists had spent the war making poisonous gas and high explosives. Democracy was another fallen idol. The idea that people should have a voice in selecting the leaders of their government enjoyed widespread support in European societies. By the early twentieth century, such sentiments had led to universal male suffrage in most societies, and after the Great War many societies also extended the franchise to women. However, many intellectuals abhorred what they viewed as weak political systems that championed the tyranny of the average person. In Germany, for example, a whole school of conservatives lamented the "rule of inferiors."

Revolutions in Physics and Psychology

The postwar decade witnessed a revolution in physics that transformed the character of science. Albert Einstein (1879–1955) struck the first blow with his theory of special relativity (1905), showing that there is no single spatial and chronological framework in the universe. According to the theory, it no longer makes sense to speak of space and time as absolutes, because the measurement of those two categories always varies with the motion of the observer. That is, space and time are relative to the person measuring them. To the layperson such notions suggested that a common-sense universe had vanished, to be replaced by a radically new one in which reality or truth was merely relative.

The Uncertainty Principle More disquieting even than Einstein's discoveries was the theory formulated by Werner Heisenberg (1901–1976), who in 1927 established the "uncertainty principle." According to Heisenberg, it is impossible to specify simultaneously the position and the velocity of a subatomic particle. The more accurately one determines

Nikolai Berdiaev (nih-koh-LYE ber-dee-ev)
Werner Heisenberg (VER-nuhr HAHY-zuyn-burg)

Albert Einstein.
One of the best-known faces of the twentieth century, Einstein was the symbol of the revolution in physics.

Sigmund Freud.
In this painted portrait, Freud presents a striking figure.

the position of an electron, the less precisely one can determine its velocity, and vice versa. In essence, scientists cannot observe the behavior of electrons objectively, because the act of observation interferes with them.

It quickly became evident that the uncertainty principle had important implications beyond physics. Indeed, Heisenberg's theory called into question established notions of truth. Likewise, objectivity as it was understood was no longer a valid concept, because the observer was always part of the process under observation. Accordingly, any observer—an anthropologist studying another society, for instance—had to be alert to the fact that his or her very presence became an integral part of the study.

Freud's Psychoanalytic Theory As equally unsettling as the advances in physics were developments in psychology that challenged established concepts of morality and values. Beginning in 1896, the Austrian medical doctor Sigmund Freud (1856–1939) embarked on research that focused on psychological rather than physiological explanations of mental disorders. Through his clinical observations of patients, Freud identified a conflict between conscious

Sigmund Freud (SIG-muhnd froid)

and unconscious mental processes that lay at the root of neurotic behavior. That conflict, moreover, suggested to him the existence of a repressive mechanism that keeps painful memories away from the conscious mind. Freud believed that dreams held the key to the deepest recesses of the human psyche. Using the free associations of patients to guide him in the interpretation of dreams, he identified sexual drives and fantasies as the most important source of repression. For example, Freud claimed to have discovered a so-called Oedipus complex, in which male children develop an erotic attachment to their mother and hostility toward their father.

In the end, Freudian doctrines shaped the psychiatric profession and established a powerful presence in literature and the arts. During the 1920s, novelists, poets, and painters acknowledged Freud's influence as they focused on the inner world of their characters. The creators of imaginative literature used Freud's bold emphasis on sexuality as a tool for the interpretation and understanding of human behavior.

Experimentation in Art and Architecture

The roots of contemporary painting go back to nineteenth-century French avant-garde artists who disdained realism and instead were concerned with freedom of expression. The aversion to visual realism was heightened by the spread of photography. When everyone could create naturalistic landscapes or portraits with a camera, it made little sense for artists to do the same with paint and brush. Thus painters began to think that the purpose of a painting was not to mirror reality but to create it.

At the beginning of the twentieth century, this new aesthetic led to the emergence of a bewildering variety of pictorial schools, all of which promised an entirely new art. Regardless of whether they called themselves expressionists, cubists, abstractionists, dadaists, or surrealists, artists generally agreed on a program "to abolish the sovereignty of appearance." Paintings no longer depicted recognizable objects from the everyday world, and beauty was expressed in pure color or shape. Some painters sought to express feelings and emotions through violent distortion of forms and the use of explosive colors; others, influenced by Freudian psychology, tried to tap the subconscious mind to communicate an inner vision or a dream.

Artistic Influences The artistic heritages of Asian, Pacific, and African societies fertilized various strains of contemporary painting. Nineteenth-century Japanese prints, for example, influenced French impressionists such as Edgar Degas (1834–1917). The deliberate violation of perspective by Japanese painters and their stress on the flat, two-dimensional surface of the picture, their habit of placing figures off center, and their use of primary colors encouraged European artists to take similar liberties with realism. In Germany a group of young artists known as the "Bridge" made a point of regularly visiting the local ethnographic museum to be inspired by the boldness and power of indigenous art. The early works of Pablo Picasso (1881–1973), the leading proponent of cubism, displayed the influence of African art forms.

By the third decade of the twentieth century, it was nearly impossible to generalize about contemporary painting. All artists were acknowledged to have a right to their own reality, and generally accepted standards that distinguished between "good" and "bad" art disappeared.

GLOBAL DEPRESSION

After the horrors and debilitating upheavals of the Great War, much of the world yearned for a return to normality and prosperity. By the early 1920s the efforts of governments and businesses to rebuild damaged economies seemed to be bearing fruit. Prosperity, however, was short-lived. In 1929 the world plunged into an economic depression that was so long-lasting, so severe, and so global that it has become known as the Great Depression. The old capitalist system of trade and finance collapsed, and until a new system took its place after 1945, a return to worldwide prosperity could not occur.

Pablo Picasso's Les demoiselles d'Avignon.
This painting (1907) was the first of what would be called cubist works. This image had a profound impact on subsequent art.

Edgar Degas (ED-gahr day-GAH)

The Great Depression

By the middle of the 1920s, most countries seemed on the way to economic recovery, and industrial productivity had returned to prewar levels. But that prosperity was fragile, perhaps false, and many serious problems and dislocations remained in the international economy.

Economic Problems The economic recovery and well-being of Europe, for example, was tied to a tangled and interdependent financial system. In essence, the governments of Austria and Germany relied on U.S. loans and investment capital to finance reparation payments to France and England. The French and British governments, in turn, depended on those reparation payments to pay off loans taken out in the United States during the Great War. Strain on any one part of the system, then, inevitably strained them all.

There were other problems as well. Improvements in industrial processes reduced worldwide demand for certain raw materials, which had devastating consequences for export-dependent areas. Technological advances in the production of automobile tires, for instance, permitted the use

The social effects of the Great Depression.
This photo by Dorothea Lange, called *Migrant Mother, Nipomo, California* (1936), is one of the most famous images of the period.

of reclaimed rubber. The resulting glut of natural rubber badly damaged the economies of the Dutch East Indies, Ceylon, and Malaysia, which relied on rubber exports. Similarly, the increased use of oil undermined the coal industry, and the growing adoption of artificial nitrogen virtually ruined the nitrate industry of Chile.

One of the nagging weaknesses of the global economy in the 1920s was the depressed state of agriculture. During the Great War, when Europe's agricultural output declined significantly, farmers in the United States, Canada, Argentina, and Australia expanded their own production. At the end of the war, European farmers resumed their agricultural activity, thereby contributing to worldwide surpluses. As production increased, prices collapsed throughout the world. By 1929 the price of a bushel of wheat was at its lowest level in four hundred years, and farmers everywhere became impoverished. The reduced income of farm families contributed to high inventories of manufactured goods, which in turn caused businesses to cut back production and to dismiss workers.

The Crash of 1929 The United States enjoyed a boom after the Great War, which prompted many people in the United States to invest their earnings and savings in speculative and risky financial ventures, particularly in stocks. By October 1929, warnings from experts that stock prices were overvalued prompted investors to pull out of the market. On Black Thursday (24 October), a wave of panic selling on the New York Stock Exchange caused stock prices to plummet. Investors who had overextended themselves through speculative stock purchases watched in agony. Thousands of people, from poor widows to industrial tycoons, lost their life savings, and by the end of the day eleven financiers had committed suicide. The crisis deepened when lenders called in loans, thereby forcing more investors to sell their securities at any price.

Economic Contraction Spreads In the wake of this financial chaos came a drastic decrease in business activity, wages, and employment. When businesses realized that shrinking consumer demand meant they could not sell their inventories, they responded with layoffs. With so many people unemployed, demand plummeted further, causing more business failures and soaring unemployment. In 1930 the slump deepened, and by 1932 industrial production had fallen to half of its 1929 level. National income had dropped by approximately half, and 44 percent of U.S. banks were out of business. Because much of the world's prosperity depended on the export of U.S. capital and the strength of U.S. import markets, the contraction of the U.S. economy created a ripple effect that circled the globe.

Most societies experienced economic difficulties throughout the 1930s. Virtually every industrialized society saw its economy shrivel, but nations that relied on exports of manufactured goods to pay for imported fuel and food—Germany and Japan in particular—suffered the most. The depression also spread to primary producing economies in Latin America, Africa, and Asia. Hardest hit were countries that depended on the export of a few primary products such as coffee, sugar, minerals, ores, and rubber.

U.S. investors, shaken by the collapse of stock prices, tried to raise money by calling in loans and liquidating investments, and Wall Street banks refused to extend short-term loans as they became due. Banking houses in Austria and Germany became vulnerable to collapse, because they had been major recipients of U.S. loans. Devastated by the loss of U.S. capital, the German economy experienced a precipitous economic slide that by 1932 resulted in 35 percent unemployment and a 50 percent decrease in industrial production. As the German economy—which had remained a leading economic power in Europe throughout the postwar years—ground to a virtual halt, the rest of Europe sputtered and stalled with it. Likewise, because of its great dependence on the U.S. market, the Japanese economy felt the depression's effects almost immediately. Unemployment in export-oriented sectors of the economy skyrocketed as companies cut back on production.

Human faces of the Great Depression.
This photograph depicts children bathing in the Ozark Mountains, Missouri, 1940.
What kinds of items signify the poverty of this family?

Economic Nationalism The Great Depression destroyed the international financial and commercial network of the capitalist economies. As international cooperation broke down, governments turned to their own resources and practiced economic nationalism. By imposing tariff barriers, import quotas, and import prohibitions, politicians hoped to achieve self-sufficiency. Yet economic nationalism invariably backfired. Each new measure designed to restrict imports provoked retaliation by other nations whose interests were affected. After the U.S. Congress passed the Smoot-Hawley Tariff Act in 1930, which raised duties on most manufactured products to prohibitive levels, the governments of dozens of other nations retaliated by raising tariffs on imports of U.S. products. The result was a sharp drop in international trade. Between 1929 and 1932, world production declined by 38 percent and trade dropped by more than 66 percent.

Despair and Government Action

By 1933 unemployment in industrial societies had reached thirty million, more than five times higher than in 1929. Both men and women lost their jobs, and over the course of the depression most governments enacted policies restricting female employment, especially for married women. Indeed, the notion that a woman's place was in the home was widespread, and some—such as the French physician Charles Richet (1850–1935)—even insisted that removing women from the workforce would solve the problem of male unemployment.

The Great Depression caused enormous personal suffering. The stark statistics documenting the failure of economies do not convey the anguish and despair of those who lost their jobs, savings, and homes. For millions of people the struggle for food, clothing, and shelter grew desperate. Shantytowns appeared overnight in urban areas, and breadlines stretched for blocks. Marriage, childbearing, and divorce rates declined, and suicide rates rose. Those simply trying to survive came to despise the wealthy, who, despite their own reduced incomes, remained shielded from the worst impact of the economic downturn. Adolescents completing their schooling faced an almost nonexistent job market.

Economic Experimentation

Classical economic thought held that capitalism was a self-correcting system that operated best when left to its own devices. Thus, in the initial stages of the depression most governments did nothing, hoping that the crisis would resolve itself. Faced with such human misery, however, some governments assumed more active roles, pursuing deflationary measures by balancing national budgets and curtailing public spending. Rather than lifting national economies out of the doldrums, however, those remedies only worsened the depression's impact. Far from self-correcting, capitalism seemed to be dying. Many people called for a fundamental revision of economic thought.

Charles Richet (shawrl ri-SHEY)

SourcesfromthePast

Franklin Delano Roosevelt: Nothing to Fear

Franklin Delano Roosevelt (1882–1945) assumed the presidency of the United States on 4 March 1933, during the very depths of the Great Depression. In his inaugural address to the nation, he conveyed both the anxiousness of the times and the seemingly unquenchable optimism that carried him—and his nation—through hard times. A vastly wealthy man serving as president during a time of devastating penury, Roosevelt nonetheless gained the admiration and respect of his people because of his warm eloquence and compassion. Although he hid his condition quite successfully during his time in public, FDR had contracted polio in the 1920s and had lost the use of his legs. This "crippled" president became a metaphor for the United States' economic collapse, but also for its ability to overcome fear itself.

I am certain that my fellow Americans expect that on my induction into the Presidency I will address them with a candor and a decision which the present situation of our Nation impels. This is preeminently the time to speak the truth, the whole truth, frankly and boldly. Nor need we shrink from honestly facing conditions in our country today. This great Nation will endure as it has endured, will revive and will prosper. So, first of all, let me assert my firm belief that the only thing we have to fear is fear itself—nameless, unreasoning, unjustified terror which paralyzes needed efforts to convert retreat into advance. In every dark hour of our national life a leadership of frankness and vigor has met with that understanding and support of the people themselves which is essential to victory. I am convinced that you will again give that support to leadership in these critical days.

In such a spirit on my part and on yours we face our common difficulties. They concern, thank God, only material things. Values have shrunken to fantastic levels; taxes have risen; our ability to pay has fallen; government of all kinds is faced by serious curtailment of income; the means of exchange are frozen in the currents of trade; the withered leaves of industrial enterprise lie on every side; farmers find no markets for their produce; the savings of many years in thousands of families are gone.

More important, a host of unemployed citizens face the grim problem of existence, and an equally great number toil with little return. Only a foolish optimist can deny the dark realities of the moment. . . .

Happiness lies not in the mere possession of money; it lies in the joy of achievement, in the thrill of creative effort. The joy and moral stimulation of work no longer must be forgotten in the mad chase of evanescent profits. These dark days will be worth all they cost us if they teach us that our true destiny is not to be ministered unto but to minister to ourselves and to our fellow men.

For Further Reflection

■ How does Roosevelt believe U.S. citizens can profit from the dark days of the Great Depression, and why is it that all they have to fear is fear itself?

Source: Franklin D. Roosevelt, First Inaugural Address, 4 March 1933, available at The Avalon Project at http://www.yale.edu/lawweb/avalon/president/inaug/froos1.htm.

Keynes John Maynard Keynes (1883–1946), the most influential economist of the twentieth century, offered a novel solution. In his seminal work, *The General Theory of Employment, Interest, and Money* (1936), he argued that the fundamental cause of the depression was not excessive supply but inadequate demand. Accordingly, he urged governments to stimulate the economy by increasing the money supply, thereby lowering interest rates and encouraging investment. He also advised governments to undertake public works projects to provide jobs and redistribute incomes through tax policy. Such intervention would result in reduced unemployment and increased consumer demand, which would lead to economic revival. These measures were necessary even if they caused governments to run deficits and maintain unbalanced budgets.

The New Deal Although Keynes's theories did not become influential with policymakers until after World War II, the administration of U.S. president Franklin Delano Roosevelt (1882–1945) anticipated his ideas. Roosevelt took aggressive steps to reinflate the economy and ease the worst of the suffering caused by the depression. His program for dealing with the national calamity—called the New Deal—included legislation designed to prevent the collapse of the banking system, to provide jobs and farm subsidies, to guarantee minimum wages, and to provide social security in old age. Its fundamental premise, that the federal government was justified in protecting the social and economic welfare of the people, represented a major shift in U.S. government policy and started a trend toward social reform legislation that continued long after the depression years.

CHALLENGES TO THE LIBERAL ORDER

Even prior to the gloom and despair of the Great Depression, some voices proclaimed the promise of an alternative to the European liberal social order in the aftermath of the Great War. Marxists, for example, believed that capitalist society was on its deathbed, and they had faith that a new and better system based on rule by the proletariat was being born out of the ashes of the Russian empire. The new rulers of Russia, Vladimir Ilyich Lenin and then Joseph Stalin, transformed the former tsarist empire into the world's first socialist society, the Union of Soviet Socialist Republics (1922). Other people, uncomfortable with socialism, found solace in fascist movements, which seemed to offer revolutionary answers to the economic, social, and political problems of the day. Among these fascist movements, the Italian and German ones figured most prominently.

Communism in Russia

In 1917 Lenin and his fellow Bolsheviks had taken power in the name of the Russian working class, but socialist victory did not bring peace and stability to the lands of the former Russian empire. After seizing power, Lenin and his supporters had to defend the world's first "dictatorship of the proletariat" against numerous internal and external enemies.

Civil War Opposition to the Bolshevik Party—by now calling itself the Russian Communist Party—erupted into a civil war that lasted from 1918 to 1920. In response, Lenin's government began a policy of terror in which 200,000 suspected anticommunists (known as Whites) were arrested, tried, and executed. In July 1918 the Bolsheviks executed Tsar Nicholas II, Empress Alexandra, and their five children because they feared that the Romanov family could strengthen counterrevolutionary forces. White terror was often equally as brutal as Red (Communist) terror. The peasantry, although hostile to the communists, largely supported the Bolsheviks, fearing that a victory by the Whites would result in the return of the monarchy.

Meanwhile, foreign powers in Britain, France, Japan, and the United States, angry over Russia's withdrawal from the Great War and inflamed by anticommunism, supported the Whites and sent a limited number of troops and

Joseph Stalin.
Here, Stalin attends a Soviet congress in 1936.

supplies to aid them. Their efforts failed, however, and in 1920 the Red Army defeated the Whites. The costs of war were devastating: estimates place the number of lives lost in the civil war at ten million, mostly from disease and starvation. Moreover, the political system that emerged from the civil war bore the imprint of political oppression, which played a significant role in the later development of the Soviet state.

War Communism Over the course of the civil war, the new rulers of Russia transformed the economy by embarking on a hasty and unplanned course of nationalization, known as war communism. After officially annulling private property, the Bolshevik government assumed control of banks, industry, and other privately held commercial properties. Landed estates and the holdings of monasteries and churches also became national property. Private trade was abolished, and the party seized crops from peasants to feed people in the cities. This last measure proved especially unpopular and caused peasants to drastically reduce their production. By 1920 industrial production had fallen to about one-tenth of its prewar level and agricultural output to about half its prewar level.

The New Economic Policy In 1921, as the Reds consolidated their military victories after the civil war, the Soviet economy was in a shambles. Workers were on strike, cities were depopulated, and factories were destroyed. Faced with economic paralysis, in the spring of 1921 Lenin decided on a radical reversal of war communism. In its place he implemented the New Economic Policy (NEP), which temporarily restored the market economy and some private enterprise in Russia. Large industries and banks remained under state control, but the government returned small-scale industries to private ownership. The government also allowed peasants to sell their surpluses at free-market prices. Other features of the NEP included a vigorous program of electrification and the establishment of technical schools to train technicians and engineers. Lenin did not live to see the success of the NEP. After suffering three paralytic strokes, he died in 1924.

Joseph Stalin After a bitter political struggle for power, Joseph Stalin (1879–1953), general secretary of the Communist Party, emerged as the new leader of the Soviet Union in 1928. A Georgian by birth, an

Thinking about TRADITIONS

Fascism and Nationalism

In the period between the world wars, fascism arose as an alternative to what appeared to be weak and failing capitalist democracies. *In what ways did the fascist states call on national traditions and characteristics in order to legitimate their authoritarian natures?*

Orthodox seminarian by training, and a Russian nationalist by conviction, Stalin indicated his unified resolve to gain power in his surname, which meant "man of steel." His first economic program, which replaced Lenin's NEP, was both ambitious and ruthless. Indeed, Stalin's First Five-Year Plan, implemented in 1929, aimed at nothing less than transforming the Soviet Union from a predominantly agricultural country to a leading industrial power. The First Five-Year Plan set targets for increased productivity in all spheres of the economy but emphasized heavy industry—especially steel and machinery—at the expense of consumer goods. As the rest of the world teetered on the edge of economic collapse, Stalin's plan offered a bold alternative to market capitalism. Stalin repeatedly stressed the urgency of this monumental endeavor, telling his people, "We are 50 to 100 years behind the advanced countries. Either we do it, or we shall go under."

Collectivization of Agriculture Integral to the drive for industrialization was the collectivization of agriculture. The Soviet state expropriated privately owned land to create collective, or cooperative, farm units whose profits were shared by all farmers. Stalin and his regime viewed collectivization as a means of increasing the efficiency of agricultural production and ensuring that industrial workers would be fed.

In some places, outraged peasants reacted to the government's program by slaughtering their livestock and burning their crops. Faced with enforced collectivization, millions of farmers left the land and migrated to cities in search of work. Those who stayed behind were often unable to meet production quotas and starved to death on the land they once owned. When Stalin called a halt to collectivization in 1931, half the farms in the Soviet Union had been collectivized. Estimates of the cost in number of peasant lives lost have fluctuated wildly, but even the most cautious place it at three million. Among them, the *kulaks*—relatively wealthy peasants who had risen to prosperity during the NEP—were nearly eliminated.

The Soviet leadership proclaimed the First Five-Year Plan a success after only four years. The Soviet Union industrialized under Stalin even though the emphasis on building heavy industry first and consumer industries later meant that citizens postponed the gratifications of industrialization. However, the scarcity or nonexistence of such consumer goods as refrigerators, radios, and automobiles was to some degree balanced by full employment, low-cost utilities, and cheap housing and food. Set against the economic collapse of the capitalist world, the ability of a centrally planned economy to create more jobs than workers could fill made it appear an attractive alternative.

The Great Purge Nevertheless, the disaster of collectivization and the ruthlessness with which it was carried out had raised doubts about Stalin's administration. As the Communist Party prepared for its seventeenth congress in 1934, the "Congress of Victors," Stalin learned of a plan to bring more pluralism back into leadership. The Congress of Victors quickly became the "Congress of Victims" as Stalin purged two-thirds of the delegates from the Communist Party. Between 1935 and 1938 Stalin removed from posts of authority all persons suspected of opposition, including more than half the army's high-ranking officers. In 1939 eight million Soviet citizens faced long-term suffering in labor camps, and three million were dead as a result of the "cleansing," as Stalin's supporters termed this process.

The outside world watched the events unfolding within the Soviet Union with a mixture of contempt, fear, and admiration. The establishment of the world's first dictatorship of the proletariat challenged the values and institutions of liberal society all over the world and seemed to demonstrate the viability of communism as a social and political system.

The Fascist Alternative

While socialism was transforming the former Russian empire, another political force swept across Europe after the Great War. Fascism, a political movement and ideology that sought to create a new type of society, developed as a reaction against liberal democracy and the spread of socialism and communism. In 1919 Benito Mussolini founded the first fascist party. Movements comparable to Italian fascism subsequently developed in many European societies, most notably in Germany in the guise of National Socialism (Nazism). Although fascism enjoyed widespread popularity in many European countries, it rarely threatened the political order and overthrew parliamentary systems only in Italy and Germany. Although potential fascist movements sprang up during the 1930s in Japan, China, and South Africa; in Latin American societies such as Brazil and Argentina; and in several Arab lands, fascism nevertheless remained basically a European phenomenon in the era between the two world wars.

During the 1920s and 1930s, fascism attracted millions of followers and proved especially attractive to middle classes and rural populations. Those groups became radicalized by economic and social crises and were especially fearful of the perceived threat from the political left. Fascism also proved attractive to nationalists of all classes. Asserting that society faced a profound crisis, fascists sought to create a new national community, which they defined either as a nation-state or as a unique ethnic or racial group. Although each fascist movement had its own unique characteristics, most nevertheless shared certain common features, such as the veneration of the state, a devotion to a strong leader, and an emphasis on ultranationalism, ethnocentrism, and militarism.

Fascist ideology consistently invoked the primacy of the state, which stood at the center of the nation's life and history. Strong and charismatic leaders, such as Benito Mussolini in Italy and Adolf Hitler in Germany, embodied the state and claimed indisputable authority. Consequently, fascists were hostile to liberal democracy, which they viewed as weak and decadent. Fascism was also extremely hostile to socialism and communism. Fascist movements emphasized a belligerent form of nationalism (chauvinism) and a fear of foreign people (xenophobia), which they frequently linked to an exaggerated ethnocentrism. The typical fascist state also embraced militarism, a belief in the rigors and virtues of military life as an individual and national ideal. In practice, militarism meant that fascist regimes maintained large and expensive military establishments, tried to organize much of public life along military lines, and generally showed a fondness for uniforms, parades, and monumental architecture.

Benito Mussolini.
In this photograph, the Italian dictator strikes a dramatic pose on horseback in 1940.

What message might Mussolini have been trying to convey with such a pose?

Italian Fascism

The first fascist movement grew in Italy after the Great War. Conditions conducive to the rise of fascism included a widespread disillusionment with uninspired political leadership and ineffective government, extensive economic turmoil and social discontent, and a growing fear of socialism. In addition, there was vast disappointment over Italy's skimpy territorial spoils from the peace settlement after the Great War.

Benito Mussolini The guiding force behind Italian fascism was Benito Mussolini, a former socialist who turned, after the Great War, to a political program that emphasized virulent nationalism, demanded repression of socialists, and called for a strong political leader. In 1919 he established the Fasci Italiani di Combattimento (Italian Combat Veteran League). Mussolini's movement gained widespread support after 1920, and by 1921 his league managed to have thirty-five fascists elected to the Italian parliament. Much of the newly found public support resulted from the effective use of violence against socialists by fascist armed squads known as Blackshirts. In 1922 Mussolini and his followers decided the time was ripe for a fascist seizure of power, and on 28 October they staged a march on Rome. While Mussolini stayed safely in Milan, thousands of his black-shirted troops converged on Rome. Rather than calling on the military to oppose the fascist threat, King Victor Emmanuel III hastily asked Mussolini on 29 October to become prime minister and form a new government. Mussolini inaugurated a fascist regime in 1922.

The Fascist State Between 1925 and 1931, Italy's fascists consolidated their power through a series of laws that transformed the nation into a one-party dictatorship. In 1926 Mussolini seized total power as dictator and subsequently ruled Italy as Il Duce ("the leader"). The regime moved

chauvinism (SHOH-vuh-niz-uhm)
xenophobia (zen-uh-FOH-bee-uh)

Thinking about ENCOUNTERS

The Global Impact of the Great Depression

When the United States stock market crashed in 1929, it caused a cascade effect that brought markets all over the world down in its wake. *Why were economies as far flung as the Americas, Europe, Asia, and Africa so intricately connected in this period, and how did failure in one set off a chain reaction in the rest?*

quickly to eliminate all other political parties, curb the freedom of the press, and outlaw free speech and association. A Special Tribunal for the Defense of the State, supervised by military officers, silenced political dissent. Marked as antifascist "subversives," thousands of Italians found themselves imprisoned or exiled on remote islands, and some faced capital punishment. Allying himself and his movement with business and landlord interests, Il Duce also crushed labor unions and prohibited strikes. In 1932, on the tenth anniversary of the fascist seizure of power, Mussolini felt confident enough to announce that "the twentieth century will be a century of fascism, the century of Italian power."

Although racism and anti-Semitism were never prominent components of Italian fascism, in 1938 the government suddenly issued a series of anti-Semitic laws. That development may have been occasioned by Mussolini's newly found friendship with fellow dictator Adolf Hitler. In 1936 Mussolini told his followers that from now on, world history would revolve around a Rome-Berlin axis. In May 1939 the leaders of fascist Italy and Nazi Germany formalized their political, military, and ideological alliance by signing a ten-year Pact of Steel.

German National Socialism

Hitler and the Nazi Party After Adolf Hitler's postwar political awakening, he came into contact with an obscure political party sympathetic to his ideas. In 1921 he became chairman of the party now known as the National Socialist German Workers' Party. National Socialism (the Nazi movement) made its first major appearance in 1923 when party members and Hitler attempted to overthrow the democratic Weimar Republic, which had replaced the German empire in 1919. The revolt was a failure, however, and Hitler was jailed. When Hitler emerged from prison in 1924, he resolved to gain power legally through the ballot box and, once successful, to discard the very instrument of his success.

The Struggle for Power National Socialism made rapid gains after 1929 because it had broad appeal. Hitler attracted disillusioned people, many of whom blamed the young German democracy for Germany's misfortunes:

a humiliating peace treaty—the Treaty of Versailles—that identified Germany as responsible for the Great War and assigned reparation payments to the Allies; the hyperinflation of the early 1920s that wiped out the savings of the middle class; and the suffering brought on by the Great Depression. Adolf Hitler promised an end to all those misfortunes by creating a new order that would lead to greatness for Germany. While anti-Semitism remained a fundamental part of Hitler's own beliefs, until he came to power in 1933 the Nazi party downplayed this aspect of its ideology in its propaganda as it attempted to gain a wide base of support among the German population. Anti-Semitism and racist doctrines were consistently important to the party's base, however, which consisted in the main of members of the lower-middle classes: ruined shopkeepers, impoverished farmers, discharged white-collar workers, and disenchanted students.

As Germany slipped into the Great Depression, the government's inability to find solutions to unemployment and impoverishment radicalized the electorate and caused them to lose faith in the democratic system. Both communists, on the far left, and fascists, on the far right, increasingly vied for the allegiance of Germans who sought alternatives to what was perceived as the failures of democracy. Between 1930 and 1932 the Nazi Party became the largest party in parliament, and the reactionary and feeble president, Paul von Hindenburg (1847–1934), decided to offer Hitler the chancellorship. Hitler lost little time in transforming the dying republic into a single-party dictatorship. He promised a German *Reich,* or empire, that would endure for a thousand years.

Consolidation of Power Under the guise of a state of national emergency, the Nazis used all available means to impose their rule. They began by eliminating all working-class and liberal opposition. The Nazis suppressed the German communist and socialist parties and abrogated virtually all constitutional and civil rights. Subsequently, Hitler made the National Socialist Party the only legal party. Between 1933 and 1935 the regime replaced Germany's federal structure with a highly centralized state. The National Socialist state then guided the destruction of trade unions and the elimination of collective bargaining, subsequently prohibiting strikes and lockouts. The Nazis also purged the judiciary and the civil service, took control of all police forces, and removed enemies of the regime—both real and imagined— through incarceration or murder.

The Racial State Once securely in power, the Nazi regime translated its racist ideology, especially the notions of racial superiority and racial purity, into practice. The leaders

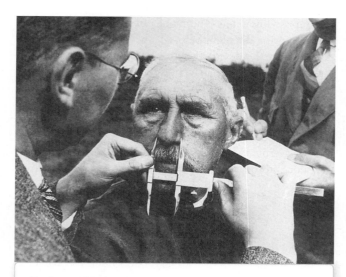

Racism under the Nazis.
A Nazi "racial expert" uses a caliper to measure the racial purity of a German.

How were the measurements of noses supposed to indicate racial purity?

Nazi Pronatalism.
"Mother and Child" was the slogan on this poster, idealizing and encouraging motherhood. The background conveys the Nazi predilection for the wholesome country life, a dream that clashed with the urban reality of German society.

of the Third Reich pursued the creation of a race-based national community by introducing eugenic measures designed to improve both the quantity and the "quality" of the German "race." Alarmed by declining birthrates, the Nazis launched a campaign to increase births of "racially valuable" children. Through tax credits, special child allowances, and marriage loans, the authorities tried to encourage marriage and, they hoped, procreation among young people. At the same time, the regime outlawed abortions, restricted birth control devices, and made it difficult to obtain information about family planning. The Nazis also became enamored of pronatalist (to increase births) propaganda and set in motion a veritable cult of motherhood. Annually on 12 August—the birth date of Hitler's mother—women who bore many children received the Honor Cross of the German Mother in three classes: bronze for those with more than four children, silver for those with more than six, and gold for those with more than eight. By August 1939 three million women carried this prestigious award, which many Germans cynically called the "rabbit decoration." In the long term, however, any efforts by the Nazis to increase the fecundity of German women failed, and the birthrate remained below replacement level.

The quantity of offspring was not the only concern of the new rulers, who were obsessed with "quality." Starting in 1933, the regime initiated a compulsory sterilization program for men and women whom the regime had identified as having "hereditarily determined" sicknesses, including schizophrenia, manic depression, hereditary blindness, hereditary deafness, and serious physical deformities. Between 1934 and 1939 more than thirty thousand men and women underwent compulsory sterilization. The mania for "racial health" culminated in a state-sponsored euthanasia ("mercy killing") program that was responsible for the murder of approximately two hundred thousand women, men, and children. Between 1939 and 1945 the Nazis systematically killed those people judged useless to society, especially the physically and mentally handicapped.

Anti-Semitism, or prejudice against Jews, was a key element in the designs to achieve a new racial order. Immediately after coming to power in 1933, the Nazis initiated systematic measures to suppress Germany's Jewish population. A flood of discriminatory laws and directives designed to humiliate, impoverish, and segregate Jews from the rest of society followed. In 1935 the notorious Nuremberg Laws deprived German Jews of their citizenship and prohibited marriage and sexual intercourse between Jews and other Germans. The Nazi party, in cooperation with government agencies, banks, and businesses, took steps to eliminate Jews from economic life and expropriate their wealth. Party authorities also supervised the liquidation of Jewish-owned businesses or argued for their purchase—at much less than their true value—by companies owned or operated by non-Jews.

The official goal of the Nazi regime was Jewish emigration. Throughout the 1930s thousands of Jews left Germany, depriving the nation of many of its leading intellectuals, scientists, and artists. The exodus gained urgency after what

came to be known as "the night of broken glass" *(Kristallnacht)*. During the night of 9–10 November 1938, the Nazis arranged for the destruction of thousands of Jewish stores, the burning of most synagogues, and the murder of more than one hundred Jews throughout Germany and Austria. This *pogrom* (a Yiddish term for devastation) was a signal that the position of Jews in Hitler's Reich was about to deteriorate dramatically. Indeed, approximately 250,000 Jews had left Germany by 1938. Those staying behind, especially the poor and the elderly, contemplated an uncertain destiny.

SUMMARY

In the decades after the Great War, European intellectuals questioned and challenged established traditions. While scientists and social thinkers conceived new theories that reshaped human knowledge and perceptions, artists forged a contemporary aesthetic. In an age of global interdependence, the U.S. stock market crash of 1929 ushered in a period of prolonged economic contraction and social misery that engulfed much of the world. As most of the industrialized world reeled under the impact of the Great Depression, the leadership of the Soviet Union embarked on a state-sponsored program of rapid industrialization that, despite causing widespread suffering, transformed the Soviet Union into a major industrial and military power.

Italians under the leadership of Mussolini rebuilt their state through fascist policies and imperial expansion. In

Germany the effects of the Great Depression paved the way for the establishment of the Nazi state, which was based on the principle of racial inequality. Although many different peoples suffered under the new regime, Jews were the principal victims of the Nazi racial state. Adolf Hitler's mission in life, envisioned in the wake of the Great War, was coming to a spectacular conclusion that culminated in another world war. That war brought both the fulfillment and the destruction of the goals and dreams he had crafted in an age of anxiety.

STUDY TERMS

Adolf Hitler (588)
agricultural collectivization (586)
Albert Einstein (579)
anti-Semitism (589)
Benito Mussolini (587)

Black Thursday (582)

Charles Richet (583)

chauvinism (587)

cubism (581)

Edgar Degas (581)

Fasci Italiani di
Combattimento (587)

fascism (586)

First Five-Year Plan (586)

Franklin Delano Roosevelt
(584)

Great Depression (582)

Great Purge (586)

John Maynard Keynes
(584)

Joseph Stalin (585)

Karl Barth (578)

Kristallnacht (590)

National Socialism (588)

New Deal (584)

New Economic Policy
(585)

Nikolai Berdiaev (579)

Nuremberg Laws (589)

pronatalism (589)

Reich (588)

Sigmund Freud (580)

Smoot-Hawley Tariff Act
(583)

war communism (585)

Werner Heisenberg (579)

xenophobia (587)

FOR FURTHER READING

Martin Broszat. *The Hitler State: The Foundation and Development of the Internal Structure of the Third Reich.* New York, 1981. An account that does justice to the complexity of the Nazi movement and its rule.

Sarah Davies and James Harris, eds. *Stalin: A New History.* New York, 2005. Reassessment of the Soviet leader based on newly available sources.

Richard Evans. *The Coming of the Third Reich.* New York, 2004. The first of a three-volume series, this work chronicles the Nazi movement's rise to power.

———. *The Third Reich in Power, 1933–1939.* New York, 2005. The second work in a three-volume series, this book starts with the Nazis' assumption of power and ends at the beginning of World War II in Europe.

Sheila Fitzpatrick. *The Russian Revolution, 1917–1932.* 2nd ed. New York, 1984. This work stands out for the author's ability to make complex processes accessible to the general reader and still instruct the specialist.

Peter Gay. *Freud: A Life for Our Time.* New York, 1988. A balanced biography of one of the most influential social thinkers of the twentieth century.

George Heard Hamilton. *Painting and Sculpture in Europe, 1880–1940.* 6th ed. New Haven, 1993. A classic that presents a discerning overview of the subject.

Ian Kershaw. *The Nazi Dictatorship: Problems and Perspectives of Interpretation.* 2nd ed. London, 1989. A superb assessment that also provides the best introduction to the enormous literature on the Third Reich.

A. J. H. Latham. *The Depression and the Developing World, 1914–1939.* London, 1981. One of the few works that look beyond the industrialized world to give a global perspective on the subject.

Robert Paxton. *The Anatomy of Fascism.* New York, 2004. A groundbreaking and fascinating history of fascism.

Nationalism and Political Identities in Asia, Africa, and Latin America

CHAPTER 31

In this cigarette advertisement from 1935, Chinese women are shown challenging traditions. They are "new women," affected by the radical changes in identity and behavior taking place after the Great War and during the Great Depression.

EYEWITNESS:
Shanfei Becomes a New Revolutionary Young Woman in China

Shanfei lived in politically exciting times. The daughter of a wealthy Chinese landowner, she grew up amid luxury and opportunity. Shanfei, however, matured into a woman who rejected the rich trappings of her youth. Her formative years were marked by the unsettling political and cultural changes that engulfed the globe in the wake of the Great War. The rise of nationalism and communism in China after the revolution of 1911 and the Russian revolution in 1917 guided the transformation of Shanfei—from a girl ruled by tradition and privilege, she became an active revolutionary.

With the exception of Shanfei's father, the members of her family in Hunan province took in the new spirit of the first decades of the twentieth century. Her brothers returned from school with compelling ideas, including some that challenged the subordinate position of women in China. Shanfei's mother, to all appearances a woman who accepted her subservience to her husband, listened quietly to her sons as they discussed new views and then applied them to her daughter. She used every means at her disposal to persuade her husband to educate their daughter. He relented but still insisted that Shanfei receive an old-fashioned education and submit to foot binding and childhood betrothal.

When Shanfei was eleven years old, her father suddenly died. Shanfei's mother took the opportunity to rip the bandages off Shanfei's feet and send her to a modern school. In the lively atmosphere of her school, Shanfei bloomed into an activist. At sixteen she incited a student strike against the administration of her school, transferred to a more modern school, and became famous as a leader in the student movement. She broke tradition in both her personal and her political life. In 1926 Shanfei abandoned her studies to join the Communist Youth, and she gave up her fiancé for a free marriage to the man she loved: a peasant leader in the communist movement.

The twists of fate that altered the destiny of Shanfei had parallels throughout the colonial world after 1914. Two major events, the Great War and the Great Depression, defined much of the turmoil of those years. Disillusion and radical upheaval marked areas in Asia, Africa, and Latin America. In Japan the ravages of the Great Depression prompted militarist leaders to build national strength through imperial expansion. Latin American states worked to alter the economic domination of their "good neighbor" to the north, and African peoples suffered a contraction in living standards along with their imperial overlords.

European empires still appeared to dominate global relations, but the Great War opened fissures within the European and American spheres of influence. Beneath colonial surfaces, resistance to foreign rule and a desire for national unity were stronger than ever. This situation was especially true in India and China, but it also pertained to those in Africa and Latin America who struggled against the domination of imperial powers.

Shanfei (shahn-fahy)

CHRONOLOGY

1912	Taft establishes "dollar diplomacy" as U.S. foreign policy
1914–1918	2.5 million African troops and carriers serve in the Great War
1919	May Fourth movement in China
1920	Noncooperation movement in India
1921	Rivera returns to Mexico to paint
1928	Socialist Party of Peru is founded
1929	Beginning of Great Depression
1930	Civil disobedience movement in India
1930s–1940s	Vargas's *estado novo* in Brazil
1931	Japanese invasion of Manchuria
1933	Roosevelt begins practice of the Good Neighbor Policy
1934	Long March by Chinese communists
1935	Government of India Act is passed
1938	Cárdenas nationalizes oil industry in Mexico

ASIAN PATHS TO AUTONOMY

The Paris peace settlement barely altered the prewar colonial holdings of Europeans, yet indirectly the Great War affected relations between Asian peoples and the imperial powers. In the decades following the Great War, nationalism developed into a powerful political force in Asia, especially in India and China. Achieving the twin ideals of independence from foreign powers and national unity became a dream of intellectuals and a goal of new political leaders. In their search for new identities untainted by the dependent past, Asians transformed and adapted European ideologies such as nationalism and socialism to fit indigenous traditions. In that sense, peoples in India and China followed in the footsteps of Japan, which had already adapted European and American economic strategies to its own advantage. Still dissatisfied with its status, Japan used militarism and imperial expansion in the interwar years to enhance its national identity.

Indian, Chinese, and Japanese societies underwent a prolonged period of disorder and struggle until a new order emerged. In India the quest for national identity focused on gaining independence from British rule but was complicated by sectarian differences between Hindus and Muslims. The Chinese path to national identity was fraught with foreign and civil war as two principal groups—the Nationalist and Communist parties—contended for power. Japanese militarists made China's quest for national unity more difficult, because Japan struggled to overcome its domestic problems through conquests that focused on China.

India's Quest for Home Rule

By the beginning of the twentieth century, Indian nationalism threatened the British empire's hold on India. The construction of a vast railway network across India to facilitate the export of raw materials contributed to national unity by bringing the people of the subcontinent within easy reach of one another. Moreover, the British had created an elite of educated Indian administrators to control and administer the vast subcontinent. A European system of education familiarized this elite with the political and social values of European society. Those values, however—democracy, individual freedom, and equality—were the antithesis of empire, and they promoted nationalist movements.

Indian National Congress Of all the associations dedicated to the struggle against British rule, the most influential was the Indian National Congress, founded in 1885. This organization, which enlisted the support of many prominent Hindus and Muslims, at first stressed collaboration with the British to bring self-rule to India, but after the Great War the congress pursued that goal in opposition to the British.

During the Great War, large numbers of Indians rallied to the British cause, and nationalist movements remained inactive. But as the war led to scarcities of goods and food, social discontent with British rule led to an upsurge in nationalist activity. Indian nationalists also drew encouragement from ideas emanating from Washington, D.C., and St. Petersburg. They read Woodrow Wilson's Fourteen

Points, which called for national self-determination, and Lenin's appeal for a united struggle by proletarians and colonized peoples. The British government responded to increased nationalism in this period with a series of repressive measures that precipitated a wave of violence and disorder throughout the Indian subcontinent.

Mohandas K. Gandhi   Into this turmoil stepped Mohandas Karamchand Gandhi (1869–1948), one of the most remarkable and charismatic leaders of the twentieth century. Gandhi grew up in a prosperous and pious Hindu household, married at thirteen, and left his hometown in 1888 to study law in London. In 1893 he went to South Africa to accept a position with an Indian firm, and there he quickly became involved in organizing the local Indian

Mohandas Gandhi (1869–1949).
This photo, which dates from about 1920, was taken several years after Gandhi's return to India from South Africa. By this time, he was a dominant force in Indian politics.

community against a system of racial segregation that made Indians second-class citizens. During the twenty-two years he spent in South Africa, Gandhi embraced a moral philosophy of tolerance and nonviolence (*ahimsa*) and developed the technique of passive resistance that he called *satyagraha* ("truth and firmness"). His belief in the virtue of simple living led him to renounce material possessions, dress in the garb of a simple Indian peasant, and become a vegetarian.

Returning to India in 1915, Gandhi became active in Indian politics and succeeded in transforming the Indian National Congress from an elitist institution into a mass organization. Gandhi's unique mixture of spiritual intensity and political activism appealed to a broad section of the Indian population, and in the eyes of many he quickly achieved the stature of a political and spiritual leader, their Mahatma, or "great soul." Although he was himself a member of the merchant caste, Gandhi was determined to eradicate the injustices of the caste system. He fought especially hard to improve the status of the lowest classes of society, the casteless Untouchables, whom he called *harijans* ("children of God").

Under Gandhi's leadership the congress launched two mass movements: the noncooperation movement of 1920–1922 and the civil disobedience movement of 1930. Convinced that economic self-sufficiency was a prerequisite for self-government, Gandhi called on the Indian people to boycott British goods and return to wearing homespun cotton clothing. Gandhi furthermore admonished his people to boycott institutions operated by the British in India, such as schools, offices, and courts. Despite Gandhi's cautions against the use of force, violence often accompanied the protest movement. The British retaliated with arrests. That the British authorities could react brutally was shown in 1919 in the city of Amritsar, where colonial troops fired on an unarmed crowd, killing 379 demonstrators.

The India Act   In the face of sustained nationalist opposition and after years of hesitation, the British parliament enacted the Government of India Act, which gave India the institutions of a self-governing state. The legislation allowed for the establishment of autonomous legislative bodies in the provinces of British India, the creation of a bicameral (two-chambered) national legislature, and the formation of an executive arm under the control of the British government. Upon the urging of Gandhi, the majority of Indians approved the measure, which went into effect in 1937.

Mohandas Karamchand Gandhi
(moh-huhn-DAHS kuhr-uhm-CHUND GAHN-dee)
ahimsa (uh-HIM-sah)
satyagraha (suh-TYA-gruh-hah)
harijan (har-i-jahn)

SourcesfromthePast

Mohandas Gandhi, *Hind Swaraj (Indian Home Rule)*

After Mohandas Gandhi completed his study of law in England, he moved to British South Africa to serve the colony's large Indian population. While there, he became outraged at British laws that discriminated against Indians. As part of his strategy of resistance to such discrimination, Gandhi developed the idea of satyagraha, *or soul-force.* Satyagraha *sought justice through love rather than violence, and its followers disobeyed unjust laws through nonviolent resistance. In 1908, Gandhi articulated his ideas about* satyagraha *in a pamphlet called* Hind Swaraj (Indian Home Rule), *which took the form of a dialogue between a reader and an editor.*

Chapter XVII: Passive Resistance

Reader: Is there any historical evidence as to the success of what you have called soul-force or truth-force? No instance seems to have happened of any nation having risen through soul-force. I still think that the evil-doers will not cease doing evil without physical punishment.

Editor: . . . The fact that there are so many men still alive in the world shows that it is based not on the force of arms but on the force of truth or love. Therefore the greatest and most unimpeachable evidence of the success of this force is to be found in the fact that, in spite of the wars of the world, it still lives on. . . . History does not and cannot take note of this fact. History is really a record of every interruption of the even working of the force of love or of the soul. . . . Soul-force, being natural, is not noted in history.

Reader: According to what you say, it is plain that instances of the kind of passive resistance are not to be found in history. It is necessary to understand this passive resistance more fully. . . .

Editor: Passive resistance is a method of securing rights by personal suffering; it is the reverse of resistance by arms. When I refuse to do a thing that is repugnant to my conscience, I use soul-force. For instance, the government of the day has passed a law which is applicable to me: I do not like it. If, by using violence, I force the government to repeal the law, I am employing what may be termed body-force. If I do not obey the law and accept the penalty for its breach, I use soul-force. It involves sacrifice of self.

Everybody admits that sacrifice of self is infinitely superior to sacrifice of others. Moreover, if this kind of force is used in a cause that is unjust, only the person using it suffers. He does not make others suffer for his mistakes.

Reader: From what you say, I deduce that passive resistance is a splendid weapon of the weak but that, when they are strong, they may take up arms.

Editor: That is gross ignorance. Passive resistance, that is, soul-force, is matchless. It is superior to the force of arms. How, then, can it be considered only a weapon of the weak? Physical-force men are strangers to the courage that is requisite in a passive resister. . . . A passive resister will say he will not obey a law that is against his conscience, even though he may be blown to pieces at the mouth of a cannon.

What do you think? Wherein is courage required—in blowing others to pieces from behind a cannon or with a smiling face to approach a cannon and to be blown to pieces? Who is the true warrior—he who keeps death always as a bosom-friend or he who controls the death of others? Believe me that a man devoid of courage and manhood can never be a passive resister.

This, however, I will admit: that even a man, weak in body, is capable of offering this resistance. One man can offer it just as well as millions. Both men and women can indulge in it. It does not require the training of an army; it needs no Jiu-jitsu. Control over the mind is alone necessary, and, when that is attained, man is free like the king of the forest, and his very glance withers the enemy.

For Further Reflection

■ Why, according to Gandhi, is soul-force stronger than physical force?

Source: Alfred J. Andrea and James H. Overfield. *The Human Record: Sources of Global History,* 3rd ed., *Vol. II: Since 1500.* Boston and New York: Houghton Mifflin, 1998.

The India Act proved unworkable, however, because India's six hundred nominally sovereign princes refused to cooperate and because Muslims feared that Hindus would dominate the national legislature. Muslims had reason for concern because they already faced economic control by Hindus, a fact underlined during the Great Depression, which had a severe impact on India. Indeed, since Muslims constituted the majority of indebted tenant farmers, during the Great Depression they found themselves increasingly unable to pay rents and debts to their Hindu landlords. As a result, many Muslims felt that they had been economically exploited by Hindus, which exacerbated tensions between the two groups. Muhammad Ali Jinnah (1876–1948), an eloquent and brilliant lawyer who headed the Muslim

Muhammad Ali Jinnah (moo-HAM-id ah-lee JIN-uh)

League—a separate nationalist organization founded in 1906 that focused on the needs of Indian Muslims—warned that a unified India represented nothing less than a threat to the Muslim faith and its Indian community. In place of one India, he proposed two states, one of which would be the "land of the pure," or Pakistan. Jinnah's proposal reflected an uncomfortable reality that society in India was split by hostility between Hindus and Muslims.

China's Search for Order

As Shanfei's life story suggested, during the first half of the twentieth century China was in a state of almost continual revolutionary upheaval. The conflict's origins dated from the nineteenth century, when the Chinese empire came under relentless pressure from imperialist powers (see chapter 28). As revolutionary and nationalist uprisings gained widespread support, a revolution in 1911 forced the Xuantong emperor, still a child (also known as Puyi), to abdicate. The Qing empire fell with relative ease. Dr. Sun Yatsen (1866–1925), a leading opponent of the old regime, became the first provisional president of what would become the new Chinese republic in 1912.

The Republic Yet the revolution of 1911 did not establish a stable government. Indeed, the republic soon plunged into a state of political anarchy and economic disintegration marked by the rule of warlords, who were disaffected generals from the old imperial Chinese army. Although the central government in Beijing ran the post office and a few other services, the warlords established themselves as provincial rulers. Because the warlords were responsible for the neglect of irrigation projects, for the revival of the opium trade, and for the decline of economic investments, they contributed to the deterioration and instability of Chinese society. Yet warlords were just one symbol of the disintegration of the political order. The relationship between native authority and foreign powers was another. Since the nineteenth century, a collection of treaties, known in China as the unequal treaties, had established a network of foreign control over the Chinese economy that permitted foreigners to intervene in Chinese society. Foreigners did not control the state, but through their privileges they impaired its sovereignty.

Chinese Nationalism After the Great War, nationalist sentiment developed rapidly in China. Youths and intellectuals, who had looked to Europe and the United States as models for Chinese reform, eagerly anticipated the results of the 1919 peace conference in Paris. They expected the U.S. government to support the termination of the treaty system and the restoration of full Chinese sovereignty. Instead, the peacemakers approved increasing Japanese interference in China. That decision gave rise to the May Fourth movement. Spearheaded by students and intellectuals in China's urban areas, all classes of Chinese protested against foreign, especially Japanese, interference. In speeches, newspapers, and novels, the movement's leaders—including student leaders such as Shanfei—pledged themselves to rid China of imperialism and reestablish national unity.

Disillusioned by the cynical self-interest of the United States and the European powers, some Chinese became interested in Marxist thought and the social and economic experiments underway in the Soviet Union. The anti-imperialist rhetoric of the Soviet leadership prompted the founding of the Chinese Communist Party (CCP) in Shanghai in 1921. Among its early members was Mao Zedong (1893–1976), a former teacher and librarian who viewed a Marxist-inspired social revolution as the cure for China's problems.

Sun Yatsen The most prominent nationalist leader at the time, Sun Yatsen, did not share the communists' enthusiasm for a dictatorship of the proletariat. Rather, Sun's basic ideology called for elimination of special privileges for foreigners, national reunification, economic development, and a democratic republican government based on universal suffrage. To realize those goals, he was determined to bring the entire country under the control of his Nationalist People's Party, or Guomindang. In 1923 members of the small CCP began to augment the ranks of the Guomindang, and by 1926 they made up one-third of the Guomindang's membership. Both organizations availed themselves of the assistance offered by the Soviet Union, whose advisors helped reorganize the Guomindang and the CCP into effective political organizations. In the process, the Soviets bestowed upon China the basis of a new political system.

Civil War After the death of Sun Yatsen in 1925, the leadership of the Guomindang fell to Jiang Jieshi (Chiang Kaishek, 1887–1975), a young general who had been trained in Japan and the Soviet Union. Before long, Jiang Jieshi launched a political and military offensive, known as the Northern Expedition, that aimed to unify the nation and bring China under Guomindang rule. Toward the end of his successful campaign, in 1927, Jiang Jieshi brutally and unexpectedly turned against his former communist allies, bringing the alliance between the Guomindang and the CCP to a bloody end. In the following year, nationalist forces occupied Beijing, set up a central government in Nanjing, and declared the Guomindang the official government of a unified and sovereign Chinese state. Meanwhile, the badly mauled communists retreated to a remote area of southeastern China to reconstitute and reorganize their forces.

Xuantong (soo-ahn-tohng)
Mao Zedong (mow zuh-doong)
Guomindang (GWOH-mihn-dahng)
Jiang Jieshi (jyahng jeh-she)

The nationalist government had to deal with many concerns, but Chinese leaders evaded one major global crisis—the Great Depression. Foreign trade in such items as tea and silk, which did decline, made up only a small part of China's economy, which was otherwise dominated by its large domestic markets. Although the new government in China generally avoided having to contend with global economic devastation, it did have to confront three major problems during the 1930s. First, the nationalists actually controlled only part of China, leaving the remainder of the country in the hands of warlords. Second, in the early 1930s communist revolution was still a major threat. Third, the Guomindang faced increasing Japanese aggression.

In dealing with those problems, Jiang Jieshi gave priority to eliminating the CCP. No longer able to ward off the relentless attacks of nationalist forces, the communists

MAP 31.1

The struggle for control in China, 1927–1936. Compare the continental territories controlled by Japan and the Guomindang in 1934.

How would the size of Japan's territories in Manchuria and Korea influence Chinese abilities to challenge Japanese expansion?

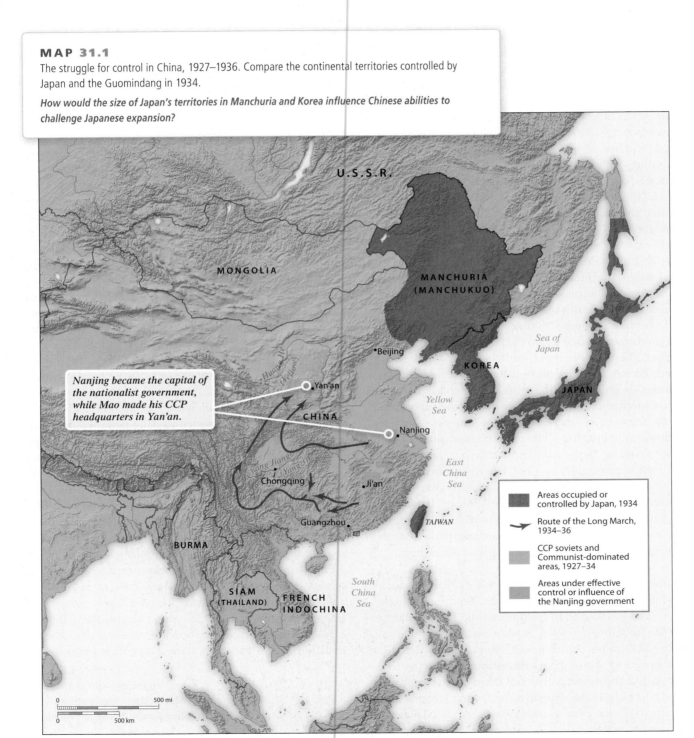

Nanjing became the capital of the nationalist government, while Mao made his CCP headquarters in Yan'an.

Areas occupied or controlled by Japan, 1934

Route of the Long March, 1934–36

CCP soviets and Communist-dominated areas, 1927–34

Areas under effective control or influence of the Nanjing government

Thinking about TRADITIONS

Combining Western Ideals with Local Traditions

During the 1920s and 1930s, colonized peoples in Asia and Africa created nationalist, anticolonial movements that were partly inspired by Western ideals of freedom and democracy or by revolutionary Marxism. *How did Asian and African nationalists modify these Western-inspired ideals with local cultural and political traditions to create unique movements of their own?*

took flight in October 1934 to avoid annihilation, and some eighty-five thousand troops and auxiliary personnel of the Red Army began the legendary Long March, an epic journey of 10,000 kilometers (6,215 miles). After traveling across difficult terrain and fighting for survival against hunger, disease, and Guomindang forces, those marchers who had not perished arrived in a remote area of Shaanxi province in northwestern China in October 1935 and established headquarters at Yan'an. During the Long March, Mao Zedong emerged as the leader and the principal theoretician of the Chinese communist movement. He came up with a Chinese form of Marxist-Leninism, or Maoism, an ideology grounded in the conviction that peasants rather than urban proletarians were the foundation for a successful revolution in China.

Imperial and Imperialist Japan

After the Great War, Japan achieved great-power status and appeared to accept the international status quo that the major powers fashioned in the aftermath of war. After joining the League of Nations as one of the "big five" powers, in 1922 the Japanese government entered into a series of international agreements whereby Japan agreed to limit naval development, pledged to evacuate the Shandong province of China, and guaranteed China's territorial integrity. In 1928 the Japanese government signed the Kellogg-Briand Pact, which renounced war as an instrument of national policy. Concerns about earlier Japanese territorial ambitions in China receded from the minds of the international community.

Japan's limited involvement in the Great War gave a dual boost to its economy. Japanese businesses profited from selling munitions and other goods to the Allies throughout the war, and they gained a bigger foothold in Asia as the war led Europe's trading nations to neglect Asian markets. Economic prosperity was short-lived, however, as the postwar economy of Japan faced a series of recessions that culminated in a giant economic slump caused by the Great Depression.

Economic contraction set the stage for social unrest and radical politics. Public demands for sweeping political and social reforms figured prominently in Japanese domestic politics throughout the 1920s. Yet conservatives blocked any major advances beyond the suffrage law of 1925, which established universal male suffrage. By the early 1930s an increasingly frustrated and disenchanted public blamed its government for the nation's continuing economic problems. Right-wing political groups called for an end to party rule, while xenophobic nationalists argued for the preservation of a unique Japanese culture and the eradication of "Western" influences. A campaign of assassinations, targeting political and business leaders, culminated in the murder of Prime Minister Inukai Tsuyoshi (1855–1932).

Inukai Tsuyoshi (ee-NO-kigh ts-yo-she)

Jiang Jieshi and Mao Zedong.
Adversaries in the struggle for power in China: at left, Jiang Jieshi (Chiang Kai-shek); at right, Mao Zedong.

Politicians who supported Japan's role in the international industrial-capitalist system faced increasing opposition from those who were inclined toward a militarist vision of a self-sufficient Japan that would dominate east Asia. Indeed, the hardships of the depression only seemed to discredit the internationalist position and make the militarist vision of self-sufficiency more attractive.

Meanwhile, militarists were setting their sights on expansion in China, where political instability made it an inviting target. In 1931 Japan's military forces began their campaign of expansion in Manchuria, which had historically been Chinese territory. The choice of Manchuria was no accident: the Japanese had significant economic interests there by the twentieth century, not least of which was the Manchurian Railroad, which they had built in 1906 and continued to maintain.

The Mukden Incident On the night of 18 September 1931, Japanese troops used explosives to blow up a few feet of rail on the Japanese-built South Manchuria Railway north of Mukden, then accused the Chinese of attacking their railroad. This "Mukden incident" became the pretext for war between Japanese and Chinese troops. Although the civilian government in Japan tried to halt this military incursion, by 1932 Japanese troops controlled all of Manchuria. The Japanese established a puppet state called Manchukuo, but in reality Japan had absorbed Manchuria into its empire, challenged the international peace system, and begun a war. In response to the Manchurian invasion, the Guomindang (Nationalist Party) leader Jiang Jieshi appealed to the League of Nations to halt Japanese aggression. The league eventually called for the withdrawal of Japanese forces and for the restoration of Chinese sovereignty. The Japanese responded by leaving the league, and nothing was done to stop the aggression. That reaction set the pattern for future responses to the actions of expansionist nations like Japan. Embarking on conquests in east Asia, Japanese militarists found a sure means of promoting a new militant Japanese national identity. They also helped provoke a new global conflagration.

AFRICA UNDER COLONIAL DOMINATION

The Great War and the Great Depression similarly complicated quests for national independence and unity in Africa. The colonial ties that bound African colonies to European powers ensured that Africans became participants in the Great War, willing or not. European states transmitted their respective animosities and their military conflicts to African soil and drew on their colonies for soldiers and carriers. The forced recruitment of military personnel led some Africans to raise arms against their colonial overlords, but Europeans generally prevailed in putting down those uprisings. African contributions to the Great War and the wartime rhetoric of self-determination espoused by U.S. president Woodrow Wilson led some Africans to anticipate a different postwar world. The peacemakers in Paris, however, ignored African pleas for social and political reform.

In the decades following the peace settlement of 1919, colonialism grew stronger on the African continent as European powers focused on the economic exploitation of their colonies. The imposition of a rapacious form of capitalism destroyed the self-sufficiency of many African economies, and African economic life became more thoroughly enmeshed in the global economy. During the decades following the Great War, African intellectuals searched for new national identities and looked forward to the construction of nations devoid of European domination and exploitation.

Africa and the Great War

The Great War had a profound impact on Africa. The conflict of 1914–1918 affected Africans because many belligerents were colonial powers with colonies in Africa. Except for Spanish-controlled territories, which remained neutral, every African colony as well as the two independent states of Ethiopia and Liberia took sides in the war.

War in Africa Although Germany had been a latecomer in the race for overseas colonies, German imperialists had managed to carve out an African empire in Togo, Cameroon, German Southwest Africa, and German East Africa. Thus, one immediate consequence of war for Africans in 1914 was that the Allies invaded those German colonies. Badly outnumbered by French and British-led troops, the Germans could not hope to win the war in Africa. Yet, by resorting to guerrilla tactics, some fifteen thousand German troops tied up sixty thousand Allied forces and postponed defeat until the last days of the war.

More than one million African soldiers participated directly in military campaigns, in which they witnessed firsthand the spectacle of white people fighting one another. The colonial powers also encouraged their African subjects in uniforms to kill the enemy "white man," whose life until now had been sacrosanct because of his skin color. Even more men, as well as women and children, served as carriers to support European armies, many of them serving involuntarily. In French colonies, military service became compulsory for all males between the ages of twenty and twenty-eight, and by the end of the war over 480,000 colonial troops had served in the French army. In British colonies, a compulsory service order in 1915 made all men aged eighteen to twenty-five liable for military service. In the Congo, the Belgians impressed more than half a million porters. Ultimately, more than 150,000 African soldiers and carriers lost their lives, and many suffered injury or became disabled.

Challenges to European Authority While the world's attention was focused on the slaughter taking place in Europe between 1914 and 1918, Africans mounted bold challenges to European colonial authority. Indeed, opportunities for rebellion and protest increased when the already thin European presence in Africa grew even thinner as commercial and administrative personnel left the colonies in large numbers to serve the war effort. The causes of those revolts varied. In some cases, as in Libya, revolts simply represented continued resistance to European rule. In other instances, religious opposition manifested itself in uprisings. The Mumbo cult in Kenya, for example, targeted Europeans and their Christian religion, declaring that "all Europeans are our enemies, but the time is shortly coming when they will disappear from our country." The major inspiration for most revolts, however, stemmed from the resentment and hatred engendered by the compulsory conscription of soldiers and carriers. No matter the cause, colonial authorities responded ruthlessly to put down the revolts.

The Colonial Economy

The decades following the Great War witnessed a thorough transformation of African economic life. Colonial powers pursued two key economic objectives in Africa: they wanted to make sure that the colonized paid for the institutions—bureaucracies, judiciary, police, and military forces—that kept them in subjugation; and they developed export-oriented economies characterized by the exchange of raw materials or cash crops for manufactured goods from abroad. In pursuit of those goals, colonial authorities imposed economic structures that altered, subordinated, or destroyed African economies by making them increasingly dependent on a European-dominated global economy. One result of this integration was that global economic downturns could spell disaster for African economies. During the Great Depression, for example, as international markets for primary products shrank, prices for African raw materials and cash crops dropped sharply and trade volume often fell by half. This, in turn, wreaked havoc on economies that had been geared almost completely toward the production of a single resource or crop.

Infrastructure Part of the process of global economic integration involved investment in infrastructures such as port facilities, roads, railways, and telegraph wires. Efficient transportation and communication networks not only facilitated conquest and rule but also linked the agricultural or mineral wealth of a colony to the outside world. Although Europeans later claimed that they had given Africa its first modern infrastructure, Europeans and their businesses were usually its main beneficiaries. Even though Africans paid for the infrastructure with their labor and taxes, Europeans designed such systems with their own needs, rather than the needs of Africans, in mind.

Farming and Mining Colonial taxation was used as an important tool to drive Africans into the labor market. To earn the money to pay colonial taxes, African farmers had to become cash-crop farmers or seek wage labor on plantations and in mines. In most colonies, farmers specialized in one or two crops destined for export to the country governing them, among them peanuts from Senegal and northern Nigeria, cotton from Uganda, cocoa from the Gold Coast, rubber from the Congo, and palm oil from the Ivory Coast and the Niger delta. In areas with extensive white settlement, such as in Kenya, Rhodesia, and South Africa, settlers expropriated African lands and grew cash crops—using African labor—themselves. In British-controlled Kenya, for example, four thousand white farmers seized seven million acres in the Kikuyu highlands, the colony's richest land.

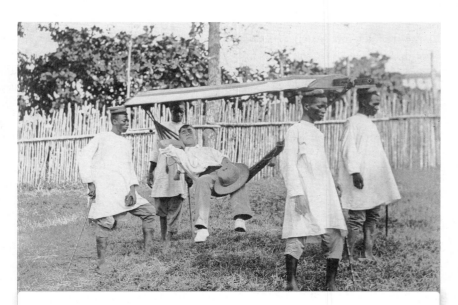

Europeans in Africa.
A European colonialist takes advantage of African labor and is "traveling in hammock," as this 1912 photograph's title suggests.

What does this photograph suggest about European attitudes toward Africans?

In South Africa, the government reserved 88 percent of all land for whites, who made up just 20 percent of the total population. Colonial mining enterprises geared toward the extraction of copper, gold, and diamonds loomed large in parts of central and southern Africa. These enterprises depended on the labor of African men who were recruited from rural areas and were paid minimal wages. Such recruitment practices set in motion a vast pattern of labor migration that persisted throughout the twentieth century. In many cases, the absence of male labor and the payment of minimal wages had the effect of impoverishing rural areas, where the women left behind could not grow enough food to feed their children and elderly relatives.

Labor Practices Where taxation failed to create a malleable native labor force, colonial officials resorted to outright forced labor and barely disguised variants of slavery. Indeed, the construction of railways and roads often depended on forced-labor regimes. When the French undertook the construction of the Congo-Ocean railway from Brazzaville to the port at Point-Noir, for example, they rounded up some ten thousand workers annually. Within a few years, between fifteen and twenty thousand African laborers had perished from starvation, disease, and maltreatment. A white settler in Kenya candidly expressed the view held by many colonial administrators: "We have stolen his land. Now we must steal his limbs. Compulsory labor is the corollary to our occupation of the country."

African Nationalism

In the decades following the Great War, many Africans were disappointed that their contributions to that conflict went unrewarded. In place of anticipated social reforms or some degree of greater political participation came an extension and a consolidation of the colonial system. Nevertheless, ideas concerning self-determination, articulated by U.S. president Woodrow Wilson during the war, gained adherents among a group of African nationalists. Those ideas influenced the growth of African nationalism and the development of incipient nationalist movements. An emerging class of native urban intellectuals, frequently educated in Europe, became especially involved in the formation of ideologies that promised freedom from colonialism and promoted new national identities.

Africa's New Elite Colonialism prompted the emergence of a new African social class, sometimes called the "new elite." This elite derived its status from European-style education and employment in the colonial state, in foreign companies, or in Christian missions. The upper echelons of this elite were high-ranking civil servants, physicians, lawyers, and writers who had studied abroad in western Europe or the United States. A case in point

was Jomo Kenyatta (1895–1978), who spent almost fifteen years in Europe, during which time he attended various schools, including the London School of Economics. An immensely articulate nationalist, Kenyatta later led Kenya to independence from the British. Below men such as Kenyatta in status stood teachers, clerks, and interpreters who had obtained a European-derived primary or secondary education. All members of the elite, however, spoke and understood the language of the colonizer and outwardly adopted the cultural norms of the colonizer, such as wearing European-style clothes or adopting European names. It was within the ranks of this new elite that ideas concerning African identity and nationhood germinated.

Forms of Nationalism Because colonialism had introduced Africans to European ideas and ideologies, African nationalists frequently embraced the European concept of the nation as a means of forging unity—as well as colonial resistance—among disparate African groups. Some nationalists looked to the precolonial past for inspiration. There they found identities based on ethnicity, religion, and languages, and they believed that any future nation must reconstitute distinctively African spiritual and political institutions. Race had provided colonial powers with one rationale for conquest and exploitation; hence it was not surprising that some nationalists used the concept of an African race as a foundation for identity, solidarity, and nation building. Indeed, race figured prominently in a strain of African nationalism known as pan-Africanism, which originated in the western hemisphere among the descendants of slaves. Representative of this pan-Africanism was the Jamaican nationalist leader Marcus Garvey (1887–1940), who thought of all Africans as members of a single race and who promoted the unification of all people of African descent into a single African state. Still other nationalists looked for an African identity rooted in geography rather than in race. That approach commonly translated into a desire to build the nation on the basis of borders that defined existing colonial states. Collectively those ideas influenced the development of nationalist movements during the 1930s and 1940s, which, after World War II, translated into demands for independence from colonialism.

LATIN AMERICAN STRUGGLES WITH NEOCOLONIALISM

The postcolonial history of Latin American states in the early twentieth century offered clues about what the future might hold for those areas in Asia and Africa still seeking independence from colonial rule. Having gained their independence in the nineteenth century, most sovereign nations in Latin America thereafter struggled to achieve political and economic stability in the midst of interference from foreign powers. The era of the Great War and the Great Depression proved crucial to solidifying and exposing to view the neocolonial structures that guided affairs in Latin America. Generally seen as a more subtle form of imperial control, neocolonialism refers to foreign economic domination, as well as military and political intervention, in states that have already achieved independence from colonial rule. In Central and South America, as well as in the Caribbean, this new imperial influence came not from former colonial rulers in Spain and Portugal but, rather, from wealthy, industrial-capitalist powerhouses such as Great Britain and the United States. Neocolonialism impinged on the political and economic development of Latin American states, but it did not fully prevent nationalist leaders from devising strategies to combat the newfound imperialism.

The Impact of the Great War and the Great Depression

The Great War, the Russian revolution, and the Mexican revolution spread radical ideas and the promise of new political possibilities throughout Latin America. The disparate ideals emerging from this time of political ferment found receptive audiences in Latin America, especially during the global economic crisis of the Great Depression. Marxism, Vladimir Lenin's theories on capitalism and imperialism, and a growing concern for the impoverished Indian masses as well as exploited peasants and workers in Latin American societies informed the outlooks of many disgruntled intellectuals and artists. The Enlightenment-derived liberalism that had shaped independence movements and the political systems of many postindependence nations no longer served as the only form of political legitimacy.

Some of the most radical responses to U.S. economic domination came from Latin American universities, whose students became increasingly politicized in this period. Many took their inspiration from the Mexican and Russian revolutions—both of which were inimical to the ideas of the United States. Indeed, universities became training grounds for future political leaders, including Cuba's Fidel Castro (1926–). In many Latin American countries, radicalism also expressed itself in the formation of political parties that either openly espoused communism or otherwise adopted rebellious agendas for change.

Diego Rivera and Radical Artistic Visions The ideological transformations apparent in Latin America became stunningly and publicly visible in the murals painted by famed Mexican artist Diego Rivera (1886–1957). Artistically trained in Mexico in his youth, Rivera went to study in Europe in 1907 and did not return to Mexico until 1921. Influenced by indigenous art forms as well as the European Renaissance artists and Cubists, Rivera's paintings reflected the turmoil and shifting political sensibilities taking place

during the Great War and its aftermath. He blended his artistic and political visions in vast public murals in Mexico's cities, because he believed that art should be on display for working people.

As a political activist, Rivera also used his art to level a pointed critique of the economic dependency and political repressiveness engendered by U.S. neocolonialism in Latin America. In the painting *Imperialism,* for example, Rivera depicted massive guns and tanks extending over the New York Stock Exchange. In the foreground and at the edges of the stock exchange are a variety of Latin American victims of this monied-military oppression. Indeed, Rivera made visible the impact of U.S. imperialism on Latin American societies, and by doing so he helped spread political activism in the Americas.

The Evolution of Economic Imperialism

Latin American states were no strangers to foreign economic domination in the nineteenth and early twentieth centuries. Their export-oriented economies had long been tied to global finances and had been subject to controls imposed by foreign investors, largely those from Great Britain and the United States. The major evolution in economic neocolonialism during this period concerned the growing predominance of the United States in the economic affairs

Diego Rivera's *Imperialism.*
This painting was one in a series on the United States and offered a visual critique of U.S. neocolonialism in Latin America.

Thinking about ENCOUNTERS

Encounters and Anticolonial Movements

As a result of physical and intellectual encounters during and after World War I, peoples in Asia, Africa, and Latin America became increasingly aware of their common exploitation by Western powers in Europe and the United States. *What encounters were most responsible for this heightened awareness, and how did they encourage the creation of nationalist and anticolonial movements in many parts of the world?*

of Latin American nations, which was sealed by the Great War. Between 1924 and 1929, U.S. banks and businesses more than doubled their financial interests in Latin America as investments grew from $1.5 billion to $3.5 billion.

That U.S. neocolonialism was meant to be largely economic became evident in the policies of President William Howard Taft (1857–1931). In his final address to Congress in 1912, Taft argued that the United States should substitute "dollars for bullets" in its foreign policy. He wanted businesses to develop foreign markets through peaceful commerce and believed that expensive military intervention should be avoided as much as possible. This new vision of U.S. expansion abroad, dubbed "dollar diplomacy" by critics, encapsulated the gist of what those in Latin America perceived as "Yankee imperialism."

The economic crisis of the Great Depression demonstrated the extent to which Latin America had become integrated into the world economy. Indeed, the Great Depression halted fifty years of economic growth in Latin America and illustrated the region's susceptibility to global economic crises. For one thing, U.S. capital investments for nascent industries and other financial concerns during the 1920s could not be maintained during this disastrous

MAP 31.2

The United States in Latin America, 1895–1941. Note the number of states where U.S. troops intervened in local politics.

On what basis did U.S. policymakers justify those interventions?

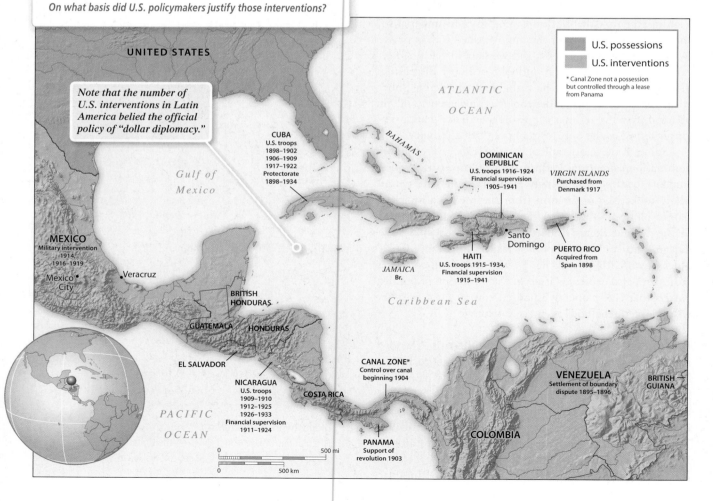

Reverberations of ● ● ● ● ● ● ● ●

The Destructive Potential of Industrial Technologies

One of the features of mid–twentieth-century nationalist movements in both Brazil and China was an emphasis on economic development through industrialization. It is easy to understand the rationale behind such plans: one of the things nationalists in Asia, Africa, and Latin America agreed upon was their objection to economic exploitation by the industrial powers of Europe, Japan, or the United States. To counter such exploitation, nationalists in this period began to seek control over their economies by producing their own industrial goods and by exploiting their own natural resources. Yet the model of industrialization established by the powers that had industrialized first was one that paid little attention to the environmental consequences of resource extraction or industrial pollution. As a result, those states seeking to industrialize in the mid–twentieth-century tended to perpetuate patterns of resource depletion, monocrop cultivation, soil erosion, and air, soil, and water pollution begun by the original industrial powers. Consider the aggregate environmental effects of this pattern of industrialization at the planetary level, especially as increasing numbers of states sought to escape economic domination through internal industrialization over the course of the twentieth century.

Social welfare initiatives accompanied industrial development, protecting workers with health and safety regulations, minimum wages, limits on working hours, unemployment compensation, and retirement benefits. Thus the Great Depression contributed in many ways to the evolution of both economic neocolonialism and economic experimentation within Latin American states.

Conflicts with a "Good Neighbor"

The "Good Neighbor Policy"   The pressures of the Great Depression and the instability of global politics led to a reassessment of U.S. foreign policy in Latin America during the late 1920s and 1930s. U.S. leaders realized the costliness and the ineffectiveness of direct interventions in Latin America, especially when committing U.S. marines as peacekeeping forces. To extricate U.S. military forces and rely more fully on "dollar diplomacy," policymakers instituted certain innovations that nonetheless called into question any true change of heart among U.S. neocolonialists. They approved "sweetheart treaties" that guaranteed U.S. financial control in the Caribbean economies of Haiti and the Dominican Republic, for example, and the U.S. Marines provided training for indigenous police forces to keep the peace and maintain law and order. This revamped U.S. approach to relations with Latin America became known as the "Good Neighbor Policy," and it was most closely associated with the administration of Franklin D. Roosevelt (1882–1945).

Under Roosevelt, the Good Neighbor Policy evolved into a more conciliatory U.S. approach to Latin American relations. The interventionist corollary to the Monroe Doctrine enunciated previously by President Theodore Roosevelt (1859–1919) was formally renounced in December 1933, when Secretary of State Cordell Hull attended the Seventh International Conference of American States in Montevideo, Uruguay. Hull signed the Convention on the Rights and Duties of States, which held that "no state has the right to intervene in the internal or external affairs of another." That proposition faced a severe challenge in March 1938 when Mexican president Lázaro Cárdenas (1895–1970) nationalized the oil industry, much of which was controlled by foreign investors from the United States and Great Britain.

Given the history of tempestuous relations between the United States and Mexico, including multiple U.S. military

economic downturn. Moreover, most Latin American states, because they exported agricultural products or raw materials, suffered from plummeting prices. Indeed, the prices of sugar from the Caribbean, coffee from Brazil and Colombia, wheat and beef from Argentina, tin from Bolivia, nitrates from Chile, and many other products fell sharply after 1929. Throughout Latin America unemployment rates increased rapidly. The drastic decline in the price of the region's exports and the drying-up of foreign capital prompted Latin American governments to raise tariffs on foreign products and impose various other restrictions on foreign trade.

Although the weaknesses of export-oriented economies and industrial development financed by foreigners became evident during the Great Depression, the international crisis also allowed Latin American nations to take alternative paths to economic development. Economic policy stressing internal economic development was most visible in Brazil, where dictator-president (1930–1945, 1950–1954) Getúlio Dornelles Vargas (1883–1954) turned his nation into an *estado novo* (new state). Ruling with the backing of the military but without the support of the landowning elite, Vargas and his government during the 1930s and 1940s embarked on a program of industrialization that created new enterprises. Key among them was the iron and steel industry. The Vargas regime also implemented protectionist policies that shielded domestic production from foreign competition, which pleased both industrialists and urban workers.

Getúlio Dornelles Vargas
(zhi-TOO-lyoo door-NE-lis VAHR-guhs)

incursions into Mexico during the revolution, it seemed there was little chance for a peaceful resolution to this provocative move on the part of Cárdenas. The reluctance of U.S. and British oil companies to grant concessions to Mexican oil workers prompted him to this drastic act. Yet despite calls for a strong U.S. and British response, Roosevelt and his administration officials resisted the demands of big businesses and instead called for a cool, calm response and negotiations to end the conflict. This plan prevailed, and the foreign oil companies ultimately had to accept only $24 million in compensation rather than the $260 million that they initially demanded.

Although the nationalization crisis in Mexico ended in a fashion that suggested the strength of the Good Neighbor Policy, a good deal of the impetus for this policy came from economic and political concerns associated with the Great Depression and the deterioration of international relations in the 1930s. The United States wanted to cultivate Latin American markets for its exports, and it wanted to distance itself from the militarist behavior of Asian and European imperial powers. The U.S. government knew it needed to improve relations with Latin America, if only to secure those nations' support in the increasingly likely event of another global war. Widespread Mexican migration to the United States during and after the Great War suggested the attractiveness of the United States for at least some Latin Americans.

Filling the migration void left by Europeans prevented from coming to the United States by the war and by the U.S. immigration restriction laws of the 1920s, Mexican men, women, and children entered the United States in the hundreds of thousands to engage in agricultural and industrial work. The migrants suffered the animosity of some U.S. citizens, who considered them "cheap Mexican labor," but the political power of agribusinesses prevented the government from instituting legal restrictions on Mexican migration. Federal and local officials managed, however, to deport thousands of Mexicans during the Great Depression.

Trying to contribute to the repairing of relations and the promoting of more positive images of Latin American and U.S. relations, Hollywood adopted a Latin American singing and dancing sensation, Carmen Miranda (1909–1955). Born in Portugal but raised from childhood

Carmen Miranda.
This Hollywood publicity photo of Carmen Miranda features the type of lively costuming that made her a colorful favorite in both the United States and Latin America.

in Brazil, Miranda found fame on a Rio de Janeiro radio station and recorded hundreds of hit songs. In the United States, she gained her greatest visibility in films produced during World War II, such as *Down Argentine Way* (1940). Carmen Miranda appeared as an exotic Latin American woman, usually clothed in sexy, colorful costumes that featured headdresses adorned with the fruits grown in Latin America—such as bananas. She softened representations of Latin Americans for audiences in the United States, providing a less threatening counterpoint to laboring migrants or women guerrilla fighters in Mexico's revolution. She also became a source of pride for Brazilians, who reveled in her Hollywood success. Hollywood's espousal of Roosevelt's Good Neighbor Policy proved a success.

SUMMARY

In the decades after the Great War, and in the midst of the Great Depression, intellectuals and political activists in Asia, Africa, and Latin America challenged the ideological and economic underpinnings of empire and neocolonialism. Often embracing the ideas and theories that were disseminated around the globe as a result of the war, including self-determination, socialism, communism, and anti-imperialism, radicals and nationalists revised understandings of political identity in the colonial and neocolonial worlds.

Japanese and U.S. imperial practices incited military and civil discord within their respective spheres, while European colonial rulers continued to limit, often brutally, the freedom of peoples in India and Africa. Like Shanfei, young intellectuals and older political leaders alike emerged transformed in these years. Their efforts to inspire nationalism and to achieve economic and political autonomy came to fruition later—after another world war had come and gone.

STUDY TERMS

ahimsa (595)
Chinese Communist Party (597)
civil disobedience movement (595)
Diego Rivera (603)
dollar diplomacy (604)
estado novo (605)
Fidel Castro (603)
Getúlio Dornelles Vargas (605)
Good Neighbor Policy (605)
Government of India Act (595)
Guomindang (597)
harijan (595)
Indian National Congress (594)
Inukai Tsuyoshi (599)
Jiang Jieshi (597)
Jomo Kenyatta (602)

Kellogg-Briand Pact (599)
Long March (599)
Manchukuo (600)
Mao Zedong (597)
Marcus Garvey (602)
May Fourth movement (597)
Mohandas Karamchand Gandhi (595)
Muhammad Ali Jinnah (596)
Mukden incident (600)
Mumbo cult (601)
Muslim League (596)
noncooperation movement (595)
pan-Africanism (602)
satyagraha (595)
Shanfei (593)
Sun Yatsen (597)
Xuantong (597)

FOR FURTHER READING

A. Adu Boahen, ed. *Africa under Colonial Domination, 1880–1935.* Berkeley, 1985. Part of the ambitious UNESCO General History of Africa (vol. 7), this work reflects how different Africans view their own history.

Victor Bulmer-Thomas, John H. Coatsworth, and Robert Cortés Conde, eds. *The Cambridge Economic History of Latin America, Vol. 2: The Long Twentieth Century.* Cambridge, 2006. Scholarly collection of essays that outlines the region's main economic trends and developments.

William Gould. *Hindu Nationalism and the Language of Politics in Late Colonial India.* New York, 2004. Political history of India on the eve of independence.

Robert E. Hannigan. *The New World Power: American Foreign Policy, 1898–1917.* Philadelphia, 2002. A detailed account of U.S. foreign relations that links class, race, and gender influences to policymakers.

Jim Masselos. *Indian Nationalism: A History.* 3rd ed. Columbia, 1998. A keen work that remains the standard, most readable introduction to Indian leaders and movements.

Michael E. Parish. *Anxious Decades: America in Prosperity and Depression, 1920–1941.* New York, 1992. A detailed portrait of the United States between the world wars, featuring treatments of foreign relations with Latin America.

Elizabeth Schmidt. *Mobilizing the Masses: Gender, Ethnicity, and Class in the Nationalist Movement in Guinea, 1939–1958.* Portsmouth, N.H., 2005. Details the emergence of lesser-known but powerful subaltern anticolonial networks that preceded formal nationalist organizations in French West Africa.

Jonathan D. Spence. *Mao Zedong.* New York, 1999. Blending history with cultural analysis, this intimate portrait of Mao is informative despite its brevity.

Odd Arne Westad. *Decisive Encounters: The Chinese Civil War, 1946–1950.* Stanford, 2003. An engagingly written work that introduces the reader to the salient political and military events that led to the eventual defeat of the Guomindang.

Louise Young. *Japan's Total Empire: Manchuria and the Culture of Wartime Imperialism.* Berkeley, 1999. An important and penetrating work on the nature of Japanese imperialism.

New Conflagrations: World War II

CHAPTER 32

Four Korean "comfort women," who were forced into prostitution by the Japanese during World War II, sit beside a rocky cliff in China at the end of the war in 1945.

EYEWITNESS:
Victor Tolley Finds Tea and Sympathy in Nagasaki

On 6 August 1945, as he listened to the armed services radio on Saipan (a U.S.-controlled island in the North Pacific), U.S. marine Victor Tolley heard the president of the United States announce that a "terrible new weapon" had been deployed against the city of Hiroshima, Japan. Tolley and the other marines rejoiced, realizing that the terrible new weapon—the atomic bomb—might end the war. A few days later Tolley heard that the city of Nagasaki had also been hit with an atomic bomb and that radio announcers suggested it might be decades before either city would be inhabitable.

Imagine Tolley's astonishment when he was assigned to the U.S. occupation forces in Nagasaki just a few weeks after the Japanese surrender. Assured that Nagasaki was "very safe," Tolley lived there for three months, during which he became very familiar with the devastation wrought by the bomb. Tolley also became acquainted with some of the Japanese survivors in Nagasaki, which proved to be an eye-opening experience. After seeing "young children with sores and burns all over," Tolley, having become separated from his unit, befriended a young boy who took Tolley home to meet his surviving family. Tolley recalled that while speaking to the boy's father about his missing son-in-law, "it dawned on me that they suffered the same as we did. They lost sons and daughters and relatives, and they hurt too."

Before his chance meeting with this Japanese family, Tolley had felt nothing except contempt for the Japanese. He pointed out, "We were trained to kill them. They asked for it and now we're gonna give it to 'em. That's how I felt until I met this young boy and his family." But after coming face-to-face with his enemies, Tolley saw only their common humanity, their suffering, and their hurt.

The civility that reemerged at the end of the war was little evident during the war years. The war began and ended with Japan. In 1931 Japan invaded Manchuria, and the United States concluded hostilities by dropping atomic bombs on Hiroshima and Nagasaki. By 1941 World War II was a truly global war. Hostilities spread from east Asia and the Pacific to Europe, north Africa, and the Atlantic. Beyond its immense geographic scope, World War II exceeded even the Great War (1914–1918) in demonstrating the willingness of societies to make enormous sacrifices in lives and other resources to achieve complete victory. Moreover, World War II redefined gender roles and relations between colonial peoples and their colonizers. The cold war and the atomic age that began almost as soon as World War II ended also inaugurated a new global order. In particular, the United States and the Soviet Union gained geopolitical strength during the early years of the cold war as they competed for global influence.

CHRONOLOGY

1937	Invasion of China by Japan
1937	Rape of Nanjing
1938	German *Anschluss* with Austria
1939	Nazi-Soviet pact
1939	Invasion of Poland by Germany
1940	Fall of France, Battle of Britain
1941	German invasion of the Soviet Union
1941	Attack on Pearl Harbor by Japan
1942	U.S. victory at Midway
1943	Soviet victory at Stalingrad
1944	D-Day, Allied invasion at Normandy
1945	Capture of Berlin by Soviet forces
1945	Atomic bombing of Hiroshima and Nagasaki
1945	Establishment of United Nations
1947	Truman Doctrine
1948	Marshall Plan
1949	Establishment of NATO
1955	Establishment of Warsaw Pact

ORIGINS OF WORLD WAR II

In 1941 two major alliances squared off against each other. Japan, Germany, and Italy, along with their conquered territories, formed the Axis powers. The Allied powers included France and its empire; Great Britain, its empire, and its Commonwealth allies (such as Canada, Australia, and New Zealand); the Soviet Union; China; and the United States and its allies in Latin America. Driven in part by a desire to revise the peace settlements that followed the Great War and compelled by the economic distress of the worldwide depression, Japan, Italy, and Germany engaged in a campaign of territorial expansion that ultimately broke apart the structure of international cooperation that had kept the world from violence in the 1920s. These revisionist powers, so called because they revised or overthrew the terms of the post–Great War peace, confronted nations that were committed to the avoidance of another world war. To expand their global influence, the revisionist nations remilitarized and conquered territories they deemed central to their needs. The Allies acquiesced to the revisionist powers' early aggressive actions, but in the late 1930s and early 1940s they decided to engage the Axis powers in a total war.

Japan's War in China

The global conflict opened with Japan's attacks on China in the 1930s: the conquest of Manchuria between 1931 and 1932 was the first step in the revisionist process of expansionism and aggression. In 1933, after the League of Nations condemned its actions in Manchuria, Japan withdrew from the League and followed an ultranationalist and promilitary policy. Four years later, Japan launched a full-scale invasion of China. Japanese troops first took Beijing and then moved south toward Shanghai and Nanjing, the capital of China. Japanese naval and air forces bombed Shanghai, killing thousands of civilians, and secured it as a landing area for armies bound for Nanjing. By December 1937 Shanghai and Nanjing had fallen, and during the following six months Japanese forces won repeated victories.

The Rape of Nanjing China became the first nation to experience the horrors of World War II: brutal warfare against civilians and repressive occupation. Chinese civilians were among the first to feel the effects of aerial bombing of urban centers; the people of Shanghai died by the tens of thousands when Japanese bombers attacked the city. What became known as the Rape of Nanjing demonstrated the brutality of the war as the residents of Nanjing became victims of Japanese troops inflamed by war passion and a sense of racial superiority. Over the course of two months, Japanese soldiers raped seven thousand women, murdered hundreds of thousands of unarmed soldiers and civilians, and burned one-third of the homes in Nanjing. Four hundred thousand Chinese lost their lives as Japanese soldiers used them for bayonet practice and machine-gunned them into open pits.

Chinese Resistance Despite Japanese military successes, Chinese resistance persisted throughout the war. Japanese aggression aroused feelings of nationalism among the Chinese that continued to grow as the war wore on. By September 1937 nationalists and communists had agreed on a "united front" policy against the Japanese, uniting themselves into standing armies of some 1.7 million soldiers. Although Chinese forces failed to defeat the Japanese, who retained naval and air superiority, they tied up half the Japanese army, 750,000 soldiers, by 1941.

Throughout the war, the coalition of nationalists and communists threatened to fall apart as the two groups competed for control of enemy territory and for political control within China. Those clashes rendered Chinese resistance less effective. While the nationalists shied away from direct military confrontation with Japanese forces and kept the Guomindang government alive by moving inland to Chongqing, the Chinese communists carried on guerrilla operations against the Japanese invaders. The guerrillas did not defeat the Japanese, but they captured the loyalty of many Chinese peasants through their resistance to the Japanese and their moderate policies of land reform. At the end of the war, the communists were poised to lead China.

The Japanese invasion of China met with intense international opposition, yet other world powers, distracted by depression and military aggression in Europe, could offer little in the way of an effective response to Japanese actions. The government of Japan aligned itself with the other revisionist nations, Germany and Italy, by signing a ten-year military and economic pact, the Tripartite Pact, in September 1940. Japan also cleared the way for further empire building in Asia and the Pacific basin by concluding a neutrality pact with the Soviet Union in April 1941, thereby precluding hostilities in

Manchuria. Japan did not face determined opposition to its expansion until it ran into conflict with the United States in December 1941.

Italian and German Aggression

Italy's expansionism helped destabilize the post–Great War peace. Italians suffered tremendously in World War I. Six hundred thousand Italian soldiers died, and the national economy was badly damaged. Many Italians expected far greater recompense and respect than they received at the conclusion of the Great War.

Italy Benito Mussolini promised to bring glory to Italy through the acquisition of territories that it had been denied after the Great War. Italy's conquest of Ethiopia in 1935 and 1936, when added to the previously annexed Libya, created an overseas empire. Italy also intervened in the Spanish Civil War (1936–1939) on the side of General Francisco Franco (1892–1975), and it annexed Albania in 1939. The invasion and conquest of Ethiopia in particular infuriated other nations, but as with Japan's invasion of Manchuria, the League of Nations offered little effective opposition.

What angered nonrevisionists about Italy's conquest of Ethiopia was not just the broken peace but also the excessive

Japanese brutalities in China.
In this photograph, Japanese soldiers prepare to execute Chinese prisoners.

use of force. Mussolini sent an army of 250,000 soldiers armed with tanks, poison gas, artillery, and aircraft to conquer the Ethiopians, who were entirely unprepared for the assault. The mechanized Italian troops mowed them down. Italy lost 2,000 soldiers, whereas 275,000 Ethiopians lost their lives.

Germany Japan and Italy were the first nations to challenge the post–World War I settlements through territorial conquest, but it was Germany that systematically undid the Treaty of Versailles and the fragile peace of the interwar years. Most Germans deeply resented the harsh terms imposed on their nation in 1919. Adolf Hitler (1889–1945) came to power in 1933, riding a wave of public discontent with Germany's postwar powerlessness and the suffering caused by the Great Depression. Hitler referred to the signing of the 1918 armistice as the "November crime" and blamed it on those he viewed as Germany's internal enemies: Jews, communists, and liberals of all sorts. Hitler's scheme for ridding Germany of its enemies and reasserting its power was remilitarization—which was legally denied to Germany under the Versailles Treaty. Hitler's aggressive foreign policy helped relieve the German public's feeling of war shame and depression trauma. Unbeknown to political leaders in Britain and France, this process was made far easier for Hitler because of the Treaty of Rapallo (1922) between Germany and the Soviet Union, in which Russians provided equipment and supplies for German military training on Russian soil—training that was clearly prohibited by the Treaty of Versailles that ended World War I. Thus, after withdrawing Germany from the League of Nations in 1933, Hitler's government was able to utilize the secret training carried out in Russia to put in motion a large-scale plan to strengthen the German armed forces. Hitler reinstated universal military service in 1935, and in the following year his troops entered the previously demilitarized Rhineland, which bordered France. In 1938 Hitler began the campaign of expansion that ultimately led to the outbreak of World War II in Europe.

Germany's forced *Anschluss* ("union") with Austria took place in March 1938. Hitler justified this annexation as an attempt to reintegrate all Germans into a single homeland. Europe's major powers, France and Britain, did nothing in response, thereby enhancing Hitler's reputation in the German military and deepening his contempt for the democracies. Soon thereafter, using the same rationale, the Nazis attempted to gain control of the Sudetenland, the western portion of Czechoslovakia, which was inhabited largely by ethnic Germans. In September 1938 Hitler demanded the immediate cession of the Sudetenland to the German Reich. Against the desires of the Czechoslovak government,

the leaders of France and Britain accommodated Hitler and allowed Germany to annex the Sudetenland. Neither the French nor the British were willing to risk a military confrontation with Germany to defend Czechoslovakian territory.

At the Munich Conference, held in September 1938, European politicians formulated the policy that came to be known as appeasement. In conceding demands to Hitler, or "appeasing" him, the British and French governments extracted a promise that Hitler would cease further efforts to expand German territorial claims. Their goal was to keep peace in Europe, even if it meant making major concessions. Britain's prime minister, Neville Chamberlain (1869–1940), arrived home from Munich to announce that the meeting had achieved "peace for our time." Unprepared for war and distressed by the depression, nations sympathetic to Britain and France also embraced peace as an admirable goal in the face of aggression by the revisionist nations.

Hitler, however, refused to be bound by the Munich agreement, and in the next year German troops occupied most of Czechoslovakia. As Hitler next threatened Poland, it became clear that the policy of appeasement was a failure, which caused Britain and France to abandon it by guaranteeing the security of Poland. By that time Joseph Stalin (1879–1953) was convinced that British and French leaders were conspiring to deflect German aggression toward the Soviet Union, which made him seek an accommodation with the Nazi regime. In August 1939 the foreign ministers of the Soviet Union and Germany signed the Russian-German Treaty of Nonaggression, an agreement that promised neutrality in the event of war with a third party and prevented the possibility of a war on two fronts. Additionally, a secret protocol divided eastern Europe into German and Soviet spheres of influence. Hitler was ready to conquer Europe.

TOTAL WAR: THE WORLD UNDER FIRE

Two months after the United States became embroiled in World War II, President Franklin Roosevelt (1882–1945) delivered one of his famous radio broadcasts, known as fireside chats. In it he explained: "This war is a new kind of war. It is warfare in terms of every continent, every island, every sea, every air lane." There was little exaggeration in FDR's analysis. Before World War II was over, almost every nation had participated in it, and virtually every weapon known to humanity had been used. More so than the Great War, this was a conflict in which entire societies engaged in warfare and mobilized every available material and human resource.

The war between Japan and China had been in progress for eight years when European nations stormed into battle

---

Anschluss (AHN-shloss)
Sudetenland (soo-DEYT-n-land)

in 1939. By 1941 nations outside Europe had also been drawn into the conflict, including the French and British colonies in Africa and India, as well as Canada, Australia, and New Zealand. As the war dragged on, only eleven countries avoided direct involvement: Afghanistan, Greenland, Iceland, Ireland, Mongolia, Portugal, Spain, Sweden, Switzerland, Tibet, and Yemen.

Blitzkrieg: Germany Conquers Europe

During World War II it became common for aggressor nations to avoid overt declarations of war. Instead, the new armed forces relied on surprise and swiftness for their conquests. Germany demonstrated the advantages of that strategy in Poland, when its air force and *Panzer* ("armored") columns moved into Poland unannounced on 1 September 1939. Within a month they had subdued its western expanses, while the Soviets took the eastern sections in accordance with the Nazi-Soviet pact. The Germans stunned the world with their *Blitzkrieg* ("lightning war") and sudden victory.

The Fall of France With Poland subdued, Germany prepared to break through European defenses. In April 1940 the Germans occupied Denmark and Norway, then launched a full-scale attack on western Europe. Their offensive against Belgium, France, and the Netherlands began in May, and again the Allies were jolted by Blitzkrieg tactics. Belgium and the Netherlands fell first, and the French signed an armistice in June. After the fall of France, Italy's Benito Mussolini entered the conflict in the hopes of reaping any potential benefits his partnership with the Germans might offer.

Before the battle for France, Hitler had boasted to his staff, "Gentlemen, you are about to witness the most famous victory in history!" Given France's rapid fall, Hitler was not far wrong. In a moment of exquisite triumph, Hitler had the French sign their armistice in the very railroad car in which the Germans had signed the armistice in 1918. Meanwhile, the British, in an attempt to rescue the remaining Allied troops in France, engineered a stunning retreat from Dunkirk across the English Channel, but it could not hide the bleak failure of the Allied troops. Britain now stood alone against the German forces.

The Battle of Britain Germany therefore launched the Battle of Britain, led by its air force, the Luftwaffe. "The Blitz," as the British called this air war, rained bombs on heavily populated metropolitan areas, especially London, and killed more than forty thousand British civilians. The Royal Air Force staved off defeat, however, forcing Hitler to abandon plans to invade Britain. Yet despite the setback in Britain, Hitler had plenty of reasons to be happy by

The fall of France.
Adolf Hitler proudly walks through conquered Paris in 1940, with the Eiffel Tower as a backdrop.

Why might it have been important to Hitler to make such a public tour of Parisian monuments?

the summer of 1941, for the swastika-bedecked Nazi flag waved from the streets of Paris to the Acropolis in Athens, and he had succeeded beyond his dreams in his quest to reverse the outcome of World War I.

The German Invasion of the Soviet Union

Flush with victory in the spring of 1941, Hitler turned his sights on the Soviet Union. This land was the ultimate German target, from which Jews, Slavs, and Bolsheviks could be expelled or exterminated to create more *Lebensraum* ("living space") for resettled Germans. Believing firmly in the bankruptcy of the Soviet system, Hitler was confident that in the Soviet Union "you only have to kick in the door, and the whole rotten structure will come crashing down."

Lebensraum (LAY-behnz-rahwm)

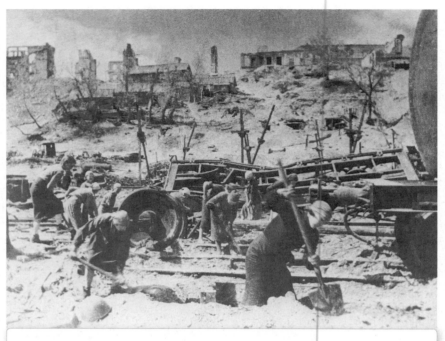

The battle of Stalingrad.
In this photograph, taken in 1942, women dig to repair train tracks damaged by German guns. The terrible destruction of the city can be seen on the hill behind them. During the long battle, men, women, and children took part in the defense of the city.

Operation Barbarossa On 22 June 1941, Adolf Hitler ordered the initiation of Operation Barbarossa, the invasion of the Soviet Union. For that, the German military assembled the largest and most powerful invasion force in history, attacking with 3.6 million soldiers, thirty-seven hundred tanks, twenty-five hundred planes, and thirty divisions from the governments of Hungary, Finland, and Romania. The invasion along a front of 3,000 kilometers (1,900 miles) took Stalin by surprise and caught the Red Army off guard. By December 1941 German troops had reached the gates of Moscow. Germany seemed assured of victory.

However, German Blitzkrieg tactics that had earlier proved so effective in Poland and western Europe failed the Germans in the vast expanses of Russia. Hitler and his military leaders underestimated Soviet personnel reserves and industrial capacity. Within a matter of weeks, for example, the 150 German divisions faced 360 divisions of the Red Army. By the time the German forces reached the outskirts of Moscow, fierce Soviet resistance had produced eight hundred thousand German casualties.

The arrival of winter—the most severe in decades—also helped Soviet military efforts. So sure of an early victory were the Germans that they did not bother to supply their troops with winter clothing and boots. One hundred thousand soldiers suffered frostbite, and two thousand of them underwent amputation. The Red Army, in contrast, prepared for winter and found further comfort in the thirteen million pairs of felt-lined winter boots sent by their new allies in the United States. By early December, Soviet counterattacks along the entire front had stopped German advances.

In the spring of 1942 the Germans briefly regained the military initiative, and by June they were approaching the city of Stalingrad. As the Germans came upon Stalingrad in September, the Russians dug in. "Not a step back," Stalin ordered. The Russians did indeed hold Stalingrad, but only at the price of waging a bloody street-by-street defense of the city until the Red Army could regroup for a counterattack.

Battles in Asia and the Pacific

Before 1941 the United States was inching toward greater involvement in the war. In 1939 it instituted a cash-and-carry policy of supplying the British, in which the British paid cash and carried the materials on their own ships. More significant was the lend-lease program initiated in 1941, in which the United States "lent" destroyers and other war goods to the British in return for the lease of naval bases. The program later extended such aid to the Soviets, the Chinese, and many others.

German victories in 1940 and Great Britain's precarious military position in Europe encouraged the Japanese to project their influence into southeast Asia in their quest for raw materials such as tin, rubber, and petroleum. Between September 1940 and July 1941, and with the blessings of the German-backed Vichy government of France, Japanese forces occupied French Indochina (now Vietnam, Laos, and Cambodia). The government of the United States—supported by Great Britain, the Commonwealth of Nations, and the Dutch East Indies—responded to this situation by freezing Japanese assets in the United States and by imposing a complete embargo on oil. To Japanese militarists faced with the alternative either of succumbing to U.S. demands—which included the withdrawal of Japanese forces from China and southeast Asia—or of engaging the United States in war, war seemed the lesser of two evils.

Pearl Harbor The Japanese hoped to destroy American naval capacity in the Pacific with an attack at Pearl Harbor. On 7 December 1941, "a date which will live in infamy," as Franklin Roosevelt concluded, more than 350 Japanese

Thinking about TRADITIONS

Nationalism and Military Service

During World War II, the force of nationalism prompted millions of people on both the Axis and Allied sides to fight for their countries. *In what ways did leaders in Japan, Germany, the United States, and Britain emphasize national traditions or characteristics as a way of encouraging active participation in wartime efforts?*

bombers, fighters, and torpedo planes struck in two waves, sinking or disabling eighteen ships and destroying more than two hundred. Except for the U.S. aircraft carriers, which were out of the harbor at the time, American naval power in the Pacific was devastated.

On 11 December 1941, though not compelled to do so by treaty, Hitler and Mussolini declared war on the United States. That move provided the United States with the only reason it needed to declare war on Germany and Italy. The United States, Great Britain, and the Soviet Union came together in a coalition that linked two vast and interconnected theaters of war, the European and Asian-Pacific theaters, and ensured the defeat of Germany and Japan. Winston Churchill (1874–1965), prime minister of Britain, expressed a vast sense of relief when he said: "So we had won after all!"

Japanese Victories Yet after Pearl Harbor the Japanese swept on to one victory after another. They coordinated their strike against Pearl Harbor with simultaneous attacks against the Philippines, Guam, Wake Island, Midway Island, Hong Kong, Thailand, and British Malaya. For the next year the Japanese military maintained the initiative in southeast Asia and the Pacific, capturing Borneo, Burma, the Dutch East Indies, and several Aleutian islands off Alaska. Australia and New Zealand were now within striking distance. Moreover, the humiliating surrender of British-held Singapore in February 1942 dealt a blow to British prestige and shattered any myths of European military invincibility.

The slogan under which Japan pursued expansion in Asia was "Asia for Asians," according to which the Japanese would lead Asian peoples to independence from the despised European imperialists. In this struggle for Asian independence, Japan required the region's resources, arguing that this was necessary to build a "Greater East Asia Co-Prosperity Sphere." The appeal to Asian independence at first struck a responsive chord among Asians, but conquest and brutal occupation soon made it obvious to most Asians that the real agenda was "Asia for the Japanese." Proponents of the Greater East Asia Co-Prosperity Sphere advocated Japan's expansion in Asia and the Pacific while cloaking their territorial and economic designs with the idealism of Asian nationalism.

Defeat of the Axis Powers

The entry of the Soviet Union and the United States into the war in 1941 was decisive, because personnel reserves and industrial capacity were the keys to the Allied victories in the European and Asian-Pacific theaters. The U.S. automotive industry alone, for instance, produced more than four million armored, combat, and supply vehicles of all kinds during the war. Not until the United States joined

Pearl Harbor.
Flames and smoke flare in the background at the United States Naval Air Station after the Japanese attack on Pearl Harbor on 7 December 1941.

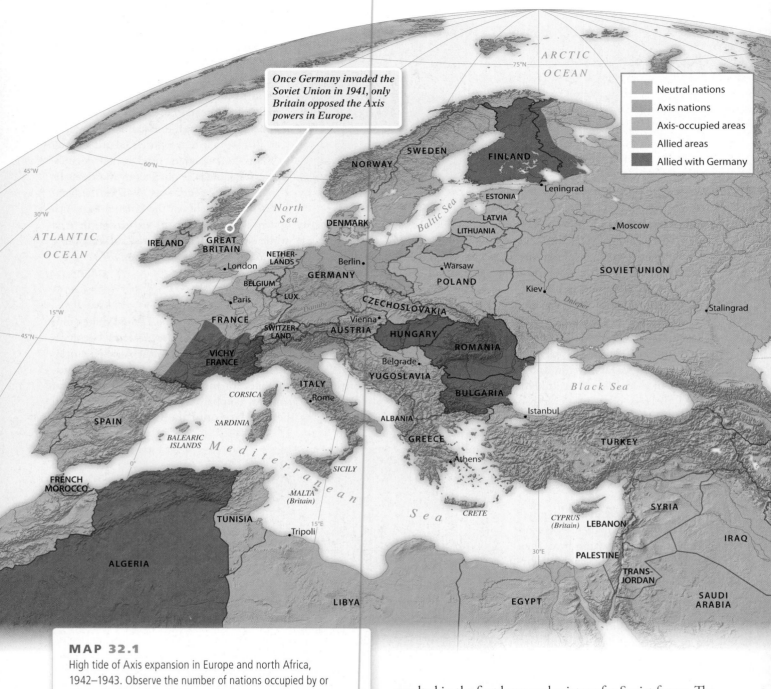

Once Germany invaded the Soviet Union in 1941, only Britain opposed the Axis powers in Europe.

Neutral nations
Axis nations
Axis-occupied areas
Allied areas
Allied with Germany

MAP 32.1

High tide of Axis expansion in Europe and north Africa, 1942–1943. Observe the number of nations occupied by or allied with the Axis powers.

Given Axis dominance in Europe, what factors finally allowed the Allies to turn the tide of war in their favor?

the struggle in 1942 did the tide in the battle for the Atlantic turn in favor of the Allies.

Allied Victory in Europe By 1943 German forces in Russia faced bleak prospects. Moscow never fell, and the battle for Stalingrad, which ended in February 1943,

resulted in the first large-scale victory for Soviet forces. The Red Army, drawing on enormous personnel and material reserves, then pushed the German invaders out of Russian territory. By April 1945 the Soviets had reached the suburbs of Berlin. At that point, the Soviets had inflicted more than six million casualties on the German enemy—twice the number of the original German invasion force. The Red Army had broken the back of the German war machine.

With the eastern front disintegrating under the Soviet onslaught, British and U.S. forces attacked the Germans from North Africa and then through Italy. In August 1944 the Allies forced Italy to withdraw from the Axis and to

D-Day landing.

Omaha Beach one week after the landing on D-Day. Troops continue to teem into the area from offshore, while ships and dirigibles offer support and protection.

What kinds of resources did the Allies have to marshal in order to put together such a massive invasion force?

strategy, capturing islands from which they could make direct air assaults on Japan. Deadly, tenacious fighting characterized these battles in which the United States and its allies gradually retook islands in the Marianas and the Philippines and then, early in 1945, moved toward areas more threatening to Japan: Iwo Jima and Okinawa.

The fighting on Iwo Jima and Okinawa was savage. On Okinawa the Japanese introduced the kamikaze—pilots who volunteered to fly planes with just enough fuel to reach an Allied ship and dive-bomb into it. In the two-month battle for Okinawa, the Japanese flew nineteen hundred kamikaze missions, sinking dozens of ships and killing more than five thousand U.S. soldiers. The kamikaze, and the defense mounted by Japanese forces and the 110,000 Okinawan civilians who died refusing to surrender, convinced many people in the United States that the Japanese would never capitulate.

join them. In the meantime, the Germans also prepared for an Allied offensive in the west, where the British and U.S. forces opened a front in France. On D-Day, 6 June 1944, British and U.S. troops landed on the French coast of Normandy and overwhelmed the Germans. With the two fronts collapsing around them and round-the-clock strategic bombing by the United States and Britain leveling German cities, German resistance faded. Indeed, the British firebombing raid on Dresden alone killed 135,000 people in February 1945. As Germans and Russians engaged in a brutal street-by-street battle in Berlin and U.S. and British forces advanced through western Germany, the Germans surrendered unconditionally on 8 May 1945. A week earlier, on 30 April, as fighting flared right outside his Berlin bunker, Hitler had committed suicide. He therefore did not live to see the Soviet red flag flying over the Berlin Reichstag, Germany's parliament building.

Turning the Tide in the Pacific

The turning point in the Pacific war came at Midway (4 June 1942), the last U.S.-controlled island in the Pacific. The victory was accomplished by a code-breaking operation known as *Magic,* which enabled a cryptographer to discover the plan to attack Midway. On the morning of 4 June, thirty-six carrier-launched dive-bombers attacked the Japanese fleet, sinking three Japanese carriers in one five-minute strike; a fourth one was sunk later in the day. After Midway, the Allies took the offensive in the Pacific. They adopted an island-hopping

Japanese Surrender The fall of Saipan in July 1944 and the subsequent conquest of Iwo Jima and Okinawa brought the Japanese homeland within easy reach of U.S. strategic bombers. The release of napalm firebombs during low-altitude sorties at night met with devastating success. The firebombing of Tokyo in March 1945 destroyed 25 percent of the city's buildings and annihilated approximately one hundred thousand people. The final blows came on 6 and 9 August 1945, when the United States used its revolutionary new weapon, the atomic bomb, against the cities of Hiroshima and Nagasaki. The atomic bombs either instantaneously vaporized or slowly killed by radiation poisoning upward of two hundred thousand people. The Soviet Union declared war on Japan on 8 August 1945, and that new threat, combined with the devastation caused by the bombs, persuaded Emperor Hirohito (1901–1989) to surrender unconditionally on 15 August. On 2 September 1945, the war officially ended.

LIFE DURING WARTIME

The widespread bombing of civilian populations during World War II, from its beginning in China to its end in Hiroshima and Nagasaki, meant that there was no safe home front during the war. So too did the arrival of often brutal occupation forces in the wake of Japanese and German

kamikaze (kah-mih-KAH-zee)

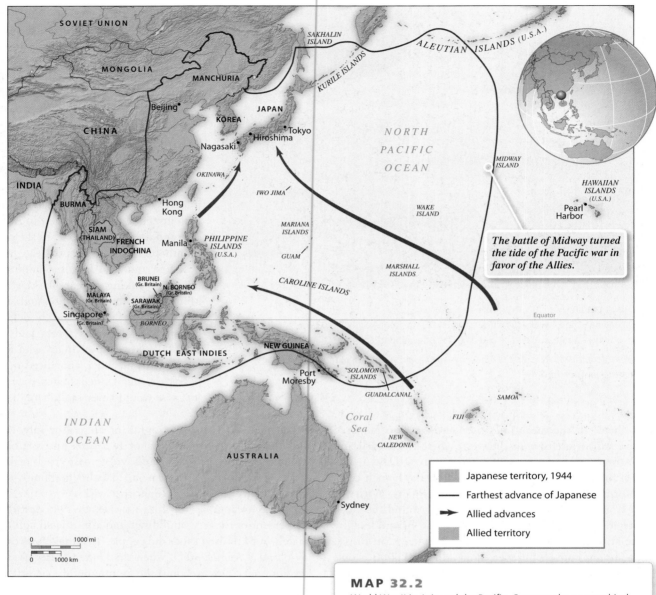

The battle of Midway turned the tide of the Pacific war in favor of the Allies.

Legend:
- Japanese territory, 1944
- Farthest advance of Japanese
- → Allied advances
- Allied territory

MAP 32.2

World War II in Asia and the Pacific. Compare the geographical conditions of the Asian-Pacific theater with those of the European theater.

What kinds of resources were necessary to win in the Asian-Pacific theater as opposed to the European theater?

conquests in Asia and Europe. In this total war, civilian death tolls far exceeded military casualties. In spite of the war's brutality, however, the human spirit endured, personified in the contributions of resistance groups and mobilized women, and in the survivors of bombings or concentration camps.

Occupation, Collaboration, and Resistance

The administration imposed on conquered territories by Japanese and German forces varied in character. In territories such as Manchukuo, Japanese-controlled China, Burma, and the Philippines, Japanese authorities installed puppet governments. Other conquered territories either were considered too unreliable for "self-rule" or were deemed strategically too important to be left alone. Thus territories such as Indochina, Malaya, the Dutch East Indies, Hong Kong, Singapore, Borneo, and New Guinea came under direct military control.

In Europe, Hitler's racist ideology played a large role in determining how occupied territories were administered. Hitler intended that most areas of western and northern

Europe—populated by racially valuable people, according to him—would become part of a Greater Germanic Empire. Accordingly, Denmark retained its elected government and monarchy under German supervision. In Norway and Holland, the Germans left the civilian administration intact. Though northern France and the Atlantic coast came under military rule, the so-called Vichy government remained the civilian authority in the unoccupied southeastern part of the country. In contrast, most conquered territories in eastern Europe and the Balkans came under direct military rule as a prelude for harsh occupation, economic exploitation, and German settlement.

Exploitation Japanese and German authorities administered their respective empires for economic gain and proceeded to ruthlessly exploit the resources of the lands under their control for their own benefit. The most notorious form of economic exploitation involved the use of slave labor. In Poland, the Soviet Union, France, Italy, and the Balkan nations, German occupiers forced millions of people to labor in work camps and war industries, and the Japanese did likewise in China and Korea. These slave laborers worked under horrific conditions and received little in the way of sustenance.

Collaboration and Resistance Reaction to Japanese and German occupation varied from willing collaboration and acquiescence to open resistance. In both Asia and Europe, local notables often joined the governments sponsored by the conquerors because collaboration offered them the means to gain power or because they thought native rule was better than foreign rule. Businesspeople and companies often collaborated because they prospered financially from foreign rule. Still other people assisted occupation forces to get revenge for past grievances.

Nevertheless, occupation and exploitation created an environment for resistance that took various forms. The most dramatic forms of resistance were campaigns of sabotage, armed assaults on occupation forces, and assassinations. Resistance fighters as diverse as Filipino guerrillas and Soviet partisans blew up ammunition dumps and destroyed communication and transportation facilities. More quietly, other resisters gathered intelligence or hid and protected refugees.

Resistance also comprised simple acts of defiance such as scribbling anti-German graffiti or walking out of bars and restaurants when Japanese soldiers entered. German and Japanese citizens faced different decisions about resistance than conquered peoples did, since they had no antiforeign axe to grind. Moreover, many institutions that might have formed the core of resistance in Japan and Germany, such as political parties, labor unions, and churches, were weak or had been destroyed. As a result, there was

little or no opposition to the state and its policies in Japan, while in Germany resistance remained generally sparse and ineffective.

Atrocities Occupation forces reacted swiftly and brutally to resistance. When in May 1942 members of the Czech resistance assassinated the Nazi official Reinhard Heydrich, the Nazis eliminated the entire village of Lidice as punishment. Likewise, when a group of officers and civilians tried to kill Adolf Hitler in July 1944, many of the conspirators were hanged with piano wire suspended from meat hooks, a process recorded on film for Hitler. The Japanese were equally brutal. When eight hundred Chinese slave laborers were captured after escaping from their camp in the small Japanese town of Hanaoka, at least fifty were beaten and tortured to death as they hung by their thumbs from the ceiling of the town hall. Yet despite such deadly retaliation meted out to people who resisted occupation, widespread resistance movements grew throughout the war.

The Holocaust

By the end of World War II, the Nazi regime and its accomplices had physically annihilated millions of Jews, Slavs, Gypsies, homosexuals, Jehovah's Witnesses, communists, and others targeted as undesirables. Jews were the primary target of Hitler's racially motivated genocidal policies, and the resulting Holocaust nearly wiped out the Jewish population of Europe.

The murder of European Jews was preceded by centuries of anti-Semitism in Europe, where Jews were routinely marked as outsiders. Thus Europeans' passive acceptance of anti-Semitism, combined with Nazi determination to destroy the Jewish population, laid the groundwork for genocide. Initially, the Nazi regime encouraged Jewish emigration. Although tens of thousands of Jews availed themselves of the opportunity to escape from Germany and Austria, many more were unable to do so because most European nations limited the migration of Jewish refugees and because German victories in Europe brought an ever-larger number of Jews under Nazi control. Early in the war, Nazi "racial experts" toyed with the idea of mass deportation of Jews, but that idea proved to be impractical as well as threatening, since the concentration of Jews in one area led to the dangerous possibility of the creation of a separate Jewish state, hardly a solution to the so-called Jewish problem in the Nazi view.

The Final Solution The German occupation of Poland in 1939 and the invasion of the Soviet Union in the summer of 1941 gave Hitler an opportunity to solve what he

Vichy (vee-SHEE)

SourcesfromthePast

"We Will Never Speak about It in Public"

On 4 October 1943, Heinrich Himmler, leader of the SS and chief of the German police, gave a three-hour speech to an assembly of SS generals in the city of Posen (Poznan), in what is now Poland. In the following excerpt, Himmler justified Nazi anti-Jewish policies that culminated in mass murder. The speech, recorded on tape and in handwritten notes, was entered into evidence at the Nuremberg war crimes trials in 1945.

I also want to mention a very difficult subject before you here, completely openly. It should be discussed amongst us, and yet, nevertheless, we will never speak about it in public. . . .

I am talking about the "Jewish evacuation": the extermination of the Jewish people. It is one of those things that is easily said. "The Jewish people is being exterminated," every Party member will tell you, "perfectly clear, it's part of our plans, we're eliminating the Jews, exterminating them, ha!, a small matter." And then along they all come, all the 80 million upright Germans, and each one has his decent Jew. They say: all the others are swine, but here is a first-class Jew.

And none of them has seen it, has endured it. Most of you will know what it means when 100 bodies lie together, when there are 500, or when there are 1000. And to have seen this through, and—with the exception of human weaknesses—to have remained decent, has made us hard and is a page of glory never mentioned and never to be mentioned. . . .

We have taken away the riches that they had, and I have given a strict order, which *Obergruppenführer Pohl* has carried out, we have delivered these riches completely to the Reich, to the State. We have taken nothing from them for ourselves. A few, who have offended against this, will be [judged] in accordance with an order, that I gave at the beginning: He who takes even one Mark of this is a dead man.

A number of SS men have offended against this order. There are not very many, and they will be dead men—WITHOUT MERCY! We have the moral right, we had the duty to our people to do it, to kill this people who wanted to kill us. But we do not have the right to enrich ourselves with even one fur, with one Mark, with one cigarette, with one watch, with anything. That we do not have. Because at the end of this, we don't want, because we exterminated the bacillus, to become sick and die from the same bacillus.

I will never see it happen, that even one bit of putrefaction comes in contact with us, or takes root in us. On the contrary, where it might try to take root, we will burn it out together. But altogether we can say: We have carried out this most difficult task for the love of our people. And we have taken on no defect within us, in our soul, or in our character.

For Further Reflection

■ Himmler argued that SS officers and soldiers "remained decent" while overseeing the extermination of the Jews; why then does he focus so much attention on punishing those who took money from the dead Jews?

(The Complete Text of the Poznan Speech), October 4, 1943, translated by Gord McFee. Translation used with permission of the Holocaust History Project (www.holocaust-history.org).

---

considered the problem of Jews throughout Europe. When German armies invaded the Soviet Union in June 1941, the Nazis dispatched three thousand troops in mobile detachments known as SS *Einsatzgruppen* ("action squads") to kill entire populations of Jews and Roma (Gypsies), and many non-Jewish Slavs in the newly occupied territories. By the spring of 1943, the special units had killed 1.4 million Jews.

Sometime during 1941 the Nazi leadership committed to the "final solution" of the Jewish question, which entailed the attempted murder of every Jew living in Europe. At the Wannsee Conference, on 20 January 1942, fifteen leading Nazi bureaucrats agreed to evacuate all Jews from Europe to camps in eastern Poland, where they would be worked to death or exterminated. Soon German forces—aided by collaborating authorities in foreign countries—rounded up Jews and deported them by rail to specially constructed concentration camps in occupied Poland. The Jewish victims packed into those suffocating railway cars never knew their destinations, but rumors of mass deportations and mass deaths spread among Jews remaining at large and among the Allied government leaders, who were apparently apathetic to the fate of Jews.

In camps such as Belzec, Treblinka, and Auschwitz, the final solution took on an organized and technologically sophisticated character. Nazi camp personnel subjected victims from all corners of Europe to industrial work, starvation, medical experiments, and outright extermination. The German commandant of Auschwitz—the largest camp, where at least one million Jews perished—explained proudly how his camp became the most efficient at killing Jews: by using the fast-acting crystallized prussic acid

Einsatzgruppen (ain-zats-groopen)

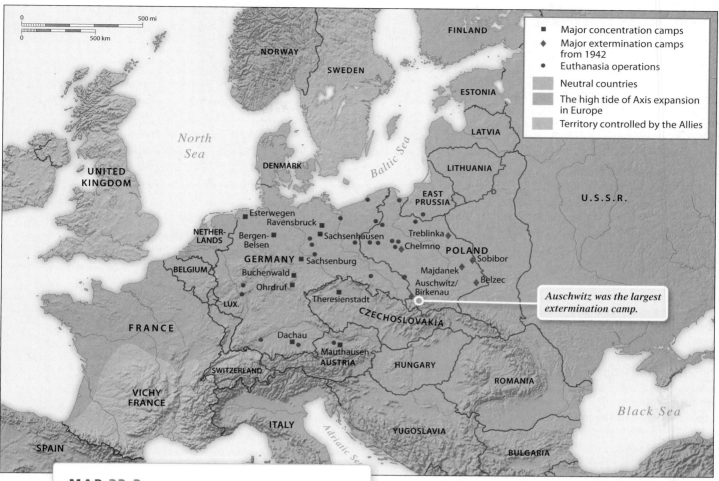

MAP 32.3

The Holocaust in Europe, 1933–1945. Observe the geographical locations of the concentration and extermination camps.

Why were there more concentration camps in Germany and more extermination camps in Poland?

Zyklon B as the gassing agent, by enlarging the size of the gas chambers, and by lulling victims into thinking they were going through a delousing process. At Auschwitz and elsewhere, the Germans also constructed large crematories to incinerate the bodies of gassed Jews and hide the evidence of their crimes. Even though Jews put up fierce resistance throughout the war, by 1945 approximately 5.7 million Jews had perished in the Holocaust.

Women and the War

Observing the extent to which British women mobilized for war, the U.S. ambassador to London noted, "This war, more than any other war in history, is a woman's war." A poster encouraging U.S. women to join the WAVES (Women Appointed for Volunteer Emergency Service in the navy)

The Holocaust.
Titled "Abyss of Human Horror," this photograph shows a survivor of the concentration camp at Nordhausen, Germany, upon its liberation by Allies in 1945.

Connecting
the Sources

Exploring perspective and neutrality in the historical interpretation of WWII

The problem More than 60 million people died in World War II. Millions more suffered intensely but ultimately survived the ordeal. Because World War II occurred within living memory, millions of individuals around the world still feel intimately connected with it—if not through their own experiences, then through those of their family members of an older generation. As a result, it is still understandably difficult for historians and non-historians alike to consider the war from a neutral perspective. Moreover, although all belligerents in the war engaged in brutalities, both the German and the Japanese states sanctioned extreme brutalities against civilian populations—which included massive campaigns of genocide, forced prostitution, forced labor, and medical experiments. These appalling events have resulted in a marked reluctance to discuss the suffering of ordinary Germans not targeted by the Holocaust or of ordinary Japanese, because doing so has been associated with cheapening the experience of the millions who suffered and died as a result of German and Japanese national policies. The implication, though not usually stated explicitly, is that not all human suffering in World War II should be explored equally. Let us consider two sources as a way of considering the ways that our own proximity to traumatic historical events might affect the ways we interpret the past.

The documents Read the documents below, and consider carefully the questions that follow.

Document 1: *Dulrahman, a Javanese farmer born in 1920, was one of approximately 250,000 laborers forced by the Japanese to work on various war-related projects in Southeast Asia during World War II. These work battalions were called* romushas. *Although* romushas *were told they would receive pay when they were recruited, instead they found themselves working without pay*

Indonesians who had been recruited by the Japanese to work as *romushas* (forced laborers).

Devastation in the aftermath of the bombing of Hiroshima.

in extremely difficult conditions and with little food. As a result, over half did not survive the war.

In June 1942, a Japanese soldier by the name of Kawakubu came to our village and asked my father if there were any people who could work, for wages, of course. My father then gave him my name. They first assigned me to help build a tunnel at Parangtritis, south of Yogya, on the coast. We didn't get paid at all, however, and they told my father they'd kill him if he'd come to fetch me. Sure, the Japanese told us repeatedly: "We've come to free you from colonial oppression." But meanwhile they forced us to work for them!

We left from Gunung Kidul for Parangtritis with about 500 people. My estimate is that about 300 survived. It's hard to be precise, for people were not buried but simply tossed into the sea. Some eight months later they shipped us out by the hundreds, including about 100 people belonging to the Gunung Kidul group. It turned out that they had taken us to Digul (in Irian Jaya, a former Dutch penal colony in what was then New Guinea) to cut trees for building a road and a prison. Compared to this place, Parangtritis had been pleasant. There at least we got a piece of cassava the size of my fist, and we could fetch water from a small mountain lake. In Digul, however, we were left to our own devices and so we had to forage for ourselves. For food, you had to look in the jungle. We ate leaves, and any snake you'd find was good for roasting.

Finally, they told us we could go home. Everybody was elated. . . . But about halfway, in the middle of the ocean, we began to ask ourselves: "Where on earth are they taking us this time?" There was no land to be seen anywhere. The voyage took a month. We finally arrived and got off the ship and that's when we panicked: Where on earth were we? This wasn't Indonesia, but then what country was it? After one week, I found out that we were in Burma.

In Burma, life for a romusha *was terrible. But compared to Digul it was better. . . . if we did anything wrong, [the Japanese would] beat us up vigorously with their rubber truncheons. That was no joke. If you got beaten with that truncheon it would remove your skin when bouncing back, and that caused a lot of pain.*

We spent exactly one year in Burma. . . . One day, our foreman let it slip that we'd be going home in two weeks. . . . When I arrived [back home], everybody cried. They thought I'd been dead long since. I certainly looked quite different. . . . During the first month, my family treated me a bit like a retiree, as it were. I was not allowed to work and they fed me very well. . . .

I still dream a lot about those days, especially about the work we did: dragging stones, that sort of thing. And about that voyage across the sea. Those high waves. That results in a nightmare once in a while, and then I find myself screaming out loud. . . . My gosh, to think that after 50 years I'm still dreaming about that!

Document 2: *Yamaoka Michiko, at fifteen years of age, worked as an operator at a telephone exchange in Hiroshima and attended girls' high school. Many young women had been mobilized for work during World War II, and they viewed even civilian work on telephone exchanges as a means of helping to protect Japan during wartime. On the morning of 6 August 1945, when the first U.S. atomic bomb used in battle devastated Hiroshima, Yamaoka Michiko had just started off for work.*

That morning I left the house at about seven forty-five. I heard that the B-29s [U.S. bomber planes] had already gone home. Mom told me, "Watch out, the B-29s might come again." My house was one point three kilometers from the hypocenter [the exact point of the atomic bomb's impact]. My place of work was five hundred meters from the hypocenter. I walked toward the hypocenter. . . . I heard the faint sound of planes. . . . I thought, how strange, so I put my right hand above my eyes and looked up to see if I could spot them. The sun was dazzling.

That was the moment. There was no sound. I felt something strong. It was terribly intense. I felt colors. It wasn't heat. You can't really say it was yellow, and it wasn't blue. At that moment I thought I would be the only one who would die. I said to myself, "Goodbye, Mom."

They say temperatures of seven thousand degrees centigrade hit me. You can't really say it washed over me. It's hard to describe. I simply fainted. I remember my body floating in the air. That was probably the blast, but I don't know how far I was blown. When I came to my senses, my surroundings were silent. There was no wind. I saw a threadlike light, so I felt I must be alive. I was under stones. I couldn't move my body. I heard voices crying, "Help! Water!" It was then I realized I wasn't the only one. . . .

"Fire! Run away! Help! Hurry up!" They weren't voices but moans of agony and despair. "I have to get help and shout," I thought. The person who rescued me was Mom, although she herself had been buried under our collapsed house. Mom knew the route I'd been taking. She came, calling out to me. I heard her voice and cried for help. . . .

My clothes were burnt and so was my skin. I was in rags. I had braided my hair, but now it was like a lion's mane. There were people, barely breathing, trying to push their intestines back in. People with their legs wrenched off. Without heads. Or with faces burned and swollen out of shape. The scene I saw was a living hell.

Mom didn't say anything when she saw my face and I didn't feel any pain. She just squeezed my hand and told me to run. She was going to rescue my aunt. Large numbers of people were moving away from the flames. My eyes were still able to see, so I made my way toward the mountain, where there was no fire. . . .

I spent the next year bedridden. All my hair fell out. When we went to relatives' houses later they wouldn't even let me in because they feared they'd catch the disease. There was neither treatment nor assistance for me. . . . It was just my Mom and me. Keloids [thick scar tissue] covered my face, my neck. I couldn't even move my neck. One eye was hanging down. I was unable to control my drooling because my lip had been burned off. . . .

The Japanese government just told us we weren't the only victims of the war. There was no support or treatment. It was probably harder for my Mom. Once she told me she tried to choke me to death. If a girl had terrible scars, a face you couldn't be born with, I understand that even a mother could want to kill her child. People threw stones at me and called me Monster. That was before I had my many operations.

Questions

- What can these documents definitively tell you about their respective situations? What **facts** can be gleaned from these brief sources?

- In Document 1, what was it like for Dulrahman to serve as a *romusha*? According to this source, how did the experience affect him after the war? Does Dulrahman's story elicit your sympathy, even though he was working in a Japanese-led work battalion? If yes, are you able to determine what factors of the story make you sympathetic? If no, are you able to determine the reasons why not?

- In Document 2, what was Yamaoka's physical condition after the bomb hit the city? Does Yamaoka's story elicit your sympathy, even though she was trying to do her part to support the Japanese war effort? If yes, what parts of her story make you feel sympathetic? If no, are you able to determine the reasons why not?

- Taking both documents together, do you believe that either Dulrahman or Yamaoka deserve more sympathy than the other? Do you find that your answer to this question is affected by the nationality of either person? Do you think it would be difficult for individuals who had experienced the war to be impartial about the suffering of individuals in enemy nations? Why or why not?

- Sources such as these make up the building blocks on which historians base their interpretations of the past. When interpreting the relatively recent past, it is especially important that historians remain aware of the ways in which their own personal and national backgrounds affect both the sources they use as well as their interpretations of them.

Source Citations: **Document 1:** http://www.opendemocracy.net/arts-photography/war_2764.jsp, from Open Democracy, Jan Banning exhibition, 2005: *Traces of War: Dutch and Indonesian Survivors.* **Document 2:** Sources from the Past, *Traditions and Encounters Brief,* 2nd ed., chapter 32, "A Hiroshima Maiden's Tale."

Reverberations of

The Destructive Potential of Industrial Technologies

World War I had demonstrated that states were willing to harness industrial technologies on a massive scale for the purpose of destroying their enemies. Many observers were horrified by this, as we know, and as a result large numbers of people around the world advocated peace as a global priority during the interwar years. But during World War II states nevertheless utilized ever more destructive industrial technologies on their enemies than they had in World War I—and now, they specifically targeted civilian populations in addition to enemy combatants. One particularly chilling example of this was Hitler's "final solution," which sought to exterminate the whole Jewish people using industrial technologies and methods. Using railways, poison gas, and a factory-like system that maximized the numbers of people who could be moved, murdered, and disposed of, the German system industrialized genocide. Consider the extent to which the use of industrial technologies during World War I might have impressed the young Adolf Hitler, who himself had fought in the war.

languishing in labor camps. Women's roles changed during the war, often in dramatic ways, but those new roles were temporary. After the war, women warriors and workers were expected to return home and assume their traditional roles as wives and mothers. In the meantime, though, women made the most of their opportunities. In Britain, women served as noncombatant pilots, wrestled with the huge balloons and their tethering lines designed to snag Nazi aircraft from the skies, drove ambulances and transport vehicles, and labored in the fields to produce foodstuffs. More than 500,000 women joined British military services, and approximately 350,000 women did the same in the United States. Meanwhile, Soviet women were the only women to serve as combatant pilots during the war. Soviet women pilots served in three aviation regiments: fighter, bomber, and night bomber—the latter known to their German adversaries as the "Night Witches."

mirrored the thought: "It's a Woman's War Too!" While hundreds of thousands of women in Great Britain and the United States joined the armed forces or entered war industries, women around the world were affected by the war in a variety of ways. Some nations, including Great Britain and the United States, barred women from engaging in combat or carrying weapons, but Soviet and Chinese women took up arms, as did women in resistance groups. In fact, women often excelled at resistance work because they were women: they were less suspect in the eyes of occupying security forces and less subject to searches. Nazi forces did not discriminate, though, when rounding up Jews for transport and extermination: Jewish women and girls died alongside Jewish men and boys.

Women's Roles Women who joined military services or took jobs on factory assembly lines gained an independence and confidence previously denied them, but so too did women who were forced to act as heads of household in the absence of husbands killed or away at war, captured as prisoners of war, or

Women in the armed forces.
An American WAVES (Women Accepted for Volunteer Emergency Service) recruitment poster proclaims "It's a Woman's War Too!"

Comfort Women Women's experiences in war were not always ennobling or empowering. The Japanese army forcibly recruited, conscripted, and dragooned as many as two hundred thousand women age fourteen to twenty to serve in military brothels, called "comfort houses" or "consolation centers." The army presented the women to the troops as a gift from the emperor, and the women came from Japanese colonies such as Korea, Taiwan, and Manchuria and from occupied territories in the Philippines and elsewhere in southeast Asia. The majority of the women came from Korea and China.

Once forced into this imperial prostitution service, the "comfort women" catered to between twenty and thirty men each day. Stationed in war zones, the women often confronted the same risks as soldiers, and many became casualties of war. Others were killed by Japanese soldiers, especially if they tried to escape or contracted venereal diseases. At the end of the war, soldiers massacred large numbers of comfort women to cover up the operation. The impetus behind the establishment of comfort houses for Japanese

Thinking about ENCOUNTERS

Unifying War, Divisive War

As a result of far-flung theaters of combat, peoples from all over Europe, Asia, Africa, the Pacific, and the Americas came into direct contact during World War II. *How and why did these encounters promote both greater understanding and greater hostility between peoples?*

soldiers came from the horrors of Nanjing, where the mass rape of Chinese women had taken place. In trying to avoid such atrocities, the Japanese army created another horror of war. Comfort women who survived the war experienced deep shame and hid their past or faced shunning by their families. They found little comfort or peace after the war.

NEITHER PEACE NOR WAR

The end of World War II produced moving images of peace, including those of Soviet and U.S. soldiers clasping hands in camaraderie at the Elbe River, celebrating their victory over the Germans. Indeed, the Soviet Union and the United States emerged as the two strongest powers after the war, and each played a central role in shaping, influencing, and rebuilding the postwar world. It quickly became clear that both powers sought to create a world in their own image. Initially, the struggle to align postwar nations on one side or the other centered on areas liberated at the end of the war. Ultimately, however, it spread to the whole world.

Postwar Settlements and Cold War

Although the peoples of victorious nations danced in the streets on Victory in Europe (V-E) Day and Victory in Japan (V-J) Day, they also gazed at a world transformed by war. At least sixty million people perished in World War II. The Soviets lost more than twenty million, one-third of whom were soldiers; fifteen million Chinese, mostly civilians, died; Germany and Japan suffered the deaths of four million and two million people, respectively; six million Poles were also dead; in Great Britain four hundred thousand people died; and the United States lost three hundred thousand. The Holocaust claimed the lives of almost six million European Jews. In Europe and Asia tens of millions of displaced persons further contributed to the difficulty of rebuilding areas destroyed by war.

At the same time, the cold war between the Soviet Union and the United States began. That long-drawn-out conflict (1947–1991) divided humans and nations as sympathetic either to the Soviet Union or to the United States. The cold war came to define the postwar era as one of political, ideological, and economic hostility between the two superpowers and affected nations around the globe.

The Origins of the Cold War Throughout most of World War II, Hitler had believed that the alliance of the communist Soviet Union, the imperialist Great Britain, and the unwarlike U.S. democracy would break up over ideological differences. Yet Hitler underestimated the extent to which opposition to his regime could unite such unusual allies. Winston Churchill had put it like this: "If Hitler invaded Hell, I would at least make favorable reference to the Devil in the House of Commons."

The necessity of defeating the Axis nations glued the Allies together, although there were tensions among them. Some of those tensions began to surface at the second wartime conference between the Allied leaders, at Yalta (4–11 February 1945), but they became obvious at the third and final wartime conference, at Potsdam (16 July–2 August 1945). By the time of the Yalta Conference, the Soviets were 64 kilometers (40 miles) from Berlin, and they controlled so much territory that Churchill and Roosevelt could do little to alter Stalin's plans for eastern Europe. They attempted to persuade Stalin to allow democracy in Poland, but Stalin's plans for Soviet-occupied nations prevailed. The Soviets suppressed noncommunist political parties and prevented free elections in Poland, Czechoslovakia, Hungary, Romania, and Bulgaria. They also installed a communist government in Poland and took similar steps elsewhere in eastern Europe.

At Yalta Stalin ensured that the Red Army's presence would dictate the future of states liberated by the Soviets, and at Potsdam Truman initiated the procapitalist, pro-democracy stance of the United States. The successful test of the atomic bomb while Truman was at Potsdam stiffened the president's resolve, and tensions over postwar settlements intensified. Having just fought a brutal war to guarantee the survival of their ways of life, neither the United States nor the Soviet Union would easily forgo the chance to remake occupied territories as either capitalist or communist allies.

In the end, all the Allies agreed on was the dismemberment of the Axis states and their possessions. The Soviets took over the eastern sections of Germany, and the United States, Britain, and France occupied the western portions. The capital city of Berlin, deep within the Soviet area, remained under the control of all four powers. In 1946, Churchill proclaimed that an "iron curtain" had come down on Europe, separating the Soviet-controlled nations of eastern Europe from the capitalist nations of western Europe. A somewhat similar division occurred in Asia. Whereas the United States alone occupied Japan,

Korea remained occupied half by the Soviets and half by the Americans.

The enunciation of the Truman Doctrine on 12 March 1947 crystallized the new U.S. perception of a world divided between free and enslaved peoples. Articulated partly in response to crises in Greece and Turkey, where communist movements seemed to threaten democracy and U.S. strategic interests, the Truman Doctrine starkly drew the battle lines of the cold war. As Truman explained to the U.S. Congress: "I believe that it must be the policy of the United States to support free peoples who are resisting attempted subjugation by armed minorities or by outside pressures." Thus the United States committed itself to an interventionist foreign policy dedicated to the "containment" of communism, which meant preventing any further expansion of Soviet influence. As a result, the world was polarized into two armed camps, each led by a superpower that provided economic and military aid to nations within its sphere of influence.

Global Reconstruction and the United Nations

The Marshall Plan   As an economic adjunct to the Truman Doctrine, the U.S. government developed a plan to help shore up the destroyed infrastructures of western Europe. The European Recovery Program, commonly called the Marshall Plan after U.S. secretary of state George C. Marshall (1880–1959), proposed to rebuild European economies to forestall Soviet influence in the devastated nations of Europe. Beginning in 1948, the Marshall Plan provided more than $13 billion to reconstruct western Europe.

In response, the Soviet Union countered with a plan for its own satellite nations. The Soviet Union established the Council for Mutual Economic Assistance (COMECON) in 1949, offering increased trade within the Soviet Union and eastern Europe as an alternative to the Marshall Plan.

NATO and the Warsaw Pact   The creation of the U.S.-sponsored North Atlantic Treaty Organization (NATO)

and the Soviet-controlled Warsaw Pact signaled the militarization of the cold war. In 1949 the United States established NATO as a regional military alliance against Soviet aggression. The original members included Belgium, Canada, Denmark, France, Great Britain, Iceland, Italy, Luxembourg, the Netherlands, Norway, Portugal, and the United States. The intent of the alliance was to maintain peace in postwar Europe through collective defense. When NATO admitted West Germany and allowed it to rearm in 1955, the Soviets formed the Warsaw Pact as a countermeasure. A military alliance of seven communist European nations, the Warsaw Pact matched the collective defense policies of NATO.

The United Nations   Despite their many differences, the superpowers were among the nations that agreed to the creation of the United Nations (UN), a supranational organization dedicated to keeping world peace. The commitment to establish a new international organization derived from Allied cooperation during the war, and in 1945 the final version of the United Nations charter was hammered out by delegates from fifty nations at the United Nations Conference in San Francisco. The United Nations was dedicated to maintaining international peace and security and promoting friendly relations among the world's nations. It offered an alternative for global reconstruction that was independent of the cold war.

It rapidly became clear, however, that international peace and security eluded both the United Nations and the superpowers. The cold war dominated postwar reconstruction efforts. It remained cold for the most part, characterized by ideological and propaganda campaigns, but it became "hot" in places, such as Korea between 1950 and 1953, and it had the potential to escalate into a war more destructive than World War II. The Soviet Union broke the U.S. monopoly on the atomic bomb in September 1949, and from that point on the world held its collective breath at the possibility of a nuclear war.

SUMMARY

At the end of World War II, it was possible for a U.S. marine to enjoy the hospitality of a Japanese family in Nagasaki, but not for Soviet and U.S. troops to continue embracing in camaraderie. World War II was a total global war that forced violent encounters between peoples and radically altered the political shape of the world. Beginning with Japan and China in 1931, this global conflagration spread to Europe and its empires and to the Pacific Ocean and the rest of Asia. Men, women, and children throughout the world became intimate with war as victims of civilian bombing campaigns, as soldiers and war workers, and as slave laborers and comfort women. When the Allies defeated the Axis powers in 1945, destroying the German and Japanese empires, the world had to rebuild as the cold war began. The cold war helped determine the new shape of the world as nations reconstructed under the auspices of either the United States or the Soviet Union, the two superpowers of the postwar era.

STUDY TERMS

Adolf Hitler (612)
Allied powers (610)
Anschluss (612)
appeasement (612)
Axis powers (610)
Battle of Britain (613)
Benito Mussolini (611)
Blitzkrieg (613)
cold war (625)
COMECON (626)
D-Day (616)
Einsatzgruppen (620)
final solution (620)
Greater East Asia
    Co-Prosperity Sphere
    (615)
Hiroshima and Nagasaki
    (617)
Holocaust (619)

Joseph Stalin (612)
kamikaze (617)
Lebensraum (613)
lend-lease (614)
Marshall Plan (626)
NATO (626)
Operation Barbarossa (614)
Pearl Harbor (614)
Rape of Nanjing (611)
Russian-German Treaty of
    Nonaggression (611)
Sudetenland (612)
Treaty of Rapallo (612)
Tripartite Pact (611)
Truman Doctrine (626)
United Nations (626)
Vichy (614)
Warsaw Pact (626)
Winston Churchill (615)

FOR FURTHER READING

Christopher Bayly and Tim Harper. *Forgotten Armies: The Fall of British Asia, 1941–1945*. Cambridge, 2005. Broad study of the impact of World War II on Britain's Asian empire.

Herbert P. Bix. *Hirohito and the Making of Modern Japan*. New York, 2001. A groundbreaking, unvarnished biography that details the strong and decisive role the emperor played in wartime operations during World War II.

Christopher R. Browning with contributions by Jürgen Matthäuss. *The Origins of the Final Solution: The Evolution of Nazi Jewish Policy, September 1939–March 1942*. Lincoln, Neb., and Jerusalem, 2004. Standard work on the evolution of Nazi anti-Jewish policies from persecution to mass murder.

Ian Buruma. *The Wages of Guilt: Memories of War in Germany and Japan*. New York, 1995. A moving account of how societies deal with the war crimes of World War II.

Haruko Taya Cook and Theodore F. Cook. *Japan at War: An Oral History*. New York, 1992. Views of World War II in the words of the Japanese who witnessed it.

Margaret Higgonet, Jane Jenson, Sonya Michel, and Margaret Weitz, eds. *Behind the Lines: Gender and the Two World Wars*. New Haven, 1987. A penetrating series of articles on women in both world wars, focusing generally on U.S. and European experiences.

Raul Hilberg. *The Destruction of the European Jews*. New York, 1967. One of the most important works on the Holocaust.

Akira Iriye. *The Origins of the Second World War in Asia and the Pacific*. New York, 1987. An examination of the Asian and Pacific origins of the war by one of the field's leading scholars.

You-Li Sun. *China and the Origins of the Pacific War, 1931–1941*. New York, 1993. An account of the origins of the war in which China takes center stage.

Gerhard Weinberg. *A World at Arms: A Global History of World War II*. Cambridge, 1994. An exhaustive look at the war from a global perspective.

The Cold War and Decolonization
CHAPTER **33**

An American air strike against Viet Cong positions results in the destruction of a Vietnamese village.

EYEWITNESS:
Ho Chi Minh Comes Face to Face with Cold War Politics

On 16 February 1946, six months after the final end of World War II in Asia, the Vietnamese revolutionary leader Ho Chi Minh wrote a letter to U.S. president Harry Truman. Ho, who had fought for decades against French imperial rule and then against the Japanese occupation of Vietnam, had reason to expect a sympathetic hearing from the American president. After all, during the war the United States had sent its own OSS (Office of Strategic Services) officers to aid Ho's Viet Minh party in their resistance against the Japanese, and the previous president (Franklin Delano Roosevelt) had been hostile to French imperialism in Asia. Thus, when Ho Chi Minh took control of Vietnam from the hated Japanese, he expected American support for his new republic. Indeed, when Ho issued his declaration of independence on 2 September 1945, some of the Vietnamese people in the huge crowd carried homemade pictures of President Harry Truman and waved American flags.

Imagine Ho's surprise when he discovered that Truman would not stand in the way of the French decision to recolonize Vietnam. As French troops landed in Vietnam and began reestablishing French authority in early 1946, Ho penned his letter to the American president, arguing that "this aggression is contrary to all principles of international law and the pledge made by the Allies during World War II. It is a challenge to the noble attitude shown before, during, and after the war by the United States Government and People. . . . [Vietnam's] security and freedom can only be guaranteed by our independence from any colonial power, and our free cooperation with all other powers. It is with this firm conviction that we request of the United States as guardians and champions of World Justice to take a decisive step in support of our independence." In fact, Ho pointed out, the Vietnamese were simply asking for the same kind of independence granted that very year to the Philippines by the United States itself.

Truman never answered Ho's letter of 16 February. Instead, as tensions between the United States and the Soviet Union became increasingly apparent by the end of World War II, the struggle between global capitalism and global communism overshadowed the way both new superpowers regarded the world around them. Although Ho had fought with the Allies in World War II, he was a founder of the French Communist Party, had lived in Moscow, and was committed to socialist ideals. With an enormous Soviet Union set to impose its will on eastern Europe in the immediate aftermath of the war, U.S. policymakers became convinced that any group with communist sympathies represented a serious threat to global security. Thus in spite of its professed anti-imperial attitude, the United States government was induced by the realities of cold war politics not only to aid the French as they tried to reconquer Vietnam, but to take on the project of eradicating communism in Vietnam once French efforts failed in 1954.

As Ho discovered, Vietnam's struggle for independence collided head-on with emerging cold war politics. Vietnam was not alone. Since decolonization and the cold war occurred simultaneously in the decades after World War II, it was almost inevitable that the wave of new nation-states that came into being as empires fell would have to face the two opposing superpowers now dominating global politics. Indeed, decolonization and

CHRONOLOGY

1947	Partition of India
1948	Creation of Israel
1948–1949	Berlin blockade and airlift
1949	Division of Berlin and Germany
1949	Establishment of People's Republic of China
1950–1953	Korean War
1954	French defeat at Dienbienphu
1955	Bandung Conference
1956	Suez crisis
1956	Uprising in Hungary
1957	Ghana gains independence
1958–1961	Great Leap Forward in China
1959	Castro comes to power in Cuba
1961	Bay of Pigs invasion
1961	Construction of Berlin Wall
1962	Cuban missile crisis
1964	Creation of Palestinian Liberation Organization (PLO)
1964	Sino-Soviet rift
1965–1973	U.S. troops to Vietnam
1968	Prague Spring
1973	U.S. defeat in Vietnam
1979	Revolution in Iran
1979	Sandinistas in power in Nicaragua
1989	Soviet withdrawal from Afghanistan
1989	Fall of Berlin Wall
1990	Reunification of Germany
1991	Collapse of Soviet Union
1991	End of cold war

social and economic systems and competing political ideologies. The geopolitical and ideological rivalry between the Soviet Union and the United States lasted almost five decades and affected every corner of the world. The cold war was responsible for the formation of military and political alliances, the creation of client states, and an arms race of unprecedented scope. It engendered diplomatic crises, spawned military conflicts, stimulated social change, and at times brought the world to the brink of nuclear annihilation. It was a contest in which neither side gave way, yet in the end the United States and the Soviet Union always avoided a direct clash of arms, hence the term *cold war.*

Like the cold war, and frequently in conjunction with it, decolonization after World War II contributed significantly to global political transformations. Decolonization, in essence the relinquishing of all colonial possessions by imperial powers, brought the world to its current international standing. Imperial agents lost control, and dozens of new independent states gained autonomy and self-determination. As cold war animosities deepened, however, the leaders of the Soviet Union and the United States often demanded that new nations take sides and choose between capitalism and communism. At times these demands compromised their independence, particularly in new nations deemed strategically important by the superpowers.

Partly as a result of cold war tensions, people in new and developing nations around the world discovered that independence was just the first step on a much longer, and often much more difficult, road to national unity and social and economic stability. Yet despite all the complications of decolonization and its aftermath, colonial peoples fought for freedom and then for security in a bipolar world. Although both decolonization and the cold war had come to an end by the late twentieth century, from their beginning to end both processes suggested that powerful new global forces were at work in the wake of World War II.

the cold war were two of the most important processes to emerge out of World War II, and both fundamentally reshaped the late-twentieth-century world—particularly in cases, such as Vietnam, where they intertwined.

The cold war was a strategic struggle that developed after World War II between the United States and its allies on the one hand and the USSR and its allied communist countries on the other. Yet the confrontation was more than an instance of power rivalry; it was also a tense encounter between rival

THE FORMATION OF A BIPOLAR WORLD

The cold war's initial arena was war-torn Europe. By the time Germany surrendered in the spring of 1945, the wartime alliance between the Soviet Union and the United States was disintegrating. With the advent of peace, the one-time partners increasingly sacrificed cooperation for their own national interests. The hostility and competition between these new adversaries resulted in a divided Europe, in powerful change within the societies of both superpowers, and ultimately in a divided world.

The Cold War in Europe

Among the first manifestations of the cold war was the division of the European continent into competing political, military, and economic blocs—one dependent on the United States and the other subservient to the USSR—separated by what Winston Churchill called an "iron curtain." In essence, each bloc adopted the political institutions, economic systems, and foreign policies of one of the two superpowers. Thus western European nations that were tied to the United States embraced parliamentary political systems and capitalist economic structures and adjusted their foreign policies to the U.S. vision of the postwar world. On the other hand, under the watchful eyes of Soviet occupation armies, the governments of eastern European states adopted Soviet political and economic institutions and supported Moscow's foreign policy goals.

MAP 33.1

Occupied Germany, 1945–1949. Locate the city of Berlin in Soviet-controlled territory.

How was it possible for the British, Americans, and French to maintain their zones of control in Berlin, given such geographical distance from western Germany?

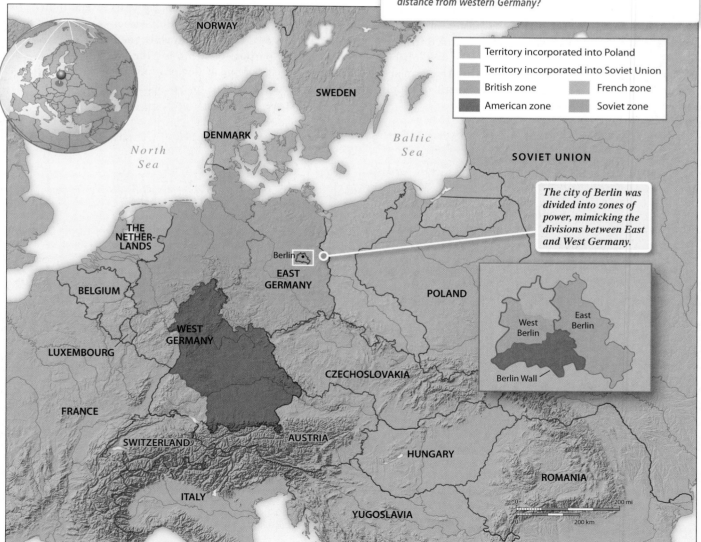

The city of Berlin was divided into zones of power, mimicking the divisions between East and West Germany.

Territory incorporated into Poland
Territory incorporated into Soviet Union
British zone
French zone
American zone
Soviet zone

A Divided Germany The fault lines of cold war Europe were first visible in Germany. There in 1948–1949 an international crisis arose when the Soviet Union pressured the western powers to relinquish their jurisdiction over Berlin. After the collapse of Hitler's Third Reich, the forces of the United States, the Soviet Union, Britain, and France occupied Germany and its capital, Berlin, both of which they divided for administrative purposes into four zones. In accordance with agreements made at Yalta, specific travel corridors running through the Soviet occupation zone of Germany gave the French, British, and Americans access from their sectors in Berlin to their respective zones of occupation in western Germany.

Blockade and Airlift When the western powers decided to merge their occupation zones in Germany—including their sectors in Berlin—into a single economic unit, however, the Soviets saw the move as a threat to their own zone of control. In retaliation, on 24 June 1948 the Soviets announced that the western powers no longer had jurisdiction in Berlin and blockaded road, rail, and water links between Berlin and western Germany. Two days later, in the first serious test of the cold war, the Americans and British responded with an airlift designed to keep the city's inhabitants alive, fed, and warm. For eleven months, American and British aircrews flew around-the-clock missions to supply West Berlin with the necessities of life. Tensions remained high during the airlift, but the cold war did not turn hot. Finally, the Soviet leadership called off the blockade in May 1949, though the airlift continued until September. Also in May of that year, the U.S., British, and French zones of occupation coalesced to form the Federal Republic of Germany (West Germany). The Soviets responded by creating the German Democratic Republic (East Germany) in their own zone. A similar process repeated itself in Berlin, which was deep within the Soviet zone. The Soviet sector formed East Berlin and became the capital of the new East Germany, while the remaining three sectors united to form West Berlin.

Berlin Wall By 1961 the communist East German state was hemorrhaging from a steady drain of refugees—nearly 3.5 million since 1949—who preferred life in capitalist West Germany. To counter this embarrassing problem, in August 1961 the communists erected a fortified wall—replete with watchtowers, searchlights, and border guards—between East and West Germany. In subsequent years several thousand East Germans escaped to West Germany, and several hundred others died trying. Meanwhile, the Berlin Wall accomplished its purpose of stemming the flow of refugees, though at the cost of openly demonstrating that the regime lacked legitimacy among its own people.

The Berlin wall.
In this 1961 photo from the Schoenholz region of Berlin, West Berliners peer over the brick and barbed-wire fence separating East and West Berlin.

Why did the Communist regime in East Germany take the drastic step of building such a wall?

Reverberations of ● ● ● ● ● ● ● ● ●

The Destructive Potential of Industrial Technologies

One of the lessons some observers took from World War I was that technological parity in weaponry and war materiel led to stalemate. The obverse of this lesson was that technological superiority could lead to victory. During World War II, the belligerent states utilized all of the industrial and scientific resources they could muster in order to create weaponry capable of leading to a decisive victory. The United States achieved this goal in 1945 with the atomic bomb, which was then used to end the war with Japan. The problem, however, was that the existence of the atomic bomb led other states to create similar weapons—especially those states, like the Soviet Union, that became rivals to the United States after the war. When the Soviets successfully tested their own atomic bomb in 1949, it became clear that industrial military technologies now made it possible for entire societies to wipe each other out with the use of a few bombs. The destructive potential of industrial technology that had seemed to reach a crescendo in World War I, then, had turned out to be only the beginning. Consider how the world's peoples lived with the possibility of nuclear holocaust even in peacetime for most of the rest of the twentieth century.

The Nuclear Arms Race A central feature of the cold war world was a costly arms race and the terrifying proliferation of nuclear weapons. The struggle between the United States and the Soviet Union led to the creation of two military blocs: the North Atlantic Treaty Organization, or NATO (1949), intended to serve as a military counterweight to the Soviet forces in Europe, and the Warsaw Treaty Organization, or Warsaw Pact (1955), established as a response to the rearming of West Germany. Because the United States was determined to retain military superiority and because the Soviet Union was equally determined to reach parity with the United States, both sides amassed enormous arsenals of thermonuclear weapons and developed a multitude of systems for deploying those weapons. By 1970, both powers had reached parity, which meant that they had acquired the capacity for mutually assured destruction, or MAD. Although the prospect of MAD was terrifying, the balance of terror had the effect of restraining the contestants and stabilizing their relationship.

Space Race During the nuclear arms race, cold war tensions accelerated when it seemed that one superpower gained a critical technological edge over the other. This was certainly the case when the Soviets took the cold war into space by announcing, on 4 October 1957, the launching into space of the first satellite, *Sputnik.* The Soviet head start in this "space race" provoked panic among U.S. citizens and politicians. U.S. panic only intensified in April 1961 when the Soviets rocketed cosmonaut Yuri Gagarin (1934–1968) into space, where he became the first man to orbit Earth. The U.S. responded to Soviet successes in space with its own, launching the satellite *Explorer I* in 1958 and sending astronaut John Glenn (1921–) into orbit in 1962. When John F. Kennedy took office in 1961, he dedicated himself and the National Aeronautics and Space Administration (NASA) to the task of landing a man on the moon. That came to fruition on 20 July 1969 when *Apollo XI* gently set down on the moon's Sea of Tranquility and thereby ensured that Americans were the first to make this "great leap for mankind." During the cold war, critical technological and scientific breakthroughs were achieved on both sides of the iron curtain as a result of intense competition between the superpowers.

Cold War Societies

The forces that split Europe into opposing blocs and created the nuclear arms race also had dramatic effects on the domestic affairs of the United States, the Soviet Union, and their European allies. Postwar social transformations in each demonstrated how domestic policies and international affairs became linked in this period.

Domestic Containment In the United States, for example, cold war concerns about the spread of communism reached deeply into the domestic sphere. Politicians, FBI agents, educators, and social commentators warned of communist spies trying to undermine the institutions of U.S. life, and Senator Joseph McCarthy (1909–1957) became infamous in the early 1950s for his unsuccessful quest to expose communists in the U.S. government. Thousands of citizens who supported any radical or liberal cause—especially those who were or once had been members of the Communist Party—lost their jobs and reputations after being deemed risks to their nation's security. Conforming to a socially sanctioned way of life and avoiding suspicion became the norm during the early, most frightening years of the cold war. Some scholars have dubbed this U.S. retreat to the home and family "domestic containment," indicating its similarity to the U.S. foreign policy of the containment of international communism. At the same time, however, people in the United States enjoyed unprecedented prosperity and leisure during the early decades of the cold war. Access to automobiles, Hollywood movies, record albums, and supermarkets therefore lessened some of the pain of atomic anxiety and international insecurity.

Soviet Society In the Soviet Union and eastern Europe, cold war ideologies also profoundly influenced domestic realities. After the war, Stalin imposed Soviet economic planning on governments in eastern Europe and expected the peoples of the Soviet Union and eastern Europe to conform to anticapitalist ideological requirements. Rebellious artists and novelists found themselves silenced or denounced in an exaggerated and reversed form of the McCarthyism that affected government workers, writers, and filmmakers in the United States in the same years. After Stalin's death in 1953, this policy of repression relaxed somewhat, as his successor—Nikita Khrushchev—pursued a slightly more liberal path with respect to domestic society. There were limits to this Soviet liberalization, though: Soviet troops cracked down on Hungarian rebels in 1956, and Soviet novelist Boris Pasternak (1890–1960), author of *Dr. Zhivago,* was not allowed to receive his Nobel Prize for Literature in 1958. In addition to political repression, social conditions and material wealth in the Soviet Union and eastern Europe differed dramatically from those in the United States and western Europe. Whereas people in the capitalist bloc enjoyed increased prosperity and access to consumer items, those in the communist bloc did not: dishwashers, automobiles, fashionable clothing, and high-quality manufactured goods remained out of the reach of most ordinary people.

Ironically, despite their intense competition and opposition, societies in the Soviet Union and the United States came to resemble one another in some ways, especially in their domestic censorship policies and their quest for cold war supremacy. There is no doubt that societies on both sides underwent dramatic transformations as a result of the international competition between capitalism and communism. Indeed, the cold war—like the world wars and the Great Depression before it—demonstrated once again that global political events had the power to shape even the day-to-day lives of ordinary people.

Confrontations in Korea and Cuba

As the tensions of the cold war were dividing Europe and spurring change within the societies of the superpowers and their allies, they also spilled out into the global arena. When hostilities broke out on the Korean peninsula in the summer of 1950, the focus of the cold war shifted to east Asia. In the previous year, the State and Defense departments in the United States had drafted the famous NSC-68 document (see Sources from the Past, this chapter), outlining the government's strident commitment to do whatever it took to block the Soviet Union from extending its control anywhere in the world. Europe had already been divided into two blocs: Korea was the first test of the policy of containment in the rest of the world.

At the end of World War II, the leaders of the Soviet Union and the United States had partitioned Korea along the thirty-eighth parallel of latitude into a northern Soviet zone and a southern U.S. zone. In 1948 they consented to the establishment of two separate Korean states: in the south, the Republic of Korea, with Seoul as its capital and the conservative anticommunist Syngman Rhee (1875–1965) as its president; in the north, the People's Democratic Republic of Korea, with Pyongyang as its capital and the revolutionary communist Kim Il Sung (1912–1995) as its leader. After arming their respective clients, each of which claimed sovereignty over the entire country, U.S. and Soviet troops withdrew.

The Korean War On the early morning of 25 June 1950, the unstable political situation in Korea came to a head. Determined to unify Korea by force, the Pyongyang regime ordered more than one hundred thousand troops across the thirty-eighth parallel in a surprise attack, capturing Seoul on 27 June. Convinced that the USSR had sanctioned the invasion, and armed with UN support, the U.S. military went into action. Within two weeks U.S. forces pushed North Koreans back to the thirty-eighth parallel. However, sensing an opportunity to unify Korea under a

The Korean War.
In August 1950, U.S. troops marched toward North Korea while South Koreans moved in the opposite direction to escape the fighting.

SourcesfromthePast

National Security Council Paper Number 68

In 1949, the cold war seemed to be going badly for the United States. The Chinese Communist Party had just taken control of China, and the Soviets had detonated their first atomic bomb. President Harry Truman, anxious over these new developments, commissioned the State and Defense departments to draft a statement on the U.S. position toward the Soviet Union and Soviet expansion. The result was National Security Council Paper Number 68, which was completed in the spring of 1950. It remained classified until the 1970s.

. . . During the span of one generation, the international distribution of power has been fundamentally altered. . . . Two complex sets of factors have now basically altered this historical distribution of power. First, the defeat of Germany and Japan and the decline of the British and French Empires have interacted with the development of the United States and Soviet Union in such a way that power has increasingly gravitated to these two centers. Second, the Soviet Union, unlike previous aspirants to hegemony, is animated by a new fanatic faith, antithetical to our own, and seeks to impose its absolute authority over the rest of the world. Conflict has, therefore, become endemic and is waged, on the part of the Soviet Union, by violent or non-violent methods in accordance with the dictates of expediency. . . .

The issues that face us are momentous, involving the fulfillment or destruction not only of this Republic but of Civilization itself. They are issues which will not await our deliberations. With conscience and resolution this Government and the people it represents must now take new and fateful decisions. . . .

Our overall policy at the present time may be described as one designed to foster a world environment in which the American system can survive and flourish. It therefore rejects the concept of isolation and affirms the necessity of our positive participation in the world community. . . .

As for the policy of "containment," it is one which seeks by all means short of war to (1) block further expansion of Soviet power, (2) expose the falsities of Soviet pretensions, (3) induce a retraction of the Kremlin's control and influence and (4) in general, so foster the seeds of destruction within the Soviet system that the Kremlin is brought at least to the point of modifying its behavior to conform to generally accepted international standards.

It was and continues to be cardinal in this policy that we possess superior overall power in ourselves or in dependable combination with other like-minded nations. One of the most important ingredients of power is military strength. . . .

Our position as the center of power in the free world places a heavy responsibility upon the United States for leadership. We must organize and enlist the energies and resources of the free world in a positive program for peace which will frustrate the Kremlin design for world domination by creating a situation in the free world to which the Kremlin will be compelled to adjust. Without such a cooperative effort, led by the United States, we will have to make gradual withdrawals under pressure until we discover one day that we have sacrificed our positions of vital interest. . . .

The whole success of the proposed program hangs ultimately on recognition by this Government, the American people, and all free peoples, that the cold war is in fact a real war in which the survival of the free world is at stake.

For Further Reflection

■ According to this document, why was the cold war so important, and how did the United States government see its role in the conflict?

Source: Alfred J. Andrea and James H. Overfield. The Human Record: Sources of Global History, 3rd ed., Volume II: Since 1500. Boston and New York: Houghton Mifflin, 1998.

pro-U.S. government, they pushed on into North Korea, occupied Pyongyang, and made advances toward the Chinese border. These advances caused the government of the People's Republic of China to issue a warning: the U.S. incursion across the thirty-eighth parallel threatened Chinese national interests and could result in Chinese intervention in the Korean conflict.

When U.S. leaders gave no indication of heeding China's warning, some three hundred thousand Chinese soldiers surged into North Korea. A combined force of Chinese

and North Koreans pushed U.S. forces and their allies back into the south, and the war settled into a protracted stalemate near the original border at the thirty-eighth parallel. After two more years of fighting that resulted in three million deaths—mostly of Korean civilians—both sides finally agreed to a cease-fire in July 1953.

The Globalization of Containment From a strategic and political standpoint, the Korean conflict was important because it had been the first test of "containment" outside of Europe. The U.S. leadership had viewed North Korean aggression as part of a larger communist conspiracy to conquer the world and thus felt obligated to act. In 1954 U.S. president Dwight D. Eisenhower (1890–1969) built on the policy of containment by articulating the famous "domino theory," which held that if one country became communist, neighboring countries would collapse to communism the way a row of dominoes falls sequentially. Thereafter, subsequent U.S. administrations extended the policy of containment to the entire world, applying it to local or imagined communist threats in Central and South America, Africa, and Asia.

Cuba: Nuclear Flashpoint Ironically, the cold war confrontation that came closest to unleashing nuclear war took place not at the expected flashpoints in Europe or Asia but on the island of Cuba. In 1959 a revolutionary movement headed by Fidel Castro Ruz (1926–) overthrew the autocratic Fulgencio Batista y Zaldívar (1901–1973), whose regime had gone to great lengths to maintain the country's traditionally subservient relationship with the United States. Denouncing American imperialism, Castro seized foreign properties and businesses, most of which were U.S. owned. He also accepted assistance from the Soviet Union. The U.S. government promptly retaliated by cutting off Cuban sugar imports to the U.S. market and imposing a severe export embargo of U.S. goods on Cuba. U.S. officials also cut diplomatic relations with Cuba and secretly began planning an invasion of the island.

The severing of ties between Cuba and the United States gave the Soviet Union an unprecedented opportunity to contest the dominant position of the United States in its own hemisphere. Castro's regime accepted a Soviet offer of massive military and economic aid, including an agreement to purchase half of Cuba's sugar production. In return for the Soviet largesse, Castro loudly declared his support for the USSR's foreign policy at the UN General Assembly on 26 September 1960.

The Bay of Pigs Cuba's alignment with the Soviet Union spurred newly elected president John F. Kennedy (1917–1963) to approve a plan to invade Cuba and overthrow Castro. In April 1961 a force of 1,500 anti-Castro Cubans trained, armed, and transported by the Central Intelligence Agency (CIA) landed on Cuba at a place called the Bay of Pigs. The invasion, however, was a complete failure and actually strengthened Castro's position in Cuba as well as his commitment to communism. It also likely encouraged Castro to accept and the Soviets to deploy nuclear missiles in Cuba as a deterrent to any future invasion.

The Cuban Missile Crisis On 22 October 1962 President Kennedy went on national television to inform the public about the U.S. discovery of offensive nuclear missiles and launch sites in Cuba. He told the public that the deployment of nuclear missiles so close to the United States represented an unacceptable threat to U.S. national security. Kennedy also called on the Soviet leadership to withdraw all missiles from Cuba and stop the arrival of additional nuclear armaments. To back up his demand, Kennedy imposed an air and naval quarantine on the island nation that went into effect two days later. The superpowers seemed poised for nuclear confrontation, and for a week the world's peoples held their collective breath.

Understanding the seriousness of a nuclear showdown over Cuba, Nikita Khrushchev agreed to Kennedy's demand that he withdraw the missiles on the condition that the United States pledge not to invade Cuba. He also received a private promise from Kennedy that U.S. missiles in Turkey would be removed. Khrushchev informed the public of the end of the crisis in a worldwide radio broadcast on 28 October, and global tension began to ebb. Nonetheless, the Cuban missile crisis revealed the dangers of the bipolar world—especially the ways in which cold war rivalries so easily drew other areas of the world into their orbit.

DECOLONIZATION AND THE GLOBAL COLD WAR

While the cold war was in the midst of dividing western Europe and the United States from eastern Europe and the Soviet Union, another global process had already begun to transform the postwar world in equally important ways: decolonization. By the end of World War II, nationalist movements devoted to the cause of independence from imperial rule had become irrepressible in both Asia and Africa. Independence came at different times in different places, depending on local circumstances and the attitude of the imperial power. In some places, the course of independence was intricately tied to the politics of the cold war because both new superpowers frequently offered support to nationalist leaders who pledged allegiance to their political and ideological agendas. While most former British colonies in both Asia and Africa avoided the complication of becoming tied up in superpower struggles for influence, others—such as Vietnam and Angola—found that they were caught squarely in the middle of nationalist and cold war politics. Yet despite sometimes long and protracted struggles, more than ninety nations became independent between the end of World War II and 1980, while others that had not been formally controlled—especially in Latin America—also sought to throw off the shackles of foreign influence.

India's Partitioned Independence

The Coming of Self-Rule After World War II, it became painfully obvious to the British government that it could not continue to bear the financial burden of governing

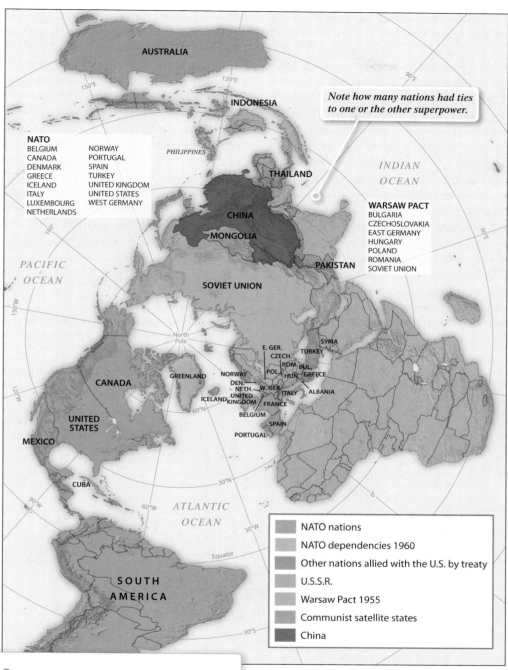

Note how many nations had ties to one or the other superpower.

NATO
BELGIUM
CANADA
DENMARK
GREECE
ICELAND
ITALY
LUXEMBOURG
NETHERLANDS
NORWAY
PORTUGAL
SPAIN
TURKEY
UNITED KINGDOM
UNITED STATES
WEST GERMANY

WARSAW PACT
BULGARIA
CZECHOSLOVAKIA
EAST GERMANY
HUNGARY
POLAND
ROMANIA
SOVIET UNION

NATO nations
NATO dependencies 1960
Other nations allied with the U.S. by treaty
U.S.S.R.
Warsaw Pact 1955
Communist satellite states
China

MAP 33.2

The cold war, 1949–1962. Note the size of the territories and the number of states allied to both sides.

Were these alliances a source of global stability or global instability?

India, particularly since nationalists made it clear that they would accept nothing less than complete independence. As the probability of Indian independence became more pronounced, the issue of Muslim separatism grew in importance, and Muslims increasingly feared their minority status in a free India dominated by Hindus. Muhammad Ali Jinnah

(1876–1948), leader of the Muslim League, felt no qualms about frankly expressing Muslim concerns and desires for a separate Muslim state. In response, Congress Party leaders like Jawaharlal Nehru (1889–1964) and Mohandas K. Gandhi urged all Indians to act and feel as one nation, undivided by what came to be known as communalism—emphasizing religious over national identity.

Partition and Violence Jinnah had his way, however, and when the British withdrew from India in 1947 two new flags were raised in place of the British Union Jack—with

Jinnah leading Pakistan and Jawaharlal Nehru leading India. Gandhi condemned the division as a "vivisection" of his homeland and prophesied that "rivers of blood" would flow in its wake. His vision came true as the terms of partition were announced and hundreds of thousands of Muslim and Hindu refugees migrated to either Muslim Pakistan (divided between parts of Bengal in the east and Punjab in the west) or Hindu India in order to escape religious persecution. By mid-1948 an estimated ten million refugees had made the tortuous journey to one or the other state, and between half a million and one million people had died in the violence that accompanied those massive migrations.

Though mired in violence, Indian independence became a reality with momentous consequences for the process of decolonization. Just as Gandhi's nonviolent resistance to British rule inspired nationalists around the globe before and after World War II, independence in India and Pakistan further encouraged anti-imperial movements throughout Asia and Africa. Moreover, once India left the British empire, there could be little doubt about the fate of Britain's remaining imperial possessions.

Nonalignment Another way in which Indian independence inspired other nations was Nehru's strategy for grappling with decolonization in the midst of a cold war. Nehru called his strategy nonalignment, arguing that "each country has not only the right to freedom but also to decide its own policy and way of life." In April 1955 leaders from twenty-three Asian and six African nations—including Nehru—met in Bandung, Indonesia to discuss nonalignment as an alternative to choosing between the United States and the Soviet Union. Besides discussing neutrality in the cold war, the Bandung Conference also stressed the struggle against colonialism and racism. Bandung was the precursor of the broader Nonaligned Movement, which held occasional meetings so that its members could discuss their relations with the United States and the Soviet Union.

MAP 33.3

Decolonization in Asia and Africa. Date is year of independence. Note the dates of independence for the colonies of Great Britain, the Netherlands, the United States, Italy, Belgium, and France.

Why did independence occur in such a short time span for most of these colonies?

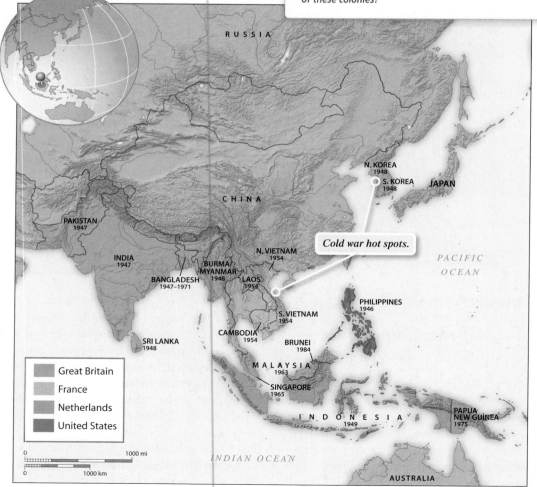

The movement's primary goal was to maintain formal neutrality. However, although theoretically nonaligned with either cold war superpower, many member states had close ties to one or the other, and this situation caused dissension within the movement. For example, the Philippines and Cuba clearly supported the U.S. and Soviet camps, respectively. Nevertheless, other individual states avoided becoming pawns in the cold war by announcing the policy of nonalignment advocated by Nehru.

Since winning its independence, India has stood out among decolonized nations not just for its advocacy of nonalignment, but also for its ability to maintain its political stability and its democratic system. Indeed, even though India has faced many of the same crises that have shaken other developing nations—ethnic and religious conflict, wars, poverty, political assassinations, and overpopulation—Nehru's heirs have remained committed to free elections and a critical press.

Nationalist Struggles in Vietnam

In contrast to India, Vietnam could not keep its nationalist struggle for independence separate from the complications of the cold war. Rather, Vietnam became deeply enmeshed in the contest between capitalism and communism, which meant that decolonization there was a long and bloody process.

Fighting the Japanese Vietnam's nationalist communist leader, Ho Chi Minh (1890–1969), had been struggling for autonomy from French imperialism for two decades when World War II broke out in Europe. Thus the Japanese invasion of his homeland after the fall of France in 1940 seemed to Ho like the replacement of one imperialist power with another. During the war, Ho fought against the Japanese and in the waning days of the war helped oust them from Vietnam altogether. With both the French and the Japanese gone, Ho took the opportunity to establish himself as leader of an independent Vietnam.

Fighting the French However, the French, humiliated by their country's easy defeat and occupation by the Germans, sought to reclaim their imperial possessions—including Vietnam—as a way of regaining their world-power status. By 1947, they seemed to have secured their power in much of the country. Yet

Ho Chi Minh.
Ho was the leader of North Vietnam from 1945 to 1969 and was one of southeast Asia's most influential communist leaders.

that security proved to be temporary. Much like the Chinese communists in their battles against the Japanese and then against the nationalists in the postwar years, the Vietnamese resistance forces, led by Ho Chi Minh and General Vo Nguyen Giap (1912–), mounted a campaign of guerrilla warfare. The Vietnamese communists increasingly regained control of their country, especially after 1949 when communist China sent aid and arms to the Viet Minh. Thus strengthened, they defeated the French at their fortress in Dienbienphu in 1954. The French had to sue for peace at the conference table.

The Geneva Conference and Partial Independence

The peace conference, held in Geneva in 1954, determined that Vietnam should be temporarily divided at the seventeenth parallel; North Vietnam would be controlled by Ho Chi Minh and the communist forces, and South Vietnam would remain in the hands of noncommunists. Leaving all of Vietnam in the hands of Ho's communists was unthinkable for the United States, especially after the globalization of the cold war that had accompanied the Korean War. The U.S. had already aided the French in their struggle against Ho—now they did the same with the government of South Vietnam. Violating the terms of the Geneva Agreements, which required elections that would likely have brought Ho to power, South Vietnam's leaders, with U.S. military support, avoided elections and sought to build a government that would prevent the spread of communism in South Vietnam and elsewhere in Asia. However, the leaders of South Vietnam did not have the support of the people, who quickly grew discontented enough to resort to arms.

Cold War Stalemate In 1960 South Vietnamese nationalists—with the aid of weapons and troops from the north—formed the National Liberation Front to fight for freedom from South Vietnamese rule and to end U.S. military interference in the area. In North Vietnam, the government received economic and military assistance from the Soviet Union and China, which in turn reinforced the U.S. military commitment in the south. The participation of three major world powers in the Vietnamese conflict ensured that the war would be a long, bloody, and expensive stalemate. Ultimately, United States forces withdrew from this unwinnable war in 1975, and in 1976 North Vietnam conquered the south, united the country, and at long last declared independence.

Thinking about TRADITIONS

The Role of Traditions in Emerging National Identities

During the process of decolonization, some emerging nations embraced the cultural traditions of the past in order to form independent national identities, while others rejected traditions in favor of new ideologies. *Provide an example of both approaches, and discuss the rationale behind each.*

Although the Vietnamese ultimately did achieve their long-awaited independence, their experience demonstrated the dangers of what could occur when independence movements became entangled with the politics and logic of the cold war.

The People's Republic of China

The birth of a communist China simultaneously ended a long period of imperialist intrusion in China and further transformed the cold war. Although China had not been formally ruled by an imperial power, many countries had impinged on its sovereignty in the nineteenth and early twentieth centuries. During the 1920s, two groups had arisen in China to reassert Chinese control over internal affairs: the nationalists and the communists. When World War II broke out, these two groups had been engaged in a civil war. After the Japanese defeat, it was clear by mid-1948 that the strategic balance favored the communists, who inflicted heavy military defeats on the nationalists throughout 1948 and 1949. With the communist People's Liberation Army controlling most of mainland China, the national government under Jiang Jieshi (Chiang Kai-shek) sought refuge on the island of Taiwan, taking along most of the nation's gold reserves. Although Jiang Jieshi continued to proclaim that the government in Taiwan was the legitimate government of all China, Mao Zedong, the chairman of the Chinese Communist Party, nevertheless proclaimed the establishment of the People's Republic of China on 1 October 1949. That declaration, much to the alarm of the United States, spawned a close relationship between China and the Soviet Union, especially since Mao sought to imitate Soviet socialism.

Social and Economic Transformations The government of the new People's Republic created new political, economic, and social organizations that completely reorganized all aspects of Chinese society. Political power was monopolized by the Communist Party and a politburo chaired by Mao, while opposition was ruthlessly repressed. In 1955 the Chinese introduced their first Five-Year Plan to encourage rapid industrialization and the collectivization of agriculture on the Soviet model. The Five-Year Plan emphasized improvements in infrastructure and the expansion of heavy industry at the expense of consumer goods. A series of agrarian laws confiscated the landholdings of rich peasants and landlords and redistributed them among the people so that virtually every peasant had at least a small plot of land. Quickly, however, state-mandated collective farms replaced private farming. In the wake of economic reforms came social reforms, many of which challenged or eliminated Chinese family traditions. Supporting equal rights for women, Chinese authorities introduced marriage laws that eliminated such practices as child or forced marriages, gave women equal access to divorce, legalized abortion, and outlawed foot binding, a symbol of women's subjugation.

Fraternal Cooperation Moscow and Beijing drew closer during the early years of the cold war, in part because of their common socialism and in part as a result of active efforts by the United States to establish anticommunist bastions throughout Asia. Most disconcerting to Soviet and Chinese leaders was the American-sponsored rehabilitation of their former enemy, Japan, and client states South Korea and Taiwan. The Chinese-Soviet partnership matured during the early 1950s and took on a distinct form when Beijing recognized Moscow's undisputed authority in world communism in exchange for Russian military equipment and economic aid.

Cracks in the Alliance As the Chinese embarked on a crash program of industrialization, the Soviet Union rendered valuable assistance in the form of economic aid and technical advisors. By the mid-1950s the Soviet Union was China's principal trading partner. Before long, however, cracks appeared in the Soviet-Chinese alliance. From the Chinese perspective, Soviet aid programs were far too modest and had too many strings attached. For example, in 1955 the Soviet Union supplied more economic aid to noncommunist countries such as Egypt and India than to China. Another source of friction was the conflict between China and India over Tibet in 1961. The Chinese were furious when the Soviets announced their neutrality in the conflict and then belied the announcement by giving a loan to India that exceeded any similar loan ever granted to China.

By the end of 1964, the rift between the Soviet Union and the People's Republic of China had become embarrassingly public, with both sides engaging in name-calling. In addition, both nations openly competed for influence in Africa and Asia, especially in the nations that had recently gained independence. The fact that the People's Republic had conducted successful nuclear tests in 1964 enhanced its prestige. An unanticipated outcome of the Chinese-Soviet split was that many countries gained an opportunity to pursue a more independent course in the global cold war by playing capitalists against communists and by playing Soviet communists against Chinese communists.

During the 1960s and 1970s, Mao succeeded in transforming European communist ideology into a distinctly Chinese communism. After 1949 he embarked on two programs designed to accelerate development in China and to distinguish Chinese communism from Soviet communism: the Great Leap Forward (1958–1961) and the Great Proletarian Cultural Revolution (1966–1976). Both were far-reaching policies that nevertheless hampered the political and economic development that Mao so urgently sought.

The Great Leap Forward Mao envisioned his Great Leap Forward as a way to overtake the industrial production of more developed nations, and to that end he worked to collectivize all land and to manage all business and industrial enterprises collectively. Private ownership was abolished, and farming and industry became largely rural and communal. The Great Leap Forward—or "Giant Step Backward" as some have dubbed it—failed. Most disastrous was its impact on agricultural production in China: the peasants could not meet quotas, and a series of bad harvests contributed to one of the deadliest famines in history. Between 1959 and 1962 as many as twenty million Chinese may have died of starvation and malnutrition in this crisis.

The Great Proletarian Cultural Revolution In 1966 Mao tried again to mobilize the Chinese and reignite the revolutionary spirit with the inauguration of the Great Proletarian Cultural Revolution. Designed to root out foreign, bourgeois, or anticommunist values in Chinese life, the Cultural Revolution subjected millions of people to humiliation, persecution, and death. The elite constituted the major targets of the Red Guards, youthful zealots empowered to cleanse Chinese society of opponents to Mao's rule. Victims were beaten and killed, jailed, or sent to corrective labor camps or to toil in the countryside. The Cultural Revolution, which cost China years of stable development and gutted its educational system, remained undiminished until after Mao's death in 1976. It fell to one of Mao's heirs, Deng Xiaoping, to heal the nation.

Deng's China Deng came to power in 1981, and the 1980s are often referred to as the years of "Deng's Revolution." Deng moderated Mao's commitment to Chinese self-sufficiency and isolation and engineered China's entry into the international financial and trading system, a move that was facilitated by the normalization of relations between China and the United States in the 1970s. To push the economic development of China, Deng opened the

The Cultural Revolution.
A 1966 poster shows Mao Zedong inspiring the Red Guards to launch the Great Proletarian Cultural Revolution.

nation to the influences that were so suspect under Mao—foreign, capitalist values. Although Deng did not hesitate to crack down on elements in Chinese society that sought democratic reform—as he did against students in Beijing's Tiananmen Square in 1989—he oversaw impressive economic growth and development by selectively opening Chinese society to global trade. In the twenty-first century, Chinese leaders have managed to maintain massive economic growth without giving up the centralized, communist political control established by Mao in the early years of the cold war.

Arab National States, the Problem of Palestine, and Islamic Resurgence

After World War II, the Arab states of southwest Asia—including Syria, Iraq, Lebanon, and Jordan—gained complete independence from the colonial powers of France and Britain. Yet significant vestiges of imperial rule impeded Arab sovereignty. The battle to rid southwest Asia of those remnants of imperialism took some twists and turns as the superpowers interfered in the region, drawn by its vast reserves of oil, the lifeblood of the cold war's military-industrial complexes. Independent states responded in various ways to superpower interference, including a turn to radical fundamentalist interpretations of Islam. Throughout, one ambiguous legacy of imperialism—Palestine—absorbed much of the region's energies and emotions.

Palestine Great Britain served as the mandate power in Palestine after the Great War, and before and during its mandate made conflicting promises both to Palestinian Arabs and to Jews who hoped to establish a secure homeland in Palestine. With the Balfour Declaration of 1917, the British government committed itself to the support of a Jewish homeland—a cause strongly advocated by Zionists, who were dedicated to combating anti-Semitism by establishing a national Jewish state. Thus the British were compelled to allow Jewish migration to Palestine under their mandate, but they also had to allay the fears of those in possession of the land—the Palestinian Arabs. The British therefore limited the migration and settlement of Jews and promised to protect the Arabs' political and economic rights.

This British attempt to balance the causes of two conflicting groups was unsuccessful, and large-scale violence was prevented only through the use of imperial military forces. The Palestinian Muslims perceived the Jews as alien interlopers in their own land. At the same time, European Jews were dangerously under attack by the Nazis, and Zionists in Palestine armed themselves to protect Jewish settlers against Arab reprisals. At the end of World War II, a battle brewed. As Arab states around Palestine gained their freedom from imperial rule, they developed a pan-Arab nationalism sparked by support for their fellow Arabs in Palestine and opposition to the possibility of a Jewish state

MAP 33.4

The Arab-Israeli conflict, 1949–1982. Compare the boundaries proposed by the UN partition of Palestine with those claimed by Israel after 1948–1949.

What were the strategic advantages of the extra territories claimed by Israel in 1948–1949?

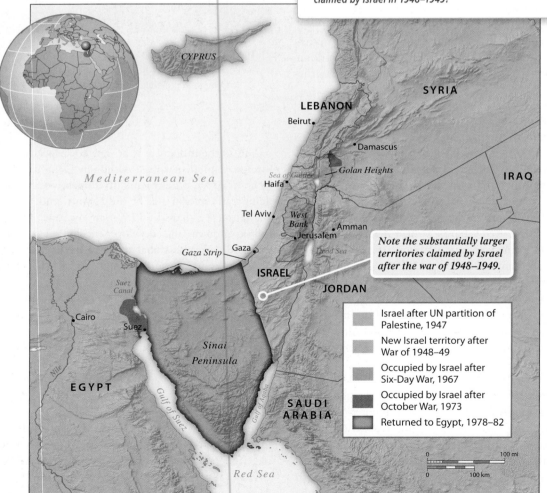

Note the substantially larger territories claimed by Israel after the war of 1948–1949.

Israel after UN partition of Palestine, 1947

New Israel territory after War of 1948–49

Occupied by Israel after Six-Day War, 1967

Occupied by Israel after October War, 1973

Returned to Egypt, 1978–82

there. The Holocaust, however, intensified the Jewish commitment to build a state capable of defending the world's remaining Jews.

The Creation of Israel

While the Arabs in Palestine insisted on complete independence under Arab rule, in 1945 the Jews embarked on a course of violent resistance to the British to compel recognition of Jewish demands for self-rule. The British could not resolve the dispute and in 1947 turned the region over to the newly created United Nations. Before the UN could implement its own plans in the region, in May 1948 the Jews in Palestine announced the creation of the independent state of Israel, claiming territories far larger than those that would have been granted by the UN. In response, the outraged Arab states of Egypt, Jordan, Syria, Lebanon, and Iraq joined Palestinians in a war to destroy the new state.

Arab attacks and campaigns, although boldly fought, were uncoordinated, and the Israelis managed to achieve a stunning victory. A truce went into effect in early 1949 under UN auspices, and the partition of Palestine resulted. Jerusalem and the Jordan River valley were divided between the new Israeli state and the kingdom of Jordan, while Israel controlled the coastal areas of Palestine and the Negev Desert to the Red Sea.

Egypt and Arab Nationalism

Meanwhile, Egyptian military leaders under the leadership of Gamal Abdel Nasser (1918–1970) committed themselves to opposing Israel and taking command of the Arab world. In July 1952 Nasser and other officers staged a bloodless coup that ended the monarchy of Egypt's King Farouk. In 1954, Nasser named himself prime minister and took control of the government. He then labored assiduously to develop Egypt economically and militarily and make it the fountainhead of pan-Arab nationalism.

The Suez Crisis

Like India's Nehru, Nasser refused to align himself with either the United States or the Soviet Union, because he believed that cold war power politics were a new form of imperialism. In fact, Nasser dedicated himself to ridding Egypt and the Arab world of imperial interference. However, Nasser sealed his reputation during the Suez crisis of 1956, when he decided to nationalize the Suez Canal and use the money for internal Egyptian projects. When he did not bow to international pressure to provide multinational control of the vital Suez Canal, British, French, and Israeli forces combined to wrest control of the canal away from him. Their military campaign was successful, but they failed miserably on the diplomatic level and tore at the fabric of the bipolar world system. They had not consulted with the United States, which strongly condemned the attack and forced them to withdraw. The Soviet Union also objected forcefully, thereby gaining a reputation for being a staunch supporter of Arab nationalism. Nasser gained tremendous prestige, and Egypt solidified its position as leader of the charge against imperial holdovers in southwest Asia and north Africa. Meanwhile, the Suez crisis further tangled cold war power politics because it divided the United States and its allies in western Europe.

Despite Nasser's successes, he did not manage to rid the region of Israel, which was growing stronger with each passing year. More wars were fought in the decades to come, and peace between the Arab states and Israel seemed not only elusive but at times impossible. Indeed, violence between Israelis and Palestinians—under the leadership of Yasser Arafat's (1929–2004) Palestinian Liberation Organization (PLO)—continued into the 1990s and beyond. A brief break in the violence occurred in 1993 and 1995, when Arafat and Israeli prime minister Yitzhak Rabin (1922–1995) signed peace treaties that advanced the notion of limited Palestinian self-rule in Israeli-occupied territories. Yet the assassination of Rabin in 1995 by a Jewish extremist who opposed the peace agreements, as well as other hurdles, blocked the peace process and led to the resumption of violence in the region.

Islamism

In southwest Asia, peace seemed a distant prospect given the political turmoil caused by the presence of Israel in the midst of Arab-Islamic states, many of which allied themselves with the Soviet Union as Israel became a staunch ally of the United States. The region could hardly be ignored by either of the superpowers, because the strategic importance of oil dictated that both superpowers vie for favor—and interfere when necessary—in the Arab states. One response to U.S. and Soviet interference in southwest Asia and north Africa was a revival of Muslim traditions, which found expression in Islamism. At the heart of Islamism was the desire for the reassertion of Islamic values in Muslim politics. Many Muslims had become skeptical about European and American models of economic development and political and cultural norms, which they blamed for economic and political failure as well as the breakdown of traditional social and religious values. The solution to the problems faced by Muslim societies lay, according to Islamists, in the revival of Islamic identity, values, and power.

The Iranian Revolution

The Iranian revolution of 1979 demonstrated the power of Islam as a means of staving off secular foreign influences. Islamist influences grew in Iran during the lengthy regime of Shah Mohammed Reza Pahlavi (1919–1980), whom the CIA helped bring to power in 1953. Money from Iran's lucrative oil industry helped finance industrialization under the shah, while the United States provided Iran with the necessary military equipment to fight communism in the region. By the late 1970s, however, opposition to the shah's government was coming from many quarters. Shia Muslims despised the shah's secular regime, Iranian small businesses detested the influence of U.S. corporations on the economy, and leftist politicians rejected the shah's repressive policies. The shah fled the country in early 1979, and power was captured by the Islamist movement under the direction of Ayatollah Ruhollah Khomeini (1900–1989).

The revolution took on a strongly anti-U.S. cast, partly because the shah was allowed to travel to the United States for medical treatment. In retaliation, Shia militants captured sixty-nine hostages at the U.S. embassy in Tehran, fifty-five of whom remained captives until 1981. In the meantime, Iranian leaders shut U.S. military bases and confiscated U.S.-owned economic ventures. This Islamic power play against a developed nation like the United States inspired other Muslims to undertake terrorist actions.

Both cold war politics and decolonization complicated events in southwest Asia in the decades following World War II. The existence of Israel—increasingly supported by the capitalist United States—encouraged the wrath of many Arab leaders who supported Palestinian rights. In addition, interference by both superpowers in the region led some Muslims in the region to turn to a fundamentalist interpretation of Islam as an alternate to the capitalist and communist worldviews.

African Nationalism and Independence

In Africa, as in most of Asia, the increase in the superpowers' global influence after World War II complicated the process of decolonization. Also complicating the decolonization process were internal divisions in African societies, which undermined attempts to forge national or pan-African identities. Tribal, ethnic, religious, and linguistic divides within and between state boundaries, all of which colonial rulers had exploited, posed a challenge to African leaders, particularly once independence came and the imperial enemy departed. Given the variety of barriers to African independence, then, it is not astonishing that independence to all the states in Africa came over the course of several decades—from the late 1950s until 1980.

African Independence   Agitation for independence in Africa took on many forms, peaceful and violent, and decolonization occurred at a different pace in different nations. Ghana became independent in 1957, but independence came much later—and after bloody conflicts—to Algeria (1962), Angola (1975), and Zimbabwe, formerly Southern Rhodesia (1980). In many instances, African nations sealed their severance from imperial control by adopting new names that

shunned the memory of European rule and drew from the glory of Africa's past empires. Ghana set the pattern, and the map of Africa soon featured similar references to precolonial African places: Zambia, Malawi, Zimbabwe.

Ghana   Ghana's success in achieving its freedom from British rule in 1957 served as a hallmark in Africa's end of empire. Under the leadership of Kwame Nkrumah (1909–1972), political parties and strategies for mass action took shape. Although the British initially subjected Nkrumah and other nationalists to jail terms and repressive control, gradually they allowed reforms and negotiated the peaceful transfer of power in their Gold Coast colony. After it became independent in 1957, Ghana emboldened and inspired other African nationalist movements. Nkrumah, as leader of the first sub-Saharan African nation to gain independence from colonial rule, became a persuasive spokesperson for pan-African unity.

Anticolonial Rebellion in Kenya   The process of attaining independence did not always prove as nonviolent as in Ghana. The battle that took place in the British colony of Kenya in east Africa demonstrated the complexity and difficulty of African decolonization. The situation in Kenya turned tense and violent in a clash between powerful white settlers and nationalists, especially the Kikuyu, one of Kenya's largest ethnic groups. Beginning in 1947, Kikuyu rebels embarked on a violent campaign against Europeans and African collaborators. The settlers who controlled the colonial government in Nairobi refused to see the uprisings as a legitimate expression of discontent with colonial rule. Rather, they branded the Kikuyu tribes as radicals—calling them Mau Mau subversives or communists—bent on a racial struggle for primacy.

In reality, Kikuyu radicalism and violence had much more to do with nationalist opposition to British colonial rule, especially land policies in Kenya. In the 1930s and 1940s, white settlers had pushed many Kikuyu off the most fertile highland farm areas and reduced them to the status of wage slaves or relegated them to overcrowded "tribal reserves." Resistance began in the early 1940s with labor strikes and violent direct-action campaigns, but attacks on white settlers and black collaborators escalated in the 1950s. In 1952 the British established a state of emergency to crush the anticolonial guerrilla movement. Unable or unwilling to distinguish violent activism from nonviolent agitation, the British moved to suppress all nationalist groups and jailed Kenya's nationalist leaders, including Jomo Kenyatta (1895–1978) in 1953. Amid growing resistance to colonial rule, the British mounted major military offenses against rebel forces, supporting their army troops with artillery, bombers, and jet fighters. By 1956 the British had effectively crushed all military resistance in a conflict that

---

Zimbabwe (zihm-BAHB-way)

The Mau Mau Rebellion.
Rebel suspects in a British internment camp, Nairobi, Kenya.

claimed the lives of tens of thousands of Africans and one hundred Europeans.

Despite military defeat, Kikuyu fighters broke British resolve in Kenya and gained increasing international recognition of African grievances. The British resisted the radical white supremacism and political domineering of the settlers in Kenya and instead responded to calls for Kenya's independence. In 1959 the British lifted the state of emergency, and as political parties formed, nationalist leaders like Kenyatta reemerged to lead those parties. By December 1963 Kenya had negotiated its independence.

Internal Colonialism in South Africa As in Kenya, the presence of large numbers of white settlers in South Africa delayed the arrival of black freedom. For decades after World War II, South Africa's majority black population remained dispossessed and disenfranchised. Anticolonial agitation thus was significantly different in South Africa than in the rest of sub-Saharan Africa: it was a struggle against internal colonialism, against an oppressive white regime that denied basic human and civil rights to tens of millions of South Africans.

Whites telephone kiosk.
The South African system of apartheid institutionalized racial segregation.

Apartheid The ability of whites to resist majority rule had its roots in the South African economy, the strongest on the continent. This strength had two sources: extraction of minerals and industrial development, which received a huge boost during World War II. In 1948, white South Africans—who feared the black activism and political reform that seemed to be stirring in the nation—brought the Afrikaner National Party to power. Under the National Party the government instituted a harsh new set of laws designed to control the restive black population. These new laws constituted the system known as apartheid, or "separateness," which was designed to divide the peoples of South Africa by skin color and ethnicity and to reserve South Africa's resources for whites.

Apartheid, however, generated tremendous resistance to white rule. The African National Congress (ANC), formed in 1912, gained new young leaders like Nelson Mandela (1918–), who inspired direct action campaigns to protest apartheid. Yet because its goals directly challenged white rule, the ANC, along with all other black activists in South Africa, faced severe repression. Indeed, protests against white rule frequently erupted into violence. One notorious incident, for example, occurred in Sharpeville in 1960, when white police killed sixty-nine black demonstrators and wounded almost two hundred others. However, even though government forces captured and imprisoned the leaders of the ANC's military unit in 1963, including Nelson Mandela, protests against the system persisted throughout the 1970s and 1980s.

The End of Apartheid Meanwhile, international opposition to oppressive white South African rule grew. Eventually, the combined effects of massive black agitation and a powerful international anti-apartheid boycott led to a growing recognition that if it were to survive, South Africa had to change. Thus, when F. W. de Klerk (1936–) became president of South Africa in 1989, he and the National Party began to dismantle the apartheid system. De Klerk released Mandela from jail in 1990, legalized the ANC, and worked with Mandela and the ANC to negotiate the end of white minority rule. Collaborating and cooperating, the National Party, the ANC, and other African political groups created a new constitution and in April 1994 held elections that were open to people of all races. The

ANC won overwhelmingly, and Mandela became the first black president of South Africa. In 1994, as president, he proclaimed his nation "free at last."

The Democratic Republic of the Congo The experience of some African countries, however, demonstrated the dangers of becoming entangled in cold war politics after World War II. This was the case in the land once known as the Belgian Congo, which was reconfigured as Zaire in 1971 and renamed the Democratic Republic of the Congo in 1997. The region won independence from Belgium in 1960 under the popular leadership of Patrice Lumumba (1925–1961), who was also a Maoist Marxist. The general Mobutu Sese Seko (1930–1997), a contender for power, killed Lumumba the very next year in a military coup supported by the United States. Although Mobutu ruled Zaire as a dictator and devastated the economy in the process of enriching himself, his government continued to receive support from the United States and other European democracies hoping to quell the growth of communism in Africa. Thus the convergence of decolonization with the politics of the cold war helped to undermine the possibilities for lasting stability in an independent Zaire.

Neoimperialism in Latin America

The uneasy path to independence in Asia and Africa also affected states on the other side of the world—states that had gained their freedom from colonial rule more than a century before postwar decolonization but that were still in many ways subject to the grasp of imperialist forces. Indeed, after World War II nations in Central and South America along with Mexico grappled with the conservative legacies of Spanish and Portuguese colonialism, particularly the political and economic power of the landowning elite of European descent. Latin America, moreover, had to deal with neocolonialism, because the United States not only intervened militarily when its interests were threatened but also had long influenced economies through investment and full or part ownership of enterprises like the oil industry.

In addition, during the cold war the establishment of communist and socialist regimes—or the instigation of programs and policies that hinted of anti-Americanism—regularly provoked a response from the United States. To be sure, the United States had insisted on the right to interfere in Latin American affairs since the enunciation of the Monroe Doctrine in 1823, and by the early 1920s Latin America had become the site of fully 40 percent of U.S. foreign investments. Yet after World War II cold war imperatives also shaped many U.S. actions in Latin America.

Nicaragua A prime example of U.S. intervention based on cold war imperatives was Nicaragua. Anastacio Somoza Garcia (1896–1956) was serving as president of Nicaragua in 1954, just as the CIA was helping Guatemalan rebels overthrow what many believed was a communist-inspired government. During that time, Somoza demonstrated himself to be a staunch U.S. ally by funneling weapons to noncommunist Guatemalan rebels and by outlawing the communist party in Nicaragua. Somoza first grasped power in the 1930s, when members of his Nicaraguan National Guard killed nationalist Augusto Cesar Sandino (1893–1934), who had led a guerrilla movement aimed at ending U.S. interference in Nicaragua. After murdering Sandino, Somoza and his sons controlled Nicaraguan politics for more than forty years, aided by U.S. financial and military support.

Iran-Contra Scandal The brutality, corruption, and pro-U.S. policies of the Somoza family alienated other Latin American nations as well as Nicaraguans. In the early 1960s, a few Nicaraguans created the Sandinista Front for National Liberation in honor of the murdered Augusto Sandino. The Sandinistas, as they became known, launched guerrilla operations aimed at overthrowing the Somozas and finally took power in 1979. Although the Sandinistas were recognized by the administration of then president Jimmy Carter, when the staunchly anticommunist Ronald Reagan came to the presidency in 1981 this recognition was reversed. Because Reagan believed that the Sandinistas were helping communist rebels elsewhere in Central America, such as El Salvador, he halted aid to Nicaragua and instituted an economic boycott of the country. Then, in 1983, Reagan offered increasing support—monetary and military—to the Contras, a CIA-trained counterrevolutionary group dedicated to overthrowing the Sandinistas. When a wary U.S. Congress imposed a two-year ban on all military aid to the Contras in 1984, Reagan went outside the law. In 1986, he provided funds for the Contras by using the profits that accrued from secretly selling weapons to Iran—a scandal that became public and highly visible in late 1986 and early 1987. Only with the help of Central American leaders such as Costa Rica's Oscar Arias Sanchez (1940–) and the presence of a UN peacekeeping force, agreed to in 1989, were the Contras effectively disarmed. In the 1990s, new elections made it clear that Sandinista power was weakened but not eliminated despite the extensive interference of the United States.

Both decolonization and the assertion of independence after decolonization were complicated infinitely by the politics and ideologies of the cold war. Indeed, nationalist leaders had to navigate the tricky business of building independent states in the context of an international arena marked by the stark division of the world into capitalist and communist blocs. In areas that attracted the attention of either of the superpowers for strategic reasons, the transition to true independence—whether in Asia, Africa, or Latin America—could be both dangerous and bloody.

FROM DISSENT TO DISSOLUTION IN THE COLD WAR

Despite the enormous power and influence of the United States and the Soviet Union, their authority was nevertheless challenged on a variety of fronts, both at home and abroad, during the cold war. Yet the desperate competition for military superiority between the two powers ultimately fell more heavily on the shoulders of the Soviet Union, and it struggled with the economic demands such competition imposed. Moreover, decades of oppression within the Soviet bloc led many under its power to desire greater freedom. When these issues converged with the leadership of Mikhail Gorbachev, who sought both economic and political reforms, the Soviet system collapsed with astonishing speed and the cold war came to an abrupt and unexpected end.

Defiance and Intervention in Europe and Beyond

De-Stalinization Some of the most serious challenges to the cold war system came from within the Soviet bloc. This was partly because of Nikita Khrushchev's policy of de-Stalinization, which entailed ending Stalin's reign of terror after his death in 1953 and allowing partial liberalization of Soviet society. Government officials removed portraits of Stalin from public places, renamed localities bearing his name, and commissioned historians to rewrite textbooks to deflate Stalin's reputation. The de-Stalinization period, which lasted from 1956 to 1964, also brought a "thaw" in government control and resulted in the release of millions of political prisoners. With respect to foreign policy, Khrushchev emphasized the possibility of "peaceful coexistence" between different social systems and the recognition that a nuclear war was more likely to lead to mutual annihilation than to victory. The peaceful coexistence that Khrushchev fostered with the United States appeared to apply to domestic Soviet and eastern European societies also and tempted communist leaders in eastern Europe to experiment with domestic reforms and seek a degree of independence from Soviet domination.

The Hungarian Challenge The most serious challenge to Soviet control in eastern Europe came in 1956 from nationalist-minded communists in Hungary. When the communist regime in Hungary embraced the process of de-Stalinization, large numbers of Hungarian citizens demanded democracy and the breaking of ties to Moscow and the Warsaw Pact. In the wake of massive street demonstrations joined by the Hungarian armed forces, communist Imre Nagy (1896–1958) gained power and visibility as a nationalist leader who announced Hungary's withdrawal from the Warsaw Pact. Yet there were limits to Soviet tolerance for reform: viewing Hungary's demands as a threat to national security, Soviet officials sent tanks into Budapest and crushed the uprising in the late autumn of 1956.

The Prague Spring Twelve years after the Hungarian uprising, Soviets again intervened in eastern Europe, this time in Czechoslovakia. In 1968 the Communist Party leader, Alexander Dubcek (1921–1992), launched a liberal movement known as the "Prague Spring" and promised his fellow citizens "socialism with a human face." But Khrushchev's successor, Leonid Ilyich Brezhnev (1906–1982), fearful that such reforms might undermine Soviet control in eastern Europe, sanctioned military intervention by the Soviet army and brought an end to the Prague Spring. Brezhnev justified the invasion of Czechoslovakia by the doctrine of limited sovereignty, better known as the "Brezhnev doctrine," which reserved the right of the Soviet Union to invade any socialist country that was deemed to be threatened by internal or external elements "hostile to socialism." The destruction of the Prague Spring served to reassert Soviet control over its satellite nations in eastern Europe and led to tightened controls within the Soviet Union.

Detente and Cooperation In spite of Soviet repression in Europe, by the late 1960s relations between the United States and the Soviet Union had actually improved. Both agreed on a policy of *detente,* or a reduction in hostility, trying to cool the costly arms race and slow their competition in developing countries. Between 1972 and 1974, U.S. and Soviet leaders exchanged visits and signed agreements calling for cooperation in areas such as health research, environmental protection, space ventures, and cultural exchange programs. The spirit of detente was most visible in negotiations designed to reduce the threat posed by strategic nuclear weapons. U.S. and Soviet negotiators concluded their Strategic Arms Limitations Talks (SALT) in 1972 with two agreements and reached another accord in 1979. The two cold war antagonists cooperated despite the tensions caused by the U.S. incursion into Vietnam, Soviet involvement in Angola and other African states, and continued Soviet repression of dissidents in eastern Europe.

The Demise of Detente The spirit of detente deteriorated markedly in the early 1980s, in large part due to Soviet intervention in Afghanistan. In 1978, a pro-Soviet coup in Afghanistan sparked widespread resistance from anticommunist Afghans. By the summer of 1979, antigovernment rebels controlled much of the Afghan countryside and were poised to oust the pro-Soviets from power. At that point the Soviet Union intervened, installing the Marxist Babrak Karmal as president. This Soviet-backed government was highly unpopular, and a national resistance movement spread throughout the country.

Thinking about ENCOUNTERS

Ideologies and Perceptions during the Cold War

Although the United States and the Soviet Union never directly confronted each other in battle during the cold war, the superpowers nevertheless encountered each other—both ideologically and through their proxies in a variety of conflicts—all over the world. *In what ways were these encounters shaped by preconceptions each held about the other?*

For nine years, well-equipped Soviet forces fought a brutal, unsuccessful campaign against Afghan mujahideen, or Islamic warriors, who gradually gained control of most of the countryside. The mujahideen were aided by weapons and money from the United States, Saudi Arabia, Iran, Pakistan, and China—all of whom wished to block Soviet influence in the area. The fact that the United States and the Soviet Union were once again in direct competition for influence—as they had been in Vietnam—crippled relations between the two powers, and U.S. military spending soared under Ronald Reagan in the 1980s. Also as with Vietnam, the participation of the superpowers in the Afghan conflict ensured a long, bloody war that could not be easily won by either side. Finally, in 1986, the Kremlin decided to pull its troops out of the seemingly unwinnable war, having damaged Soviet prestige at huge cost to itself—a cost that it could ill afford if it were to keep up with U.S. military spending. Moreover, the war in Afghanistan increased instability in that country. Five years after the Soviets finally withdrew in 1989, a fundamentalist Islamic group called the Taliban began a campaign to unify Afghanistan. In 1996 they captured the capital of Kabul after an eleven-month siege and proclaimed the Islamic State of Afghanistan.

The End of the Cold War

Between 1989 and 1991, the Soviet system in Europe collapsed with stunning speed. This was partly encouraged by U.S. president Ronald Reagan's insistence on massive military spending, which in turn forced the Soviets to spend lavishly on defense when they could least afford it. Yet while Reagan's cold war rhetoric and budgets challenged the Soviet ability to match U.S. spending, internal changes in the Soviet Union and eastern Europe worked most effectively to end communism and the cold war. Between 1989 and 1990, through a series of mostly nonviolent revolutions, the peoples of eastern and central Europe regained their independence, instituted democratic forms of government, and adopted market-based economies.

Lech Walesa (LEHK wah-LEHN-sah)

The downfall of communist regimes in Europe was the direct consequence of interrelated economic and political developments. The economic weakness of the communist regimes in eastern and central Europe and the Soviet Union became so apparent as to require reforms. The policies espoused by Soviet leader Mikhail Gorbachev (1931–), who came to power in 1985, represented an effort to address this economic deterioration, but they also unleashed a tidal wave of revolution that brought down governments from Czechoslovakia to the Soviet Union. As communism unraveled throughout eastern and central Europe, Gorbachev desperately tried to save the Soviet Union from disintegration by restructuring the economy and liberalizing society. Caught between the rising tide of radical reforms and the opposition of entrenched interests, however, there was little he could do except watch as events unfolded beyond his control. By the time the Soviet Union collapsed in 1991, the cold war system of states and alliances had become irrelevant to international relations.

Gorbachev's Impact When Gorbachev came into office, much of eastern and central Europe was seething with discontent. While early hopes for reform had been dashed in the 1950s and 1960s, Gorbachev's leadership brought new hope to many. Indeed, in light of Soviet economic stagnation and political discontent, Gorbachev had already committed himself to a restructuring of the Soviet Union and to unilateral withdrawal from the cold war. In public interviews he surprised his grim-faced hosts with the announcement that the Brezhnev doctrine was no longer in force and that from then on each country would be responsible for its own destiny. The new Soviet orientation led in rapid succession to the collapse or overthrow of regimes in Poland, Bulgaria, Hungary, Czechoslovakia, Romania, and East Germany.

Revolutions in Eastern Europe The end of communism came first in Poland, where Solidarity—a combined trade union and nationalist movement—put pressure on the crumbling rule of the Communist Party. The Polish government legalized the previously banned Solidarity movement and agreed to multiparty elections in 1989 and 1990. The voters favored Solidarity candidates, and Lech Walesa (1943–), the movement's leader, became president of Poland. In Bulgaria popular unrest forced Todor Zhivkov (1911–1998), eastern Europe's longest surviving communist dictator, to resign in November 1989. Two months later a national assembly began dismantling the communist state. In 1990 Hungarians also held free elections and launched their nation on the rocky path toward democracy and a market economy.

The disintegration of communism continued elsewhere in eastern Europe. In Czechoslovakia a "velvet revolution"—so called because it entailed little violence—swept communists out of office and restored democracy in 1990. In 1993 disagreements over the time frame for shifting to a market economy led to a "velvet divorce," breaking Czechoslovakia into two new nations, the Czech Republic and Slovakia. In Romania, by contrast, the regime of dictator Nicolae Ceauşescu (1918–1989) savagely repressed demonstrations, setting off a national uprising that ended within four days and left Ceauşescu and his wife dead.

East Germany had long been a staunchly communist Soviet satellite. Its aging leader, Erich Honecker (1912–1994), openly clung to Stalinist policies. It was too late for anything other than radical changes, however. Honecker's own party removed him from power and decided to open the Berlin Wall to intra-German traffic on 9 November 1989. The end to a divided Berlin was in sight, literally, as thousands of East and West Berliners tore down the Berlin Wall in the last weeks of 1989. In 1990 the two Germanies, originally divided by the cold war, formed a united nation.

The fall of the Berlin Wall.
Berliners climb the wall after it fell on 9 November 1989.

Why might it have been so symbolically important to stand on the wall?

The Collapse of the Soviet Union

The desire to concentrate attention and resources on urgent matters at home motivated Gorbachev's decision to disengage his nation from the cold war and its military and diplomatic extensions. Although he never intended to abolish the existing political and economic system, it proved impossible to fix parts of the system without undermining the whole.

Gorbachev's Reforms Gorbachev's reform efforts focused on the ailing economy. Antiquated industrial plants and obsolete technologies resulted in shoddy and outmoded products, and in any case the diversion of crucial resources to the military made it impossible to produce enough consumer goods. The failure of state and collective farms to feed the population compelled the Soviet government to import grains from the United States, Canada, and elsewhere. In 1990 the government imposed rationing to cope with the scarcity of essential consumer goods and food. Economic stagnation in turn contributed to the decline of the Soviet standard of living and the disintegration of the state-sponsored health care system. Funding of the educational system dropped precipitously, and pollution threatened to engulf the entire country. Demoralization affected ever larger numbers of Soviet citizens as divorce rates climbed, corruption intensified, and alcoholism became more widespread.

Perestroika and Glasnost When it was clear that the old methods of boosting productivity through bureaucratic exhortation and harassment would not work, Gorbachev contemplated different kinds of reform, using the term *perestroika,* or "restructuring," to describe his efforts to decentralize the economy. To make perestroika work, the Soviet leader linked it to *glasnost,* a term that referred to the opening of Soviet society to public criticism and admission of past mistakes.

Collapse By the summer of 1990, it was clear that Gorbachev's reforms could not halt the downward slide of industrial and agricultural production or control skyrocketing inflation. As the Soviet economy disintegrated, many minorities contemplated secession from the Soviet Union. The Baltic peoples—Estonians, Latvians, and Lithuanians—were first into the fray, declaring their independence in August 1991. In the following months the remaining twelve republics of the Soviet Union followed suit. The largest and most prominent of the Soviet republics, the Russian Soviet Federated Socialist Republic, and its recently elected president, Boris N. Yeltsin (1931–), led the drive for independence. Soviet leaders vacillated between threats of repression and promises of better treatment, but neither option could

perestroika (payr-eh-STROY-kuh)
glasnost (GLAHS-nost)

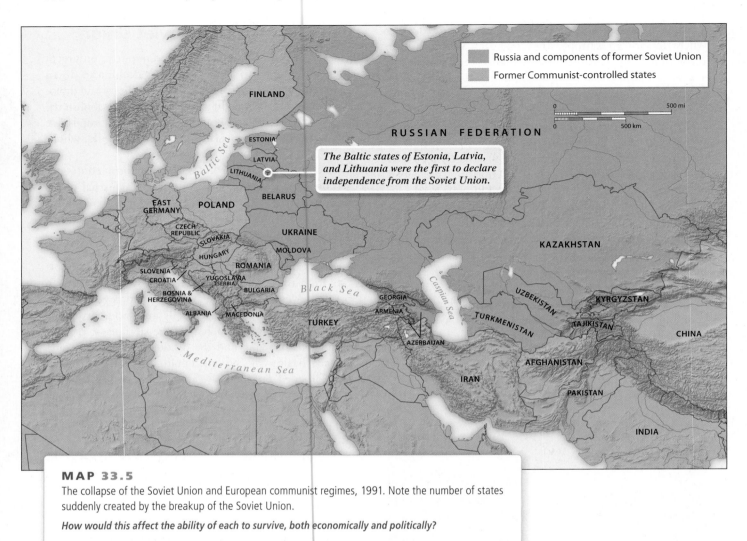

Russia and components of former Soviet Union

Former Communist-controlled states

RUSSIAN FEDERATION

The Baltic states of Estonia, Latvia, and Lithuania were the first to declare independence from the Soviet Union.

MAP 33.5

The collapse of the Soviet Union and European communist regimes, 1991. Note the number of states suddenly created by the breakup of the Soviet Union.

How would this affect the ability of each to survive, both economically and politically?

stop the movement for independence. On 25 December 1991 the Soviet flag fluttered for the last time atop the Kremlin, and by the last day of that year the Union of Soviet Socialist Republics had ceased to exist.

In many ways the cold war provided comfort to the world—however cold that comfort seemed at the time. World War II left most of the major imperialist, fascist, and militarist nations in shambles, and the United States and the Soviet Union stepped into what could have been an uncomfortable vacuum in global leadership. Perilous and controlling it may have been, but the cold war that resulted from the ideological contest between the superpowers had ordered and defined the world for almost fifty years. The

cold war also shaped how the nations and peoples of the world perceived themselves—as good capitalists fighting evil communists, as progressive socialists battling regressive capitalists, or as nonaligned peoples striving to follow their own paths. Although these perceptions placed constraints on the choices open to them, particularly given the control exerted by the United States and the USSR at the peak of their power, the choices nonetheless were familiar. At the end of the cold war, those easy choices disappeared. Indeed, the end of the cold war suggested the possibility of a radical shift in power relations, a global realignment that marked a new era of world history devoid of the categories embraced during the cold war.

SUMMARY

In the years immediately before and after World War II, a few nations controlled the political and economic destiny of much of the world. The decades following 1945 witnessed the stunning reversal of this state of affairs, as two new superpowers emerged and as European empires fell. The cold war that ensued began first in Europe but quickly spread to the world stage in places as far afield as Cuba, Vietnam, and the Congo. As European empires fell, tens of new nations struggled for independence in the midst of the cold war. While nearly every quest for independence was eventually realized, the cold war both complicated and shaped the course of events in many decolonizing and newly independent states. Yet resistance to superpower dominance occurred in many nations desiring true independence, and also from within the superpower societies themselves. These challenges put enormous strains on the cold war system, which continually demanded enormous expenditures for military defense. In the 1980s, strains within the Soviet bloc caused the sudden and unexpected collapse of the Soviet Union. With its collapse came an end to an alliance system that had dominated world affairs since the end of World War II as well as the reformation, once again, of national boundaries.

STUDY TERMS

Berlin Wall (632)
cold war (630)
containment (635)
Cuban missile crisis (636)
decolonization (636)
de-Stalinization (647)
detente (647)
domestic containment (633)
domino theory (636)
Gamal Abdel Nasser (643)
glasnost (649)
Great Leap Forward (641)
Great Proletarian Cultural
    Revolution (641)
Ho Chi Minh (639)
Iran-Contra scandal (646)
Iranian revolution (643)
iron curtain (631)
Islamism (643)
Israel (643)
Korean conflict (634)
Kwame Nkrumah (644)
Lech Walesa (648)
MAD (633)
Mao Zedong (640)
Mau Mau rebellion (645)
Mikhail Gorbachev (647)
NATO (633)
nonalignment (638)
Palestinian Liberation
    Organization (643)
perestroika (649)
Sandinistas (646)
Sputnik (633)
Suez crisis (643)
velvet revolution (649)
Warsaw Pact (633)
Zimbabwe (644)

FOR FURTHER READING

Franz Ansprenger. *The Dissolution of the Colonial Empires.* New York, 1989. A discerning and thorough treatment of the dismantling of European empires and colonies.

Nancy L. Clark and William H. Worger. *South Africa: The Rise and Fall of Apartheid.* New York, 2004. A survey of the history of the apartheid regime from 1948 to its collapse in the 1990s.

Michael J. Cohen. *Palestine and the Great Powers 1945–48.* 2nd ed. Princeton, 1992. An evenhanded assessment of the role played by the great powers in the partition of Palestine and the creation of Israel.

Prasenjit Duara, ed. *Decolonization (Rewriting Histories).* New York, 2004. The perspective of the colonized is privileged through a selection of writings by leaders of the colonizing countries.

John Lewis Gaddis. *The Cold War: A New History.* New York, 2005. A fresh and concise history of the cold war by the dean of cold war historians.

Akira Iriye. *The Cold War in Asia: A Historical Introduction.* Englewood Cliffs, N.J., 1974. A leading diplomatic historian provides an excellent introduction to the subject.

Madeline Kalb. *The Congo Cables: The Cold War in Africa— From Eisenhower to Kennedy.* New York, 1982. Proper attention for an often neglected aspect of the cold war.

Bruce Kuniholm. *The Origins of the Cold War in the Near East.* Princeton, 1980. A dissection of great power diplomacy and conflicts that focuses on Greece, Turkey, and Iran.

Thomas E. Skidmore and Peter H. Smith. *Modern Latin America.* New York, 1992. Excellent overview covering the region from the 1880s to the 1980s and supported by an extensive bibliography.

Odd Arne Westad. *The Global War: Third World Interventions and the Making of Our Times.* New York, 2005. Integrates the Third World into the history of the cold war by tracing U.S. and Soviet interventions.

A World without Borders

CHAPTER 34

This stunning digitally crafted photograph, called "Omnipotent Technology" (1999), blurs the boundaries between art and reality. Its composition of an ethnically fluid face from computer chips and hardware suggests how global identity has morphed and how computers have breached borders between humans and machines.

EYEWITNESS:

Kristina Matschat and a Falling Wall

On 9 November 1989, Kristina Matschat felt excitement and tension in the night air of Berlin. She had joined thousands of other East Germans at Checkpoint Charlie, one of the most famous crossing points in the Berlin Wall. Anticipating that the wall might come down that night, she also shivered in fear at the proximity of the *Volkspolizei* ("people's police")—the same officers who since 1961 had gunned down East Germans attempting to scale the wall and escape to freedom in West Berlin. She wore running shoes in case she needed to sprint away if shooting broke out.

She remembered that "everybody was full of fear—but also full of hope." Her hope overcame her fears, though, as she chanted with her fellow compatriots, "Tear the wall down! Open the gates!" Just before midnight East German soldiers suddenly began not only opening gates in the wall but also gently helping East Germans cross to the West, often for the first time in their lives. Her near disbelief at the swift downfall of Berlin's decades-old barricade registered in the word she heard shouted over and over again by those passing through the wall: *Wahnsinn* ("craziness").

Kristina Matschat remained at the wall until 3:00 or 4:00 A.M., celebrating with hundreds of thousands of other Berliners. While celebrating the fall of the barbed wire and mortar structure, she became aware of the significance of a world without borders: "Suddenly we were seeing the West for the first time, the forbidden Berlin we had only seen on TV or heard about from friends. When we came home at dawn, I felt free for the first time in my life. I had never been happier." The fall of the Berlin Wall brought down one of the world's most notorious borders and symbolized the breaching of all sorts of boundaries in the contemporary world.

Along with decolonization, the fall of the Berlin Wall, and the end of the cold war, many other forces were at work to create a new, more open world. One pronounced feature of this world was an increased level of economic interaction between countries and a tighter economic integration of the world. The forces driving the world economy in this direction, often referred to as *globalization,* included advances in communication technology, an enormous expansion of international trade, and the emergence of new global enterprises as well as governments and international organizations that favored market-oriented economics. Global economic interaction and integration were not new in world history, of course, but the more recent phenomenon of globalization has been different and unprecedented in both scope and speed, and it has the potential to fundamentally transform the world.

Although many formal national borders changed only after decolonization and the end of the cold war, cultural and technological developments since World War II had steadily broken down the distances between countries and peoples. Consumer goods, popular culture, television, computers, and the Internet all spread outward from advanced capitalist and industrialized nations, particularly Europe and the United States, and other societies had to come to terms with this breakdown of cultural and technological barriers.

CHRONOLOGY

1947	Establishment of GATT
1948	UN adopts Universal Declaration of Human Rights
1950	World population at 2.5 billion
1960	Introduction of birth control pill
1960	Creation of OPEC
1967	Establishment of ASEAN
1967	Birth of European Community
1981	Identification of AIDS
1992	Beginning of socialist market economy in China
1993	Establishment of NAFTA
1995	WTO supersedes GATT
2000	World population at 6 billion
2001	China joins WTO
2001	Terrorist attacks against the United States
2003	Operation Iraqi Freedom

The world's peoples also underwent changes in a world with fewer barriers. Women struggled to close the divide between the sexes, while both women and men embarked on migrations when their societies could no longer adequately support their growing populations. The populations moving around the globe revealed the diminishing significance of national boundary lines, but they also posed problems that could not be solved by any one state acting alone. International organizations such as the United Nations acknowledged that global problems like epidemic diseases, labor servitude, terrorism, and human rights crossed national boundaries and required global solutions. Indeed, as Kristina Matschat discovered at the fall of the Berlin Wall, by the late twentieth century global interconnectedness made it more difficult to maintain boundaries among the peoples and countries of the world.

THE GLOBAL ECONOMY

The global economy came into sharp focus after the spectacular collapse of communism in 1990. Economists pointed to a new economic order characterized by the expansion of trade between countries, the growth of foreign investments, the unfettered movement of capital, the privatization of former state enterprises, and the emergence of a new breed of corporations. Supporting the new global economy were technological developments in communications that have virtually eliminated geographic distances, causing an ever-faster integration of the market economy. The forces driving the world economy toward increased economic integration have been responsible for a process termed *globalization*.

Economic Globalization

Free Trade International trade proved to be a key driving force behind economic globalization. Although trade across long distances has figured prominently as an integrating force in the shaping of human history, the idea of *free trade*—meaning freedom from state-imposed limits and constraints on trade across borders—is of more recent origin. In the aftermath of World War II, leaders from industrialized nations, especially from the United States, took a decisive stand on the issue.

GATT and WTO U.S. politicians and business leaders wanted to establish an international trading system that suited their interests, and they pushed for the elimination of restrictive trading practices that stood in the way of free trade. At the Bretton Woods Conference in New Hampshire in 1944, they established the International Monetary Fund (IMF) to promote market economies, free trade, and high growth rates. However, the main vehicle for the promotion of unrestricted global trade was the General Agreement on Tariffs and Trade (GATT), which was signed by the representatives of 23 noncommunist nations in 1947. GATT members held a series of negotiations with the intent of removing or loosening barriers to free trade. After the round of negotiations that ended in 1994, the member nations of GATT (now totaling 123) signed an agreement to establish the World Trade Organization (WTO), which took over the activities of GATT in 1995. The WTO has developed into a forum for settling international trade disputes, with the power to enforce its decisions. Since the establishment of GATT, world trade has increased dramatically: world trade grew by 6.6 percent annually between 1948 and 1966 and by 9.2 percent annually between 1966 and 1977. Although trade slowed in the 1980s, by 1990 world trade exceeded six trillion U.S. dollars, roughly double the figure for 1980.

Global Corporations The emergence of a new breed of corporation played another key role in the development of the new economic order. Global corporations have increasingly replaced the more traditional international or multinational forms of corporate enterprises. Whereas multinational corporations conducted their business in several countries and had to operate within the confines of specific laws and customs of a given society, global corporations rely on a small headquarters staff while dispersing all other corporate functions across the globe in search of the lowest possible operating costs. Global corporations treat the world as a single market and act as if the nation-state no longer exists. Many multinational corporations, such as General Motors, Siemens AG, and Nestlé, have transformed themselves into global enterprises, both benefiting from and contributing to the ongoing process of globalization. Indeed, during the past twenty-five years, the transformation of the corporate landscape has resulted in the birth of some fifty thousand global corporations.

Global corporations have become the symbols of the new economy because they have transformed the political and social landscape of many societies. During the past fifty-five years, multinational corporations throughout the developed world operated under the legal constraints of the nations where they were located, which meant that they were bound by national tax laws, union agreements, and environmental regulations. Highly mobile global corporations that are no longer bound to any particular location have managed, however, to escape those obligations. For example, global corporations have moved jobs from high-wage facilities to foreign locations where wages are low and environmental laws are weak or nonexistent. The implications of this development are serious. For example, U.S. federal tax receipts show that corporations that once paid 30 percent of all federal taxes now pay only 12 percent. This trend is not confined to the United States but is visible throughout the industrialized world. In all instances, declining corporate taxes mean less money for social services and welfare programs.

Economic Growth in Asia

Globalization and the speeding up of worldwide economic integration also benefited from economic developments in east and southeast Asia, where the economies of Japan, China, and the so-called Asian tigers underwent dramatic growth.

Japan U.S. policies jump-started Japan's economic revival after its defeat in 1945, and by 1949 the Japanese economy had already attained its prewar level of productivity. Just as western European countries had benefited from the Marshall Plan, so Japan benefited from direct U.S. financial aid

Economics in art form.
This image of a "balanced world economy" (1996) artistically expresses the precariousness of economic globalization.

($2 billion), investment, and the timely abandonment of war reparations. In addition, there were no restrictions on the entry of Japanese products into the U.S. market. And, because a 1952 mutual defense treaty stipulated that Japan could never spend more than 1 percent of its gross national product on defense, Japan's postwar leaders channeled the nation's savings into economic development.

Although Japan had lost its overseas empire and was hampered by a large population and a lack of natural resources, its economic planners sidestepped those disadvantages by promoting an economic policy that emphasized export-oriented growth supported by low wages. Low wages in turn gave Japanese employers a competitive edge over international rivals.

Initially, the Japanese economy churned out labor-intensive manufactured goods such as textiles, iron, and steel slated for export to markets with high labor costs, particularly the United States. By the 1970s, however, Japanese corporations were shifting their economic resources toward technology-intensive products such as random-access memory chips, liquid crystal displays, and CD-ROM drives. By that time the label "Made in Japan," once associated with cheap manufactured goods, signified state-of-the-art products of the highest quality. Indeed, by the 1980s Japan seemed poised to overtake the United States as the world's largest economy. Even though the Japanese economy sputtered into a recession that has continued into the twenty-first century, the Japanese success story nevertheless served as an inspiration for other Asian countries.

The Little Tigers The earliest and most successful imitators of the Japanese model for economic development were Hong Kong, Singapore, South Korea, and Taiwan. Their remarkable and rapid growth rates earned them the nickname of the "four little tigers," and by the 1980s these newly industrializing countries had become major economic powers.

Like Japan, all four countries lacked natural resources and had to cope with overpopulation. But like Japan a generation earlier, they transformed apparent disadvantages into advantages through a program of export-driven industrialization. By the 1990s the four little tigers were no longer simply imitators of Japan but had become serious competitors. Before long, Indonesia, Thailand, and Malaysia joined the original tigers in their quest for economic development and prosperity.

The Rise of China China provides yet another economic success story. In the aftermath of Mao Zedong's disastrous economic policies in the 1960s and 1970s, China's leaders launched economic reforms that reversed some earlier policies and opened Chinese markets to the outside world, encouraged foreign investment, and imported foreign technology. By 1992, it was clear that the planned economic system of the past had given way to a market economy. Besides acting as a major exporter, China benefited from its large pool of cheap labor, and its enormous domestic markets have made the Chinese economy the destination of choice for foreign investment capital. In December 2001 China became a member of the World Trade Organization and moved closer to gaining global economic superpower status.

Perils of the New Economy For the supporters of the new global economy, the spectacular economic development of so many Asian societies was proof that globalization could deliver on the promise of unprecedented prosperity. However, a financial crisis that came to a head in 1997 also pointed to the perils of the new global economy. In the preceding twenty years, the developing Asian economies had started to embrace the market, opening their borders to imports and courting foreign investments. After years of generous lending and growing national debts, the international investment community suddenly lost confidence in the booming economies and withdrew support. The

crisis began in Thailand in mid-1997, when investments that once easily poured into the country now left it equally quickly, causing the Thai stock market to lose 75 percent of its value and plunging the nation into depression. From there, the financial panic spread to Malaysia, Indonesia, the Philippines, and South Korea. In each instance, the rise and fall of the individual economies resulted from their integration into the new global economy, which rewarded and punished its new participants with equal ease.

Emerging Economies in Asia and Beyond Contrary to all expectations, the nations hit so hard by the financial crisis recovered quickly. Their recovery was matched by other emerging economies, including Brazil, China, India, Mexico, Russia, eastern European nations, and several countries in Africa. In 2005 these emerging economies accounted for over half of global economic output. During the first five years of the twenty-first century, the annual growth rate of emerging economies averaged almost 7 percent—the fastest pace on record. Experts predict that by 2040 the world's ten largest economies will include Brazil, China, India, Mexico, and Russia. In addition, the IMF predicts that China will surpass the United States as the world's largest economy within the next three decades. What all this means is not only that the once-poor world is getting richer, but that the rich, developed countries no longer dominate the global economy the way they did during the nineteenth and twentieth centuries. This shift is not as astonishing as it first seems, as some of today's emerging economies—especially China and India—are simply regaining their pre–nineteenth-century preeminence.

Trading Blocs

Accepting free trade and open markets meant acknowledging global economic interdependence; no single economic power could fully control global trade and commerce. In the rapidly changing global economy, groups of nations have therefore entered into economic alliances designed to achieve advantages and greater strength for their partners in the competitive global economy.

European Union The most famous and most strongly integrated regional bloc is the European Union. In March 1957, representatives of six nations—France, West Germany, Italy, the Netherlands, Belgium, and Luxembourg—established the European Economic Community (renamed the European Community in 1967). At the heart of this new community of nations lay the dismantling of tariffs and other barriers to free trade among member nations. In 1993, the Maastricht Treaty took a further step toward economic and political integration by creating the European Union. Twenty-seven European nations have submerged much of their national sovereignty in the European Union, and since 1999 thirteen members have adopted a common currency, the euro. Although economists once predicted that this tight economic integration would lead to a European political union, serious fiscal crises in some member states in the wake of the worldwide recession of 2008—including Greece, Ireland, Italy, Portugal, and Spain—have led some pundits to wonder whether the euro itself can survive, much less as a political union.

OPEC One of the earliest and most successful economic alliances was the Organization of Petroleum Exporting Countries (OPEC), a producer cartel established in 1960 by the oil-producing states of Iran, Iraq, Kuwait, Saudi Arabia, and Venezuela, and later joined by Qatar, Libya, Indonesia, Abu Dhabi, Algeria, Nigeria, Ecuador, and Gabon. The mostly Arab and Muslim member states of OPEC sought to raise the price of oil through cooperation, but OPEC demonstrated during the Arab-Israeli War of 1973 that cooperation had

political as well as economic potential. The cartel ordered an embargo on oil shipments to the United States, Israel's ally, and quadrupled the price of oil between 1973 and 1975. The huge increase in the cost of petroleum triggered a global economic downturn, as did a curtailment of oil exports in the later 1970s. OPEC's influence diminished in the 1980s and 1990s as a result of overproduction and dissension among its members over the Iran-Iraq War and the Gulf War.

MAP 34.1

European Union membership, 2004. In 2007 the European Union celebrated the fiftieth anniversary of its founding as a supranational and intergovernmental organization that encompasses twenty-seven member states.

What major challenge faced the European Union in the twenty-first century?

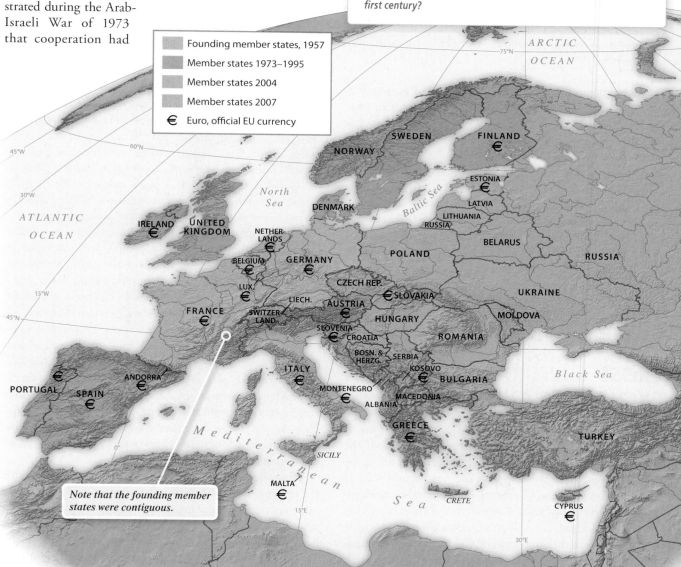

Founding member states, 1957

Member states 1973–1995

Member states 2004

Member states 2007

€ Euro, official EU currency

Note that the founding member states were contiguous.

ASEAN Another well-established economic partnership is the Association of Southeast Asian Nations, or ASEAN. Established in 1967 by the foreign ministers of Thailand, Malaysia, Singapore, Indonesia, and the Philippines, it had as its principal objectives accelerating economic development and promoting political stability in southeast Asia. In 1992 member states agreed to establish a free-trade zone and to cut tariffs on industrial goods over a fifteen-year period.

NAFTA The United States, although still home to the largest national economy in the world, also saw the need to become involved in regional trade groupings. The United States entered its own regional alliance, approving the North American Free Trade Agreement (NAFTA) with Canada and Mexico in 1993. NAFTA, which went into effect in 1994, constitutes the world's second-largest free-trade zone, but it lacks the economic coordination so typical of the European Union. There are plans to expand NAFTA to all noncommunist nations in the Americas, underscoring the increasing commitment to the elimination of tariffs and other barriers to regional and global free trade.

Globalization and Its Critics The global economy is still very much a work in progress, and it is not clear what the long-term effects will be on the economies and societies it touches. Proponents of globalization argue that the new economy is the only way to bring prosperity—the kind previously enjoyed only by industrialized nations—to the developing world. Critics of globalization, in contrast, argue that globalization diminishes the sovereignty of local and national governments and transfers that power to transnational corporations and global institutions such as the IMF and the WTO. Detractors of globalization also claim that the hallmark of globalization—rapid economic development—is responsible for the destruction of the environment, the widening gap between rich and poor societies, and the worldwide homogenization of local, diverse, and indigenous cultures.

CROSS-CULTURAL EXCHANGES AND GLOBAL COMMUNICATIONS

The demise of European colonial empires, the fall of the Berlin Wall, and the end of the cold war brought down the most obvious political barriers of the post–World War II world. Long before then, however, cultural and technological developments had started a similar process of breaching boundaries. Indeed, cultural practices have become increasingly globalized, thriving on a continuous flow of information, ideas, tastes, and values. At the turn of the twentieth century, local traditions—commonly derived from gender, social class, or religious affiliation—still determined the cultural identity of the vast majority of people. At the end of the twentieth century, thanks in part to advances in technology and communications, information and cultural practices were becoming truly global. Their impact was summarized in a jingle popularized by the Walt Disney Company during the 1964–1965 World's Fair in New York City: "It's a small world after all."

Consumption and Cultural Interaction

New communications media have tied the world together and have promoted a global cultural integration whose hallmark is consumption. Although the desire to consume is hardly new, the modern consumer culture has become a means of self-expression as well as a source of personal identity and social differentiation. The peculiar shape of this consumer culture resulted from two seemingly contradictory trends: a tendency toward homogenization of cultural products and heightened awareness of local tastes and values.

Americanization Critics sometimes refer to the homogenizing aspect of global culture as the "Americanization" or "McDonaldization" of the world. Those terms suggest that the consumer culture that developed in the United States during the mid–twentieth century has been exported throughout the world. Indeed, nothing symbolizes the global marketing of U.S. mass culture more than the spread of its food and beverage products. While Pepsi and Coca-Cola fight battles over the few places on earth that their beverages have not yet dominated, fast-food restaurants such as Burger King, McDonald's, and Starbucks sell their standardized foods throughout the world. So successful has the global spread of U.S. mass culture been that it seems to threaten local or indigenous cultures everywhere.

The export of U.S. products and services is not the sole determinant of global cultural practices, however. Because the contemporary consumer culture encourages consumers to make purchase decisions based on brand names designed to evoke particular tastes, fashions, or lifestyles, it also fosters differentiation. Indeed, global marketing often emphasizes the local value of a product. For example, genuinely Australian products, such as Foster's Lager, have become international commodities precisely because they are Australian in origin.

Experiences in Latin America have also indicated that the sharing or imposing of cultural practices is a two-way phenomenon. A trend in Latin America is Music Television (MTV) Latino, which was initially perceived by many critics as another case of foreign cultural intrusion. Yet by the 1990s many critics had relaxed their guard. They saw evidence of increased cultural sharing among Latin societies, noting that MTV and cable television have

Thinking about ENCOUNTERS

Coca-Cola and MTV

The process of globalization as it relates to culture has often been reduced to the notion of the Americanization of the globe—or to the idea of a "McWorld," given the spread of McDonald's restaurants around the world. *Are cultural exchanges so one-sided? How does the globalization of culture reveal a more complicated sharing of images, ideas, and products?*

come to serve as a means of communication and unity by making the nations of Latin America more aware of one another. While the sheer dominance and size of the U.S. entertainment-technology industry keeps cultural sharing lopsided, cultural dominance is also limited by those societies' ability to blend and absorb a variety of foreign and indigenous practices.

The Age of Access

Throughout history technological advances such as in shipbuilding have provided the means to dissolve boundaries between localities and peoples and thus allowed cultural transmission to take place. Today virtually instantaneous electronic communications have dissolved time and space. Contemporary observers have labeled our era "the age of access." Communication by radio, telephone, television, and networked computers has swept away the social, economic, and political isolation of the past. However, because it takes capital to purchase the necessary equipment, maintain and upgrade it, and train people to use it, many societies find it difficult to participate in the communications revolution. The resulting gulf between the connected and the unconnected has the potential therefore to become one border in a world without physical borders.

This new world of global interconnectedness is not without its detractors. Critics have charged, for instance, that mass media are a vehicle for cultural imperialism because most electronic media and the messages they carry emanate from advanced capitalist societies. A specific consequence is that English is becoming the primary language of

global communications systems, effectively restricting vernacular languages to a niche status.

Adaptations of Technology Yet some societies have managed to adapt European and U.S. technology to meet their needs while opposing cultural interference. Television, for example, has been used to promote state building around the world, since most television industries are state controlled. In Zaire, for example, the first television picture residents saw each day was of Mobutu Sese Seko. He especially liked to materialize in segments that pictured him walking on clouds—a miraculous vision of his unearthly power. Likewise, the revolution in electronic communications has been rigidly controlled in other societies—including Vietnam and Iraq—where authorities limit access to foreign servers on the Internet. They thus harness the power of technology for their own purposes while avoiding cultural interference.

GLOBAL PROBLEMS

By the end of the twentieth century, many traditional areas of state responsibility—whether pertaining to population policies, health concerns, or environmental issues—needed to be coordinated on an intergovernmental level. Global

Globalization.
In this photo, the golden arches of a McDonald's fast-food restaurant rise against the skyline of Shenzhen, China.

What effects might the spread of restaurants such as these have on the economies and cultures of distant lands?

Reverberations of ● ● ● ● ● ● ● ●

The Destructive Potential of Industrial Technologies

Nineteenth-century advocates of industrialization had envisioned a world in which mechanization and new technologies would lead to improvements in the human condition over the long term. Yet after only two centuries since industrialization began in Great Britain, it seems possible that the pollution associated with industrialization may have disastrous consequences for the whole planet if, as scientists predict, such pollution leads to global climate change. Think about how the issues associated with climate change are an excellent example of the ways historical events and processes can have consequences that reverberate into the future in ways that contemporaries cannot even imagine.

problems demanded global solutions, and together intergovernmental institutions have tried to compel the governments of individual states to surrender some of their sovereignty to larger international organizations such as the United Nations. Issues concerning labor servitude, poverty, epidemic diseases, terrorism, and human rights demanded attention and action on a scale greater than that of the nation-state.

Population Pressures and Environmental Degradation

The past hundred years or so have been accompanied by vast population increases. As the result of advances in agriculture, industry, science, medicine, and social organization, the world experienced a fivefold population increase over a period of three hundred years: from 500 million people in 1650 to 2.5 billion in 1950. After World War II the widespread and successful use of vaccines, antibiotics, and insecticides, along with improvements in water supplies and increased agricultural yields, caused a dramatic decline in worldwide death rates. The rapid decline in mortality among people who also maintained high levels of fertility led to explosive population growth in many areas of Asia and Africa. In some developing nations, population growth now exceeds 3.1 percent, a rate that ensures the doubling of the population within twenty-three years. In 2011 roughly 7 billion people shared the planet, and the population division of the United Nations has estimated that the earth's population will stabilize around 9 billion in 2050. In the meantime, 75 million people are joining the world's total population each year, and unless fertility declines to replacement levels—that is, two children per woman—the world's population will grow forever.

More optimistic voices, however, have pointed out that the odds of a population explosion and its dreaded consequences are exaggerated and are in fact receding. In part

this decline is the result of the AIDS crisis, which is taking a heavy demographic toll in societies where fertility rates are high. More important, fertility rates have been falling fast in the past two decades, both in rich and in poor societies.

The Planet's Carrying Capacity A large population changes the earth and its environment, raising an important question: How many people can the earth support? The exact carrying capacity of the planet is, of course, a matter of debate, but by many measures the earth seems to strain already to support the current population. Scientists and concerned citizens have become increasingly convinced that human society cannot infinitely expand beyond the physical limits of the earth and its resources. For that reason, many governments have taken action to control fertility. In fact, some eighty countries to date have adopted birth control programs.

Climate Change Indeed, the prodigious growth of the human population is at the root of many environmental problems. As people are born, pollution levels increase, more habitats and animal and plant species disappear, and more natural resources are consumed. In recent decades, two environmental issues have taken center stage: biodiversity and global warming. Biodiversity relates to the maintenance of multiple species of plants and animals. The most serious threat to biodiversity emerged from the destruction of natural habitats in the wake of urbanization, extension of agricultural activity, and exploitation of mineral and timber resources. Extinction currently threatens some 4,500 animal species.

Global warming refers to a rise in global temperature, which carries potentially dire consequences for humanity. Atmospheric pollution causes global warming because the emission of greenhouse gases prevents solar heat from escaping from the earth's atmosphere, leading to a rise in global temperatures. Even a seemingly modest rise of 1 to 3 degrees Celsius in the temperature of the atmosphere might have serious consequences, such as a rise in sea levels that would completely inundate low-lying islands and coastal areas on all continents. In the ancient Japanese capital of Kyoto, at a conference dedicated to pressing environmental problems, the delegates of 159 countries agreed in 1997 to cut greenhouse gas emissions blamed for global warming. The Kyoto protocol went into force in 2005 and imposed targets for carbon emission reductions on developed countries until 2012. The protocol did not require developing countries—some of them major polluters, such as India and China—to reduce their emissions. The world's second largest polluter after China, the United States, did not sign the protocol because it required nothing of developing countries. Since Kyoto, global carbon-dioxide emissions have risen by a third.

International efforts in dealing with climate change have been hampered by a split between developed and developing countries; only the former committed themselves to cutting emissions. Developing countries made no such promise and insisted that the rich world bear the costs of reducing emissions. In 2009, delegates from 193 countries gathered in Copenhagen, Denmark, to renew the Kyoto protocol beyond 2012, with tougher limits on emissions. They struggled to find a way to a new protocol that would include commitments from developing countries. The Copenhagen conference ended without a new protocol or binding extensions to the Kyoto agreements. The only positive outcome was that developing as well as developed countries agreed to an international monitoring of any emissions reductions they promised to pursue.

Economic Inequities and Labor Servitude

The unequal distribution of resources and income and the resulting poverty have materialized as key concerns of the contemporary world. Several hundred million people, especially in the developing areas of eastern Europe, Africa, Latin America, and Asia, struggle daily for sufficient food, clean water, adequate shelter, and other basic necessities. Malnutrition among the poor has led to starvation and death and is also responsible for stunted growth, poor mental development, and high rates of infection. Because of inadequate shelter, lack of safe running water, and the absence of sewage facilities, the poor have also been exposed disproportionately to bacteria and viruses. Poverty has correlated strongly with higher-than-average infant mortality rates and lower-than-average life expectancies.

Global Haves and Have-Nots The division between rich and poor has been a defining characteristic of all complex societies. Although relative poverty levels within a given society remain a major concern, a worldwide shortage of natural resources as well as the uneven distribution of resources has divided the world's nations into haves and have-nots. In part, the unequal distribution of resources in the world economy has resulted from five hundred years of colonialism, and it is certainly true that pervasive poverty characterizes many former colonies and dependencies. All of these developing societies have tried to raise income levels and eliminate poverty through diversified economic development,

Deforestation.
This scene from Pantanal, Brazil, depicts the massive deforestation taking place in the region. In the background, the intact forest contrasts sharply with the denuded areas of the foreground.

TABLE 34.1	Population (in Millions) for Major Areas of the World, 1900–2050				
Major Area	**1900**	**1950**	**1975**	**2005**	**2050**
Africa	133	224	416	906	1,937
Asia	947	1,396	2,395	3,905	5,217
Europe	408	547	676	728	653
Latin America	74	167	322	561	783
North America	82	172	243	331	438
Oceania	6	13	21	33	48
World (total)	1,650	2,519	4,074	6,465	9,076

Source: *World Population Prospects: The 2004 Revision. Highlights.* New York: United Nations, 2005.

but only a few, such as South Korea, Singapore, Malaysia, and Indonesia, have accomplished their aims. In the meantime, economic globalization has generated unprecedented wealth for developed nations, creating an even deeper divide between rich and poor countries.

Labor Servitude Poor economic conditions have been closely associated with forms of servitude similar to slavery. Although legal slavery no longer exists, forced and bonded labor practices continue to affect millions of poor people in the developing world. Of particular concern is child-labor servitude. Currently, more than 250 million children between ages five and fourteen work around the world, many in conditions that are inherently harmful to their physical health and emotional well-being. Child-labor servitude is most pronounced in south and southeast Asia, affecting an estimated 50 million children in India alone. Most child labor occurs in agriculture, domestic service, family businesses, and the sex trade, making it difficult to enforce existing prohibitions and laws against those practices.

Human Trafficking A growing and related global problem that touches societies on every continent is the trafficking of persons. In this insidious form of modern slavery, one to two million human beings annually are bought and sold across international and within national boundaries. In Russia and Ukraine, for example, traffickers lure victims with the promise of well-paying jobs abroad. Once the victims arrive in the countries of their destination, they become captives of ruthless traffickers who force them into bonded labor, domestic servitude, or the commercial sex industry through threats and physical brutality. Most of the victims of trafficking are girls and women, which is a reflection of the low social and economic status of women in many countries. In south Asia, for instance, it is common for poverty-stricken parents or other relatives to sell young women to traffickers for the sex trade or forced labor. The trafficking industry is one of the fastest growing and most lucrative criminal enterprises in the world, generating billions of dollars annually in profits.

Global Diseases

HIV/AIDS Since the dawn of history, disease has played a significant role in the development of human communities. Although many advances were made in the fight against epidemic disease in the twentieth century, serious threats remain. The most serious epidemic threat comes from acquired immunodeficiency syndrome (AIDS). This fatal disorder of the immune system is caused by the human immunodeficiency virus (HIV), which slowly attacks and destroys the immune system. AIDS is the last stage of HIV infection. The HIV infection is spread through sexual contact with an infected person, contact with contaminated blood, and transmission from mother to child during pregnancy and breast-feeding.

Although medical experts have discovered that AIDS originated in sub-Saharan Africa, the syndrome was identified for the first time in 1981 among homosexual men and intravenous drug users in New York and San Francisco. Subsequently, evidence for an epidemic appeared among heterosexual men, women, and children in sub-Saharan Africa, and rather quickly AIDS developed into a worldwide epidemic that affected virtually every nation. At the end of 2005, the number of people living with HIV/AIDS was 38.6 million, and over 20 million AIDS deaths had occurred since the beginning of the epidemic.

AIDS in Africa The AIDS epidemic is a serious public health threat throughout the world, but the disease has struck the developing world hardest, especially sub-Saharan Africa. Indeed, of the 38.6 million people identified with HIV/AIDS worldwide, 24.5 million of them currently live in sub-Saharan Africa. If current trends persist, AIDS deaths and the loss of future population from the demise of women in childbearing ages will lead to a 70-million drop in population by 2010. The AIDS epidemic threatens to overwhelm the social and economic fabric of African societies; the health infrastructure of most African nations cannot cope with the impact of this epidemic. Although sophisticated palliative treatments—not cures—are available, only the wealthy can afford them. When AIDS claims the lives of people in their most productive years, grieving orphans and elders must contend with the sudden loss of financial support, communities must bear the burden of caring for those left behind, and countries must draw on a diminishing number of trained and talented workers.

There are signs that HIV incidence may stabilize in sub-Saharan Africa. So many people in the sexually active population have been affected that only a small pool of people is still able to acquire the infection. In addition, successful prevention programs in a small number of countries, notably Uganda, have reduced infection rates and contributed to a regional downturn of the epidemic.

Advances in HIV Treatment Although no vaccine has yet emerged to prevent or cure HIV infection, some advances have been made. When scientists first identified AIDS, there was no treatment for the disease. By 1995, though, researchers had succeeded in developing a new class of drugs known as protease inhibitors and, in combination with some of the older drugs, they produced what is now known as highly active anti-retroviral therapy, or HAART. In most cases, HAART can prolong life indefinitely. The high cost of these sophisticated drugs initially prevented poor people from sharing in their benefits, but this too is changing. By 2007 over one million people in sub-Saharan Africa routinely received anti-AIDS drugs, and optimistic estimates suggest

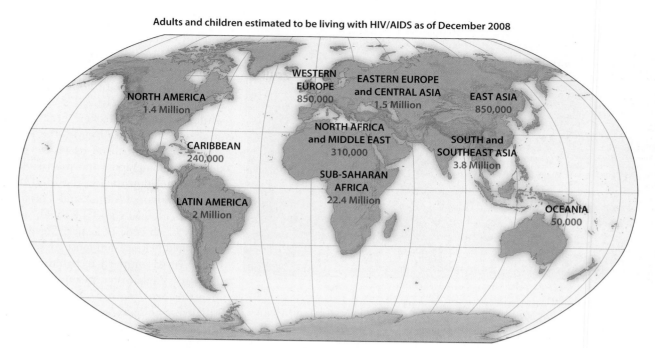

Adults and children estimated to be living with HIV/AIDS as of December 2008

NORTH AMERICA 1.4 Million

WESTERN EUROPE 850,000

EASTERN EUROPE and CENTRAL ASIA 1.5 Million

EAST ASIA 850,000

CARIBBEAN 240,000

NORTH AFRICA and MIDDLE EAST 310,000

SOUTH and SOUTHEAST ASIA 3.8 Million

LATIN AMERICA 2 Million

SUB-SAHARAN AFRICA 22.4 Million

OCEANIA 50,000

Total: 33.4 Million

MAP 34.2

Global estimates of HIV/AIDS. HIV infection in humans is one of the most destructive pandemics in recorded history, having claimed the lives of twenty-five million people since scientists first identified it in 1981.

What regions of the world have been most affected?

that by 2010 effective AIDS drugs will be available to all who might benefit from them. Although an effective vaccine remains elusive, vaginal microbicides designed to prevent the virus from entering the body and prophylactic drug regimens that create a hostile environment for any virus hold out great promise.

Global Terrorism

Terrorism has become a persistent feature of the globalized world. Although not a recent phenomenon, terrorism has attained its greatest impact in a world distinguished by rapid technological advances in transportation, communications, and weapons development. No universally agreed-on definition of terrorism exists, a fact underlined by the often-cited glib observation that "one person's terrorist is another person's freedom fighter." Most experts agree, nevertheless, that a key feature of terrorism is the deliberate and systematic use of violence against civilians, with the aim of advancing political, religious, or ideological causes. In contrast to the populations and institutions they fight, terrorists and their organizations are limited in size and resources. During the last decades of the twentieth century and the first decade of the twenty-first century, terrorism

increasingly assumed a global character because sustained terror campaigns require sophisticated financial support networks and places of sanctuary. Aside from regional initiatives such as those emanating from the European Union, however, the international community did not respond to the threat of global terrorism in a coherent or unified manner. The thorny issues of what constitutes terrorism and how to respond to it gained renewed attention, however, as a result of the terror attacks against the United States in September 2001.

9/11 On the morning of 11 September 2001, New York City and Washington, D.C., became the targets of a coordinated terrorist attack that was unprecedented in scope, sophistication, and destructiveness. Hijackers seized four passenger jetliners and used them as guided missiles. Two of the planes crashed into the World Trade Center towers, causing the collapse of the two towers and thousands of deaths. Before the morning was over, another plane crashed into the Pentagon, the nerve center of the U.S. military in Washington, D.C., and the fourth jet crashed into a field outside Pittsburgh, Pennsylvania, after passengers stormed the hijackers. As millions around the world watched events unfold on television, the U.S. government identified the

11 September 2001.
This photograph shows an aerial view of the Pentagon after terrorists hijacked a commercial airplane and crashed it into the building. The attack was part of a coordinated effort that involved the hijacking of three other airplanes.

Why did the terrorists choose the Pentagon as a target?

Islamic militant Osama bin Laden (1957–2011) as the mastermind behind the attacks. Before the dust of the collapsed World Trade towers had settled, U.S. president George W. Bush (1946–) declared war on Osama bin Laden and global terrorism itself.

War in Afghanistan and Iraq   Osama bin Laden headed al-Qaeda ("the base"), the core of a global terrorist network. Bin Laden had been a key figure in the U.S.-backed effort to aid mujahideen (Islamic warriors) who fought Soviet forces in Afghanistan, but by the end of the Persian Gulf War (1990–1991), he had begun to regard the United States and its allies with unqualified hatred. The stationing of U.S. troops on the holy soil of Saudi Arabia, the bombing of Iraq, and the support of Israel, bin Laden claimed, were tantamount to a declaration of war against God. Convinced that he was carrying out God's will, bin Laden in 1998 publicly called on every Muslim to kill Americans and their allies "wherever he finds them and whenever he can."

A related radical manifestation of Islam's resurgence was the creation of the Islamic State of Afghanistan in 1996 by the Taliban movement. The Taliban emerged out of the disorder and devastation of the Afghan-Soviet war (1979–1988) and the later civil war (see chapter 33). Dominated by Pashtuns—the majority ethnic group of Afghanistan—the Taliban under its leading mullah (male religious leader), Mohammed Omar, fought a series of holy wars against other ethnic and Muslim groups. At the same time, the Taliban provided sanctuary and training grounds for Islamist fighters in southwest and central

Asia, most notably for Osama bin Laden and al-Qaeda.

The Taliban espoused a strict brand of Islam that barred women from education and the workplace. In addition, women had to be completely veiled in burkas, while men had to eschew neckties and grow full, untrimmed beards. The Taliban also called for a ban on television, movie theaters, photographs, and most styles of music. A religious police, the Ministry of the Promotion of Virtue and Prevention of Vice, enforced these rules with an extremely harsh code of justice. Meanwhile, the United Nations and most governments in the world withheld recognition of the Taliban as Afghanistan's legitimate government, recognizing instead the Northern Alliance—an opposition force composed of the country's smaller religious and ethnic groups. The Northern Alliance became a crucial ally of the United States in its mission to find and punish those responsible for the 11 September attacks.

When the United States government announced its war against global terrorism it also pointedly targeted governments and states that supported and provided sanctuary for terrorists. The refusal of the Taliban government to surrender Osama bin Laden prompted the United States and its allies on 7 October 2001 to begin military operations against Taliban military positions and terrorist training camps. By November, U.S.-led bombardments permitted Northern Alliance troops to capture Kabul and other key Afghan cities. In a decisive military campaign, the United States' coalition smashed both the Taliban and al-Qaeda.

Another international action against terrorism came in March 2003, when President Bush coordinated what he termed "Operation Iraqi Freedom." A multinational coalition force some three hundred thousand strong, largely made up of U.S. and British troops, carried out an invasion of Iraq designed to wage further war on terrorism by ousting the regime of Saddam Hussein. One special target was Hussein's suspected stockpile of chemical and biological weapons, otherwise termed "weapons of mass destruction," which could presumably be employed by global terrorists to wreak destruction on a scale even greater than that of 11 September 2001. Coalition forces managed to establish their military supremacy in Iraq, but they did not uncover any such cache of weapons nor did they immediately control Hussein. President Bush declared an end to major battle operations on 1 May 2003, and coalition forces since that time have struggled in their efforts to occupy and stabilize Iraq. Hussein was finally caught in December 2003 and executed in 2006, but deadly resistance in Iraq persisted.

The costs of the Iraq war climbed in terms of both casualties and expenditures. Tens of thousands of Iraqi military personnel and civilians had died, as had more than 4,700 coalition soldiers, by mid-2010. The United States has spent approximately $4 billion per month to maintain troops in Iraq. While President Bush sustained the United States' willingness to pay such a price, some critics in the United States and around the globe balked at the president's aggressive approach to the war on terrorism. Dubbed by some the "Bush Doctrine of Deterrence," his preemptive strike against Iraq—which had not overtly committed a terrorist act or been proven to harbor terrorists—set a troubling precedent in U.S. foreign policy. Moreover, the increased presence of foreign military personnel in Iraq may have only served to intensify the sort of Islamist fervor already fanned by Osama bin Laden. U.S. president Barack Obama (1961–), elected in 2008, oversaw the withdrawal of U.S. troops in Iraq by the end of 2011, and authorized a reduction of 40,000 U.S. troops in Afghanistan in 2012.

Coping with Global Problems: International Organizations

Because global economic and cultural interdependence demands that political activity focus on cross-societal concerns and solutions, nations are under pressure to surrender portions of their sovereignty. The widespread recognition that the national state is ill equipped to handle problems of a global magnitude has led to an increase in the number of organizations dedicated to solving global problems through international coordination and action. Often categorized as nongovernmental international organizations and international governmental organizations, these institutions are important because they have the potential to tackle problems that do not respect territorial boundaries.

The United Nations The premier international governmental organization is the United Nations, which superseded the League of Nations (1920–1946). This association of sovereign nations attempts to find solutions to global problems and to deal with virtually any matter of concern to humanity. Under its charter a principal purpose of the UN is "to maintain international peace and security." Cynics are quick to point to the UN's apparent inability to achieve that goal, citing as evidence the eight-year war between Iraq and Iran, the civil war in Somalia, and the many years of bloodshed in Afghanistan. Yet however flawed its role as an international peacemaker, the UN has compiled an enviable record with respect to another role defined in its charter, namely, "to achieve international cooperation in solving international problems of an economic, social, cultural, or humanitarian character." Quietly and without attracting attention from the news media, the specialized agencies of the UN have achieved numerous successes.

For example, in 1980 the World Health Organization proclaimed the worldwide eradication of smallpox as a result of its thirteen-year global program. On other fronts, UN efforts resulted in a more than 50 percent decrease in both infant and child mortality rates in developing countries between 1960 and 2002.

Human Rights Governmental and nongovernmental organizations have focused much of their attention on the protection of human rights, the notion that all persons are entitled to basic rights. Universal recognition and acceptance of the concept of human rights came in the aftermath of World War II, especially with the exposure of the crimes of the Nazi regime. In the charter establishing the United Nations in 1945, fifty member nations pledged to achieve "universal respect for, and observance of, human rights, and fundamental freedoms." In 1948, the National Assembly of the UN adopted the Universal Declaration of Human Rights, which singled out specific human rights violations such as extrajudicial or summary executions, arbitrary arrest and torture, and slavery or involuntary servitude as well as discrimination on racial, sexual, or religious grounds. By the late 1980s, human rights had emerged as one of the principal themes of global politics.

Given the present level of global interaction, international coordination to solve global problems is a necessity. However, contentious issues have sometimes paralyzed the UN and its affiliated organizations, because societies at different stages of economic development have pursued sometimes conflicting social and political goals. Yet despite the shortcomings of international organizations, for the present they represent the closest thing humanity has to a global system of governance that can help the world's peoples meet the challenges of international problems.

CROSSING BOUNDARIES

Human populations also underwent radical transformations. Peoples throughout the world challenged gender definitions and embarked on large-scale migrations. Women in Europe, the United States, China, and the Soviet Union gained greater equality with men, even while women in most countries continued to be bound by traditional expectations for their sex. Meanwhile, both women and men also experienced either forced or voluntary migrations and in the process helped to create an increasingly borderless world.

Women's Traditions and Feminist Challenges

The status of women began changing after World War II. Women gained more economic, political, social, and sexual rights in highly industrialized states than in developing nations, but nowhere have they achieved full equality with

Thinking about TRADITIONS

Female Freedom and Subjugation

Despite the major transformations in the lives of women after World War II, the practice of limiting the freedom of women persisted in many areas of the world. *Why was the feminism evident in Europe and the Americas less effective and applicable elsewhere? How did women in Asia and Africa experience both freedom and subjugation?*

men. Indeed, while some women have attained high political offices or impressive leadership positions, most do not exert political power commensurate with their numbers. At the same time, the political, legal, social, and cultural rights women in some societies have gained are unprecedented in the history of the world.

Agitation for gender equality is often linked to women's access to employment, and the industrialized nations have the largest percentage of working women. For example, women constitute 40 to 50 percent of the workforce in industrial societies, compared with 20 percent or less in developing countries. In all countries, women work primarily in low-paying jobs such as teaching, service, and clerical positions. In addition, 40 percent of all farmers are women, many at the subsistence level.

Feminism and Equal Rights The discrimination that women faced in the workplace was a major stimulus for the feminist movement in industrialized nations. Women in most of those nations had gained the right to vote after the Great War, but they found that political rights did not guarantee economic or sexual equality. After World War II, when more and more women went to work, women started to protest job discrimination, pay differentials between women and men, and their lack of legal equality. In the 1960s those complaints expanded into a feminist movement that criticized all aspects of gender inequality.

Women started to expose the ways in which a biologically determined understanding of gender led to their oppression. In addition to demanding equality in the workplace, women demanded full control over their bodies and their reproductive systems. In the United States, the introduction of the birth control pill in the 1960s and legal protection of abortion in the 1970s provided a measure of sexual freedom for women even as the Civil Rights Act of 1964 prohibited discrimination on the basis of both race and sex.

Gender Equality in China Some socialist or communist societies—such as the Soviet Union, Cuba, and China—transformed their legal systems to ensure basic equality.

"Women hold up half the sky," Mao Zedong declared, and that eloquent acknowledgment of women's role translated into a commitment to fairness. In 1950 communist leaders passed a marriage law that abolished patriarchal practices such as child betrothal and upheld equal rights for men and women in the areas of work, property ownership, and inheritance.

Critics argue that despite such laws China's women have never gained true equality. Although most women in China have full-time jobs outside the home and are able to enter most professions, they do not receive wages equal to those of men. Long-standing Confucian values continue to degrade the status of women, especially in rural areas. One unintended consequence of China's population policies, which limits couples to one child, is the mysterious statistical disappearance of a half million baby girls every year. Some population experts speculate that a continued strong preference for male children causes parents to send baby girls away for adoption, to be raised secretly, or in some cases to resort to infanticide.

Although girls and women in industrial and communist nations are guaranteed basic if not fully equal legal rights and are educated in roughly the same numbers as boys and men, women in other areas of the world have long been denied access to education. In Arab and Muslim lands, women are twice as likely as men to be illiterate, and in some places nine of ten women are illiterate. In India, female literacy had reached 54 percent by 2001, and yet women remained largely confined to the home. Fewer than one-quarter of women of all ages were engaged in work, while the birthrate remained high even with the greater availability of birth control measures. This condition has ensured a life of domesticity for many Indian women, who are often completely dependent on their husbands' families and can be subject to severe domestic abuse.

Migration

Migration, the movement of people from one place to another, is as old as humanity and has shaped the formation and identity of societies throughout the world. The massive influx of outsiders has transformed the ethnic, linguistic, and cultural composition of indigenous populations. With the advent of industrialization during the eighteenth century, population experts distinguished between two types of migration: internal migration and external or international migration. Internal migration describes the flow of people from rural to urban areas within one society, whereas external migration describes the movement of people across long distances and international borders. Both types of migration result from push factors such as

Sources from the Past

China's Marriage Law, 1949

When the Chinese Communist Party came into power under Mao Zedong in 1949, the new government quickly instituted the "Marriage Law," which made Chinese men and women legal equals in marriage. This was truly revolutionary, since women traditionally held very low status in China's highly patriarchal social structure. Although actual equality was more elusive than legal equality, the Marriage Law marked a significant step toward granting women more rights in Chinese society.

Chapter I. General Principles

Article 1. The arbitrary and compulsory feudal marriage system, which is based on the superiority of man over woman and which ignores the children's interests, shall be abolished.

The new democratic marriage system, which is based on free choice of partners, on monogamy, on equal rights for both sexes, and on protection of the lawful interests of women and children, shall be put into effect.

Article 2. Bigamy, concubinage, child betrothal, interference with the remarriage of widows, and the exaction of money or gifts in connection with marriage shall be prohibited. . . .

Chapter III. Rights and Duties of Husband and Wife

Article 7. Husband and wife are companions living together and shall enjoy equal status in the home.

Article 8. Husband and wife are in duty bound to love, respect, assist, and look after each other, to live in harmony, to engage in production, to care for the children, and to strive jointly for the welfare of the family and for the building up of a new society.

Article 9. Both husband and wife shall have the right to free choice of occupation and free participation in work or in social activities.

Article 10. Both husband and wife shall have equal right in the possession and management of family property.

Article 11. Both husband and wife shall have the right to use his or her own family name.

Article 12. Both husband and wife shall have the right to inherit each other's property.

For Further Reflection

■ In what ways were these marriage laws similar to or different from the demands for gender equality made by feminists in the United States and western Europe during the 1960s and 1970s?

Source: Dennis Sherman et al. *World Civilizations: Sources, Images, and Interpretations,* 3rd ed., Volume 2. Boston and New York: McGraw-Hill, 2002.

---

population pressure or political persecution, pull factors such as better services and employment, or a combination of both.

Internal Migration The largest human migrations today are rural-to-urban flows. During the last half of the twentieth century, these internal migrations led to rapid urbanization in much of the world. Today the most highly urbanized societies are those of western and northern Europe, Australia, New Zealand, and temperate South America and North America. In these societies the proportion of people living in urban areas exceeds 75 percent; in some countries, such as Germany, it exceeds 85 percent.

Urbanization In Latin America, Africa, and south Asia, large numbers of people have migrated to metropolitan areas in search of relief from rural poverty. Once in the cities, though, they often find themselves equally destitute. More than ten million people cram the environs of cities such as Calcutta, Cairo, and Mexico City, straining those cities' resources. The few services originally available to the slum dwellers—potable water, electricity, and medical care—have diminished with the continuous influx of new people, and disease and malnutrition often run rampant.

External Migration The largest migrations in the second half of the twentieth century consisted of refugees fleeing war. For example, the 1947 partition of the Indian subcontinent into two independent states resulted in the exchange of six million Hindus from Pakistan and seven million Muslims from India. More recently, three million to four million refugees fled war-torn Afghanistan during the 1980s. According to UN estimates, at the end of 2003 there were some ten million refugees who lived outside their countries of origin and who could not return because of fear of persecution.

Many of these migrants left their home countries because they wanted to escape the ravages of war, but many others leave their country of birth in search of better jobs and more readily available health care, educational opportunities, and other services. Thus since 1960 some thirteen million "guest workers" from southern Europe, Turkey,

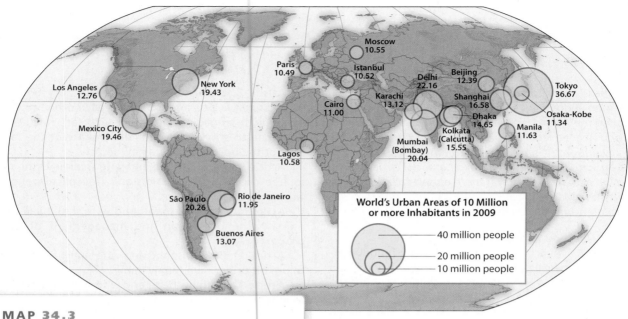

MAP 34.3
World's urban areas of 10 million or more inhabitants in 2009.

and northern Africa have taken up permanent residence in western Europe, and more than ten million permanent migrants—mostly from Mexico—have entered the United States. Worldwide, approximately 130 million people currently live outside their country of citizenship, collectively constituting a "nation of migrants" equivalent in size to Japan, the world's eighth most populous nation.

Migrant Communities International mass migrations have accelerated and broadened the scope of cross-cultural interaction. After their arrival on foreign shores, migrants established cultural and ethnic communities that maintained their social customs and native languages and transformed many cities into multicultural environments. Although the arrival of migrants has enriched societies in many ways, it has also sparked resentment and conflict. People in host countries often believe that foreigners and their ways of life undermine national identity. Beyond that, many citizens of host societies view migrants, who are often willing to work for low

wages, as competitors for jobs. As a result, governments in many countries have come under pressure to restrict immigration or even expel foreign residents. Thus, while migrants are reshaping the world outside their home countries, international mass migration poses challenges both to the migrants themselves and to the host society.

A Rio de Janeiro slum.
These shanties, built on a hillside in Rio de Janeiro, reflect the poverty of many of the city's inhabitants.

To what extent would residents be likely to have access to running water, sewers, and electricity here?

SUMMARY

By the late twentieth century, borders created by the bipolar world and European empires had dissolved, reshaping the world's landscape. Another barrier-crushing development that became visible at the end of the century was economic globalization, a process responsible for the unprecedented integration of the global economy. Globalization pointed to the new relevance of international organizations and to the increasing irrelevance of national boundaries; it signified the arrival of a world without borders. Technological and cultural developments likewise combined to break down barriers and create a global village that connected diverse peoples. Although many societies resisted cultural influences from Europe and the United States, the prevalence of communications technology and cultural diffusion made interactions and encounters inevitable. Women's efforts to achieve greater equality with men also collided with cultural traditions, while the global movement of human populations crisscrossed boundaries and contributed—for better and worse—to a more interconnected world than has ever before existed in human history.

STUDY TERMS

age of access (659)	little tigers (656)
AIDS (662)	McDonaldization (658)
al-Qaeda (664)	NAFTA (658)
ASEAN (658)	Northern Alliance (664)
biodiversity (660)	OPEC (657)
Bush Doctrine of Deterrence (665)	Operation Iraqi Freedom (664)
European Union (656)	Osama bin Laden (664)
feminist movement (666)	Saddam Hussein (664)
free trade (654)	Taliban (664)
GATT (654)	terrorism (663)
global warming (660)	United Nations (665)
globalization (654)	Universal Declaration of Human Rights (665)
HAART (662)	WTO (654)
IMF (654)	

FOR FURTHER READING

Peter Baldwin. *Disease and Democracy: The Industrialized World Faces AIDS.* Berkeley, 2005. Probing comparative history of the public health policies implemented by Western democracies to contain domestic AIDS epidemics in the 1980s and 1990s.

Jagdish Bhagwati. *In Defense of Globalization.* New York, 2004. A convincing rebuttal to popular fallacies about global economic integration.

Thomas L. Friedman. *The Lexus and the Olive Tree.* New York, 1999. A readable overview that does justice to the complexities of globalization.

Karl Gerth. *China Made: Consumer Culture and the Creation of the Nation.* Cambridge, Mass., 2003. Links notions of nationalism and consumerism in twentieth-century China.

Francis Harris, ed. *Global Environmental Issues.* New York, 2004. A clear, nontechnical introduction to a broad range of environmental issues.

Margaret Jean Hay and Sharon Stichter. *African Women South of the Sahara.* Boston, 1984. An analysis of social and economic change and how it affected African women in the twentieth century.

Nikki R. Keddie and Beth Baron, eds. *Women in Middle Eastern History: Shifting Boundaries in Sex and Gender.* New Haven, 1992. A sensitive selection of articles by the leading scholars in the field.

Joanna Liddle and Rama Doshi. *Daughters of Independence: Gender, Caste, and Class in India.* New Delhi, 1986. A work on the contemporary women's movement that covers the Indian caste system, British colonial rule, and class structure.

J. R. McNeill. *Something New under the Sun: An Environmental History of the Twentieth-Century World.* New York, 2000. A brilliant but dark tale of the past century's interaction between humans and the environment.

Joseph Stiglitz. *Globalization and Its Discontents.* New York, 2002. A former chief economist at the World Bank and the 2002 Nobel Prize winner takes aim at the institutions that govern globalization, especially the IMF.

PART 7 CONTEMPORARY GLOBAL REALIGNMENTS

Interactions and encounters between the world's peoples have been a feature of human history since ancient times. Yet in the twentieth and twenty-first centuries, the human ability to conquer space and time with technology has led to massive change at the global level and has intensified economic and cultural trends already set in motion during the industrial revolution.

Some of the most dramatic changes of the twentieth century occurred at the level of global leadership. At the beginning of the twentieth century, the world was dominated by a few major powers—especially Great Britain and France—who had used industrial technologies to conquer large empires in Asia and Africa. By midcentury, after two of the deadliest wars in the history of humankind, the great European empires were fatally weakened. In the four decades after World War II, the United States and the Soviet Union assumed global dominance, using industrial and military might to carve the world into competing capitalist and communist blocs. At the same time, nearly every colony once subject to formal imperial control struggled for and won independence—a process that necessitated the literal redrawing of the world map. Finally, by the last decade of the twentieth century the collapse of the Soviet Union brought an end to the bipolar world system, leaving an uncertain conglomeration of nation-states, regional associations, and international organizations in its place.

In addition to significant changes in global leadership, the tendency toward global economic, technological, and cultural integration accelerated dramatically during the twentieth century. Indeed, markets are now so deeply intertwined that shifts in one national stock market can affect markets in the rest of the world within hours. Global cultural habits are similarly intertwined, as people around the world now have unprecedented access to goods and services produced in distant parts of the world.

Yet while the world is more interconnected than ever before, interconnections do not always breed harmony. Many people resent the economic bullying of international organizations and argue that economic globalization has impoverished underdeveloped areas of the world. Others dislike the cultural homogenization brought about by "McDonaldization" and believe that unique cultural traditions will soon be lost forever. Indeed, the globalized world of today is replete with problems, many of which—including environmental destruction, epidemic disease, and violent conflict—are at least partly the result of accelerated connections between peoples and places. At the same time, organizations like the United Nations, international aid organizations, and regional trade networks have indicated that humans are capable of global cooperation as well. In the twenty-first century and beyond, the world's peoples will be faced with both the problems and the successes of the multiple interconnections forged in the modern world.

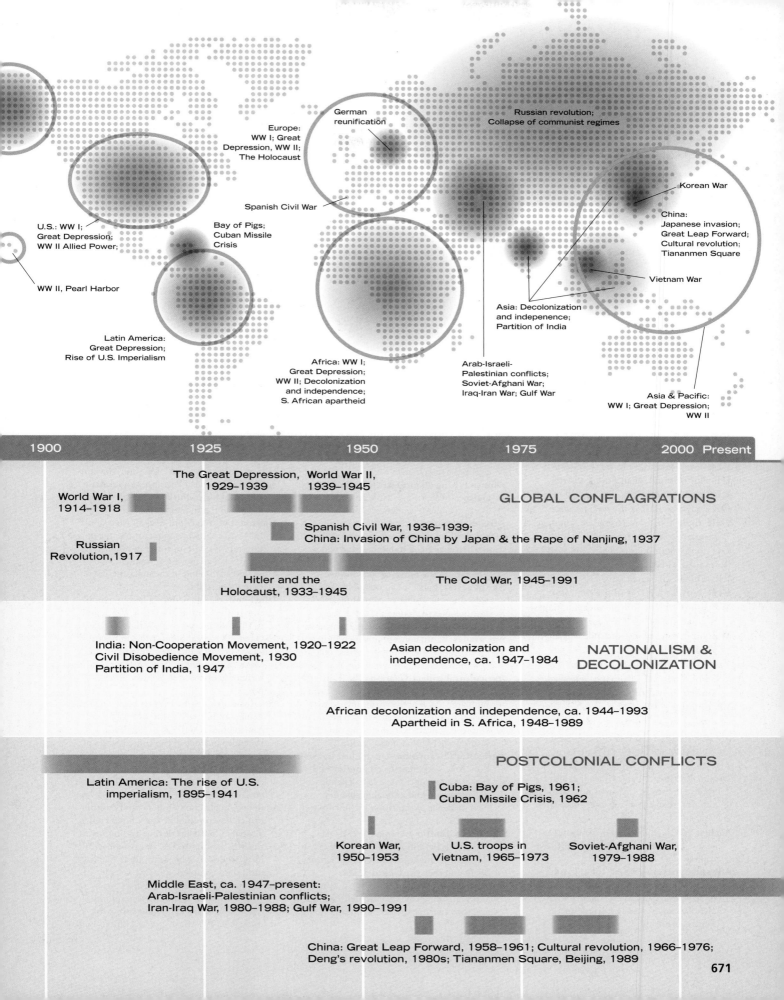

German
reunification

Europe:
WW I; Great
Depression, WW II;
The Holocaust

Russian revolution;
Collapse of communist regimes

Korean War

Spanish Civil War

China:
Japanese invasion;
Great Leap Forward;
Cultural revolution;
Tiananmen Square

U.S.: WW I;
Great Depression;
WW II Allied Power;

Bay of Pigs;
Cuban Missile
Crisis

WW II, Pearl Harbor

Vietnam War

Asia: Decolonization
and indepence;
Partition of India

Latin America:
Great Depression;
Rise of U.S. Imperialism

Africa: WW I;
Great Depression;
WW II; Decolonization
and independence;
S. African apartheid

Arab-Israeli-
Palestinian conflicts;
Soviet-Afghani War;
Iraq-Iran War; Gulf War

Asia & Pacific:
WW I; Great Depression;
WW II

| 1900 | 1925 | 1950 | 1975 | 2000 Present |

The Great Depression, World War II,
1929–1939 1939–1945

World War I,
1914–1918

GLOBAL CONFLAGRATIONS

Spanish Civil War, 1936–1939;
China: Invasion of China by Japan & the Rape of Nanjing, 1937

Russian
Revolution, 1917

Hitler and the
Holocaust, 1933–1945

The Cold War, 1945–1991

India: Non-Cooperation Movement, 1920–1922
Civil Disobedience Movement, 1930
Partition of India, 1947

Asian decolonization and
independence, ca. 1947–1984

NATIONALISM &
DECOLONIZATION

African decolonization and independence, ca. 1944–1993
Apartheid in S. Africa, 1948–1989

POSTCOLONIAL CONFLICTS

Latin America: The rise of U.S.
imperialism, 1895–1941

Cuba: Bay of Pigs, 1961;
Cuban Missile Crisis, 1962

Korean War,
1950–1953

U.S. troops in
Vietnam, 1965–1973

Soviet-Afghani War,
1979–1988

Middle East, ca. 1947–present:
Arab-Israeli-Palestinian conflicts;
Iran-Iraq War, 1980–1988; Gulf War, 1990–1991

China: Great Leap Forward, 1958–1961; Cultural revolution, 1966–1976;
Deng's revolution, 1980s; Tiananmen Square, Beijing, 1989

671

glossary&pronunciationguide

A short *a* sound, as in *asp, fat, parrot*

AH *a* sound, as in *car, father*

AHW diphthong *au* in Romance languages, similar to vowel sound in *ouch*

AHY diphthong *ai* in Romance languages, similar to vowel sound in *die*

AW diphthong *a* sound, as in *awful, paw, law*

AY long *a* sound, as in *ape, date, play*

EE long *e* sound, as in *even, meet, money*

EH short *e* sound, as in *ten, elf, berry, how, bow*

EHY diphthong *ei* in Romance languages, similar to "ay" in *day*

EW diphthong *iu* in Romance languages, similar (but shorter than) *you*

EYE long *i* sound, as in *ice, high, bite*

IH short *i* sound, as in *fit, his, mirror*

KH hard *k* sound

OH long *o* sound, as in *open, go, tone*

OHI diphthong *oi* in Romance languages, similar to "oy" in *toy*

OO long *o* sound, as in *ooze, tool, crew*

'R tapped *r* like *dd* or *tt* in *latter* and *butter*

RR trilled *r* (repeated taps)

UH short *u* sound, as in *up, cut, color*

WA diphthong *ua* in Romance languages, similar to the "wa" in *want* and *waffle*

WE diphthong *ui* in Romance languages, similar to the word *we*

Y like *ll* in *million* or *ny* in *canyon*

YA diphthong *ia* in Romance languages, similar to "ya" in *yacht*

YE diphthong *ie* in Romance languages, similar to "ye" in *yet*

YO diphthong *io* in Romance languages, similar to "yo" in the suffix *yoke*

Note on emphasis: Syllables in capital letters receive the stress. If there is no syllable in capitals, then all syllables get equal stress.

Aachen (AH-kehn) A city in western Germany; formerly Charlemagne's northern capital.

Abbasid dynasty (ah-BAH-sihd) Cosmopolitan Arabic dynasty (750–1258) that replaced the Umayyads; founded by Abu al-Abbas and reaching its peak under Harun al-Rashid.

Abolitionism Antislavery movement.

Aboriginal peoples People indigenous to an area. Commonly used in reference to the indigenous peoples of Australia.

Absolutism Political philosophy that stressed the divine right theory of kingship: the French king Louis XIV was the classic example.

Abu Bakr (ah-BOO BAHK-uhr) First caliph after the death of Muhammad.

Achaemenid empire (ah-KEE-muh-nid) First great Persian empire (558–330 B.C.E.), which began under Cyrus and reached its peak under Darius.

Aegean (ih-JEE-uhn) Bronze Age civilization that flourished near the Aegean Sea.

Aeschylus (ES-kuh-luhs) Greek tragedian, author of the *Oresteia*.

Afonso I King of Portugal (1139–1185). Won independence from Castile and established Portuguese independence.

African diaspora Africans living outside the African continent. Refers especially to Africans forced to migrate during the period of the Atlantic slave trade, from the fifteenth to the nineteenth centuries.

Age of access Label for contemporary times regarding the ability of communication technologies to change the social, economic, and political solutions of the past.

Age grades Bantu concept in which individuals of roughly the same age carried out communal tasks appropriate for that age.

Agricultural collectivization The transformation of small, individual peasant farms into large, cooperative farms owned by the state. Refers especially to the period of enforced collectivization during the 1930s in the Soviet Union under Stalin.

Agricultural transition The gradual transition from a dependence on hunting and gathering for subsistence to a dependence on cultivation and animal husbandry. First evidence of transition is from around 12,000 B.C.E.

Aguinaldo, Emilio (AH-gee-NAHL-daw, ee-MEE-lyaw) Filipino independence leader who fought for independence from Spain and then the United States.

Ahimsa (uh-HIM-suh) A Buddhist, Hindu, and Jainist doctrine that all life is sacred and that violence should be avoided at all costs.

Ahmosis (AH-moh-sis) Egyptian pharaoh (c. 1500 B.C.E.), founder of the New Kingdom.

Ahura Mazda (uh-HOORE-uh MAHZ-duh) Main god of Zoroastrianism who represented truth and goodness and was perceived to be in an eternal struggle with the malign spirit Angra Mainyu.

AIDS Acquired immune deficiency syndrome.

Akbar Mughal emperor of India (1556–1605). Known for conquering most of northern India and for his religious tolerance.

Akhenaten (ahk-eh-NAH-ton) Early ruler of Egypt who created a tradition of sun worship.

Al-Andalus (al-ahn-dah-LOOS) Islamic Spain.

Alboquerque, Afonso d' (AL-buh-kur-kee, al-FAWN-soo d') Portuguese nobleman who established the Portuguese colonial empire in the Indian Ocean.

Alexander of Macedon King of Macedonia (336–323 B.C.E.). Conqueror of large portions of Asia Minor from Egypt to India.

Ali'i nui Hawaiian class of high chiefs.

Allah (AH-lah) God of the monotheistic religion of Islam.

Allied powers The nations allied in opposition to the Central Powers in WWI, and to the Axis powers in WWII.

Al-Qaeda A radical Sunni Muslim organization dedicated to the elimination of a Western presence in Arab countries and militantly opposed to Western foreign policy.

American revolution The war between Great Britain and thirteen of its North American colonies from 1775–1783, leading to the independence of the United States of America in 1783.

Amon-Re (AH-mohn RAY) Egyptian god, combination of the sun god Re and the air god Amon.

Analects A collection of moral and ethical principles expressed by the Chinese philosopher Confucius during his lifetime in the fifth century B.C.E., and compiled by his disciples after his death in 479 B.C.E. until their completion in 221 B.C.E.

Ancestor worship Belief that dead ancestors can influence one's fortunes in this life. People who practice ancestor worship characteristically practice rituals and ceremonies to the memory or remains of their ancestors.

Ancien régime (ahn-syan rey-ZHEEM) The political and social system that existed in France before the French Revolution.

Angkor (AHN-kohr) Southeast Asian Khmer kingdom (889–1432) that was centered around the temple cities of Angkor Thom and Angkor Wat.

Angkor Thom Capital of Cambodia from the twelfth century to the mid-fifteenth century, now known as Siem Reap.

Angkor Wat Hindu temple complex built in the town of Angkor, Cambodia, in the twelfth century. One of the largest temple complexes in the world.

Anglicans Followers of the established Episcopal Church of England.

Angola Country that borders the Atlantic Ocean in southwest Africa. Colonized by the Portuguese in the sixteenth century, and achieved independence in 1975.

Anschluss (AHN-shloss) 1938 annexation of Austria into greater Germany by the Nazi regime.

Antigonus (an-TIG-uh-nuhs) A general of Alexander the Great and king of Macedonia.

Anti-Semitism Term coined in late nineteenth century that was associated with a prejudice against Jews and the political, social, and economic actions taken against them.

Antonianism African syncretic religion, founded by Doña Beatriz, that taught that Jesus Christ was a black African man and that heaven was for Africans.

Antonian movement Syncretic Christian movement founded by Beatriz Kimpa Vita between 1704 and 1706 in the African kingdom of Kongo.

Apartheid (ah-PAHR-teyed) South African system of "separateness" that was implemented in 1948 and that maintained the black majority in a position of political, social, and economic subordination.

Appeasement British and French policy in the 1930s that tried to maintain peace in Europe in the face of German aggression by making concessions.

Archaic Period Period of Greek political and artistic development between 750 and 480 B.C.E.

Arianism Early Christian heresy that centered around teaching of Arius (250–336 C.E.) and contained the belief that Jesus was a mortal human being and not coeternal with God; Arianism was the focus of the Council of Nicaea.

Aristotle (AHR-ih-stot-uhl) One of the greatest ancient Athenian philosophers and pupil of Plato.

Artha Hindu concept for the pursuit of economic well-being and honest prosperity.

Arthashastra (UHRR-th-sha-strrah) Ancient Indian political treatise from the time of Chandragupta Maurya; its authorship was

traditionally ascribed to Kautalya, and it stressed that war was inevitable.

Aryans (AYR-ee-uhns) Indo-European tribes who settled in India after 1500 B.C.E.; their union with indigenous Dravidians formed the basis of Hinduism.

Asante (uh-SAN-tee) Empire that emerged in 1670 in what is now modern Ghana.

Asceticism (uh-SET-uh-siz-uhm) Doctrine that through the renunciation of worldly pleasure one can achieve a high spiritual or intellectual state.

Ashoka (ah-SHOW-kuh) Emperor of the Mauryan empire in India (269–232 B.C.E.) and major patron of Buddhism within his realm.

Association of Southeast Asian Nations (ASEAN) Regional alliance established in 1967 by Thailand, Malaysia, Singapore, Indonesia, and the Philippines; the alliance was designed to promote economic progress and political stability; it later became a free-trade zone.

Assyrians (uh-SEER-ee-uhns) Southwest Asian people who built an empire that reached its height during the eighth and seventh centuries B.C.E.; it was known for a powerful army and a well-structured state.

Astrolabe (as-truh-leyb) Navigational instrument for determining latitude.

Atahualpa (ah-tah-WAHL-pah) The last sovereign emperor of the Inca empire, executed by the Spanish.

Aten Monotheistic god of Egyptian pharaoh Akhenaten (r. 1353–1335 B.C.E.) and arguably the world's first example of monotheism.

Athens City in and capital of Greece. One of the most powerful of the ancient Greek city-states in the fifth century B.C.E.

Atlantic slave trade Massive trade system between Europe, Africa, and the Americas between the fifteenth and nineteenth centuries that involved the capture, enforced migration, and sale of millions of African people.

Attila the Hun King of the Huns and most successful barbarian invader of the Roman empire between 406–453 C.E.

Audiencias (AW-dee-uhns-cee-ahs) Spanish courts in Latin America.

Augustus First emperor of Rome from 27 B.C.E. to 14 C.E.

Aurangzeb Mughal emperor of India from 1658–1707 C.E., known for expanding the empire and for imposing Muslim orthodoxy on his realm.

Australopithecus (ah-strah-loh-PIHTH-uh-kuhs) "Southern ape," oldest known ancestor of humans; it lived from around four million down to around one million years ago, and it could walk on hind legs, freeing hands for using simple tools.

Austronesians People who, by as early as 2000 B.C.E., began to explore and settle islands of the Pacific Ocean basin.

Avesta Book that contains the holy writings of Zoroastrianism.

Axis powers The nations allied in opposition to the Allied powers in WWII.

Axum (AHK-soom) Capital of ancient Ethiopian kingdom.

Ayllu Basic socioeconomic unit of Inca society, usually consisting of an extended family.

Azores (uh-ZAWRZ) Volcanic islands in the Northern Atlantic belonging to Portugal.

Aztec empire Central American empire constructed by the Mexica and expanded greatly during the fifteenth century during the reigns of Itzcoatl and Motecuzoma I.

Babur (BAH-ber) Founder of the Mughal dynasty in India.

Bakufu (bah-kuh-fuh) Military government under the Japanese shoguns.

Balfour Declaration British declaration from 1917 that supported the creation of a Jewish homeland in Palestine.

Bantu peoples (BAHN-too) African peoples who originally lived in the area of present-day Nigeria; around 2000 B.C.E. they began a centuries-long migration that took them to most of sub-Saharan Africa; the Bantu were very influential, especially linguistically.

Barth, Karl (1886–1968) Swiss Protestant theologian famous for opposing the Nazi regime.

Basil the Bulgar-Slayer Byzantine emperor (976–1025) who annexed Bulgaria.

Basilian monasticism Monks who follow the "Rule" of St. Basil (c. 329–379 C.E.), bishop of Caesarea in modern-day Turkey.

Battle of Britain Campaign during WWII from August to October, 1940, in which the German Luftwaffe bombed England prior to a planned invasion of Britain. The successful resistance of the British Royal Airforce led the Germans to abandon plans for invasion.

Battle of Little Big Horn Battle near the Little Bighorn River (June 25, 1876) in Montana, between the United States cavalry led by General George Custer and Native American forces inspired by Sitting Bull, in which Custer's force was defeated and many of his men were killed.

Battle of Manzikert Battle in 1071 C.E. near the town of Manzikert (modern Turkey) in which Byzantine forces were defeated by Seljuq Turks. Led to the Turkish conquest of most of Anatolia.

Bechuanaland (bech-oo-AH-nuh-land) Protectorate established in 1885 by the British in southern Africa.

Bedouins (BEHD-oh-ihnz) Nomadic Arabic tribespeople.

Belisarius (bel-uh-SAIR-ee-uhs) Byzantine general who fought against the Persians and recovered Roman territories in northern Africa.

Benefice Grant from a lord to a vassal, usually consisting of land, which supported the vassal and signified the relationship between the two.

Benin (beh-NEEN) Large precolonial African state in what is now modern Nigeria.

Berdiaev, Nikolai (ber-dee-ev, nih-koh-LYE) Late nineteenth- and early twentieth-century Russian philosopher.

Bering, Vitus Danish explorer (1681–1741) who explored the northern Pacific for the Russians, and for whom the Bering Strait is named.

Berlin Conference Meeting organized by German chancellor Otto von Bismarck in 1884–1885 that provided the justification for European colonization of Africa.

Berlin Wall Wall that separated West Berlin from East Germany.

Bessemer converter A large furnace used to convert pig iron into steel by blasting compressed air into molten iron in order to remove impurities and excess carbon.

Bezant Gold coin issued by the Byzantine empire.

Bhagavad Gita (BUHG-uh-vuhd GEE-tah) Sacred "song of god" composed in 200 B.C.E. and incorporated into the *Mahabharata*, a Sanskrit epic.

Bhakti movement (BHUK-tee) Indian movement that attempted to transcend the differences between Hinduism and Islam.

Biodiversity Diversity among and within plant and animal species in an environment.

Bismarck, Otto von (oht-toh fuhn BIZ-mahrk) German statesman under whose leadership Germany was united.

Black Hand Pre–World War I secret Serbian society; one of its members, Gavrilo Princip, assassinated Austrian archduke Francis Ferdinand and provided the spark for the outbreak of the Great War.

Black Thursday The name given to Thursday, October 24, 1929, when the New York Stock Exchange crashed, leading to the cycle of events that became the Great Depression.

Blitzkrieg German style of rapid attack through the use of armor and air power that was used in Poland, Norway, Denmark, Belgium, the Netherlands, and France in 1939–1940.

Boddhisatvas (BOH-dih-SAT-vuhs) Buddhist concept regarding individuals who had reached enlightenment but who stayed in this world to help people.

Bolívar, Simón South American soldier (1783–1830) who successfully fought for the liberation of Venezuela, Ecuador, Colombia, and Peru from the Spanish in the early nineteenth century.

Bolshevik (BOHL-shih-vehk) Russian communist party headed by Lenin.

Bolshevik revolution Revolution in November 1917 in which the Bolshevik party seized power from the provisional govern-

ment in Russia. Led to a civil war and eventual Bolshevik victory in 1922.

Bosporus Narrow strait linking the Black Sea and the Sea of Marmara, which separates European and Asian Turkey.

Bourgeoisie Middle class in modern industrial society.

Boxer rebellion Chinese uprising in 1900 aimed at pushing out all foreigners from China. Defeated by a combined European force.

Boyars (BOY-ahrs) Russian nobles.

Brahman A Hindu of the highest caste, by tradition assigned to the priesthood.

Brahmins (BRAH-minz) Hindu caste of priests.

Brazil Large country in eastern South America, ruled by the Portuguese from the sixteenth century until 1822.

Brezhnev Doctrine Policy developed by Leonid Brezhnev (1906–1982) that claimed for the Soviet Union the right to invade any socialist country faced with internal or external enemies; the doctrine was best expressed in the Soviet invasion of Czechoslovakia.

British North America Act 1867 act that created the Dominion of Canada.

Bronze An alloy of copper and tin in various proportions.

Brunelleschi, Filippo Florentine architect (1377–1446) who was one of the first and best-known architects of the Italian Renaissance.

Bubonic plague Epidemic that swept Eurasia, causing devastating population loss and economic disruption. It was known as the Black Death in Europe after around 1350 C.E.

Buddha (BOO-duh) The "enlightened one," the term applied to Siddhartha Gautama after his discoveries that would form the foundation of Buddhism.

Buddhism (BOO-diz'm) Religion, based on Four Noble Truths, associated with Siddhartha Gautama (563–483 B.C.E.), or the Buddha; its adherents desired to eliminate all distracting passion and reach nirvana.

Buenos Aires (BWE-naws AHY-res) Capital and largest city in Argentina.

Bunraku (boon-RAH-koo) A form of traditional Japanese puppet theater.

Bush Doctrine of Deterrence U.S. policy after 9/11 that preemptively attacks any supposed terrorist threat.

Bushido (BOH-shee-DOH) The "way of the warrior," the code of conduct of the Japanese samurai that was based on loyalty and honor.

Byzantine empire (BIHZ-uhn-teen) Long-lasting empire centered at Constantinople; it grew out of the end of the Roman empire, carried the legacy of Roman greatness, and was the only classical society to survive into the early modern age; it reached its early peak during the reign of Justinian (483–565).

Cacao Tropical South American tree that bears fleshy pods with many seeds that are used to make chocolate.

Caesaropapism Concept relating to the mixing of political and religious authority, as with the Roman emperors, that was central to the church versus state controversy in medieval Europe.

Cahokia (kuh-HOH-kee-uh) Large structure in modern Illinois that was constructed by the mound-building peoples; it was the third largest structure in the Americas before the arrival of the Europeans.

Caliph (KAH-leef) "deputy," Islamic leader after the death of Muhammad.

Calpulli (kal-po-lee) An organizational unit and geographical area of the Aztec capital Tenochtitlan.

Calvinists The Protestant religious group that professed faith in the doctrines of John Calvin (1509–1564), which emphasized predestination and salvation by grace alone.

Cambyses (kam-BIE-sees) Son of the Persian leader Cyrus the Great.

Canadian Pacific Railroad Transcontinental rail system that linked eastern and western Canada in the late nineteenth century.

Candomblé (kan-duhm-BLEH) African-oriented religion practiced mainly in Brazil.

Capet (KAHP-ay) Surname of the founder of the French dynasty by the same name.

Capetian (cah-PEE-shuhn) Early French dynasty that started with Hugh Capet.

Cape Town The first European city in South Africa, founded in 1652 as a supply station for the Dutch East Indies Company.

Capitalism An economic system with origins in early modern Europe in which private parties make their goods and services available on a free market.

Capitulation Highly unfavorable trading agreements that the Ottoman Turks signed with the Europeans in the nineteenth century that symbolized the decline of the Ottomans.

Caporetto (kap-uh-RET-oh) 1917 Battle of World War I in which the Italians were defeated by a combined Austro-German force.

Carolingian (kar-uh-LIHN-jee-uhn) Germanic dynasty that was named after its most famous member, Charlemagne.

Carolingian empire The realm of the Franks under the Carolingian dynasty in western and central Europe during the ninth century.

Cartels A combination of industrial or commercial enterprises designed to limit competition and to fix prices.

Carthage (KAHR-thihj) Northern African kingdom, main rival to early Roman expansion, that was defeated by Rome in the Punic Wars.

Caste system A social class system with distinctions that are transferred through generations or through occupation.

Restrictions are placed on marriage, occupation, handling of food, and other matters, according to caste. Caste usually refers to the social system of India.

Castro, Fidel (1927–) Socialist leader who staged a coup d'etat in Cuba in 1959 and established a Marxist dictatorship there.

Çatal Hüyük (chat-l-hoo-yook) Important Neolithic settlement in Anatolia (7250–6150 B.C.E.).

Cathars Medieval heretics, also known as the Albigensians, who considered the material world evil; their followers renounced wealth and marriage and promoted an ascetic existence.

Cathedral schools Schools run by cathedral clergy in Europe during the medieval period.

Catholic Reformation Sixteenth-century Catholic attempt to cure internal ills and confront Protestantism; it was inspired by the reforms of the Council of Trent and the actions of the Jesuits.

Catherine the Great (1729–1796) Empress of Russia from 1762 until 1796, who greatly increased the size of the Russian empire.

Caucasus (KAW-kuh-suhs) Mountain range between the Black and Caspian seas.

Caudillos (kahw-DEE-yohs) Latin American term for nineteenth-century local military leaders.

Central Powers World War I term for the alliance of Germany, Austria-Hungary, and the Ottoman empire.

Ceuta (SYOO-tuh) An autonomous Spanish city situated on the north African side of the Straits of Gibraltar.

Chagatai khanate Area in central Asia ruled initially by Chinggis Khan's second son, and then by the descendants of Chinggis Khan's first son, Ogodei. Mostly inhabited by nomadic Turkic peoples, the region fell to Timur in the mid-fourteenth century.

Chaghatai (chah-guh-TAHY) One of the sons of Chinggis Khan.

Chalcedon (kal-SED-n) An ancient city in northwest Asia Minor on the Bosphorus, opposite Byzantium.

Chaldiran (chahld-ih-rahn) Site of a battle between the Safavids and Ottomans in 1514, where the Safavids were badly defeated.

Chamorro (chuh-MAWR-oh) Indigenous peoples of the Mariana Islands.

Chan Buddhism (CHAHN BOO-diz'm) Most popular branch of Buddhism in China, with an emphasis on intuition and sudden flashes of insight instead of textual study.

Chanchan (chahn-chahn) Capital of the pre-Incan, South American Chimu society that supported a large population of fifty thousand.

Chandragupta Maurya (chuhn-dra-GOOP-tah MORE-yuh) Founder of the Mauryan dynasty in India and the first emperor (r. 321–297 B.C.E.) to unify most of India under one realm.

Chang'an (chahng-ahn) Ancient capital in China during the Han, Sui, and Tang dynasties.

Chariot A two-wheeled, horse-drawn battle vehicle used in ancient times.

Charlemagne (SHAHR-leh-mane) King of the Franks and the Holy Roman Emperor.

Charvaka (CHAHR-vah-kuh) Indian philosophy based on philosophical skepticism.

Châtelet, Émilie du (1706–1759) French mathematician and physicist during the Enlightenment. Translated and commented on Isaac Newton's *Principia Mathematica* with such mastery that it is still used today. Lover of Voltaire.

Chauvinism (SHOH-vuh-niz-uhm) Prejudiced belief in the superiority of one's own kind, particularly with respect to nation or biological sex.

Chavín cult Mysterious but very popular South American religion (1000–300 B.C.E.).

Chichén Itzá Ancient Mayan city in Mexico's central Yucatan, founded in the early sixth century and abandoned in the twelfth century.

Child labor The full-time employment of children, often in demanding physical jobs.

Chimu Pre-Incan South American society that fell to the Incas in the fifteenth century.

Chinampa system Style of agriculture used by Mexica (Aztecs) in which fertile muck from lake bottoms was dredged and built up into small plots.

Chinese Communist Party Political party founded in 1921 by Mao Zedong and others, which eventually took power in China in 1949 after a long struggle with the Guomindang party.

Chinggis Khan (CHIHN-gihs kahn) Conqueror of much of Eurasia in the thirteenth century, from China in the east to the Abbasid empire in the west.

Chivalry European medieval concept, a code of conduct for the knights based on loyalty and honor.

Chola kingdom Southern Indian Hindu kingdom (850–1267), a tightly centralized state that dominated sea trade.

Christianity Religious doctrine that emerged in southeast Asia in the first century C.E. and then spread through Europe, north Africa, parts of Asia, and eventually to the Americas. Central to the religion is the belief that Jesus was the son of God and sacrificed himself on behalf of humankind.

Chucuito (choo-CWE-toh) Pre-Incan South American society that rose in the twelfth century and fell to the Incas in the fifteenth century.

Churchill, Winston (1874–1965) British politician and statesman most famous for his leadership role in fighting the Axis powers in World War II.

Cicero (SIHS-ser-oh) Roman senator and bitter enemy of Marc Antony.

City-state Urban areas that controlled surrounding agricultural regions and that

were often loosely connected in a broader political structure with other city-states.

Civil disobedience movement Refusal to obey civil laws in an effort to induce governmental change, usually by using nonviolent or passive resistance.

Clemenceau, Georges (klem-uhn-SOH, jawrj) French statesman who played a key role in negotiating the Treaty of Versailles.

Coen, Jan Pieterszoon (KOH-uhn, yahn PEE-tuhr-sohn) Governor-general of the Dutch East Indies in the sixteenth century.

Cohong Specially licensed Chinese firms that were under strict government regulation.

Cold war Strategic struggle that developed after World War II between the United States and the USSR.

Collectivization Process beginning in the late 1920s by which Stalin forced the Russian peasants off their own land and onto huge collective farms run by the state; millions died in the process.

Colombo, Cristoforo (kuh-LUHM-boh, crihs-toh-for-oh) Italian navigator who discovered the Caribbean islands for Europeans while trying to find a western route to China.

Colossal heads Large stone sculptures of human heads, created by the Olmecs in what is now modern Mexico between approximately 1200–900 B.C.E.

Columbian exchange The trans-Atlantic exchange of plants, animals, and diseases that followed European contact with the Americas at the end of the fifteenth century.

Columbus, Christopher (1451–1506) Italian navigator in the service of Spain who landed in the Americas in 1492 while searching for a maritime route to China.

COMECON The Council for Mutual Economic Assistance, which offered increased trade within the Soviet Union and eastern Europe; it was the Soviet alternative to the United States's Marshall Plan.

Communalism A term, usually associated with India, that placed an emphasis on religious rather than national identity.

Communism Philosophy and movement that began in the middle of the nineteenth century with the work of Karl Marx; it has the same general goals as socialism, but it includes the belief that violent revolution is necessary to destroy the bourgeois world and institute a new world run by and for the proletariat.

Communist Manifesto A political pamphlet written by Karl Marx and Friedrich Engels in 1848, which described the history of the working-class movement and predicted the collapse of capitalism.

Confucianism (kuhn-FEW-shuhn-iz'm) Philosophy, based on the teachings of the Chinese philosopher Kong Fuzi (551–479 B.C.E.), or Confucius, that emphasizes order, the role of the gentleman, obligation to society, and reciprocity.

Congress of Vienna Gathering of European diplomats in Vienna, Austria, from October 1814 to June 1815. The representatives of the "great powers" that defeated Napoleon—Britain, Austria, Prussia, and Russia—dominated the proceedings, which aimed to restore the prerevolutionary political and social order.

Conquistadores (kohn-kees-tah-DOH-rays) Spanish adventurers like Cortés and Pizarro who conquered Central and South America in the sixteenth century.

Conservatism A political philosophy that emphasizes gradual change, continuity of traditions, and established authority. Although the word has taken on many shades of meaning, nineteenth-century conservatives generally opposed democracy and supported traditional institutions such as the church, monarchy, and nobility.

Constantine (KAHN-stuhn-teen) Emperor of Rome who made Christianity the official religion of the Roman empire in 324.

Constantinople Former capital of the Byzantine empire, founded in 330 C.E. It was captured by the Ottomans in 1453 and served as the Ottoman capital. Now known as Istanbul in modern Turkey.

Constitutionalism Movement in England in the seventeenth century that placed power in Parliament's hands as part of a constitutional monarchy and that increasingly limited the power of the monarch; the movement was highlighted by the English Civil War and the Glorious Revolution.

Containment U.S. policy to block further expansion of Soviet power.

Continental Congress The assembly of delegates from the rebellious American colonies, which sat during and after the American Revolution. Issued the Declaration of Independence in 1776 and the Articles of Confederation in 1777.

Cook, Captain James (1728–1729) English navigator who explored the Pacific Ocean and claimed the eastern portion of Australia for the British government.

Copernicus, Nicolaus (1473–1543) Polish astronomer who devised a workable model of the solar system with the sun at its center.

Coromandel (kawr-uh-MAN-dul) Southeastern coast of India.

Corporation A concept that reached mature form in 1860s in England and France; it entailed private business owned by thousands of individual and institutional investors who financed the business through the purchase of stocks.

Corpus iuris civilis (KOR-poos EW-rees sih-VEE-lees) *Body of the Civil Law,* the Byzantine emperor Justinian's attempt to codify all Roman law.

Cortés, Hernán (kawr-TEZ, er-NAHN) Spanish conquistador who defeated the Aztecs and conquered Mexico.

Cossacks (KAW-sacks) Russian "free men" recruited by Ivan III to settle conquered land in return for their freedom; the strategy eventually played a key role in Russian expansion eastward.

Council of Chalcedon The fourth of seven ecumenical councils, held in 451 C.E., that affirmed the orthodox Catholic doctrine that Christ consisted of two natures—one human and one divine—in the same person.

Council of Nicaea The first of seven ecumenical councils, held in 325 C.E., that produced the wording for the Nicene Creed and condemned Arianism as a Christian heresy.

Creole language A stable natural language that develops from two or more parent languages.

Criollos (kree-OH-lohs) The term for Spaniards born in the Americas during the Spanish colonial period.

Croesus (CREE-suhs) The last king of Lydia who died in 546 B.C.E.

Cro-Magnon (CROH MAHG-nohn) *Homo sapiens sapiens,* who appeared forty thousand years ago during the Paleolithic age and were the first human beings of the modern type.

Cross-staff Device that sailors used to determine latitude by measuring the angle of the sun or pole star above the horizon.

Crusades A series of military expeditions by Christian powers between the eleventh and thirteenth centuries to conquer the Holy Land in Palestine from Muslim powers.

Ctesiphon (TES-uh-phon) Ancient city of central Iraq on the Tigris River southeast of Baghdad.

Cuban missile crisis International crisis in October 1962 that developed when the United States government discovered that the Soviet Union had placed nuclear missiles on the island of Cuba.

Cubism Early twentieth-century artistic style that made use of abstract geometric shapes.

Cult of Osiris Cult associated with the ancient Egyptian god Osiris, god of the underworld and of the dead and husband of Isis, goddess of fertility.

Cult of Isis Cult associated with the ancient Egyptian goddess Isis, goddess of fertility and wife of Osiris, god of the underworld.

Cuneiform Written language of the Sumerians, probably the first written script in the world.

Cuzco (KOOS-koh) A town in the Andes in southern Peru; former capital of the Inca empire.

Cyrillic alphabet Alphabet developed in the ninth century, derived from the Greek alphabet and used to write Slavic languages.

Cyrus (SIGH-ruhs) King of Persia and founder of the Persian empire.

Dahomey (dah-HO-meh) Kingdom in west Africa that flourished in the eighteenth and nineteenth centuries in the area that is modern southern Benin.

Dahomey Oyo (dah-HO-meh OH-yoh) Precolonial west African empire in what is now modern Nigeria.

Daimyo (DEYEM-yoh) Powerful territorial lords in early modern Japan.

Dao Key element in Chinese philosophy that means the "way of nature" or the "way of the cosmos."

Daodejing (DOW-DAY-JIHNG) Book that is the fundamental work of Daoism.

Daoism (dow-ism) Chinese philosophical system advocating a simple, honest life and following the natural patterns of the universe.

Dar al-Islam The "house of Islam," a term for the Islamic world.

Darius I (c. 550–486 B.C.E.) King of Persia from 521–486 B.C.E., who expanded the Persian empire and developed an efficient administrative system.

D-Day Date of the Allied landing in Normandy, France on June 6, 1944, during World War II.

Declaration of Independence Drafted by Thomas Jefferson in 1776; the document expressed the ideas of John Locke and the Enlightenment, represented the idealism of the American rebels, and influenced other revolutions.

Declaration of the Rights of Man and Citizen Document from the French Revolution (1789) that was influenced by the American Declaration of Independence and in turn influenced other revolutionary movements.

Decolonization Process by which former colonies achieved their independence, as with the newly emerging African nations in the 1950s and 1960s.

Degas, Edgar (day-GAH, ED-gahr) Nineteenth- and early twentieth-century French impressionist painter.

Deism (DEE-iz'm) An Enlightenment view that accepted the existence of a god but denied the supernatural aspects of Christianity; in deism, the universe was an orderly realm maintained by rational and natural laws.

Delian League Alliance of ancient Greek city-states led by Athens, formed in c. 478 B.C.E. for mutual protection against the Persians.

Demographic transition Adjustments in the rate of births and deaths that usually accompany industrialization. The demographic transition is often triggered by improvements in health and nutrition, which result in lower death rates. Birthrates remain high initially, but after a period of rapid population growth, birthrates fall in response to the lower death rates. Eventually, in highly industrialized societies, birthrates and death rates stabilize at low levels.

Descamisados "Shirtless ones," Argentine poor who supported Juan and Eva Perón.

De-Stalinization The policy of ending Stalin's reign of terror after his death in 1953.

Détente A reduction in cold war tension between the United States and the Soviet Union from 1969 to 1973.

Devshirme Ottoman requirement that the Christians in the Balkans provide young boys to be slaves of the sultan.

Dharma (DHUHR-muh) Hindu concept of obedience to religious and moral laws and order.

Dhimmi (DIHM-mee) Islamic concept of a protected people that was symbolic of Islamic toleration during the Mughal and Ottoman empires.

Dhow Indian, Persian, and Arab ships, one hundred to four hundred tons, that sailed and traded throughout the Indian Ocean basin.

Dias, Bartolomeu (dee-as, bahr-tol-uh-MEY-oh) The first European explorer (Portuguese) to sail around the southern tip of Africa.

Diaspora (dahy-AS-per-uh) The dispersion of peoples outside their homeland.

Diaz, Porfirio (DEE-ahs, pawr-FEER-eeo) Mexican politician who became president of Mexico from 1876 to 1880 and from 1884 to 1911.

Diocletian (dah-yuh-KLEE-shuhn) Roman emperor who divided the empire into two parts, east and west, in 286 C.E.

Dionysus Greek god of wine, also known as Bacchus; Greek plays were performed in his honor.

Direct rule System of government in which the central government controls provinces or colonies.

Diula An ethnic group in west Africa.

Dollar diplomacy The use of a country's financial power to ensure favorable international relations, commonly used in reference to U.S.–Latin American relations in the early twentieth century.

Domestic containment Concern that Communist spies had infiltrated the United States.

Domino theory Theory that if one country becomes Communist, neighboring countries will also "collapse" to communism the way dominoes fall.

Doña Beatriz (1684–1786) Congolese prophet and leader of a Christian movement called Antonianism.

Doña Marina (c. 1496 or 1505–1529) Nahua woman from what is now modern Mexico who served as intermediary and interpreter for Hernan Cortes, thereby facilitating the Spanish conquest of Mexico.

Dreadnoughts A class of British battleships whose heavy armaments made all other battleships obsolete overnight.

Duma Russian parliament, established after the Revolution of 1905.

Dutch learning European knowledge that reached Tokugawa Japan.

East India Company British joint-stock company that grew to be a state within a state in India; it possessed its own armed forces.

Eastern Orthodox Church An eastern branch of Christianity that evolved after the division of the Roman empire and the subsequent development of the Byzantine empire in the east and the medieval European society in the west. The Eastern Orthodox Church acknowledged what became known as the Byzantine rite and recognized the primacy of the patriarch of Constantinople.

Edict of Milan Edict in 313 C.E. by Emperor Constantine in the western Roman empire and Licinius Augustus in the eastern Roman empire that granted religious freedom throughout the Roman empire.

Egypt A country in northeast Africa with a long and rich history.

Eight-legged essay Eight-part essays that an aspiring Chinese civil servant had to compose, mainly based on a knowledge of Confucius and the Zhou classics.

Einsatzgruppen (ain-zats-groopen) Paramilitary group run by the German SS in World War II, whose main task was to annihilate Jews, Gypsies, and Slavs as the German army moved east, invading the Soviet Union.

Einstein, Albert (1879–1955) Theoretical physicist who formulated the general theory of relativity. One of the most influential scientists of all time.

Emancipation Proclamation Announcement made by American president Abraham Lincoln on September 22, 1862, emancipating all slaves in states still rebelling against the federal republic.

Encomienda (ehn-koh-MYEN-dah) System that gave the Spanish settlers (*encomenderos*) the right to compel the indigenous peoples of the Americas to work in the mines or fields.

Engels, Friedrich (1820–1895) German socialist who co-wrote *The Communist Manifesto* with Karl Marx in 1848.

Engenho (ehn-GEN-yo) Portuguese term for a sugar mill and its facilities.

Enlightenment Eighteenth-century philosophical movement that began in France; its emphasis was on the preeminence of reason rather than faith or tradition; it spread concepts from the scientific revolution.

Epicureans (ehp-ih-KYOOR-eeuhns) Hellenistic philosophers who taught that pleasure—as in quiet satisfaction—was the greatest good.

Epidemic disease Any infectious disease that spreads rapidly to many people.

Equal-field system Chinese system during the Han dynasty in which the goal was to ensure an equitable distribution of land.

Equiano, Olaudah (ay-kwee-AHN-oh, oh-LAU-duh) An ex-slave who became deeply involved in the fight against slavery and the slave trade.

Erasmus, Desiderius (ih-raz-muhs, des-i-DEER-ee-uhs) Dutch humanist and leading Renaissance scholar in northern Europe.

Essenes Jewish sect that looked for the arrival of a savior; they were similar in some of their core beliefs to the early Christians.

Estado novo Name of the authoritarian Portuguese government installed after a coup d'etat in 1933; also the name of the authoritarian Brazilian government that lasted from 1937 to 1945, which was modeled on the Portuguese.

Estates General Political assembly of the three orders of estates in France consisting of the clergy, the nobility, and the commoners. The last meeting was in 1789, which triggered the French revolution.

Etruscans (ih-TRUHS-kuhns) Northern Italian society that initially dominated the Romans; the Etruscans helped convey Greek concepts to the expanding Romans.

Eucharist Christian ceremony commemorating the Last Supper.

Eunuch (YOO-nuhk) A castrated man.

European Community (EC) Organization of European states established in 1957; it was originally called the European Economic Community and was renamed the EC in 1967; it promoted economic growth and integration as the basis for a politically united Europe.

European Union Established by the Maastricht Treaty in 1993, a supranational organization for even greater European economic and political integration.

Factory system System of manufacturing in which goods were produced under one roof in an organized, systematic manner.

Fasci Italiani di Combattimento "Italian League of Combat." League created in 1919 by Benito Mussolini, which in 1921 became the national Italian Fascist party.

Fascism Political ideology and mass movement that was prominent in many parts of Europe between 1919 and 1945; it sought to regenerate the social, political, and cultural life of societies, especially in contrast to liberal democracy and socialism; fascism began with Mussolini in Italy, and it reached its peak with Hitler in Germany.

Fatehpur Sikri (fah-teh-poor SIH-kree) City built by the Mughal emperor Akbar to serve as the Mughal capital.

February Revolution The first phase of the Russian Revolution, when Czar Nicholas II abdicated and a provisional government took power in March 1917.

Feminist movement The movement of women in postwar industrialized nations to gain political and economic equality.

Fernando of Aragon (fer-NAWN-doh of ah-ruh-GAWN) Husband of Isabel of Castille, who jointly funded Cristoforo Colombo's expedition to search for a western trade route to China.

Ferreira, Christovão (feh-RAY-rah, chris-STOH-voh) Portuguese Jesuit who renounced his faith in Japan in 1632.

Feudalism Social system that developed in medieval Europe from the eighth century, in which nobility held lands from the Crown in exchange for military service. Under this system, peasants were obliged to live on the land of their nobles and provide both homage and a share of their agricultural produce for the upkeep of the nobles' households.

Fief (FEEF) A grant of land from a lord to a vassal.

Filial piety Idea that one is obliged to respect one's parents and ancestors, most commonly associated with Confucianism.

Final solution The Nazi policy of systematically exterminating all the Jews in Europe.

First Five-Year Plan Josef Stalin's plan for the years 1928–1932, which spelled out the economic goals for the Soviet Union.

Five Pillars of Islam The foundation of Islam; (1) profession of faith, (2) prayer, (3) fasting during Ramadan, (4) alms, and (5) pilgrimage, or hajj.

Five-year plans First implemented by Stalin in the Soviet Union in 1928; five-year plans were a staple of communist regimes in which every aspect of production was determined in advance for a five-year period; five-year plans were the opposite of the free market concept.

Floating worlds The urban, pleasure-seeking aspects of Japan in the Edo period (1600–1867).

Flying shuttle Machine invented by John Kay in 1733 that dramatically increased the speed of weaving threads.

Foot binding Custom of wrapping women's feet to make them smaller, practiced in China between the tenth and early twentieth centuries.

Forbidden City The walled imperial palaces of the Ming and Qing emperors in Beijing, China, which was formerly off limits to all commoners.

Ford, Henry (1863–1947) American automobile manufacturer who pioneered mass production.

Formal imperialism The direct conquest or annexation of lands by one power over another.

Former Han Imperial dynasty that ruled China for most of the period from 206 B.C.E. to 220 C.E.

Four Noble Truths The foundation of Buddhist thought: (1) life is pain, (2) pain is caused by desire, (3) elimination of desire will bring an end to pain, (4) living a life based on the Noble Eightfold Path will eliminate desire.

Fourteen Points The principles articulated by President Woodrow Wilson in 1918 as war aims of the United States.

Francis Ferdinand (1863–1914) Archduke of Austria and heir to Francis Joseph I who was assassinated in Sarajevo in 1914, triggering the outbreak of World War I.

Franks Group of Germanic tribes of the Rhine region in the early centuries of the Common Era.

Free trade Economic doctrine, first argued by Adam Smith in the late eighteenth century, of unrestricted trade between nations without protective tariffs or duties. Smith and his followers argue that, through free trade and competition, the forces of supply and demand will ensure that the best product is available at the best price. Free trade has gained wide acceptance since World War II.

French revolution The revolution that began in 1789 with the overthrow of the Bourbon monarchy in France and ended with Napoleon's seizure of power from the Directory in 1799.

Freud, Sigmund (froid, SIG-muhnd) Nineteenth- and early twentieth-century Austrian neurologist who developed psychoanalysis.

Front de Libération Nationale (FLN) The Algerian organization that fought a bloody guerilla war for freedom against France.

Fulani (foo-LAH-nee) Sub-Saharan African people who, beginning in the seventeenth century, began a series of wars designed to impose their own strict interpretation of Islam.

Funan An early complex society in what is now southern Vietnam between the first and sixth centuries C.E.

Fur trade Trade in animal skins and pelts, here referring to the trade carried on in the North American continent from the seventeenth to nineteenth centuries.

Galileo Galilei (1564–1642) Italian astronomer and physicist who publicly supported Nicolaus Copernicus's heliocentric theory and as a result was punished and placed under house arrest by the Catholic church.

Gandhi, Mohandas Karamchand (GAHN-dee, moh-huhn-DAHS kuhr-uhm-CHUND) Political and spiritual leader of the Indian independence movement, assassinated by a Hindu extremist in 1948.

Gao (gou) City that served as capital of the Mali empire in Africa.

Garibaldi, Giuseppe (gar-uh-BAWL-dee, juh-SEP-eh) Nineteenth-century Italian nationalist who led the Italian unification movement.

Garvey, Marcus (1887–1940) Jamaican-born black nationalist active in the United States. Advocated black separatism, the "back to Africa" movement, and black self-help.

Gathas (GATH-uhs) Zoroastrian works believed to be compositions by Zarathustra.

GATT General Agreement on Tariffs and Trade, which promoted unrestricted free trade.

Gauchos (GAHW-chohs) Argentine cowboys, highly romantic figures.

Gaugamela (GAW-guh-mee-luh) Site, in modern Iraq, of Alexander the Great's final victory over Darius III in 331 B.C.E.

Gaunahani (gwah-nah-nee) The name indigenous peoples called the island Columbus called San Salvador in the Caribbean.

Geechee (GEE-chee) See Gullah.

General Agreement on Tariffs and Trade (GATT) Free trade agreement first signed in 1947; by 1994 it had grown to 123 members and formed the World Trade Organization (WTO).

Gens de couleur A French term meaning "people of color," most commonly in reference to free people of color in the French West Indies.

German unification The formal unification of the various German states into a single nation-state that occurred in January 1871. Can also refer to the reunification of East and West Germany in 1990, after having been divided since 1945.

Ghana (GAH-nuh) Eighth- through eleventh-century empire in West Africa that grew wealthy from the trans-Saharan trade.

Ghazi (GAH-zee) Islamic religious warrior.

Ghaznavids Turkish tribe under Mahmud of Ghazni who moved into northern India in the eleventh century and began a period of greater Islamic influence in India.

Gilgamesh Legendary king of the Mesopotamian city-state of Uruk (ca. 3000 B.C.E.), subject of the *Epic of Gilgamesh,* world's oldest complete epic literary masterpiece.

Glasnost (GLAHS-nohst) Russian term meaning "openness" introduced by Mikhail Gorbachev in 1985 to describe the process of opening Soviet society to dissidents and public criticism.

Global warming The emission of greenhouse gases, which prevents solar heat from escaping the earth's atmosphere and leads to the gradual heating of the earth's environment.

Globalization The breaking down of traditional boundaries in the face of increasingly global financial and cultural trends.

Golden Horde Mongol tribe that controlled Russia from the thirteenth to the fifteenth centuries.

Good Neighbor Policy Diplomatic and foreign policy of the United States government under Franklin D. Roosevelt that encouraged good relations and mutual defense among the nations of the Americas.

Gorbachev, Mikhail Leader of the USSR in the 1980s, responsible for the opening up of the USSR in social and economic policy.

Gouges, Olympe de (gouj, oh-LIMP de) French playwright and journalist who advocated that women and men should share equal rights during the French Revolution.

Government of India Act Series of sixteen acts, beginning in 1919 and ending in 1935, passed by the British Parliament to allow greater Indian participation in the government of India. The final act in 1935 gave substantial autonomy to Indian provinces.

Gran Colombia Former South American republic formed in 1819 during the war for independence against Spain. Included the modern countries of Venezuela, Ecuador, Colombia, and Panama, and had as its first president Simón Bolívar. Dissolved in 1830 when Venezuela and Ecuador seceded.

Grand Canal Inland waterway in China more than 1,000 miles long, built between the fifth century B.C.E. and the fourteenth century C.E. to link the Yellow and Yangzi Rivers.

Great Depression The worldwide economic crisis that began in 1929 with the stock market crash in the United States and lasted through much of the 1930s.

Great Game Nineteenth-century competition between Great Britain and Russia for the control of central Asia.

Great Leap Forward The vision by Mao that planned how China could overtake the industrial production of more developed nations.

Great Proletarian Cultural Revolution Attempt by Mao to mobilize the Chinese and reignite revolutionary spirit.

Great Purge A series of political repressions and murders orchestrated by the Soviet Union's Joseph Stalin between 1936–1938, in which more than a million people were killed.

Great Wall A wall that extends 1,500 miles across northern China as a defense against the Mongols. First built in the third century B.C.E. and substantially rebuilt in the fifteenth century.

Great Zimbabwe Large sub-Saharan African kingdom in the fifteenth century.

Greater East Asia Co-Prosperity Sphere Japanese plan for consolidating Asia under their control during World War II.

Greenpeace An environmental organization founded in 1970 and dedicated to the preservation of earth's natural resources.

Gregory the Wonderworker (213–270 C.E.) Saint Gregory of Neocaesarea, who was a Christian bishop of the third century C.E.

Griot (GREE-oh) A member of a class of storytellers in west Africa who maintain a tradition of oral history.

Guadalupe Hidalgo (gwahd-i-LOOP hee-DAHL-goh) Peace treaty that ended the Mexican-American War in 1848.

Guanahani The name the indigenous people had given to the island Columbus called San Salvador when he landed there in 1492.

Guangzhou (gwahng-joh) Formerly Canton, a city in south China situated near the South China Sea.

Guangxu (wang-soo) Tenth Qing emperor who initiated the Hundred Days' Reform in 1898, but was removed from power by the Empress Dowager Cixi.

Guarani (gwahr-uh-NEE) Ethnic group of indigenous people from modern Paraguay and Bolivia, as well as their language.

Guild Organizations whose membership is based on occupation. They often regulate the production and sale of goods and serve as mutual aid societies for their members. They were particularly powerful in medieval European cities.

Gullah (GUHL-uh) Also known as Geechee, the Gullah are African Americans who live in the low country of South Carolina and Georgia. They have preserved much of their syncretic African culture from the days of slavery, including the creole Gullah language.

Gunpowder An explosive that consists of a powdered mixture of saltpeter, sulfur, and charcoal.

Guomindang (GWOH-mihn-dahng) Chinese nationalist party founded by Sun Yat-sen (1866–1925) and later led by Jiang Jieshi; it has been centered in Taiwan since the end of the Chinese civil war.

Gupta dynasty (GOOP-tah) Indian dynasty (320–550 C.E.) that briefly reunited India after the collapse of the earlier Mauryan dynasty.

HAART The active antiretroviral therapy that treats AIDS.

Habsburgs Dynasty that ruled Austria from 1298–1918.

Hacienda (ah-SYEN-dah) Large Latin American estates.

Hadith A collection of traditions containing the sayings of Muhammad.

Hagia Sophia (HAH-yah soh-FEE-uh) Greek orthodox temple constructed by the Byzantine emperor Justinian and later converted into a mosque.

Haiti A country in the Caribbean that occupies the western portion of the island of Hispaniola.

Haitian revolution A slave revolt in the French colonial possession of St. Domingue (modern Haiti). Lasted from 1791–1804, and resulted in the first successful slave revolt in the Americas.

Hajj (HAHJ) Pilgrimage to Mecca.

Hammurabi's Code (hahm-uh-RAH-beez cohd) Sophisticated law code associated with the Babylonian king Hammurabi (r. 1792–1750 B.C.E.).

Han dynasty Dynasty that ruled China for most of the period between 206 B.C.E. and 220 C.E.

Han Feizi (hahn fay-zi) Chinese philosopher who developed the doctrine of Legalism.

Han Wudi (hahn woo-dee) Seventh emperor of the Han dynasty who developed a strong, centralized, Confucian state.

Hanseatic League (han-see-AT-ik) A commercial and defensive confederation of free cities in northern Germany and surrounding areas in the thirteenth and fourteenth centuries.

Harappan (huh-RUHP-puhn) Early brilliant Indian society centered around Harappa and Mohenjo-Daro.

Harijans (har-i-jahns) Literally meaning the "children of God," very low-status Indian people who are outside the caste system.

Harsha Indian ruler from 606–647 C.E. who forged most of northern India into an empire, and became a devout Buddhist.

Harun al-Rashid (c. 763–809) The fifth and most famous Arab Abbasid caliph.

Hatshepsut (hat-SHEP-soot) Queen of Egypt (1505 B.C.E.) who shared her throne with her nephew Tuthmosis III.

Hebrews Semitic-speaking nomadic tribe influential for monotheistic belief in Yahweh.

Heian Japan (HAY-ahn) Japanese period (794–1185), a brilliant cultural era notable for the world's first novel, Murasaki Shikibu's *The Tale of Genji*.

Heisenberg, Werner (HAHY-zuyn-burg, VER-nuhr) Twentieth-century German theoretical physicist responsible for the development of uncertainty theory.

Hellenic Era First phase in Greek history (ca. 2000–328 B.C.E.), which was highlighted by the Golden Age of Athens in the fifth century B.C.E.

Hellenistic Era Second phase in Greek history (328–146 B.C.E.), from the conquest of Greece by Philip of Macedon until Greece's fall to the Romans; this era was a more cosmopolitan age facilitated by the conquests of Alexander the Great.

Herzl, Theodore (HER-tsuhll, TEY-aw-dohr) Hungarian Jewish journalist and author of the book *Judenstaat*, he is considered by many to be the father of modern Zionism.

Hidalgo, Miguel de (hee-DHAHL-goh, mee-GEL de) Priest and leader of the Mexican War of Independence in 1810–1821.

Hieratic (hahy-uh-RAT-tik) A cursive form of Egyptian hieroglyphics.

Hieroglyphics (heye-ruh-GLIPH-iks) Ancient Egyptian written language.

Hijra (HIHJ-ruh) The migration of Muhammed and his followers to the city of Medina in 622 C.E.

Hinayana Buddhism (HEE-nah-yah-nuh) Branch of Buddhism known as the "lesser vehicle," also known as Theravada Buddhism; its beliefs include a strict, individual path to enlightenment, and it is popular in south and southeast Asia.

Hinduism Main religion of India, a combination of Dravidian and Aryan concepts; Hinduism's goal is to reach spiritual purity and union with the great world spirit; its important concepts include dharma, karma, and samsara.

Hippodrome An arena for equestrian and other spectacles in ancient Greece or Rome.

Hiroshima and Nagasaki The two Japanese cities that became the target of the first atomic bombs, dropped by United States forces on August 6 and 9, 1945.

Hitler, Adolf (1889–1945) German Nazi dictator who came to power during the Great Depression and precipitated the Second World War in Europe.

Hittites An ancient people who lived in Anatolia and northern Syria from about 2000–1200 B.C.E.

Ho Chi Minh Leader of Vietnam during revolution.

Holocaust German attempt in World War II to exterminate the Jews of Europe.

Holy Roman Empire A confederation of states mostly in central and western Europe. It began in 962 C.E. with the crowning of Otto I by the pope.

Home front Term made popular in World War I and World War II for the civilian "front" that was symbolic of the greater demands of total war.

Hominid (HAW-mih-nihd) A creature belonging to the family Hominidae, which includes human and humanlike species.

Homo erectus (HOH-moh ee-REHK-tuhs) "Upright-walking human," which existed from 1.5 million to two hundred thousand years ago; *Homo erectus* used cleavers and hand axes and learned how to control fire.

Homo sapiens (HOH-moh SAY-pyans) "Consciously thinking human," which first appeared around two hundred fifty thousand years ago and used sophisticated tools.

Homo sapiens sapiens (HOH-moh SAY-pyans SAY-pyans) First human being of the modern type, which appeared roughly one hundred thousand years ago; Cro-Magnon falls into this category.

Hong Xiuquan (hoong shee-OH-chew-an) The leader of the nineteenth-century Taiping Rebellion.

Hongwu (hawng-woo) The first Ming emperor, who overthrew the Yuan dynasty in 1368.

Huitzilopochtli (we-tsee-loh-POCK-tlee) Sun god and patron deity of the Aztecs.

Hülegü (Hoo-LAY-goo) Grandson of Chinggis Khan and leader of the Ilkhan khanate, who was responsible for the destruction of Baghdad.

Humanism Cultural movement during the Renaissance that drew inspiration from the humanities, that is, literature, history, philosophy, and the arts. In contrast to medieval theologians, humanists argued that one could live a moral life and still be actively engaged in the affairs of the world.

Hundred Days of Reform Chinese reforms of 1898 led by Kang Youwei and Liang Qichao in their desire to turn China into a modern industrial power.

Hunting/gathering culture Any culture whose primary means of subsistence is through hunting and gathering from the environment. Humans survived this way for millions of years before the agricultural transition, and some hunting/gathering cultures persisted into the twenty-first century C.E.

Hürrem Sultana (c. 1500–1558) Favorite concubine slave of Süleyman the Magnificent, who became queen of the Ottoman empire. Also known as Roxelana.

Hussein, Saddam President of Iraq before the U.S. operation in 2003.

Hyksos (HICK-sohs) Invaders who seized the Nile delta and helped bring an end to the Egyptian Middle Kingdom.

Ibn Battuta (ih-bun BAH-too-tah) A famous fourteenth-century traveler and historian of Africa and Asia.

Ibn Rushd (IB-uhn RUSHED) A twelfth-century Muslim philosopher, born in Cordoba in modern Spain, whose philosophy influenced European thought.

Iconoclasts (eye-KAHN-oh-klasts) Supporters of the movement, begun by the Byzantine emperor Leo III (r. 717–741), to destroy religious icons because their veneration was considered sinful.

Ife (EE-fehy) Eighth- to tenth-century kingdom in what is now modern Nigeria.

Ilkhanate (EEL-kahn-ate) Mongol state that ruled Persia after abolition of the Abbasid empire in the thirteenth century.

Ilkhan Ghazan (1271–1304) Seventh emperor of the Mongol empire's ilkhanate, which included modern Iran and Iraq. Most famous for converting to Islam in 1295 as he became emperor.

Ilkhans Mongol khanate founded by the Hülegü dynasty, which extended over modern Iran and Iraq.

IMF International Monetary Fund.

Imperialism Term associated with the expansion of European powers and their conquest and colonization of African and Asian societies, mainly from the sixteenth through the nineteenth centuries.

Inca empire Powerful South American empire that would reach its peak in the fifteenth century during the reigns of Pachacuti Inca and Topa Inca.

Indentured labor Labor source in the Americas; wealthy planters would pay the European poor to sell a portion of their working lives, usually seven years, in exchange for passage.

Indian National Congress Indian political party founded in 1885. Began as a reformist party, but by the second decade of the twentieth century supported complete Indian independence from Great Britain.

Indian Removal Act of 1830 Law signed by U.S. president Andrew Jackson that forced the removal and relocation of the Choctaw, Seminole, Creek, Cherokee, and other Indian nations.

Indirect rule A system of government in which one state rules over another while the ruled state retains certain administrative and legal powers.

Indo-Europeans Series of tribes from southern Russia who, over a period of millennia, embarked on a series of migrations from India through western Europe; their greatest legacy was the broad distribution of Indo-European languages throughout Eurasia.

Indra Early Indian god associated with the Aryans; Indra was the king of the gods and was associated with warfare and thunderbolts.

Indus (IN-duhs) A river with its source in Tibet that flows southwest through India to the Bay of Bengal.

Informal imperialism When one state has strong military or fiscal influence over another but does not gain political sovereignty.

Intelligentsia Refers to an educated and literate class in Russia that often advocated social and political reform. In the late nineteenth century the Russian intelligentsia became frustrated when reform efforts failed, and many turned to anarchism and violence. Some members of the intelligentsia supported the Bolshevik rise to power in the revolution of 1917.

Inti (ihn-tee) The Inca sun god.

Investiture (ihn-VEHST-tih-tyoor) The granting of church offices by a lay leader; one aspect of the medieval European church versus state controversy.

Iran-Contra scandal Political scandal over arms for hostages in Iran and funding for Nicaraguan contras.

Iranian revolution Islamist revolution to throw out the U.S.-backed shah in 1979.

Iron curtain Dividing line between the two blocs of Europe, with one supported by the USSR and the other by the United States.

Iroquois (EER-uh-kwah) Eastern American Indian confederation made up of the Mohawk, Oneida, Onondaga, Cayuga, and Seneca tribes.

Isabel of Castile (IHZ-uh-bel of ka-steel) Queen of Castile and Leon and wife of Fernando II of Aragon, who together funded Cristoforo Colombo's expedition to discover a westerly route to China.

Islam Monotheistic religion of the prophet Muhammad (570–632); influenced by Judaism and Christianity, Muhammad was considered the final prophet because the earlier religions had not seen the entire picture; the Quran is the holy book of Islam.

Islamic slave trade Slave trade dominated by Muslim Arabs that brought sub-Saharan Africans across the Sahara desert to the Arab world after the eighth century C.E.

Islamism The reassertion of Islamic values in Muslim politics.

Israel A Jewish state created after World War II.

Israelites Ethnic group claiming descent from Abraham and Isaac.

Istanbul (iss-TAHN-bull) Capital city of the Ottoman Empire, built on the site of the capital city of the Byzantine empire, Constantinople.

Isthmus of Kra (ihs-muhs of krah) A narrow isthmus linking the Malay peninsula to the Asian mainland.

Italian unification The political and social movement that led to the unification of the Italian states in 1870.

Itzcóatl (tsee-ko-atl) The name of the fourth emperor of the Aztecs who ruled from 1427 to 1440.

Jahangir (1569–1627) Mughal emperor of India from 1605–1627. Continued his father Akbar's program of expansion in the Indian subcontinent.

Jainism (JEYEN-iz'm) Indian religion associated with the teacher Vardhamana Mahavira (ca. 540–468 B.C.E.) in which every physical object possessed a soul; Jains believe in complete nonviolence to all living beings.

Janissaries Soldiers in the Ottoman emperor's personal military guard from the fourteenth century to 1826. Individuals were selected from Christian Ottoman territories as boys and converted to Islam.

Jati Indian word for a Hindu subcaste.

Jenne (jehn-neh) City in what is now modern Mali, famous for its role in the trans-Saharan trade and for its mud-brick mosque.

Jesuits Members of the Society of Jesus, a Roman Catholic order of priests founded by St. Ignatius Loyola in 1534 for the purpose of missionary work.

Jesus of Nazareth (c. 4 B.C.E.–c. 30 C.E.) Teacher and prophet born in Bethlehem around whom the basis of Christianity was formed.

Jewish War An anti-Roman uprising in the Roman province of Judea from 66–73 C.E., sparked by abuses by the Roman procurator.

Jiaozhou (jyou-joh) A city in the Shandong province of China.

Jieshi, Jiang (jeh-she, jyahng) Also known as Chiang Kai-shek, Jiang became leader of the Kuomintang party after the death of Sun Yat-sen in 1925. After the communist victory in 1949, Jiang and the Kuomintang retreated to the island of Taiwan.

Jihad Arabic word meaning "struggle." In Islam this word is understood to be one's duty to struggle on behalf of the faith. Although this struggle might be a personal and spiritual effort, it has frequently been a call for holy war against perceived enemies. In recent years, radical Islamists such as al-Qaeda have called for a *jihad* against the United States and other "nonbelievers."

Jinnah, Muhammad Ali (moo-HAM-id ah-lee JIN-uh) Indian statesman and founder of the state of Pakistan.

Jizya (JIHZ-yuh) Tax in Islamic empires that was imposed on non-Muslims.

Joint-stock company Early forerunner of the modern corporation; individuals who invested in a trading or exploring venture could make huge profits while limiting their risk.

Juárez, Benito (WAHR-ez, beh-nee-toh) Important Mexican liberal (1806–1872) who served as president from 1857–1872. He came from a peasant family with Zapotec Indian origins.

Judaism The monotheistic religion of the Jewish people that traces its origins to Abraham (ca. 2000 B.C.E.).

Judenstaat (juh-dehn-STAHT) 1896 book written by Theodore Herzl advocating the creation of a Jewish state.

Julius Caesar (100–44 B.C.E.) Roman general and statesman, conqueror of Gaul. Best known for his role in transforming the Roman republic into the Roman empire.

Junzi (juhn-zee) Confucian idea of the ideal human, who lives according to virtue.

Jurchen (JUHR-chehn) A people who inhabited Manchuria until the seventeenth century.

Justinian (483–565 C.E.) Byzantine emperor from 527–565, known for codifying Roman law in 529.

Ka'ba (KAH-bah) Main shrine in Mecca, goal of Muslims embarking on the hajj.

Kabuki (kah-BOO-kee) Japanese theater in which actors were free to improvise and embellish the words.

Kama Hindu concept of the enjoyment of physical and sexual pleasure.

Kamakura period Period in Japan from 1186–1336, when the court was situated in the city of Kamakura.

Kamikaze (KAH-mih-kah-zee) A Japanese term meaning "divine wind" that is related to the storms that destroyed Mongol invasion fleets; the term is symbolic of Japanese isolation and was later taken by suicide pilots in World War II.

Kangxi (kahng-shee) The third emperor of the Qing dynasty, famous for his learning and work ethic.

Kanun (KUH-noon) Laws issued by the Ottoman Süleyman the Magnificent, also known as Süleyman Kanuni, "the Lawgiver."

Kapu Hawaiian concept of something being taboo.

Karakorum (kahr-uh-KOR-uhm) Capital of the Mongol empire in the thirteenth century.

Karma (KAHR-mah) Hindu concept that the sum of good and bad in a person's life will determine his or her status in the next life.

Kautalya (KAHT-ahl-yah) A minister of Chandragupta, founder of the Mauryan dynasty in India.

Kebra Negast (kee-brah NAH-gahst) A book written in the priestly Ethiopian language Ge'ez, that traces the Solomonic origins of the Ethiopian emperors.

Kellogg-Briand Pact 1928 treaty, also known as the Pact of Paris, that attempted to outlaw war. By 1933, sixty-five nations had signed the pact.

Kemal, Mustafa (kuh-MAHL, MOOS-fah) Turkish statesman and World War I hero who abolished the caliphate and established Turkey as a modern secular state.

Kenyatta, Jomo (1893–1978) Kenyan statesman who became the first president of independent Kenya in 1964.

Kepler, Johannes (1571–1630) German astronomer best known for first stating the laws of planetary motion.

Keynes, John Maynard (1883–1946) British economist who advocated that governments use monetary and fiscal policy to maintain full employment. Profoundly influenced the practice of modern macroeconomics.

Khan Title given to Mongol, Tatar, Turkish, and other Central Asian leaders in the medieval period.

Khanate of Chaghatai Region in central Asia ruled by Chaghatai Khan, second son of Genghis Khan, from the 1220s until the seventeenth century.

Khanbaliq (Kahn-bah-LEEK) Name of the capital of the Yuan dynasty in China.

Khans of the Golden Horde Mongol khanate established in Russia from the thirteenth to the fifteenth century.

Khartoum (khar-TOOM) The capital of Sudan, located at the confluence of the Blue Nile and the White Nile.

Khoikhoi (KOI-koi) An ethnic group in southern Africa.

Khubilai Khan (KOO-bih-lie kahn) Prominent Mongol ruler in the thirteenth century and founder of the Yuan dynasty.

Kilwa (KILH-wah) A thriving Swahili city-state in east Africa between the twelfth and sixteenth centuries.

Kin-based society A society that governs itself primarily through family and clan relationships; many existed in sub-Saharan Africa throughout history.

Kongo Central African state that began trading with the Portuguese around 1500; although their kings, such as King Afonso I (r. 1506–1543), converted to Christianity, they nevertheless suffered from the slave trade.

Korean conflict The Korean War between North and South Korea.

Koumbi-Saleh Important trading city along the trans-Saharan trade route from the eleventh to the thirteenth centuries.

Kowtow (kou-tou) A former Chinese custom of bowing the forehead to touch the ground as an act of submission.

Kristallnacht "Crystal Night" or Night of the Broken Glass, which occurred on 9 November 1938 when the Nazi party coordinated an attack on Jewish people and property in Germany and German-controlled lands.

Kshatriyas (SHUHT-ree-uhs) Hindu caste of warriors and aristocrats.

Kulaks Land-owning Russian peasants who benefited under Lenin's New Economic Policy and suffered under Stalin's forced collectivization.

Kush (kuhsh) An ancient African state of the Nile River Valley, also known as Nubia.

Kushan empire Empire that formed in the first century C.E. in Bactria, in an area that now includes northern Afghanistan.

Kwarazm shah Dynasty that ruled central Asia and Iran from 1077 C.E. until its fall to the Mongols in 1231.

Lamaist Buddhism (LAH-muh-ihst BOO-diz'm) Branch of Buddhism that was similar to shamanism in its acceptance of magic and supernatural powers.

Laozi Sixth-century B.C.E. Chinese philosopher regarded as the founder of Daoism, and who is thought to have authored the *Daodejing*.

Lapita (Lah-PEE-tah) The pottery style of an ancient Pacific Ocean culture.

La Reforma Political reform movement of Mexican president Benito Juárez (1806–1872) that called for limiting the power of the military and the Catholic church in Mexican society.

Later Han Chinese dynasty founded in 947 C.E. and lasting until 951, known for being one of the shortest-lived Chinese dynasties.

Latifundia (lah-tee-FOON-dya) Huge state-run and slave-worked farms in ancient Rome.

La Venta Village in southeastern Mexico, where the remains of a culture that existed from about 500 B.C.E.–600 C.E. were found.

League of Nations Forerunner of the United Nations, the dream of American president Woodrow Wilson, although its potential was severely limited by the refusal of the United States to join.

Lebensraum (LAY-behnz-rahwm) German term meaning "living space"; the term is associated with Hitler and his goal of carving out territory in the east for an expanding Germany.

Legalism Chinese philosophy from the Zhou dynasty that called for harsh suppression of the common people.

Legazpi, Miguel Lopez de (le-GAHS-pee, mee-GEHL LOH-pess de) Spanish conquistador who established one of the first European settlements in the East Indies.

Leif Ericsson (leef ER-ik-suhn) A Norse explorer who probably landed in North America in the eleventh century.

Lend-lease System engineered by the United States in 1941 in which nations fighting Germany were provided with equipment and services.

Lenin, Vladimir Ilyich (LEHN-in, VLAD-uh-meer IL-yich) Founder of the Bolshevik party, leader of the Russian Revolution, and first leader of the Soviet Union from 1917 to 1924.

Leonardo da Vinci (lee-uh-NAHR-doh duh VIHN-chee) Italian artist and scientist of the Italian Renaissance.

Leopold II (1865–1909) King of Belgium from 1876 to 1904, who also ruled the Congo Free State. Best known for the brutal regime he sponsored in the Congo, in which millions of Congolese died, and because of which he was forced to abdicate in 1904.

Levée en masse (leh-VAY ahn MAS) A term signifying universal conscription during the radical phase of the French revolution.

Lex talionis (lehks tah-LYO-nihs) "Law of retaliation," laws in which offenders suffered punishments similar to their crimes; the most famous example is Hammurabi's Laws.

Li (LEE) Confucian concept, a sense of propriety.

Liaodong peninsula (lyou-dawng) A peninsula in northeastern China that extends into the Yellow Sea.

Liberalism A political philosophy inspired by John Locke and the ideals of the Enlightenment that advocated individual liberty, constitutional government, and free trade. Nineteenth-century liberals favored representative government but not necessarily democracy.

Liberation theology The beliefs of Christian thinkers and social activists who emphasize Jesus' role in helping those who were oppressed, a view that gained wide support in Latin America in the late twentieth century. Liberation theologians question the historic role of the church in supporting traditional regimes.

Lili'uokalani (lee-lee-oo-oh-kah-LAH-nee) The last monarch of Hawaii before it was annexed by the United States.

Lincoln, Abraham (1809–1865) Sixteenth United States president who served during the American Civil War, issued the Emancipation Proclamation in 1863, and was assassinated by John Wilkes Booth in 1865.

Linear A Minoan written script.

Linear B Early Mycenaean written script, adapted from the Minoan Linear A.

Little tigers Asian countries that followed the Japanese model for economic development.

Liu Bang (256–195 B.C.E.) Founder of China's Han dynasty in 206 B.C.E.

Locke, John (1632–1704) English philosopher who believed that all knowledge comes from sensory experience.

Long March Six thousand mile march led by Mao Zedong from southeast to northeast China in 1934–1935 after his Communist party was attacked by the Kuomintang.

Louis (LOO-ee) French name for many of the Capetian kings.

Louis XIV (1638–1715) King of France from 1643–1715. Known as the Sun King, whose reign was characterized by a magnificent court, absolute rule, and the expansion of French influence in Europe.

Louis XVI (1754–1793) King of France from 1774–1792. Summoned the Estates General of France in 1789 to solve the state's financial difficulties, which triggered the French revolution. Louis was executed in 1792.

Luddites Early-nineteenth-century artisans who were opposed to new machinery and industrialization.

Macdonald, John A. (1815–1891) First prime minister of Canada.

Macedon (MAS-ih-don) The ancient kingdom of Alexander the Great in the southeastern Balkans.

Machismo (mah-CHEEZ-moh) Latin American social ethic that honored male strength, courage, aggressiveness, assertiveness, and cunning.

MAD Mutually Assured Destruction. Refers to a military strategy developed by the United States at the end of President John F. Kennedy's administration in which the use of nuclear force by one of the two Cold War powers would result in the complete annihilation of both.

Madeiras (muh-DEER-uhs) A group of islands in the Atlantic Ocean to the west of Morocco.

Madrasas (MAH-drahs-ahs) Islamic institutions of higher education that originated in the tenth century.

Magellan, Ferdinand (muh-JEHL-uhn, FUR-dih-nand) Portuguese navigator who commanded an expedition that was the first to circumnavigate the world.

Magnetic compass A compass that indicates magnetic north.

Magyars (MAH-jahrs) Hungarian invaders who raided towns in Germany, Italy, and France in the ninth and tenth centuries.

Mahabharata (mah-hah-BAH-rah-tah) Massive ancient Indian epic that was developed orally for centuries; it tells of an epic civil war between two family branches.

Mahayana Buddhism (mah-huh-YAH-nah) The "greater vehicle," a more metaphysical and popular northern branch of Buddhism.

Mahmud of Ghazni (mah-muhd of gahz-nee) Founder of the Ghaznavid empire in what is now Afghanistan.

Mahmud II (mah-MOOD) The thirtieth sultan of the Ottoman Empire, famous for instituting extensive military and legal reforms.

Maize Also known as corn. Grain domesticated by indigenous peoples of Mesoamerica in prehistoric times.

Majapahit (mah-jah-PAH-hit) An Indianized kingdom of eastern Java, powerful from the late thirteenth to the end of the fourteenth century.

Maji-Maji rebellion Violent African resistance to German colonial rule in East Africa from 1905–1907.

Mali empire (MAH-lee) West African kingdom founded in the thirteenth century by Sundiata; it reached its peak during the reign of Mansa Musa.

Malindi (mah-LIN-dee) East African town on the Indian Ocean.

Malintzin (mal-een-tzeen) Also known as La Malinche, Malintzin was an indigenous woman who acted as interpreter and guide for Hernán Cortés during his conquest of Mexico.

Manchukuo Puppet state set up by the Japanese empire in Manchuria from 1931–1945.

Manchus Manchurians who conquered China, putting an end to the Ming dynasty and founding the Qing dynasty (1644–1911).

Mandarins Powerful bureaucrats in imperial China.

Mandate of Heaven Chinese belief that the emperors ruled through the mandate, or approval, of heaven contingent on their ability to look after the welfare of the population.

Mandate system System that developed in the wake of World War I when the former colonies ended up as mandates under European control, a thinly veiled attempt at continuing imperialism.

Mande An ethnic group in west Africa.

Mani (c. 216– c. 276) Persian prophet who founded Manichaeism.

Manichaeism (man-ih-KEE-iz'm) Religion founded by the prophet Mani in the third century c.e., a syncretic version of Zoroastrian, Christian, and Buddhist elements.

Manifest destiny The idea, popular in the United States in the mid-nineteenth century, that the North American continent was intended by God to be settled by white Americans. This notion helped justify the Mexican war of 1846–1848 and the Indian wars of the 1870s and 1880s.

Manila galleons Spanish trading ships that travelled once or twice a year from Acupulco, New Spain (present-day Mexico) to Manila, Philippines from 1565–1815.

Manioc A starch made by leaching and drying the cassava plant that became a staple food in the tropics.

Manor Large estates of the nobles during the European middle ages, home for the majority of the peasants.

Mansa Musa (MAHN-suh MOO-suh) Emperor of the kingdom of Mali in Africa who made a famous pilgrimage to Mecca.

Maodun (1896–1981) Chinese literary critic and author who became minister of culture under Mao Zedong from 1949–1964.

Mao Zedong (mow zuh-doong) Revolutionary leader of the Chinese Communist Party, who came to power in 1949 and ruled until 1976.

Maori (MAY-oh-ree) Indigenous peoples of New Zealand.

Marae Polynesian temple structure.

Marathon Battlefield, scene of the Athenian victory over the Persians in 490 b.c.e.

Mare nostrum "Our Sea." The name the Romans called the Mediterranean Sea.

Maroons Runaway African slaves.

Marshall Plan U.S. plan, officially called the European Recovery Program, that offered financial and other economic aid to all European states that had suffered from World War II, including Soviet bloc states.

Marx, Karl (1818–1883) German political economist and political theorist who is credited as the founder of modern communism.

Massacre at Wounded Knee Massacre inflicted by United States troops on Lakota Native Americans at Wounded Knee, South Dakota on December 29, 1890. Approximately 200 men, women, and children were killed.

Masulipatam (mahsu-lih-pah-tahm) Ancient port town in east-central India.

Mau Mau rebellion Revolution in Kenya, forcing out the British.

Maurya, Chandragupta (MORE-yuh, chuhn-drah-GOOP-tah) Founder of the Indian Mauryan empire.

Mauryan dynasty Indian dynasty (321–185 b.c.e.) founded by Chandragupta Maurya and reaching its peak under Ashoka.

May Fourth Movement Chinese movement that began 4 May 1919 with a desire to eliminate imperialist influences and promote national unity.

Maya (MY-uh) Brilliant Central American society (300–1100) known for math, astronomy, and a sophisticated written language.

Mazzini, Giuseppe (maht-TSEE-nee, joo-ZEP-pe) Italian nationalist whose writings spurred the movement for a unified Italy in the nineteenth century.

McDonaldization The term for cultural homogenization created by globalization.

Mecca City in western Saudi Arabia. Muslims believe it to be the holiest city of Islam, as it was the city in which the prophet Muhammad was born. Site of annual pilgrimages by Muslims.

Medes (meeds) Indo-European branch that settled in northern Persia and eventually fell to another branch, the Persians, in the sixth century.

Medina City in western Saudi Arabia, north of Mecca, considered the second holiest city of Islam. Contains Muhammad's tomb.

Mehmed the Conqueror (1432–1481) Sultan of the Ottoman empire who conquered Constantinople in 1453.

Meiji restoration (MAY-jee) Restoration of imperial rule under Emperor Meiji in 1868 by a coalition led by Fukuzawa Yukichi and Ito Hirobumi; the restoration enacted western reforms to strengthen Japan.

Melaka (may-LAHK-ah) Southeast Asian kingdom that was predominantly Islamic.

Mencius (MEN-shi-us) Chinese philosopher who refined the ideas of Confucius and spread them across China.

Menes (mee-neez) The Egyptian pharoah who unified Egypt in 3100 b.c.e.

Meroitic writing Language of the inscriptions of Meroe in the Middle Nile from the second half of the first millennium b.c.e. to the early centuries c.e.

Mesoamerica (mez-oh-uh-MER-i-kuh) The region comprising Mexico and Central America.

Mesopotamia Term meaning "between the rivers," in this case the Tigris and Euphrates; Sumer and Akkad are two of the earliest societies.

Mestizo (mehs-TEE-soh) Latin American term for children of Spanish and native parentage.

Metallurgy The process of extracting metal from ores, or purifying metals, and of creating objects from metals.

Métis (may-TEE) Canadian term for individuals of mixed European and indigenous ancestry.

Mexica (meh-SHEE-kah) An indigenous people of the Valley of Mexico who became the rulers of the Aztec empire.

Mexican-American War War that occurred between 1846–1848 between the United States and Mexico, after the United States annexed Texas in 1845.

Michelangelo Buonarotti (mik-uhl-AN-juh-loh baw-nahr-RAW-tee) Famous Italian Renaissance painter, sculptor, and architect.

Middle class The social group between the upper and working classes.

Middle Kingdom A period of ancient Egyptian history from 2040–1640 b.c.e.

Middle Passage The journey taken by slave ships from West Africa to the Americas during the Atlantic slave trade from the sixteenth through the nineteenth centuries.

Millet An autonomous, self-governing community in the Ottoman empire.

Mindanao (min-duh-NAH-oh) Second largest island in the Philippines.

Ming dynasty Chinese dynasty (1368–1644) founded by Hongwu and known for its cultural brilliance.

Minoan (mih-NOH-uhn) Society located on the island of Crete (ca. 2000–1100 b.c.e.) that influenced the early Mycenaeans.

Missi dominici (MEE-see doh-mee-NEE-chee) "Envoys of the lord ruler," the noble and church emissaries sent out by Charlemagne.

Mission civilisatrice (mee-see-on sih-vihl-ihs-a-trihs) Belief by French colonial rulers in the duty to bring Western civilization to colonized subjects.

Mita system A Spanish colonial system in which colonized subjects had to work a prescribed number of days for their colonial overlords.

Mithradates (mihth-rah-DAY-teez) Ancient king of Pontus who expanded his kingdom by defeating the Romans.

Mithraism (MIHTH-rah-iz'm) Mystery religion based on worship of the sun god Mithras; it became popular among the Romans because of its promise of salvation.

Mochica (moh-CHEE-kah) Pre-Incan South American society (300–700) known for their brilliant ceramics.

Moksha Hindu concept of the salvation of the soul.

Mongols A people from Mongolia who conquered vast swaths of Eurasia between the thirteenth and sixteenth centuries.

Monotheism (mah-noh-THEE-iz'm) Belief in only one god, a rare concept in the ancient world.

Monroe Doctrine American doctrine issued in 1823 during the presidency of James Monroe that warned Europeans to keep their hands off Latin America, and that expressed growing American strength and also growing American imperialistic views regarding Latin America.

Motecuzoma (mo-tec-oo-ZO-ma) Aztec emperor who ruled when Hernán Cortés conquered Mexico.

Motecuzoma II (c. 1466–1520) The last Aztec emperor, who was overthrown by Hernán Cortés.

Mozambique (moh-zam-BEEK) A country on the southeast coast of Africa that became independent from Portugal in 1975.

Mughal (MOO-guhl) Islamic dynasty that ruled India from the sixteenth through the eighteenth centuries; the construction of the Taj Mahal is representative of their splendor; with the exception of the enlightened reign of Akbar, the increasing conflict between Hindus and Muslims was another of their legacies.

Muhammad (muh-HAHM-mahd) Prophet of Islam (570–632).

Mukden incident Japanese bombing of train tracks in Manchuria on September 18, 1931, which the Japanese used as the pretext for invading and occupying Manchuria.

Mulattoes Persons of mixed European and African ancestry.

Mumbo cult Cult in Kenya during the second decade of the twentieth century that rejected Christianity and predicted the disappearance of Europeans from the African continent.

Mummification The process of embalming, drying, and wrapping a dead body with linen cloths.

Mumtaz Mahal (moom tahz muh-HAHL) Beloved wife of the Mughal emperor Shah Jahan, whose death inspired him to build the Taj Mahal.

Muromachi period Period in Japanese history from the fourteenth to the sixteenth centuries marked by military rule by the bakufu.

Muslim A follower of Islam.

Muslim League Political organization in India and Pakistan founded in 1906 to secure the rights of Muslims living in India. Under the leadership of Muhammed Ali Jinnah after 1940 the League demanded a separate Muslim state.

Mussolini, Benito (1883–1945) Italian Fascist dictator from 1922–1945.

Mutsuhito (MOO-tsoo-HEE-taw) Emperor of Japan who encouraged the modernization of Japan after the Meiji restoration.

Mycenaean society (meye-suh-NEE-uhn) Early Greek society on the Peloponese (1600–1100 B.C.E.) that was influenced by the Minoans; the Mycenaeans' conflict with Troy is immortalized in Homer's *Odyssey*.

NAFTA North American Free Trade Agreement. A trade agreement between the United States, Canada, and Mexico implemented in 1994 that encourages free trade among these countries.

Nahuatl (na-watl) Ancient language of the Valley of Mexico, and language of the Aztec empire.

Nam Viet Ancient kingdom from c. 207 B.C.E. to 111 B.C.E. that comprised most of present-day Vietnam and the Chinese provinces of Kwangtung and Kwangsi.

Nan Madol A series of artificial islands linked by canals built around 1500 C.E. near the island of Pohnpei in present-day Federated States of Micronesia in the Pacific Ocean.

Napoleon Bonaparte (nuh-POH-lee-uhn BOH-nuh-pahrt) French general who became emperor of the French from 1804 until his defeat by enemy European powers in 1815.

Nara period Japanese period (710–794), centered around city of Nara, that was the highest point of Chinese influence.

Nasser, Gamal Abdel Leader of Egypt and founder of pan-Arab nationalism.

National Assembly The elected legislature in France that was created during the first phase of the French revolution, from 1789–1791.

Nationalism A form of extreme patriotic feeling and devotion to a state.

National Policy Nineteenth-century Canadian policy designed to attract migrants, protect industries through tariffs, and build national transportation systems.

National Socialism The political doctrine of the Nazi party of Germany.

NATO The North Atlantic Treaty Organization, which was established by the United States in 1949 as a regional military alliance against Soviet expansionism.

Navajo (NAH-vah-ho) Native American group that settled in what is now Arizona, New Mexico, and Utah.

Ndebele (uhn-duh-BEE-lee) A people of South Africa that split from King Shaka of the Zulu in the 1820s.

Ndongo (n'DAWN-goh) Angolan kingdom that reached its peak during the reign of Queen Nzinga (r. 1623–1663).

Neandertal (nee-ANN-duhr-tawl) Early humans (100,000 to 35,000 years ago) who were prevalent during the Paleolithic period.

Nebuchadnezzar (neb-uh-kud-NEZ-er) Chaldean king of Babylon.

Negritude (NEH-grih-tood) "Blackness," a term coined by early African nationalists as a means of celebrating the heritage of black peoples around the world.

Neo-Confucianism (nee-oh-kuhn-FYEW-shuhn-iz'm) Philosophy that attempted to merge certain basic elements of Confucian and Buddhist thought; most important of the early Neo-Confucianists was the Chinese thinker Zhu Xi (1130–1200).

Neolithic (nee-uh-LITH-ik) New Stone Age (10,000–4000 B.C.E.), which was marked by the discovery and mastery of agriculture.

Nestorian (neh-STOHR-eeuhn) Early branch of Christianity, named after the fifth-century Greek theologian Nestorius, that emphasized the human nature of Jesus Christ.

New Babylonian empire Period of Mesopotamian history from 626 B.C.E.–529 B.C.E. during which the Babylonians reconquered most of the Assyrian empire.

New Deal Economic measures introduced by United States president Franklin D. Roosevelt in 1933 to combat the worst effects of the Great Depression.

New Economic Policy (NEP) Plan implemented by Lenin that called for minor free market reforms.

New Kingdom Period of ancient Egyptian history comprising the eighteenth–twentieth dynasties, from about 1580–1090 B.C.E.

New Spain The name the Spanish gave to the viceroyalty in the Americas from the sixteenth to the nineteenth centuries that included present-day Mexico, part of Central America, the southwest United States, some Caribbean islands, and the Philippines.

Newton, Isaac (1642–1727) English mathematician and physicist who developed the theory of the law of gravitation and the laws of motion.

New Zealand Wars (1845–1872) A series of armed conflicts that took place between European settlers and indigenous Maori peoples over land rights.

Nian (neen) An armed uprising that occurred in China in 1851 contemporaneously with the Taiping rebellion.

Nicaea (nahy-SEE-uh) The first ecumenical council in 325 C.E. that produced the wording of the Nicene Creed and condemned heresy.

Nile River River that flows northward through eastern Africa and empties in the Mediterranean. At 4,150 miles, it is the longest river in the world.

Ninety-five Theses The theses of Martin Luther (1483–1546) against the sale of indulgences by the Roman Catholic Church, commonly credited with beginning the Protestant Reformation.

Nirvana (ner-VAHN-nah) Hindu belief in the state of having transcended the cycle of reincarnation and ending the human cycle of desire and suffering.

Nkrumah, Kwame The leader of Ghana who gained freedom from Britain for Ghana.

Noble Eightfold Path Final truth of the Buddhist Four Noble Truths that called for leading a life of balance and constant contemplation.

No-man's-land The land between the trenches of the Allies and the Central Powers on the Western Front during World War I.

Nonalignment Countries not associated with the two powers in the cold war, the USSR and the United States.

Noncooperation movement Nonviolent movement organized by Mohandas Gandhi from 1920–1922 to induce the British to grant self-government to India.

Normans People of mixed Scandinavian and Frankish origin who settled the area of Normandy (present-day France) in about 912 C.E.

North American Free Trade Agreement (NAFTA) Regional alliance established in 1993 between the United States, Canada, and Mexico; it formed the world's second largest free-trade zone.

Northern Alliance A multiethnic coalition in Afghanistan opposed to the Taliban.

Northwest Rebellion Armed uprising of metis and Native peoples led by Louis Riel in Canada's district of Saskatchewan in 1885, for the purpose of forcing the Canadian government to recognize their rights.

Nostrum (NAHS-truhm) Latin word for "our."

Nubia (NOO-bee-uh) Area south of Egypt; the kingdom of Kush in Nubia invaded and dominated Egypt from 750 to 664 B.C.E.

Nuremburg Laws Anti-Semitic laws introduced by the Nazi party after the annual Nuremburg Rally for the party in 1935.

Nurhaci (NOOR-hacheh) Founding father of the Manchu state.

Nzinga Mbemba (IN-zinga MEHM-bah) Also called King Afonso I, he was ruler of the kingdom of Kongo in the first half of the sixteenth century.

Oaxaca (wah-hah-kah) A city in southeastern Mexico.

Oceania Term referring to the Pacific Ocean basin and its lands.

Odovacer (AHD-oh-vah-cer) Germanic general and first non-Roman ruler after 476.

Old Kingdom Period of ancient Egyptian history from about 3000–2100 B.C.E. comprising the third through sixth dynasties. The pyramids were built during this period.

Olmecs Early Central American society (1200–100 B.C.E.) that centered around sites at San Lorenzo, La Venta, and Tres Zapotes and that influenced later Maya.

Olympic Games Ancient Greek festival featuring athletic and other competitions held every four years at the city of Olympia from 776 B.C.E. to 393 C.E.

Omdurman (om-door-MAHN) 1898 battle in the Sudan in which a British and Egyptian force defeated the Sudanese.

OPEC Organization of Petroleum Exporting Companies. Founded in 1960, a collection of states that decided to collaborate on managing their oil exports to the rest of the world.

Operation Barbarossa The code-name for the surprise German attack on the Soviet Union on June 22, 1941.

Operation Iraqi Freedom The Iraq War.

Opium War War between China and Britain between 1839–1842 over the Chinese refusal to allow the British to trade opium in China. Resulted in a defeat for China that began a long period of unequal treaties between European countries and China.

Oprichnina (oh-PREEK-nee-nah) A Russian term meaning the "land apart," Muscovite territory that the Russian tsar Ivan IV (r. 1533–1584) demanded to control; the tsar created a new class of nobles called the *oprichniki* for this territory.

Oracle bones Chinese Shang dynasty (1766–1122 B.C.E.) means of foretelling the future.

Organization of African Unity (OAU) An organization started in 1963 by thirty-two newly independent African states and designed to prevent conflict that would lead to intervention by former colonial powers.

Organization of Petroleum Exporting Countries (OPEC) An organization begun in 1960 by oil-producing states originally for purely economic reasons but that later had more political influence.

Osama bin Laden Founder of al-Qaeda and terrorist wanted for 9/11 attack on the United States.

Osiris Ancient Egyptian god that represented the forces of nature.

Osman Bey (oz-MAHN) Founder of the dynasty that ruled the Ottoman empire from 1289–1923.

Otto of Saxony (912–973 C.E.) Became the first Holy Roman Emperor since Charlemagne.

Ottoman empire Powerful Turkish empire that lasted from the conquest of Constantinople (Istanbul) in 1453 until 1918 and reached its peak during the reign of Süleyman the Magnificent (r. 1520–1566).

Owen, Robert (1771–1858) Welsh social reformer and one of the founders of utopian socialism.

Oyo An ethnic group in west Africa.

Pachacuti (pah-cha-KOO-tee) Ruler of Inca society from 1438 to 1471, whose military campaigns greatly extended Inca control.

Paleolithic (pey-lee-oh-LITH-ik) Old Stone Age, a long period of human development before the development of agriculture.

Palestinian Liberation Organization (PLO) Ruling party of the Palestinian territories occupied by Israel.

Pan-Africanism Social and political movement founded around 1900 that sought equal rights, independence, and unity among peoples of African descent in Africa and in the world.

Panama Canal A fifty-one-mile canal across the isthmus of Panama that connects the Caribbean with the Pacific Ocean. The canal was completed by the United States in 1914.

Paper money Legal tender in the form of paper bank notes.

Paris Peace Accords Agreement reached in 1973 that marked the end of the United States' role in the Vietnam War.

Paris Peace Conference Meeting in 1919–1920 that set the peace terms at the end of World War I.

Parsis (pahr-SEES) Indian Zoroastrians.

Parthians Persian dynasty (247 B.C.E.–224 C.E.) that reached its peak under Mithradates I.

Pasargadae (pah-SAR-gah-dee) Capital city of ancient Persia.

Pasion (pahs-ee-on) Fourth-century B.C.E. Athenian slave who eventually became a wealthy Athenian citizen.

Pataliputra (pah-tal-ih-puh-trah) Capital city of the Indian Mauryan and Gupta empires.

Paterfamilias (PAH-tehrr-fah-MEE-lyas) Roman term for the "father of the family," a theoretical implication that gave the male head of the family almost unlimited authority.

Patriarch (PAY-tree-ahrk) Leader of the Greek Orthodox church, which in 1054 officially split with the Pope and the Roman Catholic church.

Patriarchy A system of social organization in which males dominate the family and in which the public institutions and descent and succession are traced through the male line.

Patricians Roman aristocrats and wealthy classes.

Pax Americana "American Peace," a term that compares American domination in the years after World War II with the power of Rome at its peak.

Pax romana (Pahks roh-MAH-nah) "Roman Peace," a term that relates to the period of political stability, cultural brilliance, and economic prosperity beginning with unification under Augustus and lasting through the first two centuries C.E.

Peace of Westphalia The peace treaty that ended the Thirty Years' War in 1648.

Pearl Harbor Site of the United States naval base that was bombed in a surprise attack by the Japanese on December 7, 1941. The attack brought the United States into World War II.

Peloponnesian (pell-uh-puh-NEE-suhn) A large peninsula in southern Greece.

Peloponnesian War War between the Greek city states of Athens and its allies, and Sparta and its allies from 431–404 B.C.E., which ended in defeat for Athens.

Peloponnesus (pell-uh-puh-NEE-suhs) See Peloponnesian.

Peninsulares (peh-neen-soo-LAH-rehs) Latin American officials from Spain or Portugal.

Perestroika (PAYR-eh-stroy-kuh) Economic policy adopted by the USSR to increase labor efficiency.

Pericles (PEH-rih-kleez) Athenian orator and statesman whose leadership contributed to the political and cultural supremacy of Athens.

Perry, Commodore Matthew C. (1794–1858) Commodore in the United States Navy who fought in the War of 1812 and the Mexican-American War. Known for delivering the message to the Japanese government in 1854 that it would have to open up to the West or fight.

Persepolis (per-SEP-uh-lis) Ancient capital of the Persian empire.

Persian Royal Road Ancient highway rebuilt by the Persian king Darius I of the Achaemenid empire in the fifth century B.C.E.

Persian Wars The wars fought between Greece and Persia from 550–469 B.C.E.

Peru Country in southwest South America on the Pacific coast. The site of the Inca empire from the twelfth–sixteenth centuries, then a territory of the Spanish empire until its independence in 1824.

Petrarca, Francesco (pe-TRAHRK-a, frahn-CHES-kaw) Fourteenth-century Italian poet famous for his love poems.

Petrarch (1304–1374) Italian scholar and poet known as the "father of humanism."

Pharaohs (FARE-ohs) Egyptian kings considered to be gods on earth.

Philosophes (fil-uh-sofs) Enlightenment intellectuals who sought to apply the methods of science to the improvement of society.

Phoenicians (fi-NEE-shins) Inhabitants of ancient Phoenicia, a narrow coastal plain north of Palestine between the Mediterranean Sea and the Lebanon Mountains.

Piri Reis (pir-ree reys) An Ottoman Turkish admiral and cartographer famous for his maps and charts.

Pizarro, Francisco (1471–1541) Spanish conquistador who conquered the Inca empire.

Plantation An estate on which cash crops are grown for commercial purposes.

Plato (427–347 B.C.E.) Greek philosopher and mathematician who was the student of Socrates and the teacher of Aristotle.

Plebeians (plih-BEE-uhns) Roman common people.

Poison gas Gas or vapor used in chemical warfare. First used effectively on the battlefield in World War I.

Polis (POH-lihs) Greek term for the city-state.

Polo, Marco (1254–1324) Venetian merchant and traveler who explored Asia in the thirteenth century and served the Chinese emperor Khubilai Khan.

Polynesians People from the islands in the eastern part of Oceania.

Pope The head of the Roman Catholic Church.

Pope Gregory I (c. 540–604) Pope from 590–604, most known for strengthening the authority of the papacy, centralizing the church, and enforcing rules for the clergy.

Pope Urban II (1035–1099) Pope from 1088–1099, most famous for inspiring the First Crusade.

Popol Vuh (poh-pohl VOO) Mayan creation epic.

Porcelain A white, nearly translucent hard ceramic. Also called "china" because the ceramic style originated there.

Potosi (paw-taw-SEE) City in what is now Bolivia, where Spanish conquerors discovered one of the richest silver veins in the world in 1545.

Power loom A mechanical loom for weaving yarn into fabric.

Prehistory The period before the invention of writing.

Prince Henry the Navigator (1394–1460) Prince of Portugal, noted for his patronage of exploratory voyages along the coast of west Africa.

Prince Vladimir of Kiev (956–1015) First Christian ruler in Russia.

Procopius (proh-KOH-pee-uhs) Roman member of the Constantinian dynasty.

Proletariat Urban working class in a modern industrial society.

Pronatalism Beliefs and policies that encourage and promote childbearing.

Protestant Reformation Sixteenth-century European movement during which Luther, Calvin, Zwingli, and others broke away from the Catholic church.

Ptolemaic (tawl-oh-MAY-ihk) Term used to signify both the Egyptian kingdom founded by Alexander the Great's general Ptolemy and the thought of the philosopher Ptolemy of Alexandria (second century C.E.), who used mathematical formulas in an attempt to prove Aristotle's geocentric theory of the universe.

Pueblo (PWEB-loh) Native American groups native to what is now the southwestern United States, called such because they lived in communal adobe homes called pueblos.

Punic Wars Three wars between Rome and Carthage extending from 264–146 B.C.E. that led to the destruction of Carthage and the domination of Rome in the western Mediterranean.

Putting-out system Method of getting around guild control by delivering unfinished materials to rural households for completion.

Pyramids Pyramid-shaped masonry tombs built between 3000–2100 B.C.E. in ancient Egypt.

Qadi (KAH-dee) An Islamic judge.

Qanat (kah-NAHT) Persian underground canal.

Qi (chee) Chinese concept of the basic material that makes up the body and the universe.

Qianlong (chyahn-lawng) The fifth Qing emperor of China who ruled at the end of the eighteenth century and was famous for his erudition.

Qin dynasty (chihn) Chinese dynasty (221–207 B.C.E.) that was founded by Qin Shihuangdi and was marked by the first unification of China and the early construction of defensive walls.

Qin Shihuangdi (chin she-huang-dee) Founder of the Qin dynasty.

Qing dynasty (chihng) Chinese dynasty (1644–1911) that reached its peak during the reigns of Kangxi and Qianlong.

Qizilbash (gih-ZIHL-bahsh) Term meaning "red heads," Turkish tribes that were important allies of Shah Ismail in the formation of the Safavid empire.

Quanzhou (chwahn-joh) Chinese city-port established during the Tang dynasty.

Quechua (keh-CHUA) South American ethnic group of Peru who were once the ruling people of the Inca empire.

Queen Nzinga (1583–1663) Monarch of the Mbundu people in central Africa in the region the Portuguese called Angola. Famous for resisting Portuguese control and defeating a Portuguese army in 1647.

Quetzalcoatl (keh-tzahl-koh-AHT'l) Aztec god, the "feathered serpent," who was borrowed originally from the Toltecs; Quetzalcoatl was believed to have been defeated by another god and exiled, and he promised to return.

Quiché (keesh-AY) Mayan ethnic group of south-central Guatemala.

Quilon (kee-yawn) A city in the southwest corner of India in the modern state of Kerala.

Quinto (KEEN-toh) The one-fifth of Mexican and Peruvian silver production that was reserved for the Spanish monarchy.

Quipu (KEE-poo) Incan mnemonic aid comprised of different colored strings and knots that served to record events in the absence of a written text.

Quran (koorr-AHN) Islamic holy book that is believed to contain the divine revelations of Allah as presented to Muhammad.

Rabban Sauma (c. 1220–1294) Nestorian Christian monk of Turkic/Mongol origin best known for his travels to western Europe.

Railroad time Name given to the standardized time created by the English Great Western Railway Company in 1840, in which a variety of local times were synchronized and standardized for the purpose of maintaining railroad time schedules.

Raja (RAH-juh) A prince or king in India.

Ramanuja (c. 1017–1137) Indian Hindu theologian and philosopher.

Ramayana (rah-MAHY-yuh-nah) Ancient Indian masterpiece about the hero Rama that symbolized the victory of *dharma* (order) over *adharma* (chaos).

Rape of Nanjing Japanese conquest and destruction of the Chinese city of Nanjing in the 1930s.

Realpolitik (ray-AHL-poh-lih-teek) The Prussian Otto von Bismarck's "politics of reality," the belief that only the willingness to use force would actually bring about change.

Reconquista (ray-kohn-KEES-tah) Crusade, ending in 1492, to drive the Islamic forces out of Spain.

Reconstruction System implemented in the American South (1867–1877) that was designed to bring the Confederate states back into the union and also extend civil rights to freed slaves.

Reich The government or territory of a German state. Most commonly used with regard to Germany's Third Reich, the Nazi regime that lasted from 1933–1945.

Reign of terror A period between 1793 and 1794 during the French revolution, when thousands of people were executed by guillotine for being anti-revolutionary.

Relic Part of a holy person's body or belongings that is kept as an object of religious reverence after death.

Remus (REE-muhs) Along with his brother Romulus, one of the twin founders of Rome.

Ren Confucian value of humaneness and altruism.

Renaissance (ren-uh-SAHNS) A period of European history between the fourteenth and mid-seventeenth century in which culture and the arts experienced a rebirth.

Repartimiento (ray-pahrr-tee-MYEN-toh) Spanish labor system in Latin America, supposed to replace the *encomienda* system, in which native communities were compelled to provide laborers for the farms or mines and the Spanish employers were expected to pay fair wages.

Rhodes, Cecil (rhohdz, see-sihl) British financier and statesman in Southern Africa who made his fortune in gold and diamonds.

Ricci, Matteo (REET-chee, maht-TAY-oh) Italian Jesuit priest famous for his service in China during the sixteenth century.

Richelieu (RISH-uh-loo) French statesman and principal minister to king Louis XIII of France.

Richet, Charles (ri-SHEY, shawrl) French physiologist in the late nineteenth and early twentieth centuries.

Rivera, Diego (1886–1957) Mexican painter best known for creating large murals espousing socialist ideals.

Robespierre, Maximilien (1758–1794) An important figure in the French revolution who was a member of the Committee of Public Safety and crucial in instigating the reign of terror from 1793 until his own execution in 1794.

Roman Catholic Church Since the Reformation in the sixteenth century, the Christian church that acknowledges the Pope as its spiritual head.

Romanov (ROH-muh-nawf) The Russian imperial dynasty that ruled from 1613 to 1917.

Romulus (ROM-yuh-luhs) Along with his brother Remus, one of the twin founders of Rome.

Roosevelt Corollary Theodore Roosevelt's 1904 corollary to the Monroe Doctrine, which stated that the United States would consider military action against any European country that interfered in the affairs of any American republic.

Roosevelt, Franklin Delano (1882–1945) The thirty-second president of the United States, who was elected four times. Led the country through the Great Depression and World War II.

Rosas, Juan Manuel de (roh-sahs, HWAHN mahn-WEL de) A conservative Argentine politician who ruled the country from 1829 to 1852.

Rousseau, Jean-Jacques (1712–1778) Swiss-born French philosopher and writer whose ideas influenced the Enlightenment and the French revolution.

Rubaiyat (ROO-beye-aht) "Quatrains," famous poetry of Omar Khayyam that was later translated and transformed by Edward Fitzgerald.

Russian-German Treaty of Nonaggression Treaty between the Soviet Union and Germany signed on August 23, 1939, effectively dividing eastern Europe between them.

Russo-Japanese War War between Russia and Japan over Manchuria from 1904–1905, from which Japan emerged victorious.

Sacraments In Christian churches, any of the religious rituals (such as baptism) that confer grace on the participants.

Safavid (SAH-fah-vihd) Later Persian empire (1501–1722) that was founded by Shah Ismail and that became a center for Shiism; the empire reached its peak under Shah Abbas the Great and was centered around the capital of Isfahan.

Saint-Domingue (san doe-MANG) French colony in the Caribbean in what is now the republic of Haiti.

Sakk Letters of credit that were common in the medieval Islamic banking world.

Saljuqs (sahl-JYOOKS) Turkish tribe that gained control over the Abbasid empire and fought with the Byzantine empire.

Samsara (suhm-SAH-ruh) Hindu term for the concept of transmigration, that is, the soul passing into a new incarnation.

Samurai (SAM-uhr-eye) A Japanese warrior who lived by the code of *bushido*.

Sandinistas A socialist Nicaraguan political party in the 1960s and 1970s looking to overthrow the government.

San Lorenzo Town in Veracruz state, Mexico, near which Olmec ruins were found.

Sanskrit (SAHN-skriht) An ancient classical language of India.

Santa Anna, Antonio Lopez (1794–1896) Mexican general and political leader who was president of Mexico many times over the course of his political career.

Santeria (sahn-tuh-REE-uh) A syncretic Afro-Caribbean religion.

São Jorge de Mina (Sou hor-hay day meena) The first Portuguese trading post built on the Gulf of Guinea, which later became an important site for the Atlantic slave trade.

São Tomé (SOU tuh-MEY) Island in the Atlantic west of Africa's Kongo kingdom, used by the Portuguese beginning in the fifteenth century to produce sugar.

Saramaka (sar-ah-mah-kah) A group of Maroons (runaway slaves) who established themselves in the interior of Suriname.

Sargon of Akkad (r. 2334–2279 B.C.E.) King of Mesopotamia who conquered Sumeria to found the Akkadian empire.

Sasanids (suh-SAH-nids) Later powerful Persian dynasty (224–651) that would reach its peak under Shapur I and later fall to Arabic expansion.

Sati (suh-TEE) Also known as *suttee*, Indian practice of a widow throwing herself on the funeral pyre of her husband.

Satraps (SAY-traps) Persian administrators, usually members of the royal family, who governed a satrapy.

Satyagraha (suh-TYA-gruh-hah) "Truth and firmness," a term associated with Gandhi's policy of passive resistance.

Schlieffen plan (SHLEE-fn) Early twentieth-century German plan for fighting a continental European war on two fronts.

Scholar-bureaucrats Describes the administrative apparatus of China created by the Ming dynasty (1368–1644) and continued by the Qing dynasty (1644–1911). Under this system, Confucian scholars, chosen through a highly competitive series of examinations, ran the country. This system meant that China was a meritocracy, but a very conservative one.

Scholasticism Medieval attempt of thinkers like St. Thomas Aquinas to merge the beliefs of Christianity with the logical rigor of Greek philosophy.

Scientific racism Nineteenth-century attempt to justify racism by scientific means; an example would be Gobineau's *Essay on the Inequality of the Human Races*.

Scientific revolution Seventeenth-century intellectual movement based on discoveries in physics and astronomy, which challenged earlier established views about the origins and nature of the universe.

Sebiumeker (sehb-ih-meh-kur) Ancient Nubian creator god.

Seleucid (sih-LOO-sid) A successor state of Alexander the Great that comprised modern Syria, Iraq, and Iran in the Hellenistic era.

Self-determinism Belief popular in World War I and after that every people should have the right to determine their own political destiny; the belief was often cited but ignored by the Great Powers.

Self-Strengthening Movement Chinese attempt (1860–1895) to blend Chinese cultural traditions with European industrial technology.

Semitic (suh-MIHT-ihk) A term that relates to the Semites, ancient nomadic herders who spoke Semitic languages; examples of Semites were the Akkadians, Hebrews, Aramaics, and Phoenicians, who often interacted with the more settled societies of Mesopotamia and Egypt.

Senate An assembly or council with legislative power.

Seneca Falls Convention Women's rights convention held in Seneca Falls, New York in July 1848. The convention issued a decree declaring that men and women are created equal.

Sengoku (sehn-goh-koo) Also called the "Warring States" period, a time in Japan of social upheaval and military conflict between the fifteenth and seventeenth centuries.

Sepoy Rebellion Uprising in 1857 of Indian soldiers in the British East India Company's Bengal Army in north and north-central India.

Sepoys Indian troops who served the British.

Seppuku A Japanese term for ritual suicide committed by the samurai when he had been dishonored.

Serfs Peasants who, while not chattel slaves, were tied to the land and who owed obligation to the lords on whose land they worked.

Seven Years' War War between Britain and Prussia on the one hand, and France and Austria on the other between 1756–1763. The war was fought in Europe, India, and the Americas.

Shah Abbas the Great (1571–1629) Shah of Persia from 1588 to his death. Considered one of the greatest Safavid rulers, and was responsible for moving the capital of the empire to the city of Isfahan.

Shah Ismail (shah IZ-may-el) Founder of the Safavid dynasty that ruled Persia in the sixteenth and seventeenth centuries.

Shah Jahan (shah jah-han) Mughal emperor of India, famous for building the Taj Mahal in memory of his beloved wife.

Shamanism (SHAH-mah-niz'm) Belief in shamans or religious specialists who possessed supernatural powers and who communicated with the gods and the spirits of nature.

Shanfei (shahn-fahy) Twentieth-century communist revolutionary in China.

Shang A Chinese dynasty that ruled from its capital at Anyang from 1766–1122 B.C.E.

Shapur I (226–272) The second ruler of the Persian Sassanid empire.

Sharia (shah-RREE-ah) The Islamic holy law, drawn up by theologians from the Quran, and accounts of Muhammad's life.

Shaykh Salim Chishthi (sheyk sah-LEEM CHEESH-tee) Sufi saint whose correct prophecy to Akbar prompted the Mughal emperor to move his capital to Fatehpur Sikri.

Shia (SHEE-ah) Islamic minority in opposition to the Sunni majority; their belief is that leadership should reside in the line descended from Ali.

Shiism Branch of Islam that rejects the first three caliphs and regards Ali and his descendants as the only legitimate successors of Muhammad.

Shinto Japanese religion marked by ancestor worship and veneration of nature spirits.

Shintoism (SHIHN-toh) Indigenous Japanese religion that emphasizes purity, clan loyalty, and the divinity of the emperor.

Shiva (SHIH-vuh) Hindu god associated with both fertility and destruction.

Shogun (SHOH-gun) Japanese military leader who ruled in place of the emperor.

Shudras (SHOO-druhs) Hindu caste of landless peasants and serfs.

Siddhartha Gautama (sih-DHAR-thuh GAHW-tah-mah) Indian *kshatriya* who achieved enlightenment and became known as the Buddha, the founder of Buddhism.

Sikhs (SIHKS) Indian syncretic faith that contains elements of Hinduism and Islam.

Silk roads Ancient trade routes that extended from the Roman empire in the west to China in the east.

Silla dynasty Kingdom in Korea that unified the three existing kingdoms in the region from 668–935 C.E., and which organized itself on the Chinese bureaucratic model.

Sima Qian (139–86 B.C.E.) Han dynasty prefect known as the greatest historian of China in ancient times.

Sinan Pasha (sih-NAHN pah-cha) Ottoman military commander who was appointed governor of Egypt in 1569.

Singosari (sihng-oh-sah-ree) Thirteenth-century kingdom in east Java.

Sioux (soo) Native North American tribe that ranged from Lake Michigan to the Rocky Mountains.

Skeptics Ancient Greek philosophy that claimed true knowledge of things was impossible.

Smoot-Hawley Tariff Act Law enacted in the United States after the onset of the Great Depression that raised import tariff rates almost 50 percent, causing other countries to retaliate and enact similar legislation.

Social Darwinism Nineteenth-century philosophy, championed by thinkers such as Herbert Spencer, that attempted to apply Darwinian "survival of the fittest" to the social and political realm; adherents saw the the elimination of weaker nations as part of a natural process and used the philosophy to justify war.

Socialism Political and economic theory of social organization based on the collective ownership of the means of production; its origins were in the early nineteenth century, and it differs from communism by a desire for slow or moderate change compared to the communist call for revolution.

Society of Jesus The official name of the clerical order of the Jesuits, founded by St. Ignatius Loyola in 1534.

Socrates (SAHK-rah-teez) Ancient Athenian philosopher and teacher of Plato.

Solidarity Polish trade union and nationalist movement in the 1980s that was headed by Lech Walesa.

Song dynasty (SOHNG) Chinese dynasty (960–1279) that was marked by an increasingly urbanized and cosmopolitan society.

Song Taizu (sawng tahy-zoo) Founder of the tenth-century Song dynasty in China.

Songhay empire (song-AHY) Fifteenth-through sixteenth-century empire in west Africa specializing in the gold trade.

Son of Heaven Designation given to Chinese emperors.

South African War War fought from 1899–1902 between Great Britain and two republics of Dutch-descended settlers (Transvaal and the Orange Free State) over resources and territory.

Soviets Russian elected councils that originated as strike committees during the 1905 St. Petersburg disorders; they represented a form of local self-government that went on to become the primary unit of government in the Union of Soviet Socialist Republics. The term was also used during the cold war to designate the Soviet Union.

Spanish-Cuban-American War War between Spain and the United States in 1898, which resulted in the independence of Cuba in 1902 and the cession of the United States of Puerto Rico, Guam, and the Philippines.

Spanish Inquisition Institution organized in 1478 by Fernando and Isabel of Spain to detect Protestant heresy and the secret practice of Judaism or Islam.

Sparta City-state of ancient Greece that reached its height in influence in the sixth century B.C.E. Known for its militarism and the athletic and disciplined lifestyle of its inhabitants.

Spartacus (SPAHR-tah-cus) A Roman slave who became the leader of an uprising meant to overthrow the Roman Republic.

Spheres of influence A region dominated by an outside power. Generally refers to the intrusion of western imperial powers into China in the late nineteenth century. China, although technically a sovereign state, was divided into "spheres," each one occupied by a European state that had license to conduct business without any interference.

Spinning mule Spinning machine invented by Samuel Crompton in 1779, which allowed large-scale production of thread for the textile industry.

Sputnik The first manmade satellite to orbit Earth, made by the USSR.

Srivijaya (sree-vih-JUH-yuh) Southeast Asian kingdom (670–1025), based on the island of Sumatra, that used a powerful navy to dominate trade.

Stalin, Joseph (1878–1953) Leader of the Soviet Union after the death of Vladimir Lenin, who created a brutal totalitarian state by purging all opposition through execution or imprisonment.

Stanton, Elizabeth Cady (1815–1902) American abolitionist, activist, and leader of the early women's movement for suffrage.

Stateless societies Term relating to societies such as those of sub-Saharan Africa after the Bantu migrations that featured decentralized rule through family and kinship groups instead of strongly centralized hierarchies.

Stephenson, George (1781–1848) British inventor who built the first passenger railway in 1825.

Stoicism A Hellenistic philosophy that emphasized strict adherence to duty and personal self-discipline. It became very popular among the Roman upper classes.

Stoics (STOH-ihks) Hellenistic philosophers who encouraged their followers to lead active, virtuous lives and to aid others.

Strabo (STRAH-boh) Greek geographer (first century C.E.).

Strategic Arms Limitations Talk (SALT) Agreement in 1972 between the United States and the Soviet Union.

St. Augustine (354–430) Latin-speaking philosopher and theologian who lived in Roman North Africa, whose writings were influential in the development of Christianity.

St. Benedict of Nursia (480–547) Italian monk who founded the Benedictine order.

St. Dominic (c. 1170–1221) Spanish priest who founded a monastic order that came to be known as the Dominicans.

St. Francis of Assisi (1181–1226) Roman Catholic monk who founded the Franciscan order of friars.

St. Scholastica (skuh-LAS-tih-kah) The twin sister of St. Benedict of Nursia, the compiler of *The Rule of St. Benedict,* which provided a guide to monastic living based on poverty, obedience, and service. St. Scholastica (480–547 C.E.) is believed to have spread the *Rule* among communities of nuns.

St. Thomas Aquinas (uh-KWAHY-nuhs) Thirteenth-century Italian theologian best remembered for his attempt to reconcile faith and reason in Christian theology.

Stupas (STOO-pahs) Buddhist shrines.

Sudetenland (soo-DEYT-n-land) The name used to describe the western regions of Czechoslovakia inhabited mostly by ethnic Germans.

Suez Canal A shipping canal, completed in 1869, that connects the Mediterannean Sea with the Red Sea.

Suez crisis When Britain, France, and Israel attacked Egypt in 1956 to regain the Suez Canal.

Sufis (SOO-fees) Islamic mystics who placed more emphasis on emotion and devotion than on strict adherence to rules.

Sugarcane The tropical plant whose sap is used to produce commercial sugar and molasses.

Sui dynasty (SWAY) Chinese dynasty (589–618) that constructed the Grand Canal, reunified China, and allowed for the splendor of the Tang dynasty that followed.

Sui Yangdi (sway-yahng-dee) Second emperor of the Sui dynasty, famous for completing the Grand Canal and reconstructing the Great Wall in the early seventh century.

Süleyman (SOO-lehy-mahn) Ottoman Turkish ruler Süleyman the Magnificent (r. 1520–1566), who was the most powerful and wealthy ruler of the sixteenth century.

Sultan A Muslim sovereign.

Sultanate of Delhi The various Muslim dynasties that ruled in north India from 1210–1526.

Sumerians (soo-MEHR-ee-uhns) Earliest Mesopotamian society.

Sundiata (soon-JAH-tuh) Founder of the Mali empire (r. 1230–1255), also the inspiration for the *Sundiata,* an African literary and mythological work.

Sunni (SOON-nee) "Traditionalists," the most popular branch of Islam; Sunnis believe in the legitimacy of the early caliphs, compared to the Shiite belief that only a descendant of Ali can lead.

Sunni Ali (soon-ee ah-lee) First great king of the Songhay empire in West Africa.

Sun Yatsen (1866–1925) Chinese revolutionary, leader of the Kuomintang party, and first president of the Republic of China in 1911.

Surat (soo-RAHT) Port city on India's northwest coast with an important historical role in trade.

Suriname (SOOR-uh-nahm) Former Dutch colony in northeastern South America that achieved independence in 1975.

Suu Kyi, Aung San (SOO KEE, AWNG SAHN) Opposition leader (1945–) in Myanmar; she was elected leader in 1990 but she was not allowed to come to power; she was a Nobel Peace Prize recipient in 1991.

Swahili (swah-HEE-lee) East African citystate society that dominated the coast from Mogadishu to Kilwa and was active in trade.

Taino (tah-EE-noh) A Caribbean tribe who were the first indigenous peoples from the Americas to come into contact with Christopher Columbus.

Taiping rebellion (TEYE-pihng) Rebellion (1850–1864) in Qing China led by Hong

Xiuquan, during which twenty to thirty million were killed; the rebellion was symbolic of the decline of China during the nineteenth century.

Taliban A fundamentalist Islamic militia in Afghanistan.

Tamerlane (1336–1405) Mongol-Turkic ruler who conquered a huge swath of territory in west, central, and south Asia.

Tang dynasty Chinese imperial dynasty that lasted from 618–907.

Tang Taizong (TAHNG TEYE-zohng) Chinese emperor (r. 627–649) who founded the Tang dynasty (618–907).

Tanzimat (TAHNZ-ee-MAT) A period of reform in the Ottoman Empire between 1845 and 1876.

Temple of the Giant Jaguar Name given to one of the largest structures at Tikal, a site of ancient Mayan civilization located in present-day Guatemala.

Temüjin (TEM-oo-chin) Mongol conqueror (ca. 1167–1227) who later took the name Chinggis Khan, "universal ruler."

Tenochtitlan (teh-noch-tee-TLAHN) Capital of the Aztec empire, later Mexico City.

Teotihuacan (tay-oh-tee-wa-KAHN) Central American society (200 B.C.E.–750 C.E.); its Pyramid of the Sun was the largest structure in Mesoamerica.

Terrorism The use of violence against civilians in order to gain political or religious goals.

Tetrarchs Governors of the four main divisions of the Roman empire.

Teutonic Knights Crusading European order that was active in the Baltic region.

Texcoco (TEHS-co-co) A major city-state in the Valley of Mexico during the Aztec period, and a member of the Aztec Triple Alliance.

Tezcatlipoca (tehs-cah-tlee-poh-cah) A central deity in the Aztec religion.

Theme system System of administrative divisions in the Byzantine empire, initiated in the seventh century and lasting in some form until its dissolution.

Theodora (500–548) Wife of Justinian, Byzantine emperor.

Theodosius (thee-uh-DOH-see-uhs) The last emperor of a united Roman empire. He became a Christian in 391 C.E.

Theravada Buddhism (thehr-ah-VAH-dah) One of two schools of Buddhism emphasizing personal salvation through one's own efforts.

Third Rome Concept that a new power would rise up to carry the legacy of Roman greatness after the decline of the Second Rome, Constantinople; Moscow was referred to as the Third Rome during the fifteenth century.

Thirty Years' War Major European conflict from 1618–1648 between Protestants and Catholics, and also between the Holy Roman Empire and other European powers.

Three Principles of the People Philosophy of Chinese Guomindang leader Sun Yat-sen

(1866–1925) that emphasized nationalism, democracy, and people's livelihood.

Tian (TEE-ehn) Chinese term for heaven.

Tian Shan (tyahn shahn) A mountain range located in central Asia.

Tikal (tee-KAHL) Maya political center from the fourth through the ninth centuries.

Timbuktu (tim-buhk-TOO) A city in what is now central Mali, famous for its historical role in the gold trade.

Timur-i lang (tee-MOOR-yee LAHNG) "Timur the Lame," known in English as Tamerlane (ca. 1336–1405), who conquered an empire ranging from the Black Sea to Samarkand.

Tlacopan (tee-laaa-co-pawn) A major city-state in the Valley of Mexico during the Aztec period, and a member of the Aztec Triple Alliance.

Tlatelolco (tl-tay-LOL-ko) Once a separate island city in Lake Texcoco, it was later incorporated into the Aztec capital of Tenochtitlan.

Tobacco Plant native to the Americas, which can be chewed or smoked and contains the addictive substance nicotine. Was disseminated around the world beginning in the sixteenth century.

Tokugawa Ieyasu (1543–1616) Founder and first shogun (military leader) of the Tokugawa shogunate, which ruled Japan from 1600–1867.

Tokugawa shogunate (TOH-koo-GAH-wah) Last shogunate in Japanese history (1600–1867); it was founded by Tokugawa Ieyasu who was notable for unifying Japan.

Toltecs Central American society (950–1150) that was centered around the city of Tula.

Topkapi (TOHP-kah-pih) A palace in Istanbul that was the main residence of the Ottoman sultans from 1465 to 1853.

Total war Military conflict in which the opposing sides mobilize all of their military and civilian resources to achieve victory.

Toussaint Louverture (1743–1803) Haitian military and political leader who led the Haitian revolution and was instrumental in establishing the first black republic in the Americas.

Trade unions Organization of workers in the same or similar trades whose purpose is to collectively advocate for worker interests.

Trail of Tears Forced relocation of the Cherokee from the eastern woodlands to Oklahoma (1837–1838); it was symbolic of U.S. expansion and destruction of indigenous Indian societies.

Trans-Saharan trade Trade across the Sahara between North Africa and sub-Saharan Africa, which reached a peak between the eighth and sixteenth centuries.

Treaty of Brest-Litovsk Peace treaty signed on March 3, 1918, between the Central Powers and Soviet Russia, in which Russia ceded many of its European territories.

Treaty of Lausanne The final peace treaty settling terms after WWI, signed in 1923 between Turkey and the former Allied powers.

Treaty of Rapallo Treaty signed between Germany and the Soviet Union in 1922, which normalized relations between the two powers in the aftermath of WWI.

Treaty of Sèvres (SEV-ruh) The peace treaty (1920) between the Ottoman empire and the Allies after World War I.

Tres Zapotes (TRACE-zah-POE-tace) Ancient Olmec city in what is now Veracruz state in Mexico.

Triangular trade Trade between Europe, Africa, and the Americas that featured finished products from Europe, slaves from Africa, and American products bound for Europe.

Tribute system A system in which subordinate peoples or governments demonstrate their subordination and respect by sending goods or labor to the superordinate government.

Tripartite Pact Agreement signed on September 27, 1940, between Germany, Italy, and Japan pledging military and economic assistance to one another for a period of ten years.

Triple Alliance Pre–World War I alliance of Germany, Austria-Hungary, and Italy.

Triple Entente (ahn-TAHNT) Pre–World War I alliance of England, France, and Russia.

Truman Doctrine U.S. policy instituted in 1947 by President Harry Truman in which the United States would follow an interventionist foreign policy to contain communism.

Trusts A combination of firms for the purpose of controlling prices or reducing competition within an industry.

Tsar (ZAHR) Old Russian term for king that is derived from the term *caesar*.

Tsar Alexander II (1818–1881) Russian tsar who emancipated Russia's serfs in 1861.

Tsuyoshi, Inukai (ts-yo-she, ee-NO-kigh) Prime minister of Japan from December 1931 to May 1932.

Tungan (tuhn-gahn) A term used to describe a Muslim people of Chinese origin.

Turkish peoples Ethnic group originating in Central Asia who speak one of the Turkic languages.

Tuthmosis (tuh-MOE-sis) Egyptian pharaoh from the eighteenth dynasty.

Twelver Shiism (SHEE'i'zm) Branch of Islam that stressed that there were twelve perfect religious leaders after Muhammad and that the twelfth went into hiding and would return someday; Shah Ismail spread this variety through the Safavid empire.

Twenty-one Demands Ultimatum presented by Japan to China in 1915 that would have given Japan special privileges in China.

Tyre (tah-yer) A port in what is now southern Lebanon, formerly an important Phoenician city for trade in silk.

Uighurs (WEE-goors) Turkish tribe.

Ukiyo Japanese word for the "floating worlds," a Buddhist term for the insignificance of the world that came to represent the urban centers in Tokugawa Japan.

Ulaanbaatar (OO-lahn-bah-tahr) Mongolian city.

Ulama (oo-lah-MAH) Islamic officials, scholars who shaped public policy in accordance with the Quran and the *sharia*.

Umayyad dynasty (oo-MEYE-ahd) Arabic dynasty (661–750), with its capital at Damascus, that was marked by a tremendous period of expansion to Spain in the west and India in the east.

Umma (UM-mah) Islamic term for the "community of the faithful."

Unequal treaties Series of treaties between China and other powers, beginning in 1842 at the end of the Opium War, in which China was forced to cede both territory and some of its sovereign rights.

United Nations (UN) Successor to the League of Nations, an association of sovereign nations that attempts to find solutions to global problems.

United States Civil War (1861–1865) Massive civil conflict in the United States between the northern and the southern states, in which the North emerged victorious.

Universal Declaration of Human Rights United Nations bill of rights protecting all human beings.

Unrestricted submarine warfare A type of marine warfare in which military vessels sink merchant or civilian ships without warning. Important in bringing the United States into World War I against Germany in 1917.

Untouchables Members of a group considered outside and inferior to the four castes in Hinduism.

Upanishads (oo-pan-NIH-shuhds) Indian reflections and dialogues (800–400 B.C.E.) that reflected basic Hindu concepts.

Urdu (OOR-doo) A language that is predominant in Pakistan.

Uruk (OO-rook) Ancient Mesopotamian city from the fourth millennium B.C.E. that was allegedly the home of the fabled Gilgamesh.

Vaishyas (VEYESH-yuhs) Hindu caste of cultivators, artisans, and merchants.

Vaqueros (bah-KEH-rohs) Latin American cowboys, similar to the Argentine gaucho.

Vardhamana (vahr-duh-MAH-duh) Indian sage who developed the central tenets of Jainism.

Vargas, Getúlio Dornelles (VAHR-guhs, zhi-TOO-lyoo door-NE-lis) Twentieth-century Brazilian statesman who ruled Brazil as a virtual dictator.

Varna (VUHR-nuh) Hindu word for caste.

Varuna (vuh-ROO-nuh) Early Aryan god who watched over the behavior of mortals and preserved the cosmic order.

Vasco da Gama (VAS-koh duh GAM-uh) Portuguese explorer who was the first to sail directly from Europe to India in 1498.

Vedas (VAY-duhs) "Wisdom," early collections of prayers and hymns that provide information about the Indo-European Aryans who migrated into India around 1500 B.C.E.; *Rig Veda* is the most important collection.

Vedic age Period in India between the second and first millennium B.C.E. and the sixth century B.C.E. in which the sacred texts of the Indo-Aryans were being composed.

Velvet revolution A term that describes the nonviolent transfer of power in Czechoslovakia during the collapse of Soviet rule.

Venta, La (BEHN-tah, lah) Early Olmec center (800–400 B.C.E.).

Venus figurines Small Paleolithic statues of women with exaggerated sexual features.

Vernacular (ver-NA-kyoo-lar) The language of the people; Martin Luther translated the Bible from the Latin of the Catholic church into the vernacular German.

Versailles (vehr-SEYE) Palace of French King Louis XIV.

Viceroy A ruler of a colony who exercises authority on behalf of a monarch.

Vichy (vee-SHEE) A city in France that served as the capital of unoccupied France during World War II.

Viet Minh North Vietnamese nationalist communists under Ho Chi Minh.

Vijayanagar kingdom (vih-juh-yuh-NUH-guhr) Southern Indian kingdom (1336–1565) that later fell to the Mughals.

Villa, Francisco (VEE-uh, frahn-SEES-kow) General in the Mexican Revolution, also known as "Pancho Villa."

Viracocha (veer-rah-coh-chah) A deity in the Inca religion believed to have been responsible for the creation of civilization.

Virgin of Guadalupe (gwah-dah-LOO-pay) Iconic image of the Virgin Mary who appeared to a peasant in Mexico in 1531, after which a shrine was built to commemorate the vision. It is an enduring symbol of Mexican national identity.

Vishnu (VIHSH-noo) Hindu god, preserver of the world, who was often incarnated as Krishna.

Visigoths People from a western group of Goths who invaded the Roman empire in the fourth century C.E.

Vittore Emmanuele III (1869–1947) The last king of Italy, who supported Benito Mussolini's Fascist dictatorship. Abdicated in 1946.

VOC Vereenigde Oost-Indische Compagnie, or United East India Company. Dutch chartered company that both traded and ruled in Asia from its founding in 1602 until its dissolution in 1800.

Volksgeist (FOHLKS-geyest) "People's spirit," a term that was coined by the German philosopher Herder; a nation's volksgeist would not come to maturity unless people studied their own unique culture and traditions.

Volta do mar (VOHL-tah doh MAHR) "Return through the sea," a fifteenth-century Portuguese sea route that took advantage of the prevailing winds and currents.

Von Herder, Johann Gottfried (fuhn HER-duhr, YOH-hahn GAWT-freet) Eighteenth-century German philosopher who advocated the power of intuition over reason.

Von Metternich, Klemens (fuhn MET-er-nik, kleh-mens) German-Austrian politician who was critical in the negotiations of the Congress of Vienna after the end of the Napoleonic wars.

Voudou (voo-doo) A polytheistic West African religion that traveled with African slaves and was adapted to conditions in the Caribbean, particularly on the island of Haiti.

Wahhabi (wuh-HAH-bee) Orthodox Sunni Muslim sect from Saudi Arabia that rejects any changes in Islam after the third century of its existence.

Waldensians Twelfth-century religious reformers who criticized the Roman Catholic church and who proposed that the laity had the right to preach and administer sacraments; they were declared heretics.

Walesa, Lech (WAH-lehn-sah, LEHK) Leader of the Polish Solidarity movement.

Wang Mang (45 B.C.E.–23 C.E.) Han dynasty official who overthrew the Liu family and established the Xin dynasty. Ruled from 9–23 C.E.

Wanli (wahn-LEE) Chinese Ming emperor (r. 1572–1620) whose refusal to meet with officials hurried the decline of Ming dynasty.

War communism The Russian policy of nationalizing industry and seizing private land during the civil war.

War of 1812 Conflict between the United States and Great Britain from 1812–1814, fought mainly along the Canadian border. Ended in a relative stalemate.

Warsaw Pact Warsaw Treaty Organization, a military alliance formed by Soviet bloc nations in 1955 in response to rearmament of West Germany and its inclusion in NATO.

Washington, George (1732–1799) Commander-in-chief of the Continental Army during the American Revolutionary War and first president of the United States.

Waterloo A town in central Belgium where Napoleon was finally defeated in 1815.

Watt, James (1736–1819) Scottish engineer and inventor whose improvements to the steam engine led to its wide use in industry.

Western front The theater of battle in western Europe during World War I.

Westphalia (west-FEY-lee-uh) Peace treaties that ended the Thirty Years' War.

Whitney, Eli (1765–1825) American inventor of the cotton gin, which allowed cotton to be more easily separated from the seed.

Wilberforce, William An English politician (1759–1833) known for his leadership of the movement to end the slave trade and abolish slavery in British territories.

William the Conqueror Duke of Normandy (1027–1087), who led the Norman invasion of England, defeated English forces at the Battle of Hastings in 1066, and became the first Norman king of England.

Wind wheels Prevailing wind patterns in the Atlantic and Pacific Oceans north and south of the equator; their discovery made sailing much safer and quicker.

Witte, Sergei (VIHT-tee, SAYR-gay) Late-nineteenth-century Russian minister of finance who pushed for industrialization.

Wollstonecraft, Mary English writer (1797–1851) who advocated equal education and rights for women.

World Health Organization (WHO) United Nation organization designed to deal with global health issues.

World Trade Organization (WTO) An organization that was established in 1995 with more than 120 nations and whose goal is to loosen barriers to free trade.

Wuwei (woo-WAY) Daoist concept of a disengagement from the affairs of the world.

Xavier, Francis (ZEY-vee-er, fran-sis) Jesuit missionary who introduced Christianity to Japan.

Xenophobia (zen-uh-FOH-bee-uh) A fear of foreigners or strangers.

Xerxes King of Persia from 486–465 B.C.E. who led a vast army against Greece. His army destroyed Athens in 480 B.C.E., but his navy was defeated at Salamis the same year, and his army was defeated a year later in 479 B.C.E.

Xhosa (KOH-suh) An agriculturalist people in southeast South Africa who speak a Bantu language.

Xia (shyah) Early Chinese dynasty (2200–1766 B.C.E.) that is known mainly from legend.

Xi'an (shee-ahn) One of the oldest cities in Chinese history, and one of the capitals of the Zhou, Qin, Han, Sui, and Tang dynasties.

Xianyang (SHYAHN-YAHNG) Capital city of Qin empire.

Xiao (SHAYOH) Confucian concept of respect for one's parents and ancestors.

Xinjiang (shin-jyahng) Western Chinese province.

Xiongnu (SHE-OONG-noo) A nomadic people of Central Asia who frequently invaded Han dynasty China.

Xuantong (soo-ahn-tohng) Also known as Puyi, the twelfth and final Qing emperor to rule China.

Xuanzang (SHWEN-ZAHNG) Seventh-century Chinese monk who made a famous trip to India to collect Buddhist texts.

Xunzi (SHOON-dzuh) Chinese philosopher who lived during the Warring States period, who believed human nature was essentially bad.

Yahweh (YAH-way) God of the monotheistic religion of Judaism that influenced later Christianity and Islam.

Yang Jian (yahng jyahn) Late-sixth-century founder of the Sui dynasty who brought all of China under centralized imperial rule.

Yangshao (YAHNG-shahw) Early Chinese society (2500–2200 B.C.E.).

Yangzi (YAHNG-zuh) River in central China.

Yellow River Second longest river in China, famous for its many floods that have caused significant death and destruction.

Yellow Turban rebellion Rebellion against the Han dynasty from 184–204 C.E. by a Chinese secret society whose members wore yellow headdresses, which contributed to the fall of the Han.

Yemelian Pugachev (yehm-eel-ian puh-gah-chehf) Leader of a major Cossack rebellion during the reign of Catherine II in eighteenth-century Russia.

Yongle (YAWNG-leh) Chinese Ming emperor (r. 1403–1424) who pushed for foreign exploration and promoted cultural achievements such as the *Yongle Encyclopedia*.

Young Italy A political society founded in 1831 to promote the unification of Italy.

Young Turk Party Nineteenth-century Turkish reformers who pushed for changes within the Ottoman empire, such as universal suffrage and freedom of religion.

Yu (yoo) Legendary founder of the Xia dynasty (ca. 2200 B.C.E.).

Yuan dynasty (yoo-AHN) Chinese dynasty (1279–1368) that was founded by the Mongol ruler Khubilai Khan.

Yucatan (yoo-kah-TAN) Peninsula in Central America, home of the Maya.

Yurts (yuhrts) Tents used by nomadic Turkish and Mongol tribes.

Zacatecas (sah-kah-TEH-kahs) The capital of the Mexican state of Zacatecas.

Zahir al-Din Muhammad (zah-here ahl-dihn muh-HAHM-mud) Also known as Babur, founder of the Mughal dynasty in India.

Zaibatsu (zeye-BAHT-soo) Japanese term for "wealthy cliques," which are similar to American trusts and cartels but usually organized around one family.

Zambos (SAHM-bohs) Latin American term for individuals born of indigenous and African parents.

Zamudio, Adela (sah-MOO-dyo, ah-DEH-lah) Nineteenth-century Bolivian poet, author of "To Be Born a Man."

Zanj revolt (zahn-jee) Slave revolt led by Ali bin Muhammed in 869 C.E. The rebels successfully captured Basra in Mesopotamia and established a state in the region until they were defeated by the Abbasid empire fourteen years later.

Zapata, Emiliano (zuh-PAH-tuh, eh-mee-LYAH-no) Revolutionary who was a leading figure in the Mexican Revolution of 1910.

Zarathustra (zar-uh-THOO-struh) Persian prophet (ca. 628–551 B.C.E.) who founded Zoroastrianism.

Zemstvos (ZEHMST-voh) District assemblies elected by Russians in the nineteenth century.

Zen Buddhism Japanese version of Chinese Chan Buddhism, with an emphasis on intuition and sudden flashes of insight instead of textual study.

Zhang Qian (jung-chen) Imperial envoy during the Han dynasty in the second century B.C.E., who was the first to bring reliable information about central Asia back to the emperor.

Zheng He (jung ha) Chinese eunuch mariner who commanded the famous Seven Voyages from 1405 to 1433.

Zhou (JOH) Chinese dynasty (1122–256 B.C.E.) that was the foundation of Chinese thought formed during this period: Confucianism, Daoism, Zhou Classics.

Zhu Xi (ZHOO-SHEE) Neo-Confucian Chinese philosopher (1130–1200).

Zhuangzi (joo-wong-dz) Fourth-century B.C.E. Chinese philosopher who developed the Hundred Schools of Thought tradition.

Ziggurats (ZIG-uh-rahts) Mesopotamian temples.

Zimbabwe (zihm-BAHB-way) Former colony of Southern Rhodesia that gained independence in 1980.

Zionism A national movement that supports the return of the Jewish people to the land of Israel and the establishment of a national home there.

Zoroastrianism (zohr-oh-ASS-tree-ahn-iz'm) Persian religion based on the teaching of the sixth-century B.C.E. prophet Zarathustra; its emphasis on the duality of good and evil and on the role of individuals in determining their own fate would influence later religions.

A.D. 1325–1354, 4 vols. Cambridge: Hakluyt Society, 1958–1994, 2: 374–77. Reprinted by permission of David Higham Associates, Ltd. **Photo Credits Opener:** © Explorer/Photo Researchers, Inc.; **p. 273:** Photograph © 1979 Dirk Bakker; **p. 276:** © Marc and Evelyne Bernheim/Woodfin Camp and Associates; **p. 277:** © Peter Guttman/Corbis; **p. 280:** © Werner Forman/Art Resource, NY; **p. 281:** © British Library/HIP/Art Resource, NY; **p. 282:** © Great Zimbabwe/Woodfin Camp and Associates.

CHAPTER 16

Text Credits p. 294: Henry Yule and Henri Cordier, eds. *Cathay and the Way Thither,* 2nd ed., 4 vols. London: Hakluyt Society, 1913–16, 3:151–55. (Translation slightly modified.) **Photo Credits Opener:** © Scala/Art Resource, NY; **p. 290:** © Erich Lessing/Art Resource, NY; **p. 293:** © British Library/HIP/Art Resource, NY; **p. 295:** © Bodleian Library, University of Oxford (MS Bodl. 264, fol. 218r); **p. 297:** © Erich Lessing/Art Resource, NY; **p. 299:** © The Pierpont Morgan Library/Art Resource, NY; **p. 300:** © Royalty-Free/Corbis; **p. 303:** © Bibliothèque Nationale, Paris, France/The Bridgeman Art Library.

CHAPTER 17

Text Credits p. 321: Teuira Henry and others, Dennis Kawaharada, ed., *Voyaging Chiefs of Havai'i,* pp. 138–39, 144–46. Copyright © 1995 Kalamaka Press. Reprinted by permission. **Photo Credits Opener:** © Private Collection/Jean-Pierre Courau/The Bridgeman Art Library; **p. 310:** © Bodleian Library, University of Oxford (MS Arch. Selden, A.1, fol. 31r); **p. 312:** © Biblioteca Nazionale Centrale, Florence/Index S.A.S.; **p. 313:** © Georg Gerster/Photo Researchers, Inc.; **p. 315:** © Jim Zuckerman/Corbis RF; **p. 316:** © Collection of the New-York Historical Society, USA/The Bridgeman Art Library; **p. 319:** © Honolulu Academy of Arts, Gift of George R. Carter, 1927 (5945); **p. 320:** © Douglas Peebles Photography/Alamy RF.

CHAPTER 18

Text Credits p. 330: Henry Yule and Henri Cordier, eds. *Cathay and the Way Thither,* 4 vols. London: Hakluyt Society, 1913–1916, 3:45–50. (Translation slightly modified.); **p. 332, Document 1:** Francesco Petrarca: *Ad Seipsum* (To Himself) (*Epistola Metrica I,* 14: lines 1–55). http://www.brown.edu/Departments/Italian_Studies/dweb/plague/perspectives/petrarca2.php; **p. 332, Document 2:** John Aberth, *The First*

Horseman: Disease in Human History (Upper Saddle River, N.J.: Pearson Prentice Hall, 2007), pp. 42–43. **Photo Credits Opener:** © The Philadelphia Museum of Art/Art Resource, NY; **p. 331:** © Biblioteca Monasterio del Escorial, Madrid, Spain/Index/The Bridgeman Art Library; **p. 333:** © bpk, Berlin/Kupferstichkabinett, Staatliche Museen/Joerg P. Anders/Art Resource, NY; **p. 334:** With permission of the Royal Ontario Museum © ROM; **p. 336:** © Medioimages/Getty Images RF; **p. 337:** © Scala/Art Resource, NY; **p. 341:** With permission of the Royal Ontario Museum © ROM.

PART 5

Photo Credits 347 (left): © Collection Rijksmuseum, Amsterdam; **p. 347 (right):** Courtesy of the Hispanic Society of America, New York.

CHAPTER 19

Text Credits p. 355: *Diario of Christopher Columbus's First Voyage to America,* 1492–1493, by Christopher Columbus, edited by Oliver C. Dunn and James E. Kelley, Jr. University of Oklahoma Press, 1989. Used by permission of University of Oklahoma Press. **Photo Credits Opener:** © Banco Nacional Ultramarino, Portugal/Giraudon/The Bridgeman Art Library; **p. 351:** © Bildarchiv, ÖNB, Wien; **p. 357:** © National Maritime Museum, Greenwich, UK; **p. 360:** © Maritiem Museum, Rotterdam. P-2161-31; **p. 364:** © President and Fellows of Harvard College, Peabody Museum of Archaeology and Ethnology, 2004.24.29636; **p. 365:** © Stapleton Collection/Corbis; **p. 366:** From the James Ford Bell Library, University of Minnesota, Minneapolis, Minnesota; **p. 367:** © Bettmann/Corbis.

CHAPTER 20

Text Credits p. 386: Galileo Galilei, "Letter to the Grand Duchess Christina," excerpt from *Discoveries and Observations of Galileo,* translated and edited by Stillman Drake. Copyright © 1957 by Stillman Drake. Reprinted by permission of Random House. **Photo Credits Opener:** © Erich Lessing/Art Resource, NY; **p. 374:** © Bildarchiv Preussischer Kulturbesitz, Berlin/Kupferstichkabinett, Staatliche Museen/Joerg P. Anders/Art Resource, NY; **p. 377:** © Bridgeman-Giraudon/Art Resource, NY; **p. 378:** © The Granger Collection, NYC; **p. 379:** © Bridgeman-Giraudon/Art Resource, NY; **p. 383:** © The Granger Collection, NYC; **p. 385:** © The

Granger Collection, NYC; **p. 387:** © World History Archive/Alamy.

CHAPTER 21

Text Credits p. 395: Bernardino de Sahagún. *Florentine Codex: General History of the Things of New Spain,* 13 vols. Trans. by Arthur J. O. Anderson and Charles E. Dibble. Salt Lake City: University of Utah Press, 1950–1982, 13:19–20. (Translation slightly modified). Used by permission of the University of Utah Press. **Photo Credits Opener:** © The Granger Collection, NYC; **p. 393:** © The New York Public Library/Art Resource, NY; **p. 394:** © Bridgeman-Giraudon/Art Resource, NY; **p. 398:** © Art Resource, NY; **p. 399:** © Museo Nacional de Historia, Mexico City, Mexico/Giraudon/The Bridgeman Art Library; **p. 402:** © The New York Public Library/Art Resource, NY; **p. 403:** © The Bridgeman Art Library; **p. 404:** © Christie's Images/Corbis.

CHAPTER 22

Text Credits p. 415: Basil Davidson. *The African Past.* Boston: Little, Brown, 1964, pp. 191–93. Copyright © 1964 by Basil Davidson. Reprinted by permission of Curtis Brown, Ltd., and Andre Deutsch.; **p. 420, Document 1:** This advertisement comes from the *New London Summary* (Connecticut) on March 30, 1764. http://www.yale.edu/glc/citizens/stories/module1/documents/runaway_slave.html; **p. 420, Document 2:** This broadside advertisement was posted in Charlestown, South Carolina, in 1769. http://www.pbs.org/wgbh/aia/part1/1h304.html. **Photo Credits Opener:** © North Wind Picture Archives; **p. 411:** © Bibliothèque Nationale, Paris, France/The Art Archive at Art Resource, NY; **p. 413:** From *Description de l'Afrique* by Olifert Dapper, 1686; **p. 417:** © National Maritime Museum, Greenwich, UK; **p. 419:** © The New York Public Library/Art Resource, NY; **p. 420:** © America's Historical Newspapers, an Archive of Americana Collection, published by Readex, a division of NewsBank.com; **p. 421:** © American Antiquarian Society; **p. 423:** From Debret, *Voyages Pittoresque et Historiques au Bresil,* 1816–1831; **p. 425:** © National Portrait Gallery, Smithsonian Institution/Art Resource, NY.

CHAPTER 23

Text Credits p. 437: J. O. P. Bland. *Annals and Memoirs of the Court of Peking.* Boston: Houghton Mifflin, 1914, pp. 325–31. (Translation slightly modified.) **Photo**

Credits Opener: © Erich Lessing/Art Resource, NY; **p. 431:** © David Noton/Aurora Photos; **p. 433:** The Metropolitan Museum of Art, Rogers Fund, 1942. (42.141.2). Photograph © 1980 The Metropolitan Museum of Art/Art Resource, NY; **p. 436:** Detail from a vase depicting silk weaving (ceramic), Chinese School, Ming Dynasty (1368–1644)/Golestan Palace, Tehran, Iran. © Giraudon/The Bridgeman Art Library; **p. 438:** © The New York Public Library/Art Resource, NY; **p. 442:** © The Granger Collection, NYC; **p. 443:** © The Trustees of the British Museum. All rights reserved.

CHAPTER 24

Text Credits p. 452: "Sultan Selim I, Letter to Shah Ismail of Persia," Reprinted with the permission of Simon & Schuster, Inc., from THE MUSLIM WORLD ON THE EVE OF EUROPE'S EXPANSION, translated and edited by John J. Saunders. Copyright © 1966 by Prentice Hall. All rights reserved. **Photo Credits Opener:** © Andrea Pistolesi/The Image Bank/Getty Images; **p. 450:** © Bridgeman-Giraudon/Art Resource, NY; **p. 452:** © The British Library Board. All rights reserved 01/2013/OR.3248, f. 55v; **p. 453:** © V&A Images, London/Art Resource, NY; **p. 455:** © Private Collection/The Stapleton Collection/The Bridgeman Art Library; **p. 457 (left):** © Harvey Lloyd; **p. 457 (right):** © Robert Harding/Robert Harding World Imagery/Corbis; **p. 458:** © Gavin Hellier/Robert Harding World Imagery/Corbis; **p. 460:** © Topkapi Palace Museum.

PART 6

Photo Credits 465 (left): © Eileen Tweedy/The Art Archive at Art Resource, NY; **p. 465 (right):** © Bettmann/Corbis.

CHAPTER 25

Text Credits p. 474: "Declaration des droits de l'homme et du citoyen" Translated by Jerry H. Bentley. **Photo Credits Opener:** © Bridgeman-Giraudon/Art Resource, NY; **p. 471:** Architect of the Capitol; **p. 474:** © Gianni Dagli Orti/The Art Archive at Art Resource, NY; **p. 476:** © The Granger Collection, NYC; **p. 478:** © Art Resource, NY; **p. 482:** © Erich Lessing/Art Resource, NY; **p. 485 (left):** © Schloss Friedrichsruhe/The Bridgeman Art Library; **p. 485 (right):** © Scala/White Images/Art Resource, NY.

CHAPTER 26

Text Credits p. 499: "Testimony for the Factory Act of 1833: Working Conditions in England," Commission for Inquiry into the Employment of Children in Factories, *Second Report, with Minutes of Evidence and Reports by the Medical Commissioners,* vol. V, Session 29 January–20 August, 1833 (London: His Majesty's Printing Office, 1833), pp. 5, 26–28. **Photo Credits Opener:** © The Art Archive at Art Resource, NY; **p. 494:** © Science Museum, London/The Bridgeman Art Library; **p. 495:** © Ann Ronan Picture Library/HIP/The Image Works; **p. 497:** © Guildhall Library, Corporation of London/The Bridgeman Art Library; **p. 500:** © Hulton-Deutsch Collection/Corbis; **p. 501:** © Bettmann/Corbis; **p. 503:** © Deutsches Historisches Museum, Berlin; **p. 505:** Library of Congress; **p. 507:** © The Granger Collection, NYC.

CHAPTER 27

Text Credits p. 527: "Letter from Jourdan Anderson to P.H. Anderson, August 7, 1865." Published in the *Cincinnati Commercial* and reprinted in the *New York Tribune,* August 22, 1865. **Photo Credits Opener:** © Underwood & Underwood/Corbis; **pp. 514–515:** Library of Congress; **p. 519:** © Lake County Museum/Corbis; **p. 520:** © The Mariners' Museum/Corbis; **p. 521:** © Museum of the City of New York/Corbis; **p. 523:** © Corbis; **p. 524:** © Bettmann/Corbis.

CHAPTER 28

Text Credits p. 541: A standard treaty of the British Royal Niger Company, 1880's; **p. 548, Document 1:** Eva March Tappan, ed., *China, Japan, and the Islands of the Pacific,* Vol. I of *The World's Story: A History of the World in Story, Song, and Art,* (Boston: Houghton Mifflin, 1914), p. 197. http://www.fordham.edu/halsall/mod/1842canton.asp; **p. 549, Document 2:** G. M. Theal, ed., *Records of Southeastern Africa* (Capetown: Government of Capetown, 1898–1903). http://www.fordham.edu/Halsall/mod/1858basuto.asp. **Photo Credits Opener:** © Erich Lessing/Art Resource, NY; **p. 531:** © Baldwin H. Ward & Kathryn C. Ward/Corbis; **p. 533:** © V&A Images, Victoria and Albert Museum; **p. 537:** © Historical Picture Archives/Corbis; **p. 540:** © Anti-Slavery International/Panos; **p. 544:** © Brown Brothers; **p. 546:** © Chris Hellier/Corbis; **p. 548:** © National Maritime Museum, London/The Image Works; **p. 549:** Source: *A Short History of Lesotho* by Stephen Gill.

PART 7

Photo Credits Page 554: Courtesy of the Australian War Memorial; **p. 555 (left):** © National Archives, London, Great Britain/HIP/Art Resource, NY; **p. 555 (right):** © David & Peter Turnley/Corbis.

CHAPTER 29

Text Credits p. 568: Edmund Blunden, ed., *The Poems of Wilfred Owen.* London: Chattus & Windus, 1933, p. 66. **Photo Credits Opener:** © Detail. Imperial War Museum (Art. IWM ART 1921); **p. 559:** © Christel Gerstenberg/Corbis; **p. 561:** © Imperial War Museum (CO 2246); **p. 562:** © akg-images, London; **p. 563:** © The Art Archive at Art Resource, NY; **pp. 565–567:** National Archives; **p. 569:** © Hulton-Deutsch Collection/Corbis; **p. 570:** © Imperial War Museum (Q 353).

CHAPTER 30

Text Credits p. 585: Franklin D. Roosevelt, *First Inaugural Address, 4 March 1933,* available at The Avalon Project at http://www.yale.edu/lawweb/avalon/president/inaug/froos1.htm. **Photo Credits Opener:** © Scala/Art Resource, NY and © 2006 The Munch Museum/The Munch-Ellingsen Group/Artists Rights Society (ARS), NY; **p. 579:** © Bettmann/Corbis; **p. 580 (left):** © Culver Pictures/The Art Archive at Art Resource, NY; **p. 580 (right):** © Bettmann/Corbis; **p. 581:** © The Museum of Modern Art/Licensed by Scala/Art Resource, NY and © 2012 Estate of Pablo Picasso/Artists Rights Society (ARS), NY; **p. 582:** Courtesy of the Oakland Museum of California; **p. 583:** Library of Congress; **p. 585:** © Bettmann/Corbis; **p. 587:** © Hulton-Deutsch Collection/Corbis; **p. 589 (left):** © Henry Guttmann/Getty Images; **p. 589 (right):** © akg-images, London.

CHAPTER 31

Text Credits p. 596: Mohandas Gandhi, *Hind Swaraj* (Indian Home Rule) published in the Gujarati columns of *Indian Opinion,* 11th and 18th December, 1909. No rights reserved. The International Printing Press, Phoenix, Natal, 1910. **Photo Credits Opener:** © Swim Ink/Corbis; **pp. 595–599:**